A Learners' Cornish Dictionary

in the

Standard Written Form

Second edition (revised)

Edited by

Steve Harris, Dee Harris, Peter Harvey, Raël Harvey

Published by Ors Sempel, 2019

Published by Ors Sempel, 2019

Typeset in LATEX using TEX Gyre Pagella

Cover design by Dee Harris

Pryntys gans BookPrintingUK

Printed by BookPrintingUK

ISBN 978-0-9930764-3-5

Acknowledgements

We are once again grateful to everyone who supported the production of this dictionary.

Special thanks are due to Roger Henley, Pol Hodge and Esmé Tackley for their invaluable and extensive contributions.

Thanks are also due to Ray Chubb, Jan Edmondson, John Gillingham, Tony Hak, Loveday Jenkin, Kath Jones and Maureen Pierce for their work on specific sections of this second edition.

Feedback from our users has been very important to us, so lastly we offer our thanks to everyone who made any contribution, no matter how small, to the quality of this new publication.

Steve Harris, Dee Harris, Peter Harvey, Raël Harvey.

Contents

Introduction

Introduction to the second edition

The editors were gratified to receive many positive comments about the first edition of *A Learners' Cornish Dictionary*, which also received the Holyer an Gof 2017 Publishers' Award in the category *Cornish Language Books for Teaching*. We hope that this new edition will prove equally useful to students of the Standard Written Form.

This second edition contains improvements and updates from the first. Many new words and definitions have been added, and errors and inconsistencies removed. Any remaining flaws are the responsibility of the editors.

A number of sections have been added or extended:

- **New: Possessive adjectives.** A table of possessive adjective contractions has been added. See page 9.

- **Expanded: Verbs.** The verb **y'm beus** has been added to the list. See page 11.

- **New: Decimal numbers.** In addition to the traditional system, a modern decimal counting system similar to the one used in Welsh is described which it is hoped will make working with numbers in Cornish much more accessible. See page 27.

- **New: Prefixes and suffixes.** A range of prefixes and suffixes are listed to make it easier to determine the meanings of existing words and to help with coining neologisms. See page 31.

- **New: Gendered occupations.** Readers are encouraged to take note of the new section on gender equality in Cornish and how it is treated in this new edition. See page 39.

- **New: Idiomatic phrases.** A new section containing examples of Cornish idioms. See page 41.

- **Expanded: Example sentences.** This section has been expanded to include asking questions in Cornish. See page 49.

- **Expanded: The natural world.** Among the new words in this edition is a wide range of common plant names and an expanded selection of bird names in Cornish. Where only collective nouns for plants are given, the feminine singular can be made by adding **-en** to the end of the name (or first word in the name).

It was proposed that we include Cornish placenames in the dictionary but we suggest that readers instead visit the Akademi Kernewek website where there is a regularly-updated list.[a]

This 2019 second edition (revised) contains minor corrections.

Introduction to the first edition

The revival of the Cornish language received a major boost in 2002 when it was officially recognised by the UK government under the European Charter for Regional or Minority Languages. The desire to see Cornish used more widely in public life and in education subsequently led to the setting up of the Cornish Language Partnership and Maga in 2005, which in turn oversaw a consultation and discussion process with the aim of gathering the support of as much of the language community as possible behind a single orthography. That process guided the development of the Standard Written Form in 2008, and its review, which was published in 2014.

All of the major language groups agreed that the Standard Written Form (SWF) – in Cornish **Furv Skrifys Savonek** – was to be used in public life, by Cornwall Council, and within education. An online dictionary was set up[b] with an accompanying PDF download.

---

[a]http://www.akademikernewek.org.uk/

[b]http://www.cornishdictionary.org.uk/

Frequent requests from students for a printed SWF dictionary have inspired the production of this volume.

This dictionary aims to provide the learner with enough vocabulary to use Cornish in a variety of situations. It is not an academic reference containing etymologies and recommended pronunciations, nor does it contain every single known word in Cornish, but it should provide the student learning the Standard Written Form of Cornish with a good grounding in the language. Those who progress further will find it useful to use other publications in addition to this volume. As few learners of Cornish are familiar with the IPA phonetic symbols, the passing on of good pronunciation has been left to teachers and audio resources.

To ensure that this dictionary is as easy to use as possible by children, other learners, and those producing material for use in public life, there are no spelling variants. SWF dictionaries under development by other publishers will provide alternative spellings for those who wish to use them.

Alongside the two dictionary sections, there is a mutation table, a selection of pronominal prepositions, a collection of useful and representative verbs, a selection of numbers, example sentences and a list of resources available in the SWF.

Mutation Table

Like all Celtic languages, Cornish has a regular system of initial letter modification known as *mutation*. Some words modify the initial letter of the following word, and this is indicated in the dictionary by a superscript number showing which type of mutation is caused, e.g. **dhe²**.

A full description of the causes of mutation can be found in Cornish grammars.

Original	2nd	3rd	4th	5th	5th(a) ('th)
B	V		P	F	V
Ch	J				
D	Dh		T	T	T
G+a G+e G+i G+y	-		K	H	H
G+l G+r	-		K		
Gw	W		Kw	Hw	W
G+o G+u G+ro G+ru	W		K	Hw	W
K	G	H			
M	V			F	V
P	B	F			
T	D	Th			

Prepositions

In Cornish, a large number of prepositions, that is, words indicating relationships such as *to*, *from*, *before*, *after*, *on*, *under*, can have personal forms (aka *pronominal* or *inflected prepositions*). These generally have regular final letters similar to those in the present tense of the verb **bos**, so are usually recognisable. Irregular inflected prepositions' endings only vary slightly from these:

1s **-v**; *2s* **-s**; *3sm* **-o**; *3sf* **-i**; *1p* **-n**; *2p* **-owgh**; *3p* **-a**.

A few prepositions are required for the first two grades of language exams as set by Kesva an Taves Kernewek, and these are included in the representative list below. Personal forms of prepositions are listed in the main part of the dictionary. A full list of prepositions and their personal forms is available in other publications.

Note that inflected forms of prepositions do not cause mutation.

a^2 – *of, from*

1s	**ahanav**	*of me, from me*
2s	**ahanas**	*of you, from you*
3sm	**anodho**	*of him, from him*
3sf	**anedhi**	*of her, from her*
1p	**ahanan**	*of us, from us*
2p	**ahanowgh**	*of you, from you (pl)*
3p	**anedha**	*of them, from them*

gans – *with, by*

1s	**genev**	*with me, by me*
2s	**genes**	*with you, by you*
3sm	**ganso**	*with him, by him*
3sf	**gensi**	*with her, by her*
1p	**genen**	*with us, by us*
2p	**genowgh**	*with you, by you (pl)*
3p	**gansa**	*with them, by them*

dhe^2 – *to*

1s	**dhymm**	*to me*
2s	**dhis**	*to you*
3sm	**dhodho**	*to him*
3sf	**dhedhi**	*to her*
1p	**dhyn**	*to us*
2p	**dhywgh**	*to you (pl)*
3p	**dhedha**	*to them*

heb – *without*

1s	**hebov**	*without me*
2s	**hebos**	*without you*
3sm	**hebdho**	*without him*
3sf	**hebdhi**	*without her*
1p	**hebon**	*without us*
2p	**hebowgh**	*without you (pl)*
3p	**hebdha**	*without them*

orth – *at*

1s	**orthiv**	*at me*
2s	**orthis**	*at you*
3sm	**orto**	*at him*
3sf	**orti**	*at her*
1p	**orthyn**	*at us*
2p	**orthowgh**	*at you (pl)*
3p	**orta**	*at them*

war[2] – *on*

1s	**warnav**	*on me*
2s	**warnas**	*on you*
3sm	**warnodho**	*on him*
3sf	**warnedhi**	*on her*
1p	**warnan**	*on us*
2p	**warnowgh**	*on you (pl)*
3p	**warnedha**	*on them*

rag – *for*

1s	**ragov**	*for me*
2s	**ragos**	*for you*
3sm	**ragdho**	*for him*
3sf	**rygdhi**	*for her*
1p	**ragon**	*for us*
2p	**ragowgh**	*for you (pl)*
3p	**ragdha**	*for them*

yn – *in*

1s	**ynnov**	*in me*
2s	**ynnos**	*in you*
3sm	**ynno**	*in him*
3sf	**ynni**	*in her*
1p	**ynnon**	*in us*
2p	**ynnowgh**	*in you (pl)*
3p	**ynna**	*in them*

The personal forms of some prepositions are formed in a different way, by using possessive adjectives as shown for **yn kever** below. Note that the possessive adjectives cause mutation of the preposition in the usual way.

yn kever – *about, regarding*

1s	**yn ow[3] hever**	*about me*
2s	**yn dha[2] gever**	*about you*
3sm	**yn y[2] gever**	*about him*
3sf	**yn hy[3] hever**	*about her*
1p	**y'gan kever**	*about us*
2p	**y'gas kever**	*about you (pl)*
3p	**y'ga[3] hever**	*about them*

Possessive adjectives

Possessive adjectives *my*, *our*, *their*, etc. are sometimes contracted in Cornish, which can give them an unfamiliar appearance to students. To help clarify this, the contractions are tabulated below. The reader will find a few examples of these amongst the Example Sentences and Idioms.

English	Corn.	of/from a^2	to dhe^2	and ha	nor na	by re^2	in yn
my	ow^3	a'm	dhe'm	ha'm	na'm	re'm	y'm
your sg.	dha^2	a'th^{5a}	dhe'th^{5a}	ha'th^{5a}	na'th^{5a}	re'th^{5a}	y'th^{5a}
his/its	y^2	a'y^2	dh'y^2	ha'y^2	na'y^2	re'y^2	yn y^2
her/its	hy^3	a'y^3	dh'y^3	ha'y^3	na'y^3	re'y^3	yn hy^3
our	agan	a'gan	dh'agan	ha'gan	na'gan	re'gan	y'gan
your pl.	agas	a'gas	dh'agas	ha'gas	na'gas	re'gas	y'gas
their	aga^3	a'ga^3	dh'aga^3	ha'ga^3	na'ga^3	re'ga^3	y'ga^3

Verbs

Regular Cornish verbs are conjugated by adding a suffix representing the tense and person to the verb's stem. A selection of common, useful and representative verbs is given in the follcwing pages, including the auxiliary verbs **gallos, gul** and **mynnes** and the common irregular verbs **bos, dos, godhvos** and **mos**. Also included are these paradigms of regular verbs: **berrhe, kara, ponya, prena** and **tybi**. The verb **y'm beus** is included for more advanced students.

berrhe – *to shorten*

present

1s	**berrhav**
2s	**berrhydh**
3s	**berrha**
1p	**berrhyn**
2p	**berrhowgh**
3p	**berrhons**
0	**berrhir**

present subjunctive

1s	**berrhahiv**
2s	**berrhahi**
3s	**berrhaho**
1p	**berrhahyn**
2p	**berrhahowgh**
3p	**berrhahons**
0	**berrhaher**

preterite

1s	**berrhis**
2s	**berrhasys**
3s	**berrhas**
1p	**berrhasyn**
2p	**berrhasowgh**
3p	**berrhasons**
0	**berrhas**

imperfect subjunctive

1s	**berrhahen**
2s	**berrhahes**
3s	**berrhaha**
1p	**berrhahen**
2p	**berrhahewgh**
3p	**berrhahens**
0	**berrhahys**

imperfect

1s	**berrhyn**
2s	**berrhys**
3s	**berrhi**
1p	**berrhyn**
2p	**berrhewgh**
3p	**berrhens**
0	**berrhys**

imperative

1s	-
2s	**berrha**
3s	**berrhes**
1p	**berrhyn**
2p	**berrhewgh**
3p	**berrhens**
0	-

pluperfect

1s	**berrhasen**
2s	**berrhases**
3s	**berrhasa**
1p	**berrhasen**
2p	**berrhasewgh**
3p	**berrhasens**
0	**berrhasys**

bos – *to be*

present

1s	ov/esov
2s	os/esos
3s	yw/yma/eus/usi
1p	on/eson
2p	owgh/esowgh
3p	yns/ymons/esons
0	or/eder

present subjunctive

1s	biv
2s	bi
3s	bo
1p	byn
2p	bowgh
3p	bons
0	ber

imperfect

1s	en/esen
2s	es/eses
3s	o/esa
1p	en/esen
2p	ewgh/esewgh
3p	ens/esens
0	os/eses

imperfect subjunctive

1s	ben
2s	bes
3s	be
1p	ben
2p	bewgh
3p	bens
0	bes

habitual imperfect

1s	bedhen
2s	bedhes
3s	bedha
1p	bedhen
2p	bedhewgh
3p	bedhens
0	bedhes

imperative

1s	-
2s	bydh
3s	bedhes
1p	bedhen
2p	bedhewgh
3p	bedhens
0	-

preterite

1s	beuv
2s	beus
3s	beu
1p	beun
2p	bewgh
3p	bons
0	beus

pluperfect

1s	bien
2s	bies
3s	bia
1p	bien
2p	biewgh
3p	biens
0	bies

future

1s	bedhav
2s	bedhydh
3s	bydh
1p	bedhyn
2p	bedhowgh
3p	bedhons
0	bedher

dos – *to come*   *past participle:* **devedhys**

present

1s	**dov**
2s	**deudh**
3s	**deu**

1p	**deun**
2p	**dewgh**
3p	**dons**

0	**deer**

perfect

1s	**deuvev**
2s	**deuves**
3s	**deuva**

1p	**deuven**
2p	**deuvewgh**
3p	**deuvons**

0	**deuves**

preterite

1s	**deuth**
2s	**deuthys**
3s	**deuth**

1p	**deuthen**
2p	**deuthewgh**
3p	**deuthons**

0	**deuthes**

present subjunctive

1s	**dyffiv**
2s	**dyffi**
3s	**deffo**

1p	**dyffyn**
2p	**dyffowgh**
3p	**deffons**

0	**deffer**

imperfect

1s	**den**
2s	**des**
3s	**do**

1p	**den**
2p	**dewgh**
3p	**dens**

0	**des**

imperfect subjunctive

1s	**deffen**
2s	**deffes**
3s	**deffa**

1p	**deffen**
2p	**deffewgh**
3p	**deffens**

0	**deffes**

pluperfect

1s	**dothyen**
2s	**dothyes**
3s	**dothya**

1p	**dothyen**
2p	**dothyewgh**
3p	**dothyens**

0	**dothyes**

imperative

1s	-
2s	**deus**
3s	**des**

1p	**deun**
2p	**dewgh**
3p	**dens**

0	-

gallos – *to be able to. Auxiliary verb.*   *past participle: -*

present

1s	gallav
2s	gyllydh
3s	gyll

1p	gyllyn
2p	gyllowgh
3p	gyllons

0	gyllir

present subjunctive

1s	gylliv
2s	gylli
3s	gallo

1p	gyllyn
2p	gyllowgh
3p	gallons

0	galler

preterite

1s	gyllis
2s	gyllsys
3s	gallas

1p	gyllsyn
2p	gyllsowgh
3p	gallsons

0	gallas

imperfect subjunctive

1s	gallen
2s	galles
3s	galla

1p	gallen
2p	gallewgh
3p	gallens

0	galles

imperfect

1s	gyllyn
2s	gyllys
3s	gylli

1p	gyllyn
2p	gyllewgh
3p	gyllens

0	gyllys

imperative

1s	-
2s	-
3s	-

1p	-
2p	-
3p	-

0	-

pluperfect

1s	gallsen
2s	gallses
3s	gallsa

1p	gallsen
2p	gallsewgh
3p	gallsens

0	gallses

godhvos – *to know*

past participle: godhvedhys

present

1s	gonn
2s	godhes
3s	gor
1p	godhon
2p	godhowgh
3p	godhons
0	godhor

present subjunctive

1s	godhviv
2s	godhvi
3s	godhvo
1p	godhvyn
2p	godhvowgh
3p	godhvons
0	godher

preterite

1s	godhvev
2s	godhves
3s	godhva
1p	godhven
2p	godhvewgh
3p	godhvons
0	godhves

imperfect subjunctive

1s	godhven
2s	godhves
3s	godhve
1p	godhven
2p	godhvewgh
3p	godhvens
0	godhves

imperfect

1s	godhyen
2s	godhyes
3s	godhya
1p	godhyen
2p	godhyewgh
3p	godhyens
0	godhyes

imperative

1s	-
2s	godhvydh
3s	godhvedhes
1p	godhvedhyn
2p	godhvedhewgh
3p	godhvedhens
0	-

pluperfect

1s	godhvien
2s	godhvies
3s	godhvia
1p	godhvien
2p	godhviewgh
3p	godhviens
0	godhvies

future

1s	godhvedhav
2s	godhvedhydh
3s	godhvydh
1p	godhvedhyn
2p	godhvedhowgh
3p	godhvedhons
0	godhvedher

gul – *to do. Auxiliary verb.*

past participle: gwrys

present

1s	gwrav
2s	gwredh
3s	gwra

1p	gwren
2p	gwrewgh
3p	gwrons

| 0 | gwrer |

preterite

1s	gwrug
2s	gwrussys
3s	gwrug

1p	gwrussyn
2p	gwrussowgh
3p	gwrussons

| 0 | gwrug |

imperfect

1s	gwren
2s	gwres
3s	gwre

1p	gwren
2p	gwrewgh
3p	gwrens

| 0 | gwres |

pluperfect

1s	gwrussen
2s	gwrusses
3s	gwrussa

1p	gwrussen
2p	gwrussewgh
3p	gwrussens

| 0 | gwrussys |

present subjunctive

1s	gwrylliv
2s	gwrylli
3s	gwrello

1p	gwryllyn
2p	gwryllowgh
3p	gwrellons

| 0 | gwreller |

imperfect subjunctive

1s	gwrellen
2s	gwrelles
3s	gwrella

1p	gwrellen
2p	gwrellewgh
3p	gwrellens

| 0 | gwrellys |

imperative

1s	-
2s	gwra
3s	gwres

1p	gwren
2p	gwrewgh
3p	gwrens

| 0 | - |

kara – *to love*

past participle: **kerys**

present

1s	**karav**
2s	**kerydh**
3s	**kar**
1p	**keryn**
2p	**kerowgh**
3p	**karons**
0	**kerir**

present subjunctive

1s	**kyrriv**
2s	**kyrri**
3s	**karro**
1p	**kyrryn**
2p	**kyrrowgh**
3p	**karrons**
0	**karrer**

preterite

1s	**keris**
2s	**kersys**
3s	**karas**
1p	**kersyn**
2p	**kersowgh**
3p	**karsons**
0	**karas**

imperfect subjunctive

1s	**karren**
2s	**karres**
3s	**karra**
1p	**karren**
2p	**karrewgh**
3p	**karrens**
0	**kyrrys**

imperfect

1s	**karen**
2s	**kares**
3s	**kara**
1p	**karen**
2p	**karewgh**
3p	**karens**
0	**kerys**

imperative

1s	-
2s	**kar**
3s	**kares**
1p	**keryn**
2p	**kerewgh**
3p	**karens**
0	-

pluperfect

1s	**karsen**
2s	**karses**
3s	**karsa**
1p	**karsen**
2p	**karsewgh**
3p	**karsens**
0	**kersys**

mos – *to go*

present

1s	av
2s	edh
3s	a
1p	en
2p	ewgh
3p	ons
0	er

perfect

1s	galsov
2s	galsos
3s	gallas
1p	galson
2p	galsowgh
3p	galsons
0	-

preterite

1s	yth
2s	ethys
3s	eth
1p	ethen
2p	ethewgh
3p	ethons
0	es

present subjunctive

1s	ylliv
2s	ylli
3s	ello
1p	yllyn
2p	yllowgh
3p	ellons
0	eller

imperfect

1s	en
2s	es
3s	e
1p	en
2p	ewgh
3p	ens
0	es/os

imperfect subjunctive

1s	ellen
2s	elles
3s	ella
1p	ellen
2p	ellewgh
3p	ellens
0	elles

pluperfect

1s	gylsen
2s	gylses
3s	galsa
1p	gylsen
2p	gylsewgh
3p	gylsens
0	-

imperative

1s	
2s	ke/a
3s	es
1p	deun
2p	kewgh/ewgh
3p	ens
0	-

mynnes – *to want. Auxiliary verb.*

past participle: -

present

1s	**mynnav**
2s	**mynnydh**
3s	**mynn**
1p	**mynnyn**
2p	**mynnowgh**
3p	**mynnons**
0	**mynnir**

present subjunctive

1s	**mynniv**
2s	**mynni**
3s	**mynno**
1p	**mynnyn**
2p	**mynnowgh**
3p	**mynnons**
0	**mynner**

preterite

1s	**mynnis**
2s	**mynsys**
3s	**mynnas**
1p	**mynsyn**
2p	**mynsowgh**
3p	**mynsons**
0	**mynnas**

imperfect subjunctive

1s	**mynnen**
2s	**mynnes**
3s	**mynna**
1p	**mynnen**
2p	**mynnewgh**
3p	**mynnens**
0	**mynnys**

imperfect

1s	**mynnen**
2s	**mynnes**
3s	**mynna**
1p	**mynnen**
2p	**mynnewgh**
3p	**mynnens**
0	**mynnys**

imperative

not used

pluperfect

1s	**mynsen**
2s	**mynses**
3s	**mynsa**
1p	**mynsen**
2p	**mynsewgh**
3p	**mynsens**
0	**mynsys**

ponya – *to run*

present

1s	ponyav
2s	ponydh
3s	poon
1p	ponyn
2p	ponyowgh
3p	ponyons
0	ponir

preterite

1s	ponis
2s	ponsys
3s	ponyas
1p	ponsyn
2p	ponsowgh
3p	ponsons
0	ponyas

imperfect

1s	ponyen
2s	ponyes
3s	ponya
1p	ponyen
2p	ponyewgh
3p	ponyens
0	ponys

pluperfect

1s	ponsen
2s	ponses
3s	ponsa
1p	ponsen
2p	ponsewgh
3p	ponsens
0	ponsys

present subjunctive

1s	ponniv
2s	ponni
3s	ponnyo
1p	ponnyn
2p	ponnyowgh
3p	ponnyons
0	ponnyer

imperfect subjunctive

1s	ponnyen
2s	ponnyes
3s	ponnya
1p	ponnyen
2p	ponnyewgh
3p	ponnyens
0	ponnys

imperative

1s	-
2s	poon
3s	ponyes
1p	ponyn
2p	ponyewgh
3p	ponyens
0	-

prena – *to buy*

present

1s	prenav
2s	prenydh
3s	pren
1p	prenyn
2p	prenowgh
3p	prenons
0	prenir

preterite

1s	prenis
2s	prensys
3s	prenas
1p	prensyn
2p	prensowgh
3p	prensons
0	prenas

imperfect

1s	prenen
2s	prenes
3s	prena
1p	prenen
2p	prenewgh
3p	prenens
0	prenys

pluperfect

1s	prensen
2s	prenses
3s	prensa
1p	prensen
2p	prensewgh
3p	prensens
0	prensys

present subjunctive

1s	prenniv
2s	prenni
3s	prenno
1p	prennyn
2p	prennowgh
3p	prennons
0	prenner

imperfect subjunctive

1s	prennen
2s	prennes
3s	prenna
1p	prennen
2p	prennewgh
3p	prennens
0	prennys

imperative

1s	-
2s	pren
3s	prenes
1p	prenyn
2p	prenewgh
3p	prenens
0	-

tybi – *to think*

past participle: tybys

present

1s	**tybav**
2s	**tybydh**
3s	**tyb**
1p	**tybyn**
2p	**tybowgh**
3p	**tybons**
0	**tybir**

present subjunctive

1s	**typpiv**
2s	**typpi**
3s	**typpo**
1p	**typpyn**
2p	**typpowgh**
3p	**typpons**
0	**typper**

preterite

1s	**tybis**
2s	**tybsys**
3s	**tybis**
1p	**tybsyn**
2p	**tybsowgh**
3p	**tybsons**
0	**tybis**

imperfect subjunctive

1s	**typpen**
2s	**typpes**
3s	**typpa**
1p	**typpen**
2p	**typpewgh**
3p	**typpens**
0	**typpys**

imperfect

1s	**tybyn**
2s	**tybys**
3s	**tybi**
1p	**tybyn**
2p	**tybewgh**
3p	**tybens**
0	**tybys**

imperative

1s	-
2s	**tyb**
3s	**tybes**
1p	**tybyn**
2p	**tybewgh**
3p	**tybens**
0	-

pluperfect

1s	**tybsen**
2s	**tybses**
3s	**tybsa**
1p	**tybsen**
2p	**tybsewgh**
3p	**tybsens**
0	**tybsys**

y'm beus – *to have*

present

1s	y'm beus
2s	y'th eus
3sm	y'n jeves
3sf	y's teves

1p	y'gan beus
2p	y'gas beus
3p	y's teves

preterite

1s	y'm beu
2s	y'feu
3sm	y'n jeva
3sf	y's teva

1p	y'gan beu
2p	y'gas beu
3p	y's teva

imperfect

1s	y'm bo
2s	y'th o
3sm	y'n jevo
3sf	y's tevo

1p	y'gan bo
2p	y'gas bo
3p	y's tevo

pluperfect

1s	y'm bia
2s	y'fia
3sm	y'n jevia
3sf	y's tevia

1p	y'gan bia
2p	y'gas bia
3p	y's tevia

present subjunctive

1s	y'm bo
2s	y'fo
3sm	y'n jeffo
3sf	y's teffo

1p	y'gan bo
2p	y'gas bo
3p	y's teffo

imperfect subjunctive

1s	y'm be
2s	y'fe
3sm	y'n jeffa
3sf	y's teffa

1p	y'gan be
2p	y'gas be
3p	y's teffa

future

1s	y'm bydh
2s	y'fydh
3sm	y'n jevydh
3sf	y's tevydh

1p	y'gan bydh
2p	y'gas bydh
3p	y's tevydh

habitual imperfect

1s	y'm bedha
2s	y'fedha
3sm	y'n jevedha
3sf	y's tevedha

1p	y'gan bedha
2p	y'gas bedha
3p	y's tevedha

Numbers

Traditional numbers

1	onan; unn[c]	28	eth warn ugens
2	dew^2 *m*; diw^2 *f*	29	naw warn ugens
3	tri^3 *m*; teyr^3 *f*	30	deg warn ugens
4	peswar *m*; peder *f*	31	unnek warn ugens
5	pymp	32	dewdhek warn ugens
6	hwegh	33	tredhek warn ugens
7	seyth	34	peswardhek warn ugens
8	eth	35	pymthek warn ugens
9	naw	36	hwetek warn ugens
10	deg	37	seytek warn ugens
11	unnek	38	etek warn ugens
12	dewdhek	39	nownsek warn ugens
13	tredhek	40	dew ugens; dewgens
14	peswardhek	41	onan ha dew ugens
15	pymthek	42	dew ha dew ugens
16	hwetek	43	tri ha dew ugens
17	seytek	44	peswar ha dew ugens
18	etek	45	pymp ha dew ugens
19	nownsek	46	hwegh ha dew ugens
20	ugens	47	seyth ha dew ugens
21	onan warn ugens	48	eth ha dew ugens
22	dew warn ugens	49	naw ha dew ugens
23	tri warn ugens	50	deg ha dew ugens; hanterkans
24	peswar warn ugens	51	unnek ha dew ugens
25	pymp warn ugens	52	dewdhek ha dew ugens
26	hwegh warn ugens	53	tredhek ha dew ugens
27	seyth warn ugens		

---

[c]**onan** is used when counting; **unn** is used when specifying the number of items. **unn** causes the same mutations as **an**.

54	peswardhek ha dew ugens	89	naw ha peswar ugens
55	pymthek ha dew ugens	90	deg ha peswar ugens
56	hwetek ha dew ugens	91	unnek ha peswar ugens
57	seytek ha dew ugens	92	dewdhek ha peswar ugens
58	etek ha dew ugens	93	tredhek ha peswar ugens
59	nownsek ha dew ugens	94	peswardhek ha peswar ugens
60	tri ugens		
61	onan ha tri ugens	95	pymthek ha peswar ugens
62	dew ha tri ugens	96	hwetek ha peswar ugens
63	tri ha tri ugens	97	seytek ha peswar ugens
64	peswar ha tri ugens	98	etek ha peswar ugens
65	pymp ha tri ugens	99	nownsek ha peswar ugens
66	hwegh ha tri ugens	100	kans
67	seyth ha tri ugens	115	kans ha pymthek
68	eth ha tri ugens	177	kans, seytek ha tri ugens
69	naw ha tri ugens	200	dew kans[d]
70	deg ha tri ugens	300	tri hans
71	unnek ha tri ugens	400	peswar kans
72	dewdhek ha tri ugens	500	pymp kans
73	tredhek ha tri ugens	1 000	mil^2
74	peswardhek ha tri ugens	1 293	mil, dew kans, tredhek ha peswar ugens
75	pymthek ha tri ugens		
76	hwetek ha tri ugens	2 000	dew vil
77	seytek ha tri ugens	3 000	tri mil
78	etek ha tri ugens	4 000	peswar mil
79	nownsek ha tri ugens	5 000	pymp mil
80	peswar ugens	10 000	deg mil
81	onan ha peswar ugens	100 000	kans mil
82	dew ha peswar ugens	1 000 000	milvil
83	tri ha peswar ugens	10 000 000	deg milvil
84	peswar ha peswar ugens	100 000 000	kans milvil
85	pymp ha peswar ugens	1 000 000 000	bilvil
86	hwegh ha peswar ugens	10 000 000 000	deg bilvil
87	seyth ha peswar ugens	100 000 000 000	kans bilvil
88	eth ha peswar ugens	1 000 000 000 000	trilvil

[d]Note that **dew** does not mutate **kans** to prevent confusion with **dewgens** (40)

Decimal numbers

In traditional Cornish, numbers and parts of numbers less than 100 were counted using a base-20 (*vigesimal*) system, as described in the preceding pages. In the Cornish texts there are very few large numbers, and those that are mentioned are round multiples of a thousand or a million, which merely implies a non-specific large number. Nowhere do we find a precise large number such as 6,421,793, and until very recently such numbers would have never occurred during most people's daily lives. In modern times, however, people regularly deal in large figures, for example when buying a car or a house, and children use maths at school in a way which has outpaced the evolution of the traditional Cornish counting system. In modern Welsh a decimal system is now widely used which makes working with large numbers and mathematical and scientific calculations much easier, and there is increasing support for a similar system for Cornish.

On the following pages the previous selection of numbers (pp. 25-26) is repeated using a modern decimal counting system designed to make numbers easier to construct and to work with. In this system, when numbers 11-19 stand alone, these are the same as the traditional system. When they are the final part of a larger number such as 4,319, they are broken down as **unn deg unn**, **unn deg dew**, **unn deg tri** etc., as shown in the examples. Only the masculine versions of 2, 3 and 4 are used for counting, but duals of feminine nouns retain **diw**[2]. In conversational Cornish, as in spoken Welsh, larger numbers such as years can be simplified even more by just saying each digit in turn, with 2018 becoming **dew, mann, onan, eth**.

When specifying the number of an item, the number is followed by **a**[2] and the plural noun, e.g. *324 dogs*: **tri hans, dew dheg peswar a geun**. Below are example numbers comparing the old and new systems:

893:
   Trad.:   **eth kans, tredhek ha peswar ugens**
   Dec.:   **eth kans, naw deg tri**
25,377:
   Trad.:   **pymp mil warn ugens, tri hans, seytek ha tri ugens**
   Dec.:   **dew dheg pymp a vilyow, tri hans, seyth deg seyth**

1	onan; unn	38	tri deg eth
2	dew^2	39	tri deg naw
3	tri^3	40	peswar deg
4	peswar	41	peswar deg onan
5	pymp	42	peswar deg dew
6	hwegh	43	peswar deg tri
7	seyth	44	peswar deg peswar
8	eth	45	peswar deg pymp
9	naw	46	peswar deg hwegh
10	deg	47	peswar deg seyth
11	unnek	48	peswar deg eth
12	dewdhek	49	peswar deg naw
13	tredhek	50	pymp deg
14	peswardhek	51	pymp deg onan
15	pymthek	52	pymp deg dew
16	hwetek	53	pymp deg tri
17	seytek	54	pymp deg peswar
18	etek	55	pymp deg pymp
19	nownsek	56	pymp deg hwegh
20	dew dheg	57	pymp deg seyth
21	dew dheg onan	58	pymp deg eth
22	dew dheg dew	59	pymp deg naw
23	dew dheg tri	60	hwegh deg
24	dew dheg peswar	61	hwegh deg onan
25	dew dheg pymp	62	hwegh deg dew
26	dew dheg hwegh	63	hwegh deg tri
27	dew dheg seyth	64	hwegh deg peswar
28	dew dheg eth	65	hwegh deg pymp
29	dew dheg naw	66	hwegh deg hwegh
30	tri deg	67	hwegh deg seyth
31	tri deg onan	68	hwegh deg eth
32	tri deg dew	69	hwegh deg naw
33	tri deg tri	70	seyth deg
34	tri deg peswar	71	seyth deg onan
35	tri deg pymp	72	seyth deg dew
36	tri deg hwegh	73	seyth deg tri
37	tri deg seyth	74	seyth deg peswar

75	seyth deg pymp	99	naw deg naw
76	seyth deg hwegh	100	kans
77	seyth deg seyth	115	kans, unn deg pymp
78	seyth deg eth	177	kans, seyth deg seyth
79	seyth deg naw	200	dew kans[e]
80	eth deg	300	tri hans
81	eth deg onan	400	peswar kans
82	eth deg dew	500	pymp kans
83	eth deg tri	1 000	mil^2
84	eth deg peswar	1 293	mil, dew kans, naw deg tri
85	eth deg pymp		
86	eth deg hwegh	2 000	dew vil
87	eth deg seyth	3 000	tri mil
88	eth deg eth	4 000	peswar mil
89	eth deg naw	5 000	pymp mil
90	naw deg	10 000	deg mil
91	naw deg onan	100 000	kans mil
92	naw deg dew	1 000 000	milvil
93	naw deg tri	10 000 000	deg milvil
94	naw deg peswar	100 000 000	kans milvil
95	naw deg pymp	1 000 000 000	bilvil
96	naw deg hwegh	10 000 000 000	deg bilvil
97	naw deg seyth	100 000 000 000	kans bilvil
98	naw deg eth	1 000 000 000 000	trilvil

---

[e]The traditional exception of not mutating **kans** after **dew** is maintained to prevent **dew gans onan** being mistaken for the addition $2 + 1$. There is no confusion in this system with 40, which is **peswar deg**.

Prefixes and suffixes

In Cornish a wide selection of prefixes and suffixes can be added to words to change their meaning in different ways, for example to strengthen or weaken or reverse the meaning, or to produce a noun from an adjective, or an adjective from a noun. A selection of the more common prefixes and suffixes are gathered below. Readers are encouraged to use them when coining new words of their own.

Note that some prefixes cause different types of mutation, and some cause mutations irregularly; this information can be found detailed in *A Grammar of Modern Cornish* by Wella Brown, 3rd ed. §§268-273.

In the lists which follow, the Cornish prefixes and suffixes are shown with their English equivalents and example words containing them.

Prefixes

Prefix	*Meaning(s)*	Example
an-	*un-* *non-*	**ankrysadow**: *unbelievable* **anweladow**: *invisible*
ar- **dar-**	*fore-* *pre-*	**arvor**: *coast* **dargan**: *forecast*
das-	*re-*	**dasskrifa**: *rewrite*

di-	*not-* *without-*	**diannedh**: *uninhabited* **dilagha**: *lawless*

dis-	*un-*	**diswrys**: *done for; undone; unmade*

drog- **drok-**	*bad* *mis-*	**drogbrederys**: *malicious* **droktemprys**: *bad-tempered*

go-	*diminutive*	**gobrena**: *hire; rent*

gor-	*over-* *super-*	**gordhybri**: *overeat* **gorvarghas**: *supermarket*

gorth-	*anti-*	**gorthpryv**: *insecticide*

gour- **gor-**	*male-*	**gorvleydh**: *werewolf*

hanter-	*half-* *semi-*	**hanter-dydh**: *midday* **hanterkylgh**: *semicircle*

he-	*-able*	**hedor**: *breakable; fragile.* See suffix **-adow**

is-	*sub-* *under-*	**isetholans**: *by-election* **islavrek**: *underpants; knickers*

kamm-	*wrong* *bent*	**kammwrians**: *error* **kammneves**: *rainbow*

ke-	*con-* *com-*	**keheveli**: *compare* **kehevelus**: *comparative*

ken-	*co-; con-* *mutual*	**kendegi**: *conduct* (*electricity*) **kentrevek**: *neighbour*

kes-	*co-* *inter-* *together, joint*	**kesordenans**: *coordination* **kesrosweyth**: *internet* **keskerdh**: *march*

kev-	*co-* *together*	**kevals**: *joint* (*articulation*) **kevro**: *contribution*

korr-	*micro-* *mini-*	**korrbryv**: *microbe* **korrdon**: *microwave*

kowl- **kol-**	*do completely*	**kowlleski**: *incinerate* **kollenwel**: *fill up*

kowr-	*macro-* *mega-*	**kowrvargh**: *camel* **kowrgarow**: *elk*

kyn(s)-	*pre-*	**kynsskrif**: *preface* **kynser**: *apprentice*

les-	*step-*	**lesflogh**: *stepchild*
mann-	*petty*	**mannbluv**: *down (feathers); fluff* **mannvona**: *petty cash*
meur-	*great- major*	**meurgolonnek**: *great-hearted* **meurgerys**: *beloved*
om-	*reflexive*	**omwolghi**: *wash oneself* **omlusek**: *self-adhesive*
penn-	*chief principal*	**pennmenyster**: *prime minister* **pennlinen**: *headline*
rag- rak-	*pre- fore-*	**ragbreder**: *precaution* **rakhanow**: *pronoun*
ter-	*intermittent or feeble action*	**tergoska**: *sleep fitfully*
treus-	*trans-*	**treusplansa**: *transplant*
try-	*triple*	**tryflek**: *threefold; treble; triple* **trymis**: *trimester*
ugh- ughel-	*high; over- up-*	**ughradha**: *upgrade* **ughkarg**: *upload*

un-	*mono-*	**undon**: *monotonous*
	uni-	**unfordh**: *one-way*

yn-	*in-*	**ynkleudhyas**: *inter (bury)*

Suffixes

Suffix	Meaning(s)	Example
-adow	*-able*	**bewbodradow**: *biodegradable* See prefix **he-**
-ans **-yans**	*masc. noun suffix*	**darlesans**: *broadcast* **redyans**: *reading*
-as	*-ful*	**gwedrennas**: *glassful* **platas**: *plateful; serving*
-der **-ter**	*makes masc. noun* *from adj.*	**tewder**: *thickness* **tekter**: *beauty*
-di; -ji; **-ti**	*building*	**jynnji**: *engine house* **arghantti**: *bank*
-edh	*masc. abstract* *noun suffix*	**meuredh**: *majesty*
-ek	*adj. ending* *from noun*	**kussulyek**: *advisory* **gossenek**: *rusty; abounding in rust*
-el; -en; **-yn**	*diminutive*	**porghel**: *young pig* **hwegyn**: *sweet*

-ell	*denotes tools and appliances (fem.)*	**yeynell**: *fridge* **trogentrell**: *screwdriver*
-en	*a single item derived from a collective (fem.)*	**gwedhen**: *tree*
-er **-yer**	*human agent*	**gesyer**: *joker* **skoodhyer**: *supporter; fan*
-es	*female suffix*	**dyskadores**: *female teacher*
-eth	*fem. abstract noun suffix*	**eseleth**: *membership*
-gweyth	*times*	**diwweyth**: *twice*. Takes a feminine number if there is one.
-ieth **-onieth**	*study or science (fem.)*	**dororieth**: *geology* **steronieth**: *astronomy*
-ik	*diminutive*	**fleghik**: *small child*. **-ik** sometimes has a double plural **fleghesigow**, *small children*
-neth	*makes a fem. noun from adj.*	**yowynkneth**: *youth*

-us	*-ous* *adj. ending*	**hwarthus**: *humorous*
-va	*a place for* *something (fem.)*	**gerva**: *vocabulary* **meythrinva**: *nursery*
-ys	*-ed* *past participle*	**tremenys**: *passed*

Gendered occupations

Different European languages have come to express gender equality in different ways. In English it is increasingly common to use a single word for both genders: the word *actress*, for example, has been largely replaced by *actor*, and *poetess* universally replaced by *poet*. In German, on the other hand, it is considered impolite not to use a feminine version if one exists. Welsh, by contrast, has only a handful of distinct feminine forms. In historic Cornish the situation is less clear because few traditional names for professions and other roles where both sexes performed the same duties have come down to us in both masculine and feminine forms.

In revived Cornish there has been a tendency to create both masculine and feminine versions of all new job descriptions and other roles, and to invent feminine forms for old words where none previously existed. However, the female Grand Bards of Cornwall have taken the title **Bardh Meur** not **Bardhes Veur**, and the only female Archdruid of the Welsh Gorsedd to date took the masculine title *Archdderwydd*.

The language community itself will ultimately decide the future development of Cornish, however in this second edition of *A Learners' Cornish Dictionary*, the editing committee have decided after considerable discussion to remove most of the feminine forms from the main body leaving only those commonly found in exam situations, and to suggest that the remaining masculine/gender neutral forms be used for both sexes. For those who wish to continue to use distinct feminine forms, the table below shows a variety of masculine/gender neutral endings, and how to create the corresponding feminine forms.

Gender-specific word endings with examples

	sing.	plur.	example	plural	*English*
M	**-an**	**-anyon**	**Alban**	**Albanyon**	*Scot*
F	*-anes*	*-anesow*	*Albanes*	*Albanesow*	
M	**-ek**	**-ogyon**	**benfisek**	**benfisogyon**	*beneficiary*
F	*-oges*	*-ogesow*	*benfisoges*	*benfisogesow*	
M	**-er**	**-oryon**	**askorrer**	**askorroryon**	*producer*
F	*-eres*	*-eresow*	*askorreres*	*askorerresow*	
M	**-er**	**-oryon**	**brager**	**bragoryon**	*brewer*
F	*-ores*	*-oresow*	*bragores*	*bragoresow*	
M	**-ner**	**-oryon**	**difenner**	**difenoryon**	*defendant*
F	*-ores*	*-oresow*	*difenores*	*difenoresow*	
M	**-or**	**-oryon**	**hwedhlor**	**hwedhloryon**	*narrator*
F	*-ores*	*-oresow*	*hwedhlores*	*hwedhloresow*	
M	**-rer**	**-roryon**	**hwithrer**	**hwithroryon**	*inspector*
F	*-ores*	*-oresow*	*hwithrores*	*hwithroresow*	
M	**-ser**	**-soryon**	**arghanser**	**arghansoryon**	*banker*
F	*-sores*	*-soresow*	*arghansores*	*arghansoresow*	
M	**-sik**	**-sigyon**	**arvethesik**	**arvethesiges**	*employee*
F	*-siges*	*-sigesow*	*arvethesigyon*	*arvethesigesow*	
M	**-yas**	**-ysi**	**arvreusyas**	**arvreusysi**	*critic*
F	*-yades*	*-yadesow*	*arvreusyades*	*arvreusyadesow*	
M	**-ydh**	**-ydhyon**	**awenydh**	**awenydhyon**	*genius*
F	*-ydhes*	*-ydhesow*	*awenydhes*	*awenydhesow*	
M	**-yer**	**-yers**	**beggyer**	**beggyers**	*beggar*
F	*-yores*	*-yoresow*	*beggyores*	*beggyoresow*	
M	**-yer**	**-yoryon**	**iskaderyer**	**iskaderyoryon**	*vice-chair*
F	*-yores*	*-yoresow*	*iskaderyores*	*iskaderyoresow*	

Idiomatic phrases

This new section for the second edition is intended to help learners use more idiomatic Cornish from the outset and to rely less on direct translations from English. Some are traditional expressions and some have become common since the revival, but all are examples of good Living Cornish and may be used with confidence. Please note that the idioms below are not always translated word-for-word from Cornish, but rather give an equivalent meaning in English.

Readers seeking a detailed explanation of the grammar found in this section and/or word-for-word direct translations of idioms should consult their teacher or an appropriate work from the list of resources.

Idioms for beginners:

Some of these idioms have plural forms. If used to address more than one person the second form (following the forward slash) should be used:

Hello!	Dydh da!
Please.	Mar pleg.
Thanks.	Meur ras.
Thank you.	Meur ras dhis. / Meur ras dhywgh.
Thank you very much.	Meur ras dhis yn feur. / Meur ras dhywgh yn feur.
Excuse me.	Gav dhymm. / Gevewgh dhymm.
Slower, please!	Lenta, mar pleg!
Again, please!	Arta, mar pleg!
I don't know.	Ny wonn.
I don't understand.	Ny wonn konvedhes.
No matter!	Na fors!
It doesn't matter!	Ny vern!
No problem!	Kudyn vyth!
Yn hwir?	Really?
Gwir!	Really!
Don't worry!	Na vydh prederus! / Na vedhewgh prederus!
Good idea!	Tybyans da!
Of course!	Heb mar!
Great!	Splann!
Brilliant!	Bryntin!
Goodbye!	Dha weles! / Agas gweles!
Goodbye!	Duw genes! / Duw genowgh!

Idioms for first and second grade:

Using **ass yw**…

Isn't the weather great!
Isn't the room cold tonight!
Isn't he happy now!

Ass yw an gewer splann!
Ass yw yeyn an stevel haneth!
Ass yw ev lowen lemmyn!

Using **da yw**…/**gwell yw**… etc.:

Do you like bananas?
I like bananas.
I prefer oranges.
Don't you like apples?
I don't like apples.
I hate strawberries.
I must eat.
You'd better eat now, then!

Yw da genes bananas?
Da yw genev bananas.
Gwell yw genev owravalow.
A nyns yw da genes avalow?
Nyns yw da genev avalow.
Kas yw genev sevi.
Res yw dhymm dybri.
Gwell yw dhis dybri lemmyn, ytho!

43

Using **yma ...dhe** and **yma ...gans**:

I am hungry.	Yma nown dhymm.
I am very thirsty.	Yma seghes bras dhymm.
I have a dog.	Yma ki dhymm.
I have a dog with me.	Yma ki genev.
I have homework.	Yma ober tre dhymm.
I have my homework with me.	Yma ow ober tre genev.

Using **dell...**

That's not true, I think.	Nyns yw henna gwir, dell brederav.
That's the way, I think.	Honn yw an fordh, dell dybav.
I'm wrong, it seems.	Kamm ov, dell hevel.
You're not wrong, it seems to me.	Nyns os ta kamm, dell hevel dhymm.
He's dead, I believe.	Marow yw ev, dell grysav.
But she'll be okay, they hope.	Mes da lowr vydh hi, dell waytyons.

44

Using **nans yw**...

I saw him a week ago.
I went there three years ago.

My a wrug y weles nans yw seythen.
My eth ena nans yw teyr bledhen.

Using **yma...war:**

I have a cold.
He has a headache.
She had a sore throat.

Yma anwos warnav.
Yma drog penn warnodho.
Yth esa briansen glav warnedhi.

Using **gwynn ...bys:**

I passed, fortunately for me!
You were fortunate indeed!

My a wrug seweni, gwynn ow bys!
Gwynn dha vys yn tevri!

45

A selection of idioms beyond second grade:

Using **ha my** …

As I was going to St Ives …
As they were crossing the road …
When I was a girl, I lived in Camborne.
While I was there I saw my uncle.

Ha my ow mos dhe Borthia …
Hag i ow treusi an fordh …
Ha my mowes, trigys en vy yn Kammbronn.
Ha my ena, y hwelis ow ewnter.

Using some traditional similies:

The night was as black as coal.
The witch was as old as the mountains.
The roses were as white as snow.
His shoes were as expensive as saffron.

An nos o mar dhu avel glow.
Mar goth avel an menydhyow o an wragh.
Mar wynn avel ergh o an rosennow.
Y eskisyow o mar ger avel safran.

Using **namna²(g)** …

I nearly forgot!
It was nearly broken!
It's nearly finished now!

Namna ankevis vy!
Namna veu terrys!
Namnag yw gorfennys lemmyn!

46

Using **yma … dhe … a …**

I need to go to the doctor's surgery.	**Yma edhom dhymm a vos dhe'n vedhegva.**
I'd like [desire] to stop for a while.	**Yma hwans dhymm a hedhi pols.**
I long for home.	**Yma hirneth dhymm a dre.**
I fancy some crisps.	**Yma si dhymm a gresigow.**
I've an idea [notion] to go to Truro tomorrow.	**Yma sians dhymm a vos dhe Druru a-vorow.**
I'm keen to go with her.	**Yma mall dhymm a vos gensi.**
I've a craving for a pasty and a pint.	**Yma ewl dhymm a basti ha pinta.**
I regret going.	**Yma edrek dhymm a vos.**
I regret that I didn't go.	**Yma edrek dhymm na wrug vy mos.**

Using **skant ny …**

I can hardly believe it!	**Skant ny'n krysav!**
I can hardly believe he did it!	**Skant ny grysav ev dh'y wul!**
She can hardly wait!	**Skant ny yll hi gortos!**
He could hardly wait to leave.	**Skant ny ylli cv gortos diberth.**

A final miscellany:

I have a mind like a sieve.	Yma ympynnyon dhymm avel rider.
According to the forecast, it'll be dry today.	*Hervydh an dhargan* y fydh sygh hedhyw.
It's different *these days*.	Ken yw y'n jydh hedhyw.
It'll be *a week today*.	Y fydh an jydh ma war seythen.
He did it *straight away*.	Ev a'n gwrug kettooth h'an ger.
He worked *ceaselessly*.	Ev a oberi mo ha myttin.
To my mind …	Orth ow brys vy …
In my opinion …	Dhe'm breus vy …
Excuse me, would you *kindly* help me, *please?*	Gav dhymm, a alles ow gweres, *my a'th pys?*
Would you make my coffee, *pretty please?*	A alles pareusi ow hoffi, *dell y'm kyrri?*
Whatever!	Pypynag!
I'll do it *as fast as I can.*	My a'n gwra skaffa gylliv.
There's nothing like it *anywhere.*	Nyns eus travyth a'y bar yn tir hag yn mor.
I *promised* I'd do it.	*Yn-dann ambos* yth esen vy dh'y wul.
She did it *secretly*.	Hi a'n gwrug yn-dann gel.
It was *locked up safely*.	*Yn-dann naw alhwedh* yth esa.
To my knowledge it's okay to do that.	*A'm godhvos* y vos da lowr dhe wul henna.
I'll do it *to the best of my ability*.	My a'n gwra dhe'm gallos.
Tell me *what happened*.	Lavar dhymm an pyth a hwarva.

48

Example sentences

The following pages contain a selection of sentences constructed using several common tenses of Cornish encountered during the first and second grades of study, with some examples of more advanced grammar included for comparison. Most are 'nominal' sentences, which means that the person (**my**/**ty** etc.) can be substituted without changing the following verbal form. Further, most of the early examples also use auxiliary verbs for simplicity.

In this second edition a wide selection of example questions phrased in Cornish is given for the use of students as they advance through the grades of study. Please note that the example sentences and questions are not always word-for-word translations of the English, but are examples of good Living Cornish which learners may use and adapt for their own purposes.

Readers seeking a detailed explanation of the grammar found in this section and/or word-for-word direct translations of the examples should consult their teacher or an appropriate work from the list of resources.

Using **mynnes**:

I want/intend to do that straight away. — My a vynn gul henna a-dhistowgh.
I wanted/intended to do that but it was too late. — My a vynnas gul henna mes re dhiwedhes o.
I've wanted to do that for ages. — My re vynnas gul henna dres termyn hir.
I used to want to do that but not any more. — My a vynna gul henna mes namoy.
I'd wanted to do that once. — My re vynsa gul henna unweyth.
I want/intend to do that next week. — My a vynn gul henna seythen a dheu.

Using **gul**:

I see John every Saturday. — My a wra gweles Yowan pub dy' Sadorn.
I saw John last Saturday. — My a wrug gweles Yowan dy' Sadorn usi passyes.
I have seen John every day this week. — My re wrug gweles Yowan pub dydh an seythen ma.
I used to see John every Saturday. — My a wre gweles Yowan pub dy' Sadorn.
I had seen John in November. — My re wrussa gweles Yowan mis Du.
I will see John next weekend. — My a wra gweles Yowan an bennseythen a dheu.

I work in Truro. — My a wra oberi yn Truru.
I worked in Truro once last Christmas. — My a wrug oberi yn Truru unweyth Nadelik usi passyes.
I have worked in Truro from time to time. — My re wrug oberi yn Truru a dermyn dhe dermyn.
I used to work in Truro for a while. — My a wre oberi yn Truru pols.
I had worked in Truro at that time. — My re wrussa oberi yn Truru dhe'n prys na.
I will work in Truro next year. — My a wra oberi yn Truru nessa bledhen.

Using **gallos**, and differentiating beween some English meanings of *should* and *could*:

I can do that if you want.	**My a yll gul henna mar mynnydh.**
I was able to do that for him.	**My a allas gul henna ragdho.**
I used to be able to do that when I was young.	**My a ylli gul henna pan en vy yowynk.**
I could do that at one time.	**My a ylli gul henna yn termyn eus passyes.**
I could do that if I wanted.	**My a allsa gul henna mar mynnen vy.**
He could do that if he wanted.	**Ev a allsa gul henna mar mynna ev.**

(Note that in the above sentences the verb following the conjunctions *when* and *if* must be conjugated for person, and the correct declension must be used following the preposition **rag**.)

I should (ought to) do that soon.	**Y tegodh dhymm gul henna a verr spys.**
I should (it would benefit me to) do that now.	**Y tal dhymm gul henna lemmyn.**

(Note that in the above two sentences the verb differs depending on the English meaning of the word *should*.)

Using **mos** both with the auxiliary verb **gul** and as a main verb, shown in pairs. Note that the unpaired sentences require the long form of **bos**, inflected for person, prior to the use of **ow mos** meaning *going*:

I go to the town every Thursday.
I go to the town every Thursday.

My a wra mos dhe'n dre pub dy' Yow.
My a dhe'n dre pub dy' Yow.

I am going to the town now.

Yth esov vy ow mos dhe'n dre lemmyn.

I was going to the town but the train was late.

Yth esen vy ow mos dhe'n dre mes diwedhes veu an tren.

I went to the town last Thursday.
I went to the town last Thursday.

My a wrug mos dhe'n dre dy' Yow usi passyes.
My eth dhe'n dre dy' Yow usi passyes.

I have been to the town this week.
I have been to the town this week.

My re wrug mos dhe'n dre an seythen ma.
My res eth dhe'n dre an seythen ma.

I used to go to the town every Thursday.
I used to go to the town every Thursday.

My a wre mos dhe'n dre pub dy' Yow.
My e dhe'n dre pub dy' Yow. (*Rarely used.*)

I had been to the town with Morwenna.
I had been to the town with Morwenna.

My re wrussa mos dhe'n dre gans Morwenna.
My re alsa dhe'n dre gans Morwenna. (*Rarely used.*)

I will be in the town next Thursday.

My a vydh y'n dre dy' Yow a dheu.

I will go to the town every Thurday in future.
I will go to the town every Thursday in future.

My a wra mos dhe'n dre pub dy' Yow y'n termyn a dheu.
My a dhe'n dre pub dy' Yow y'n termyn a dheu.

52

Using some parts of **bos** in nominal sentences:

I am always busy these days.	**My yw bysi pub prys y'n jydh hedhyw.**
I was angry all day yesterday.	**My o serrys dres oll an jydh de.**
I have been happy this week.	**My re beu lowen dres an seythen ma.**
I had been sad before winter came.	**My re bia trist kyns an gwav dhe dhos.**
I will be excited when spring comes.	**My a vydh yntanys pan dheu an gwenton.**

(Note the infinitive construction following **kyns** and that **pan** must be followed by a verb conjugated for person.)

That's great!	**Ass yw henna splann!**
That would be great!	**Henna a via splann!**
I would really like that!	**Henna a via pur dha genev vy!** (*Inflect* **gans** *for person.*)

Using imperatives, called out to one/more than one person:

Come in!	Deus/dewgh a-ji!
Look out!/Be careful!	Bydh/bedhewgh war!
Look at that!	Mir/mirewgh orth henna!
Go away!	Ke/kewgh dhe-ves!
Get going!/Start now!	Dallath/dallethewgh lemmyn!
Send me an email soon!	Danvon/danvenewgh dhymm e-bost a verr spys!
Stand up!	Sav/sevewgh yn-bann!
Sit down!	Esedh!/Esedhewgh!
Shut the door, please!	Dege an daras, mar pleg!
Come back soon!	Dehwel/dehwelewgh yn skon!
Show me that right now!	Diskwa/diskwedhewgh dhymm henna a-dhistowgh!
Eat your dinner!	Deber dha ginnyow!/Debrewgh agas kinnyow!
Drink your coffee!	Yv dha goffi!/Evewgh agas koffi!
Hurry up!	Fisten!/Fistenewgh!

Using imperatives, always in the plural:

Let's go!	Deun yn-rag!
Let's go!	Gwren ni mos!

Don't do that!
Wait a minute!
Listen to me, please!
Help me!
Stop!
Open the window, please!
Sing louder!
Speak more quietly, please!
Take care!
Listen!
Sleep well!
One, two, three, jump!
Boil the kettle, please!
Give me that!
Be quiet!
Pass me that, please!

Na wra/wrewgh henna!
Gorta/gortewgh pols!
Goslow/goslowewgh orthiv, mar pleg!
Gweres/gweresewgh vy!
Hedh!/Hedhewgh!
Ygor an fenester, mar pleg!
Kan/kenewgh ughella!
Kows/kewsewgh isella, mar pleg!
Kemmer/kemerewgh with!
Klew!/Klewewgh!
Kosk/koskewgh yn ta!
Onan, dew, tri, lamm/lemmewgh!
Gorr/gorrewgh an galter dhe vryjyon, mar pleg!
Ro/rewgh dhymm henna!
Taw/tewewgh taves!
Ystyn/ystynewgh dhymm henna, mar pleg!

Asking questions:

Using **fatel** and **fatla**:

How are you?
How is Maria?
How were your mother and father?
How were they when you saw them?
What's the weather like today?
What's the pub like?
What's her new house like?

Fatla genes?
Fatla gans Maria? / Fatel yw Maria?
Fatel o dha vamm ha dha das?
Fatel ens pan y's gwelsys?
Fatel yw an gewer hedhyw?
Fatel yw an diwotti?
Fatel yw hy chi nowydh?

Using **pandra**:

What do you want?
What do you want to drink?
What would you like to drink?
What would you like to eat tonight?
What shall we do tomorrow?

Pandr'a vynnydh? / Pandr'a vyn'ta?
Pandr'a vyn'ta dhe eva?
Pandr'a garses eva?
Pandr'a garses dybri haneth?
Pandr'a wren ni a-vorow?

Using **piw**:

Who are you?   Piw os ta?
Who is she/he?   Piw yw hi/ev?
Who did that?   Piw a wrug henna?
Who wrote this book?   Piw a skrifas an lyver ma?
By whom was this book written?   Gans piw y feu skrifys an lyver ma?

Using **pes**:

How many miles is it from here to Penzance?   Pes mildir alemma dhe Bennsans?
How many days will you stay with him?   Pes dydh y hwre'ta triga ganso?

Using **p'eur** and **py eur**. Note the difference between usages:

What time is it?   Py eur yw hi?
What time was it when we arrived?   Py eur o hi pan dheuthen?
What time will it be when we leave?   Py eur fydh hi pan dhiberthyn?
When will the meeting be?   P'eur fydh an kuntelles?
When did we arrive?   P'eur hwrussen ni dos?
When will we leave?   P'eur hwren diberth?

Using **ple**:

Where are you?
Where are they?
Where is Tamsin?
Where is the post box?
Where are the gent's toilets?

Where did I leave my keys?

Ple'th esos ta?
Ple'mons i?
Ple'ma Tamsin?
Ple'ma an gisten bost?
Ple'ma'n privedhyow gwer?
(Note that the contraction of ple'ma and **an** is optional.)
Ple hwrug vy gasa ow alhwedhow?

Using **prag** and **praga**:

Why?
Why not?
Why did you do that?
Why didn't you do it?
Why must we do that?
Why can't I come?
Why didn't you go?
Why is she shouting at him?
Why isn't he shouting at her?

Praga?
Prag na?
Prag y hwruss'ta henna?
Prag na'n gwruss'ta?
Prag yth yw res dhyn gul henna?
Prag na allav dos?
Prag na wrussowgh hwi mos?
Prag yma hi ow karma orto?
Prag nag usi ev ow karma orti?

58

Using **py**:

What cat?	**Py kath?**
What people?	**Py tus?**
Which team is your favourite?	**Py para yw an gwella genes?**
Which one is that?	**Py huni yw henna?**
Which biscuits can the children eat?	**Py tesennow kales a yll an fleghes aga dybri?**
Which ones are they?	**Py re yns?**
How many do you have, please?	**Py lies eus genes, mar pleg?**
What sort of biscuits are they?	**Py par tesennow kales yns?**

Note that **py par** may be interchanged with **py eghen, py kinda** or **py sort.**

What place is that?	**Py tyller yw henna?**

Note that **py tyller** may be interchanged with **py plas.**

What day is Jori's party?	**Py dydh y fydh kevewi Jori?**

Using **pygemmys**:

How many are there?
How many people will be going to Jori's party?
How many went to Jori's party?

Pygemmys eus?
Pygemmys tus a wra mos dhe gevewi Jori?
Pygemmys eth dhe gevewi Jori?

Using **pyneyl**:

Which one do you want?
Which one would you like?
Which one is the shorter?
Which one of his dogs died?

Pyneyl a vynnydh?
Pyneyl a garses?
Pyneyl yw an berra?
Pyneyl a'y geun a verwis?

Using **pyth**:

What?
What was that?
What's the reason for that?
What was the best plan?

Pyth?
Pyth o henna?
Pyth yw an acheson rag henna?
Pyth o an gwella towlen?

Note that question words are often used in English as part of a statement. The same is not true of Cornish:

This is *what* I want.	**Hemm yw *an pyth* a vynnav.**
When grandad was a small boy…	***Pan* o tas gwynn maw byghan…**
It was the one *which* he had chosen himself.	**An huni *hug* a dhewisas ev y honan o.**
That was *why* I did it.	**Henn o *an praga* ma'n gwrug vy.**
	Henn o *an acheson* ma'n gwrug vy.
He's the man *who* did it!	**Ev yw an den *neb* a'n gwrug!**
She found it *where* she'd left it last night.	**Hi a'n kavas y'n *le may* hwrug hi y asa nyhewer.**
That's *how* to do it!	**Honn yw *an fordh* dh'y wul!**
Now I see *what* house that is.	**Lemmyn y hwelav *pana* ji yw henna.**
Tell me *what* things are on special offer here.	**Lavar dhymm *pana* re yw gwerthys omma avel kynnik arbennek.**
What a view!	***Pana* wel!**

But:

I don't know *when* I will see her.	**Ny wonn *p'eur* y's gwelav.**

Resources

This list contains most of the published resources in the Standard Written Form at the time of going to print, in no particular order. Further publications will be available in future.

Note that some of these titles were published before the SWF review in 2014 and may therefore contain slight spelling differences from this volume.

For children

Kronek - An Pyski Kernewek, Wendy Simpson. Kowethas an Yeth Kernewek, 2017. *ISBN 9-781899-342792*

Ple'ma Spot, Eric Hill (1980). Kowethas an Yeth Kernewek, 2012. *ISBN: 978-1-899342-68-6*

Spot ha'y Lyver Bras a Gynsa Geryow, Eric Hill (1988). Kowethas an Yeth Kernewek, 2014. *ISBN: 978-1-899342-71-6*

Topsy ha Tim a wra kampya, Jean and Gareth Adamson (2007). Kowethas an Yeth Kernewek, 2013. *ISBN: 978-1-899342-74-7*

Topsy ha Tim ha'n Kevywi Penn-bloodh, Jean and Gareth Adamson (1995). Kowethas an Yeth Kernewek, 2013. *ISBN: 978-1-899342-72-3*

Topsy ha Tim war an Bargen-Tir, Jean and Gareth Adamson (1995). Kowethas an Yeth Kernewek, 2013. *ISBN: 978-1-899342-73-0*

Kanow Flehes, B. Carne et al. Book and CD. Kowethas an Yeth Kernewek, 2009. *ISBN: 978-1-899342-60-0*

First Thousand Words, Graham Sandercock. Kowethas an Yeth Kernewek, 2013. *ISBN: 978-1-908965-06-6*

Keur Kernewek, booklet of songs and CD for pre-school children. Movyans Skolyow Meythrin, 2012.

Steren an Kolyn Kernow, Ann Jenkin. Bilingual. Noonvares Press, 2008. *ISBN: 978-0-9524601-7-6*

Stories

Briallen ha'n Alyon, Steve Harris. Bilingual. Ors Sempel, 2014. *ISBN: 978-0-9930764-0-4*

Hwedhlow a Flogholeth ha Yowynkneth, h.e., John Prowse. Bilingual. Lyvrow Avalennek, 2016. *ISBN: 978-1-326-52675-7*

Hwedhlow Nowydh ha Koth, John Page. Kesva an Taves Kernewek, 2012. *ISBN: 978-1-908965-00-4*

Keskowsow Istorek ha Keskowsow, John Parker. Kowethas an Yeth Kernewek, 2009. *ISBN: 978-1-899342-75-4*

Tri yw Niver Hudel: An Kelegel, Ray Clemens. Kowethas an Yeth Kernewek, 2018. *ISBN 978-1-899342-80-8*

Reference books

Cornish Grammar for Beginners, John Page. Kesva an Taves Kernewek, 2010. *ISBN: 978-1-902917-75-7*

Cornish Grammar Intermediate, John Page. Kesva an Taves Kernewek, 2011. *ISBN: 978-1-902917-95-5*

Bora Brav, Polin Prys. Kesva an Taves Kernewek, 2011. *ISBN: 978-1-902917-86-3*

Skeul an Tavas, Ray Chubb. Agan Tavas, 2010. *ISBN: 978-1-901409-13-0*

Other

Cornish-English phrase book: Lyver Lavarow, Pol Hodge. Kesva an Taves Kernewek, 2015. *ISBN: 978-1-899342-76-1*

Scryfer - RV Walling, Ann Trevenen Jenkin and Stephen Gadd. Gorsedh Kernow and Kesva an Taves Kernewek, 2016. *ISBN: 978-1-903668-13-9*

Taves an Tir - The Tongue of the Land. A Resources and Information Pack for Schools and Families, ed. Pat Parry. Activities in English and Cornish. Kowethas an Yeth Kernewek, 2016. *ISBN: 978-1-899342-78-5*

Taves an Tir: Place-Names of Lanivet Parish and its People, ed. Nev Meek. Kesva an Taves Kernewek, 2015. *ISBN: 978-1-908965-16-5*

Taves an Tir: Place-Names of Heamoor, Madron and its People, ed. Nev Meek. Kesva an Taves Kernewek, 2016. *ISBN: 978-1-908965-21-9*

Taves an Tir: Place-Names of Redruth Parish and its People, ed. Nev Meek. Kesva an Taves Kernewek, 2016. *ISBN: 978-1-908965-24-0*

Special note for advanced students

The only comprehensive Cornish grammar currently available is in the Kernewek Kemmyn orthography. Advanced students are advised to study its contents.

A Grammar of Modern Cornish, 3rd ed., Wella Brown. Kesva an Taves Kernewek, 2001. *ISBN: 978-1-902917-00-6*

Abbreviations

The following abbreviations are used with verbs and prepositions:

1s	first person singular	*I*
2s	second person singular	*you*
3s	third person singular	*he/she/it*
3sm	third person singular, masculine	*he/it*
3sf	third person singular, feminine	*she/it*
1p	first person plural	*we*
2p	second person plural	*you*
3p	third person plural	*they*
0	impersonal form of verb	-

The following abbreviations are used throughout the dictionary:

abbrev	abbreviation
adj	adjective
adv	adverb
anat	anatomical
arch	archaic
biol	biology
cnj	conjunction
coll	collective
colloq	colloquial
contr	contraction
eccles	ecclesiastic
excl	exclamation
f	feminine
fig	figurative
idiom	idiomatic phrase
int	interjection
m	masculine

med	medical term
n	noun
n.coll	collective noun
n.dl	dual noun
n.f	feminine noun
n.m	masculine noun
n.pl	plural noun
name	name
num	number
part	particle
pl	plural
poss	possessive
ppt	past participle
prfx	prefix
prn	pronoun
prp	preposition
sffx	suffix
sg	singular
top	toponym
top n.f	feminine toponym
top n.m	masculine toponym
top n.pl	plural toponym
vb	verb

Cornish - English

A

a *int* ah; oh

a² **(1)** *prp* of; from. **a bris** outstanding; renowned. **a vri** famous; prominent; relevant; significant; renowned. *Personal forms: 1s ahanav, 2s ahanas, 3sm anodho, 3sf anedhi, 1p ahanan, 2p ahanowgh, 3p anedha*

a² **(2)** *part* (*vocative particle; sometimes lenites following names*) o

a² **(3)** *part* (*verbal particle; used after the subject or direct object*)

a⁴ *cnj* if. **a pe henna gwir** if that were true

a-ban² *cnj* since

a-barth *prp* in the name of; on behalf of; for the sake of; in favour of. **a-barth a-woles** down below. **a-barth Duw** for God's sake. **a-barth dyghow dhe²** on the right side of. **a-barth kledh dhe²** on the left side of. **a-barth woles dhe²** on the bottom of

abas *n.m* **abasow** abbot

abasel *adj* abbatial

abases *n.f* **abasesow** abbess

abatti *n.m* **abattiow** abbey

abecedari *n.m* **abecedaris** alphabet

abel *adj* able

a-bell *adv* afar. **galow a-bell** *n.m* long-distance call

aber *n.m* **aberyow** river-mouth

a-berth *prp* within. **a-berth yn** within

a-bervedh *adv* indoors; inside. **gorra a-bervedh** *vb* insert

a-bervedh yn *prp* inside

abhorrya *vb* abhorr

a-ble⁵ *adv* whence

a-borpos I *adj* deliberate; intentional **II** *adv* deliberately; intentionally; on purpose; purposely

abostol *n.m* **abesteli** apostle

a-boynt I *adj* punctual **II** *adv* punctually; promptly

abrans *n.m* **abransow**, *dl* **dewabrans** eyebrow

a-brys *adv* early; on time; timely

absolut *adj* absolute

abusya *vb* abuse

acheson *n.m* **achesonys, achesonyow** motive; occasion; reason. **acheson rag skonya** *n.m* objection

a-dal *prp* facing; opposite

adamant *n.m* **adamantys, adamantow** diamond. **shap adamant** *n.m* lozenge

adamantek *adj* adamant

addyans *n.m* **addyansow** addition

aden *n.f* **adenyow** cover

a-denewen *adv* aside; aloof; sidelong. **gorra a-denewen** set aside; reserve

a-der I *adv* rather than **II** *prp* outside; except

a-derdro *adv* all around

a-dermyn *adv* in time; on time

a-dhann² *prp* from beneath; from under. *Personal forms: 1s a-dhannov, 2s a-dhannos, 3sm a-dhanno, 3sf a-dhanni, 1p a-dhannon, 2p a-dhannowgh, 3p a-dhanna*

a-dhedro *adv* round about

a-dhelergh *adv* aft; at the back; behind

a-dhelergh dhe² *prp* at the back of; behind

a-dherag I *adv* in front of **II** *prp* before. *Personal forms: 1s a-dheragov, 2s a-dheragos, 3sm a-dheragdho, 3sf a-dherygdhi, 1p a-dheragon, 2p a-dheragowgh, 3p a-dheragdha*

a-dhesempis *adv* (= **'dhesempis**) at once; forthwith; immediately; instantly

a-dhewis I *adj* optional **II** *adv* optionally

a-dhia² *prp* from; since. **a-dhia ban²** *cnj* since

a-dhistowgh *adv* immediately

a-dhiwedhes I *adj* recent; late **II** *adv* recently; lately

adhves *adj* mature; mellow; ripe

adhvesi *vb* mature; ripen; grow up

adhvetter *n.m* ripeness

a-dhyghow *adv* on the right.
a-dhyghow dhe² to the right of

a-dhyghowbarth *adv* on the south side

adhyskans *n.m* **adhyskansow** education

adhyskansek *adj* educational

adhyski *vb* educate

a-dhywar² *prp* from on, from over, from on top of. *Personal forms: 1s a-dhywarnav, 2s a-dhywarnas, 3sm a-dhywarnodho, 3sf a-dhywarnedhi, 1p a-dhywarnan, 2p a-dhywarnowgh, 3p a-dhywarnedha*

adla *n.m* **adlyon** outcast; outlaw; rogue

-adow *sffx* -able

a-dre *adv* from home

a-dreus *adv* across. **a-dreus dhe²** *prp* across. **kewsel a-dreus** argue; interrupt

a-dro I *adv* about; around **II** *prp* **a-dro dhe²** about; around; concerning; (*of clothing*) on. **an eskisyow a-dro dhe'th treys** the shoes on your feet. **mos a-dro** get about

a-droos *adv* on foot

a-dryv *adv* behind. **a-dryv dhe²** *prp* behind

adverb *n.m* **adverbow** adverb

affirmya *vb* affirm

affordya *vb* afford

affordyadow *adj* affordable

afia *vb* affirm

afina *vb* adorn; beautify; decorate; illuminate; ornament; refine

afinus *adj* decorative; ornamental

afinuster *n.m* **afinusterow** cosmetic; make-up

afinys *adj* refined

Afrika *top n.m* Africa

Afrikan *n.m* **Afrikans** African

afrikan *adj* African

afydhya *vb* assure; confirm

afydhys *adj* accredited

aga³ *poss. adj* their. **aga re** *prn* (*pl*) theirs

agan *poss. adj* our. **Agan Tavas** (*name of organisation*) Our Tongue. **agan honan** *prn* ourselves

agas *poss. adj* your (*pl*). **agas honan** *prn* yourselves

a'gas *contr* (*object*) you (*pl*)

ages *prp* (= **es** (**2**)) than. **moy ages kans** over a hundred. *Personal forms: 1s agesov, 2s agesos, 3sm agesso, 3sf agessi, 1p ageson, 2p agesowgh, 3p agessa*

a-gevres *adj* serial

agh (**1**) *int* oh; fie

agh (**2**) *n.f* **aghow** offspring; race

aghel (**1**) *n.f* **aghlow** axle

aghel (**2**) *adj* racial

aghskrif *n.m* **aghskrifow** pedigree

a-gledh *adv* on the left. **a-gledh dhe²** *prp* to the left of

a-gledhbarth *adv* on the north side

agnostek I *adj* agnostic **II** *n.m* **agnostogyon** agnostic

agorafobia *n.m* agoraphobia (*med*)

a-gynnik *adj* tentative

a-gynsow *adv* recently; a little while ago; lately

ahanan *prn* from us; of us

a-has *adj* severe; stressful

ahwer *n.m* anxiety; trouble. **heb ahwer** readily. **na borth ahwer!** don't worry!

ahwerek *adj* sorrowful

ahwesydh *n.m* **ahwesydhes** lark; skylark

a-hys *adv* along

AIDS *abbrev* AIDS (*med*). **Syndrom Immunodifyk Akwirys** Acquired Immune Deficiency Syndrome

a-is *adv* lower

a-ji *adv* indoors; inside. **a-ji dhe²** *prp* within

akademek I *adj* academic **II** *n.m*
akademogyon academic
akademi *n.m* **akademiow** academy
akont *n.m* **akontys, akontow** account.
akont arghantti *n.m* bank account.
akont arghow *n.m* deposit account.
akont kesres *n.m* current account.
fugya an akontys *vb* cook the books
akontya *vb* account
akontyadow *adj* accountable
akontydh *n.m* **akontydhyon**
accountant
akord *n.m* accord; agreement;
understanding. **yn akord gans**
consistent with
akordus *adj* conciliatory
akordya *vb* accord; agree. **akordya**
gans, akordya orth agree with
akordys *adj* agreed
akrylek I *adj* acrylic **II** *n.m* **akrylogyon**
acrylic
aktivita *n.m* **aktivitys** activity
akwytya *vb* discharge; pay off
akwytyans *n.m* **akwytyansow** receipt
alamand *n.m* **alamandys, alamandow**
almond. **toos alamandys** *n.m*
marzipan
alargh *n.m* **elergh** swan
alarm *n.m* **alarmow** (*warning device*)
alarm. **alarm ladron** *n.m* burglar
alarm. **alarm tan** *n.m* fire alarm
Alban I *n.m* **Albanyon** Scot **II** *top n.m*
Scotland
albanek *adj* Scottish
Albani *top n.f* Albania
Albanian *n.m* **Albanians** Albanian
Albaniek *n.m* Albanian language
albaniek *adj* Albanian
albom *n.m* **albomow** album
alemma *adv* hence; from here. **alemma**
rag from now on. **pell alemma** a
long way from here. **termyn pell**
alemma long ago
a-lemmyn *adv* present
alena *adv* from there

a-lergh *adv* recently; lately
a-les *adv* apart
algi *n.coll* algae
alhwedh *n.m* **alhwedhow** (*lock*) key.
alhwedh korkyn *n.m* corkscrew.
alhwedh know *n.m* spanner; wrench.
ger alhwedh *n.m* keyword. **toll**
alhwedh *n.m* keyhole
alhwedha *vb* lock
alhwedhell *n.f* **alhwedhellow**
keyboard
alhwedhen *n.f* **alhwedhennow**
(*typing*) key
alhwedhor *n.m* **alhwedhoryon**
treasurer
alibi *n.m* **alibis** alibi
alinya *vb* align
alinyans *n.m* **alinyansow** alignment
aljebra *n.m* algebra
alkan *n.m* **alkenyow** metal
alkemi *n.m* alchemy
alkohol *n.m* alcohol
allergedh *n.m* **allergedhow** allergy
allergek *adj* allergic
alligator *n.m* **alligators** alligator
Alman *n.m* **Almanyon** German
Almayn *top n.m* Germany. **Republik**
Keffrysek Almayn *top n.m* Federal
Republic of Germany
Almaynek *n.m* German language
almaynek *adj* German
aloes *n.pl* aloes
alowa *vb* allow; permit
Alpys *top n.pl* Alps
als *n.f* **alsyow** cliff
alten *n.f* **altennow** razor
altrewen *n.f* **altrewenyow** stepmother
altrow *n.m* **altrowyon** stepfather
aluminiom *n.m* (*element*) aluminium
alusen *n.f* **alusenow** alms; charity
aluseneth *n.f* **alusenethow**
(*organisation*) charity
alyon *n.m* **alyons** alien; stranger
a'm (1) *contr* (*object*) me
a'm (2) *contr* of my

amal *n.m* **emlow** border; edge; margin; periphery; side; verge

amalek *adj* marginal; peripheral

amalgam *n.m* **amalgamys** amalgam

amanyn *n.m* **amanynnow** butter

amanynna *vb* butter

amari *n.f* **amaris** cupboard; locker. **amari gweli** *n.f* bedside cabinet

amber *n.m* **ambrys** amber

ambos *n.m* **ambosow** agreement; contract; obligation; pact; promise. **ambos demedhyans** *n.m* engagement

ambosa *vb* promise

ambosys *adj* engaged. **gour ambosys** *n.m* fiancé. **benyn ambosys** *n.f* fiancée

ambulans *n.m* **ambulansys** ambulance

amendya *vb* make right; make amends; revise

amendyans *n.m* **amendyansow** reform. **amendyansow ledan** *n.pl* sweeping reforms

amendys *n.pl* amends. **gul amendys** make amends

Amerika *top n.m* America

Amerikan *n.m* **Amerikanyon** American

amerikanek *adj* American. **pel droos amerikanek** *n.m* American football

amethel *adj* agricultural

amethi *vb* farm

amevys *adj* agitated

amkan *n.m* **amkanow** goal; aim; objective

amkanus *adj* resourceful

amm *n.m* **ammow** kiss

amma *vb* kiss. **amma dhe² nebonan** kiss somebody

ammeth *n.f* agriculture; farming. **ammeth organek** *n.f* organic farming

amnesti *n.m* **amnestis** amnesty

amontya *vb* count. **jynn-amontya** *n.m* computer. **ny amont** it is of no avail

amovya *vb* agitate

amovyans *n.m* **amovyansow** emotion

amser *n.f* **amseryow** tense. **amser a-lemmyn** *n.f* present tense. **amser anperfydh** *n.f* imperfect tense. **amser berfydh** *n.f* perfect tense. **amser worberfydh** *n.f* pluperfect tense. **amser a dheu** *n.f* future tense. **amser dremenys** *n.f* preterite tense

amseryow *n.pl* menstruation; period

amstyryus *adj* ambiguous

amyttya *vb* admit; accept; acknowledge

amyttyans *n.m* **amyttyansow** admission

an *art* the. **an … ma** *adj* (*demonstrative*) this; these. **an … na** *adj* (*demonstrative*) that; those

a'n (1) *contr* of the

a'n (2) *contr* (*object*) him; it

a'n golon *adj* cardiac. **astel kolon** *n.m* cardiac arrest

an- *prfx* un-; non-

anadhves *adj* immature; unripe

anal *n.f* breath

analladow *adj* impossible

anallans *n.m* respiration

analog *adj* analogue

analogieth *n.f* **analogiethow** analogy

ananedhadow *adj* uninhabitable

ananedhys *adj* uninhabited

anarvethys *adj* redundant (*from employment*)

anaswonys *adj* unrecognised; unfamiliar

anbarghus *adj* temporary

andharganadow *adj* unpredictable

andhemedhys *adj* unmarried; single

andhesiradow *adj* undesirable

andheskrifadow *adj* indescribable

andhiblans *adj* imprecise; indistinct; unclear

andhidro *adj* indirect

andhien *adj* incomplete

andhiogel *adj* insecure; unreliable

andhiogeledh *n.m* **andhiogeledhow**
insecurity
andhoutys *adj* undoubted
androw *n.m* **androwyow** afternoon
androweyth *n.m* **androweythyow**
afternoon-time
anedhadow *adj* habitable; inhabitable
anedhel *adj* residential
anedhi (1) *prn* from her; of her
anedhi (2) *vb* inhabit
anedhyans *n.m* **anedhyansow**
occupation
anedhyas *n.m* **anedhysi** inhabitant
anedhys *adj* inhabited; residential. **heb
bos anedhys** non-residential
aneffeythus *adj* ineffective; inefficient
anella *vb* breathe
anemek *adj* anaemic
anemia *n.m* (*med*) anaemia
anerys *adj* (*unploughed*) fallow
anes I *adj* uneasy; uncomfortable **II** *n.m*
disquiet
aneth *n.m* **anethow** marvel
anethek *adj* fabulous; amazing
anetholys *adj* unelected
anevadow *adj* undrinkable
anewn *adj* unfair; incorrect; unjust
anfalladow *adj* unfailing
anfel *adj* naive
anfeus *n.m* misfortune
anfeusik *adj* wretched; unfortunate;
unlucky
anformel *adj* casual; informal
anfur *adj* unwise
angespos *n.m* **angesposow** imbalance
Anglikan I *adj* Anglican **II** *n.m*
Anglikanyon Anglican
Anglikanieth *n.f* Anglicanism
angos *n.m* anguish
anhedhadow *adj* inaccessible
anhedhek I *adj* perpetual **II** *adv*
perpetually
anhegol *adj* sceptical
anhun *n.m* insomnia (*colloq*)
anhunek *adj* insomniac

anhwek *adj* unkind; unfriendly
ania *vb* annoy; disturb; irk; worry (a
person or animal). **parys dhe ania**
disruptive
anion *n.m* **anions** anion
anjust *adj* unjust
anjustis *n.m* injustice
ankablus *adj* innocent; not guilty
ankarus *adj* reclusive
ankelmys *adj* unrelated
ankemeradow *adj* unacceptable
ankemmyn *adj* uncommon
ankempen *adj* untidy
anken *n.m* **ankenyow** grief; misery
ankensi *adj* grievous; painful
ankerys *adj* unpopular
ankespar *adj* unalike
ankevi *vb* forget. **gwra y ankevi!** forget
it! no way!
ankewar *adj* inaccurate; incorrect
ankewerder *n.m* inaccuracy
ankler *adj* unclear; obscure
ankombra *vb* bother; hamper;
inconvenience; disturb
ankombrus *adj* embarrassing;
inconvenient
ankombrynsi *n.m* bother; difficulty;
embarassment; inconvenience.
ankombrynsi euthyk *n.m* an awful
drag
ankombrys *adj* embarrassed
ankompes *adj* uneven
ankonvedhadow *adj* incomprehensible
ankor *n.m* **ankoryow** anchor
ankorva *n.f* **ankorvaow** anchorage
ankorya *vb* anchor
ankoth *adj* unknown; strange
ankov *n.m* **ankovyow** forgetfulness;
oversight
Ankow *n.m* (*personified*) Death
ankres *n.m* unrest; disquiet
ankresya *vb* disturb; disquiet
ankresyans *n.m* **ankresyansow**
disturbance
ankrydor *n.m* **ankrydoryon** atheist

ankryjyk *adj* unbelieving

ankrysadow *adj* unbelievable; incredible

anlaghel *adj* illegal; unlawful

anlehadow *adj* irreducible

anles *n.m* **anlesow** disadvantage. **gorra nebonan yn-dann anles** disavantage somebody

anlettrys *adj* illiterate

anlettryseth *n.f* illiteracy

anlowen *adj* unhappy

anlowr *adj* insufficient

annaghadow *adj* undeniable; irrefutable

annedh *n.f* **anedhow** abode; dwelling. **annedh witha** *n.f* **anedhow gwitha** care home

annorel *adj* unearthly

anodho *prn* from him; of him

anorak *n.m* **anorakys** anorak

anoreksek *adj* anorexic (*med*)

anoreksia nervosa *n.m* anorexia nervosa (*med*)

anorganek *adj* inorganic

anoyntya *vb* anoint

anperfydh *adj* imperfect. **amser anperfydh** *n.f* imperfect tense

anplegadow *adj* unsatisfactory

anporthadow *adj* unbearable; intolerable

anposek *adj* unimportant; trivial

anpossybyl *adj* impossible

anpythek *adj* abstract

anresnadow *adj* unreasonable

anreyth *adj* abnormal

-ans *sffx* masculine noun suffix

ansans *adj* unholy

anserghek *adj* independent

anserghogeth *n.f* independence

ansertan *adj* uncertain

ansodhogel *adj* unofficial

anstag *adj* unattached; untethered

ansur *adj* uncertain

ansurneth *n.f* **ansurnethow** uncertainty

Antarktek *top n.m* Antarctic

antavadow *adj* untouchable; legally immune

antempna *n.m* **antempnys, antempnow** anthem

anterrys *adj* unbroken

antowlek *adj* aimless

antryghadow *adj* unbeatable; invincible

anusadow *adj* unusual

anvarwel *adj* immortal

anvas *adj* immoral

anvaseth *n.f* **anvasethow** immorality

anvateryel *adj* abstract

anvenowgh *adj* infrequent

anvlasus *adj* tasteless

anvodhek *adj* reluctant

anwaytys *adj* unexpected

anweladewder *n.m* invisibility

anweladow *adj* invisible

anweythresek *adj* inactive

anwir *adj* untrue

anwirder *n.m* untruth

anwiw *adj* improper; unsuitable; unqualified; unworthy

anwoderrys *adj* uninterrupted

anwodhvedhys *adj* unknown

anwoheladow *adj* unavoidable

anwos *n.m* **anwosow** (*infection*) cold; chill

anwosek *adj* (*infection*) chilly

anwosi *vb* to catch cold

anwovenek *adj* hopeless

anyagh *adj* unwell; unhealthy

anygerys *adj* unopened

apa *n.m* **apys** ape

aparel *n.m* apparel; gear; outfit; tackle

apert *adj, adv* apparent; candid; evident; obvious; openly; patent; plainly; plain to see

apertya *vb* lay open

aperya *vb* impair

apoyntya *vb* appoint; ordain

apoyntyans *n.m* **apoyntyansow** appointment

app *n.m* **appow** (*IT*) app

appel *n.m* **appelyow** (*law*) appeal

appla *adj* (**see: abel**) more able

apposya *vb* examine; test by questions; interrogate

apposyans *n.m* **apposyansow** examination. **apposyans skrifys** *n.m* written examination. **apposyans war anow** *n.m* oral examination

apron *n.m* **apronnyow** apron

ar- *prfx* pre-; fore-

Arab *n.m* **Arabyon** Arab

Arabek *n.m* Arabic

arabek *adj* Arabian

Arabi *top n.m* Arabia

arader *n.m* **ereder** plough

araderor *n.m* **araderoryon** ploughman

aradow *adj* arable

a-rag I *adj* front II *adv* forward; in front; on III *prp* in front of; in the presence of. **an keyn a-rag** back to front. *Personal forms: 1s **a-ragov**, 2s **a-ragos**, 3sm **a-ragdho**, 3sf **a-rygdhi**, 1p **a-ragon**, 2p **a-ragowgh**, 3p **a-ragdha***

aral *pl* **erel** I *adj* another; other; alternative II *prn* another

aras *vb* plough

aray *n.m* **arayys, arayow** arrangement; layout; order. **yn aray diyskynnus** in descending order. **yn aray yskynnus** in ascending order. **yn aray termyn** in chronological order

araya *vb* arrange; bring in order; put in order; structure

arbeniger *n.m* **arbenigoryon** specialist

arbennek *adj* distinctive; particular; special. **yn arbennek** especially

arbrevi *vb* experiment

arbrov *n.m* **arbrovow** experiment

arbrovel *adj* experimental

arbrovji *n.m* **arbrovjiow** laboratory

ardak *n.m* **ardagow** delay

ardh *n.m* **ardhow** height; high place

ardhek *adj* lofty

ardyghtya *vb* cope (with)

arenebedh *n.m* **arenebedhow** area

arenebel *adj* superficial

arenep *n.m* **arenebow** surface

areth *n.f* **arethyow** lecture; oration

arethek *adj* rhetorical

arethor *n.m* **arethoryon** lecturer; orator

arethva *n.f* **arethvaow** platform

arethya *vb* lecture

argas *n.m* **argasow** aggression

argasor *n.m* **argasoryon** aggressor

argasreydh *n.f* **argasreydhow** rape

argasreydher *n.m* **argasreydhoryon** rapist

argasreydhya *vb* rape

argasus *adj* aggressive

arge *n.m* **argeow** dam

argel *n.f* **argelyow** refuge; retreat; secluded place. **bos trigys yn argel** live at the back of beyond

argelys *adj* secluded

argemmyn *n.m* **argemynnow** advertisement; notice

argemynna *vb* advertise. **garm-argemynna** *n.f* advertising slogan

argemynnans *n.m* **argemynansow** publicity

argerdh *n.m* **argerdhow** process

argerdhes *vb* process

argevri *vb* donate

argevro *n.m* **argevrohow** donation

argh *n.f* **arghow** ark; bin; chest; coffer. **argh dhillas** *n.f* chest of drawers. **argh lyvrow** *n.f* bookcase. **argh vona** *n.f* money box

arghadow *n.m* **arghadowyow** command; order; commandment. **an Deg Arghadow** the Ten Commandments

arghans *n.m* (*element*) silver; money. **arghans byw** *n.m* (*element*) mercury; quicksilver. **arghans-gweres** *n.m* subsidy

arghansek *adj* silvery

arghansel *adj* financial

arghanser *n.m* **arghansoryon** banker

Arghantina *top n.f* Argentina

Arghantinan *n.m* **Arghantinans**
Argentinian

arghantinek *adj* Argentinian

arghantti *n.m* **arghanttiow** bank.
    akont arghantti *n.m* bank account.
    kespos arghantti *n.m* bank balance.
    kostow arghantti *n.m* bank charges

arghas *n.m* **arghasow** fund

arghasa *vb* fund

arghasans *n.m* funding

arghel *n.m* **argheledh** archangel

arghena *vb* put on shoes

arghepskop *n.m* **arghepskobow**
    archbishop

arghpedrevan *n.m* **arghpedrevanes**
    dinosaur

argol *n.m* perdition; risk

argollus *adj* hazardous

argraf *n.m* **argrafyow** impression

argrevell *n.f* **argrevellow** amplifier

argya *vb* argue. **argya orth** argue with.
    argya erbynn argue against

argyans *n.m* **argyansow** argument

arholyas *n.m* **arholysi** examiner

arhwilas *vb* audit; scan

arhwilell *n.f* **arhwilellow** scanner.
    arhwilell weli flatbed scanner

arhwilyans *n.m* **arhwilyansow** audit;
    scan

arhwithra *vb* survey

arhwithrans *n.m* **arhwithransow**
    survey

arlenans *n.m* **arlenansow** adhesion

arlenwel *vb* top up

arliw *n.m* **arliwyow** tint

arliwa *vb* tint

arlodh *n.m* **arlydhi** lord; master. **Chi
    an Arlydhi** House of Lords

arlodhes *n.f* **arlodhesow** lady; mistress.
    arlodhes kadys *n.f* drag queen

arlodhesow noth *n.pl* amaryllis (*Jersey
    lily*)

arlottes *n.m* jurisdiction

arlotteth *n.f* **arlottethow** domain

armatur *n.m* **armaturyow** armature

armel *n.m* **armels** bracelet

arnewa *vb* storm; damage by weather

arnewys *adj* storm-damaged

arnowydh *adj* modern

arnowydhhe *vb* modernise

arnowydhheans *n.m*
    arnowydhheansow modernisation

arsenyk *n.m* (*element*) arsenic

arta *adv* again; back. **arta mar pleg**
    please repeat it. **unweyth arta** once
    more

artydh *n.m* **artydhyon** artist

arv *n.f* **arvow** arm; weapon. **den
    arvow** *n.m* man-at-arms. **kota arvow**
    n.m coat-of-arms. **mos dhe arvow**
    take up arms

arva *vb* arm

arvedh *vb* insult

arvedhen *n.f* **arvedhennow** insult

arvedhus *adj* insulting

arveth I *n.m* **arvethow** hire **II** *vb*
    employ; hire

arvethesik *n.m* **arvethesigyon**
    employee

arvethor *n.m* **arvethoryon** employer

arvor I *adj* maritime **II** *n.m* **arvoryow**
    coast

arvorel *adj* coastal; littoral

arvreus *n.f* **arvreusow** criticism

arvreusi *vb* criticise; evaluate

arvreusyans *n.m* **arvreusyansow**
    evaluation

arvreusyas *n.m* **arvreusysi** critic

arvwisk *n.m* armour

arwask *n.m* **arwaskow** oppression

arwaska *vb* oppress

arwedhya *vb* symbolise

arwodh *n.f* **arwodhyow** emblem;
    symbol; sign; signal; symptom. **post
    arwodh** *n.m* sign-post

arwodhek *adj* symbolic; emblematic

arwodhik *n.m* **arwodhigow** badge;
    (*computer desktop*) icon

arwodhogeth *n.f* symbolism
arwostel *n.m* **arwostlow** pledge
arwostla *vb* pledge
-as *sffx* **-asow** -ful
a's (1) *contr (object)* her; it
a's (2) *contr (object)* them
ascendya *vb* ascend
ASD *abbrev* ASD *(med)*. **Disordyr
Spektrom Awtysm** Autism
Spectrum Disorder
asen (1) *n.m* **asenes** donkey. **margh
asen** *n.m* jackass
asen (2) *n.f* **asennow** radius
asen (3) *n.f* **asennow** rib
asennek *adj* ribbed
Asi *top n.f* Asia
Asian *n.m* **Asians** Asian
asiek *adj* Asian
askal *n.coll* thistles
askallen *n.f* **askallennow** thistle
askallen bras *n.f* **askallennow pras**
field thistle
askallen leth *n.f* **askallennow leth**
milk thistle
askallen vogh *n.f* **askallennow mogh**
sow thistle
askel *n.f* **eskelli** fin; wing. **askel
groghen** *n.f* bat
askellek *adj* winged
asklos *n.coll* chips
asklosen *n.f* **asklosennow** chip
asklosi *vb* chip
asklotti *n.m* **asklottiow** chip shop
askor *n.m* produce
askorn *n.m* **eskern** bone. **askorn keyn**
n.m backbone. **askorn bolonjedh**
wishbone
askornek *adj* skinny
askorra *vb* produce
askorrans *n.m* production
askorras *n.m* **askorrasow** product
askorrer *n.m* **askorroryon** producer
askrifa *vb* attribute
askrifys *adj* attributed
askus *n.m* **askusyow** excuse

askusya *vb* excuse
aslam *n.m* **aslammow** bounce
aslamma *vb* bounce
aslea *vb* replace
asnodhow *n.pl* resources
asow *n.coll* ribs
asowen *n.f* **asowennow** rib
asper *adj* grim
aspia *vb* observe; scout
aspians *n.m* **aspiansow** observation;
surveillance; espionage
aspier *n.m* **aspioryon** scout
asran *n.f* **asrannow** department
asrannel *adj* departmental
ass *int* how. **ass ywa teg!** how sweet it
is!
assa[2] *int* how
assay *n.m* **assays** attempt; effort; essay;
exercise; rehearsal; try
assaya *vb* attempt; endeavour; exercise;
try
assentya *vb* agree; assent; consent.
assentya gans agree with; take the
side of. **assentya dhe** agree to
assessadow *adj* assessable
assoyladow *adj* soluble
assoylya *vb* absolve; solve
astel (1) I *n.m* stoppage; suspension **II**
vb abort; cease; suspend; *(transitive)*
stop. **astel ober** strike *(suspension of
work)*. **astel kolon** cardiac arrest
astel (2) *n.f* **estyl** plank; shingle; splint.
astel an oles *n.f* mantelpiece
astelwolya *vb* go windsurfing
astelwolyans *n.m* windsurfing
astewisyans *n.m* **astewisyansow**
adoption
asthma *n.m* *(med)* asthma
asthmatek *adj* *(med)* asthmatic
astiveri *vb* compensate; make amends;
restore
astiveryans *n.m* **astiveryansow**
compensation
astranj *adj* strange

asvaba *vb* adopt. **maynorieth-asvaba**
n.f adoption agency
asvabans *n.m* **asvabansow** adoption
Asvens *n.m* Advent
aswa *n.f* **aswaow** breach; gap
aswiwa *vb* adapt
aswiwer *n.m* **aswiworyon** adapter
aswon *vb* know; be familiar with;
realise; recognise; acknowledge.
sevel orth aswon ignore
aswonvos *n.m* knowledge;
acknowledgement; acquaintance
aswonys *adj* familiar; known
atal *n.coll* junk; mine waste; refuse;
rubbish. **atal mor** *n.coll* flotsam and
jetsam
atalgist *n.f* **atalgistyow** dustbin;
waste-paper basket
a'th[5a] *contr* (*object*) you (*sg*)
athlet *n.m* **athletys** athlete
athletek I *adj* athletic **II** *n.f* athletics
atlantek *adj* Atlantic. **Keynvor**
Atlantek *n.m* Atlantic Ocean
atom *n.m* **atomow** atom
atomek *adj* atomic
attal *n.m* **attelyow** repayment. **yn attal**
as repayment
attamya *vb* broach; tackle
attendya *vb* attend; pay attention;
make out; note
attendyans *n.m* **attendyansow**
attendance; attention
attent *n.m* **attentys** attempt; endeavour
attes *adj* comfortable; easy
attesva *n.f* **attesvaow** lavatory; toilet
atti *n.m* malice; spite. **rag atti** out of
spite
attyli *vb* repay
a-ugh I *adv* above **II** *prp* **a-ugh dhe**[2]
above; over. *Personal forms: 1s*
a-ughov, 2s a-ughos, 3sm a-ughto,
3sf a-ughti, 1p a-ughon, 2p
a-ughowgh, 3p a-ughta
aval *n.m* **avalow** apple. **aval briansen**
n.m Adam's apple. **aval dor** *n.m*

potato. **aval dor brewys** *n.m* mashed
potato. **avalow dor ha kig** *n.coll*
hot-pot. **avalow dor ha losow** *n.coll*
vegetable hot-pot. **aval gwlanek** *n.m*
peach. **aval kerensa** *n.m* tomato. **aval**
lagas *n.m* eyeball. **aval paradhis** *n.m*
grapefruit. **aval saben** *n.m* pine-cone
avalen *n.f* **avalennow** apple tree
avalennek *n.f* **avalenegi** orchard
avallan *n.f* **avallannow** orchard
avalowa *vb* gather apples
avalwedhen *n.f* **avalwedhennow**
apple tree
avalwydh *n.coll* apple trees
avan *n.coll* raspberries
avanen *n.f* **avanennow** raspberry
a-vann *adv* aloft
a-varr *adv* early
avaylya *vb* avail
avel *adv* as; like. **my a'n gwrug avel**
ges I did it as a joke. *Personal forms:*
1s avelov, 2s avelos, 3sm avello, 3sf
avelli, 1p avelon, 2p avelowgh, 3p
avella
aven *n.m* **avenyow** image
aventur *n.m* **aventurys, aventuryow**
adventure; venture; speculation
aventurus *adj* adventurous
aventurya *vb* speculate (*financially*)
a-ves *adj* external; outside. **a-ves dhe**[2]
prp outside of
avi (1) *n.m* jealousy; enmity; malice.
perthi avi orth be jealous of; bear
malice against
avi (2) *n.m* **aviow** liver
avis *n.m* **avisyow** advice; opinion;
motion
avisya *vb* note; observe; superintend
avisyer *n.m* **avisyoryon**
superintendant
avius *adj* jealous
avlan *adj* unclean
avlavar *adj* mute
avlenter *adj* matt; drab
avochya *vb* vouch

a-vodh *adj* voluntary

avodya *vb* (= **avoydya**) avoid; distance oneself; go away

avokado *n.m* **avokados** avocado

avon *n.f* **avonyow, avenow** river

avonsya *vb* (*intransitive*) advance; progress; (*transitive*) promote

avonsyans *n.m* **avonsyansow** advance; progress; promotion; headway

a-vorow *adv* tomorrow

avoutrer *n.m* **avoutrers, avoutroryon** adulterer

avoutri *n.m* adultery

avowa *vb* admit; accept; acknowledge; confess; justify. **res yw avowa** admittedly

avowadow *adj* justifiable

avowans *n.m* **avowansow** confession

avoydya *vb* (= **avodya**) avoid; distance oneself; go away

avresnel *adj* preposterous

avresonus *adj* unreasonable

avrewlys *adj* irregular

a-vusur *adj* bespoke; custom-made

a-wartha *adv* on top. **a-wartha dhe**^{2} *prp* on top of. (**an pyth**) **a-wartha dhe-woles** upside-down

awedhya *vb* influence

awedhyans *n.m* **awedhyansow** influence

awel *n.f* **awelyow** wind; weather; gale. **awel glor** *n.f* breeze. **hager-awel** *n.f* bad weather

awelek *adj* windy

awen (1) *n.f* imagination; inspiration; muse

awen (2) *n.f* **awenow** *dl* **diwawen** jaw

awenek *adj* creative

awenekter *n.m* creativity

aweni *vb* inspire

awenydh *n.m* **awenydhyon** genius

aweyl *n.f* **aweylys, aweylyow** gospel

awgrym *n.m* mathematics

a-woles *adv* below; downstairs; lower; on the bottom. **a-woles dhe**^{2} *prp*

below; under. **a-barth a-woles** down below. **leur a-woles** *n.m* ground floor

awos *cnj* because of; for the sake of; in spite of; on account of. **awos Duw** for crying out loud; for God's sake

a-wosa *adv* afterwards

awotta *int* behold! **awott an trobel!** there's the rub!

awra *n.m* **awra** aura

awtomatek *adj* automatic

awtorita *n.m* **awtoritas** authority. **an awtoritas** *n.pl* the powers that be

awtoritaus *adj* authoritarian

awtoritauster *n.m* authoritarianism

awtour *n.m* **awtours** author

awtysm *n.m* autism (*med*)

awtystek *adj* autistic (*med*)

ayr *n.m* air. **y'n ayr** in flight; airborne

ayra *vb* air

ayrborth *n.m* **ayrborthow** airport

ayrbost *n.m* airmail. **der ayrbost** by airmail

ayr-degys *adj* (*e.g. disease*) air-borne

ayredh *n.m* **ayredhow** climate

ayrek *adj* aerial

ayrell *n.f* **ayrellow** ventilator

ayrella *vb* ventilate

ayrellans *n.m* **ayrellansow** ventilation

ayren *n.f* **ayrennow** aeroplane; plane (*aircraft*)

ayrewnans *n.m* **ayrewnansow** air conditioning

ayrgregi *vb* hang-glide

ayrgylgh *n.m* atmosphere

ayrgylghyek *adj* atmospheric

ayrlinen *n.f* **ayrlinennow** airline

ayrlorgh *n.f* (*m*) **ayrlorghow** aerial

ayrobek *adj* aerobic

ayrosol *n.m* **ayrosolys** aerosol

ayrsketh *n.m* **ayrskethow** airstrip

ayrstanch *adj* airtight

aysel *n.m* vinegar

azalea *n.m* **azaleas** azalea

B

baban *n.m* babanes baby
babi *n.m* babiow baby
bacheler *n.m* bachelers bachelor
bachelerieth *n.f* bacheleriethow
  bachelor's degree
backen *n.m* bacon
badh (1) *n.m* badhys bath
badh (2) *n.m* badhes boar
badhya *vb* bathe
badminton *n.m* badminton
badus *adj* (*offensive*) lunatic
bagas *n.m* bagasow band; bunch; gang;
  group. bagas gwaskas *n.m* pressure
  group; lobby. gorra yn bagas *vb*
  group together
bagasik *n.m* bagasigow batch
bagh (1) *n.f* baghow cell
bagh (2) *n.f* baghow hook
bagha *vb* trap
bakteriom *n.m* bakteria bacterium
bal *n.m* balyow mine. den bal *n.m* tus
  val miner
balegva *n.f* balegvaow balcony
balek *adj* jutting
balgh *adj* arrogant
ball *n.f* ballow pest; plague
ballad *n.m* ballads ballad
balweyth *n.m* mining
balyer *n.m* balyeryow barrel. kravas
  goles an balyer scrape the bottom of
  the barrel
banadhel *n.coll* (*plant*) broom; besom
banadhlek *n.f* banadhlegi
  broom-brake
banadhlen *n.f* banadhlennow (*plant*)
  broom; besom
banana *n.m* bananas banana
baner *n.m* baneryow, baners flag;
  standard; banner
Bangladesh *top n.m* Bangladesh
banken *n.f* bankennow bank
banket *n.m* bankettys banquet

bann *n.m* bannyow prominence
banna I *n.m* banaghow drop; bit II *adv*
  at all
bannek *adj* prominent
banow *n.f* banowes, bynewi sow
bara *n.m* bread. bara byghan *n.m* roll.
  bara gwaneth *n.m* wheaten bread.
  bara leun *n.m* wholemeal bread.
  bara sugal *n.m* rye bread. losowen
  an bara *n.f* coriander. torth (a) vara
  n.f loaf of bread
baramanyn *n.m* baramanynnow
  sandwich
barbakoa *n.m* barbakoas barbecue
barbarek *adj* barbaric
barbour *n.m* barbours barber
bardh *n.m* berdh bard; poet
bardhek *adj* bardic
bardhonek *n.m* bardhonogow poem
bardhonieth *n.f* poetry
bargen *n.m* bargennyow bargain; deal.
  bargen tir *n.m* farm
bargesi *vb* hover
bargos *n.m* bargoses buzzard
bargynnya *vb* bargain; deal; negotiate;
  engage in horse-trading
barkado *n.m* barkados densely packed
  pile of fish for curing
barlen *n.f* barlennow lap
barlennell *n.f* barlenellow laptop
barlys *n.coll* barley
barlysen *n.f* barlysennow grain of
  barley
barna *vb* judge
barner *n.m* barnoryon, barneryow
  judge; critic
barometer *n.m* barometrow barometer
barr (1) *n.m* barrow summit
barr (2) *n.m* barrys bar; pub
barrek *adj* twiggy
barren *n.f* barrennow twig; sprig.
  barren spas *n.f* space bar

barrgod *n.m* **barrgodys** bar-code

barthusek *adj* marvellous; miraculous; wonderful

barv *n.m* **barvow** beard. **barv gaver** *n.m* goatee

barvus I *adj* bearded **II** *n.m* **barvusi** cod

bas *adj* shallow

basa *vb* stun

basar *n.m* **basars** bazaar; jumble sale

bashe *vb* abate; become shallow

Bask *n.m* **Baskyon** Basque

Baskek *n.m* Basque language

baskek *adj* Basque

basket *n.m* **baskettys** basket

basnet *n.m* **basnettys, basnettow** helmet

basnet gwithyas *n.m* Himalayan balsam

bason *n.m* **basonys** basin

bastard *n.m* **bastardyon** bastard

batalyas *vb* do battle; fight. **batalyas orth** fight against

batel *n.f* **batalyow** battle

bath *n.m* **bathow** coin

bath arghans *n.m* (*plant*) honesty

bathva *n.f* **bathvaow** mint (*for money*)

batri *n.m* **batriow** (*electric*) battery

batt *n.m* **battys; battow** bat

batti *n.m* **battiow** mint (*for money*)

bay *n.m* **bayow** kiss

baya (1) *vb* kiss

baya (2) *n.m* **bayys** bay

bayros *n.coll* oleander

bayrosen *n.f* **bayrosennow** oleander

bayt *n.m* **baytys** byte

baywedhen *n.f* **baywedhennow** bay-tree

baywydh *n.coll* bay-trees

bedh *n.m* **bedhow** grave; tomb. **men bedh** *n.m* grave-stone

bedha *vb* dare; presume; venture

bedhas *n.m* **bedhasow** dare

bedhek *adj* daring

bedhekter *n.m* **bedhekteryow** presumption

bedhros *n.f* **bedhrosow** graveyard

bedhygla *vb* bellow

begel (1) *n.m* **begelyow** navel

begel (2) *n.m* **begelyow** nuisance; annoying person

beggya *vb* beg

beggyer *n.m* **beggyers** beggar

begh *n.m* **beghow** burden; load

beghus *adj* burdensome; onerous

beghya *vb* burden; impose upon; load

bejeth *n.f* **bejethow** face; visage. **liw bejeth** *n.m* make-up; cosmetic

Belarus *top n.m* Belarus

Belarussek *n.m* Belarussian language

belarussek *adj* Belarussian

Belarussian *n.m* **Belarussians** Belarussian

beler *n.coll* cress

beler dowr *n.coll* watercress

beleren *n.f* **belerennow** cress plant

beler hwerow *n.coll* hairy bitter cress

beler lowarth *n.coll* garden cress

Belg *n.m* **Belgyon** Belgian. **Pow Belg** *top n.m* Belgium

belgek *adj* Belgian

bell *n.m* war. **gostla bell** *vb* wage war

ben (1) *n.m* **benyow** foot; base; trunk (*tree*)

ben (2) *n.f* woman. **an eyl...hy ben** *n.f* (*only use of the word* **ben**) one another

benelegor *n.m* **benelegoryon** feminist

benelegorieth *n.f* feminism

benelek *adj* feminist

benenes *n.pl* ladies

benesikter *n.m* sanctity

benfisek I *adj* beneficiary **II** *n.m* **benfisogyon** beneficiary

bengalji *n.m* **bengaljiow** bungalow

bengorfonieth *n.f* gynaecology

bengorfoniethel *adj* gynaecological

bengorfydh *n.m* **bengorfydhyon** gynaecologist

bennath *n.f* **benathow** blessing

benow *adj* female; feminine

ben'vas *n.f* **benenes mas** housewife

benyga *vb* bless

benygys *adj* blessed; hallowed

benyn *n.f* **benenes** woman. **benyn ambosys** *n.f* fiancée. **benyn bries** *n.f* bride. **benyn jentyl** *n.f* gentlewoman

benynreydh *n.f* **benynreydhow** female; womankind

bern (1) *n.m* **bernyow** heap; mound; pile

bern (2) *n.m* **bernyow** source of concern; interest

bern (3) *vb* (*3s only*) concerns; matters. **ny vern** it doesn't matter

bernya *vb* matter

berr (1) *n.f* **berrow** calf (*of leg*)

berr (2) *adj* short; brief

berranal *n.m* shortness of breath

berranellek *adj* short of breath

berrhe *vb* abbreviate; shorten; (*garment*) take up

berrheans *n.m* **berrheansow** abbreviation

berrik *adj* fatty; obese; plump

berrskrif *n.m* **berrskrifow** abstract; summary

berrskrifa *vb* summarise

berrwelyek *adj* short-sighted

berya *vb* run through; stab

besont *n.m* **besons** bezant

besow *n.coll* birches

besowen *n.f* **besowennow** birch-tree **besowen Hav** *n.f* maypole

best *n.m* **bestes** animal; beast. **best hwel** *n.m* working animal

besydh *n.m* **besydhyow** baptism

besydhven *n.m* **besydhveyn** font

besydhya *vb* christen; baptise

besydhyans *n.m* **besydhyansow** christening

besyel *adj* digital

besyon *n.m* **besyons** vision

betys *n.coll* beet. **betys rudh** *n.coll* beetroot. **betys sugra** *n.coll* sugar beet

betysen *n.f* **betysennow** beet. **betysen rudh** *n.f* beetroot

beudhi *vb* drown; swamp

bever *n.m* **bevers** beaver

bewa *vb* live; be alive. **bewa orth neppyth** live on something

bewbodradow *adj* biodegradable

bewder *n.m* liveliness; agility

bewedh *n.m* **bewedhow** lifestyle

bewek *adj* lively; vital

bewin *n.m* beef

bewles hwerow *n.coll* biting stonecrop

bewnans *n.m* **bewnansow** life; living. **dendyl bewnans** earn a living

bewonieth *n.f* biology

bewoniethel *adj* biological

bewskrif *n.m* **bewskrifow** biography

bewva *n.f* **bewvaow** habitat

Bibel *n.m* **Biblow** Bible

biblek *adj* biblical

bibyn bubyn *n.m* **bibynes bubyn** prawn; shrimp

bilen I *adj* villainous; thuggish II *n.m* **bilens** villain; gangster; thug. **bilen pur** *n.m* an accomplished villain

bili *n.coll* pebbles

bilien *n.f* **biliennow** pebble

bilvil[2] *num, n.m* (10^9) **bilvilyow** billion

bis *n.f* **bisyow** (*tool*) vice

bismer *n.m* **bismeras** scandal; infamy. **gul bismer dhe**[2] scandalise

blam *n.m* **blamys** blame

blamya *vb* blame; find fault with. **blamya nebonan rag ev dhe wul neppyth** blame somebody for doing something

blas *n.m* **blasow** smell; odour; flavour; taste

blasa *vb* smell; taste. **blesys da** palatable

blaser *n.m* **blasers** blazer

bledhen *n.f* **bledhynnyow** year.
bledhen lamm *n.f* leap year. **kyns penn bledhen** before the year is out.
nessa bledhen next year

bledhynnyek *adj* annual; yearly.
kummyas bledhynnyek *n.m* annual leave

bleudh *adj* delicate; tender; soft

bleudhder *n.m* delicacy; tenderness; softness

bleudhya *vb* soften; weaken

bleujen *n.f* **bleujyow** blossom; flower

bleujen an gog *n.f* bluebell

bleujen an gwyns *n.f* wood anemone
(*windflower; thimbleweed*)

bleujen an howl *n.f* sunflower

bleujen ergh *n.f* **bleujennow ergh** snowdrop

bleujen fosow *n.f* wallflower

bleujen gevnisen *n.f* red campion

bleujen gevnisen wynn *n.f* white campion

bleujen gool Mighal *n.f* autumn aster; Michaelmas daisy

bleujen tulyfant *n.f* tulip

bleujyowa *vb* blossom; flower

bleujyowek *n.f* **bleujyowegi** flower bed

bleujyow ergh *n.coll* snowdrop

bleus *n.m* **bleusyow** flour. **bleus hesken** *n.m* sawdust. **bleus leun** *n.m* wholemeal

bleusek *adj* floury

blew *n.coll* hair. **blew lagas** *n.coll* eyelashes. **liw blew lagas** *n.m* mascara

blewek *adj* hairy; long-haired. **kath vlewek** *n.f* hairy caterpillar

blewen *n.f* **blewennow** (*strand of*) hair

bleydh *n.m* **bleydhi** wolf

bleyn *n.m* **bleynyow** point; tip; peak

bleynya *vb* sharpen; point; tip

blogh *adj* bald

blonegek *adj* greasy

blonek *n.m* **blonegow** fat; grease; lard

bloodh *n.m* years of age (*no plural*)

bobba *n.m* **bobbys** idiot; fool

bocka *n.m* **bockas, bockyas** gnome; goblin; scarecrow; bogeyman. **bocka dov** *n.m* familiar. **bocka du** *n.m* bad ghost. **bocka gwynn** *n.m* good ghost. **bocka lugarn** *n.m* genie

bockla *vb* buckle

bockyl *n.m* **bocklys** buckle

bodh *n.m* **bodhow** wish; will; consent.
orth bodh y vrys intentionally

bodhar *adj* deaf

bodhara *vb* become deaf or hearing impaired

bodharek I *adj* hearing impaired **II** *n.m*
bodharogyon person with hearing impairment

bodharhe *vb* deafen

bodhegi *vb* volunteer

bodhek I *adj* willing; voluntary **II**
bodhogyon *n.m* volunteer

bodhel *adj* consensual

bodhesik I *adj* amateurish **II** *n.m*
bodhesigyon amateur

Bodisatva *n.m* **Bodisatvaow**
Boddhisattva

bogalek *adj* vocalic

bogalen *n.f* **bogalennow** vowel

bogh (1) *n.f* **boghow**, *dl* **diwvogh**
cheek. **liw diwvogh** *n.m* blusher

bogh (2) *n.m* **boghes** he-goat

boghes *adj* few; little; slight

boghosek I *adj* poor; destitute;
impoverished **II** *n.m* **boghosogyon**
poor person

boghosekhe *vb* impoverish

boghosogneth *n.f* poverty; destitution

bojet *n.m* **bojettys** budget

boksusi *vb* box; punch

bolder *n.m* audacity; boldness

bolgh *n.m* **bolghow** breach; gap;
opening

bolgha *vb* breach

bolghen *n.f* **bolghennow** boll; capsule.
klout bolghen *n.m* tripe

bolimek *adj* bulimic (*med*)

bolimia nervosa *n.m* bulimia nervosa (*med*)

boll *adj* transparent

bolla *n.m* **bollys** bowl

bollen *n.f* **bollennow,** lightbulb

bollyn *n.m* **bollynnow,** bulletin

bolonjedh *n.m* **bolonjedhow** wish; will

bomm *n.m* **bommyn** blow; bump; crash; punch; slam

bommell *n.f* **bomellow** buffer

bommen *n.f* **bomennow** stroke; (*strike*) buffet

bond *n.m* **bondys, bondow** band. **bond ledan** *n.m* broadband. **hesken vond** *n.f* bandsaw

bonden *n.f* **bondennow** tyre

bones *vb* (= **bos**) be

bonk *n.m* **bonkys** bang; knock

bonkya *vb* bump; knock. **kerri bonk** *n.pl* dodgems

bonnik *n.m* **bonniges** meadow pipit

bonus *n.m* **bonusys** bonus

bool *n.f* **bolyow** axe

boos *n.m* **bosow** food; meal; fare. **boos atal** *n.m* junk food

boosa *vb* feed

boos nader *n.m* greater stitchwort

bora *n.m* **boraow** dawn

boragweyth *n.f* **boragweythyow** morning twilight

bord *n.m* **bordys, bordow** board; tabletop. **bord du** *n.m* blackboard. **bord gwynn** *n.m* whiteboard. **bord-hornella** *n.m* ironing board. **bord lestri** *n.m* sideboard. **bord-mordardha** *n.m* surfboard

boreles *n.m* **borelesyow** chrysanthemum

borger *n.m* **borgers** burger. **borger bewin** *n.m* beef burger

Borlowen *n.f* morning star; Venus

borr *adj* overweight

bos *vb* be; become; exist. **bos ena** attend. **bos war** beware; take care. **dos ha bos** become. **mos ha bos** become. **na yll bos** impossible

bosek *adj* bushy

Bosni *top n.f* Bosnia

Bosnian *n.m* **Bosnians** Bosnian

bosniek *adj* Bosnian

bost *n.m* **bostys, bostow** boast

bosti *n.m* **bostiow** restaurant

bostya *vb* boast

bostyans *n.m* **bostyansow** swank

bostyer *n.m* **bostyoryon** boaster

bosva *n.f* **bosvaow** existence

botas *n.coll* boots. **botas palvek** *n.coll* flippers

botasen *n.f* **botasennow** boot

botel *n.m* **botellow** bottle

botella *vb* bottle

botellas *n.m* **botellasow** bottleful

both *n.f* **bothow** hump

bothek *adj* protuberant

bothel *n.f* **bothellow** blister

bothen *n.f* **bothennow** lump; swelling; hump

bothfurvek *adj* convex

boton *n.m* **botonyow** button; game counter

boton owr *n.m* **botonyow owr** tansy

bouben *n.f* **boubennow** wick

Bouddiek *adj* buddhist

Bouddieth *n.f* Buddhism

Bouddydh *n.m* **Bouddydhyon** Buddhist

bowji *n.m* **bowjiow** cowshed

bownder *n.f* **bownderyow** lane

bra *n.m* **bras** bra

brag *n.m* **bragow** malt

braga *vb* brew

brager *n.m* **bragoryon** brewer

braggya *vb* menace; threaten

bragji *n.m* **bragjiow** brewery

brall *n.m* **brallow** dent

brallya *vb* dent

bramm *n.m* **bremmyn** fart. **bramm an gath!** *int* fiddlesticks!

bramma *vb* fart

bran *n.f* **brini** crow. **bran vras** *n.f*, **brini bras** raven. **bran dre** *n.f*, **brini tre** rook

bras (1) *adj* big; bulky; large. **dre vras** *adv* generally; mainly; for the most part. **yn fras** *adv* greatly

bras (2) *n.m* **brasow** conspiracy; plot

brasa *vb* conspire; plot

braser *n.m* **brasoryon** conspirator; plotter

brashe *vb* enlarge

Brasil *top n.m* Brazil

braslavar *n.m* **braslavarow** boast; threat

brasoberys *adj* magnificent

brassa *adj* bigger; major. **(an) brassa** (the) biggest

braster *n.m* **brasterow** size; bulk

brastereth *n.f* majesty

brastir *n.m* **brastiryow** continent. **dryftyans an brastiryow** *n.m* continental drift

brastiryel *adj* continental

brath *n.m* **brathow** bite

bratha *vb* bite

brathles *n.m* scarlet pimpernel

brav *adj* fine; grand

bre *n.f* **breow** hill

brederedh *n.m* brotherhood

bregh *n.f* **breghow**, *dl* **diwvregh** arm

breghel *n.m* **bregholow** sleeve

breghellik *n.m* **breghelligow** bracelet

breghys *adj* spotted

bregys *adj* brewed

brendya *vb* frown

brenigen *n.f* **brenigennow** limpet

brennik *n.coll* limpets

brennyas *n.m* **brenysi** mate (*on a ship*)

bresel *n.f* **breselyow** dispute; war. **garm vresel** *n.f* battle cry

breselek *adj* militant

breseler *n.m* **breseloryon** militant

breseli *vb* go to war

breselyans *n.m* warfare

brest (1) *n.m* brass

brest (2) *n.m* **brestys** breast; chest

Breten *top n.f* Britain. **Breten Veur** *top n.f* Great Britain. **Breten Vyghan** *top n.f* Brittany

Bretenborth *n.f* Brexit

bretennek *adj* British

Bretmes *n.m* Brexit

Breton *n.m* **Bretonyon** Breton

Bretonek *n.m* Breton language

bretonek *adj* Breton

breus *n.f* **breusow** judgement; doom; opinion; sentence; verdict. **breus ughel** *n.f* high esteem. **ri breus** give an opinion. **Dydh Breus** Judgement Day

breusel *adj* critical; judgmental

breusi *vb* judge; sentence; criticise; doom

breuslys *n.f* **breuslysow** court of law

breusyans *n.m* **breusyansow** critique; review

breusyas *n.m* **breusysi** judge

brew I *adj* bruised **II** *n.m* **brewyon** bruise. **kresten vrew** *n.f* shortcrust. **tesen vrew** *n.f* shortbread

brewgik *n.m* minced meat

brewi *vb* bruise; crumble; mash. **aval dor brewys** *n.m* mashed potato

brewvos *n.m* mincemeat (*sweet*)

brewyon *n.coll* crumbs

brewyonen *n.f* **brewyonennow** crumb

breyn *adj* rotten; putrid

breyna *vb* decay; rot

breynans *n.m* **breynansow** decay

breynder *n.m* rot

bri *n.f* distinction; esteem; importance; relevance; reputation; value; prominence. **a vri** famous; prominent; relevant; renowned; significant. **gul vri a²** take notice of. **heb bri** irrelevant. **heb meur a vri**

mediocre. **meur y vri, meur hy bri** outstanding

briallen *n.f* **briallennow** wild primrose

briallen an gog *n.f* cowslip

briallen lowarth *n.f* polyanthus; garden primrose

brialli *n.coll* wild primrose

briansen *n.f* **briansennow** throat

brigad *n.m* **brigadow** brigade

brin *n.m* **brinyow** brine

brith I *adj* streaked; striped **II** *n.coll* tartan

britha *vb* mottle; dapple; streak

brithel *n.m* **brithyli** mackerel

brithen *n.f* **brithennow** freckle

brithennek *adj* freckled

brithlen *n.f* **brithlennow** tapestry

brithweyth *n.m* **brithweythyow** mosaic

brithys *adj* dappled; mottled

bro *n.f* **broyow** country; land

brocha *n.m* **brochys** brooch

broder *n.m* **breder** brother. **broder da** *n.m* brother-in-law. **hanter-broder** *n.m* half-brother

brogh *n.m* **broghes** badger

broghki *n.m* **broghkeun** dachshund

broklo *n.m* **broklos** broccoli

bronkitis *n.m* bronchitis (*med*)

bronn (1) *n.f* **bronnow**, *dl* **diwvron** breast; hill

bronn (2) *n.coll* rushes (*plant*)

bronna *vb* breast-feed

bronnen *n.f* **bronennow** (*plant*) rush

bronnvil *n.m* **bronnviles** mammal

bronnvilek *adj* mammalian

brons *n.m* bronze

bros (1) *adj* searing hot

bros (2) *n.m* **brosow** goad; prick

bros (3) *n.m* **brosow** stew

brosa *vb* goad; prick; provoke

brosans *n.m* **brosansow** provocation

brosweyth *n.m* embroidery

brosya *vb* stitch; embroider

brottel *adj* brittle; frail; transitory. **brottel y jer** moody

browagh *n.m* terror

broweghereth *n.f* terrorism

broweghi *vb* terrify; terrorise

broweghus *adj* alarming

broweghyas *n.m* **broweghysi** terrorist

brows *n.coll* crumbled material

browsi *vb* crumble

browsyon *n.coll* crumbs

browsyonen *n.f* **browsyonennow** crumb

Brussel *top n.m* Brussels

brybour *n.m* **brybours** vagabond

bryck *n.m* **bryckys** brick

brygh *n.f* **breghi** pox; smallpox. **brygh Almayn** *n.f* German measles. **brygh rudh** *n.f* measles. **brygh yar** *n.f* chicken-pox

bryghlin *n.m* **bryghlinyow** vaccine

bryghlina *vb* vaccinate

bryghlinans *n.m* **bryghlinansow** vaccination

bryjyon *vb* boil. **gorra an galter dhe vryjyon** put the kettle on

bryjys *adj* boiled. **oy bryjys** *n.m* boiled egg

brykedh *n.coll* apricots

brykedhen *n.f* **brykedhennow** apricot

brynk *n.coll* (*respiratory organ*) gills

brynken *n.f* **brynkennow** (*respiratory organ*) gill

bryntin *adj* grand; great; superb

brys (1) *n.m* **brysyow** intention; mind; opinion; psyche. **orth bodh ow brys** intentionally. **orth ow brys** to my mind; in my opinion. **dhe'm brys vy** to my mind; in my opinion

brys (2) *n.m* **brysyow** uterus; womb

brysel *adj* mental

brysonieth *n.f* psychology

brysoniethel *adj* psychological

brysonydh *n.m* **brysonydhyon** psychologist

Brython *n.m* **Brythonyon** Briton

Brythonek *adj* Brythonic
bryton *n.coll* sea pink; thrift
bryvya *vb* bleat
bual *n.m* **bualyon** bison; buffalo
buan *adj* quick; lively
budh *n.m* **budhow** profit
budhek *adj* victorious. **karten vudhek** *n.f* trump card
budhogel *adj* victorious
budhyn *n.m* **budhynnow** meadow
budji *n.m* **budjies** budgerigar
buffe *n.m* **buffes** (*food counter*) buffet
bugel *n.m* **bugeledh** shepherd; pastor
bugeles *n.f* **bugelesow** shepherdess
bugelya *vb* herd
bugh *n.f* **bughes** cow. **bugh-godra** *n.f* dairy cow. **gwelen vughes** *n.f* cattle prod
bughik *n.f* **bughigesow** little cow
bughik Dhuw *n.f* **bughigesow Duw** ladybird
bughwas *n.m* **bughwesyon** cowboy. **fylm bughwas** *n.m* Western (*film genre*)
Bulgarek *n.m* Bulgarian language
bulgarek *adj* Bulgarian
Bulgari *top n.f* Bulgaria
Bulgarian *n.m* **Bulgarians** Bulgarian
bulhorn *n.m* **bulhornes** snail
bulugen *n.f* **bulugennow** earthworm
buluk *n.coll* earthworms
burjes *n.m* **burjysi** citizen; townsman
burjesek *adj* bourgeois
burjeseth *n.f* bourgeoisie
burjestra *n.f* **burjestrevow** borough; municipality
burm *n.coll* yeast
burokrat *n.m* **burokratyon** bureaucrat
burokratieth *n.f* bureaucracy
burow *n.m* **burowyow** bureau; office
busel *n.m* cow dung
bush *n.m* **bushys** crowd; mass. **bush a²** masses of
but *n.m* **butys** (*archery*) butt

byghan *adj* little; small. **an dus vyghan** the fairies
byghanhe *vb* reduce; make smaller
byghanna *adj* smaller
byjyon *n.m* **byjyons** rubbish tip; midden
bykken *adv* ever. **bys vykken** forever
bynari *adv* ever. **bys vynari** forever; evermore
bynitha *adv* ever. **bys vynitha** forever. **rag nevra vynitha** forever
bynk *n.f* **bynkyow** platform; workbench
bynner *adv* (*negative optative*) never. **bynner re wrello…** may he never do…
byrla *vb* embrace; hug
byrlans *n.m* **byrlansow** hug
bys (1) *n.m* **besies** digit; finger. **bys bras** *n.m* thumb. **bys rag** *n.m* index finger. **bys kres** *n.m* middle finger. **bys bysow** *n.m* ring finger. **bys byghan** *n.m* little finger. **bys troos** *n.m* toe
bys (2) *n.m* **bysow** world. **dres oll an bys** all over the world; worldwide
bys (3) *prp* until; till. **bys dhe²** *prp* up to. **bys di** to the place. **bys may⁵** *cnj* until; till. **bys pan²** *cnj* until; till. **bys yn** *prp* (*with nouns*) until; till; (*places*) all the way to. **bys vynitha** forever. **bys yn** *adv* all the way to
bysi *adj* busy; important; pressing. **bysi yw dhymm** I must
byskon *n.f* **byskonyow** thimble. **byskon mes** *n.f* acorn cup
bysow *n.m* **bysowyer** ring. **bys bysow** *n.m* ring finger. **bysow skovarn** *n.m* earring
bysowek *n.f* **bysowegi** keyboard
bystel *n.f* bile; gall
bystyon *adj* nasty
byth *adv* ever. **byth moy** nor yet; still more. **byth pan²** whenever

bythkweth *adv* ever (in the past);
never (in the past)
bythkwethek *adj* everlasting; eternal
bythlas *adj* evergreen
bytt *n.m* **byttys; byttow** (*IT*) bit
byttegyns *adv* however; nevertheless
byttele *adv* nonetheless
byw *adj* active; agile; alive; lively;
living; switched on. **arghans byw**
n.m mercury. **goli byw** *n.m* ulcer.
Kernewek Byw *n.m* Living Cornish.
yn fyw (*of an event*) live
bywhe *vb* activate; animate
bywheans *n.m* **bywheansow**
activation; animation
bywhes *adj* activated; animated

C

celder *n.m* **celders** cellar
cellulos *n.m* cellulose
celluloyd *n.m* celluloid
centimeter *n.m* **centimetrow**
centimetre
certan *adj* certain. **yn certan** *adv*
certainly
certifia *vb* certify
certifiys *adj* certified
cessya *vb* cease; give over
chal *n.m* **chalys** jowl; jaw
chalenj *n.m* **chalenjys** challenge; claim
chalenjya *vb* challenge
challa *n.m* **challys** jawbone; mandible
chambour *n.m* **chambours** bedroom
chanj *n.m* **chanjyow** change. **kevradh**
chanj *n.m* exchange rate
chanjus *adj* variable
chanjya *vb* alter; change; modify
chanjyans *n.m* **chanjyansow**
modification
chanjyell *n.f* **chanjyellow** (*software*)
editor
chapel *n.m* **chapelyow** chapel
charj *n.m* **charjys** charge; undertaking;
responsibility
charjya *vb* charge
chartour *n.m* **chartours** charter; deed.
An Darn Chartour The Charter
Fragment
chassya *vb* chase
chastia *vb* chastise; restrain

chatelydh *n.m* **chatelydhyon** capitalist
chatelydhieth *n.f* capitalism
chayn *n.m* **chaynys** chain
chaynya *vb* chain
checken *n.f* **checkennow** cheque.
checken ygor *n.f* blank cheque
checkva *n.f* **checkvaow** checkpoint
checkya *vb* check
Chek *n.m* **Chekyon** Czech
chek (1) *n.m* **chekys** cauldron; kettle.
chek te *n.m* tea kettle
chek (2) *adj* Czech. **Repoblek Chek**
n.f Czech Republic
Chekek *n.m* Czech language
chenon *n.m* **chenons** canon
cher *n.m* **cheryow** mood; state of mind;
cheer. **fekyl cher** hypocritical.
gwellha dha jer! cheer up! **brottel y**
jer moody
cher isel *n.m* depression (*colloq*)
cherita *n.m* charity
chersya *vb* cherish; fondle; pet. **chersya**
re pamper
cherya *vb* cheer up
chevalri *n.m* chivalry
chevisya *vb* borrow
chi *n.m* **chiow, treven** house. **chi dolli**
n.m doll's house. **chi golyow** *n.m*
holiday home. **chi gweder** *n.m*
greenhouse. **chi tiek** *n.m* farmhouse.
chi unnik *n.m* detached house
chif *n.m* **chifys** chief

chikog *n.f* **chikoges** house martin
chilader *n.m* **chiladron** burglar
chiladrans *n.m* **chiladransow** burglary
China *top n.f* China
Chinek *n.m* Chinese language
chinek *adj* Chinese
chogha *n.m* **choghys** jackdaw
choklet *n.m* **choklets** chocolate
chons *n.m* **chonsyow** chance; luck; odds; opportunity. **chons da!** good luck! **chons vyth!** no chance! nothing doing! **towl chons** *n.m* stroke of luck
chonsus *adj* casual; random

chonsya *vb* chance. **chonsya dhe**[2] (+ *verb*) happen to
chorl *n.m* **chorlys** (*offensive*) pleb; prole
churra nos *n.m* **churrys nos** nightjar
chyften *n.m* **chyftens** chieftain
chymbla *n.m* **chymblys** chimney
cider *n.m* **ciders** cider
cidi *n.m* **cidis** CD; compact disc
cigar *n.m* **cigarow** cigar
cigarik *n.m* **cigarigow** cigarette
cinema *n.m* **cinemas** cinema
cirk *n.m* **cirkow** circus
cita *n.f* **citys** city
civil *adj* civil

D

da *adj* good. **da lowr** OK; all right; mediocre. **bos da gans** be liked by
dader *n.m* goodness
dadhel *n.f* **dadhlow** argument; discussion; dispute
dadhelor *n.m* **dadheloryon** orator; debater
dadhelva *n.f* **dadhelvaow** debate
dadhla *vb* argue; discuss; debate
daffar *n.m* equipment; gear; kit; material; provision; stuff. **daffar ilow** *n.m* musical instrument. **daffar ladhva** *n.m* ammunition. **daffar lymm** *n.m* cutlery
dager *n.m* **dagrow** (*weep*) tear. **devera dagrow, skollya dagrow** shed tears. **skollya liv a dhagrow** cry one's eyes out
dagerles *n.m* betony (*wood; purple; bishop's wort*)
dagren *n.f* **dagrennow** teardrop
dagrewi *vb* weep; shed tears
dalgh *n.m* **dalghow** content
dalghasedh *n.m* capacitance
dalghedh *n.m* volume

dalghen *n.f* **dalghennow** grasp; grip; hold
dalghenna *vb* arrest; grasp; grip; lay hands on; seize
dalghennans *n.m* **dalghenansow** chemical suspension
dalghennas *n.m* **dalghenasow** arrest; holding
dalghennus *adj* absorbing (*interesting*)
dalghus *adj* inclusive
dalghuster *n.m* inclusivity; capacity
dall *adj* blind. **fordh dhall** *n.f* cul-de-sac; dead end
dalla *vb* blind
dallathvos *n.m* **dallathvosow** beginning; onset; origin
dalleth I *n.m* **dallethow** beginning; inception; opening; origin; start **II** *vb* begin; originate; set in; verb. **dalleth triga** set up house
dallether *n.m* **dallethoryon** beginner; novice
dallhe *vb* blind; dazzle
dalva *n.f* **dalvaow** quarrel
dama *n.f* **damyow** dame; mother. **dama wynn,** *n.f* grandmother

damach *n.m* **damajys** damage
dama goth *n.f* black sea bream
dampnya *vb* damn
damsel *n.f* **damsels** (*girl*) miss
Dan *n.m* **Danyon** Dane
Danek *n.m* Danish language
danek *adj* Danish
danjer *n.m* **danjeryow** danger; scruple.
  heb danjer *adj* safely
Danmark *top n.m* Denmark
dans *n.m* **dens** tooth. **dans dhelergh**
  n.m back tooth. **dans keyn** *n.m*
  wisdom tooth. **dans lagas** *n.m* canine
  tooth. **dans lew** *n.m* dandelion. **dans**
  olifans *n.m* ivory. **dans rag** *n.m* front
  tooth. **dans-sugna** *n.m* milk tooth.
dansell *n.f* **dansellow** cog
danvon *vb* dispatch; send
danvonadow *n.m* transmission;
  instructions
da-ober *n.m* **da-oberow** good deed
dar *n.m* **deri** oak
dar! *int* why! what!
dar- *prfx* pre-; fore-
daras *n.m* **darasow** door. **war dharas**
  through a door
darasik *n.m* **darasigow** wicket
darbar *n.m* **darbarow** preparation;
  provision
darbarer *n.m* **darbaroryon** assistant
darbari *vb* equip; prepare
darbarys *adj* equipped; prepared
darbolla *vb* convince
dardhyghtya *vb* dictate (*to a secretary*)
dargan *n.f* **darganow** forecast;
  prediction; prophecy. **herwydh an**
  dhargan according to the forecast
dargana *vb* forecast; predict
darganadow *adj* predictable
darlesa *vb* broadcast; televise
darlesans *n.m* **darlesansow** broadcast
darleverel *vb* predict
darn *n.m* **darnow** bit; fragment; part;
  piece. **darn paper** *n.m* slip of paper
darnas *n.m* **darnasow** portion

daromdak *n.m* **daromdagow** traffic
  jam
daromres I *n.m* **daromresow** traffic;
  intercourse; oscillation. **daromres**
  karnal *n.m* sexual intercourse **II** *vb*
  frequent
darsewya *vb* prosecute
darsewyans *n.m* **darsewyansow**
  prosecution
darsewyas *n.m* **darsewysi** prosecutor
darvos I *n.m* **darvosow** event **II** *vb*
  happen
darweri *vb* forewarn
das *n.f* **deys** stack; rick. **das wora** *n.f*
  haystack
das- *prfx* re-; again
dasa *vb* stack
dasanedhi *vb* resettle
dasarvedh *vb* retaliate
dashenwel *vb* rename
dashwithra *vb* review; re-examine
dashwithrans *n.m* **dashwithransow**
  review; re-examination
daskarga *vb* reload
daskavos *vb* recover; get back
daskelwel *vb* recall; call back
daskemeres *vb* resume
daskenedhlegys *adj* renationalized
dasknias *vb* chew cud
daskor *vb* restore; give up; give back
daskwertha *vb* retail
daskwerthans *n.m* **daskwerthansow**
  retail
daskwerther *n.m* **daskwerthoryon**
  retailer
daslev *n.m* **daslevow** echo
dasleverel *vb* say again; repeat
dasliv *n.m* feedback
dasliva *vb* feedback
dasoberi *vb* react
dasoberor *n.m* **dasoberoryon** reactor.
  dasoberor nuklerek *n.m* nuclear
  reactor
dasoberyans *n.m* **dasoberyansow**
  reaction

daspren *n.m* **dasprenyow** ransom; redemption

dasprena *vb* buy back; ransom; redeem

daspryntya *vb* reprint

daspryntyans *n.m* **daspryntyansow** reprint

dasseni *vb* echo

dasserghi *vb* revive; resurrect. **Kernewek Dasserghys** *n.m* Revived Cornish

dasserghyans *n.m* **dasserghyansow** revival; resurrection

dassettya *vb* reset

dassev *n.m* rehab

dassevelyans *n.m* rehabilitation

dasskrif *n.m* **dasskrifow** rewrite; copy

dasskrifa *vb* rewrite; copy

dasson *n.m* **dassonyow** echo

dastardh *n.m* **dastardhow** resurgence

dastarlesans *n.m* **dastarlesansow** (*broadcasting*) repeat

dastewynnya *vb* reflect

dastrehevel *vb* reconstruct

dastrehevyans *n.m* **dastrehevyansow** reconstruction

dasunya *vb* reunify

dasunyans *n.m* **dasunyansow** reunification

daswel *n.f* **daswelyow** review; revision

dasweles *vb* review; revise

daswerth *n.f* **daswerthow** resale. **pris daswerth** *n.m* resale price. **toll dhaswerth** *n.f* value added tax

daswertha *vb* resell

daswerther *n.m* **daswerthoryon** reseller

daswrians *n.m* **daswriansow** remake; reproduction

daswriansek *adj* iterative

daswul *vb* redo; remake

dates *n.coll* (*fruit*) dates

datesen *n.f* **datesennow** (*fruit*) date

davas *n.f* **deves** sheep; ewe. **kig davas** *n.m* mutton

de I *n.m* yesterday II *adv* yesterday. **de vyttin** yesterday morning

debatya *vb* debate; discuss; argue

debisya *vb* debit; charge

deboner *adj* gracious

debreni *vb* itch

debron *n.m* **debronow** itch

dedhewadow *n.m* **dedhewadowyow** promise. **an Tiredh a Dhedhewadow** *n.m* the Promised Land

dedhewi *vb* promise. **dedhewys heb keweras** an unkept promise

dedhwi *vb* lay (*eggs*)

dedhya *vb* date (*a document*)

dedhyas *n.m* **dedhyasow** (specific) date. **dedhyas diwedh** *n.m* date of expiry

dedhyek *adj* daily

defendya *vb* defend; eliminate; erase

defendyans *n.m* **defendyansow** erasure

defens *n.m* defence; resistance

defia *vb* defy

defians *n.m* **defiansow** defiance

defolya *vb* defile; pollute

defolyans *n.m* **defolyansow** defilement; pollution

defolyer *n.m* **defolyoryon** polluter

defowt *n.m* **defowtow** default; defect; failing; failure

deg *num* ten

dega *n.m* **degedhow** tithe

degadow *adj* portable

degea *vb* close; enclose

degedhek *n.m* **degedhogow** decimal

degemeres *vb* accept; receive; take up. **degemeres a-berth** admit

degemerus *adj* hospitable

degemerva *n.f* **degemervaow** reception area

degemeryans *n.m* **degemeryansow** reception

deges *adj* shut

degevi *vb* pay tithe

deghesi *vb* cast; fling; hurl; throw violently

degi *vb* (= **don**) carry; bear

deglena *vb* shiver

degoodh *vb* is due; is fitting

degowek I *adj* teenage **II** *n.m* **degowogyon** teenager

degre *n.m* **degrys** degree; rank

degves *num* tenth. **degves ha tri ugens** seventieth. **degves ha peswar ugens** ninetieth

degvledhen *n.f* **degvledhynnyow** decade

degynsywa *vb* impend

degynsywek *adj* imminent; impending

dehen *n.m* **dehennow** cream. **dehen howl** *n.m* sun cream. **dehen rew** *n.m* ice cream. **dehen molys** *n.m* clotted cream. **tesen dhehen** *n.f* cream cake

dehwelans *n.m* **dehwelansow** (= **dehwelyans**) return; comeback

dehweles *vb* return; come back; go back; turn back

dehwelyans *n.m* **dehwelyansow** (= **dehwelans**) return; comeback

deklarya *vb* announce; declare

deklaryans *n.m* **deklaryansow** declaration

deklinya *vb* decline

deklinyans *n.m* **deklinyansow** declension

del *n.coll* leaves. **del bleujyow** *n.coll* petals

dela *n.f* **deledhow** yardarm

delanwes *n.m* **delanwesow** influence

delatya *vb* defer; delay; postpone; put back; drag one's feet; procrastinate

delay *n.m* **delays** delay

delek *adj* leafy

delen *n.f* **delyow** leaf. **delen vleujen** *n.f* petal

delennek *adj* leafy

delenwel *vb* influence

deleva *vb* yawn

delinya *vb* draw; represent

delinyans *n.m* **delinyansow** drawing; layout

delit *n.m* **delitys** fun; delight; pleasure

delitya *vb* delight

delivra *vb* deliver; free. **delivra dhyworth** deliver from; free from. **delivra dhe²** deliver up. **delivra dhe wari** liberate; set free

delivrans *n.m* **delivransow** deliverance; riddance

delk *n.m* **delkow** necklace

dell² *cnj* how; as. **dell hevel** as it seems; **dell grysav** as I believe. **dell y'm kyrri** be so kind as to

dellni *n.m* blindness; vision impairment

delow *n.f* **delowyow** statue; icon

delvrys *n.m* **delvrysyow** ideal

delvrysek *adj* ideal

delwedh *n.m* imagery

delyowek *adj* leafy

demedhi *vb* marry

demedhyans *n.m* **demedhyansow** marriage

demedhys *adj* married

dementia *n.m* dementia (*med*)

demma *n.m* **demmys** dime; halfpenny

Demokrat *n.m* **Demokratyon** (*member of US Democratic party*) Democrat

demokratek *adj* democratic

demokratieth *n.f* **demokratiethow** democracy

demondya *vb* demand

den *n.m* **tus** man; guy; human; person. **den bal** *n.m* miner. **den ergh** *n.m* snowman. **den jentyl** *n.m* gentleman. **den mas** *n.m* good man. **den vyth** nobody. **den y'n bys** nobody at all

dena *vb* absorb; suck

denagha *vb* withdraw; retract; refuse; reject

denans *n.m* absorption

dendyl *vb* deserve; earn; merit. **dendyl bewnans** earn a living. **dendylys yn ta** well deserved

denel *adj* human

dengerensedhek *adj* humanitarian

dengibya *vb* abduct; kidnap

dengibyans *n.m* **dengibyansow** abduction; kidnapping

denladh *n.m* **denladhow** homicide; manslaughter

denladha *vb* commit manslaughter

denladra *vb* abduct; kidnap

denladrans *n.m* **denladransow** abduction; kidnapping

denledhyas *n.m* **denledhysi** killer; assassin; murderer

densa *n.m* good man

densek I *adj* jagged; toothy; dental **II** *n.m* **densoges** (*fish*) hake

densek dowr *n.m* **densoges dowr** (*fish*) pike

densel *vb* munch; crunch

denses *n.m* humanity

dentethyel *adj* delicious

denti *adj* dainty; delicate; fastidious; fussy. **tamm denti** *n.m* (*food*) delicacy

der (= **dre²**) *prp* (*before a vowel*) through; by means of; per. **der anow** verbal. *Personal forms: 1s* **dredhov**, *2s* **dredhos**, *3sm* **dredho**, *3sf* **dredhi**, *1p* **dredhon**, *2p* **dredhowgh**, *3p* **dredha**

-der *sffx* makes a masculine noun from an adjective

deray *n.m* **derays** chaos; disorder; mess

deraylya *vb* rail

derivador *n.m* **derivadoryon** reporter

derivadow *n.m* account; manifesto. **Derivadow an Gemynegoryon** *n.m* the Communist Manifesto

derivas I *n.m* **derivasow** account; narration; report; statement **II** *vb* inform; tell; relate; report. **derivas dhe² nebonan, derivas orth nebonan** inform somebody. **derivas ledan** *n.m* a sweeping statement

dermatologieth *n.f* dermatology

dermatologydh *n.m* **dermatologydhyon** dermatologist

dernigel *adj* fragmentary

derow (1) *n.m* **derowyow** beginning; start. **derow nos** *n.m* nightfall

derow (2) *n.coll* oaks

derowel *adj* original

derowen *n.f* **derow** oak tree

dervyn *vb* deserve; merit

derwen *n.f* **derow** oak tree

desedha *vb* adapt; adjust; fit; locate; suit

desedhans *n.m* situation; adjustment

desedhva *n.f* **desedhvaow** set (*in theatre*)

desegha *vb* dry out; dry up

desempis *adj* abrupt; immediate; instant. **koffi desempis** *n.m* instant coffee. **messach desempis** *n.m* instant message

deserth *adj* precipitous

desev *n.m* **desevow** assumption

desevos *vb* assume; expect; imagine; speculate

desin *n.m* **desinyow** design

desiner *n.m* **desinoryon** designer

desinya *vb* design

desiradow *adj* desirable

desk *n.m* **deskys, deskow** desk

deskerni *vb* snarl, grin

deskrifa *vb* describe

deskrifans *n.m* **deskrifansow** description

deskrifus *adj* descriptive

desper *n.m* despair

despit *n.m* **despityow** contempt; despite; insult. **despit heb y dyli** undeserved contempt. **yn despit dhe²** in despite of. **yn despit dhe'n fowtow** warts and all

despitya *vb* insult

desta *vb* testify; certify; witness

destna *vb* destine

destnans *n.m* fate

destnys *adj* destined

destryppya *vb* strip

destys *adj* certified

determya *vb* determine. **bos determys dhe**[2] be determined to; have decided upon

determys *adj* determined

deur *vb* concerns; *(3s only)* interests

deuv *n.m* **deuvyon** son-in-law

devarow *adj* stone-dead

devedhyans *n.m* **devedhyansow** arrival; advent; origin; source

devedhys *ppt* come (past participle of *dos*)

dever *n.m* **deverow** duty

devera *vb* drip; leak; trickle; shed. **devera dagrow** shed tears. **devera goos** lose blood

deverel *adj* watery

deverell dre withien *n.f* **deverellow dre withien** drip *(intravenous therapy; med)*

devis *n.m* **devisyow** device; notion

deviser *n.m* **devisoryon** inventor

devisya *vb* devise; invent; plan; scheme

devnydh *n.m* **devnydhyow** use; material; ingredient; stuff. **gul devnydh a**[2] make use of; utilise. **gul devnydh da a**[2] put to good use. **devnydh-tardha** *n.m* explosive

devnydhya *vb* utilise

devnydhyer *n.m* **devnydhyoryon** user

devnydhys *adj* used

devorya *vb* devour

devos *n.f* **devosow** ritual

devosek *adj* ritual

devosel *adj* ritual

devrek *adj* watery

devri I *adj* definite II *adv* **yn tevri** certainly; definitely; indeed; seriously

devyn *n.m* **devynnow** quote; quotation. **merk devyn** *n.m* quotation mark

devynna *vb* quote

dew[2] *num, n.m* two. **an dhew** *adj, prn* both

dewabrans *n.dl* (pair of) eyebrows

dewana *vb* penetrate; permeate

dewblek *adj* double

dewblekhe *vb* double

dewbries *n.m* married couple

dewdhegves *num* twelfth

dewdhek I *num* twelve II *n.m* **dewdhegow** dozen. **dewdhek person** *n.pl* jury

dewdhen *n.m* couple; pair

dewdhorn *n.dl* (pair of) fists; hands

dewdros *n.dl* (pair of) feet

dewek *adj* binary

dewelin *n.dl* (pair of) elbows

dewer *n.dl* (pair of) temples *(anat)*

dewfrik *n.dl* nostrils; muzzle; nose. **ughel y dhewfrik** stuck up

dewgorn *n.dl* (pair of) horns

dewgroch *n.dl* (pair of) crutches

dewi *vb* kindle

dewis I *n.m* **dewisyow** choice; option; pick; selection II *vb* choose; pick; select. **dre dhewis** optional. **ken dewis** *n.m* alternative

dewisek *adj* choosy

dewisel *adj* optional

dewisyans *n.m* **dewisyansow** *(IT)* preference

dewlagas *n.dl* (pair of) eyes

dewlin *n.dl* (pair of) knees

Dewnens *top n.m* Devon

dewufern *n.dl* (pair of) ankles

dew ugens *num* forty

dew ugensves *num* fortieth

dewweder *n.dl* (pair of) glasses; spectacles

dewyn *n.m* **dewynnow** ray. **dewyn-X** *n.m* X-ray

dewynnek *adj* radiant; glittering

dewynnell *n.f* **dewynellow** radiator

dewynnya *vb* radiate

dewynnyans *n.m* **dewynyansow** radiation

dha[2] *poss. adj* your *(sg)*

dh'aga[3] *contr* to their

dh'agan *contr* to our

dh'agas *contr* to your *(pl)*

dhe^2 *prp* to; for; at. **dhe dhiw eur androweyth** at two in the afternoon. **dhe wari** liberated. **spit dhe**^{2} in spite of. *Personal forms: 1s* **dhymm**, *2s* **dhis**, *3sm* **dhodho**, *3sf* **dhedhi**, *1p* **dhyn**, *2p* **dhywgh**, *3p* **dhedha**

dhe-denewen *adv* to one side

dhe-dre *adv* homewards

dhe-hys *adv* at length

dhe'm *contr* (= **dh'ow**^{3}) to my

dhe'n *contr* to the

dherag *prp* before. **dherag dorn** beforehand. *Personal forms: 1s* **dheragov**, *2s* **dheragos**, *3sm* **dheragdho**, *3sf* **dherygdhi**, *1p* **dheragon**, *2p* **dheragowgh**, *3p* **dheragdha**

'dhesempis *adv* (= **a-dhesempis**) forthwith; immediately

dhe'th^{5a} *contr* to your (*sg*)

dhe-ves *adv* away; off. **ke dhe-ves!** go away! (*sg*)

dhi *adv* to there, thither

dh'ow^3 *contr* (= **dhe'm**) to my

dh'y^2 *contr* to his; to its

dh'y^3 *contr* to her; to its

dhywar^2 *prp* (= **dywar**^{2}) from on, from over, from on top of. *Personal forms: 1s* **dhywarnav**, *2s* **dhywarnas**, *3sm* **dhywarnodho**, *3sf* **dhywarnedhi**, *1p* **dhywarnan**, *2p* **dhywarnowgh**, *3p* **dhywarnedha**

dhywarlinen *adj, adv* offline

dhyworth *prp* (= **dyworth**) from. *Personal forms: 1s* **dhyworthiv**, *2s* **dhyworthis**, *3sm* **dhyworto**, *3sf* **dhyworti**, *1p* **dhyworthyn**, *2p* **dhyworthowgh**, *3p* **dhywortha**

di *adv* to there, thither. **bys di** up to the place. **pan dhyffiv di** when I get there

di-^{2} *prfx* un-; -less; non-; without

-di *sffx* building; house

diabetes mellitus *n.m* diabetes mellitus (*med*)

diabetik I *adj* diabetic **II** *n.m* **diabetigyon** diabetic

diagnosa *vb* diagnose

diagnosans *n.m* **diagnosansow** diagnosis

dial *n.m* revenge; retribution

diala *vb* avenge; take revenge

dialar *adj* without grief

dialhwedha *vb* unlock

diallos *adj* incapable; incompetent; powerless; unable

diambos *adj* unaccountable

diamovyans *adj* emotionless; clinical

dianal *adj* breathless

diank I *n.m* **diankow** escape **II** *vb* escape; run away

diannedh *adj* uninhabited; unoccupied; homeless. **person diannedh** *n.m* homeless person

dianowi *vb* yawn

diantel I *adj* dangerous; unsteady; unstable **II** *vb* (*trap*) set off

diarghen *adj* barefoot

diaskellek *adj* wingless

dibalster *n.m* **dibalsteryow** austerity

dibarder *n.m* **dibarderyow** inequality

dibarow I *adj* unique; without equal; (*numbers*) odd **II** *adv* separately

dibarth *n.f* **dibarthow** departure; separation

dibayn *adj* painless

dibenn *adj* endless; eternal

dibenna *vb* behead; crop; top

diber *n.m* **dibrow** saddle. **diber dowr** *n.m* broad-brimmed hat

dibersonel *adj* impersonal

diberth *vb* (*intransitive*) depart; leave; part; (*transitive*) segregate; separate

diberthva *n.f* **diberthvaow** ward. **diberthva vamoleth** *n.f* maternity ward

diberthys *adj* separate

dibita *adj* heartless; pitiless; ruthless

diblans *adj* distinct; distinctive; separate; unrelated

diblanseth *n.f* distinctiveness; separateness

dibobel *adj* deserted; depopulated

diboll *adj* senseless

diboltra *vb* dust (off)

diboos *adj* unimportant

dibowes *adj* restless

dibra *vb* saddle

dibreder *adj* careless; irresponsible; rash; unwise

dibries *adj* unmarried

dibystik *adj* unharmed; unhurt

didakla *vb* dismantle

didal *adj* gratis

didhan I *adj* entertaining **II** *n.m* **didhenyow** amusement; entertainment

didhana *vb* amuse; delight; entertain

didhanedh *n.m* entertainment

didhaner *n.m* **didhanoryon** entertainer

didhanus *adj* amusing

didhehenna *vb* (*of milk*) skim

didhelen *adj* leafless

didhemedhi *vb* divorce

didhemedhyans *n.m* **didhemedhyansow** divorce

didhemedhys *adj* divorced

didheurek *adj* interesting

didhiwedh *adj* endless; infinite

didhiwedhter *n.m* infinity

didhoth *adj* tactless; uncivil

didhregynnus *adj* harmless

didhuw *adj* atheistic, godless

didhuwieth *n.f* atheism

didhuwydh *n.m* **didhuwydhyon** atheist

didhynnargh *adj* inhospitable; unwelcome

didoll *adj* tax-free

didon *adj* tuneless

didor *adj* continuous

didorreth *n.m* continuity

didowl *adj* unintentional

didreylya *vb* avert; divert

didro *adj* direct; straightforward

didrogentra *vb* unscrew

didros *adj* silent; noiseless

didrueth *adj* merciless

diduel *adj* neutral

diegi *n.m* laziness; lethargy; sloth

diek *adj* idle; lazy

diekter *n.m* laziness; indolence

dieli *adj* incurable

dielvenna *vb* analyse

dielvennans *n.m* **dielvenansow** analysis

dien *adj* complete; entire; thorough; utter. **yn tien** *adv* completely; wholly; utterly; thoroughly

dienebys *adj* unopposed

dieneth *n.f* completeness

dierbynna *vb* encounter

dieskis *adj* barefoot

dieth *n.m* shame. **dieth yw** it's a shame

difardella *vb* unpack

difastya *vb* unfasten

difen *vb* forbid; prohibit

difenner *n.m* **difenoryon** defendant

difennys *adj* prohibited

difeyth I *adj* barren; waste **II** *n.m* **difeythyow** wasteland; desert

difeythtir *n.m* **difeythtiryow** desert

difinweth *adj* unlimited

diflows *adj* straightforward; homely

difres I *n.m* **difresow** relief **II** *vb* defend; protect; relieve; save. **difres nebonan a neppyth** relieve somebody of something

difresek *adj* spare

difresyans *n.m* **difresyansow** protection; relief

difresyas *n.m* **difresysi** defender

difreth *adj* insipid; dull

difreudh *adj* non-violent

difron *adj* unrestrained

difudhell *n.f* **difudhellow** extinguisher

difudhi *vb* put out; extinguish

difun *adj* awake; sleepless. **pur dhifun** wide awake

difuna *vb* wake up. **heb difuna** dormant

difunell *n.f* **difunellow** alarm clock

difygas *n.m* **difygasow** deficit

difygel *adj* deficient

difygya *vb* cease; fail; fall short; run out (*of something*)

difyk *n.m* **difygyow** deficiency; eclipse

digelmi *vb* resolve; disentangle; untie

digelmys *adj* untied; (*e.g. a knot*) undone

digempen *adj* untidy

digemusur *adj* asymmetrical

digemyska *vb* sort

digessenyans *n.m* **digessenyansow** anomaly; dissonance

digeudh *adj* carefree

diglevesi *vb* disinfect

diglon I *adj* desperate; (*cheerless*) desolate **II** *n.f* desperation

diglos *adj* exposed

dignas *adj* unnatural; unkind

digodenni *vb* decode; decipher

digolenni *vb* depress; discourage

digolennys *adj* disheartened

digolm *n.m* **digolmow** solution

digolonna *vb* core

digolonnus *adj* discouraging

digommol *adj* cloudless

digompes *adj* irregular; uneven

digomposter *n.m* **digomposteryow** irregularity

digorf *adj* ethereal

digosk *adj* sleepless

digoswiga *vb* deforest

digoweth *adj* lonely; friendless

digreft *adj* inexpert; unskilled

digresennans *n.m* devolution

digresenni *vb* devolve; decentralise

digudh *adj* unconcealed

diguv *adj* unkind; unfriendly

dihanow *adj* anonymous; nameless

dihares I *n.m* **diharesow** apology **II** *vb* apologise. **diharesow!** *int* sorry!

diharesek *adj* apologetic

dihaval *adj* different; unlike. **different from** dihaval orth

dihevelebi *vb* alter; disfigure

dihevelepter *n.m* **dihevelepterow** difference

dihwans *adv* straight away

dilagha *adj* lawless

dilasek *adj* non-alcoholic

dilavar *adj* speechless

dilea *vb* abolish; cancel; delete; eliminate; remove

dileans *n.m* **dileansow** abolition; deletion; elimination

diles *adj* profitless; useless

dilestra *vb* disembark

dillas *n.coll* clothes; suit. **dillas-gwia** *n.coll* knitwear. **dillas nos** *n.coll* pyjamas. **dillas-neuvya** *n.coll* swimsuit. **dillas-omvadhya** *n.coll* bathing suit

dillasen *n.f* **dillasennow** item of clothing

dillasva *n.f* **dillasvaow** wardrobe

dilowr *adj* unsatisfactory

dilughya *vb* demist

din *n.m* **dinyow** fort

dinam *adj* flawless; spotless

dinas *n.m* **dinasow** fort

dinasydh *n.m* **dinasydhyon** civilian

dinatur *adj* abnormal; unnatural

dinek *adj* fortified (*of a building*)

diner *n.m* **dinerow** penny

dineren *n.f* **dinerennow** penny coin

dinerth *adj* forceless; powerless

dinythi *vb* generate; give birth

dinythor *n.m* **dinythoryon** generator. **dinythor tredan** *n.m* electric generator

dinythyans *n.m* generation; birth; reproduction

diod *n.m* **diodys** diode

diogel *adj* secure; reliable; certain. **diogel rag gossen** rustproof. **diogel ha kosel** safe and sound

diogeledh *n.m* security. **grugys diogeledh** *n.m* safety belt

diogeli *vb* secure; safeguard

diomborth *adj* unbalanced

diown *adj* fearless

diownekter *n.m* fearlessness

diplomen *n.f* **diplomennow** diploma

diras *adj* graceless

diredhya *vb* degrade

direson *adj* irrational

direwi *vb* defrost

direwl I *adj* irregular; anarchic **II** *n.m* irregularity; anarchy

direwlyas *n.m* **direwlysi** anarchist

direydh *adj* neuter

direyth *adj* illegitimate

dirolya *vb* unroll

diruska *vb* peel; skin; flay

diruskell *n.m* **diruskellow** (*tool*) peeler

dis *n.m* **disyow** dice

dis- *prfx* un-

disakord *n.m* **disakordow** disagreement

disakordya *vb* disagree

disawor *adj* unpleasant

discernya *vb* discern; discriminate

discernyans *n.m* **discernyansow** taste

disebilya *vb* unplug

disegha *vb* refresh; quench (*thirst*)

disegher *n.m* **diseghoryon** wiper; windscreen wiper

disel *n.m* diesel

disenor *n.m* **disenors** dishonour

disenora *vb* dishonour

diserri *vb* placate

dises *n.m* **disesys** disease; disquiet; inconvenience

disesya *vb* make ill at ease; molest

disevel *vb* upset; trip; throw down

disfavera *vb* discriminate against

disfaverus *adj* unfavourable

diskansa *vb* scale (*a fish*)

diskar *n.m* **diskarow** collapse

diskara *vb* collapse; fall apart

diskarga *vb* unload; discharge; unpack

diskargans *n.m* **diskargansow** discharge

diskevelsi *vb* dislocate (*a joint*)

diskeverans *n.m* **diskeveransow** outing

diskevra *vb* uncover

diskians *adj* unintelligent

diskler *adj* indistinct; opaque; unclear; vague. **kows diskler** *n.m* mumble

disklerya *vb* declare

diskleryans *n.m* **diskleryansow** declaration

disklos *adj* homeless

diskont *n.m* **diskontow** discount

diskontentys *adj* discontented; unsatisfied

diskontya *vb* discount

diskortes *adj* impolite; rude

diskryjyk I *adj* sceptical **II** *n.m* **diskryjygyon** sceptic

diskudha *vb* discover; expose; reveal; uncover; disclose

diskudhans *n.m* **diskudhansow** discovery; revelation; dislosure

diskwedhes *vb* show; appear. **diskwedhes an meus** thumb a lift

diskwedhyans *n.m* **diskwedhyansow** exhibition; show; revelation

diskwedhyn *n.f* **diskwedhynnow** exhibit

diskwir *adj* non-standard

diskwitha *vb* relax; repose; rest

diskwithans *n.m* relaxation

diskwithus *adj* relaxing

dislen *adj* faithless; unfaithful

dislenni *vb* unveil

disliw *adj* pale; dull; drab

disliwa *vb* fade

dismaylya *vb* unwrap

dismygel *adj* imaginary

dismygi *vb* figure out; find out; guess; imagine; invent

dismygriv *n.m* **dismygrivow** estimate

dismygwari I *n.m* **dismygwariow** improvisation **II** *vb* improvise

dismygyans *n.m* **dismygyansow** imagination; invention

dismyk *n.m* **dismygow** riddle (*puzzle*)

disobaya *vb* disobey

dison I *adj* quiet; soundless **II** *adv* forthwith; without another word

disonest *adj* dishonest

disonester *n.m* dishonesty

disordyr bipolar *n.m* bipolar disorder (*med*)

disordyr dybri *n.m* eating disorder

Disordyr Gorgemeryansek Omherdhys *n.m* Obsessive Compulsive Disorder; OCD

Disordyr Gwask wosa Trawma *n.m* Post-traumatic Stress Disorder; PTSD

disordyr personoleth *n.m* personality disorder (*med*)

Disordyr Spektrom Awtysm *n.m* Autism Spectrum Disorder; ASD

dispar *adj* unequal

displegel *adj* developing

displegya *vb* develop; explain; unfold. **heb displegya** undeveloped

displegyans *n.m* **displegyansow** development; explanation

displegyansek *adj* explanatory

displesour *n.m* **displesours** displeasure

displesya *vb* displease

displesyans *n.m* displeasure

displesys *adj* displeased

displetya *vb* display; unfold

displetyans *n.m* **displetyansow** display

disposya *vb* dispose

dispresya *vb* despise; look down on; neglect; slight

dispresyans *n.m* **dispresyansow** contempt; neglect; slight

disprevi *vb* disprove

disputya *vb* argue; dispute. **disputya orth** argue with. **disputya erbynn** argue against

disrannen *n.f* **disranennow** denominator

dissembla *vb* dissemble

dissent *n.m* dissent

dissentya *vb* dissent; disagree

dissentyer *n.m* **dissentyoryon** non-conformist

distag *adj* detached

distaga *vb* (*intransitive*) come away; (*transitive*) detach. **distaga dhyworth** come away from

distagyn *n.f* **distagynnow** military detail

distempra *vb* upset

distemprys *adj* upset

disto *adj* homeless

distowgh *adv* suddenly; staight away; directly

distrui *vb* destroy; do for

distruyans *n.m* **distruyansow** destruction

distyr *adj* insignificant; of no account

diswar *adj* unwary; unaware; unconscious

diswaytus *adj* disappointing

diswaytyans *n.m* **diswaytyansow** disappointment

diswaytyas *vb* disappoint

diswaytys *adj* disappointed

diswrians *n.m* **diswriansow** ruin; destruction; undoing

diswrys *adj* done for; undone; ruined

diswul *vb* undo; spoil; dismantle

disynklevya *vb* disinfect

disynklevyans *n.m* **disynklevyansow** disinfection

disynklevyas *n.m* **disynklevysi** disinfectant

divagli *vb* disentangle; separate

divaren *n.f* **divarennow** constant

divarva *vb* shave. **ewon-divarva** *n.coll* shaving foam

divedhow *adj* sober

diveri *vb* pour

divern *adj* unconcerned; carefree

divers *adj* diverse; miscellaneous; varied; various

diversita *n.m* **diversitys** diversity

diveth *adj* shameless

divlam *adj* blameless; irreproachable

divlas *adj* disgusting; gross; offensive; revolting; unpleasant

divlasa *vb* (*transitive*) disgust; offend; (*intransitive*) be disgusted; feel revulsion

divroa *vb* migrate

divroans *n.m* **divroansow** migration

divroek *n.m* **divroegyon** migrant

divroyas *n.m* **divroysi** emigrant

divyn *vb* chop; mince

diw^2 *num, n.f* two. **an dhiw** *adj, prn* both

diwarr *n.dl* (pair of) legs

diwawen *n.dl* jaws

diwbedren *n.dl* (pair of) buttocks

diwedh *n.m* **diwedhow** end; outcome. **dedhyas diwedh** *n.m* date of expiry. **heb dhiwedh** eternal. **war an diwedh** at long last; in the long term

diwedha *vb* end; expire

diwedhans *n.m* **diwedhansow** expiry

diwedhes *adj* late

diwedhva *n.f* **diwedhvaow** ending

diwedhyn *adj* stiff; inflexible

diwedhynder *n.m* **diwedhynderyow** inflexibility

diwedhys *adj* over; ended

diwen *n.dl* jaws

diweres *adj* helpless

diwerth *adj* valueless; worthless

diwes *n.m* **diwosow** drink

diwessa *vb* go drinking

diwettha *adj* last; later; latest; latter; extreme

diweyth *adj* unemployed

diweythieth *n.f* unemployment. **gober diweythieth** *n.m* unemployment benefit

diwgasel *n.dl* (pair of) armpits

diwgell *n.dl* (pair of) testicles

diwglun *n.dl* (pair of) hips

diwgoloren *n.dl* (pair of) collar-bones

DiWi *n.m* WiFi

diwirhaval *adj* unlikely; improbable

diwiska *vb* undress; take off

diwiskieth *n.f* nudism

diwiskydh *n.m* **diwiskydhyon** naturist; nudist

diwith *adj* unprotected

diwiver *adj* wireless

diwla *n.dl* (pair of) hands

diwleuv *n.dl* (pair of) hands

diwodhav *adj* intolerable

diwosa *vb* (*transitive*) bleed

diwotti *n.m* **diwottiow** pub; tavern

diwreydhek *adj* bisexual

diwreydhya *vb* eradicate; stamp out

diwros *n.f* **diwrosow** bicycle

diwrosa *vb* cycle; ride a bike

diwroser *n.m* **diwrosoryon** cyclist

diwskodh *n.dl* (pair of) shoulders

diwskovarn *n.dl* (pair of) ears

diwvogalen *n.f* **diwvogalennow** diphthong

diwvogh *n.dl* (pair of) cheeks

diwvordhos *n.dl* (pair of) thighs

diwvregh *n.dl* (pair of) arms

diwvron *n.dl* (pair of) breasts

diwvronner *n.m* **diwvronoryon** bra

diwweus *n.dl* (pair of) lips

diwwewen *n.dl* (pair of) heels

diwweyth *adv* twice. **diwweyth mar dha** twice as good

diwyethek *adj* bilingual

diwyethogeth *n.f* bilinguialism

diwysyans *n.m* **diwysyansow** industry

diwysyansel *adj* industrial

diwysygneth *n.f* diligence

diwysyk *adj* conscientious; diligent; earnest; hard-working; industrious; zealous; observant

diwysykter *n.m* zeal

diyskynna *vb* descend; go down; alight

diyskynnus *adj* descending. **yn aray diyskynnus** in descending order

dogen *n.m* **dognow** dose

dognya *vb* dose

dognyans *n.m* **dognyansow** dosage

dogvennek *adj* documentary

dohajydh *n.m* **dohajydhyow** afternoon. **dohajydh da** good afternoon

dohajydhweyth *adv* afternoon-time

doktour *n.m* **doktours** (*title*) doctor

doktourieth *n.f* doctorate

dol *n.m* dole

dolli *n.f* **dolliow** doll

dolor *n.m* **dolors** pain

domhwel *vb* revolt; overthrow

domhwelans *n.m* **domhwelansow** (*political*) revolution; revolt

domhweler *n.m* **domhweloryon** revolutionary

domhwelus *adj* revolutionary

domino *n.m* domino

don *vb* (= **degi**) carry; bear

dones *vb* (= **dos**) come; arrive

doneson *n.m* **donesonow** donation

dons *n.m* **donsyow** dance

donsya *vb* dance

donsyer *n.m* **donsyoryon** dancer

doos *adj* dense

dooth I *adj* prudent; sage II *n.m* **dothyon** (*wise person*) sage

dor *n.m* **doryow** earth; ground. **dhe'n dor** down; to the ground. **dor bras** *n.m* mainland. **know dor** *n.coll* peanuts; groundnuts

dorge *n.m* **dorgeow** earthwork

dorgel *n.m* **dorgellow** cellar; vault

dorgrys *n.m* **dorgrysyow** earthquake

dorhok *n.m* **dorhokys** nightjar

dorn *n.m* **dornow**, *dl* **dewdhorn** fist; hand. **dhe dhorn** nearby; near at

hand. **dherag dorn** beforehand. **dre dhorn** manual(ly). **fardellow dorn** *n.pl* hand-luggage. **padel dhorn** *n.f* saucepan

dorna *vb* bash; beat; punch; strike; thrash; thump

dornas *n.m* **dornasow** fistful; handful

dornbel *n.f* **dornbelyow** handball

dornel *adj* manual

dornell *n.f* **dornellow** whisk

dornella *vb* whip (*cream*)

dornla *n.m* **dornleow** handle

dornlyver *n.m* **dornlyvrow** handbook; manual

dornskrif *n.m* **dornskrifow** manuscript

dornskrifa *vb* write by hand

dornskrifans *n.m* **dornskifansow** handwriting

dornweyth *n.m* **dornweythyow** handicraft

doronieth *n.f* geography

doroniethel *adj* geographical

dororieth *n.f* geology

dororiethel *adj* geological

dororydh *n.m* **dororydhyon** geologist

dos *vb* come; arrive. **dos erbynn** encounter. **dos dhe weles** come and see. **dos ha** happen to. **dos ha bos** become. **dos nes** come close; approach. **dos yn-rag** come on

dosedh *n.m* **dosedhow** (*in physics*) density

doth *adj* discreet; tactful; well behaved

dothenep *n.m* tact

dothter *n.m* prudence; tact

dotya *vb* dote; go mad

dour *adj* intensive; rigorous

dourwith *n.m* intensive care

doust *n.m* dust

dout (1) *cnj* lest. **kemmer with dout ty dhe godha** mind you don't fall

dout (2) *n.m* **doutys** doubt; scruple. **heb dhout** without doubt; of course; undoubtedly

doutus *adj* doubtful

doutya *vb* doubt; fear

doutys *adj* jittery

dov *adj* tame; pet. **eneval dov** *n.m* pet animal. **bocka dov** *n.m* familiar (*demon or spirit*)

dova *vb* tame

dover *n.m* **dovoryon** tamer. **dover lewyon** *n.m* lion tamer

dovhe *vb* tame

down *adj* deep

downder *n.m* **downderyow** depth

downfria *vb* deep-fry

downhe *vb* deepen

downrewi *vb* deep-freeze

dowr *n.m* **dowrow** water; (*in names of rivers*) river. **a'n dowr** aquatic. **dowr ewonek** *n.m* mineral water. **dowr sall** *n.m* salt water. **Dowr Tamar** *n.m* River Tamar. **dowr tomm** *n.m* brandy. **dowr tomm molas** *n.m* rum. **dowr tomm Alban** *n.m* whisky. **dowr tomm Iwerdhon** *n.m* whiskey. **dowr tonek** *n.m* tonic water

dowra *vb* water; (*crash-land in water*) ditch

dowrargh *n.m* **dowrarghow** water tank

dowrdredanek *adj* hydroelectric

dowrek *adj* watery; aquatic

dowrfols *n.m* **dowrfolsyow** leak

dowrgi *n.m* **dowrgeun** otter

dowrgleudh *n.m* **dowrgleudhyow** canal

dowrhe *vb* irrigate; water

dowrlam *n.m* **dowrlammow** waterfall

dowrliw *n.m* **dowrliwyow** water-colour

dowrrath *n.f* **dowrrathes** water vole

dowrvargh *n.m* **dowrvergh** hippopotamus

dowrya *vb* moisten

dowryar *n.f* **dowryer** coot

dragon *n.f* **dragones** dragon

dralva *n.f* **dralvaow** scrap heap

drama *n.m* **dramas** drama

dramasek *adj* dramatic

dramasydh *n.m* **dramasydhyon** dramatist

dramatydh *n.m* **dramatydhyon** playwright

drayl *n.m* (*pull*) **draylyow** drag

draylell *n.f* **draylellow** sleigh

draylya *vb* drag

draylyer *n.m* **draylyoryon** trailer

dre[2] *prp* (= **der**) (*before a consonant*) through; by means of; per. **dre happ** by chance; incidentally. **dre lev** vocal. **dre reson** because. **dre vras** generally; mainly; for the most part. **dre wythien** intravenous. *Personal forms: 1s* **dredhov**, *2s* **dredhos**, *3sm* **dredho**, *3sf* **dredhi**, *1p* **dredhon**, *2p* **dredhowgh**, *3p* **dredha**

drefen *cnj* because of; on account of

dregyn *n.m* **dregynnow** harm; mischief

dregynna *vb* wrong

dregynnus *adj* harmful; mischievous

drehedhes *vb* reach; access; arrive

drehedhyans *n.m* **drehedhyansow** attainment; reach

drehevel *vb* build; construct; erect; lift; raise

drehever *n.m* **drehevoryon** builder

drehevyans *n.m* **drehevyansow** building; construction; erection

dremedal *n.m* **dremedales** dromedary

dren *n.m* **dreyn** thorn; fishbone

drenek *adj* thorny

dres *adv, prp* beyond; over; through; during; past; in the course of. **dres an jydh** all day long. **dres henna** besides. **dres keyn** afterwards. **dres oll** particularly; primarily. **dres eghen** *adj* extraordinary; *adv* extraordinarily. **dres musur** extremely. **dres nivera** redundant (*supernumerary*). **dres nos** overnight. **dres penn ha diwskovarn** head over heels. **dres pols** temporarily. *Personal forms: 1s* **dresov**,

2s **dresos**, 3sm **dresto**, 3sf **dresti**, 1p
  dreson, 2p **dresowgh**, 3p **dresta**
dreslemmel *vb* jump over. **dreslemmel**
  an lost jump the queue
drewedhek *adj* druidical
dreweskel *vb* buffet
drewydh *n.m* **drewydhyon** druid
dreys *n.coll* brambles
dreysa *vb* tangle
dreysen *n.f* **dreysennow** bramble
dri *vb* bring; persuade
drivya *vb* drive. **drivya yn-mes** drive
  out
drog I *adj* bad; evil; invalid; naughty;
  wicked; nasty **II** *n.m* **drogow** bad; ill;
  harm; hurt. **drog dans** *n.m* toothache.
  drog penn *n.m* headache. **drog dres**
  eghen abysmal. **drog pes** *adj*
  displeased; dissatisfied; in a bad
  mood. **drog yw genev** I'm sorry
droga *vb* wrong
drogbrederys *adj* malicious
drogdybi *vb* suspect
drogedh *n.m* **drogedhow** (*moral*
  weakness) vice
drogfara *vb* behave badly
drogg *n.m* **droggys** drug
drog gerys *adj* infamous
droghandla *vb* mishandle; abuse
droglam *n.m* **droglammow** accident;
  crash; mishap
drog-ober *n.m* **drog-oberow** crime;
  bad deed
drogoberor *n.m* **drogoberoryon**
  criminal; culprit
drog-polat *n.m* **drog-polatys** rascal;
  scoundrel
drogura *vb* smear
drogurans *n.m* **droguransow** smear
drogwas *n.m* **drogwesyon** rogue;
  delinquent
drokoleth *n.f* wrong; wickedness
droktavosek *adj* foul-mouthed
droktemprys *adj* bad-tempered
drokter *n.m* wickedness

drolla *n.m* **drollys** folk tale; story; yarn.
  derivas drolla spin a yarn
droppya *vb* drop
droppys kogh *n.coll* fuchsia
droug *n.m* **drougow** drug
drudh *adj* cherished; favourite;
  precious
drumm *n.m* **drummyow** ridge
dryftbren *n.m* **dryftbrennyer**
  driftwood
dryftya *vb* drift
dryftyans *n.m* **dryftyansow** drift.
  dryftyans an brastiryow *n.m*
  continental drift
drylsi *n.m* monotonous, annoying
  noise
Du *n.m* November
du *adj* black. **pur dhu** pitch black
duhe *vb* blacken
duik *adj* blackish
duk *n.m* **dukys** duke
dukes *n.f* **dukesow** duchess
duketh *n.f* **dukethow** duchy
dulas *adj* dark green
dur *n.m* steel
Durdadhewhi *idiom* good day
Durnostadha *idiom* good night
Dursona *idiom* God bless!
durya *vb* last; continue; endure
duryadow *adj* lasting; durable
duryer *n.m* **duryoryon** survivor
dustuni *n.m* **dustuniow** evidence;
  testimony; witness
dustunia *vb* testify; witness
dustunier *n.m* **dustunioryon** witness
Duw *n.m* (Jewish, Christian & Muslim)
  God. **awos Duw** for crying out loud;
  for God's sake. **molleth Duw!** damn!
duw *n.m* **duwow** god
duwena *vb* sadden; grieve
duwenhe *vb* grieve; sadden
duwenhes *adj* grieved; saddened
duwenus *adj* depressing
duwenys *adj* depressed (*colloq*)
duwes *n.f* **duwesow** goddess

duwon *n.m* grief; sadness; sorrow

duwonieth *n.f* theology

duwonydh *n.m* **duwonydhyon** theologian

dy' *abbrev* day. **dy'gol** *n.m* holiday; vacation; feast-day. **dy'Lun** *n.m* Monday. **dy'Meurth** *n.m* Tuesday. **dy'Mergher** *n.m* Wednesday. **dy'Yow** *n.m* Thursday. **dy'Gwener** *n.m* Friday. **dy'Sadorn** *n.m* Saturday. **dy'Sul** *n.m* Sunday

dybradow *adj* edible

dybri *vb* eat

dydh *n.m* **dedhyow** day; date. **dres an jydh** all day long. **hanter-dydh** *n.m* midday; noon. **hunros dydh** *n.m* daydream; reverie. **unweyth y'n jydh** once a day

dydhlyver *n.m* **dydhlyvrow** diary

dydhweyth *n.m* daytime

dyegrans gonisogeth *n.m* culture shock

dyegri *vb* dazzle; shock

dyegrys *adj* shocked; terrified; thunderstruck

dyena *vb* pant; gasp

dyffrans **I** *adj* different; divergent; various **II** *n.m* **dyffransow** difference; distinction

dyghow *adj* (*opposite of left*) right; right-handed

dyghowbarth *n.f* south. **a'n dhyghowbarth** southern

dyghtya *vb* treat; dictate; manage; serve; trim. **dyghtya kreghyn** tan leather

dyghtyans *n.m* **dyghtyansow** procedure; treatment; therapy; management. **dyghtyans kemmyn** routine procedure

dyghtyer *n.m* **dyghtyoryon** manager. **dyghtyer galar** *n.m* **dyghtyoryon alar** funeral director

dyghtys *adj* treated; processed. **keus dyghtys** *n.m* processed cheese

dy'gol *n.m* **dy'golyow** feast-day; holiday; vacation. **dy'gol kemmyn** *n.m* bank holiday. **dy'gol arghantti** *n.m* bank holiday. **Dy'gol Maria Mis Meurth** *n.m* The Feast of the Annunciation. **Dy'gol Stefan** Boxing Day

dy'Gwener *n.m* Friday. **dy'Gwener dhe nos** Friday night. **dy'Gwener an Grows** *n.m* Good Friday

dy'gweyth *n.m* **dedhyow gweyth** weekday

dygynsete **I** *adv* on the day before yesterday; **II** *n.m* the day before yesterday

dyji *n.m* **dyjiow** small cottage

dyjyn *n.m* **dyjynnow** dot; speck; mite; little piece. **dyjynnow an veusva** *n.pl* dots per inch; DPI

dyllans *n.m* **dyllansow** edition; issue; release

dyller *n.m* **dylloryon** publisher

dyllo *vb* issue; release; leak; publish

dy'Lun *n.m* Monday. **dy'Lun dhe nos** Monday night. **dy'Lun Penkost** Whitmonday

dy'Mergher *n.m* Wednesday. **dy'Mergher dhe nos** Wednesday night

dy'Meurth *n.m* Tuesday. **dy'Meurth dhe nos** Tuesday night

dynamegieth *n.f* dynamics

dynamek *adj* dynamic

dynamit *n.m* dynamite

dynamitya *vb* dynamite

dynamo *n.m* **dynamoyow** dynamo

dynedh *n.m* inductance

dynerghi *vb* greet; welcome

dynita *n.m* dignity

dynnargh *n.m* **dynarghow** greeting; welcome

dynya *vb* fascinate; entice

dynyans *n.m* **dynyansow** fascination

dynyansek *adj* fascinating; tempting

dynyek *adj* tempting

dyowl *n.m* **dyowlow** (= **jowl**) devil

dy'Sadorn *n.m* Saturday. **dy'Sadorn dhe nos** Saturday night

dysforia reydhedh *n.m* gender dysphoria

dyskador *n.m* **dyskadoryon** (*male*) teacher; trainer; instructor; tutor

dyskadores *n.f* **dyskadoresow** (*female*) teacher; trainer; instructor; tutor

dyskans *n.m* **dyskansow** lesson; instruction; tuition; tutorial. **ri dyskans dhe²** educate. **feow dyskans** *n.pl* tuition fees. **fowt dyskans** *n.m* **fowtow dyskans** ignorance. **heb dyskans** *adj* ignorant

dyskansus *adj* tutorial

dyskas *n.m* **dyskasow** teaching; doctrine

dysker *n.m* **dyskoryon** learner

dyskevres *n.m* **dyskevresow** syllabus

dyski *vb* (*intransitive*) learn; (*transitive*) teach; train; instruct. **dyski gans** learn from. **dyski dhe nebonan gul neppyth** teach/train somebody to do something

dysklyver *n.m* **dysklyvrow** text-book

dyskybel *n.m* **dyskyblon** pupil; disciple; adherent

dyskybeleth *n.f* **dyskybelethow** discipline

dyskys *adj* learned; educated; erudite. **dyskys bras** scholarly

dysleksia *n.m* dyslexia (*med*)

dy'Sul *n.m* Sunday. **dy'Sul dhe nos** Sunday night

dysmorfia *n.m* dysmorphia (*med*)

dyth *n.m* **dythow** recitation; saying

dythya *vb* recite

dywar² *prp* (= **dhywar²**) from on, from over, from on top of. *Personal forms: 1s* **dywarnav**, *2s* **dywarnas**, *3sm* **dywarnodho**, *3sf* **dywarnedhi**, *1p* **dywarnan**, *2p* **dywarnowgh**, *3p* **dywarnedha**

dyworth *prp* (= **dhyworth**) from. *Personal forms: 1s* **dyworthiv**, *2s* **dyworthis**, *3sm* **dyworto**, *3sf* **dyworti**, *1p* **dyworthyn**, *2p* **dyworthowgh**, *3p* **dywortha**

dy'Yow *n.m* Thursday. **dy'Yow dhe nos** Thursday night

E

ea! *int* yes!

ebel *n.m* **ebeli** colt

ebil *n.m* **ebilyow, ebilyer** bolt; peg. **ebil horn** *n.m* iron bolt

ebilya *vb* plug

ebilyer *n.m* **ebilyer, ebilyorow** (*electrical*) plug

ebost *n.m* **ebostow** email

ebostya *vb* email

Ebrel *n.m* April

ebron *n.f* **ebronyow** sky

-edh *sffx* (*abstract noun suffix*)

edhel *n.coll* aspen

edhen *n.f* **ydhyn** bird

edhlen *n.f* **edhlennow** aspen

edhom *n.m* **edhommow** necessity; want; need. **edhom a'm beus anodho** I need it. **dres edhom** superfluous

edhommek I *adj* needy **II** *n.m* **edhomogyon** needy person

edrega *vb* regret

edregus *adj* regretful; repentant

edrek *n.m* **edregow** regret. **edrek a'm beus, yma edrek dhymm** I regret

edrygys *adj* sorry

efan *adj, adv* broad; vast; plainly; wide

efander *n.m* range; latitude; space (*in general*)

efani *vb* expand

efanvos *n.m* (*astronomy*) space

efanyans *n.m* expansion

effeyth *n.m* **effeythyow** effect. **effeyth Doppler** *n.m* Doppler effect. **effeyth chi gweder** *n.m* greenhouse effect

effeythadewder *n.m* efficiency

effeythadow *adj* efficient

effeythi *vb* effect

effeythus *adj* effective

eghek *n.m* **eghoges, eghogyon** salmon

eghel *n.f* **eghelow** axis

eghen *n.f* **eghennow** kind; sort; species; type; variety; genre. **a lies eghen** varied; heterogeneous. **a unn eghen** uniform. **awos eghen** at all costs. **dres eghen** exceedingly; outstanding; extremely. **eghen beryllys** *n.f* endangered species

eghoka *vb* fish for salmon

egin *n.m* **eginyow** shoot (*of plant*); bacterium

egina *vb* germinate; sprout; shoot (*growing plant*)

eglos *n.f* **eglosyow** church

Ejyp *top n.m* Egypt

Ejyptek *n.m* Egyptian language

ejyptek *adj* Egyptian

Ejyptyon *n.m* **Ejyptyonyon** Egyptian

-ek *sffx* adj. ending from noun

ekologieth *n.f* ecology

ekologydh *n.m* **ekologydhyon** ecologist

ekonomieth *n.f* economy

ekonomydh *n.m* **ekonomydhyon** economist

eksamnya *vb* examine; check; inspect

eksamnyer *n.m* **eksamnyoryon** examiner

eksekutya *vb* execute; run (*a program; IT*)

eksekutyans *n.m* **eksekutyansow** execution

eksistya *vb* exist

ekskludus *adj* exclusive

ekskludya *vb* exclude

eksotek *adj* exotic

eksperyans *n.m* **eksperyansow** experience

eksperyansys *adj* experienced

ekspres *adj* express

el *n.m* **eledh** angel

-el (1) *sffx* -al; -ile

-el (2) *sffx* (*verbal noun suffix*)

elastek *adj* elastic

elek *adj* angelic

elektron *n.m* **elektrons** electron

elektronek *adj* electronic

elester *n.coll* yellow flag iris

elestren *n.f* **elestrennow** (*plant*) iris

elgeth *n.f* **elgethyow** chin

eli *n.m* **eliow** balm; ointment; salve. **eli gweus** *n.m* lip balm; lip salve

elia *vb* anoint

eli lymmaval *n.m* lemon balm

elin *n.m* **elinyow** *dl* **dewelin** elbow; angle. **elin pedrek** *n.m* right angle

elinek *adj* angular

-ell *sffx* (*denotes tools and appliances*)

ellas *int* alas

elow *n.coll* elms

elowek *n.f* **elowegi** elm grove

elowen *n.f* **elowennow** elm

els *n.m* **elsyon** stepson

elses *n.f* **elsesow** stepdaughter

elven *n.f* **elvennow** element; factor; spark

elvennek *adj* basic; elementary

elvennel *adj* elemental

emayl *n.m* enamel

emaylhe *vb* enamel

emperes *n.f* **emperesow** empress

emperour *n.m* **emperours** emperor

emperouregek *adj* imperialistic

emperouregieth *n.f* imperialism

emperoureth *n.f* **emperourethow** empire

emperourethek *adj* imperial

emskemuna *vb* ban; excommunicate

-en *sffx* a feminine single item derived from a collective

ena *adv* there; then

enamel *n.m* enamel

enamelhe *vb* enamel

enebi *vb* face; oppose

enebieth *n.f* opposition

enep *n.m* **enebow** face

enesega *vb* insulate

enesek I *adj* insular **II** *n.f* **enesegi** archipelago

enesik *n.f* **enesigow** islet

enev *n.m* **enevow** soul. **daskor y enev** give up one's ghost

eneval *n.m* **enevales** animal. **eneval dov** *n.m* pet

ennwydh *n.coll* ash tree

eno *adv* over there; yonder

enor *n.m* **enorys** honour

enora *vb* honour

enoradow *adj* honourable

enorys *adj* honourable; honoured

enos *adj, adv* over there; yonder

enowell *n.f* **enowellow** lighter

enowi *vb* kindle; switch on

enowys *adj* lit

ensampel *n.m* **ensamplys, ensamplow** example; instance. **rag ensampel (r.e.)** for instance; for example (e.g.)

ensaym *n.m* **ensaymyow** enzyme

entra *vb* enter. **entra a-ji** go inside. **entra dhe² neb le, entra yn neb le** enter some place

entrans *n.m* **entransow** entrance

envi *n.m* enemy

enwydhen *n.f* **enwydhennow** ash tree

enys *n.f* **enesow** island. **Enys Morris** *top n.f* Mauritius. **Enys Vanow** *top n.f* Isle of Man. **Enesow Syllan** *top n.pl* Isles of Scilly

enysegans *n.m* **enysegansow** insulation

enysekter *n.m* (state of) isolation; remoteness

enyshe *vb* isolate

enysheans *n.m* **enysheansow** (process of) isolation

enyshes *adj* isolated

eos *n.f* **eosow** nightingale

epilepsi *n.m* (*med*) epilepsy

epskobeth *n.f* **epskobethow** bishopric

epskop *n.m* **epskobow** bishop

epyk I *adj* epic **II** *n.m* **epygys** epic

epystyl *n.m* **epystlys** epistle

er (1) *n.m* **eryon, eres** eagle

er (2) *n.m* **erys** heir; successor

er (3) *n.m* **eryow**, *dl* **dewer** (*anat*) temple

er (4) *n.m* challenge; defiance; heresy; insistence; stubbornness

-er *sffx* human agent

erba *n.m* **erbys** herb

erber *n.m* **erberow, erbers** kitchen garden; arbour

erbynn *prp* against; versus; in preparation for; by. **erbynn Nadelik** by Christmas. **dos erbynn** encounter; fall on. **erbynn an gwias** against the grain. **erbynn an lagha** against the law. *Personal forms: 1s* **er ow fynn**, *2s* **er dha bynn**, *3sm* **er y bynn**, *3sf* **er hy fynn**, *1p* **er agan pynn**, *2p* **er agas pynn**, *3p* **er aga fynn**

erbynner *n.m* **erbynoryon** opponent

erbys *n.m* **erbysyow** thrift (*saving money*)

erbysek *adj* economic

erbysi *vb* save (money); economise

erbysiedh *n.m* **erbysiedhow** economy

erbysieth *n.f* economics

erbysus *adj* economical

erbysyas *n.m* **erbysysi** miser

erbysydh *n.m* **erbysydhyon** economist

erbysyon *n.pl* savings

ergh *n.coll* snow. **den ergh** *n.m* snowman. **karow ergh** *n.m* reindeer. **gul ergh** *vb* snow

erghek *adj* snowy

erghen *n.f* **erghennow** snowflake

erghi *vb* bid; command; decree; order; require. **erghi der an post** mail order

erghslynk *n.m* **erghslynkys, erghsklynkow** avalanche

erita *vb* inherit

erna[2] **(g)** *cnj* until; till. **erna vo klewys neppyth ken** until further notice

erotek *adj* erotic

erow *n.f* **erewi** acre

ertach *n.m* **ertajys** heritage. **Ertach Kernow** *n.m* Cornish Heritage

erthygel *n.m* **erthyglow** (*text*) article

ervin *n.coll* turnips

ervinen *n.f* **ervinennow** turnip

ervinik *n.m* **ervinigow** rapeseed (*oilseed rape*)

ervira *vb* decide; resolve

ervirans *n.m* **erviransow** decision; verdict

ervirus *adj* decisive

ervirys *adj* determined

ervys *adj* armed. **ervys bys y'n dhiwen** armed to the teeth

erya *vb* challenge; defy; fly in the face of

erys *adj* ploughed

es (1) I *adj* easy II *n.m* ease; comfort

es (2) *cnj* (= **ages**) than. **moy es kans** over a hundred. *Personal forms: 1s esov, 2s esos, 3sm esso, 3sf essi, 1p eson, 2p esowgh, 3p essa*

-es *sffx* **-esow** (*female suffix*)

esedh *n.f* **esedhow** seat. **esedh fenester** *n.f* window seat. **esedh gasel** *n.f* aisle seat. **grugys esedh** *n.m* seat belt

esedha *vb* sit; take a seat. **esedha war skavel an gow** slander; gossip

esedhek *n.m* **esedhogow** session

esedhva *n.f* **esedhvaow** living room; lounge; sitting room

esedhvos *n.m* **esedhvosow** session; eisteddfod

esedhys *adj* seated

esel *n.m* **eseli** member. **esel senedh** *n.m* member of parliament (MP). **galar eseli** *n.m* rheumatism. **kleves eseli** *n.m* rheumatism

eseleth *n.f* **eselethow** membership

eskar *n.m* **eskerens** adversary; enemy

eskarek *adj* hostile

eskarogeth *n.f* enmity

eskerensa *n.f* enmity

eskis *n.f* **eskisyow** shoe. **eskis sport** *n.f* trainer

esknians *n.m* erosion

eskorra *vb* output

eskorrans *n.m* **eskorransow** output

eskravus *adj* abrasive

esoterek *adj* esoteric

esperthi *vb* export

esporth *n.m* **esporthow** export

essensek *adj* essential **yn essensek** *adv* essentially

Est *n.m* August

est *n.m* east. **a'n est** eastern

estem *n.m* admiration; esteem

estemya *vb* admire; esteem; estimate

ester *n.coll* oysters

estewlel *vb* eject; expel

estewlys *vb* expelled

esthetek *adj* aesthetic

Estoni *top n.f* Estonia

Estonian *n.m* **Estonians** Estonian

Estoniek *n.m* Estonian language

estoniek *adj* Estonian

estren (1) *n.f* **estrennow** oyster

estren (2) I *adj* alien; foreign; strange II *n.m* **estrenyon** alien; outsider; stranger; foreigner

estrek *n.f* **estregi** oyster-bed

estren I *adj* alien; strange II *n.m* **estrenyon** alien; outsider; stranger

estrenya *vb* alienate

estriger *n.m* **estrigoryon** absentee

estrigys *adj* absent. **perghen estrigys** *n.m* absentee landlord; second-home owner

estrik *n.m* **estrigow** absence

estyllen *n.f* **estyllennow** shelf

esya (1) *adj (comparative of es)* easier

esya (2) *vb* ease; put at ease; accommodate; facilitate

esyans *n.m* **esyansow** accommodation

etegves *num* eighteenth

etek *num* eighteen

eth (1) *num* eight

eth (2) *n.m* **ethow** odour; scent

eth (3) *vb* went (*3s pret*)

eth (4) *n.m* **ethys** hearth

-eth *sffx (abstract noun suffix)*

ethegel *adj* ethical

ethek *n.f* ethics

ethen *n.f* **ethennow** odour; scent; steam

ethenna *vb* evaporate; steam

ethnek *adj* ethnic. **karth ethnek** *n.m* ethnic cleansing

ethol *n.m* **etholow** choice

etholans *n.m* **etholansow** ballot; election

etholer *n.m* **etholoryon** elector

etholi *vb* elect

etholys *adj* elected

ethves I *n.m* **ethvesow** octave; eighth **II** *num* eighth

eur *n.f* **euryow** hour; o'clock. **pub eur** always. **py eur yw?** what is the time? **war euryow** now and then

eurdal *n.m* **eurdalow** hourly rate

Europa *top n.m* Europe

European *n.m* **Europeanyon** European

europek *adj* European. **Unyans Europek (UE)** *n.m* European Union (EU)

Eurosenedh *n.m* European Parliament

euryador *n.m* **euryadoryow** timetable

euryor *n.f* **euryoryow** watch

eus *vb (3s. pres. long form of bos; used with indefinite subjects)* there is; is. **eus mona genes?** do you have any cash on you?

euth *n.m* horror; panic. **kemeres euth** panic

euthanisya *vb* euthanise

euthega *vb* terrify

euthekter *n.m* terror

euthvil *n.m* **euthviles** monster

euthwrians *n.m* **euthwriansow** atrocity

euthwriansek *adj* atrocious

euthyk I *adj* awful; frightful; ghastly; horrible; terrible; terrific **II** *adv* awfully; horribly; terribly

euver *adj* futile; valueless; worthless

ev *prn* he; him

eva *vb* drink; absorb

evadow *adj* drinkable

evredh *n.m* **evredhyon** person with disability

evredhder dyski *n.m* **evredhderow dyski** learning disability (*med*)

evredhek *adj* disabled; handicapped

evy *prn (emphatic)* me

ewin (1) *n.m* **ewines** claw; fingernail; talon; toenail. **ewin kennin** *n.m* clove of garlic. **gwernis ewin** *n.f* nail varnish

ewin (2) *n.coll* yews

ewinen *n.f* **ewinennow** yew

ewinrew *n.m* numbness

ewinrewys *adj* numb

ewl *n.f* **ewlow** craving. **ewl voos** *n.f* appetite

ewn *adj* fair; correct; just; proper; right; accurate. **yn ewn** fairly

ewna *vb* correct; make right; mend; repair

ewnans *n.m* **ewnansow** correction; repair

ewnder *n.m* fairness; justice

ewngryjyk *adj* orthodox

ewnhe *vb* fix; repair

ewnheans *n.m* **ewnheansow** repair

ewnhynsek *adj* just; upright; virtuous **ewnhynseth** *n.f* integrity; fairness

ewnran *n.f* **ewnrannow** ration

ewnranna *vb* ration

ewnter *n.m* **ewntres** uncle

ewon *n.coll* foam; froth. **ewon-divarva** *n.coll* shaving foam

ewonek *adj* foamy; frothy. **dowr ewonek** *n.m* mineral water

ewonen *n.f* **ewonennow** foam

ewoni *vb* froth

eyl *prn* one of two; second. **an eyl y gila** *n.m* one another (*male*); mutual. **an eyl hy ben** *n.f* one another (*female*); mutual. **an eyl wosa y gila** successive

eyles *n.coll* sundew

eylesen *n.f* **eylesennow** sundew

eylgylghya *vb* recycle

eylgylghyans *n.m* recycling

eylskrif *n.m* **eylskrifow** copy; facsimile

eylskrifa *vb* copy

eylya *vb* second

Eynda *top n.f* India

Eyndek *n.m* **Eyndogyon** Indian

eyndek *adj* Indian. **Keynvor Eyndek** *n.m* Indian Ocean

eyrin *n.coll* sloes

eyrinen *n.f* **eyrinennow** sloe

eythin *n.coll* furze; gorse

eythinen *n.f* **eythinennow** furze; gorse

F

faborden I *adj* bass **II** *n.m* **fabordenyon** bass. **gitar faborden** *n.m* bass guitar

fagel *n.f* **faglow** flame; inflammation

fagla *vb* inflame

faglen *n.f* **faglennow** torch

fakt *n.m* **faktys** fact

falghun *n.m* **falghunes** falcon

fall *n.m* **fallow** failure; loss

falladow *n.m* **falladowyow** failure. **heb falladow** without fail; doubtless

fals *adj* false; cheating; insincere; treacherous; adulterous. **fekyl fals** *n.m* hypocrite

falsgober *n.m* **falsgobrow** bribe

falsgobra *vb* bribe

falshe *vb* falsify

falsuri *n.m* insincerity; treachery

falswas *n.m* **falswesyon** cheater; fraud; impostor

famya *vb* starve

fangla *vb* contrive

fantasi *n.m* **fantasis** fantasy

fantasiek *adj* fantastic

fanya *vb* fan

fara I *n.m* conduct; behaviour **II** *vb* behave; fare

fara gorgemeryansek *n.m* obsessive behaviour

fardel *n.m* **fardellow** package; parcel. **fardellow** *n.pl* luggage

fardella *vb* pack; package

fardellik *n.m* **fardelligow** packet

fardellow *n.pl* luggage. **roos fardellow** *n.f* luggage rack

Faro *n.m* **Faros** Pharaoh

farwell *n.m* farewell; goodbye

fas *n.m* **fassow** face; visage. **sawya fas** save face

faskor I *adj* fascist **II** *n.m* **faskoryon** fascist

fast *adj* stable; steady; permanent

faster *n.m* stability

fasthe *vb* ratify

fastheans *n.m* **fastheansow** ratification

fastya *vb* attach; confirm; establish; fasten; tighten; secure

fastyans *n.m* **fastyansow** confirmation

fasya *vb* boast; brag

fatel[2] *adv* how

fatla *adv* how

fav *n.coll* beans

faven *n.f* **favennow** bean

favera *vb* favour; discriminate in favour of

faverus *adj* favourable

favour *n.m* **favours** favour

faw *n.coll* beeches

fawen *n.f* **fawennow** beech

fay (1) *n.m* faith

fay (2) *n.f* **fayys** fairy

fayntys *n.m* hypocrisy

fe (1) *n.m* **feow** fee. **feow dyskans** *n.pl* tuition fees. **feow-parkya** *n.pl* parking fees

fe (2) *n.m* **feow** feudal estate; fief

federal *adj* federal

fekla *vb* (*transitive*) flatter; (*intransitive*) pretend

feklans *n.m* flattery

fekler *n.m* **fekloryon** hypocrite

fekyl I *adj* flattering; perfidious **II** *n.m* hypocrite. **fekyl cher** hypocritical

fel *adj* astute; crafty; sly; shrewd

felder *n.m* slyness

felgh *n.f* **felghyow** spleen

felghell *n.f* **felghellow** mower

felghya *vb* mow

fell *adj* grim; cruel; mean

fella *adj* (= **pella**) (*mutated form of* ***pella*** *following* **na**) further

fellder *n.m* **fellderyow** cruelty

felon *n.m* **felons** felon; delinquent

felshyp *n.m* **felshyps** fellowship; company

fenester *n.f* **fenestri** window. **esedh fenester** *n.f* window seat

fenestrek *adj* windowed

fenna *vb* overflow

fenoghel *n.m* fennel

fenoghel mor *n.m* rock samphire

fensya *vb* (*receive or sell stolen goods*) fence

fenten *n.f* **fentynnyow** fountain; spring; well

fer *n.m* **feryow** fair

ferla *n.m* **ferleow** fairground

fernoth *adj* barelegged

ferror *n.m* **ferroryon** farrier

fers *adj* fierce

feryl *n.m* **ferylyow** alchemist

fesont *n.m* **fesons** pheasant

fest *adv* extremely; indeed

fesya *vb* cast out; chase off

feth *n.m* **fethow** fact

fetha *vb* beat; conquer; defeat; overcome; top; vanquish

fethans *n.m* **fethansow** conquest; defeat

fethek *adj* victorious

fether *n.m* **fethoryon** conqueror; victor

fethesik *n.m* **fethesigow** victim

fethus *adj* smart; luxuriant

fethyel *adj* factual

fethys *adj* beaten; defeated; overcome

feus *n.m* chance; luck

feusik *adj* fortunate; lucky

fewdal *adj* feudal

feyth *adj* fertile

fi *int* fie

fia (1) *vb* flee; run away. **fia dhe'n fo** take flight

fia (2) *vb* despise; disdain

fiadow *adj* despicable

fians *n.m* contempt

fienas *n.m* **fienasow** anxiety

fienasow *n.pl* anxiety; suspense; fret

figur *n.m* **figurys** figure

figura *vb* figure

figys *n.coll* figs

figysen *n.f* **figysennow** fig

filosofek *adj* philosophical

filosofer *n.m* **filosofers** philosopher

filosofieth *n.f* **filosofethow** philosophy

fin (1) *n.f* **finyow** end; limit

fin (2) *adj* fine; astute; delicate; refined; sensitive

finder *n.m* sensibility

findhyskys *adj* cultured

finek *adj* final

finel *adj* final

finsya *vb* finish; end

finweth *n.f* **finwethow** limit. **finweth tooth** *n.f* speed limit. **heb finweth** unlimited

finwetha *vb* limit

fion *n.coll* narcissi

fionen *n.f* **fionennow** narcissus

fisegel *adj* physical

fisten *n.m* hurry; haste

fistena *vb* hurry; make haste; rush

flamek *n.m* **flameges** flamingo

flamm *n.m* **flammow** flame

flammgos an howl *n.m* sun spurge

flammgos an ke *n.m* wood spurge

flammgos an mor *n.m* sea spurge

flappya *vb* flap

flattra *vb* delude; wind up; have on

fleghik *n.m* **fleghesigow, fleghigyow** infant

fler *n.m* **fleryow** smell; odour; stench; stink

flerya *vb* stink; smell

flerys *adj* pungent; stinking

flock *n.m* **flockys** flock

flogh *n.m* **fleghes** child; kid. **flogh byghan** *n.m* baby. **flogh besydh** *n.m* godchild. **flogh gwynn** *n.m* grandchild. **flogh yn-dann oos** *n.m* minor. **flogh stret** *n.m* street child. **gans flogh** pregnant

floghek *adj* childlike

floghel *adj* puerile

floghgovia *vb* baby-sit

floghgovier *n.m* **floghgovioryon** baby-sitter

floghva *n.f* **floghvaow** crèche

floren *n.f* **florennow** door-lock

florennik *n.f* **florenigow** locket

flosh *n.m* **floshys** flush

floshya *vb* flush

flou *n.f* influenza; flu

flour (1) *n.m* **flourys** flower

flour (2) *adj* perfect; eminent

flour (3) *n.m* **flouryow** deck

flows *n.m* nonsense; idle talk

flowsa *vb* waffle

flyckra *vb* flicker

flyckrans *n.m* **flyckransow** flicker

flynt *n.m* **flyntys** flint

flyrtya *vb* flirt

fo *n.m* flight (*only used in expression* **fia dhe'n fo**)

fobia *n.m* phobia (*med*)

foesik I *adj* fugitive; runaway **II** *n.m* **foesigyon** fugitive; runaway

fog *n.f* **fogow** focus; furnace; hearth. **mes a fog** out of focus. (*fog lew*) sharp focus

fogella *vb* focus

fogellys *adj* focussed

fol I *adj* foolish; mad; absurd **II** *n.m* (*offensive*) **felyon** madman

folen *n.f* **folennow** page; leaf; sheet

folenep *n.m* **folenebow** foolish face; foolishness; folly

folenna *vb* paginate

folennans *n.m* pagination

folennik *n.f* **folenigow** brochure; flyer; leaflet; pamphlet

folneth *n.f* folly; foolishness

fols *n.m* **folsyow** cleft; fissure; rift; split **folsa** *vb* split. **folsa blew** nit-pick; quibble

folsa *vb* cleave; split

folsans *n.m* **folsansow** splitting. **folsans blew** *n.m* quibble

fondya *vb* found; establish; lay foundations

fondyans *n.m* **fondyansow** establishment; foundation

fong *n.m* **fongow** fungus

fongalgi *n.coll* lichen

font *n.m* **fontys** *in church* font

foon *n.m* new-mown hay

fordh *n.f* **fordhow** way; road; manner. **dhe hanter an fordh** midway. **fordh a-dro** *n.f* (*traffic*) roundabout. **fordh dhall** *n.f* cul-de-sac; dead end. **fordh dhibarth** *n.f* junction. **fordh dremen** *n.f* bypass. **fordh lan** *n.f* thoroughfare. **fordh-skapya** *n.f* fire escape; escape route. **fordh veur** *n.f* highway. **fowt fordh aral** as a last resort. **heb fordh** trackless. **klerfordh** *n.f* clearway. **mos y'n fordh** be on one's way. **war ow fordh hir** in the long run; in the end. **y'n fordh aral** on the other hand. **y'n fordh ma** in this way. **yn neb fordh** anyway

fordhlett *n.m* **fordhlettys, fordhlettow** road-block

forgh *n.f* **fergh** fork

forlell *n.f* **forlellow** whisk

forlya *vb* whip; whisk

form (1) *n.m* (*f*) **formys** bench

form (2) *n.m* (*f*) **formys** (= **furv**) form; figure; mould; shape

formel *adj* formal

formya *vb* (= **furvya**) form; figure; shape

formyer *n.m* **formyoryon** creator

forn *n.f* **fornow** oven. **forn gorrdon** *n.f* microwave oven. **forn byng** *n.f* microwave oven (*colloq*)

fornya *vb* bake

fors *n.m* **forsow** force; heed. **na fors** never mind; no matter. **na fors pyneyl** irrespective of; no matter if

forsakya *vb* abandon; desert; forsake

forsedh *n.m* (*in physics*) force

forster *n.m* **forstoryon** forester

fortun *n.m* **fortunnyow** fortune

fos *n.f* **fosow** wall

fosforos *n.m* (*element*) phosphorus

fouton *n.m* **foutonyow** futon

fow *n.f* **fowys** cave

fowt *n.m* **fowtys, fowtow** deficiency; fault; lack. **fowt bri** *n.m* insignificance. **fowt dyskans** *n.m* ignorance. **fowt fordh aral** as a last resort. **fowt perthyans** *n.m* intolerance. **fowt styr** *n.m* insignificance. **yn despit dhe'n fowtow** warts and all

fram *n.m* **framyow** frame

framweythel *adj* structural

framya *vb* frame; formulate; put together; structure

franchis *n.m* **franchisow** franchise

frank *adj* frank; free; candid

frankedh *n.m* liberty

frankincens *n.m* frankincense

franklondya *vb* smuggle

frankres *adj* free-range. **oy frankres** *n.pl* free-range egg. **yar frankres** *n.f* free-range hen

frappya *vb* beat; knock; strike

frappyans *n.m* percussion

frappyansek *adj* percussive

fraws *n.m* fraud

frawsus *adj* fraudulent

fres *n.m* freight

fresk *adj* fresh (*not food*)

freth *adj* eager; fluent; outspoken

frethter *n.m* eagerness; fluency

freudh *n.m* **freudhow** commotion; violence

freudha *vb* unravel; fray

freudhek *adj* violent

freudhi *vb* brawl

fria *vb* fry. **oy friys** *n.m* fried egg

frig *n.m* **frigow**, *dl* **dewfrik** nostril. **frigow** *n.pl* nose. **ughel y dhewfrik** stuck up

frigow *n.pl* (= **frig**) nose

frikhwyth *n.m* **frikhwythow** sniff

frikhwytha *vb* sniff

friys *adj* fried. **oy friys** *n.m* fried egg

frommus *adj* edgy

fronn *n.f* **fronnow** brake; restraint. **gweskel an fronn** slam on the brakes

fronna *vb* brake; restrain; restrict

fronnans *n.m* **fronansow** restriction

frooth *n.coll* fruit. **sugen frooth** *n.m* fruit juice

fros *n.m* **frosow** current; flow. **fros tredan** *n.m* electric current

frosa *vb* flow

frothen *n.f* **frothennow** fruit

frothus *adj* fertile

frowsya *vb* defraud

frut *n.m* **frutys** fruit

Frynk *n.m* **Frynkyon** French person

Frynkek *n.m* French language

frynkek *adj* French

fug I *adj* counterfeit; fake **II** *n.m*
  fugyow feint; forgery. **hanow fug** *n.m*
  incognito

fug-[2] *prfx* pseudo-

fugieth *n.f* fiction

fugya *vb* counterfeit; fake; feign; forge.
  fugya an akontys cook the books

fugyans *n.m* **fugyansow** forgery

fumado *n.m* **fumados** sardine
  (*preserved*)

fun *n.f* **funyow** cable

fur *adj* sensible; prudent; well advised;
  wise

furneth *n.m* wisdom

furv *n.f* **furvow, furvyow** (= **form**
  (**2**)) form; figure; mould; shape

furvas *n.m* **furvasow** (*IT*) format

furvasa *vb* (*IT*) format

furvya *vb* (= **formya**) form; figure;
  shape

furvyer *n.m* **furvyoryon** creator

fusen *n.f* **fusennow** rocket

fust *n.f* **fustow** club; cudgel

fusta *vb* beat (with a club); batter;
  thresh

fydh *n.f* **fedhyow** faith. *excl* **re'm fydh!**
  by my faith!

fydhya *vb* trust. **fydhya war**[2] rely on

fydhyans *n.m* confidence; trust

fydhyansek *adj* confident

fyll *n.m* **fyllys, fyllow** fiddle; violin

fyllel *vb* fail; miss; be missing; lose; fall
  short. **fyllel a**[2] lack. **fyllel dhe**[2] fail
  somebody. **fyllel gweles** overlook;
  fail to notice

fyller *n.m* **fylloryon** fiddler (*musician*)

fyllya *vb* fiddle (*play musical
  instrument*)

fylm *n.m* **fylmow** film; movie (*US*) .
  fylm bughwas *n.m* Western

fylmya *vb* film

Fynn *n.m* **Fynnys** Finn

Fynndir *n.m* Finland

Fynnek *n.m* Finnish language

fynnek *adj* Finnish

fyrv *adj* firm

fysegieth *n.f* physics

fysek *n.f* medicine

fysk I *adj* impulsive; hasty; rushed **II**
  n.m haste; hurry; rush

fyski *vb* rush; hurry; dash; bustle

fysla *vb* fidget; fuss

fyslek *adj* annoying; fussy;
  troublesome

fytt *n.m* **fyttys, fyttow** sports match

fyttya *vb* prepare

G

'ga[3] *prn* (*infixed*) them; (*poss. adj*) their

gahen *n.f* henbane

gaja *n.m* **gajys** pledge

gal *n.m* **galyon, galow** villain; outcast

galar *n.m* **galarow** grief. **galar eseli**
  n.m rheumatism

galarans *n.m* **galaransow** funeral

galarek *adj* miserable

galari *vb* grieve; lament; mourn

galarow *n.pl* agony

galladewder *n.m* **galladewderyow**
  potential

galladow *adj* potential; possible

gallon *n.m* **gallons** gallon

gallos I *n.m* **gallosow** ability;
  capability; might; power **II** *vb* can; be
  able

gallosedh *n.m* (*in physics*) power

gallosegi *vb* enable

gallosek *adj* capable; competent; mighty; potent; powerful

galow *n.m* **galowyow** call; calling; appeal; invitation; vocation. **galow a-bell** *n.m* long-distance call. **galow pellgows** *n.m* telephone call

galwansek *adj* vocational

galwen *n.f* **galwennow** call. **galwen bellgows** *n.f* telephone call

galwesigeth *n.f* **galwesigethow** profession; calling; vocation

galwesik I *adj* professional **II** *n.m* **galwesigyon** professional

galweyth *n.m* **galweythow** crime

galweythel *adj* criminal

galwydh *n.m* **galwydhyon** pager

gam *n.m* game (*hunting target*)

'gan *prn* (*infixed*) us; (*poss. adj*) our

ganow *n.m* **ganowow** mouth; (*of a gun*) muzzle. **der anow, war anow** verbal

ganowas *n.m* **ganowasow** mouthful

ganowek I *adj* big-mouthed **II** *n.m* anchovy

gans *prp* with; by. **gans ganow** by word of mouth. **gans golow** alight; lit. **gans tan** on fire. *Personal forms: 1s genev, 2s genes, 3sm ganso, 3sf gensi, 1p genen, 2p genowgh, 3p gansa*

garan *n.f* **garanes** crane (*bird and machine*). **koll garan** *n.coll* cranberries

garen *n.f* **garennow** stalk

garlont *n.f* **garlons** wreath

garm *n.f* **garmow** shout; whoop; yell. **garm-argemynna** *n.f* advertising slogan. **garm wormola** *n.f* ovation. **garm vresel** *n.f* battle cry. **pas garm** *n.m* whooping cough

garma *vb* cry out; shout; whoop; yell. **garma yn lowen** cheer

garnisyon *n.m* **garnisyons** garrison

garow *adj* brutal; coarse; crude; fierce; grim; harsh; rough; savage

garowder *n.m* roughness; violence; brutality

garr *n.f* **garrow**, *dl* **diwarr** leg

garren *n.f* **garrennow** calf (*of leg*)

garth *n.m* **garthow** courtyard; enclosure; yard. **garth-gwari** *n.m* **garthow-gwari** playground

garwa *adj* rougher. **an garwa** the roughest

gass *n.m* **gassys** gas

'gas *prn* (*infixed, pl*) you; (*poss. adj, pl*) your

gasa *vb* allow; leave; set off; let; permit; abandon. **gasa mewgh** jump bail. **gasa spas dhe²** make way for. **gas dha son!** shut up! **gesewgh ni dhe weles!** (*periphrastic imperative*) let's see!

gasadow *n.m* **gasadowyow** balance (of a bank account); residue

gast *n.f* **gesti** bitch; female dog

gastritis *n.m* (*med*) gastritis

gava *vb* forgive; pardon. **gava dhe nebonan** forgive somebody. **gav dhymm** excuse me; pardon me

gavel *n.f* **gavelyow** grasp; capacity

gavelieth *n.f* capacitance

gaver *n.f* **gever** goat. **barv gaver** *n.m* goatee. **gaver hal** *n f* snipe. **gaver vor** *n.f* crayfish

gelforn *n.f* **gelfornow** forge

gell *adj* (light) brown. **gell kesten** *adj* chestnut brown

gellburpur *adj* puce

gellik *adj* brownish

gellrudh *adj* auburn

gelvin *n.m* **gelvines** beak; bill

gelvinek *n.m* **gelvinoges, gelvinogyon** curlew

gelvin garan *n.m* crane's-bill

gelwel *vb* call; appeal; invite; summon

gemm *n.m* **gemmow** gem

gemmweyth *n.m* jewellery

gen *n.f* **genyow**, *dl* **diwen** jaw. **ervys bys y'n dhiwen** armed to the teeth. **serr dha dhiwen!** shut up!

genesigeth *n.f* **genesigethow** birth

genesik I *adj* native **II** *n.m* **genesigyon** native

genn *n.m* **gennow** wedge

genna *vb* wedge

Genver *n.m* January

genynnek *adj* genetic

genys *adj* born. **genys orth** born of. **nowydh genys** newborn

ger *n.m* **geryow** word. **ger alhwedh** *n.m* keyword. **ger da** *n.m* good reputation. **ger kesstyr** *n.m* synonym. **ger mell** *n.m* article (*grammar*). **ger rag ger** *idiom* literal; word for word. **ger-tremena** *n.m* password. **ger herwydh son** *n.m* onomatopoeia

gerda *n.m* fame

gerennek *adj* verbose

gerenogeth *n.f* verbosity

gerlyver *n.m* **gerlyvrow** dictionary; lexicon

gerva *n.f* **gervaow** vocabulary

gerya *vb* babble; be verbose

geryel *adj* verbal

gerys-da *adj* well spoken of; famous; popular; renowned

ges *n.m* **gesyow** joke; jeer; mockery; ridicule. **ges a'n jydh** *n.m* **gesyow a'n jydh** satire. **gul ges** *vb* joke. **gul ges a**^{2} lampoon; mock; ridicule

'ges *prp* (= **ages**) than

gesedh *n.f* **gesedhow** irony

gesya *vb* jeer; mock

gesyer *n.m* **gesyoryon** comedian; joker

gesys *adj* left

getto *n.m* **gettos** ghetto

gevel (1) *n.m* **gevellyon, gevellas** twin

gevel (2) *n.f* **gevelyow** tongs

geveligow *n.pl* pliers

gevelji *n.m* **geveljiow** semi-detached house

gevella *vb* twin (*towns*)

gevellys *adj* twinned (*of towns*)

gevyans *n.m* **gevyansow** forgiveness; pardon

gew *n.m* **gewow** woe

gid *n.m* **gidys** guide

gidlyver *n.m* **gidlyvrow** guidebook

gidya *vb* guide; conduct. **gidya menestrouthi** conduct an orchestra

gigabayt *n.m* **gigabaytys** gigabyte; *abbrev* GB

gik *n.m* **gikys** peep. **heb gul gik na mik** stock-still. **na gik na mik** not a sound

gil *n.m* guile; deceit. **heb toll na gil** sincerely

gis *n.m* **gisyow** fashion; guise; style; (*grammar*) mood. **herwydh an gis** stylish; fashionable. **gis islavarek** *n.m* subjunctive mood. **gis menegek** *n.m* indicative mood. **gis-skrifa** *n.m* literary style

giswisk *n.m* fancy dress

gisyer gols *n.m* **gisyoryon wols** hair stylist

gitar *n.m* **gitaryow** guitar. **gitar tredanek** *n.m* electric guitar

glan I *adj* clear; clean; pure **II** *adv* quite. **fordh lan** *n.f* thoroughfare

glanhe *vb* clean

glann *n.f* **glannow** bank. **glann fordh** *n.f* roadside verge. **glann gales** *n.f* hard shoulder. **glann vedhel** *n.f* soft shoulder

glanyth *adj* tidy

glas *adj* blue; green; grey

glas an niwl *n.m* love-in-a-mist

glasa *vb* flourish (*plants*); become green/blue

glasik (1) *adj* bluish

glasik (2) *n.m* cornflower

glasneth *n.f* vegetation

glasrudh *adj* purple

glaswenon *n.m* devil's bit scabious

glaveri *vb* drivel; drool; slobber

glavor *n.m* drivel; drool; slobber

glavorek *adj* slobbering

glaw *n.m* rain. **gul glaw** *vb* rain

glawas *n.m* rainfall

glawek *adj* rainy

glawen *n.f* **glawennow** drop of rain

glawlen *n.f* **glawlennow** umbrella

gledh *n.m* chickweed

glena *vb* stick; adhere. **glena orth** stick to; adhere to

glenus *adj* adhesive

glenysen *n.f* **glenysennow** sticker

glesin *n.m* **glesinyow** lawn. **jynn glesin** *n.m* lawn-mower

glesin an koos *n.m* (*plant*) bugle

glew *adj* sharp; intense; vivid

glewder *n.m* **glewderyow** intensity

glin *n.m* **glinyow**, *dl* **dewlin** knee. **penn glin** *n.m* knee-cap. **war benn glin** kneeling

gloos *n.f* **glosow** ache; anguish; pang; spasm

gloosa *vb* hurt (*instrans*); smart

glori *n.m* glory

gloryus *adj* glorious

glow *n.coll* coal

glowbren *n.f* **glowbrennyer** charcoal

glowen *n.f* **glowennow** lump of coal

glowor *n.m* **gloworyon** collier

glowva *n.f* **glowvaow** colliery

glus *n.m* **glusow** gum; adhesive; glue. **glus gwedhyn** *n.m* rubber

glusa *vb* glue

glusek *adj* sticky; adhesive

gluth *n.m* **gluthow** dew

gluthvelhwen *n.f* **gluthvelhwennow** slug

gluthyans *n.m* condensation

glyb *adj* moist; damp; wet

glybor *n.m* moisture; damp; wetness

glybya *vb* moisten; wet

glynn *n.m* **glynnow** deep wooded valley; glen

gnas *n.f* **gnasow** character; nature; quality

gnasek *adj* natural

gnasen *n.f* **gnasennow** trait

go *int* woe. **go vy!** woe is me!

gobalas *vb* skim (*in digging or mining*)

gobans *n.m* **gobansow** dingle; hollow

gober *n.m* **gobrow** income; pay; salary; reward; wage; remuneration. **gober ispoyntel** *n.m* minimum wage. **gober kleves** *n.m* sick pay. **gober omdennans** *n.m* pension. **gober tew** *n.m* gross pay. **gober ylyn** *n.m* net pay

goblegi *vb* imply

gobra *vb* reward; remunerate. **gobrys yn ta** well paid

gobrena *vb* rent

gobrener *n.m* **gobrenoryon** tenant

gocki I *adj* daft; foolish; stupid; absurd II *n.m* **gockies** fool

gockia *vb* behave foolishly

gockineth *n.f* stupidity; folly

goderri *vb* interrupt, disrupt

goderrys *adj* interrupted

godevesik *adj* adolescent

godewl *adj* dim; dusky

godh *n.f* **godhow** mole

Godhal *n.m* **Godhyli** Irishman; Gael

Godhalek *n.m* Gaelic language

godhalek *adj* Gaelic

godhan *n.m* **godhanes** moth

godhav *vb* suffer; bear; tolerate

godhen *n.m* **godhnow** sole

godhes *n.m* **godhosow** dregs; grounds; sediment

godhesa *vb* deposit sediment

godhevek *adj* passive. **ranngemeryans godhevek** *n.m* passive participle

godhevel *vb* suffer; bear; tolerate

godhevus *adj* patient; passive

godhevyans *n.m* suffering

godhevyas *n.m* **godhevysi** patient

godhik *n.m* **godhigow** gosling

godhoniador *n.m* **godhoniadoryon** encyclopaedia

godhonieth *n.f* **godhoniethow** science

godhoniethek *adj* scientific

godhonydh *n.m* **godhonydhyon** scientist

godhosek *adj* sedimentary

godhvedhys *adj* known

godhvewnans *n.m* wildlife

godhvil *n.m* **godhviles** wild animal

godhvos I *n.m* **godhvosow** ability; knowledge; know-how **II** *vb* know; be qualified to; can; acknowledge. **a wodhes ta kewsel Kernewek?** can you speak Cornish? **godhvos a²** know about. **godhvos gras a²** give thanks for

godhynya *vb* tempt

godom *adj* lukewarm

godor *n.m* **godorrow** interruption

godra *vb* milk

godramm *n.m* **godrammow** cramp

godreghi *vb* trim

godrek *n.m* first milk; colostrum

godrev *n.f* **godrevi** small farm

godrevedh *adv* in three days time; the third day from now

godriga *vb* visit

godriger *n.m* **godrigoryon** visitor

godrik *n.m* **godrigow** visit

godros I *n.m* **godrosow** threat **II** *vb* threaten

godrosus *adj* threatening

godybi *vb* hypothesise

godybieth *n.f* **godybiethow** hypothesis

goghi *n.coll* wasps

goghien *n.f* **goghiennow** wasp

gogledh *n.f* north

gogosk *n.m* **gogoskow** nap

gogoska *vb* nap

gogow *n.f* **gogowyow** cave

gogrys *n.m* suspicion

gogrysek I *adj* suspect **II** *n.m* **gogrysogyon** suspect

gogrysi *vb* to be suspicious; suspect

gogrysus *adj* suspicious

gohasa *vb* dislike

goheladow *adj* avoidable

goheles *vb* avoid. **sevel orth goheles** face up to

gohelus *adj* bashful; shy; timid

gohydh *n.f* **gohydhow** daughter-in-law

goi *vb* digest

gol *n.m* **golyow** goal

golan *n.f* **golanes** gull; seagull

golans *n.m* **golansow** small valley

goleder *n.f* **goledrow** incline; tilt; tip

golegi *vb* edit

goles *n.m* **golesow** bottom; base. **kravas goles an balyer** scrape the bottom of the barrel

golesen *n.f* **golesennow** petticoat

golewder *n.m* **golewderyow** brightness; glory

golf *n.m* golf

golgh *n.m* **golghow** washing; wash

golghadow *adj* washable

golghas *n.m* **golghasow** washing

golghi *vb* wash; bathe

golghlin *n.m* **golghlinyow** washing-up liquid

golghti *n.m* **golghtiow** laundry

golghva *n.f* **golghvaow** bathroom; washing place. **golghva gerri** *n.f* car wash

golgi *n.m* **golgeun** watchdog

goli *n.m* **goliow** injury; sore; wound. **goli byw** *n.m* ulcer

golia *vb* wound

goliadow *adj* vulnerable

goliesik *n.m* **goliesigow** casualty

golinyans *n.m* **golinyansow** diagram

gologhas *n.m* worship

gologva *n.f* **gologvaow** outlook

golok *n.f* look; presence. **golok war-dhelergh** *n.f* retrospect

golow I *adj* luminous **II** *n.m* **golowys** light; glow. **gans golow** alight. **krevder golow** *n.m* luminous intensity

Golowan *n.m* Midsummer

golowboyntya *vb* highlight

golowbren *n.m* **golowbrennyer** lamp-post

golowi *vb* illuminate; glow; light up; lighten; shine

golowji *n.m* **golowjiow** lighthouse

golowyans *n.m* enlightenment; lighting

golowyn *n.m* **golowynnow** ray

golowys *adj* lit

gols *n.coll* hair. **kempenner gols** *n.m* hairdresser

golusek I *adj* rich; wealthy **II** *n.m* **golusogyon** rich person; wealthy person

golvan *n.m* **golvanes** sparrow

golvan chi *n.m* **golvanes chi** house sparrow

golvanek kors *n.m* **golvanoges kors** reed bunting

golvan ke *n.m* **golvanes ke** dunnock (*hedge sparrow*)

golya (1) *vb* sail. **skath-wolya** *n.f* sailing boat

golya (2) *vb* feast

golyas *vb* keep watch

golyer *n.m* **golyoryon** sailor

gommon *n.coll* kelp; seaweed

gomonen *n.f* **gomonennow** strand of kelp; seaweed

gomonna *vb* gather seaweed

gonedhys *adj* cultivated (*of land*)

gonis I *n.m* **gonisyow** service; work **II** *vb* cultivate; labour. **gonis has** *vb* sow seed. **gonis tir** *vb* farm. **Gonis Yeghes** *n.m* Health Service

gonisek *n.m* **gonisogyon** servant. **gonisek civil** *n.m* civil servant

gonisogeth *n.f* **gonisogethow** culture

gonisogethel *adj* cultural

gonn *n.m* **gonnys** gun. **gonn hir** *n.m* rifle

gonner *n.m* **gonoryon** gunner

goodh (1) *adj* wild; fierce

goodh (2) *n.f* **godhow** goose

gool (1) *n.m* **golyow** fair; festival; feast; vigil; wake. **chi golyow** *n.m* holiday home. **Gool Enys** *n.m* carnival

gool (2) *n.m* **golyow** sail

goon (1) *n.f* **gonyow** down; moor

goon (2) *n.m* **gonyow** (*garment*) habit

goos *n.m* **gosow** blood; bloodline. **devera goos** lose blood; bleed. **tomm y woos** hot-blooded

gooth (1) *n.m* pride

gooth (2) *n.f* **gothi** vein; channel

gor- *prfx* over-

gora *n.m* hay

gorambos *n.m* **gorambosow** (*financial*) bond

goraswonek I *adj* celebrity **II** *n.m* **goraswonogyon** celebrity

gorawen *n.f* ecstasy

gorawena *vb* gloat

gorawenus *adj* ecstatic

gorbassya *vb* surpass

gorbeblys *adj* overpopulated

gorberfydh *adj* pluperfect

gorbeski *vb* spoil

gorbollek I *adj* genius bordering on madness **II** *n.m* **gorbologyon** mad person

gorcita *n.f* **gorcitys** metropolis

gordermyn *n.m* overtime

gordevi *vb* overgrow

gordevys *adj* overgrown

gordhroglam *n.m* **gordhroglammow** catastrophe

gordhroglammek *adj* catastrophic

gordhya *vb* worship; respect; adore

gordhyans *n.m* glory; worship; adoration

gordhybri *vb* overeat

gordhyllo *vb* dismiss; fire

goredhom *n.m* **goredhommow** emergency

gorer *n.m* **goreryow** adverb

goresek *vb* jog

goreser *n.m* **goresoryon** jogger

gorewnter *n.m* **gorewntres** great-uncle

gorfen *n.m* **gorfennow** conclusion; finish

gorfenna *vb* finish; terminate

gorfennys *adj* ended; finished; over

gorfordh *n.f* **gorfordhow** motorway

gorfrosa *vb* overflow

gorfydhyans *n.m* **gorfydhyansow** overconfidence

gorfydhyansek *adj* overconfident

gorge *n.m* **gorgeow** low hedge

gorgemeryans *n.m* obsession

gorgemerys *adj* obsessed

gorgevren *n.f* **gorgevrennow** hyperlink

gorgi *n.m* **gorgeun** male dog

gorgomolek *adj* overcast

gorgoynt *adj* bizarre

gorgudha *vb* overlap

gorgudhans *n.m* **gorgudhansow** overlap

gorhana *vb* enchant

gorharga *vb* overcharge; overload

gorhel (1) *n.m* **gorholyon** ship. **gorhel kenwerth** *n.m* merchant ship. **gorhel golyow** *n.m* sailing ship. **gorhel tan** *n.m* steamship. **gorhel trethysi** *n.m* passenger ship

gorhel (2) *adj* lavish

gorhelas *n.m* **gorhelasow** shipload; shipment

gorhemmyn I *n.m* **gorhemynnow** command; order **II** *vb* order

gorhemynadow *n.pl* greetings; regards. **gorhemynadow a'n gwella** best regards; kind regards

gorhemynnek *adj* prescriptive

gorher *n.m* **gorheryow** cover; lid

gorheri *vb* cover

gorholeth *n.m* **gorholethow** demand

gorjersya *vb* pamper

gorladhva *n.f* **gorladhvaow** massacre

gorlanwes (1) *n.m* **gorlanwesow** spring-tide

gorlanwes (2) *n.m* **gorlanwesow** luxury

gorlanwesek *adj* luxurious

gorlavurus *adj* labour intensive

gorleski *vb* incinerate; scorch

gorlewin *n.f* West

gorliwa *vb* exaggerate

gorliwans *n.m* **gorliwansow** exaggeration

gorliwys *adj* gaudy; garish

gorlosk *n.m* incineration

gorloskell *n.f* **gorloskellow** incinerator

gorlost *n.coll* earwigs

gorlosten *n.f* **gorlostennow** earwig

gorm *adj* (dark) brown

gormel *vb* applaud; praise

gormesi *vb* bully

gormesyer *n.m* **gormesyoryon** bully

gormola *n.f* **gormoledhow** applause; praise; glory. **garm wormola** *n.f* ovation

gormoledhek *adj* triumphant; jubilant; glorious

gornaturel *adj* supernatural

gorour *n.m* **gorwer** hero

gorow *adj* male; masculine

gorra *vb* put; place; set. **gorra a-bervedh** insert. **gorra a-denewen** set aside; reserve. **gorra dhe**[2] apply (paint etc.). **gorra dhe-ves** take away. **gorra marth yn** amaze. **gorra own yn** alarm. **gorra poos war**[2] stress. **gorra war**[2] apply (paint etc.). **gorra yn bagas** group. **gorra yn geryow** put into words; express. **gorra yn-mes** expel; put out

gorrans *n.m* **gorransow** lift (in a car); ride. *vb* **ri gorrans** give a lift

gorreydh *n.m* male

gorsav *n.m* **gorsavow** station

gorsedh *n.f* **gorsedhow** gorseth; meeting of bards. **Gorsedh Kernow** *n.f* The Cornish Gorseth

gorspena *adj* overspend

gorth *adj* obstinate; perverse; stubborn; uppity

gorth- *prfx* anti-

gorthargyadow *adj* controversial

gorthargyans *n.m* **gorthargyansow** controversy

gorthebi *vb* answer; counter; respond; reply. **gorthebi yn tont** answer back

gorthebus *adj* responsive

gortheneba *vb* counter; oppose

gorthenep *n.m* **gorthenebow** reverse side; opposite side

Gortheren *n.m* July

gorthnaswedhek *adj* anti-clockwise

gorthpryv *n.m* **gorthpryvyow** insecticide

gorthter *n.m* opposition; stubbornness

gorthtreylya *vb* reverse

gorthtro *n.f* **gorthtroyow** inversion

gorthugher *n.m* **gorthugherow** evening. **gorthugher da** good evening

gorthugherweyth *adv* evening time

gorthwedh *n.f* **gorthwedhow** contrast

gorthyp *n.m* **gorthebow** answer; response

gortos *vb* await; wait; remain. **ha henna ow kortos** in the meantime

gorughel *adj* sublime; supreme

goruvel *adj* obsequious

gorvarghas *n.f* **gorvarghasow** supermarket

gorvarthys *adj* stupendous

gorvegh *n.m* **gorveghyow** overload

gorveghya *vb* overload

gorvewek *adj* hyperactive

gorvodrep *n.f* **gorvodrebedh** great-aunt

gorvok *n.m* **gorvogow** exhaust

gorvynnek *adj* jealous

gorwedha *vb* (= **growedha**) lie; couch; recline

gorwedhva *n.f* **gorwedhvaow** (= **growedhva**) couch

gorwel *n.f* **gorwelyow** horizon

gorweles *vb* oversee; supervise

gorwelyek *adj* horizontal

gorwir *adj* surreal

gorwitha *vb* mind

gorwiw *adj* fantastic

gorwolok *n.f* **gorwologow** overview

gorwolyas *n.m* **gorwolysi** monitor; overseer; supervisor

gorwul *vb* overdo

gorylla *n.m* **gorylles** gorilla

goryskyn *n.m* **goryskynnow** invasion

gosa *vb* (*intransitive*) bleed

gosek *adj* bloody; gory; (*of meat*) rare

goskes *n.m* shade

goskeusi *vb* shade; harbour

goskotter *n.m* shade

goslowes *vb* listen. **goslowes orth** listen to

goslowva *n.f* **goslowvaow** hearing (*legal*)

goslowyas *n.m* **goslowysi** listener

gosogen *n.f* **gosogennow** black pudding. **gosogen wynn** *n.f* **gosogennow gwynn** hog's pudding

gossen *n.f* rust. **diogel rag gossen** rustproof

gossenek *adj* rusty

gosseni *vb* rust

gostel *n.m* **gostlow** hostage; pawn

gostla *vb* pawn; wage. **gostla bell** wage war. **gostla neppyth a**^{2} pawn something for (a certain price)

gostydh *adj* susceptible

gostyth *adj* obedient

gostytter *n.m* obedience

Gothek *n.m* Gothic language

gothek *adj* Gothic. **pennserneth wothek** *n.f* Gothic architecture

gothus *adj* arrogant; proud

gour *n.m* **gwer** male (man); husband. **gour ambosys** *n.m* fiancé

gour-^{2} *prfx* male

gourel *adj* manly; masculine

gour pries *n.m* **gwer bries** bridegroom

gourti *n.m* husband

gourvleydh *n.m* **gourvleydhes** werewolf

gov *n.m* **govyon** smith; blacksmith

govedhow *adj* tipsy

govel *n.f* **goveli** forge

govelya *vb* forge

govenek *n.m* **govenegow** hope; petition

gover *n.m* **goverow** brook; stream

governa *vb* govern; administer

governans *n.m* **governansow** government

govis *n.m* **govisyon** regard

govryjyon *vb* simmer

govyn I *n.m* **govynnow** question; query; request II *vb* ask; inquire; query; question; request. **govyn orth nebonan** ask a question of somebody

govynador *n.m* **govynadoryon** questionnaire

govynadow *n.m* enquiry; inquiry

govynnus *adj* curious; inquisitive

govynnuster *n.m* curiosity

govynva *n.f* **govynvaow** enquiry office

gow *n.m* **gowyow** lie; untruth. **gow diveth** barefaced lie. **heb wow** really; truly. **leverel gow** tell a lie

gowek I *adj* lying; dishonest; treacherous II *n.m* **gowygyon** liar

gowelek *adj* partially sighted

gowir *adj* virtual

gowl *n.f* **gowlow** fork; crotch

gowlek *adj* forked

gowleverel *vb* lie; tell a lie

gowli *n.m* perjury

gowlia *vb* perjure

gownagh *n.f* **gownaghes** calfless cow

goyeyn *adj* cool; chilly

goyeynder *n.m* chill

goyeynhe *vb* cool

grabalyas *vb* cling; clutch

gradh *n.m* **gradhow** degree; grade; step. **gradh ughella** *n.m* superlative

gradhegi *vb* grade

gradhel *adj* gradual

gradhesik *n.m* **gradhesigyon** graduate

gradhya *vb* graduate

gradhyans *n.m* **gradhyansow** graduation

grafegel *adj* graphical

grafek *n.f* **grafegow** graphics

graghel *n.f* **graghellow** heap

graghellys *adj* heaped

gral *n.m* grail

gramasek I *adj* grammatical II *n.f* **gramasegow** grammar

gramer *n.m* **grameryow** grammar. **skol ramer** *n.f* grammar school

gramm *n.m* **grammow** gram

grappa *n.m* **grappys, grappow** grape

gras *n.m* **grassow** grace; thanks. **meur ras a**^{2} thanks for. **meur ras dhe**^{2} thanks to. **meurastaji** thank you

grasek *adj* grateful

grassa *vb* thank. **grassa dhe**^{2} **nebonan a**^{2} **neppyth** thank somebody for something

grassyes *adj* graceful; gracious

grastal *n.m* **grastalyow** (*money*) tip

gravath *n.f* **gravathow** barrow; litter; stretcher. **gravath ros** *n.f* wheelbarrow

gravedh *n.m* **gravedhow** gravity

gravya *vb* engrave; sculpt

gravyans *n.m* **gravyansow** sculpture

gravyer *n.m* **gravyoryon** sculptor

gre (1) *n.f* **greow** flock; herd

gre (2) *n.m* **greys** position; status

grega *vb* cackle

Grek *n.m* **Grekys** Greek person

grek *adj* Greek. **Pow Grek** *n.m* Greece

Greka *n.m* Greek language

Gres *top n.f* Greece

greun *n.coll* grain. **ris greun berr** *n.coll* short grain rice. **ris greun hir** *n.coll* long grain rice

greun an Jowl *n.coll* black bryony

greunaval *n.m* **greunavalow** pomegranate

greunek *adj* cereal

greunen *n.f* **greunennow** single seed of grain

greunji *n.m* **greunjiow** granary; grange

greunva *n.f* **greunvaow** granary

greunvos *n.m* **greunvosow** cereal

greuv *n.m* **greuvow** face; front

grev *n.m* **grevow** bother; distress

grevons *n.m* **grevonsys** bother; distress; grudge; grievance

grevus *adj* distressing

grevya *vb* bother; distress; grieve; give trouble. **grevya dhe² nebonan** give somebody trouble

grija *n.m* **grijow** starry ray; thornback

gris *n.m* **grisyow, grisys** step; stair

grommya *vb* growl

grommyans *n.m* **gromyansow** growl

grond *n.m* **grondys, grondow** foundation; base; basis

grondya *vb* ground; found; lay foundations

gronn *n.m* **gronnow** bunch; bundle

gronna *vb* amass

gronnedh *n.m* (*in physics*) mass

gront *n.m* **grontys, grontow** grant; permission

grontya *vb* accord; grant

grot *n.m* **grotys** (*silver coin*) groat

grow *n.coll* gravel

growan *n.m* **growenyow** granite

growedha *vb* (= **gorwedha**) lie; couch; recline

growedhva *n.f* **growedhvaow** (= **gorwedhva**) couch

growen *n.f* **growennow** piece of gravel

grows *n.coll* gooseberries

growsen *n.f* **growsennow** gooseberry

growsvos *n.m* **growsvosow** gooseberry bush

growynnek *adj* gravelly; gritty

grudh *n.f* **grudhow** jaw; mandible

grug *n.m* **grugow** heath; heather; ling

grugyar *n.f* **grugyer** partridge

grugys *n.m* **grugysyow** belt; girdle. **grugys diogeledh** *n.m* safety belt. **grugys esedh** *n.m* seat belt. **grugys-sawya** *n.m* lifebelt

gryll *n.m* **grylles** crayfish; (*insect*) cricket

gryllya *vb* chirp

grysel *adj* frightful

grysla *vb* bare one's teeth; grin; snarl

gul *vb* do; create; make. **gul bos unverhes** reconcile. **gul devnydh a²** make use of. **gul dhe glamdera** stun. **gul dhe² nebonan gul neppyth** make somebody do something. **gul ges** joke; kid; mock. **gul hwel** work. **gul lost** queue. **gul tronkys** have a bath. **gul war-lergh** imitate

guw *n.m* **guwow** spear

guwa *vb* spear

gwag I *adj* blank; empty; hollow; hungry; unoccupied; unfurnished; vacant **II** *n.m* **gwagyon** cave

gwagen *n.f* **gwagennow** blank

gwagla *n.m* **gwagleow** vacancy

gwagren *n.f* **gwagrennow** gland

gwagva *n.f* **gwagvaow** vacuum

gwakhe *vb* vacate; empty

gwakter *n.m* **gwakteryow** emptiness; vacuum

gwalgh *n.m* fill; repletion. **kavos y walgh a²** have one's fill of

gwall *n.m* **gwallow** accident; defect; neglect. **dre wall** by accident

gwaluster *n.m* casualty

gwan *n.f* **gwanyow** sting; jab; prick

gwana *vb* pierce; stab; sting

gwander *n.m* weakness

gwandra *vb* wander; hike

gwandrans *n.m* **gwandransow** hike; range (*of an animal*)

gwandrek *adj* wandering

gwandryas *n.m* **gwandrysi** wanderer; nomad

gwaneth *n.coll* wheat

gwann *adj* faint; frail; weak. **gwann y golon** weak-hearted. **hanow gwann** *n.m* adjective

gwanna *vb* weaken

gwannhanow *n.m* **gwannhenwyn** insulting nickname; rude name

gwannhe *vb* weaken

gwannliwek *adj* pale

gwar *adj* chaste

gwara *n.coll* goods; merchandise; wares. **gwara boos** *n.coll* groceries

gwaraji *n.m* **gwarajiow** warehouse

gwarak *n.m* **gwaregow** arc; bow; arch; (*in street signage*) crescent. **hesken warak** *n.f* bow saw

gwareger *n.m* **gwaregoryon** archer

gwaregieth *n.f* archery

gwaren *n.f* **gwarennow** item of merchandise

gwari I *n.m* **gwariow** game; fun; pastime; play **II** *vb* play; act. **delivra dhe wari** liberate; set free. **garth-gwari** *n.m* playground. **gwari bord** *n.m* board game. **gwari dall** *n.m* lottery. **gwari gans gwelen dhewblek** play a double game. **gwari gwydhyow** *n.m* video game. **gwari ilow** *n.m* musical. **gwari kan** *n.m* opera; musical. **gwari kartennow** *n.m* card game. **gwari mildam** *n.m* jigsaw puzzle. **gwari mir** *n.m* miracle play. **gwari mus** *n.m* pantomime. **Gwariow Olympek** *n.pl* Olympic Games. **gwari pelyow** *n.m* bowling. **gwari rann** *n.m* role playing game (RPG). **gwari sagh** *n.m* raffle. **gwari sebon** *n.m* soap opera. **gwari war eryow** *n.m, vb* pun. **plen an gwari** *n.m* playing place

gwariell *n.f* **gwariellow** toy. **gwerthji gwariellow** *n.m* toy-shop

gwarier *n.m* **gwarioryon** actor; player; performer

gwariji *n.m* **gwarijiow** theatre

gwarijiel *adj* theatrical

gwariva *n.f* **gwarivaow** theatre; stage

gwarnya *vb* warn; proclaim; notify

gwarnyans *n.m* **gwarnyansow** warning; proclamation

gwarr *n.f* **gwarrow** curve

gwartha *adj* higher; upper; top

gwarthek *n.coll* horned cattle

gwarthevya *vb* dominate

gwarthevyans *n.m* **gwarthevyansow** domination; supremacy

gwarthevyek *adj* dominant

gwas *n.m* **gwesyon** chap; fellow; guy; servant; jack (playing card); knave (playing card). **gwas hwel** *n.m* workman. **gwas ti** *n.m* homemaker. **yn kettep gwas** to the last man

gwask *n.f* **gwaskow** press; stress; nip. **an Wask** *n.f* the Press. **gwask-pryntya** *n.m* printing press

gwaska *vb* press; lobby; nip. **gwaska yn-mes** squeeze out; express

gwaskans *n.m* **gwaskansow** impression; squeezing

gwaskedh *n.m* (*in physics*) pressure

gwaskell *n.f* **gwaskellow** compressor

gwast *adj* waste

gwastas *adj* (*of land*) flat; open; plain

gwastel *n.f* **gwastellow** sweet cake

gwastya *vb* waste

gwav *n.m* **gwavow** winter. **dres an gwav** all winter. **y'n gwav** in winter

gwavek *adj* wintry

gwavi *vb* pass the winter

gwavos *n.f* **gwavosow** winter dwelling

gwaya I *n.m* **gwayow** move **II** *vb* move

gwayadow *adj* movable

gwayans *n.m* **gwayansow** movement; motion

gwayn *n.m* **gwaynyow** gain; win; winning

gwaynya *vb* gain; procure; profit; win

gwaynyer *n.m* **gwaynyoryon** winner

gwaytyas *vb* watch out; mind; expect; hope (for). **gwayt** + *verbal noun* see that you …! (*sg*). **gwaytyewgh** + *verbal noun* see that you …! (*pl*)

gwaytys *adj* expected; due

gwayvya *vb* go away quickly; get out; scarper; waive. **gwayv ow golok!** get out of my sight! buzz off!

gweder *n.m* **gwedrow** glass. **gweder-mires** *n.m* mirror. **dewweder** *n.dl* glasses; spectacles

gwedh *n.f* **gwedhow** phase (*e.g. of the Moon*)

gwedhan *n.m* **gwedhanes** weevil

gwedhek *n.f* **gwedhegi** woodland

gwedhen *n.f* **gwedhennow** tree

gwedhow I *adj* widowed **II gwedhowyon** *n.m* widower. **gour gwedhow** *n.m* widower. **benyn wedhow** *n.f* widow

gwedhra *vb* wither

gwedhrys *adj* withered

gwedhwes *n.f* **gwedhwesow** widow

gwedhyn *adj* flexible; pliable; elastic; supple

gwedhynder *n.m* **gwedhynderow** flexibility; elasticity; suppleness

gwedren *n.f* **gwedrennow** drinking glass

gwedrennas *n.f* **gwedrenasow** glassful

gwedrik *n.m* **gwedrigow** lens. **gwedrik kestav** *n.m* contact lens

gwegbys an park *n.coll* common vetch

gwegbys melyn *n.coll* yellow vetch

gwel (1) *n.m* **gwelyow** field. **gwel golf** *n.m* golf course

gwel (2) *n.f* **gwelyow** sight; view; vision; scene

gwel (3) *n.coll* canes; poles; rods; sticks

gweladewder *n.m* visibility

gweladow *adj* visible

gwelen *n.f* **gwelynni** cane; rod; pole; stick; wand. **gwelen-byskessa** *n.f* fishing rod. **gwelen gala** *n.f* straw. **gwelen garr** *n.f* pole (*of a cart*). **gwelen hus** *n.f* magic wand. **gwelen vughes** *n.f* cattle prod. **gwelen vusur** *n.f* dipstick. **gwelen ski** *n.f* ski pole. **gwelen vaglen** *n.f* gearstick

gwelennik *n.f* **gwelenigow** chopstick

gweles *vb* see. **dha weles** goodbye; see you (*sg*). **agas gweles** goodbye; see you (*pl*). **skonya gweles** turn a blind eye

gweles aperys *adj* sight impaired

gwelesek *adj* visual

gwelesigeth *n.f* **gwelesigethow** vision

gweli *n.m* **gweliow** bed. **gweli ros** *n.m* pram. **gweli bonk** *n.m* bunk bed. **arhwilell weli** *n.f* flatbed scanner

gwelivedhes *n.f* **gwelivedhesow** midwife

gwelivesi *vb* go into labour

gwelivos *n.m* labour

gwell *adj, adv* (**see: da**) better; superior. **bos gwell gans** be preferred by. **gwell es** better than; superior to

gwella *adj, adv* (**see: da**) best

gwellhe *vb* improve; (*intransitive*) get well; (*transitive*) make well; enhance; upgrade

gwellheans *n.m* **gwellheansow** improvement

gwels *n.coll* grass

gwelsek *adj* grassy

gwelsen *n.f* **gwelsennow** blade of grass

gwelsigow *n.pl* scissors. **gwelsigow ewin** *n.pl* nail scissors

gwelsow *n.pl* shears

gwelva *n.f* **gwelvaow** viewpoint

gwenen *n.coll* bees. **kowel gwenen** *n.m* beehive

gwenenen *n.f* **gwenenennow** bee

Gwener *n.f* Friday; Venus

gwenn *n.m* **gwennow** anus

gwennel *n.f* **gwenili** (*bird*) swallow

gwennel dhu *n.f* **gwenili du** (*bird*) swift

gwennen *n.f* **gwenennow** blister

gwenogen *n.f* **gwenogennow** wart

gwenolles *n.m* greater celandine

gwenon *n.m* **gwenenyow** poison

gwenonek *adj* poisonous; toxic

gwenton *n.m* spring

gwentonel *adj* vernal

gwer (1) *adj* green. **an Parti Gwyrdh** the Green Party. **an Re Wyrdh** the Greens

gwer (2) *n.pl* men; husbands

gwer (3) *n.pl* (*signage*) gents

gwerem *n.m* gweremmow emerald

gweres (1) I *n.m* help; aid; assistance
II *vb* help; aid; assist. arghans-gweres
n.m subsidy. gweres nebonan ow kul
neppyth help somebody do
something

gweres (2) *n.m* gweresow ground; soil

gweresek *adj* accessory; helpful;
subsidiary

gwereser *n.m* gweresoryon accessory;
helper

gwerghes *n.f* gwerghesow virgin

gwerik *adj* greenish

gwerin *n.f* common people; folk;
proletariat. kan werin *n.f* folk song.
yeth an werin *n.f* informal meeting
of Cornish speakers

gwerinek *adj* proletarian

gwerinel *adj* democratic

gwerinieth *n.f* gweriniethow
democracy

gweriniether *n.m* gweriniethoryon
democrat

gwerinor *n.m* gwerinoryon peasant

gwern (1) *n.f* gwernow mast

gwern (2) *n.coll* marshlands; swamp

gwern (3) *n.coll* alder trees

gwernek *adj* marshy; swampy

gwernen (1) *n.f* gwernennow marsh;
swamp

gwernen (2) *n.f* gwernennow alder
tree

Gwernenys *top n.f* Guernsey

gwernis *n.f* gwernisyow varnish.
gwernis ewin *n.f* nail varnish

gwernisya *vb* varnish

gwers *n.f* gwersyow verse; stanza

gwersella *vb* encamp

gwersellans *n.m* gwersellansow
encampment

gwerth *n.f* gwerthow sale; price.
reken gwerth *n.m* bill of sale

gwertha *vb* sell; vend. gwertha a² sell
for

gwerthas *n.f* gwerthasow sale

gwerther *n.m* gwerthoryon
salesperson; seller; vendor. gwerther
jornalys *n.m* newsagent. gwerther
leth *n.m* milkman. gwerther losow
n.m greengrocer

gwerthji *n.m* gwerthjiow shop; store.
gwerthji gwariellow *n.m* toy-shop.
gwerthji lyvrow *n.m* bookshop.
gwerthji hwegennow *n.m* sweetshop

gwerthveurhe *vb* appreciate

gwerthveurheans *n.m*
gwerthveurheansow appreciation

gwerwyn *adj* light green

gweskel *vb* beat; hit; strike. gweskel an
fronn slam on the brakes. gweskel
nebonan gans pellen shoot
somebody with a bullet. gweskel
nebonan gans seth shoot somebody
with an arrow. gweskel tabour beat a
drum; drum

gweskys *adj* (*struck*) beaten

gwester *n.m* gwestoryon guest

gwesti *n.m* gwestiow guesthouse

gwestva *n.f* hospitality

gweth *adj, adv* (see: drog) worse;
inferior

gwethafor I *adj* pessimistic II *n.m*
gwethaforyon pessimist

gwethaforieth *n.f* pessimism

gwethhe *vb* aggravate; deteriorate;
worsen

gwethheans *n.m* gwethheansow
deterioration

gwettha *adj* worst (see: drog)

gweun *n.m* gossamer

gweus *n.f* gweusyow, *dl* diwweus lip.
eli gweus *n.m* lip balm; lip salve.
lenter gweus *n.m* lip gloss. liw
gweus *n.m* lipstick

gwevya *vb* wave; flourish (*a sword*)

gwevyans *n.m* gwevyansow wave
(*hand*)

gwewen *n.f* gwewennow *dl*
diwwewen heel

gweyth (1) *n.f* **gweythyow** instance; occasion

gweyth (2) *n.f* **gweythyow** work; work-day

-gweyth (3) *sffx* times (*takes feminine 2, 3, 4*)

gweytha *vb* apply; set to work

gweythor *n.m* **gweythoryon** worker; workman

gweythresans *n.m* **gweythresansow** activation; implementation

gweythresek *adj* active; functional

gweythva *n.f* **gweythvaow** factory

gwia *vb* knit; weave

gwiader *n.m* **gwiadoryon** weaver

gwias *n.m* **gwiasow** web; fabric; consistency. **erbynn an gwias** against the grain. **gwias kevnis** *n.m* cobweb; spider web

gwiasedh *n.m* **gwiasedhow** texture

gwiaspost *n.m* **gwiaspostow** webmail

gwiasva *n.f* **gwiasvaow** website

gwiasvester *n.m* **gwiasvestrysi** webmaster

gwibes *n.coll* midges; gnats

gwibesen *n.f* **gwibesennow** midge; gnat

gwibessa *vb* waste time (*lit.* to hunt gnats)

gwiek *adj* webbed

gwig *n.f* **gwigow** village

gwighal *vb* squeak

gwikor *n.m* **gwikoryon** merchant; peddler; trader. **gwikor frank** *n.m* smuggler

gwin *n.m* **gwinow** wine. **gwin gwynn** *n.m* white wine. **gwin rudh** *n.m* red wine. **gwin skaw** *n.m* elderberry wine

gwinbren *n.m* **gwinbrennyer** vine, grape-vine

gwinlan *n.f* **gwinlannow** vineyard

gwinwel *n.coll* maple trees

gwinwelen *n.f* **gwinwelennow** maple

gwir I *adj* true; genuine; real; right; actual **II** *n.m* **gwiryow** right; truth.

dhe wir really. **gwiryow kemmyn** *n.pl* civil rights. **yn hwir** actually

gwirbryntyans *n.m* **gwirbryntyansow** copyright

gwirhaval *adj* likely; plausible; probable

gwirhe *vb* verify

gwirhevelepter *n.m* likelihood; plausibility

gwir-pryntya *n.m* **gwiryow-pryntya** copyright

gwirvos *n.m* **gwirvosow** reality. **gwirvos gowir** virtual reality

gwirvosek *adj* realistic

gwirya *vb* verify

gwiryon *adj* genuine; truthful

gwiryonedh *n.m* **gwiryonedhow** truth

gwiryonedhek *adj* factual

gwis *n.f* **gwisi** sow

gwisk *n.m* **gwiskow** clothes. **gwisk horn** *n.m* iron armour

gwiska *vb* clothe; dress; wear

gwiskas *n.m* **gwiskasow** costume; layer; coating

gwiskti *n.m* **gwisktiow** vestry

gwiskva *n.f* **gwiskvaow** changing room

gwith *n.m* care; custody; guard; retention. **yn-dann with** care of; c/o. **gwith an kreslu** *n.m* police custody. **kemmer with!** (*sg.*) take care!

gwitha *vb* guard; keep; nurse (sick people); preserve; protect; reserve; retain; safeguard. **gwitha rag** preserve from; protect from. **gwitha war²** look after; watch over

gwithans *n.m* conservation

gwithti *n.m* **gwithtiow** museum

gwithva *n.f* **gwithvaow** reserve; storehouse. **gwithva natur** *n.f* nature reserve

gwithyas *n.m* **gwithysi** chaperone; custodian; guard; guardian; keeper; retainer; warden. **gwithyas gol** *n.m* goalkeeper. **gwithyas kres** *n.m* police officer. **gwithyas klevyon** carer (*of sick people*). **kummyas gwithyas** *n.m* carer's leave

gwithyasel *adj* conservative

gwius *adj* intricate

gwiver *n.coll* wires

gwivren *n.f* **gwivrennow** wire

gwiw *adj* appropriate; fit; suitable

gwiwder *n.m* fitness; worthiness

gwiwer *n.m* **gwiweres, gwiwerow** squirrel

gwlan *n.coll* wool

gwlanek I *adj* woollen; woolly **II** *n.m* **gwlanogow** jersey; jumper; pullover. **aval gwlanek** *n.m* peach

gwlanik *n.m* great mullein (*common; woolly; Aaron's rod*)

gwlas *n.f* **gwlasow** country; land

gwlasek *adj* pertaining to a country

gwlaskar *adj* patriotic

gwlaskarer *n.m* **gwlaskaroryon** patriot

gwlaskerensa *n.f* patriotism

gwlaskor *n.f* **gwlaskordhow** kingdom; realm. **Gwlaskor Unys** United Kingdom

gwledh *n.f* **gwledhow** banquet

gwlyghi *vb* soak

gwradhel *adj* radial

gwragh *n.f* **gwraghes** hag; witch; (*fish*) wrasse. **gwragh oles** *n.f* woodlouse

gwrannen *n.f* **gwranennow** wren

gwreck *n.m* **gwreckys** wreck

gwreg *n.f* **gwragedh** wife

gwregel *adj* feminine

gwresek *adj* ardent; enthusiastic

gwre'ti *n.f* homemaker; housewife

gwreydh *n.coll* roots

gwreydhek *adj* original

gwreydhen *n.f* **gwreydhennow** root. **gwreydhen bedrek** *n.f* square root

gwreydhyel *adj* radical. **gul gwreydhyel** *vb* radicalise

gwreydhyoleth *n.f* radicalism

gwreydhyolydh *n.m* **gwreydhyolydhyon** radical

gwri *n.m* **gwriow** stitch

gwrians *n.m* **gwriansow** act; activity; action; deed; manufacture; creation. **gwrians dres eghen** *n.m* feat. **gwrians war-lergh** *n.m* imitation; impression

gwrias *vb* stitch; sew. **jynn-gwrias** *n.m* sewing machine

gwrier *n.m* **gwrioryon** creator; maker; manufacturer

gwruthyl *vb* (=**gul**) build; carry out; create; make; manufacture; perform

gwryghonek *adj* sparkling

gwrynnya *vb* wring; squeeze

gwrys (1) *adj* done; made

gwrys (2) *n.m* **gwrysow** crystal

gwrysegans *n.m* **gwrysegansow** crystallization

gwrysven *n.m* **gwrysveyn** feldspar

gwryth *n.f* **gwrythow** performance; deeds

gwrythyans *n.m* **gwrythyansow** performance

gwydh *n.coll* trees. **gwydh Nadelik** *n.coll* Christmas trees

gwydhbol *n.m* chess

gwydhvos *n.coll* honeysuckle

gwydhvosen *n.f* **gwydhvosennow** honeysuckle

gwydhyel *adj* wooded

gwydhyow *n.m* **gwydhyowyow** video

gwyles *n.m* **gwylesow** lovage

gwylgos *n.m* **gwylgosow** jungle

gwyll *n.m* **gwyllyow** (*offensive*) tramp; vagrant

gwyls I *adj* wild; fierce; savage; violent **II** *n.m* **gwylsyon** savage

gwylvos *n.m* **gwylvosow** wilderness

gwynder *n.m* whiteness

gwynk *n.m* **gwynkow** wink

gwynkya *vb* wink

gwynn I *adj* white; fair; blessed **II** *n.m* **gwynnow** white. **gwynn oy** *n.m* egg white

gwynnek *n.m* **gwynoges** whiting

gwynnel *vb* struggle
Gwynngala *n.m* September
gwynnik *adj* whitish
gwynnrudh *adj* pale pink
gwynnvys *adj* blessed; fortunate; lucky.
  gwynn ow bys! how lucky I am!
gwyns (1) *n.m* **gwynsow** wind. **gwyns
  a-dro** *n.m* cyclone. **skew wyns** *n.f*
  windscreen
gwyns (2) *n.f* **gwynsys** winch
gwynsek *adj* windy
gwynsell *n.f* **gwynsellow** fan

gwynsella *vb* fan
gwyrdh *adj* green
gwyrgh *adj* virgin
gwythi *n.coll* veins
gwythiek *adj* bloodshot
gwythien *n.f* **gwythiennow** vein.
  gwythien an konna jugular vein
gyki *vb* peep
gyllys *adj* gone
gymnastek *n.m* gymnastics
gyth *n.m* **gythyow** complaint

H

habadolya *n.m* racket; uproar
hackya *vb* hack; chop. **hackya dhe-ves**
  hack off
ha(g) *cnj* and; plus; (*before present
  participle*) while. **hag ev owth oberi**
  while he was working. **war-tu ha(g)**
  prp toward(s). **Onan hag Oll** One
  and All
ha'ga[3] *contr* and their
ha'gan *contr* and our
ha'gas *contr* and your (*pl*)
hagensoll *adv* moreover
hager *adj* (*precedes the noun*) bad;
  hideous; nasty
hager-awel *n.f* **hager-awelyow** storm;
  squall; tempest
hager-bryv *n.m* **hager-breves,
  hager-brevyon** serpent (*in the book of
  Genesis*)
hager-dowl *n.m* **hager-dowlow** stroke
  of bad luck
hager-dros *n.f* **hager-drosow**
  cacophony
hager-gowas *n.f* **hager-gowasow**
  deluge; downpour
hager-ober *n.m* **hager-oberow** crime
hager-vargen *n.m* a bad deal;
  something gone wrong. **hager-vargen**

yw hemma! this has gone all wrong!
hager-viaj *n.m* bad business
hagoll *adv* moreover
hagra *vb* disfigure; make ugly; uglify
hakkra *adj* uglier; ugliest
hakter *n.m* ugliness; eyesore
hal *n.f* **halow** marsh; moor. **gaver hal**
  n.f snipe
halya *vb* haul; heave; tow
halyans *n.m* **halyansow** haulage; heave
ha'm *contr* and my
hamster *n.m* **hamsters** hamster
ha'n *contr* and the
hanaf *n.m* **hanafow** cup; beaker
hanafas *n.m* **hanafasow** cupful
hanas *n.m* **hanasow** murmur; sigh;
  groan; whisper
hanasa *vb* murmur; sigh; groan;
  whisper
handla *vb* handle; manipulate; sort out.
  handla yn harow manhandle
handlans *n.m* **handlansow** handling;
  manipulation
haneth *adv* this evening; tonight.
  haneth dhe nos just before night falls
hanow *n.m* **henwyn** name; noun;
  substantive. **hanow gwann** *n.m*
  adjective. **hanow gwari** *n.m* stage

name. **hanow restren** *n.m* filename.
hanow kynsa *n.m* forename. **hanow**
pluven *n.m* pen name. **hanow teylu**
n.m surname. **kavos hanow** gain a
reputation. **pyth yw dha hanow?**
what is your (sg.) name? **yn hanow**
nominally
hanow-verb *n.m* **henwyn-verb**
infinitive
hansel *n.m* **hanselyow** breakfast
hanter *n.m* **hanteryow** half. **dhe hanter**
an fordh midway. **hanter-broder** *n.m*
half-brother. **hanter-dydh** *n.m*
midday; noon. **hanter-hwor** *n.f*
half-sister. **hanter-mis** *n.m* fortnight.
hanter-nos *n.f* midnight. **hanter-our**
n.m half-hour
hanter- *prfx* half-; hemi-; semi-
hantera *vb* halve
hanterbogalen *n.f* **hanterbogalennow**
semi-vowel
hanterbrev *n.m* **hanterbrevow**
semibreve
hanter-dydh *n.m* **hanter-dedhyow**
midday; noon
hantergwari *n.m* **hantergwariow**
semifinal
hanterkans *num* fifty
hanterkansves *num* fiftieth
hanterkylgh *n.m* **hanterkylghyow**
semicircle
hanter-nos *n.f* **hanter-nosow** midnight
hanwans *n.m* **hanwansow** religious
denomination
happ *n.m* **happys, happow** chance;
luck. **dre happ** by chance; incidentally
happriv *n.m* **happrivow** random
number
hapwari *vb* gamble
harber *n.m* **harbers** asylum; haven;
place of refuge
harbereth *n.f* asylum. **harbereth**
wlasek *n.f* political asylum
hardh *adj* bold; brave; fearless; game;
strict

hardhder *n.m* audacity; boldness
hardigras *n.m* severity
hardlych *adv* stringently
harmonika *n.f* **harmonikas**
harmonica; mouth organ
harow *int* help!
harth *n.m* **harthow** bark (of a dog);
baying
hartha *vb* bark; bay
has *n.coll* seed; sperm
hasa *vb* sow
hasen *n.f* **hasennow** seed; sperm
haslet *n.m* **haslettow** contraceptive;
condom
haslettyans *n.m* **haslettyansow**
contraception
ha'th[5a] *contr* and your (*sg*)
hatt *n.m* **hattys, hattow** hat. **hatt**
bowler *n.m* bowler. **hatt howl** *n.m*
sunhat
hav *n.m* **havow, havyow** summer.
besowen Hav *n.f* maypole
haval *adj* alike; like; similar;
resembling. **haval dhe**[2] like; similar
to. **bos haval dhe**[2] resemble
havalreydhek *adj* homosexual; gay
havalreydhor *n.m* **havalreydhoryon**
homosexual person
havek *adj* summery
havi *vb* pass the summer. **tyller havi**
n.m holiday resort
havos *n.f* **havosow** summer dwelling;
holiday home
havyas *n.m* **havysi** summer tourist
hay *n.f* **hayow** enclosure
ha'y[2] *contr* and his
ha'y[3] *contr* and her
haylya *vb* greet; hail
he- *prfx* -able
heb *prp* without; un-. **heb danjer** safely.
heb difuna dormant. **heb dhout**
without doubt; of course;
undoubtedly. **heb fordh** trackless.
heb gul gik na mik stock-still. **heb**
hedhi continually; perpetually;

non-stop. **heb kost** free of charge. **heb lett** incessantly. **heb mar** without doubt; of course. **heb mebel** unfurnished. **heb par** unequalled. **heb styryans** unaccountable. **heb toll na gil** sincerely. **heb tyli** unpaid. **heb wow** truly. *Personal forms: 1s **hebov**, 2s **hebos**, 3sm **hebdho**, 3sf **hebdhi**, 1p **hebon**, 2p **hebowgh**, 3p **hebdha***

hebask *adj* calm; serene; peaceful. **Keynvor Hebask** *n.m* Pacific Ocean

hebaskhe *vb* calm; put to rest; soothe; pacify

heblek *adj* folding

hebleth *adj* flexible; supple; pliable

hedardh *adj* explosive

hedeuth *adj* soluble

hedh *n.m* **hedhow** halt; pause; respite

hedhadow *adj* accessible; reachable

hedhas *n.m* **hedhasow** access

hedhes *vb* achieve; attain; manage; reach

hedheuryer *n.m* **hedheuryerow** stopwatch

hedhi *vb* cancel; cease; halt; pause. **heb hedhi** perpetually; continually; non-stop

hedhlor *n.m* **hedhloryon** ploughman

hedhyans *n.m* **hedhyansow** accomplishment; attainment

hedhyw *adv* today. **hedhyw vyttin** this morning. **y'n jydh hedhyw** nowadays

hedor *adj* fragile

Hedra *n.m* October

hedre² *cnj* while; as long as. **hedre vewiv** as long as I live

hedro *adj* changeable; fickle

hedrogh *adj* cuttable

hefordh *adj* navigable; passable

hegar *adj* affectionate; kind; kindly; amicable

hegaredh *n.m* affection

hegas *adj* wretched

heglew *adj* audible; loud; resonant

hegol *adj* credulous; superstitious

hegoledh *n.m* **hegoledhow** superstition

hegos *adj* ticklish

hegov *adj* memorable

hel (1) *n.f* **helyow** hall. **hel an dre** *n.f* the town hall. **hel sport** *n.f* gymnasium

hel (2) *adj* benevolent; generous; hospitable; liberal

helder *n.m* benevolence; generosity; hospitality

heledh *n.m* **heledhow** amplitude

helergh *adj* late

helerghell *n.f* **helerghellow** detector

helerghi *vb* detect; track

helerghyas *n.m* **helerghysi** detective. **helerghyas privedh** *n.m* private detective; private eye

helgh *n.m* **helghow** hunt; chase; frantic search

helghi *vb* hunt; chase

helghor *n.m* **helghoryon** hunter

helghya *vb* hunt; chase; drive out

helghyas *n.m* **helghysi** pursuer

helgi *n.m* **helgeun** hound (*for hunting*)

helgik *n.m* (*meat*) game. **ladra helgik** poach

hell *adj* reluctant

helosk *adj* flammable

helygen *n.f* **helygennow** willow

helygles *n.coll* willowherb

helygles denti *n.coll* hoary willowherb

helygles ledan *n.coll* broad-leaved willowherb

helyk *n.coll* willow-trees

hembrenkyas *n.m* **hembrenkysi** leader; conductor

hembronk *vb* lead

hemm *prn* (*used before* **yw** *and* **o**) this *m*

hemma *prn* this (one) *m*

hen *adj* (*precedes the noun*) old; long-standing; archaic; ancient

henavek I *adj* elder; elderly II **henavogyon** *n.m* elder; senior. **tus henavek** *n.pl* elderly people

henbyth *n.m* **henbythow** antique

hendas *n.m* **hendasow** ancestor; forefather

hendedhyow *n.pl* the olden days. **an hendedhyow brav** *n.pl* the good old days

hendhillas *n.coll* jumble; old clothes

hendhillasen *n.f* **hendhillasennow** old item of clothing

hendhyskonieth *n.f* archaeology

hendhyskoniethel *adj* archaeological

hendhyskonydh *n.m* **hendhyskonydhyon** archaeologist

hendra *n.f* **hendrevow** home farm

henedh *n.m* **henedhow** generation

henfordh *n.f* **henfordhow** ancient track

hengov *n.m* **hengovyow** tradition

hengovek *adj* traditional

henhwedhel *n.m* **henhwedhlow** legend

henlavar *n.m* **henlavarow** proverb

henlavarek *adj* proverbial

henn *prn* (*used before* **yw** *and* **o**) that *m*. **henn yw** namely

henna *prn* that (one) *m*. **wosa henna** after that; later

henwel *vb* name

henwys *adj* named

henys *n.m* old age

hepatitis *n.m* (*med*) hepatitis

hepfordh *adj* impassable; trackless

hepken *adv* just; only

hepkor *vb* abandon; do without; give up; relinquish; yield

heptu *adj* neutral; non-aligned

heptueth *n.f* neutrality

her *n.m* **heryon** heir

herdhya *vb* push; shove. **kador-herdhya** *n.f* **kadoryow-herdhya** push-chair. **herdhys war-barth** crowded together

herdhyans *n.m* **herdhyansow** push

hermesek *adj* hermetic; airtight

hern *n.coll* pilchards; sardines. **hern gwynn** herrings

hernen *n.f* **hernennow** pilchard; sardine

hernes *n.m* **hernessow** harness

hernessya *vb* put on a harness; put on equipment; equip

hernya *vb* shoe (*a horse*)

herwydh *prp* according to; on the authority of. **herwydh an dhargan** according to the forecast. **herwydh an lagha** lawful. **herwydh an our** hourly. **herwydh reson** logical. **herwydh usadow** as usual. **yn herwydh** adjoining; in the vicinity of *Personal forms: 1s* **yn ow herwydh**, *2s* **yn dha herwydh**, *3sm* **yn y herwydh**, *3sf* **yn hy herwydh**, *1p* **y'gan herwydh**, *2p* **y'gas herwydh**, *3p* **y'ga herwydh**

herya *vb* inherit

hes *n.f* **hesow** flock; shoal; swarm

hesk *n.coll* saw-grass; sedge. **hesk an tewes** *n.coll* marram grass

hesken *n.f* **heskennow** saw; blade of saw-grass. **bleus hesken** *n.m* sawdust. **hesken gadon** *n.f* chainsaw. **hesken vond** *n.f* bandsaw. **hesken warak** *n.f* bow saw

heskenna *vb* saw (*wood, etc.*)

hester *n.m* **hesteryow** trough

hesya *vb* flock

heudh *adj* glad; joyful; merry

heudhadow *adj* enjoyable

heudhi *vb* be glad

heudhik *adj* glad

heuthhe *vb* ease; be eased; gladden; be gladdened

heveladow *adj* apparent

hevelenep *n.m* **hevelenebow** likeness

hevelep I *adj* like; similar II *n.m* likeness; resemblance; image. **yn hevelep a²**, **yn hevelep dhe²** in the likeness of

hevelepter *n.m* similarity; correspondence

heveli *vb* (*intransitive*) seem; come across as; (*transitive*) liken; compare. **dell hevel** as it seems; probably

hevis *n.m* **hevisyow** blouse

hevlena *adv* this year

hevleni *adv* this year

hewel *adj* conspicuous; manifest; noticeable; obvious

heweledh *n.m* **heweledhow** manifestation

heweres *adj* helpful; auxiliary; user-friendly

hewol *adj* attentive; vigilant

hewul *adj* practical

heyjik *n.m* **heyjigow** duckling

heyl *n.m* **heylyow** estuary; river-mouth

heylyn *n.m* **heylynnow** creek

hi *prn* she

hick *n.m* **hickow** hiccup

hickas *vb* hiccup

hidrojen *n.m* (*element*) hydrogen

hidrolek *adj* hydraulic

higen *n.f* **higennow** hook; fish-hook

higenna *vb* hook

hil *n.f* **hilyow** ethnicity; race

hilgasek *adj* racist

hilgasieth *n.f* racism

hilgasydh *n.m* **hilgasydhyon** racist person

hin *n.f* **hinyow** climate

Hindieth *n.f* Hinduism

hinek *adj* climatic

hir *adj* long. **hir y vlew** long-haired. **hir y gows** long-winded

hirbedrek I *adj* rectangular; oblong **II** *n.m* **hirbedrogow** rectangle

hirbrederi *vb* contemplate

hirbren *n.m* **hirbrenyow** hire purchase. **yn hirbren** on hire purchase

hirbrena *vb* buy on hire purchase

hirder *n.m* tallness; length

hireth *n.f* **hirethow** longing; loneliness; nostalgia; yearning

hirethek *adj* homesick; lonely; longing; yearning

hirgorn *n.m* **hirgern** trumpet

hirgren *adj* cylindrical

hirgrennen *n.f* **hirgrenennow** cylinder

hirgylgh *n.m* **hirgelghyow** ellipse; oval

hirgylghek *adj* elliptical; oval

hirhe *vb* lengthen

hirneth *n.f* a very long time; tedium

hirra *adj* longer. **an hirra** longest

hirskeusen *n.f* **hirskeusennow** frieze

hirviga *vb* procrastinate

hirvryjyon *vb* stew

hirwelyek *adj* long-sighted

HIV *abbrev* HIV (*med*). **Virus Immunodifyk Denel** Human Immunodeficiency Virus

hoba *n.m* **hobas** pony

hobadolya *n.m* **hobadolyas** clamour; row

hobi *n.m* **hobis** hobby

hobihors *n.m* **hobihorsys** hobby-horse

hocki *n.m* hockey

hockya *vb* falter; hesitate. **heb hockya** without further ado

hockyans *n.m* **hockyansow** hesitation

hod *n.m* **hodys** hood

hodik *n.m* **hodigow** hoodie

hodya *vb* injure

hodys *adj* injured

hogen (1) *adv* even; still

hogen (2) *n.f* **hogennow** pie; oggy; pastry. **hogen vewin ha loneth** *n.f* steak and kidney pie

hogh *n.m* **hoghes** hog; pig; swine. **hogh Gyni** *n.m* Guinea pig

hok *n.m* **hokys** hawk. **hok karyn** *n.m* vulture

holan *n.coll* salt

holanek *adj* salty

holanen *n.f* **holanennow** grain of salt

holograf *n.m* **holografow** holograph

holya *vb* follow

holyans *n.m* **holyansow** sequence

holyer *n.m* **holyoryon** follower

homeli *n.m* **homelis** homily

homm *prn* (*used before* **yw** *and* **o**) this *f*

homma *prn* this (one) *f*

honan *prn* oneself; self; alone; one's own. **ow honan** myself. **dha honan** yourself. **y honan** himself. **hy honan** herself. **agan honan** ourselves. **agas honan** yourselves. **aga honan** themselves

honangonstrinus *adj* compulsive

honanieth *n.f* **honaniethow** identity. **honanieth usyer** *n.m* user identity

honanus *adj* selfish

honanuster *n.m* selfishness

hond *n.m* **hons** (*used as terms of abuse*) hound

honn *prn* (*used before* **yw** *and* **o**) that *f*

honna *prn* that (one) *f*

hons *adv* yonder; over there

hopys *n.coll* hops

hopysen *n.f* **hopysennow** (*plant*) hop

hora *n.f* **horys** prostitute

hordh *n.m* **hordhes** ram

horji *n.m* **horjiow** brothel

horn *n.m* (*element*) iron. **gwisk horn** *n.m* iron armour. **horn margh** *n.m* horseshoe. **lorgh horn** *n.f* (*m*) crowbar

hornek *adj* iron; ferric

hornell *n.f* **hornellow** (pressing) iron

hornella *vb* iron

horner *n.m* **hornoryon** ironmonger

horsen *n.m* **horsens** son-of-a-bitch

hos *n.m* **heyji** duck

hoskerdhes *vb* waddle

hostelri *n.m* **hostelriow** inn; tavern

hou *int* hello; hi

howl *n.m* **howlyow** sun. **towl howl** *n.m* sunstroke. **liw howl** *n.m* suntan; tan

howldrehevel *n.m* **howldrehevelyow** (= **howldrevel**) sunrise; east. **an Howldrehevel** *n.m* the Orient. **a'n howldrehevel** eastern

howlek *adj* solar

howllen *n.f* **howllennow** parasol

howlleski *vb* tan

howlleskys *adj* sunburnt; tanned

howllosk *n.m* **howlloskow** sunburn

howlsedhes *n.m* **howlsedhesow** West; sunset. **a'n howlsedhes** *adj* western

howlwedrow *n.pl* sunglasses

howlyek *adj* sunny

howtyn *adj* haughty; arrogant

hudel *adj* magical

huder *n.m* **hudoryon** magician

hudhygel *n.m* soot

hudhyglek *adj* sooty

huk *n.f* **hukys** riding hood. **Huk Vyghan Rudh** *n.f* Little Red Riding Hood

hulla *n.m* **hullevow** (= **hunlev**) nightmare

hunegen *n.f* **hunegennow** dormouse

hunek *n.coll* dormice

hungan *n.f* **hunganow** lullaby

Hungarek *n.m* Hungarian language

hungarek *adj* Hungarian

Hungari *top n.m* Hungary

Hungarian *n.m* **Hungarians** Hungarian

huni *prn* one. **kettep huni** everyone. **lies huni** many a one. **pub huni** everyone

hunlev *n.m* **hunlevow** (= **hulla**) nightmare

hunros *n.m* **hunrosow** dream. **hunros dydh** *n.m* daydream; reverie

hunrosa *vb* dream

hunyek *adj* sleepy

hurlya (1) *vb* hurl

hurlya (2) *n.m* hurling (*game*)

hurlyer *n.m* **hurlyoryon** hurler

hus *n.m* **husow** charm; enchantment; illusion; magic; spell; sorcery; glamour

husa *vb* charm; enchant; create an illusion

huskoskek *adj* hypnotic

husys *adj* spellbound, enchanted

hwaff (1) *n.m* **hwaffys** gust

hwaff (2) *n.m* **hwaffys** punch
hwaffa *vb* punch
hwann *n.coll* fleas
hwannen *n.f* **hwanennow** fleas
hwans *n.m* **hwansow** desire; want;
wish
hwansa *vb* desire
hwansek *adj* desirous; keen. **bos**
hwansek wish
hwar *adj* meek; mild; tame
hware *adv* immediately; at once;
directly; presently
hwarhe *vb* civilise; domesticate
hwarheans *n.m* **hwarheansow**
civilisation
hwarhes *adj* civilised; domesticated
hwarth *n.m* **hwarthow** laugh; laughter
hwarthus *adj* comic; homorous;
laughable; ludicrous; ridiculous
hwarthuster *n.m* humour
hwarvedhyans *n.m* **hwarvedhyansow**
incident; occurrence
hwarvos I *n.m* **hwarvosow** event;
happening **II** *vb* happen; occur; come
to pass; take place. **pandr'a hwer?**
what's going on? what's up?
hwarvosek *adj* incidental
hwath *adv* still; yet. **na hwath** not yet
hwattya *vb* slap
hwedh *n.m* **hwedhow** swelling;
tumour
hwedhel *n.m* **hwedhlow** tale; story;
narrative
hwedhi *vb* swell
hwedhla *vb* narrate; tell tales
hwedhlans *n.m* **hwedhlansow**
narration
hwedhlek *adj* narrative
hwedhlor *n.m* **hwedhloryon** narrator
hwedner *n.m* sixpence
hweg *adj* sweet; dear; gentle; kind; nice;
pleasant; pleasing. **pompyon hweg**
n.m melon
hwegen *n.f* **hwegennow** darling; pet;
sweet; lozenge

hweger *n.f* **hwegrow** mother-in-law
hwegh *num* six
hweghkorn *n.m* **hweghkernow**
hexagon
hweghmis *n.m* **hweghmisyow**
semester
hweghves *num* sixth
hwegol I *adj* darling; delightful;
sweetest **II** *n.m* darling
hwegron *n.m* **hwegronyon**
father-in-law
hwegyn *n.m* **hwegennow** sweet
hwegys *n.coll* maize
hwegysen *n.f* **hwegysennow** grain of
maize
hwejalen *n.f* **hwejalennow** boil (*med*)
hwekhe *vb* sweeten
hwel *n.m* **hwelyow** work; mine-work;
labour. **best hwel** *n.m* working
animal. **gul hwel** work. **hwel ober**
n.m industry
hweldro *n.f* **hweldroyow** (*mechanical*)
revolution
hwelji *n.m* **hweljiow** workshop
hwenn *n.coll* weeds
hwennek *adj* weedy
hwennen *n.f* **hwenennow** weed;
nipple; teat
hwerow *adj* bitter; harsh; sharp
hwerow-hweg *adj* bitter-sweet
hwerthin *vb* laugh. **sevel orth**
hwerthin keep a straight face. **ynter**
hwerthin hag ola half laughing half
crying
hwesker *n.coll* insects
hweskeren *n.f* **hweskerennow** insect
hweskeronieth *n.f* entomology
hwetegves *num* sixteenth
hwetek *num* sixteen
Hwevrel *n.m* February
Hwevrer *n.m* February
hwi *prn* (*pl*) you; (*enclitic, pl*) you
hwiban *n.m* whistle
hwibana *vb* whistle

hwibanans *n.m* **hwibanansow** whistle (*sound*)

hwibanowl *n.f* **hwibanowlow** whistle (*instrument*)

hwigen *n.f* **hwigennow** breadcrumb

hwil *n.m* **hwiles** beetle. **hwil du** *n.m* cockroach. **hwil tan** *n.m* moped

hwilas *vb* seek; look for; attempt; try; search

hwilva *n.f* **hwilvaow** laboratory

hwiski *n.m* **hwiskiow** whisky

hwithra *vb* examine; inspect; investigate; look into; probe; search

hwithrans *n.m* **hwithransow** check-up; inspection; research; search; quest. **hwithrans medhek** *n.m* medical examination

hwithrer *n.m* **hwithroryon** inspector; researcher

hwithrus *adj* observant; investigative

hwor *n.f* **hwerydh** sister. **hanter-hwor** *n.f* half-sister

hwyflyn *adj* blustering

hwyja *vb* vomit; throw up

hwymm-hwamm *adj* haphazard; slapdash

hwypp *n.m* **hwyppys, hwyppow** whip

hwyppya *vb* whip

hwyrni *vb* hum

hwys *n.m* sweat. **gwagren hwys** *n.f* sweat gland

hwysa *vb* sweat; perspire

hwystra *vb* whisper

hwystren *n.f* **hwystrennow** whisper

hwyth *n.m* **hwethow** breath; puff

hwytha *vb* blow; breathe; inflate; puff; play a wind instrument

hwythans *n.m* **hwythansow** (*with gas*) inflation

hwythek *adj* puffy

hwythell *n.f* **hwythellow** (*instrument*) whistle

hwythennek *adj* bubbly

hwythfi *vb* bubble

hy[3] *poss. adj* her

hyg *n.f* **hygow** trick; fiddle; swindle

hyga *vb* cheat; fiddle; swindle; trick

hyli *n.m* salt water

hymna *n.m* **hymnys** hymn

hyns *n.m* **hensyow** course; path; road; way. **hyns horn** *n.m* railway. **Hyns Sen Jamys** *n.m* Milky Way. **hyns-tira** *n.m* runway

hynsa *n.pl* fellows; peers

hynsledan pymp gwythien *n.m* ribwort plantain

hynt *n.m* **hyntys** hint

hyntya *vb* hint

hys *n.m* extent; length. **hys-ha-hys** altogether; end to end

I

i *prn* they; (*enclitic*) they

idhyow *n.coll* ivy

idhyowen *n.f* **idhyowennow** ivy-strand

-ieth *sffx* study of; science of

-ik *sffx* diminutive

ikon *n.m* **ikonys** icon

ikonek *adj* iconic

ilewydh *n.m* **ilewydhyon** musician

ilow *n.f* music

ilowari *n.m* **ilowariow** musical

ilowek *adj* musical

imach *n.m* **imajys** image; picture; statue

immun *adj* (*med*) immune

immunedh *n.m* (*med*) immunity

immunhe *vb* (*med*) immunise

immunheans *n.m* (*med*) immunisation

inocent I *adj* (*naive*) innocent **II** *n.m*
  inocens innocent
insomnia *n.m* insomnia (*med*)
ion *n.m* **ions** ion
ionek *adj* ionic
ironek *adj* ironic
is- *prfx* lower; deputy; vice; sub-
isel *adj* low; modest; vulgar. **a bris isel**
  cheap
Iseldiryas *n.m* **Iseldirysi** Dutch person
Iseldiryek *n.m* Dutch language
iseldiryek *adj* Dutch
Iseldiryow *top n.pl* Netherlands
iselhe *vb* lower; decrease
iselheans *n.m* **iselheansow** lowering;
  decrease
isella *adj* lower; lowest; inferior
iselweyth *n.m* **iselweythyow**
  depression (*med; economic*)
isetholans *n.m* **isetholansow**
  by-election
isframweyth *n.m* amenity;
  infrastructure
iskaderyer *n.m* **iskaderyoryon**
  vice-chairperson; deputy chairperson
iskarg *n.m* **iskargow** download
iskarga *vb* download
iskevresek *adj* subsequent
iskowethyans *n.m* **iskowethyansow**
  subsidiary
Islam *n.m* Islam
Islamek *adj* Islamic; Muslim
islavarek *adj* subjunctive. **gis islavarek**
  n.m subjunctive mood
islavrek *n.m* **islavrogow** underpants;
  knickers
islewydh *n.m* **islewydhyon**
  vice-president
islinya *vb* underline
islonk *n.m* **islonkow** abyss; gorge

islonkel *adj* abyssal
ismegen *n.f* **ismegennow** salve
ismek *n.coll* salves
isobar *n.m* **isobarow** isobar
isogloss *n.m* **isoglossow** isogloss
isotop *n.m* **isotopow** isotope
isotopek *adj* isotopic
ispan *n.m* **ispannow** lining
ispoynt *n.m* **ispoyntys, ispoyntow**
  minimum
ispoyntegieth *n.f* minimalism
ispoyntel *adj* minimal. **gober**
  ispoyntel *n.m* minimum wage
isradhek *adj* undergraduate
isradhesik *n.m* **isradhesigyon**
  undergraduate
Israel *top n.m* Israel
Israelyas *n.m* **Israelysi** Israeli
israelyek *adj* Israeli
isrudh *adj* infrared
issavonek *adj* substandard
isskrif *n.m* subscript
isskrifik *n.m* **isskrifigow** caption
istenna *vb* subtract
istennans *n.m* **istenansow** subtraction
istitel *n.m* **istitlow, istitlys** subtitle
istitla *vb* subtitle
istorek *adj* historical
istori *n.m* **istoris** history
istorior *n.m* **istorioryon** historian
isyeth *n.f* **isyethow** slang
Italek I *n.m* Italian language **II** *adj*
  (*font*) italic
italek *adj* Italian
Itali *top n.f* Italy
Italian *n.m* **Italians** Italian
Iwerdhon *top n.f* Ireland
Iwerdhonek *n.m* Irish language
iwerdhonek *adj* Irish

J

jagg *n.m* **jaggys** jar; jolt; shock. **jagg tredan** *n.m* electric shock
Jakka a'n ke *n.m* Jack-by-the-hedge; garlic mustard
jangal *n.m* **janglow** jungle
jarrik *n.m* **jarrigow** small jar
jayler *n.m* **jaylers** jailer; gaoler
jazz *n.m* jazz
jell *n.m* **jellow** gel; gelatine
jentyl *adj* gentle; pleasing. **den jentyl** *n.m* gentleman. **benyn jentyl** *n.f* gentlewoman
jentylys *n.m* graciousness
jerkyn *n.m* **jerkynnow, jerkyns** jerkin; jacket. **jerkyn strooth** *n.m* straight-jacket
Jersenys *top n.f* Jersey
jest *n.m* **jestys** jest
jestya *vb* jest
jett *n.m* **jettys, jettow** jet plane
jevan *n.m* **jevanow** fiend; demon
jevanek *adj* demonic, fiendish
-ji *sffx* building; house
jins *n.pl* jeans
jip *n.m* **jipys** jeep
jiraf *n.m* **jirafes** giraffe
jogler *n.m* **joglers, jogloryon** juggler
joglya *vb* juggle
jolif *adj* jolly
jornal *n.m* **jornalys** journal. **gwerther jornalys** *n.m* newsagent. **jornal seythennyek** *n.f* weekly
jornalyas *n.m* **jornalysi** journalist
jouta *n.m* jute
Jovyn *n.m* Jupiter
jowdyn *n.m* **jowdyns** rascal
jowel *n.m* **jowelys** jewel
jowl *n.m* **jowlow** (= **dyowl**) (*found after* **unn** *and* **an**) devil. **jowl-lemmel** *n.m* jack-in-the-box. **lo an jowl** *n.f* trapdoor. **re'n jowl** by the devil
joy *n.m* **joyys** joy; bliss

Jubyter *n.m* Jupiter
judo *n.m* judo
junya *vb* (*transitive*) connect; join; link. **junya dhe, junya orth** connect to; join with
junyans *n.m* **junyansow** connection; joining-up
justifia *vb* justify
justis *n.m* **justisyow** justice; magistrate
justisek *adj* juridical
jy *prn* (*enclitic, sg*) you
jyg *n.m* **jygyow** jig
jynevra *n.m* **jynevrys** gin
jynjer *n.coll* ginger
jynjyber *n.coll* ginger
jynn *n.m* **jynnys, jynnow** engine; machine; motor. **jynn-amontya** *n.m* computer. **jynn diwros** *n.m* motorcycle. **jynn ebron** *n.m* aeroplane; plane (*aircraft*). **jynn-fusta** *n.m* thresher. **jynn glesin** *n.m* lawn-mower. **jynn-golghi** *n.m* washing machine. **jynn-gorthebi** *n.m* answering machine. **jynn-gwrias** *n.m* sewing machine. **jynn-krommgentra** *n.m* stapler. **jynn lestri** *n.m* dishwasher. **jynn-palas** *n.m* digger. **jynn-plottya** *n.m* plotter. **jynn-rolya** *n.m* roller. **jynn skeusen** *n.m* camera. **jynn-skrifa** *n.m* typewriter. **jynn tan** *n.m* fire engine. **jynn-tenna** *n.m* tractor. **jynn-tewel** *n.m* projector. **jynn tokyn** *n.m* ticket machine. **jynn-tomma** *n.m* heater. **jynn-yskynna** *n.m* escalator
jynner *n.m* **jynoryon** mechanic
jynnji *n.m* **jynnjiow** engine house
jynnskrifa *vb* type; typewrite
jynnskrifer *n.m* **jynnskriforyon** typist
jynnweyth *n.f* **jynnweythow** machinery; mechanism
jynnweythek *adj* mechanical

140

jynnweythor *n.m* **jynnweythoryon** mechanic

Jypson *n.m* **Jypsonyon** Gypsy

jypsonek *adj* gypsy

K

kabel *n.m* **kablow** accusation; blame; libel

kabinet *n.m* **kabinettys** (*government*) cabinet

kabla *vb* blame; accuse; libel

kabli *vb* criticise; find fault with; revile

kablus *adj* guilty

kabluster *n.m* (*legal*) guilt

kaboli *vb* mix up; stir

kabolva *n.f* **kabolvaow** mix; mix-up

kachya *vb* catch

kachyans *n.m* **kachyansow** catch; take

kaderya *vb* chair; preside

kaderyer *n.m* **kaderyoryon** chairperson

kadon *n.f* **kadonyow** chain; mountain range. **hesken gadon** *n.f* chainsaw. **kadon baper** *n.f* paper chain

kadona *vb* chain

kador *n.f* **kadoryow** chair; seat. **kador dreth** *n.f* deck-chair. **kador-herdhya** *n.f* push-chair. **kador ros** *n.f* wheelchair. **kador vregh** *n.f* armchair. **kador-yskynna** *n.f* chairlift

kagla *vb* spatter with filth; soil

kaja *n.f* **kajow** daisy

kaja vras *n.f* **kajow bras** ox-eye daisy

kaktus *n.m* **kaktusow** cactus

kala *n.coll* straw. **gwelen gala** *n.f* straw stalk

kala gweli *n.coll* yellow bedstraw; lady's bedstraw

kala hweg *n.coll* sweet woodruff

kalan *n.m* **kalannow** first of the month; calends. **Kalan Genver** *n.m* New Year's Day. **Kala' Me** *n.m* May Day. **Kalan Gwav** *n.m* All Hallows

kalaven *n.f* **kalavennow** straw stalk. **kalaven-eva** *n.f* **kalavennow-eva** drinking straw

kalder *n.m* cunning; slyness

kalender *n.m* **kalenderyow** calendar

kales *adj* hard; tough; difficult. **penn kales** obstinate; stubborn. **lyver kudhlen gales** *n.m* hardback

kalesen *n.f* **kalesenrow** (*toy*) marble

kalesweyth *n.m* hardware

kalesyans *n.m* (*4th state mutation*) provection

kaletter *n.m* **kaletterow** hardness; difficulty

kaletter dyski *n.m* **kaletterow dyski** learning difficulty (*med*)

kaletter redya *n.m* **kaletterow redya** reading difficulty

kalgh (1) *n.m* limestone

kalgh (2) *n.f* **kalghyow** penis

kalkor *n.m* **kalkoryon** calculator

kalkya *vb* calculate

kall (1) *adj* cunning; sly

kall (2) *n.m* **kallow** wolframite

kalmydh *n.m* **kalmydhyon** tranquiliser

kalmynsi *n.m* calm; tranquility

kalori *n.m* **kaloris** calorie

kals *n.m* **kalsow** heap; abundance

kalter *n.f* **kaltoryon** kettle. **gorra an galter dhe vryjyon** put the kettle on

kamera *n.m* **kameras** camera

kalteras *n.m* **kalterasow** kettleful

kamfor *n.m* camphor

kamil *n.coll* chamomile

kamilen *n.f* **kamilennow** chamomile plant

kamm (1) **I** *adj* bent; crooked; erroneous; wrong **II** *n.m* **kammow** error; wrong. **war an tu kamm** offside

kamm (2) *n.m* **kammow** pace; step; track

kamm- *prfx* wrong; bent

kamma *vb* curve

kammamseren *n.f* **kammamserennow** anachronism

kammamseryek *adj* anachronistic

kammas *n.f* **kamasow** bay; bend

kammdremena *vb* trespass

kammdremener *n.m* **kammdremenoryon** trespasser

kammdreylya *vb* zigzag

kammdro *n.f* **kammdroyow** zigzag

kammdybi *vb* err. **kammdybi war**[2] think wrong of

kammdybyans *n.m* **kammdybyansow** error

kammdybys *adj* mistaken

kammen (1) *adv* in no way; not at all. **kammen vyth** in no way at all

kammen (2) *n.f* **kamennow** pace; step

kammgemeryans *n.m* **kammgemeryansow** mistake

kammgemerys *adj* mistaken; wrong

kammgonvedhes *vb* misunderstand

kammgrysyans *n.m* **kammgrysyansow** delusion (*med*)

kammhynsek *adj* unjust; unrighteous; wicked

kammledya *vb* mislead

kammneves *n.f* **kammnevesow** rainbow

kammusya *vb* misuse

kammvreusi *vb* misjudge

kammweyth *n.m* misdeed; trespass

kammwonis I *n.m* **kammwonisyow** blunder **II** *vb* blunder

kammwrians *n.m* **kammwriansow** error

kammwul *vb* err

kamp *n.m* **kampow** camp

kampol *n.m* comment; mention

kampolla *vb* comment; mention

kampollans *n.m* **kampollansow** reference

kampollys *adj* mentioned. **an pyth kampollys diwettha** the latter. **an pyth kampollys kynsa** the former

kampva *n.f* **kampvaow** encampment

kampya *vb* camp; encamp

kan *n.f* **kanow** song; poem. **gwari kan** *n.m* opera; musical. **kan werin** *n.f* folk song

kana *vb* sing

kanabys *n.coll* cannabis. **porven ganabys** *n.f* (*cannabis cigarette*) joint; reefer

Kanada *top n.m* Canada

kanadek *adj* Canadian

Kanadian *n.m* **Kanadians** Canadian

kanari *n.m* **kanaris** canary

kanasa *vb* delegate

kanasedh *n.m* **kanasedhow** *n.m* delegation; deputation

kanasedhi *vb* (*electorate*) represent

kanaseth *n.f* **kanasethow** mission; (*mission*) embassy

kanatti *n.m* **kanattiow** (*building*) embassy

kanel (1) *n.f* **kanolyow** channel. **kanel bellwolok** *n.f* television channel

kanel (2) *n.coll* cinnamon. **gwelen ganel** *n.f* cinnamon stick

kaner *n.m* **kanoryon** singer

kangarou *n.m* **kangarous** kangaroo

kanik *n.f* **kanigow** ditty; jingle

kanister *n.m* **kanisters** canister

kanker *n.m* **kankres** crab; cancer

kann (1) *adj* bright white

kann (2) *n.m* fluorite; fluorspar

kanna *n.m* **kannys, kannow** can

kannas *n.f* **kanasow** ambassador; messenger

kannlagas *n.m* eyebright

kannven *n.m* **kannveyn** quartz

kanon *n.m* **kanonyow** cannon

kanou *n.m* **kanouyow** canoe

kanrol *n.f* **kanrolyow** playlist

kans *num* **kansow** hundred

kanskradh *n.m* **kanskradhow** centigrade

kanskweyth *adv* a hundred times

kansplek *adv* hundredfold

kansran *n.f* **kansrannow** percent; percentage

kanstel *n.f* **kanstellow** basket. **pel ganstel** *n.f* basketball

kansves *num* hundredth

kansvledhen *n.f* **kansvledhynnyow** century

kantol *n.f* **kantolyow** candle

kantolbren *n.m* **kantolbrennyer** candlestick

kapel *n.m* **kaplys** cable

kappa *n.m* **kappys, kappow** cap

kappa kornhwilen *n.m* **kappys kornhwilen** nasturtium

kapten *n.m* **kaptens, kaptenow** captain

kapyas *n.m* **kapyasow** writ of arrest

kar *n.m* **kerens** parent; relation; (*male*) relative

kara *vb* love; like; care for. **dell y'm kyrri** be so kind as to

karadow *adj* beloved; fond; loving

karamel *n.m* **karamels** caramel

karate *n.m* karate

karavan *n.m* **karavans** caravan

karbohydrat *n.m* **karbohydratow** carbohydrate

karbon *n.m* (*element*) carbon. **karbon dioxid** carbon dioxide

kardamon *n.coll* cardamom

kardigan *n.m* **kardigans, kardiganow** cardigan

karer *n.m* **karoryon** (*male*) lover; boyfriend

kares *n.f* **karesow** girlfriend; relation; (*female*) relative

karetys *n.coll* carrots

karetysen *n.f* **karetysennow** carrot

karg *n.m* **kargow** burden; cargo; freight; load

karga *vb* load; charge

kargedh *n.m* **kargedhow** electric charge

karghar *n.m* **kargharow** fetter; shackle. **karghar prenn** *n.m* pillory; stocks

karghara *vb* detain; fetter; imprison; incarcerate; pillory, shackle

kargharans *n.m* **kargharansow** incarceration; detention; imprisonment

karigell *n.f* **karigellow** trolley

karleyth *n.f* **karleythow** ray

karn (1) *n.m* **karnow** rock-pile; tor

karn (2) *n.m* **karnow** hoof. **karn kollan** *n.m* knife-handle

karnal *adj* carnal; sexual. **daromres karnal** *n.m* sexual intercourse

karnedh *n.m* **karnedhow** cairn

karnedhek *adj* rocky

karnek *adj* rocky

karnival *n.m* carnival

karolli *vb* dance

karores *n.f* **karoresow** (*female*) lover; girlfriend

karow *n.m* **kerwys** stag; deer. **karow ergh** *n.m* reindeer

karr *n.m* **kerri** car. **gwelen garr** *n.f* pole (of a cart). **kerri bonk** *n.pl* dodgems. **karr klavji** *n.m* ambulance. **karr heb lewyer** *n.m* driverless car. **karr kreslu** *n.m* police car. **karr-resek** *n.m* racing car. **karr slynk** *n.m* sleigh. **karr stret** *n.m* tram. **karr tan** *n.m* motor-car. **yn karr** by car

karrek *n.f* **kerrek, karrygi** rock

karrji *n.m* **karrjiow** garage

karrostel *n.m* **karrostelyow** motel

karten *n.f* **kartennow** card. **karten benn-bloodh** *n.f* birthday card. **karten bost** *n.f* postcard. **karten gresys** *n.f* credit card. **karten vona** *n.f* cash card. **karten vudhek** *n.f* trump card. **sewt kartennow** *n.m* suit of cards

karth *n.m* **karthyon** cleansing; purge. **karth ethnek** *n.m* ethnic cleansing

kartha *vb* clean out; cleanse; rid; purge; flush; scrub

karven *n.f* **karvenow** wagon

karya *vb* carry; transport

karyans *n.m* **karyansow** transport. **karyans poblek** *n.m* public transport

karyn *n.m* **karynyes** carrion. **hok karyn** *n.m* vulture

kas (1) *n.f* **kasow** battle; armed conflict

kas (2) *n.m* **kasys** case; circumstance. **y'n gwella kas** ideally. **y'n kas** under the circumstances. **y'n kas arbennek ma** in this particular case. **yn neb kas** anyway; in any case; at any rate

kas (3) *n.m* hate; hatred; dislike. **kas yw genev** I hate

kasa *vb* hate; dislike

kasadow *adj* hateful; revolting

kas a gethreydh *n.f* homophobia (*hate of*; cf. *own a gethreydh*)

kas a venynreydh *n.f* misogyny

kasegor a gethreydh *n.m* **kasegoryon a gethreydh** homophobe (*hater of*; cf. *ownegor a gethreydh*)

kasegor benynreydh *n.m* **kasegoryon venynreydh** misogynist

kasek *n.f* **kasegi** mare

kasek a gethreydh *adj* homophobic (*hateful of*; cf. *ownek a gethreydh*)

kasek koos *n.f* **kasegi koos** woodpecker

kasek koos bras *n.f* **kasegi koos bras** great spotted woodpecker

kasek koos byghan *n.m* **kasegi koos byghan** lesser spotted woodpecker

kasel *n.f* **kaselyow**, *dl* **diwgasel** armpit; aisle. **esedh gasel** *n.f* aisle seat

kashya *vb* cash

kaskyrgh *n.m* **kaskyrghow** campaign

kaskyrgher *n.m* **kaskyrghoryon** campaigner

kaskyrghes *vb* campaign

kasor *n.m* **kasoryon** fighter

kasorek *adj* militant; military

kast *n.m* **kastys** trick (*dodge*)

kastek *adj* tricky

kastel *n.m* **kastylli, kestel** castle; hill fort. **kastel tewes** *n.m* sandcastle

kastiga *vb* flog

kastya *vb* trick

kasyer *n.m* **kasyerow** large sieve

Katalan *n.m* **Katalans** Catalan

katalonek *adj* Catalan

Kataloni *top n.f* Catalonia

kath *n.f* **kathes** cat. **kath vlewek** *n.f* hairy caterpillar. **prena kath yn sagh** buy a pig in a poke. **losow an gath** *n.coll* catmint; catnip

kathek *adj* feline

kathik *n.m* **kathigow** kitten

Katholigieth *n.f* Catholicism

Katholik I *adj* Catholic **II** *n.m* **Katholigyon** Catholic

kation *n.m* **kations** cation

kavadow *adj* available

kavanedhi *vb* occupy

kavanskeusa *vb* evade

kavas *n.m* **kavasow** (*container*) tin

kavos *vb* find; acquire; get; have; obtain; procure. **kavos chons dhe**[2] get round to. **kavos hanow** gain a reputation

kavylek *adj* argumentative; contentious

kawdarn *n.m* **kawdarns** cauldron

kawgh *n.m* dung; excrement; faeces; shit

kawgha *vb* defecate; shit

kawghans *n.m* excretion

kaws *n.m* **kawsys** cause; reason

kawsya *vb* cause

kay *n.m* **kayys, kayow** quay; dock; jetty; pier; platform. **kay peulyow** *n.m* pier

kayak *n.m* **kayakys, kayagow** kayak

ke *n.m* **keow** hedge; fence. **war an ke** abstaining; on the fence

ke- *prfx* con-; com-

keas *vb* hedge; fence; enclose with a hedge; enclose with a fence. **keas mes** exclude

kebren *n.f* **kebrennow** rafter

kechap *n.m* ketchup

kedhel *n.m* **kedhlow** tale

kedhla *vb* inform; tell

kedhlow *n.pl* information

kedhor *n.coll* pubic hair

kedhorek *adj* pubic

kedhoren *n.f* **kedhorennow** a pubic hair

kedhorieth *n.f* puberty

kedhorva *n.f* **kedhorvaow** groin; pubis

kedhow *n.m* (*plant*) white mustard (*yellow*); (*condiment*) mustard

kedrynn *n.f* **kedrynnow** dispute; quarrel; trouble

kedrynna *vb* quarrel; dispute; bicker

keek *adj* hedged

keffrys *adv* also; likewise; moreover

keffrysek *adj* federal

keffrysyans *n.m* **keffrysyansow** alliance

keffrysyas *n.m* **keffrysysi** ally

keffrysys *adj* allied

kegi *vb* cook

kegin (1) *n.f* **keginow** kitchen

kegin (2) *n.f* **kegines** jay

kegina *vb* cook

keginer *n.m* **keginoryon** chef

keginieth *n.f* cookery

kegis *n.coll* hemlock. **kegis hweg** *n.coll* celery

kegis an mogh *n.coll* hogweed

kegis an vugh *n.coll* cow parsley

kegisen *n.f* **kegisennow** hemlock plant

kehaval *adj* alike; equal

kehavalen *n.f* **kehavalennow** equation

keher *n.coll* muscles

keherek *adj* burly; muscular

keheren *n.f* **keherennow** muscle

keheveli *vb* compare; equate

kehevelus *adj* comparative

kehevelyans *n.m* **kehevelyansow** comparison

kehys *adj* of the same length. **kehys ha** of the same length as

kehysedh *n.m* **kehysedhow** circumference; equator

kehysnos *n.f* **kehysnosow** equinox

kekemmys *adv* as many as; as much as

kekesow *n.coll* Cornish heath

kel I *adj* hidden; secret **II** *n.m* **kelyow** hideout. **yn-dann gel** in secret; secretly

kelegel *n.m* **keleglow** chalice

keler *n.coll* pignut

keles *vb* conceal; hide

kelester *n.m* **kelesteryow** pebble; flint

kell *n.f* **kellow, kellyow,** *dl* **diwgell** cell; testicle

kelli (1) *vb* lose. **kelli liw** *vb* pale

kelli (2) *n.f* **kelliow** grove

kelligen *n.f* **kelligennow** razor fish

kellik *n.coll* razor fish

kellyllik *n.f* **kellylligow** pocket knife

kellyn *n.coll* duckweed

kellynnen *n.f* **kellynennow** duckweed plant

kellys *adj* lost

kelmi *vb* bind; knot; tie. **kelmi X orth Y** tie X to Y

kelmys *adj* related

kelorn *n.m* **kelern** bucket; pail

Kelt *n.m* **Keltyon** Celt

Keltek *adj* Celtic

kelus *adj* cagey

kelyfydhys *adj* confidential

kelyn *n.coll* hollies

kelynnen *n.f* **kelynennow** holly tree

kelyon *n.coll* flies. **kelyon garan** *n.coll* craneflies. **kelyon kig** *n.coll* bluebottle flies. **kelyon margh** *n.coll* gadflies

kelyonen *n.f* **kelyonennow** fly

Kembra *top n.f* Wales

Kembrek *n.m* Welsh language

kembrek *adj* Welsh

Kembres *n.f* **Kembresow** Welshwoman

Kembro *n.m* **Kembroyon** Welshman

kemel *n.f* **kemellow** clause

kemeneth *n.f* **kemenethow** community. **kresen gemeneth** *n.f* community centre

kemeradow *adj* acceptable

kemeres *vb* take; receive; subtract. **kemeres dy'gol** take a day off. **kemeres euth** panic. **kemeres merci a²** have mercy on. **kemeres meth** be ashamed. **kemeres own rag** take fright from. **kemeres rann** take part; participate. **kemeres truedh a²** have pity on. **kemeres with** take care; take heed. **kemeres X a² Y** subtract X from Y

kemeryans *n.m* **kemeryansow** reception

kemmyn *adj* common; ordinary; routine; vulgar. **gwiryow kemmyn** *n.pl* civil rights. **mona kemmyn** *n.coll* currency

kemmys *adv* as many as; as much as; equivalent

kemmysk *n.m* **kemyskow** mix; jumble

kempen *adj* neat; tidy

kempenna *vb* set in order; tidy

kempenner *n.m* **kempenoryon** orderly. **kempenner gols** *n.m* hairdresser

kemper *n.m* **kemperyow** confluence; junction of streams

kemusur I *adj* symmetrical II *n.m* **kemusuryow** proportion; symmetry

kemusurel *adj* proportional

kemynegor *n.m* **kemynegoryon** communist. **Derivadow an Gemynegoryon** *n.m* the Communist Manifesto

kemynegorek *adj* communist

kemynegoreth *n.f* communism

kemynskrif *n.m* **kemynskrifow** will

kemyska *vb* mingle; mix; jumble; blend

kemyskans *n.m* **kemyskansow** mixture

kemyskell *n.f* **kemyskellow** mixer

kemysker *n.m* **kemyskoryon** mixer

kemyskys *adj* mixed; blended; confused

ken (1) I *adj* other; else; different; alternative II *adv* else; otherwise

ken (2) *n.m* **kenyow** lawsuit

ken- *prfx* co-; con-; mutual

kendegi *vb* (*electricity*) conduct

kenderow *n.m* **kenderwi** cousin

kendon *n.f* **kendonow** debt; liability. **kavos kendon** borrow. **kodha yn kendon** get into debt. **mos a-berth yn kendon** run into debt. **ri kendon** lend. **ri neppyth yn kendon dhe nebonan** lend something to someone

kenedhel *n.f* **kenedhlow** nation. **an Kenedhlow Unys** *n.pl* the United Nations

kenedhlegi *vb* nationalise

kenedhlegieth *n.f* nationalism

kenedhlegys *adj* nationalised

kenedhlek *adj* national. **Servis Kenedhlek an Yeghes (NHS)** *n.m* the National Health Service (NHS). **Trest Kenedhlek** *n.m* National Trust

kenedhloger *n.m* **kenedhlogoryon** nationalist

kenedhlogeth *n.f* **kenedhlogethow** nationality

kenertha *vb* boost

kenerthas *n.m* **kenerthasow** booster

kengrel *n.f* **kengrellow** girdle

kenhanow *n.m* **kenhenwyn** alias

keninen *n.f* **keninennow** bulb of garlic; garlic plant

keniver I *adj* as many; so many II *prn* everyone; everybody. **keniver den** everyone. **keniver dydh** every day. **keniver onan** every single one

kenn *n.m* **kennow** peel; scum; skin

kenna *vb* coat with film
kennek *adj* scummy
kennen *n.f* **kenennow** film;
  membrane; cataract (*of eye*)
kennin *n.coll* (*plants*) garlic. **ewin**
  kennin *n.m* clove of garlic. **kennin**
  sevi *n.coll* chives
kennin trihornek *n.coll* three cornered
  leek; wild garlic
kenn lynn *n.coll* duckweed
kennys *adj* canned
kenreydhek *adj* heterosexual
kenreydhor *n.m* **kenreydhoryon**
  heterosexual
kenskrif *n.m* **kenskrifow** brief
kentel *n.m* **kentelyow** event; lesson.
  pub kentel on every occasion
kenter *n.f* **kentrow** nail; spike
kentra *vb* nail; spike; tack. **kentra X**
  orth Y nail X to Y
kentrevek *n.m* **kentrevogyon**
  neighbour
kentreveth *n.f* **kentrevethow**
  neighbourhood
kentrewi *vb* nail with many nails
kentrik *n.m* **kentrigow** tack. **kentrik**
  spis *n.m* clove
kenwerth *n.m* **kenwerthow** commerce;
  trade
kenwertha *vb* trade
kenwerthel *adj* commercial
kenwes *n.m* **kenwesow** feast
kenwostel *n.m* **kenwostlow** bet; wager
kenwostla *vb* bet; wager
kenwra *n.m* **kenwraow** prototype
kepar *adv* like; alike. **kepar dell**[2] just as.
  kepar ha like. **kepar dell**[2] **via** as it
  were. **yn kepar maner** similarly
ker (1) *adj* dear; precious
ker (2) *n.f* **kerow, keryow** fort;
  fortress; hill fort; city
kerdh *n.m* **kerdhow** walk; journey.
  yn-kerdh *adv* away
kerdher *n.m* **kerdhoryon** walker;
  pedestrian. **kerdher lovan** *n.m*

tightrope walker. **treusva**
  gerdhoryon *n.f* pedestrian crossing
kerdhes *vb* walk; get along (*move*)
kerdhin *n.coll* rowan trees
kerdhinen *n.f* **kerdhinennow** rowan
  tree
kerdhva *n.f* **kerdhvaow** footpath;
  promenade
keredhi *vb* scold; reproach; tell off;
  rebuke
kerens *n.pl* parents
kerensa *n.f* love; charity. **kerensa**
  gudhys *n.f* affair. **klav dre gerensa**
  love-sick. **rag kerensa** for the sake of;
  for the love of
kerensedhek *adj* loving
kerensel *adj* parental. **kummyas**
  kerensel *n.m* parental leave
keres *n.coll* cherries
keresen *n.f* **keresennow** cherry
keresik I *adj* darling; dear **II** *n.m*
  keresigyon darling; sweetheart
kergh *n.coll* oats
kerghen *n.f* **kerghennow** oat flake
kerghes *vb* fetch; get
kerghydh *n.f* **kerghydhyon** heron
kerghyn *n.m* **kerghynnow** environs;
  vicinity
kerghynedhel *adj* environmental
kerghynedhor *n.m* **kerghynedhoryon**
  environmentalist
kerghynna *vb* surround
kerghynnedh *n.m* **kerghynedhow**
  environment
kergys *adj* loaded
Kerneweger *n.m* **Kernewegoryon**
  Cornish speaker
Kernewek *n.m* Cornish language.
  Kernewek Byw Living Cornish
kernewek *adj* Cornish
Kernewekhe *vb* Cornicise
Kernewes *n.f* **Kernewesow**
  Cornishwoman
Kernow I *top n.f* Cornwall **II** *n.m*
  Kernowyon Cornishman

kernya *vb* hoot
kerrik *n.m* **kerrigow** cart; carriage.
  kerrik flogh *n.m* baby carriage
kert *n.m* **kertys, kertow** cart; lorry;
  truck
kerth *n.f* **kerthow** property
kertik *n.m* **kertigow** van
kervya *vb* carve
keryn *n.f* **kerynyow** butt; tub; vat
kes- *prfx* co-; con-; mutual
kes *adj* hedged
kesakordyans *n.m* **kesakordyansow**
  consensus
kesareth *n.f* **kesarethyow** seminar
kesassoylyans *n.m* **kesassoylyansow**
  compromise
keschanj *n.m* **keschanjyow** exchange;
  interchange; swap
keschanjadow *adj* interchangeable
keschanjya *vb* exchange; interchange;
  swap
keser *n.coll* hail. **gul keser** *vb* hail
keseren *n.f* **keserennow** hailstone
kesfurvya *vb* conform
kesfurvyans *n.m* conformity
kesfurvyas *n.m* **kesfurvysi** conformist
keskal *n.m* **keskalyon** accomplice
keskan *n.f* **keskanow** (*vocal*) concert
keskar I *n.m* dispersion; parting;
  scattering; separation **II** *vb* disperse;
  part; scatter
keskarieth *n.f* separatism
keskarydh *n.m* **keskarydhyon**
  separatist
keskelmi *vb* relate; liaise; link. **liase
  with** keskelmi orth
keskeltek *adj* inter-Celtic
keskerdh *n.m* **keskerdhow** march;
  procession
keskerdhes *vb* march
keskeverek *adj* convergent
keskeverya *vb* converge
keskeveryans *n.m* **keskeveryansow**
  convergence
keskewsel *vb* converse; chat

keski *vb* tell off; exhort
keskiansek *adj* conscientious
kesklappya *vb* chat. **kesklappya yn
  unn sklandra** gossip
kesknius *adj* corrosive
keskodhevek *adj* sympathetic
keskolon *adj* unanimous
keskolonekter *n.m* sympathy
keskolonnek *adj* sympathetic
keskomunya *vb* communicate
keskomunyans *n.m* **keskomunyansow**
  communication
keskorra *vb* (*transitive*) assemble;
  collate; put together
keskoweth *n.m* **keskowetha** partner
keskowethyans *n.m*
  keskowethyansow partnership.
  Keskowethyans an Yeth Kernewek
  n.m (*name of organisation*) The
  Cornish Language Partnership
keskows *n.m* **keskowsow** chat;
  conversation; dialogue
keskowsva *n.f* **keskowsvaow** chat
  room
keskreuni *vb* concentrate
keskussulyans *n.m* **keskussulyansow**
  conference
keslinek *adj* cognate; parallel
keslowena *n.f* congratulations
keslowenhe *vb* congratulate
keslytherennans *n.m* alliteration
kesoberek *adj* cooperative
kesoberi *vb* cooperate; go along
kesoberyans *n.m* cooperation
kesordena *vb* coordinate
kesordenans *n.m* **kesordenansow**
  coordination. **kesordenans
  dorn-lagas** *n.m* hand-eye
  coordination
kesordenek I *adj* coordinate **II** *n.m*
  kesordenogyon coordinate
kesow *n.coll* turf. **kesen** *n.f* sod of turf
kespar *n.m* **kesparow** partner
kesplegadow *adj* compatible

kespos *n.m* **kesposow** balance; equilibrium. **kespos arghantti** bank balance

kesrann *n.f* **kesrannow** component

kesresek *adj* serial. **niver kesresek** *n.m* serial number

kesrosweyth *n.m* internet

kessedhek *n.m* **kessedhogow** committee

kessenegow *n.pl* harmonics

kesseni *vb* accord; harmonise

kessenyans *n.m* **kessenyansow** harmony

kesservyas *n.m* **kesservysi** attendant

kesskol *n.f* **kesskolyow** comprehensive school

kesskoodhya *vb* support together

kesskoodhyans *n.m* mutual support

kesskrifa *vb* (*writing*) correspond

kesskrifans *n.m* **kesskrifansow** correspondence; exchange of letters

kesskrifer *n.m* **kesskriforyon** correspondent

kesskwat *n.m* **kesskwattow** collision

kesskwattya *vb* collide

kesson *adj* harmonious

kessonen *n.f* **kessonennow** consonant

kessonennel *adj* consonantal

kesstrif *n.m* **kesstrifow** contest; competition. **kesstrif-tenna** *n.m* tug-of-war. **kesstrif treghi konna** *n.m* cut-throat competition

kesstriver *n.m* **kesstrivoryon** competitor

kesstrivus *adj* competitive

kesstrivya *vb* compete; keep up

kesstrotha *vb* compact

kesstrothys *adj* compact

kesstudh *n.m* **kesstudhyow** circumstance. **y'n kesstudhyow** under the circumstances

kesstyr *adj* synonymous. **ger kesstyr** *n.m* synonym

kessydhya *vb* punish

kessydhyans *n.m* **kessydhyansow** punishment

kestav *n.m* **kestavow** contact. **gwedrik kestav** *n.m* contact lens

kestava *vb* contact; get in touch; keep in touch. **kestava gans** keep in touch with

kesten *n.coll* chestnuts

kestenen *n.f* **kestenennow** chestnut

kestenwedhen *n.f* **kestenwedhennow** chestnut tree

kestenwydh *n.coll* chestnut trees

kesteudhans *n.m* **kesteudhansow** fusion

kestevyn *n.m* **kestevynnow** concrete

kestew *n.m* **kestewow** batter

kestrevesik *n.m* **kestrevesigyon** compatriot

kesunses *n.m* **kesunsesow** amalgam

kesunya *vb* merge; amalgamate; unite; combine

kesunyans *n.m* **kesunyansow** union; league; combination. **kesunyans lavur** *n.m* trade union

kesva *n.f* **kesvaow** assembly; board. **Kesva an Taves Kernewek** *n.f* (*name of organisation*) the Cornish Language Board

kesvargynnya *vb* barter

kesvewa *vb* live together

kesvewek *adj* interactive

keswel *n.f* **keswelyow** interview

kesweles *vb* interview

kesweyth *n.m* **kesweythow** structure

kesweythel *adj* structural

keswlasek *adj* international. **politegieth keswlasek** *n.f* international politics

kesyewa *vb* conjugate

kesyewans *n.m* **kesyewansow** conjugation

keth (1) *adj* same. **an keth ha** the same as. **an keth onan** the same one

keth (2) I *adj* captive; servile **II** *n.m* **kethyon** captive; slave

kethneth *n.f* captivity; slavery

kethreydhek *adj* homosexual; gay

kethreydhor *n.m* **kethreydhoryon** homosexual person

kethsam *adj* identical

kethsonek *n.f* **kethsonegow** homophone

kettel[2] *adv* as soon as

kettep *adj* each; every. **kettep huni** everyone. **yn kettep gwas** to the last man

kettermyn *n.m* meantime. **yn kettermyn** in the meantime; at the same time

kettermynegi *vb* synchronise

kettermynyek *adj* simultaneous

kettesten *n.f* **kettestennow** context

kettooth *adv* as soon. **kettooth ha** as quickly as; as soon as. **kettooth ha'n ger** no sooner said than done; instantly

kettost *adj* as soon. **kettost ha** as soon as

kettres *n.m* **kettresow** contour

kettuel *adj* parallel

kettuelen *n.f* **kettuelennow** parallelogram

keudh *n.m* **keudhow** grief

keudhesik *adj* sorry

keudhi *vb* (*intransitive*) grieve; (*transitive*) make sorry

keun *n.pl* dogs

keunegen *n.f* **keunegennow** bog; reed bed

keunva *n.f* **keunvaow** kennels

keunys *n.coll* firewood; fuel

keunysen *n.f* **keunysennow** piece of firewood

keunyssa *vb* gather firewood

keur *n.m* **keuryow** choir

keus *n.m* **keusyow** cheese. **tesen geus** *n.f* cheesecake. **keus dyghtys** *n.m* processed cheese

keuswask *n.f* **keuswaskow** cheese press

kev- *prfx* co-; together

kevals *n.m* **kevalsyow** joint

kevambos *n.m* **kevambosow** contract; treaty

Kevardhu *n.m* December

kevarghewi *vb* invest

kevarghow *n.m* **kevarghowyow** investment

kevarwodha *vb* direct; guide; indicate

kevarwodher *n.m* **kevarwodhoryon** guide; director

kevasran *n.f* **kevasrannow** faculty

kevelek *n.m* **keveloges** woodcock

kevelin *n.m* **kevelinyow** cubit; half a yard

kevenna *vb* memorise

keverang *n.f* **keverangow** (*administrative division*) Hundred

kevernya *vb* compile

kevernyans *n.m* **kevernyansow** compilation

kevewi *n.m* **kevewiow** party; feast

kevewya *vb* party; celebrate

keveylya *vb* accompany

keveylyans *n.m* **keveylyansow** accompaniment

kevnis *n.coll* spiders. **gwias kevnis** *n.m* cobweb; spider web

kevnisen *n.f* **kevnisennow** spider

kevogas *adj* adjacent

kevos *adj* contemporary

kevothek *adj* powerful

kevradh *n.m* **kevradhow** rate. **kevradh chanj** *n.m* exchange rate. **kevradh mernans** *n.m* death rate. **kevradh oker** *n.m* interest rate. **kevradh toll** *n.m* tax rate

kevrannor *n.m* **kevranoryon** shareholder

kevren *n.f* **kevrennow** bond; link; share

kevrenna *vb* share

kevrennek I *adj* participating **II** *n.m* **kevrenogyon** participant;

stakeholder. **bos kevrennek a²** share in; partake in; participate in

kevres *n.m* **kevresyow** series; suite; sequence

kevresek *adj* serial; sequential

kevreyth *n.m* **kevreythyow** system

kevri *vb* contribute

kevrin *n.m* **kevrinyow** mystery; secret

kevrinek *adj* secret; esoteric; mysterious

kevrinva *n.f* **kevrinvaow** lodge; secret meeting place

kevriv *n.m* **kevrivow** tally

kevriva *vb* tally

kevriyas *n.m* **kevriysi** contributor

kevro *n.m* **kevrohow** contribution

kevrol *n.f* **kevrolyow** (*book*) volume

kevryllys *adj* corrugated

kew *n.f* **kewyow** hollow

kewar *adj* accurate; exact

kewargh *n.coll* (*plant*) Indian hemp

kewarghen *n.f* **kewarghennow** (*plant*) Indian hemp

kewer *n.f* weather. **kewer deg** *n.f* fine weather

kewera *vb* fulfil; keep a promise

keweras *n.m* fulfilment; perfection. **dedhewys heb keweras** an unkept promise

kewerder *n.m* accuracy

keweronieth *n.f* meteorology

keweroniethel *adj* meteorological

kewni *n.coll* moss; mildew

kewniek *adj* mossy

kewnien *n.f* **kewniennow** lump of moss

keworra *vb* add; supplement

keworrans *n.m* **keworransow** addition

keworransel *adj* additional

keworransus *adj* supplementary

kewsel *vb* speak; talk. **kewsel a-dreus** interrupt. **kewsel yn tiskler** mumble. **kewsel orth** speak to; address

kewydh rudh *n.coll* escallonia

keyn *n.m* **keynow** back; keel; ridge. **an keyn a-rag** back to front. **a'n keyn** spinal. **askorn keyn** *n.m* backbone. **dres keyn** afterwards. **keyn lomm** *adj* bare-backed. **keyn to** *n.m* ridge (of a house). **mell keyn** *n.m* spine. **payn keyn** *n.m* backache

keynres *n.m* **keynresyow** torrent

keynvor *n.m* **keynvoryow** ocean. **Keynvor Atlantek** *n.m* Atlantic Ocean. **Keynvor Eyndek** *n.m* Indian Ocean. **Keynvor Hebask** *n.m* Pacific Ocean

ki *n.m* **keun** dog. **ki bleydh** *n.m* German shepherd dog

kibel *n.f* **kibellow** bath; skip

kibya *vb* snatch

ki du *n.m* depression (*colloq*)

kig *n.m* **kigyow** meat; flesh. **kig bewin** *n.m* beef. **kig davas** *n.m* mutton. **kig dens** *n.m* (*anat*) gum. **kig divynys** *n.m* minced meat. **kig mogh** *n.m* pork. **kig yar** *n.m* chicken meat. **avalow dor ha kig** *n.coll* hot-pot. **yn kig yn kneus** in the flesh

kiger *n.m* **kigoryon** butcher

kigliw *adj* pink (*flesh-coloured*)

kigti *n.m* **kigtiow** butcher's shop

kiji *n.m* **kijiow** kennel

kil *n.m* **kilyer** back; nape of neck; nook; reverse

kila (1) *n.m* companion. **an eyl...y gila** *n.m* (*only use of the word kila*) one another (masc.); mutual. **an eyl wosa y gila** successive

kila (2) *vb* recede

kilans *n.m* **kilansow** recession

kilden *n.m* **kildennow** retreat

kildenna *vb* back off; retreat; withdraw

kildennans *n.m* **kildenansow** withdrawal

kildhans *n.m* **kildhens** molar

kildro *n.f* **kildroyow** backward turn; reversal

kilfia *vb* desert; jump ship

kilgi *n.m* **kilgeun** coward
kilgieth *n.f* cowardice
kilobayt *n.m* **kilobaytys** kilobyte
kilogram *n.m* **kilogrammow**
  kilogramme
kilokalori *n.m* **kilokaloris** kilocalorie
kilometer *n.m* **kilometrow** kilometre
kilva *n.f* **kilvaow** background
kilwagren *n.f* **kilwagrennow** tonsil
kinda *n.m* **kindys** kind
kinetyk *adj* kinetic
kinnyow *n.m* **kinyewow** dinner
kinyewel *vb* dine
kiogh *n.f* **kioghyon** (*bird*) snipe
kiosk *n.m* **kioskys** kiosk
kist *n.f* **kistyow** box; chest. **kist**
  lytherow *n.f* letterbox
kisten *n.f* **kistennow** small box. **kisten**
  danbren *n.f* matchbox. **kisten**
  liwyow *n.f* paint box
kisya *vb* damage
kisyans *n.m* **kisyansow** damage
kius *adj* canine
klamder *n.m* **klamderyow** faint; swoon
klamdera *vb* faint; fall unconscious;
  lose consciousness; swoon. **gul dhe**
  glamdera stun
klamderek *adj* liable to faint;
  unconscious
klamderus *adj* anaesthetic
klamderyas *n.m* **klamderysi**
  anaesthetic
klapp *n.m* chatter. **syns dha glapp!**
  shut up!
klappkodh *n.f* **klappkodhow**
  cell-phone; mobile phone
klappya *vb* chatter; gabble; talk
klass *n.m* **klassys, klassow** category;
  class. **stevel an klass** *n.f* classroom
klassa *vb* classify
klassans *n.m* **klassansow** classification
klassek *adj* classical
klassya *vb* class
klatter *n.m* chatter
klattra *vb* chatter

klav I *adj* ill; sick; invalid II *n.m*
  klevyon sick person; invalid. **kodha**
  klav fall ill
klavder *n.m* sickness; illness
klavji *n.m* **klavjiow** hospital
klavjior *n.m* **klavjioryon** nurse
klavor *n.m* leprosy
klavorek *n.m* **klavorogyon** leper
klawstrofobia *n.m* claustrophobia
  (*med*)
kledh *adj* left
kledha *n.m* **kledhedhyow** sword.
  kledha meur *n.m* claymore. **kledha**
  kromm *n.m* scimitar
kledhbarth *n.f* north. **a'n gledhbarth**
  northern
kledhek *adj* left-handed; awkward;
  clumsy
kledhren *n.f* **kledhrennow** rail
kledhya *vb* wield a sword
klefni *n.m* lameness
kleger *n.m* **klegrow** cliff; crag;
  precipice
klegh an eos *n.pl* harebell
klegh an kowr *n.pl* Canterbury bells
kleghi *n.coll* icicles
kleghien *n.f* **kleghiennow** icicle
kleghik *n.m* **kleghigow** small bell
kleghti *n.m* **kleghtiow** belfry
klem *n.m* **klemys** plea
kler *adj* clear. **yn kler** *adv* clearly
klerder *n.m* clarity
klerfordh *n.f* **klerfordhow** clearway
klerhe *vb* brighten; clarify
klerheans *n.m* **klerheansow**
  clarification
klerya *vb* clear
klesa *vb* shelter
kleudh *n.m* **kleudhyow** ditch
kleudhik *n.m* **kleudhigow** groove
kleudhya *vb* dig a trench; ditch;
  excavate
kleves *n.m* **klevesow** illness; malady;
  medical complaint. **kleves Alzheimer**
  n.m Alzheimer's disease. **kleves an**

myghtern *n.m* scrofula. **kleves bras** *n.m* leprosy. **kleves eseli** *n.m* rheumatism. **kleves kogh** *n.m* scarlet fever. **kleves marghogyon** *n.m* haemorrhoids; piles. **kleves melyn** *n.m* jaundice. **kleves melys** *n.m* diabetes mellitus. **kleves seson** *n.m* ague

klevesans *n.m* **klevesansow** infection

klevesi *vb* infect

klevesus *adj* infectious

klevesys *adj* infected

klew *n.m* hearing

klewadow *adj* audible

klewell *n.f* **klewellow** hearing aid

klewes *vb* hear; feel; sense; perceive. **klewes a²** hear about. **klewes gans** hear from

klewes aperys *adj* hearing impaired

klewwelyek *adj* audio-visual

kliens *n.m* **kliensow** client

klock *n.m* **klockys, klockow** clock

klog *n.f* **klogow** cliff; crag

klogh *n.m* **klegh** bell. **klogh meur** *n.m* church bell

klogh an eos *n.m* harebell

kloghbren *n.m* **kloghbrennyer** gallows

klok *n.m* **klokys** cloak

kloos *n.f* **klosyow** fence; rack

klopen *n.m* **klopennow** skull

kloppek I *adj* lame; limping **II** *n.m* **kloppogyon** person with a limp

kloppya *vb* limp

klor *adj* mild; moderate; modest; meek

klorder *n.m* modesty

klorek *n.m* **klorogyon** clergyman; clerk

klorin *n.m* (*element*) chlorine

klos I *adj* close; stuffy; secluded **II** *adv* closely. **skath klos** *n.f* raft. **tyller klos** *n.m* secluded spot

klosya *vb* harrow

klott *n.m* **klottys, klottow** wad of spit

klout *n.m* **kloutys** patch; wad; (*blow*) clout. **klout bolghen** *n.m* tripe. **klout skav** *n.m* flip

kloutya *vb* (*strike*) clout; patch

klub *n.m* **klubys** club. **klub nos** *n.m* nightclub

klubya *vb* go clubbing

klun *n.f* **klunyow**, *dl* **diwglun** hip

klyckya *vb* click

klyji *n.coll* toffees

klyjien *n.f* **klyjiennow** toffee

klys *adj* cosy; snug

klysa *vb* make snug

kneus *n.coll* skin. **yn kig yn kneus** in the flesh

knew *n.m* **knewyow** fleece

knias *vb* chew

knouk *n.m* **knoukys** knock

knoukya *vb* knock

knoukyer *n.m* **knoukyers** gnome; mine spirit; knocker

know *n.coll* nuts. **know dor** *n.coll* peanuts; groundnuts. **know Frynk** *n.coll* walnuts. **know koll** *n.coll* hazelnuts. **know koko** *n.coll* coconuts. **know muskat** *n.coll* nutmeg. **know toos** *n.coll* doughnuts

knowa *vb* gather nuts

knowdhel *n.coll* gillyflower; stock

knowen *n.f* **knowennow** nut

knyvyas *vb* shear (*fleece*)

kober *n.m* (*element*) copper

kocha *n.m* **kochys** carriage. **kocha-dybri** *n.m* dining car

kod *n.m* **kodys** code. **kod post** *n.m* postcode

koden *n.f* **kodennow** code

kodenni *vb* encode

kodh *n.m* **kodhow** fall; tumble. **kodh glaw** *n.m* rainfall. **kodh ergh** *n.m* snowfall

kodha *vb* fall; tumble. **kodha dhelergh** fall back. **kodha klav** fall ill

kodhans *n.coll* precipitation

kofen *n.f* **kofennow** container

kofer *n.m* **kofrow** coffer; chest; trunk. **kofer saw** *n.m* safe

koffi *n.m* **koffiow** coffee

koffiji *n.m* **koffijiow** café
koffiva *n.f* **koffivaow** cafeteria
kofhe *vb* remind; (*transitive*) remember
kofrik *n.m* **kofrigow** small coffer.
  kofrik erbys *n.m* piggy bank; money
  box
kofryn *n.m* **kofrynnow** casket
kog (1) *n.m* **kogow** cook; chef
kog (2) *n.f* **koges** cuckoo. **bleujen an
  gog** *n.f* bluebell. **les an gog** *n.m*
  marigold
kogforn *n.f* **kogfornow** cooker
kogh (1) *adj* blood-red; crimson;
  scarlet; (*of meat*) lean. **kleves kogh**
  n.m scarlet fever
kogh (2) *n.m* **koghow** bonnet; hood;
  hull
koghyn *n.m* **koghynnow** coffin mine
kogrenni *vb* meander
K.O.K. *abbrev* **Kyns Osweyth
  Kemmyn** B.C.E.; B.C.
kok (1) *n.m* (*beverage*) Coke
kok (2) *n.coll* coke; treated coal
kok (3) *n.m* **kokow** fishing boat
Koka-Kola *n.m* Coca-Cola; Coke
kokayn *n.m* cocaine
koklys *n.coll* cockles
koklysen *n.f* **koklysennow** cockle
kol- *prfx* (=**kowl-**) whole; wholly
kola *vb* heed; trust. **kola orth nebonan**
  trust somebody. **kol orthiv!** heed my
  words! (*sg*)
kolenki *vb* swallow
koler *n.m* rage
kolgh *n.m* **kolghow** spike
kolghes *n.f* **kolghesow** duvet; quilt
kolji *n.m* **koljiow** college
koll (1) *n.m* **kollow** loss. **mos dhe goll**
  be lost; go missing
koll (2) *n.coll* hazel-trees. **koll garan**
  n.coll cranberries (*plants*)
kollaj *n.m* **kollajow** collage
kolldhel *adj* deciduous
kollell *n.f* **kellylli** knife. **kollell bleg**
  n.f penknife. **kollell-lesa** *n.f* octopus

kollen *n.f* **kollennow** hazel tree
kollen aran *n.f* **kollennow garan**
  cranberry (*plants*)
kollenwel *vb* fulfil; achieve;
  accomplish; complete; fill up.
  kollenwel an tank fill up (*with petrol*)
kolles *n.f* **kollesow** loss
kollor *n.m* **kolloryon** loser
kollverk *n.m* **kollverkys** apostrophe
kolm *n.m* **kolmow** knot; bind; link; tie.
  kolm konna *n.m* necktie. **kolm goos**
  (*familial*) relationship
kolm an askorn *n.m* comfrey
kolmek *adj* knotty
kolmen *n.f* **kolmennow** knot
kolodhyon *n.coll* guts
kolodhyonen *n.f* **kolodhyonennow**
  gut
kolom *n.f* **kelemmi** dove; pigeon
kolon *n.f* **kolonnow** heart. **gwann y
  golon** weak-hearted. **astel kolon** *n.m*
  cardiac arrest. **shora kolon** *n.m* heart
  attack. **tan y'n golon** *n.m* enthusiasm
kolonekter *n.m* courage; valour
kolonnek *adj* brave; cordial;
  courageous; fearless; hearty; kindly
kolonnen *n.f* **kolonennow** core
kolonwythiek *adj* cardiovascular
koloren *n.f* **kolorennow** *dl*
  diwgoloren collar-bone
koloven *n.f* **kolovennow** column;
  pillar
kolpes *n.m* **kolpesow** lever
kolpon *n.m* **kolpons** coupon
kolter *n.m* **koltrow** coulter
kolva *n.f* **kolvaow** state of loss
kolyek *n.m* **kolyogyon** fortune-teller
kolyn *n.m* **kelyn** cub; puppy
komedi *n.m* **komedis** comedy
komendya *vb* introduce; present;
  recommend; approve
komendyadow *adj* commendable
komendyans *n.m* **komendyansow**
  introduction; recommendation;
  approval

komendys *ppt* approved
komik *n.m* **komigow** comic; cartoon
komma *n.m* **kommas** comma. **poynt ha komma** semicolon
kommol *n.coll* clouds. **komolen sugra** *n.f* candy-floss
komner *n.m* **komners** commoner; plebeian
komodyta *n.m* **komodytys** facility
komolek *adj* cloudy
komolen *n.f* **komolennow** cloud
komparek *adj* specific
komparriv *n.m* **komparrivow** ratio
komparya *vb* compare
komparyans *n.m* **komparyansow** simile
kompassus *adj* comprehensive
kompes *adj* even; level; plain; right (*morally*). **bos kompes gans** be level with
komplegeth *n.f* complexity
komplekhe *vb* complicate
kompleth *adj* complex; complicated
komposa *vb* fulfil; level; sort out; validate; verify
komposter *n.m* **komposteryow** correctness; equilibrium; validity
komposya *vb* compose; put together
komposyans *n.m* **komposyansow** composition
komposydh *n.m* **komposydhyon** composer
komprehendya *vb* include
kompressa *vb* oppress
kompressyans *n.m* **kompressyansow** oppression
komptyer *n.m* **komptyoryon** counter
komunya *vb* take Communion
kon *n.f* **konyow** dinner
kona *vb* dine
koncevya *vb* conceive; imagine
konduk *n.m* conduct
konegeth *n.f* expertise
koneri *vb* rage
koneryek *adj* furious; rabid

konfessor *n.m* **konfessors** confessor
konfessya *vb* confess
konfirmya *vb* confirm
konfondya *vb* confound
konfort *n.m* **konforts** comfort
konfortya *vb* comfort
konin *n.m* **konines** rabbit
konjorya *vb* implore
konkludya *vb* conclude; refute
konkwerrya *vb* conquer; beat; defeat; vanquish
konna *n.m* **konaow** neck. **gwythien an konna** jugular vein. **kolm konna** *n.m* necktie. **konna tir** *n.m* peninsula. **treghi konna** cut-throat
konna bregh *n.m* **konaow bregh** wrists
konna gwynn *n.m* **konaow gwynn** whitethroat
konnar *n.f* fury; mania; rage. **gorra konnar yn** *vb* enrage
konnyk I *adj* clever; cunning; gifted; skilled **II** *n.m* cunning; wits **III** *n.m* **konygyon** expert
kons (1) *n.m* **konsys, konsow** pavement; causeway
kons (2) *n.f* **konsow, konsyow** vagina
konsel *n.m* **konsels** council. **Konsel Kernow** *n.m* Cornwall Council. **Konsel Stenegow Kernow** *n.m* The Cornish Stannary Parliament
konseler *n.m* **konseloryon** councillor. **konseler a'n dre** *n.m* town councillor
konsolen *n.f* **konsolennow** console. **konsolen wariow** *n.f* video game console
konstrina *vb* constrain; compel
konstrinus *adj* compulsory
konsumya *vb* consume
konsumyans *n.m* **konsumyansow** consumption
konsumyer *n.m* **konsumyoryon** consumer
konsya *vb* pave
konsyans *n.m* **konsyansow** conscience
konsystya *vb* consist

konter I *adj* opposite II *n.m* **konters** opposite

konternot *n.m* descant

konteth *n.f* **kontethow** county

kontradia *vb* contradict

kontradians *n.m* **kontradiansow** contradiction

kontradiek *adj* contradictory

kontrari I *adj* contrary II *adv* otherwise III *n.m* **kontraris** opposite. **dhe'n kontrari** on the contrary. **y'n kontrari part** on the other hand

kontrewaytya *vb* ambush; intercept

kontrewaytyans *n.m* **kontrewaytyansow** ambush; interception

kontrolya *vb* control

kontron *n.coll* maggots

kontronen *n.f* **kontronennow** maggot

konvedhadow *adj* comprehensible

konvedhes I *n.m* understanding II *vb* understand; realise

koog *adj* worthless; vain

koog linas *n.coll* deadnettle

kool *n.f* **kolyow** omen

koos *n.m* **kosow** wood; forest

koos kennin *n.coll* ramsons; wild garlic

kooth *adj* excellent

kopel *n.m* **koplow** couple; pair

kopia *vb* copy

kor (1) *n.coll* wax. **koren** *n.f* cake of wax

kor (2) *n.m* **korow** manner; style; work shift. **war neb kor** somehow

kora *vb* wax

Korawys *n.m* Lent. **lili Korawys** *n.coll* daffodils

korbel *n.m* **korblys** bracket

kord *n.m* **kordys** chord

korden *n.f* **kerdyn** cord

kordh *n.m* **kordhow** tribe

Korea *top n.f* Korea. **Korea Gledh** *top n.f* North Korea. **Korea Dhyghow** *top n.f* South Korea

Korean *n.m* **Koreans** Korean

Koreek *n.m* Korean language

koreek *adj* Korean

koren *n.f* **korennow** cake of wax

korev *n.m* **korevow** beer; ale. **korev gwann** *n.m* lager

korf *n.m* **korfow** body; person. **korf lagha** *n.m* constitution

korfek *adj* corpulent, portly, bodily

korf-laghel *adj* constitutional

korflan *n.f* **korflannow** cemetery; graveyard

korfleski *vb* cremate

korfliw *n.m* **korfliwyow** tattoo

korfloskans *n.m* **korfloskansow** cremation

korforeth *n.f* **korforethow** corporation. **korforeth lieskenedhlek** *n.f* multinational corporation

koriander *n.m* coriander

korkyn *n.m* **korkynnow** cork

korkynna *vb* cork

korn (1) *n.m* **kern**, *dl* **dewgorn** horn. **korn-kewsel** *n.m* megaphone

korn (2) *n.m* **kernow** corner **kornel** *n.f* **kornellow** corner

kornek *adj* horned

kornella *vb* corner

kornet *n.m* **kornettow** corner

kornya *vb* butt

korr *n.m* **korryon** dwarf; midget

korr- *prfx* micro-; mini-; miniature

korrbryv *n.m* **korrbryves, korrbryvyon** germ; microbe

korrdon *n.f* **korrdonnow** microwave. **forn gorrdon** *n.f* microwave oven

korrgowsell *n.f* **korrgowsellow** microphone

korrigan *n.m* **korriganes** elf

korrik *n.m* **korrigow** gnome. **korrik lowarth** *n.m* garden gnome

korrvanadhel owr *n.coll* dyer's greenweed

korrvarvus *n.m* **korrvarvusi** haddock

korrwelek *adj* microscopic

korrwelell *n.f* **korrwelellow**
microscope

kors (1) *n.m* **korsow** course;
movement (*in music*); spell (*period of
time*). **kors-dyski** *n.m* curriculum

kors (2) *n.coll* reeds

korsek I *adj* reedy **II** *n.f* **korsegi** reedy
marsh; reed bed

korsen *n.f* **korsennow** reed; cable

korsen Eynda *n.f* bamboo

korset *n.m* **korsettys** corset

korsyer *n.m* **korsyoryon** cruiser

kort *n.f* **kortys** court of law

kortes *adj* courteous; polite

kortesi *n.m* **kortesis** courtesy

kortesies *n.m* **kortesiesow** compliment

korynt *n.m* **koryns** currant. **korynt du**
n.m blackcurrant

kos *n.f* **kosow** itch

kosa *vb* itch

kosek *adj* woody (*many trees*)

kosel *adj* calm; quiet; non-violent;
restful. **yn kosel** *adv* calmly; gently

koselek *adj* calm

koselhe *vb* lull; pacify; placate; soothe;
quieten

kosfinel *n.coll* wild thyme

kosfinellen *n.f* **kosfinellennow** wild
thyme plant

kosin *n.m* **kosins** cousin; good friend

kosk (1) *n.m* (*fungus*) mould

kosk (2) *n.m* sleep. **yn kosk** asleep;
dormant

koska *vb* sleep; go mouldy.
sagh-koska *n.m* sleeping bag

koskkerdhes *vb* sleepwalk (*colloq*)

koskor *n.pl* troop; retinue; suite

koskti *n.m* **kosktiow** dormitory

kosmek *adj* cosmic

kosmetek *adj* cosmetic

kosmonieth *n.f* cosmology

kosmos *n.m* cosmos

kosoleth *n.f* quiet; quietness;
tranquility

kost (1) *n.m* **kostys, kostow** cost;
charge; expense. **heb kost** free of
charge. **kostow arghantti** *n.pl* bank
charges. **kostow mentons** *n.pl*
maintenance costs

kost (2) *n.m* **kostys** coast; district

kostek *adj* costly; expensive; dear

kosten *n.f* **kostennow** goal; target

kostenna *vb* target

kostrel *n.m* **kostrels** flask. **kostrel
gwakter** *n.m* vacuum flask

kostrelas *n.m* **kostrelasow** flaskful

kostya *vb* cost

koswik *n.f* **koswigow** forest. **koswik
law** *n.f* rain forest

kota *n.m* **kotys, kotow** coat. **kota glaw**
n.m raincoat

koth *adj* old. **lavar koth** *n.m* proverb

kothe *vb* shorten; abridge

kotheans *n.m* **kotheansow** contraction;
shortening. **heb kotheans**
unabridged

kothes *adj* abridged

kothhe *vb* age; grow old

kothman *n.m* **kothmans** comrade;
friend; mate

kothni *n.f* old age

koton *n.m* **kotenyow** cotton. **gwlan
koton** *n.coll* cotton wool

kott *adj* short; brief. **skrif kott** *n.m*
abstract

kottha *adj* older; elder; senior. **an
kottha** oldest; eldest

kough damawynn *n m* aquilegia;
columbine

koukou *n.f* **koukous** cuckoo

kov *n.m* **kovyow** memory; recollection.
er kov in memory of. **kyv kov** *n.m*
memory stick. **men kov** *n.m*
monument; memorial. **perthi kov a**[2]
vb recall; recollect

kovadh *n.m* **kovadhow** record

kovadha *vb* record

kovaytya *vb* covet

kovaytys *n.m* selfishness

kovia *vb* cherish; incubate

kovnotya *vb* minute (*a meeting*)

kovnotyans *n.m* **kovnotyansow** minute (*of a meeting*)

kovro *n.m* **kovrohow, kovroyow** keepsake; memento; souvenir

kovskrifa *vb* register

kovskrifans *n.m* **kovskrifansow** registration. (**niver**) **kovskrifans karr** *n.m* car registration (number)

kovskrifla *n.m* **kovskrifleow** registry

kovva *n.f* **kovvaow** (= **kudhva**) hideout; lair

kow I *adj* hollow **II** *n.f* **kowyow** hollow

kowa *vb* excavate

kowal I *adj* entire; thorough; utter **II** *adv* entirely; thoroughly; utterly

kowan *n.f* **kowannow** owl

kowans *n.m* **kowansow** excavation

kowas *n.f* **kowasow** shower. **kowas wyns** *n.f* gust. **kowas niwl** *n.f* thick mist. **men kowas** *n.m* meteorite

kowasek *adj* showery

kowbal *n.m* **kowbalow** ferry

kowbalhyns *n.m* **kowbalhensyow** ferry crossing

kowel *n.m* **kowellow** basket; cage. **kowel gwenen** *n.m* beehive. **kowel kankres** *n.m* crab-pot. **kowel lesk** *n.m* cradle

kowella *vb* cage

kowesi *vb* shower

kowesik *adj* hollowed

koweth *n.m* **kowetha** (*male*) companion; comrade; friend; mate

kowethas *n.m* **kowethasow** association; fellowship. **Kowethas an Yeth Kernewek** *n.m* (*name of organisation*) The Cornish Language Fellowship. **kowethas yowynkneth** *n.m* youth club

kowethasek *adj* social

kowethegeth *n.f* friendship

kowethek *adj* friendly

kowethes *n.f* **kowethesow** (*female*) companion; comrade; friend; mate

kowethlyver *n.m* **kowethlyvrow** manual; handbook

kowethus *adj* gregarious

kowethya *vb* associate. **kowethya gans** associate with

kowethyadow *adj* sociable

kowethyans *n.m* **kowethyansow** company; communion (of saints); organisation; relationship. **Kowethyans an Kenedhlow Unys (KKU)** *n.m* United Nations Organisation (UNO)

kowethyas *n.m* **kowethysi** colleague

kowfordh *n.f* **kowfordhow** tunnel

kowgrom *adj* concave

kowl (1) *n.coll* cabbage; kale

kowl (2) *n.m* **kowlow** soup

kowl- *prfx* (=**kol-**) whole; wholly

kowla *vb* clot; congeal; congest; curdle

kowlans *n.m* **kowlansow** congestion

kowlbrena *vb* buy up

kowldevys *adj* full-grown

kowlek *adj* gluttonous

kowlen *n.f* **kowlennow** cabbage; kale

kowlennik *n.f* **kowlenigow** brussels sprout

kowlen S. Padrek *n.f* London pride

kowles *n.coll* curd; jelly. **kowles lymmaval** *n.coll* lemon curd

kowlesen *n.f* **kowlesennow** a curd; a jelly

kowlik *n.m* **kowligow** brussels sprout

kowllehe *vb* (*IT*) minimise

kowlleski *vb* burn up; consume by fire; incinerate

kowlniver *n.m* **kowlniverow** integer

kowlvleujen *n.f* **kowlvleujennow** cauliflower

kowlvoghhe *v* (*IT*) maximise

kowlwerth *adj* wholesale

kowlwertha *vb* sell wholesale

kowlwrians *n.m* **kowlwriansow** accomplishment; achievement

kowlwrys *adj* accomplished

kowlwul *vb* accomplish; achieve; complete; execute; fulfil; implement

kowlys *adj* clotted; curdled. **leth kowlys** *n.m* curdled milk

kownans *n.m* **kownansow** gorge; ravine

kowr *n.m* **kewri** giant

kowr- *prfx* macro-; mega-; giant

kowrek *adj* enormous; giant; gigantic; king size; immense; massive

kowrgarow *n.m* **kowrgerwys** elk

kowrogeth *n.f* **kowrogethow** enormity

kowrvalow *n.m* **kowrvalowyow** hibiscus

kowrvargh *n.m* **kowrvergh** camel

kows *n.m* **kowsow** talk; speech. **kows diskler** *n.m* mumble. **kows unn den** *n.m* monologue

kowser *n.m* **kowsoryon** speaker

kowses *n.m* **kowsesyow** conscience; conviction

kowva *n.f* **kowvaow** cavity

koynt *adj* odd; weird; curious; peculiar; quaint

koyntys *n.f* **koyntysyow** curiosity; oddity; weirdness

kraban *n.m* **krabanow** claw

kraban an ors *n.m* hellebore

krack *n.m* **krackys** crack; crunch

kracker *n.m* **krackers** cracker (*Christmas*)

krackya *vb* break; crack. **krackya konna** *adj* breakneck

kraf I *adj* greedy; miserly **II** *n.m* **krefyon** miser

krag *n.coll* sandstone

kragen *n.f* **kragennow** (*individual*) sandstone

kragh *n.m* **kreghi** scab

krambla *vb* climb; mount; scale

krambler *n.m* **krambloryon** climber

krampoth *n.coll* pancakes. **krampoth mowysi** *n.coll* pennywort. **krampoth oyow** *n.coll* omelettes

krampothen *n.f* **krampothennow** pancake

krampothen vowysi *n.f* **krampothennow mowysi** navelwort; pennywort

krampoth mowysi *n.coll* navelwort; pennywort

kramvil *n.m* **kramviles** reptile

kramvilek *adj* reptilian

kramya *vb* crawl; creep; grovel

kramyerik *n.m* **kramyeriges** treecreeper (*bird*)

krann *n.coll* bracken; scrub

krannek *adj* scrubby

krannen *n.f* **krannennow** bracken

krapp *n.m* grip

kras I *adj* crisp; parched; toasted **II** *n.coll* toast

krasa *vb* parch; toast

krasell *n.f* **krasellow** toaster

krasen *n.f* **krasennow** (slice of) toast

kravas I *n.m* **kravasow** scratch **II** *vb* claw; scrape; scratch. **kravas goles an balyer** scrape the bottom of the barrel

kravell *n.f* **kravellow** hoe

kravellas *vb* hoe; scrape

kravlost *n.m* **kravlostow** (*mine spirit*) knocker

kraw *n.m* **krawyow** perforation; socket

kreador *n.m* **kreadors** creator

krebogh *adj* wrinkled; decrepit

krefhe *vb* strengthen

krefhes *adj* fortified (*strengthened*)

krefni *n.f* greed

kreft *n.f* **kreftow** trade; craft; workmanship

krefter *n.m* **krefteryow** strength; stability

kreftor *n.m* **kreftoryon** craftsperson

kreftus *adj* artificial. **skians kreftus** *n.m* artificial intelligence

kreg *adj* hoarse

kregans *n.m* **kregansow** suspension

kregi *vb* hang; suspend. **kregi war²** depend on

krellas *n.m* **krellow** rough or ruined hut

kren *n.m* **krenyow** shake. **kavos kren** have a fit

krena *vb* tremble; shiver; shake; vibrate

krenans *n.m* **krenansow** vibration

Krener *n.m* **Krenoryon** Quaker

krenn *adj* round

krer *n.m* **kreryow** relic (*of saint*)

krerva *n.f* **krervaow** shrine

kres (1) I *adj* central; mid II *n.m* **kresyow** centre; middle; waist. **tommheans kres** *n.m* central heating

kres (2) *n.m* peace

kresek I *adj* average; medium II *n.m* **kresogow** average

kresel *adj* central

kresen *n.f* **kresennow** centre (building or institution). **kresen-brenassa** *n.f* shopping centre. **kresen gemeneth** *n.f* community centre. **kresen yowynkneth** *n.f* youth centre

kresenna *vb* centralise

kresfoesik *adj* centrifugal

kreshwilus *adj* centripetal

kresik *n.m* **kresigow** (*potato*) crisp

kreslu *n.m* police. **gwith an kreslu** *n.m* police custody. **sodhva greslu** *n.f* police station

kresosel *adj* medieval

kresriv *n.m* **kresrivow** median

kressya *vb* increase

kressys *adj* increased

kresten *n.coll* crusts. **kresten vrew** *n.f* shortcrust

krestennek *n.m* **krestenogyon** crustacean

krestennen *n.f* **krestennennow** crust

Kresvor *n.m* Mediterranean Sea

kresvorek *adj* Mediterranean

kreswas *n.m* **kreswesyon** centre (*rugby*)

kreswedhek *adj* medium

kresydh *n.m* **kresydhyon** pacifist

kresydhieth *n.f* pacifism

kresys (1) *adj* toasted

kresys (2) *n.m* **kresysow** credit. **karten gresys** *n.f* credit card

kreun *n.m* **kreunyow** reserve; reservoir; stockpile

kreunell *n.f* **kreunellow** accumulator

kreuni *vb* accumulate; congest

kreunyer *n.m* **kreunyoryon** accumulator

krev *adj* strong; forceful; powerful; robust; substantial

krevder *n.m* **krevderyow** strength; intensity. **krevder golow** *n.m* luminous intensity

krey *n.m* **kreyow** chalk

kreyon *n.m* **kreyonyow** crayon

kreyth *n.coll* scars

kreythen *n.f* **kreythennow** scar

kreythya *vb* scar

kri *n.m* **kriow** call; cry; shout; yell

kria *vb* call; cry; shout; yell

krib *n.f* **kribow** comb; reef

kribas *vb* comb

kribellow *n.pl* teasel

kriben *n.f* **kribennow** ridge. **kriben vel** *n.f* honeycomb

krin *adj* arid

krina *vb* become dry or brittle

kris *n.m* vigour. **gans meur a gris** vigorously

krisek *adj* enthusiastic

Krist *n.m* Christ

Kristonedh *n.m* Christianity

kristonhe *vb* christen

Kristyon I *adj* Christian II *n.m* **Kristonyon** Christian

kriv *adj* raw; crude; fresh; uncooked; unripe. **leth kriv** *n.m* unpasteurised milk

krivder *n.m* rawness; crudity

kro *adj* (*of food*) fresh

kroadur *n.m* **kroaduryon** creature

Kroat *n.m* **Kroatyon** Croat

Kroatek *n.m* Croatian language

kroatek *adj* croatian

Kroati *top n.f* Croatia

kroban *n.m* **krobanes** tortoise

kroch *n.m* **krochys, krochow,** *dl* **dewgroch** crutch

krochet *n.m* **krochetow** crochet

kroder *n.m* **krodrow** riddle; strainer; coarse (garden) sieve. **kroder kroghen** *n.m* bodhran; holdall

krodhek *adj* grumbling

krodhvol *n.m* **krodhvolyow** complaint; grumble; protest

krodhvolas *vb* complain; grumble; moan; protest

krodra *vb* sift

krog *n.f* **krogow** hang; suspension; tug

krogbren *n.m* **krogbrennyer** gallows

krogen *n.f* **kregyn** shell. **krogen benn** *n.f* skull. **krogen brierin** *n.f* scallop

kroghen *n.f* **kreghyn** hide. **dyghtya kreghyn** tan leather. **kroghen lagas** *n.f* eyelid. **medhek kroghen** *n.m* dermatologist. **tew y groghen** insensitive

kroghena *vb* skin

kroghendanow *adj* sensitive

krogla *n.m* **krogleow** gibbet

kroglen *n.f* **kroglennow** curtain

krokodil *n.m* **krokodiles** crocodile

kromatek *adj* chromatic

kromm *adj* curved; rounded

kromma *vb* bend; curve

krommen *n.f* **kromennow** crescent; curve

krommlegh *n.f* **krommleghow** cromlech; dolmen

krommvagh *n.f* **krommvaghow** bracket; parenthesis

kronegyn *n.m* **kronegynnow** little toad. **kronegyn hager du** *n.m* ugly black little toad

kronek I *adj* skinny **II kronoges** *n.m* toad. **kronek ervys** *n.m* tortoise. **kronek ervys mor** *n.m* turtle. **kronek du** *n.m* toad. **skavel gronek** *n.f* toadstool; mushroom

kronk *n.m* **kronkys** stroke; thump; wallop

kronkya *vb* beat; bash; strike; tan; thump; wallop

kronogas *vb* hop

kropya *vb* penetrate; probe

kroth *n.f* **krothow** (*bird's*) crop

kroust *n.m* **kroustys, kroustyow** lunch; picnic; snack

krow (1) *n.m* **krowyow** hut; shed; sty. **krow deves** *n.m* sheep-cot. **krow mogh** *n.m* pigsty. **krow prenn** *n.m* chalet. **krow yer** *n.m* chicken shed

krow (2) *n.m* bloodshed; gore

krowd *n.m* **krowdys** violin

krowdra *vb* loiter

krowji *n.m* **krowjiow** cabin

krowles melyn *n.m* yellow loosestrife

krowles purpur *n.m* purple loosestrife

krows *n.f* **krowsow** cross. **y'n krows** on the cross

krowsek *adj* cross-shaped; cross-tempered; irritable; testy

krowseryow *n.pl* crossword

krowsfordh *n.f* **krowsfordhow** crossroads

krowslinek *adj* diagonal

krowslinen *n.f* **krowslinennow** diagonal

krowsya *vb* crucify

krug *n.m* **krugow** mound; tumulus

krullya *vb* curl

krullys *adj* curly. **kudyn krullys** *n.m* curl

kruskyn *n.m* **kruskynnow** mug

krycket *n.m* (*sport*) cricket

krygha *vb* crimp; rumple; wrinkle

kryghias *vb* neigh

kryghlam *n.m* **kryghlammow** jig

kryghylli *vb* jolt

kryjyans *n.m* **kryjyansow** religion; belief

kryjyk *adj* religious

kryllas *n.m* **kryllasow** ruin (*of a dwelling*)

krys *n.m* **krysyow** shirt. **krys nos** *n.m* nightshirt. **krys T** *n.m* T-shirt

krysadow *adj* credible

krysi *vb* believe

kryspows *n.f* **kryspowsyow** waistcoat

krytika *vb* criticise

krytykel *adj* critical

kub *n.m* **kubow** cube. **kub rew** *n.m* ice cube

kubek *adj* cubic

kudh *adj* hidden; secret; concealed

kudha *vb* conceal; hide. **kudha rag** hide from

kudhlen *n.f* **kudhlennow** cover; veil. **lyver kudhlen gales** *n.m* hardback. **lyver kudhlen vedhel** *n.m* paperback

kudhoberys *adj* underhand

kudhva *n.f* **kudhvaow** (= **kovva**) hideout; lair

kudhys *adj* veiled

kudyn *n.m* **kudynnow** lock of hair; problem. **kudyn krullys** *n.m* curl

kugol *n.m* **kugollow** hood

kugol an managh *n.m* monkshood; wolf's bane

kuhudha *vb* accuse; allege

kuhudhans *n.m* **kuhudhansow** accusation; allegation

kuhudhys *adj* alleged

kukomber *n.m* **kukomberyow** cucumber

kul *adj* narrow

kuldremenva *n.f* **kuldremenvaow** corridor

kulyek *n.m* **kulyoges** cockerel

kumin *n.coll* cumin

kummyas *n.m* **kumyasow** leave; licence; permission; permit. **kummyas bledhynnyek** *n.m* annual leave. **kummyas-entra** *n.m* admittance. **kummyas-lewya** *n.m* driving licence. **kummyas gwithyas** *n.m* carer's leave. **kummyas mamoleth** *n.m* maternity leave. **kummyas tasoleth** *n.m* paternity

leave. **kummyas tregeredhus** *n.m* compassionate leave

kuner *n.m* **kunoryon** lighter

kuntel I *n.m* **kuntellow** collection **II** *vb* collect; gather; pick; accumulate

kunteller *n.m* **kuntelloryon** collector; gatherer

kuntelles *n.m* (*f*) **kuntellesow** assembly; congress; meeting

kuntellyans *n.m* **kuntellyansow** congregation

kuntilow *n.m* **kuntilowyow** music album

kur *n.m* **kurys, kuryow** cure

kuriek *n.m* **kuriogas, kuriegi** pimple; spot

kurri *n.m* **kurris** curry

kurun *n.f* **kurunyow** crown. **kurun spern** *n.f* crown of thorns; hangover

kurunik (1) *n.f* **kurunigow** tiara

kurunik (2) *n.f* carnation

kurunyans *n.m* **kurunyansow** coronation

kussul *n.f* **kussulyow** advice; council; counsel; opinion; suggestion. **Cussel an Tavas Kernôwek** *n.f* (*name of organisation*) the Cornish Language Council

kussulya *vb* advise; consult; suggest. **bos kussulys a**² be advised that

kussulyans *n.m* **kussulyansow** consultation

kussulyek *adj* advisory

kussulyer *n.m* **kussulyoryon** adviser

kustard *n.m* custard

kuv I *adj* dear; kind; amicable **II** *n.m* **kuvyon** darling; beloved. **kuv kolon** *n.m* sweetheart

kuvder *n.m* kindness

kwackya *vb* quack

kwadrant *n.m* **kwadrantys** quadrant

kwalifia *vb* qualify

kwalifians *n.m* **kwalifiansow** qualification

kwarel *n.m* **kwarels** pane

kwarter *n.m* **kwartrys** quarter
kwartrona *vb* quarter; cut in four
kwaver *n.m* **kwaveryow** quaver
kweth *n.f* **kwethow** cloth. **kweth ponn**
  n.f duster. **kweth lestri** *n.m* dishcloth
kwetha *vb* cover with a cloth; clothe
kwethyn *n.m* **kwethynnow** napkin
kwilkyn *n.m* **kwilkynnyow** frog
kwit *adv* deservedly
kwoffi *vb* gorge; overeat; binge
kwoffys *adj* swollen, bloated
kwys *n.m* **kwysyow** quiz
kwytya *vb* quit
kwytyans *n.m* **kwytyansow** exit
kyf *n.m* **kyfyon** log
kyfeyth *n.m* **kyfeythyow** jam;
  confection; preserves. **kyfeyth**
  owraval *n.m* orange marmalade
kyfeythya *vb* preserve (*foods*)
kyfya *vb* confide
kyfyans *n.m* confidence
kyfyansek *adj* confident
kygel *n.f* **kygelyow** distaff
kyhwedhel *n.m* **kyhwedhlow** rumour;
  gossip
kyhwedhla *vb* gossip
kyjya *vb* unite; copulate; fuck; have
  sexual intercourse; screw
kyjyans *n.m* **kyjyansow** sexual
  intercourse; fuck
kylasenna *vb* (*roof with*) slate
kylgh *n.m* **kylghyow** circle; hoop; ring;
  round
kylghek *adj* circular
kylghigow *n.pl* hoop-la
kylghlavar *n.m* **kylghlavarow**
  circumlocution
kylghresek *vb* circulate
kylghvusur *n.m* **kylghvusuryow**
  perimeter
kylghya *vb* encircle

kyllas *n.coll* slates
kyllasen *n.f* **kyllasennow** slate
kymygen *n.f* **kymygennow** chemical
kymygieth *n.f* chemistry
kymygiethel *adj* chemical. **arwodh**
  gymygiethel *n.f* chemical symbol
kymygydh *n.m* **kymygydhyon**
  scientific chemist
kymyk *adj* chemical
kymyst (**1**) *n.m* **kymystyon**
  dispensing chemist; pharmacist
kymyst (**2**) *n.m* chemist's shop
kyn[5] (**th**) *cnj* although; though
kyngel *n.f* **kynglow** girdle
kyni *vb* lament; moan; mourn; wail
kynnik I *n.m* **kynigow** offer; bid **II** *vb*
  offer; bid
kynnyav *n.m* autumn
kyns I *adj* former; previous; sooner **II**
  adv formerly; rather **III** *prp* before.
  kyns lemmyn before now; hitherto.
  kyns ena before that. **kyns oll**
  notably
kynsa I *num* first; initial. **hanow kynsa**
  n.m forename. **y'n kynsa le** primarily
  II *adj* primary
kynseghwa *n.m* forenoon
kynser *n.m* **kynseri** apprentice
kynserneth *n.m* **kynsernethow**
  apprenticeship
kynsistorek *adj* prehistoric
kynsskrif *n.m* **kynsskrifow** preface
kynvan *n.m* **kynvannow** lament;
  lamentation; moan; mourning
kynwel *n.f* **kynwelyow** preview
kynweres *n.m* first aid
kynyas *vb* harvest
kynyavel *adj* autumnal
kyttrin *n.m* **kyttrinyow** bus
kyttrinva *n.f* **kyttrinvaow** bus stop

L

labedha *vb* stone
label *n.m* labelyow label
labol *adj* striped
lader *n.m* ladron thief; robber. **alarm ladron** *n.m* burglar alarm
ladha *vb* kill; murder; slaughter
ladher *n.m* ladhoryon killer; murderer
ladhva *n.f* ladhvaow killing; slaughter. **daffar ladhva** *n.m* ammunition
ladra *vb* rob. **ladra helgik** poach
ladrans *n.m* ladransow theft; robbery
ladrynsi *n.m* theft; robbery
lagas *n.m* lagasow *dl* dewlagas eye. **aval lagas** *n.m* eyeball. **blew lagas** *n.coll* eyelashes. **kroghen lagas** *n.f* eyelid. **liw lagas** *n.m* eye-shadow. **medhegieth lagasow** *n.f* ophthalmology. **pyncel lagas** *n.m* eye-liner. **yn lagas an bys** in the limelight
lagasek *adj* big-eyed; goggle-eyed
lagasow kathes *n.pl* lesser stitchwort
lagatta *vb* stare; eye
lagen *n.f* lagennow pond; puddle
lagha *n.f* laghys law. **herwydh an lagha** lawful. **lagha an lovan** *n.f* lynch law. **sewya dre lagha** sue
laghel *adj* legal; lawful
laghyas *n.m* laghysi lawyer; attorney
lagya *vb* splash
lagyans *n.m* splash
lagyar *n.f* lagyer moorhen
lakka *adj* (see: **drog**) worse; worst
lamm *n.m* lammow jump; hop; leap. **bledhen lamm** *n.f* leap year
lamma *vb* jump; hop; leap
lammer *n.m* lamoryon jumper (*athlete*)
lammleder *n.f* lammledrow precipice
lammlen *n.f* lammlennow parachute
lank I *adj* adolescent II *n.m* lankyow adolescent
lann *n.f* lannow holy enclosure; yard

lannergh *n.m* lanerghi glade
lantern *n.m* lanterns lantern
lanwes *n.m* lanwesow flood; abundance; fill. **lanwes mor** *n.m* tide
lappa *n.m* lappys lobe; flap
lappya *vb* perform gymnastics
lappyans *n.m* gymnastics
lappyer *n.m* lappyoryon acrobat
lapya *vb* lap; lick
larchwedhen *n.f* larchwedhennow larch
larchwydh *n.coll* larches
larynjitis *n.m* (*med*) laryngitis
larynks *n.m* larynx
las (1) *n.m* lasow lace
las (2) *n.m* lasow alcohol; liquor
laseger *n.m* lasegoryon alcoholic
lasek *adj* alcoholic
las Myghternes Anna *n.m* Queen Anne's lace; wild carrot
lasnagher *n.m* lasnaghoryon teetotaller
lasnaghus *adj* teetotal
lasogeth *n.f* alcoholism (*med*)
lastedhes *n.m* scum; filth; vermin
lasya *vb* lace
lath *n.f* lathow staff; stick; yard
latimer *n.m* latimers interpreter
Latin *n.m* Latin language
latinek *adj* Latin
latti *n.m* lattiow abattoir
Latvi *top n.f* Latvia
Latvian *n.m* Latvians Latvian
Latviek *n.m* Latvian language
latviek *adj* Latvian
lava *n.m* lava
lavant *n.m* lavender
lavar *n.m* lavarow expression; idiom; sentence; utterance. **lavar koth** *n.m* proverb; saying
lavaren *n.f* lavarennow phrase

lavasos *vb* claim; dare; presume; venture

lavrek *n.m* **lavrogow** trousers. **lavrek berr** *n.m* shorts

lavur *n.m* **lavuryow** labour; toil; work. **kesunyans lavur** *n.m* trade union. **lavur tre** *n.m* housework

lavurus *adj* laborious

lavurya *vb* labour; work; toil; slave

lavuryans *n.m* toil

lavuryas *n.m* **lavurysi** labourer

lavurys *adj* worn-out

law *adj* miserable

lawd *n.m* **lawdys** laud

lawdya *vb* laud

lawen krib owr *n.m* **lawenes krib owr** goldcrest

lawen melyn *n.m* **lawenes melyn** chiffchaff

lay *n.f* **layys** religious law

le (1) *n.m* **leow** place; position; situation; venue. **yn le** in place of; instead of *Personal forms: 1s* **yn ow le**, *2s* **yn dha le**, *3sm* **yn y le**, *3sf* **yn hy le**, *1p* **yn agan le**, *2p* **yn agas le**, *3p* **yn aga le**

le (2) *adj, adv, prn* less; lesser; minor; smaller

lea *vb* site

lebanek *adj* Lebanese

Lebanon *top n.m* Lebanon

Lebanyas *n.m* **Lebanysi** Lebanese

lecher *n.m* **lechers** frying pan

led *n.m* **ledyow** electrical lead

ledan *adj* broad; wide. **amendyansow ledan** *n.pl* sweeping reforms. **bond ledan** *n.m* broadband. **lo ledan** *n.f* ladle

ledanhe *vb* widen

leder *n.f* **ledrow** slope

ledher *n.m* **ledhrow** leather

ledhrek *adj* leather

ledhyas *n.m* **ledhysi** killer. **ledhyas lowena** *n.m* killjoy

ledhys *adj* killed; murdered

ledrek *adj* sloping

ledri *vb* slope

ledrys *adj* stolen

ledya *vb* lead; conduct

ledyer *n.m* **ledyoryon** leader

leel *adj* local

leelieth *n.f* localism

leftenant *n.m* **leftenants** lieutenant

leg I *adj* lay **II** *n.m* **legyon** lay person

legessa *vb* catch mice

legest *n.m* **legesti** lobster

legh *n.coll* slates

leghen *n.f* **leghennow** slate; (*IT*) tablet

legras *n.m* **legrasow** corruption; decadence

legri *vb* corrupt

legrys *adj* corrupted

lehe *vb* lessen; mitigate; reduce; shrink; zoom out

lel *adj* faithful; genuine; loyal; reliable; trusty. **dhis yn lel** yours sincerely

lelder *n.m* loyalty

Lelyas *n.m* **Lelysi** Loyalist

le may⁵ (th) *cnj* where

lemen *cnj* but; only; save

lemmel *vb* jump; hop; leap. **lemmel lovan** skip (*with a rope*)

lemmyn *adv* now

len *adj* faithful

lenes *n.f* **lenesow** nun; ling-fish

lenji *n.m* **lenjiow** nunnery

lenki *vb* swallow; absorb

lenn *n.f* **lennow** cloth; blanket. **lenn dhu** *n.f* blind (*window*)

lenna *vb* read aloud

lenner *n.m* **lenoryon** reader

lenni *vb* cover

lennus *adj* legible

lens *n.m* **lensys, lensow** lens

lent *adj* slow. **yn lent** *adv* slowly

lenter *n.m* gloss; shine. **lenter gweus** *n.m* lip gloss

lenthe *vb* slow down

lentri *vb* gleam

lentrus *adj* gleaming

lentvil *n.m* **lentviles** sloth
lenwel *vb* fill. **lenwel a²** fill with
leowta *n.m* loyalty
leper *n.m* **lepers** leper
lergh *n.m* **lerghow** trace; track; trail
les (1) *n.m* **lesow** advantage; gain; benefit; interest; importance; profit; utility; welfare. **dhe les** *adj* advantageous; interesting. **meur y les** absorbing; beneficial. **stat an les** *n.m* the welfare state
les (2) *n.m* **lesyow** plant
les (3) *n.m* **lesyow** breadth; width
les (4) *cnj* in case
lesa *vb* expand; spread; unfold
les an gog *n.m* **losow an gog** calendula; common marigold
lesans *n.m* **lesansow** expansion; spread
lesbenigys an dowr *n.m* water avens
lesbenigys an koos *n.m* wood avens
lesbian *adj* lesbian
lesbianes *n.f* **lesbianesow** lesbian
lesderth *n.m* feverfew
lesek *adj* interesting; profitable
lesel *adj* beneficial
lesflogh *n.m* **lesfleghes** stepchild
lesh *n.m* **leshyow** leash; lead
leshanow *n.m* **leshenwyn** pseudonym
leshwor *n.f* **leshwerydh** stepsister
leshyans *n.m* **leshyansow** licence
les hynsledan *n.m* **losow hynsledan** broad-leaved plantain
lesk *n.m* **leskow** swing. **lesk lovan** *n.m* swing
leska *vb* rock; swing. **margh-leska** *n.m* rocking horse
lesken *n.f* **leskennow** fuse
leski *vb* burn
leskys *adj* burnt
leslen *n.f* **leslennow** spreadsheet
leslesa *n.m* speedwell
les loos *n.m* horehound
lesranna *vb* distribute

lesrannans *n.m* **lesranansow** distribution
lesrennyas *n.m* **lesrenysi** distributor
les Robin *n.m* herb-Robert
les serghek *n.m* greater burdock
les serghek byghan *n.m* cleavers; goosegrass (*sticky willy*)
lesta *vb* prevent; thwart. **lesta nebonan rag gul neppyth** prevent somebody from doing something
lestans *n.m* prevention
lestas *n.m* **lestasow** stepfather
lester (1) *n.m* **lestri** vessel; dish; ship. **lester-gwari** *n.m* yacht. **lester bleujyow, lester flourys** *n.m* vase. **lester-sedhi** *n.m* submarine. **mes a'n lester** *adv* overboard. **porth lestri** *n.m* dock
lester (2) *n.m* width
lestrier *n.m* **lestrieryow** dresser; kitchen dresser
lestriva *n.f* **lestrivaow** dockyard
lestryn *n.m* **lestrynnow** container
lesvam *n.f* **lesvammow** stepmother
lesvroder *n.m* **lesvreder** stepbrother
leswedh *n.m* **leswedhow** frying pan
lesyeth *n.f* **lesyethow** regional accent
leth *n.m* **lethow** milk. **leth didhehen** *n.m* skimmed milk. **leth kowlys** *n.m* curdled milk. **leth kriv** *n.m* unpasteurised milk
lethles *n.m* common milkwort
lethwas *n.m* **lethwesyon** milkman
lethwreg *n.f* **lethwragedh** milkmaid
leti *n.m* **letiow** dairy
lett *n.m* **lettys, lettow** barrier; check; obstacle; obstruction. **heb lett** incessantly
lettrys *adj* literate
lettryseth *n.f* literacy
lettya *vb* block; check; hinder; impede; prevent
letus *n.coll* lettuce
letusen *n.f* **letusennow** lettuce
leugh *n.m* **leughi** calf

leun *adj* full; complete; thorough. **leun a²** full of. **leun a dus** crowded. **leun a styr** meaningful

leunder *n.m* fullness; fill

leunhe *vb* fill

leur *n.m* **leuryow** floor; ground; storey. **leur a-woles** *n.m* ground floor

leurlen *n.f* **leurlennow** carpet

leurnedh *n.m* **leurnedhow** area

leuv *n.f* **leuvyow**, *dl* **diwleuv, diwla** hand. **shackya leuv** shake hands

leuvtosa *vb* massage

leuvtosans *n.m* **leuvtosansow** massage

leuvvedhegel *adj* surgical

leuvvedhegneth *n.f* **leuvvedhegnethow** surgery. **leuvvedhegneth kosmetek** *n.f* cosmetic surgery

leuvvedhek *n.m* **leuvvedhogyon** surgeon

leuvwelen *n.f* **leuvwelynni** baton

lev *n.m* **levow** voice. **dre lev** vocal

leva *vb* cry out

levbost *n.m* **levbostow** voicemail

leven *adj* level; plain

levena *vb* smooth

levenek *n.f* **levenegow** smoothie

levenhe *vb* level

leverel *vb* say; tell; pronounce

leveryans *n.m* **leveryansow** pronunciation

levna *vb* press

levrith *n.m* sweet milk

levyel *adj* vocal

lew (1) *n.m* **lewyow** rudder

lew (2) *n.m* **lewyon** lion

lewa *vb* drive

lewd *adj* lewd; indecent; obscene

lewdnes *n.m* **lewdnessys** obscenity

lewen losow *n.f* **lewennow losow** aphid

lewes *n.f* **lewesow** lioness

lewik *n.m* **lewigow** lion cub

lew losow *n.coll* aphids

lewpard *n.m* **lewpardes** leopard

lewsel *vb* free; loosen

lewya *vb* drive

lewyader *n.f* **lewyadoryon** pilot

lewydh *n.m* **lewydhyon** helmsman; president; director

lewyer *n.m* **lewyoryon** driver. **lewyer kyttrin** *n.m* bus driver. **lewyer tren** *n.m* train driver

leys *n.m* **leysyow** mud; slime

leysek I *adj* muddy **II** *n.f* **leysegi** mire

leyth *adj* humid; moist

leytha *vb* moisten

li (1) *n.f* **livyow** (= **liv (3)**) lunch

li (2) *n.m* **liow** oath

lia *vb* swear; take an oath

lien (1) *n.m* **lienyow** linen cloth; kerchief. **lien baban** *n.m* nappy. **lien diwla** *n.m* napkin. **lien dorn** *n.m* handkerchief. **lien gweli** *n.m* bedsheet. **lien konna** *n.m* scarf. **lien paper** *n.m* paper tissue. **lienyow gweli** *n.pl* bedding

lien (2) *n.m* **liennow** literature. **lien gwerin** *n.m* folklore

liennek *adj* literary

lies *adj, prn* many; lots (many of); numerous. **a lies eghen** varied; heterogeneous. **pana lies, py lies** how many

lies- *adj* multi-

liesek *adj* various; multiple; plural

liesgonisogethek *adj* multicultural

lieshe *vb* multiply. **lieshes gans** multiplied by

liesheans *n.m* **liesheansow** multiplication

liesheor *n.m* **liesheoryon** multiplier

lieskenedhlek *adj* multinational. **korforeth lieskenedhlek** *n.f* multinational corporation

lieskonnyk *adj* versatile

lieskweyth *adv* many times; often

lieskweythresek *adj* multifunctional

liesleur *adj* multi-storey

liesliw *adj* multicoloured

liesplek I *adj* multiple **II** *n.m*
liesplegow plural
liesporpos *adj* multipurpose
liesroasek I *adj* multi-talented **II** *n.m*
liesroasogyon polymath
liesskrif *n.m* **liesskrifow** photocopy
liesskrifa *vb* photocopy
liesskrifell *n.f* **liesskrifellow**
photocopier
liester *n.m* **liesteryow** abundance;
multiplicity; plurality
liestu *adj* multilateral
liesyethek *adj* multilingual
lili *n.coll* lilies
lili Korawys *n.coll* daffodils
lilien *n.f* **liliennow** lily
lilien gledha *n.f* **liliennow kledha**
gladiolus
lili kledha *n.coll* gladiolus
lim *n.m* cement
limaval *n.m* **limavalow** lime
lin (1) *n.coll* linen; flax
lin (2) *n.m* **linyow** fluid; liquid; lotion.
lin sebon *n.m* detergent; washing-up
liquid
lin (3) *n.m* **linyow** line. **lin goles** *n.m*
bottom line
lin gwyls *n.m* common toadflax
(*yellow*)
linas *n.coll* nettles
linasek *n.f* **linasegi** bed of nettles
linasen *n.f* **linasennow** nettle
linek rudh *n.f* **linoges rudh** linnet
linen (1) *n.f* **linennow** linen; flax plant
linen (2) *n.f* **linennow** line. **linen
denewen** *n.f* touch-line. **linen
dermyn** *n.f* time-line
linenna *vb* sketch
linennans *n.m* **linenansow** sketch
linennell *n.f* **linenellow** straight-edge;
rule
linenner *n.m* **linenoryon** linesman
linyek *adj* linear
linyel *adj* fluid; liquid
lion *n.m* **lions** lion

lisiw *n.m* **lisiwyow** washing powder
lisliwen *n.f* **lisliwennow** alkali
liter *n.m* **litrow** litre
lith *n.f* **lithes** plaice
lithiom *n.m* (*element*) lithium
Lithuani *top n.f* Lithuania
Lithuanian *n.m* **Lithuanians**
Lithuanian
Lithuaniek *n.m* Lithuanian language
lithuaniek *adj* Lithuanian
liv (1) *n.f* **livyow** file
liv (2) *n.m* **livyow** flood. **skollya liv a
dhagrow** cry one's eyes out
liv (3) *n.f* **livyow** (= **li (1)**) lunch
liva *vb* flood; swamp
livra *vb* liberate; release
livrel *adj* (*politically*) liberal. **Parti
Livrel Gwerinel** *n.m* Liberal
Democratic Party
livreson *n.m* **livresons** delivery;
liberation; release. **livreson uskis** *n.m*
express delivery
LivWer *adj, abbrev* LibDem. **an re
LivWer** *n.pl* the LibDems
livwolowys *n.pl* floodlights
livya (1) *vb* lunch
livya (2) *vb* file; scrape
livyet *n.f* **livyetow** floodgate
liw *n.m* **liwyow** colour; dye; paint.
kelli liw blanch; turn pale. **liw
bejeth** *n.m* make-up. **liw blew lagas**
n.m mascara. **liw diwvogh** *n.m*
blusher. **liw gweus** *n.m* lipstick. **liw
howl** *n.m* suntan; tan. **liw lagas** *n.m*
eye-shadow. **liw rudh** *n.m* blush
liwa *vb* colour; dye; paint
liwans *n.m* **liwansow** painting
liwek *adj* coloured; dyed
liwus *adj* colourful
liwvord *n.m* **liwvordow** palette
liwyans *n.m* **liwyansow** picture;
painting
liwys *adj* coloured; dyed
lo *n.f* **loyow** spoon. **lo an jowl** *n.f*
trapdoor. **lo-balas** *n.f* trowel. **lo de** *n.f*

teaspoon. **lo ledan** *n.f* ladle. **lo vras** *n.f* tablespoon

loder *n.m* **lodrow** stocking. **lodrow nilon** *n.pl* nylons

lodhen *n.m* **lodhnow** (**lonn**) bullock; young ox

lodrik *n.m* **lodrigow** sock

log *n.f* **logow** cell

logel *n.m* **logelyow** coffin; tomb

logh (1) *n.m* **loghow** inlet

logh (2) *adj* lax

logheth *n.f* laxity

logos *n.coll* mice

logosen *n.f* **logosennow** mouse

logystek *n.f* logistics

lojyk *n.m* logic. **herwydh lojyk** logical; logically

lok *n.m* presence. **y'm lok** in my presence

lokust *n.m* **lokustes** locust

lolla *vb* lull

lomder *n.m* bareness

lomm *adj* bare; naked

lommas *n.m* **lomasow** small bream

lommhe *vb* bare; strip bare

lonchya *vb* launch

londer *n.m* **londrys** gutter

loneth *n.f* **lonethi** kidney. **hogen vewin ha loneth** *n.f* steak and kidney pie

longya *vb* belong

lonn *n.m* **lonnow** (**lodhen**) bullock; young ox

loor *n.f* **loryow** moon

loos *adj* grey; mouldy

loos les *n.coll* mugwort

looth *n.m* **lothow** tribe

lorden *n.m* **lordenyon** clown

lorek I (*offensive*) *adj* lunatic **II** *n.m* **lorogyon** lunatic; maniac

lorel (1) *n,m* **lorels** vagrant; rascal

lorel (2) *adj* lunar

lorell *n.f* **lorellow** satellite

lorgh *n.f* (*m*) **lorghow** staff; cane; pole. **lorgh horn** *n.f* (*m*) crowbar

los *adj* soiled

losanj *n.m* **losanjys** lozenge. **losanj pas** *n.m* cough lozenge; cough sweet

loselwas *n.m* **loselwesyon** (*offensive*) tramp

losi *vb* go mouldy

losk *n.m* **loskow** burn

loskaberth *n.m* **loskaberthow** holocaust

loskadow *adj* flammable

loskrians *n.m* **loskriansow** arson

loskrias *n.m* **loskriysi** arsonist

loskven *n.m* (*element*) **loskveyn** sulphur

loskvenydh *n.m* **loskvenydhyow** volcano

loskvenydhyek *adj* volcanic

losonieth *n.f* botany

losoniethek *adj* botanical

losow *n.coll* herbs; plants

losowa *vb* gather plants

losow an bara *n.coll* coriander

losow an bleydh *n.coll* wolf's bane; monkshood

losow an Drynsys *n.f* heartsease; wild pansy

losow an gath *n.coll* catmint; catnip

losow an hav *n.coll* lily of the valley

losowedh *n.m* vegetation

losoweger *n.m* **losowegoryon** vegetarian

losowek *adj* vegetarian

losow eledh *n.coll* angelica (*wild celery*)

losowen *n.f* **losowennow** herb; plant

losow lagas *n.coll* celandine

losow S. Jowan *n.coll* St John's Wort

losow troos ebel *n.coll* coltsfoot

lost *n.m* tail; queue. **gul lost** *vb* queue

lost an gath *n.m* reedmace

lostek *adj* big-tailed; bushy-tailed

losten *n.f* **lostennow** skirt. **losten albanek, losten vrith** *n.f* kilt. **losten vrith kernewek** *n.f* Cornish kilt

lostledan *n.m* **lostledanes** beaver

lostleverel *vb* prompt

lost margh *n.m* horsetail
lostya *vb* queue; form a queue
losvelyn *adj* beige
lothel *adj* tribal
loub *n.m* **loubyow** sludge
louba *vb* lubricate
loubek *adj* slimy
Loundres *top n.m* London
lovan *n.f* **lovanow** rope. **lagha an lovan** *n.f* lynch law. **skeul lovan** *n.f* rope ladder
lovrek *adj* mangy
lovryjyon *n.pl* leprosy
lowarn *n.m* **lewern** fox
lowarnik *n.m* **lewernigow** fox cub
lowarth *n.m* **lowarthyow** garden. **lowarth losow** *n.m* market garden
lowartha *vb* garden
lowarther *n.m* **lowarthoryon** gardener
lowen *adj* glad; happy. **pur lowen** delighted
lowena *n.f* **lowenedhow** happiness; bliss; cheer; joy. **lowena dhis/dhywgh!** greetings!
lowender *n.m* mirth; celebration; enjoyment. **Lowender Peran** *n.m* 'Perran's Mirth' (*Celtic music festival*)
lowenek *adj* cheerful; gay; happy; jolly; joyful; merry
lowenhe *vb* (*intransitive*) rejoice; (*transitive*) make happy; delight
lower *adj* many; much
lown *n.m* **lownyow** blade; flake
lownek *adj* flaky
lownya *vb* flake
lowr I *adj* adequate; ample; considerable; enough; plenty; sizeable **II** *adv* quite; sufficiently. **da lowr** OK; all right. **lowr a²** enough of; galore. **lowr a bewasow** prizes galore
lows *adj* loose
lu *n.m* **luyow** army; military; troop. **lu lestri** *n.m* fleet
lugarn *n.m* **lugern** lamp; lantern. **bocka lugarn** *n.m* genie

lughes *n.coll* lightning
lughesen *n.f* **lughesennow** bolt of lightning; flash
lughesi *vb* flash
lughwrians *n.m* photosynthesis
lulyn *n.f* **lulynnow** anchorage
Lun *n.m* Monday
lust *n.m* **lustys** lust
lusu *n.coll* ashes
lusuegyn *n.m* **lusuegynnow** ashtray
lusuek *adj* ashen
lusuen *n.f* **lusuennow** piece of ash
lut *n.m* **lutys** lute
lyha *adj* least; minimal; minimum. **dhe'n lyha** at least
lyjyon *n.m* **lyjyons** legion
lymm *adj* acute; sharp; keen; piercing. **daffar lymm** *n.m* cutlery
lymma *vb* sharpen
lymmaval *n.m* **lymmavalow** lemon
lymmelin *n.m* **lymmelinyow** acute angle
lymna *vb* illustrate; paint
lymnans *n.m* **lymnansow** illustration; painting; picture
lymner *n.m* **lymnoryon** painter; artist; illustrator
lynn *n.f* **lynnyn** lake
lys *n.f* **lysow** court
lyskanasedh *n.m* diplomacy
lyskanasek *adj* diplomatic
lyskannas *n.f* **lyskanasow** diplomat
lysten *n.f* **lystennow** bandage
lystenna *vb* bandage
lyther *n.m* **lytherow** letter. **kist lytherow** *n.f* letterbox. **lyther nowodhow** *n.m* newsletter
lytherdol *n.m* **lytherdollow** postage
lytheren *n.f* **lytherennow** letter; character
lytherenans *n.m* **lytherenansow** spelling
lytherenieth *n.f* orthography
lytherenna *vb* spell
lytherennek *n.f* **lytherenegi** alphabet

lythervowes *n.f* **lythervowysi** postwoman
lytherwas *n.m* **lytherwesyon** postman
lyver *n.m* **lyvrow** book. **argh lyvrow** *n.f* bookcase. **lyver akontow** *n.m* account book. **lyver dedhyow** *n.m* calendar. **lyver kudhlen gales** *n.m* hardback. **lyver kudhlen vedhel** *n.m* paperback. **lyver kuntel** *n.m* album. **lyver notennow** *n.m* notebook. **lyver**

skol *n.m* schoolbook. **lyver termyn** *n.m* magazine; periodical
lyverji *n.m* **lyverjiow** bookshop
lyvermerk *n.m* **lyvermerkyow** bookmark
lyverva *n.f* **lyvervaow** library
lyveryas *n.m* **lyverysi** librarian
lyvrik *n.m* **lyvrigow** booklet
lyvryn *n.f* **lyvrynnow** booklet

M

'm *prn* (*infixed*) me; (*poss. adj*) my
ma *adj* (*demonstrative*) this. **an gath ma** this cat
-ma *prn* (*enclitic pronoun*) I; me
mab *n.m* **mebyon** son. **mab den** *n.m* humankind. **mab meythrin** *n.m* foster-son. **mab wynn** *n.m* grandson. **Mebyon Kernow** *n.pl* Sons of Cornwall (*party*)
maban *n.m* **mebyn** little son
mab-gov *n.m* **mebyon-gov** smith's apprentice
mabyar *n.f* **mabyer** chick
madama *n.f* **madamys** madam; milady
madra *n.m* **madrow** groundsel
madra bras *n.m* **madrow bras** ragwort
maga *vb* feed; foster; nourish; nurse; nurture; raise; rear
maga[5] *cnj* as. **maga ta** as well; also
ma'gan *contr* so that we
ma'gas *contr* so that you (*pl*)
magereth *n.f* nurture
maghteth *n.f* **maghtethyon** maid; maiden
maglen *n.f* **maglennow** (*mechanical*) gear; trap. **maglen dhelergh** *n.f* reverse gear
maglenna *vb* trap; tangle; change gear. **maglenna 'bann** change up. **maglenna 'nans** change down

magli *vb* tangle
magor *n.f* **magoryow** ruin
magores *n.f* **magoresow** nanny
magus *adj* nutritious
majenta *adj* magenta
Makedoni *top n.f* Macedonia
Makedonian *n.m* **Makedonians** Macedonian
Makedoniek *n.m* Macedonian language
makedoniek *adj* Macedonian
mal *int* pest
mala *vb* grind
malan *n.m* **malanes** devil
malaria *n.m* (*med*) malaria
malbew *int* plague. **malbew damm** plague take
malell *n.f* **malellow** (*tool*) grinder
maler *n.m* **maloryon** grinder
mall *n.m* **mallow** haste; keenness; eagerness. **mall yw genev hy metya** I am eager to meet her
mallborth *n.m* **mallborthow** emergency exit
malow *n.coll* common mallow
malowen *n.f* **malowennow** common mallow
malowen geunek *n.f* **malowennow keunek** marsh mallow
malow keunek *n.coll* marsh mallow

malow lowarth *n.coll* hollyhock

Malta *top n.m* Malta

Maltek *n.m* Maltese language

maltek *adj* Maltese

Maltyas *n.m* **Maltysi** Maltese

mamm *n.f* **mammow** mother; mum. **mamm vesydh** *n.f* godmother. **mamm wynn** *n.f* grandmother

mammel *adj* maternal

mammeth *n.f* **mamethow** wet nurse

mammfurv *n.f* **mammfurvow, mammfurvyow** original; original version

mammik *n.f* **mamigow** mummy

mammrewl *n.f* **mammrewlys** matriarchy

mammskrif *n.m* **mammskrifow** original text

mammvro *n.f* **mammvroyow** mother country; motherland

mammyeth *n.f* mother tongue

mamoleth *n.f* motherhood; maternity. **kummyas mamoleth** *n.m* maternity leave. **diberthva vamoleth** *n.f* maternity ward

mamveth *n.f* **mamvethow** foster-mother

managh *n.m* **menegh** monk

managhek *adj* monastic

managhti *n.m* **managhtiow** monastery

mandragora *n.m* mandrake

manek (1) *adj* manic (*med*)

manek (2) *n.f* **manegow** glove. **manek blat** *n.f*, **manegow plat** gauntlet

manek lowarn *n.f* **manegow lowarn** foxglove

maner (1) *n.f* **maners, manerow** manner; custom; way. **maners, manerow** *n.pl* morals. **yn ken maner** otherwise. **yn kepar maner** similarly. **y'n keth vaner** similarly

maner (2) *n.m* **maners, manoryow** manor

manerji *n.m* **manerjiow** manor house

manerus *adj* affected

maneruster *n.m* affectation

manga *n.m* **mangas** manga; Japanese comic

mango *n.m* **mangos** mango

mania *n.m* mania (*med*)

mann I *n.m* nothing; nil; nought **II** *num* zero **III** *adv* at all

mann-² *prfx* petty

mannbluv *n.coll* down; fine feathers; fluff

mannbluvek *adj* fluffy

mannbluven *n.f* **mannbluvennow** fine feather

mannvona *n.coll* petty cash

Manow *top n.f* Isle of Man; Man

Manowek *n.m* Manx language

manowek *adj* Manx

mansyon *n.m* **mansyons** mansion

mantedh *n.coll* stones (*in the body*)

mantel *n.f* **mantylli** cloak; coat; mantle. **mantel nos** *n.f* dressing gown. **mantel law** *n.f* raincoat

mantol *n.f* **mantolyow** balance; scales

manykyn *n.m, n.f* **manykyns** mannequin

manylya *vb* detail

manylyon *n.pl* details

mappa *n.m* **mappys, mappow** map

mappalyver *n.m* **mappalyvrow** atlas

mar *n.m* doubt. **heb mar** without doubt; of course

mar² *adv* as; so. **mar² … avel** (*used with a noun or pronoun*) as … as. **mar² … dell²** (*used with a verb*) as … as

mar⁴ *cnj* if. **mar pleg** (if you) please

mara⁴ *cnj* if

maras *cnj* if

marbel *n.m* (*rock*) marble

marblen *n.f* **marblennow** (*toy*) marble

marchont *n.m* **marchons** merchant; salesman; trader

margarin *n.m* margarine

margh *n.m* **mergh** horse. **margh asen** *n.m* jackass. **margh dall** *n.m* blind man's buff. **margh-leska** *n.m* rocking

horse. **margh-skrifa** *n.m* easel. **nader**
margh *n.f* dragonfly

marghador *n.m* **marghadoryon**
merchant

marghas *n.f* **marghasow** market.
marghas puskes *n.f* fish market.
marghas stock *n.f* stock market

marghasa *vb* market; (*at a market*) shop;
trade

marghasadow *adj* marketable

marghasans *n.m* marketing

marghasva *n.f* **marghasvaow** market
place

marghek *n.m* **marghogyon** knight;
rider

marghnerth *n.m* **marghnerthow**
horse-power

marghogeth I *n.f* **marghogethow** ride
on a horse; riding **II** *vb* ride a horse

marghredenen *n.f* male fern

marghredik *n.m* **marghredigow**
horseradish

marghti *n.m* **marghtiow** stable

marghvran *n.f* **marghvrini** raven

marksydh *n.m* **marksydhyon** Marxist

marksydhek *adj* Marxist

Marksydhieth *n.f* Marxism

markyans *n.m* **markyansow** marking

marnas *cnj* except; unless

marner *n.m* **marners, marnoryon**
mariner; sailor; seaman

marow I *adj* dead; switched off **II** *n.m*
re varow dead person

marowvor *n.m* neap-tide

mars *cnj* if

martesen *adv* maybe; perhaps; possibly

marth *n.m* **marthow** amazement;
surprise; wonder. **marth yw genev,**
yma marth dhymm I am surprised.
gorra marth yn amaze

marthek *adj* remarkable

marthus *n.m* **marthusyon, marthusi,**
marthusow marvel; miracle

marthys I *adj* amazing; fabulous;
marvellous; remarkable; terrific;

wonderful **II** *adv* amazingly;
fabulously; marvellously; remarkably;
surprisingly; wonderfully

marvor *n.m* neap-tide

marwel *adj* deadly; mortal

marwostel *n.m* **marwostlow** mortgage

marwostla *vb* mortgage

mas *adj* good; respectable; moral. **yn**
fas *adv* properly

maseth *n.f* **masethow** morality

mask *n.m* **maskow** mask

maskot *n.m* **maskotys** mascot

mason *n.m* **masons** mason

masvresek *adj* well-intentioned

mater *n.m* **maters, materyow** issue;
matter. **pandr'yw an mater?** what's
the matter?

matras *n.m* **matrassow** mattress

maw *n.m* **mebyon** boy; lad

may[5] **(th)** *prn* which. **(rag) may**[5] *cnj* so
that

maylya *vb* wrap; bind

maylyans *n.m* **maylyansow** wrapping

maylyer *n.m* **maylyers** envelope

mayn *n.m* **maynys** means; agency;
instrument; mediator

maynek *adj* instrumental

mayni I *n.m* **mayniow** crew;
household; troop; staff (*employees*) **II**
a'n mayni *adj* domestic

maynor *n.m* **maynoryon** agent

maynorieth *n.f* **maynoriethow** agency.
maynorieth-asvaba *n.f* adoption
agency

maystri *n.m* control; mastery. **gul**
maystri war[2] exercise control over;
face down; tyrannise

Me *n.m* May

mebel *n.m* furniture. **heb mebel**
unfurnished

mebla *vb* furnish

medalen *n.f* **medalennow,** medal.
medalen vras *n.f* medallion

meder *n.m* **medrow** aim

medh *n.m* mead; hydromel. **medh oy** *n.m* egg flip

medhador *n.m* **medhadoryon** mediator

medhegel *adj* medical

medhegieth *n.f* medical science. **medhegieth lagasow** *n.f* ophthalmology

medhegiethel *adj* medicinal

medhegneth *n.f* **medhegnethow** medicine; medication

medhegva *n.f* **medhegvaow** clinic; doctor's surgery

medhegvael *adj* clinical

medhek *n.m* **medhogyon** doctor; physician. **hwithrans medhek** *n.m* medical examination. **medhek brys** *n.m* psychiatrist. **medhek dens** *n.m* dentist. **medhek fleghes** *n.m* paediatrician. **medhek kroghen** *n.m* dermatologist. **medhek lagasow** *n.m* ophthalmologist. **medhek mayni** *n.m* general practitioner

medhel I *adj* soft. **lyver kudhlen vedhel** *n.m* paperback **II** *adj* non-alcoholic

medhelhe *vb* soften; lenite; absorb (*a shock or blow*)

medhelheans *n.m* **medhelheansow** lenition

medhelweyth *n.m* software

medhles *n.m* meadowsweet

medhoges an gors *n.f* all-heal; common valerian

medhoges las *n.f* self-heal

medhow *adj* drunk; intoxicated

medhwenep *n.m* drunkenness; intoxication

medhwi *vb* make drunk; intoxicate

medhwynsi *n.m* drunkenness

medra *vb* aim

medras *n.m* **medrasow** aim; goal; object

medynor *n.f* **medynoryow** hinge

megabayt *n.m* **megabaytys** megabyte

meghin *n.m* bacon

megi *vb* smoke; fume. **megi difennys** no smoking

megrim *n.m* migraine

megyans *n.m* nutrition

megys *adj* nourished; reared. **megys orth** nourished by

mekanek *n.f* mechanics

Meksikan *n.m* **Meksikans** Mexican

meksikan *adj* Mexican

Meksiko *top n.m* Mexico

mel *n.m* honey

mela *vb* gather honey

melder *n.m* **melderyow** sweetness; darling; (*terms of endearment*) love

melhwen *n.f* **melhwennow** slug

melhwes *n.coll* snails; slugs

melhwesek *adj* snail-like

melhwesen *n.f* **melhwesennow** snail; slug

melhwessa *vb* catch snails

melhwioges *n.f* **melhwiogesow** tortoise

melin *n.f* **melinyow** mill. **melin buber** *n.f* pepper mill. **melin dhowr** *n.f* water mill. **melin wyns** *n.f* windmill

meliner *n.m* **melinoryon** miller

melinji *n.m* **melinjiow** millhouse

melion *n.coll* violet

melion an gors *n.coll* marsh violet

melion an ki *n.coll* dog violet

melionen *n.f* **melionennow** violet

melionen velyn *n.f* **melionennow melyn** yellow pansy

melionen velyseth *n.f* **melionennow melyseth** sweet violet

melion lowarth *n.coll* garden pansy

melion melyn *n.coll* yellow pansy

melion melyseth *n.coll* sweet violet

mell *n.m* **mellow** joint; link; connection. **mell dorn** *n.m* knuckle. **mell keyn** *n.m* spine

mellek *adj* jointed

mellya *vb* meddle; interfere

mellyans *n.m* **mellyansow** interference

mellyer *n.m* **mellyoryon** meddler; busybody. **mellyer dader** *n.m* do-gooder

mellyon *n.coll* clover

mellyon an Werghes *n.coll* field rocket (*yellow rocket*)

mellyonen *n.f* **mellyonennow** clover. **mellyonen beder delen** *n.f* four-leaf clover

melodi *n.m* **melodis** melody

melodius *adj* melodious

melon *n.m* **melonyow** melon

melyas *vb* grind

melyn *adj* yellow; fair; blonde. **kleves melyn** *n.m* jaundice. **melyn hy blew** *n.f* blonde

melynek banal *n.m* **melynoges banal** greenfinch

melynek eythin *n.m* **melynoges eythin** yellowhammer

melynek gwern *n.m* **melynoges gwern** siskin

melynek penn rudh *n.m* **melynoges penn rudh** goldfinch

melynik *adj* yellowish; jaundiced

melyn oy *n.m* **melynyow oy** egg yolk

melys *adj* very sweet; honeyed

melyshe *vb* sweeten

melyssand *n.m* **melyssandys** dessert; pudding

melysugen *n.m* **melysugenyow** syrup

men *n.m* **meyn** stone. **men bedh** *n.m* gravestone; tombstone. **men bras** *n.m* megalith. **men du** *n.m* jet. **menhir** *n.m* **menhiryon** longstone; menhir. **men kov** *n.m* monument; memorial. **men kowas** *n.m* meteorite. **men-pobas** *n.m* griddle

menedhorieth *n.f* mountaineering

menedhyek *adj* mountainous

menedhyer *n.m* **menedhyoryon** mountaineer

menegek *adj* indicative. **gis menegek** *n.m* indicative mood

meneges *vb* admit; confess; indicate; mention; state

meneghi *n.m* **meneghiow** asylum; refuge

meneghiji *n.m* **meneghijiow** place of asylum; sanctuary

menegva *n.f* **menegvaow** index; catalogue

menegyans *n.m* **menegyansow** statement

menek *n.m* **menegow** indication; mention

menestrouthi *n.m* (instrumental) music; minstrelsy

mengleudh *n.m* **mengleudhyow** quarry

mengleudhyer *n.m* **mengleudhyoryon** quarry worker

menhe *vb* petrify

menhesen *n.f* **menhesennow** fossil

menopos *n.m* menopause

menowes *n.f* **menowesow** awl

menowgh *adj* frequent; often. **boghes venowgh** *adv* seldom. **yn fenowgh** *adv* frequently; regularly

menowghedh *n.m* (*physics*) **menowghedhyow** frequency

menowghter *n.m* **menowghteryow** frequency

menoyl *n.m* **menoylys** petrol

menstrel *n.m* **menstrels** musician; minstrel

menta *n.f* mint

menta an dowr *n.f* water mint

menta aval *n.f* apple mint

menta riel *n.f* pennyroyal

menta wuwdhel *n.f* spearmint

mentena *vb* maintain

mentenour *n.m* **mentenouryon, mentenours** maintainer; conservative

mentenya *vb* maintain

mentons *n.m* maintenance. **kostow mentons** *n.pl* maintenance costs

menweyth *n.m* masonry

menydh *n.m* **menydhyow** mountain; hill. **war venydh** on a mountain; uphill

menyster *n.m* **menystrys, menystroryon** minister

menystra *vb* administer; manage; supervise

menystrans *n.m* **menystransow** administration; management; ministry; supervision

menystrek *adj* administrative

menystrer *n.m* **menystroryon** administrator

meppik *n.m* **meppigow** little son

mer (1) *n.m* **meryon** mayor

mer (2) *n.m* (*bone*) marrow

mera *vb* snivel

merci *n.m* mercy. **kemeres merci a²** have mercy on. **kria merci war nebonan** beg mercy from somebody

Mergher *n.m* Mercury, **dy'Mergher** Wednesday

mergherles fug *n.m* dog's mercury

meridian I *adj* meridian II *n.m* **meridians** meridian

merit *n.m* **meritys** merit

merji *n.m* **merjiow** home of the mayor

merk *n.m* **merkys** mark. **merk devyn** *n.m* quotation mark.

merkya *vb* mark; note; perceive; notice

merkyl *n.m* **merklys** miracle

merlosow *n.coll* asparagus

merlosowen *n.f* **merlosowennow** asparagus plant

mernans *n.m* **mernansow** death. **kevradh mernans** *n.m* death rate. **ronk mernans** *n.m* death rattle

merther *n.m* **mertheryon** martyr

mertherya *vb* martyr

merwel *vb* die; decease; pass away; (*light, flame*) go out

meryw *n.coll* junipers

merywen *n.f* **merywennow** juniper

mes (1) *cnj* but

mes (2) I *adv* out; outside II *n.m* **mesyow** open country. **keas mes** exclude. **mes a'n lester** overboard. **mes a'y skians** out of his mind

mes (3) *n.coll* acorns. **byskon mes** *n.f* acorn cup

mesa *vb* gather acorns

mesen *n.f* **mesennow** acorn

meskel *n.coll* mussels

meskist *n.f* (*email*) outbox

meskla *vb* gather mussels

mesklen *n.f* **mesklennow** mussel

mesporth *n.m* **mesporthow** exit. **mesporth tan** *n.m* fire exit

messach *n.m* **messajys** message. **messach desempis** *n.m* instant message. **messach tekst** *n.m* text message

messajya *vb* message

messianek *adj* messianic

messias *n.m* **messiasow** messiah

Mester *n.m* Mr

mester *n.m* **mestrysi** master; mister; boss. **mester cirk** *n.m* ringmaster

Mestres *n.f* **Mestresow** Ms; Miss (*adult woman*)

mestres *n.f* **mestresow** mistress; (*female*) boss

Mestresik *n.f* **Mestresigow** Miss (*girl*)

mestrev *n.f* **mestrevow** suburb

mestronieth *n.f* **mestroniethow** master's degree

mestrynses *n.m* dominion

mesya *vb* field

metaboledh *n.m* **metaboledhow** metabolism

metabolek *adj* metabolic

metafor *n.m* **metaforow** metaphor

metelyek *adj* metallic

meter *n.m* **metrow** metre

meth *n.f* **methow** shame. **kemeres meth** be ashamed. **rag meth!** for shame!

methardak *n.m* **methardagow** stalemate

methek *adj* ashamed

Metheven *n.m* June

method *n.m* **methodys** method

Methodek *adj* Methodist

methodek *adj* methodical

Methodydh *n.m* **Methodydhyon** Methodist

methus *adj* shameful; embarassing

methys *adj* shamed

metol *n.m* **metelyow** metal

metya *vb* meet; encounter. **metya nebonan** meet somebody. **metya gans nebonan** meet with somebody. **metya orth nebonan** encounter somebody

metyans *n.m* **metyansow** meeting; encounter

meur *adj* great; grand; large; substantial. **Breten Veur** *n.f* Great Britain. **meur a**^{2} lots (many of); many; much. **meurastaji** thank you. **meur y golon** magnanimous. **tir meur** *n.m* mainland. **yn mar veur dell**^{2} for as much as. **yn feur** greatly

meur-^{2} *prfx* great-; major

meuredh *n.m* majesty

meuredhek *adj* majestic

meurgerys *adj* beloved

meurgolonnek *adj* great-hearted

meurlith *n.f* **meurlithes** halibut

Meurth *n.m* March; Mars

meurthek *adj* martian

meus *n.m* **meusi** thumb. **diskwedhes an meus** thumb a lift

meusva *n.f* **meusvaow** inch

meusya *vb* hitchhike

mewgh *n.m* **mewghyow** guarantee; bail; bond. **gasa mewgh** jump bail

mewghya *vb* guarantee; stand bail

mewl *n.m* bad luck. **re'gas bo mewl!** bad luck to you! (*pl*)

meyl *n.m* **meyli** (*fish*) mullet

meythrin *vb* foster; raise (a child); rear. **mab meythrin** *n.m* foster-son. **myrgh**

veythrin *n.f* foster-daughter. **skol veythrin** *n.f* nursery school

meythrinva *n.f* **meythrinvaow** nursery

mik *n.m* **mikow** squeak. **heb gul gik na mik** stock-still. **na gik na mik** not a sound

mil *n.m* **miles** animal

mil^2 *num, n.m* **milyow** thousand

milblek *adj* thousandfold

mildam *n.m* jigsaw

mildir *n.m* **mildiryow** mile

miliga *vb* curse

milimeter *n.m* **milimetrow** millimetre

milonieth *n.f* zoology

miloniethel *adj* zoological

milus *adj* brutal

miluster *n.m* brutality

milva *n.f* **milvaow** zoo

milvedhegiethel *adj* veterinary

milvedhek *n.m* **milvedhogyon** vet, veterinary surgeon

milves *num* thousandth

milvil^2 *num* **milvilyow** million

milvilves *num* millionth

milvilwas *n.m* **milvilwesyon** millionaire

milvilweyth *adv* a million times

milvledhen *n.f* **milvledhynnyow** millennium

milwell *adj* far better

milweth *adj* far worse

milweyth *adv* a thousand times

milyon *num* **milyonow** million

mim *n.m* **mimyow** mime; mimic

mimya *vb* mime; mimic

min *n.m* **minow, minyow, minyon** mouth

minfel *n.m* yarrow

mingow *adj* lying; dishonest

mingreft *n.m* make-up; cosmetic

minhwarth *n.m* **minhwarthow** smile

minhwerthin *vb* smile

minliw *n.m* **minliwyow** lipstick

minor *n.m* **minors** minor

minoryta *n.m* **minorytys** minority

minvlew *n.coll* moustache

minvlewen *n.f* **minvlewennow** whisker

minya *vb* nuzzle

miow *n.m* meow

miowal *vb* meow; mew

mir *n.m* **mirow** appearance; look. **gwari mir** *n.m* miracle play

miraj *n.m* **mirajys** mirage

mirer *n.m* **miroryon** spectator

mires *vb* look; behold. **mires dhe**^{2} watch over. **mires orth** look at (a specific object or person); regard. **mires orth an bellwolok** watch television. **mires stark orth** stare at. **mires war**^{2} look upon; consider; contemplate

mirva *n.f* **mirvaow** gallery; exhibition room

mis *n.m* **misyow** month. **hanter mis** *n.m* fortnight. **mis Genver** *n.m* January. **mis Hwevrer, mis Hwevrel** *n.m* February. **mis Meurth** *n.m* March. **mis Ebrel** *n.m* April. **mis Me** *n.m* May. **mis Metheven** *n.m* June. **mis Gortheren** *n.m* July. **mis Gwynngala** *n.m* September. **mis Hedra** *n.m* October. **mis Du** *n.m* November. **mis Kevardhu** *n.m* December. **mis mel** *n.m* honeymoon

misek *adj, adv* monthly

mistal *n.m* **mistalyow** monthly rate

misyek *adj, adv* monthly

misyow *n.pl* menstruation

mo *n.m* **moyow** dusk

model gis *n.m* **modelys is** model (*fashion*)

modem *n.m* **modems** modem

modrebik *n.f* **modrebigow** auntie

modrep *n.f* **modrebedh** aunt

mog *n.m* smoke; fume

moga *vb* choke

mogh *n.pl* pigs; swine. **kig mogh** *n.m* pork

moghhe *vb* amplify; augment; increase; zoom in

mol *n.m* **molyow** hardened blood

mola *vb* clot

Moldavek *n.m* Moldavian language

moldavek *adj* Moldavian

Moldavian *n.m* **Moldavians** Moldavian

Moldova *top n.f* Moldova

moldra *vb* murder

moldrans *n.m* **moldransow** murder

moldrer *n.m* **moldroryon** murderer

moldrys *adj* murdered

molekulen *n.f* **molekulennow** molecule

molgh *n.f* **molghi** thrush

molgh dhu *n.f* **molghi du** blackbird

molgh las *n.f* **molghi glas** fieldfare

molgh loos *n.f* **molghi loos** song thrush

molgh gerdhin *n.f* **molghi kerdhin** mistle thrush

molgh dhowr *n.f* **molghi dowr** dipper

molleth *n.f* **mollothow** curse. **molleth Duw!** damn!

mollethi *vb* curse

mollothek *adj* cursed

molys *adj* clotted. **dehen molys** *n.m* clotted cream

momentom *n.m* momentum

mon *n.m* manure

mona *n.coll* cash; change; money. **mona kemmyn** *n.coll* currency

mones *vb* (= **mos**) go; become

monesek *adj* monetary

mong *n.f* **mongow** mane

mongel *n.f* **mongellow** collar

mongleudh *n.m* **mongleudhyow** opencast mine

monopolegieth *n.f* monopoly

monopoli *n.m* **monopolis** monopoly

mool *adj* bald; bare

moon (1) *adj* thin; slim; slender

moon (2) *n.m* **monyow** mineral

moos *n.f* **mosow** table. **settya moos** set the table

mooth *n.m* **mothow** breakdown

mor (1) *n.coll* berries. **mor du** *n.coll* blackberries

mor (2) *n.m* **moryow** sea. **atal mor** *n.coll* flotsam and jetsam. **dres mor** overseas; abroad. **mor Adriatek** *n.m* Adriatic. **mor bras** *n.m* ocean. **gaver vor** *n.f* crayfish. **pleg mor** *n.m* bay. **yn mor** at sea

mora (1) *vb* put to sea

mora (2) *vb* gather berries

morben *n.m* **morbennow** mallet

morblek *n.m* **morblegow** gulf

mordardh *n.m* surf

mordardha *vb* surf

mordhos *n.f* **mordhosow**, *dl* **diwvordhos** thigh; haunch. **mordhos hogh** *n.f* ham

Mordir Nowydh *top n.m* New Zealand

mordon *n.f* **mordonnow** sea-wave

mordrik *n.m* low tide

mordu *adj* navy (*colour*)

moredh *n.m* **moredhow** melancholy

moredhek *adj* melancholic; miserable; sorrowful

morek *adj* maritime

morel (1) *adj* jet-black

morel (2) *n.m* belladonna; deadly nightshade

moren (1) *n.f* **morenyon** lass; wench

moren (2) *n.f* **morennow** berry

moren bries *n.f* **morenyon pries** bridesmaid

moren dhu *n.f* **morennow du** blackberry

moresk *n.coll* sea-sedge

moresken *n.f* **moreskennow** sea-sedge

morfordh *n.f* **morfordhow** seaway

morgaryans *n.m* lighterage

morgelyn *n.coll* eryngo; sea holly

morgi *n.m* **morgeun** dogfish

morgowl *n.coll* seakale

morgowles *n.coll* jellyfish

morgowlesen *n.f* **morgowlesennow** jellyfish

morgroban *n.m* **morgrobanes** turtle

morhogh *n.m* **morhoghes** porpoise

morlader *n.m* **morladron** pirate

morladrynsi *n.m* piracy

morlanow *n.m* **morlanowyow** high tide

morlu *n.m* **morluyow** navy

mornaswydh *n.f* **mornaswydhow** sea compass

morrep *n.m* **morrebow** seashore

morsort *n.m* **morsortes** sea urchin

morthol *n.m* **mortholyow** hammer

mortholya *vb* hammer

mortholys *adj* hammered

mortid *n.m* **mortidys** tide

morverk *n.m* **morverkys** buoy

morviaj *n.m* **morviajys, morviajyow** sea journey; cruise

morviajya *vb* cruise

morvil *n.m* **morviles** whale

morvleydh *n.m* **morvleydhes** shark

morvoren *n.f* **morvoronyon** mermaid

morvran *n.f* **morvrini** cormorant

morvugh *n.f* **morvughes** walrus

morwas *n.m* **morwesyon** mariner

moryon *n.coll* ants

moryonen *n.f* **moryonennow** ant; (*offensive*) tourist

mos *vb* go; become. **mos dhe arvow** take up arms. **mos dhe goll** be lost; go missing. **mos dhe-ves** go away. **mos ha bos** become. **mos re bell** go too far; exaggerate. **mos war-barth ha** accompany someone. **mos y'n fordh** be on one's way. **mos yn-mes** go out. **mos yn-mes gans** date (*a person*)

mosegi *vb* stink; smell

mosek *adj* stinking; pungent; rank

mosen *n.f* **mosennow** table (*tabular data*). **An Vosen Beriodek** The Periodic Table

mosk *n.m* **moskow** mosque

moskito *n.m* **moskitos** mosquito**

Moslem I *n.m* **Moslemyon** Muslim **II** *adj* Muslim

mosokter *n.m* stink; pungency

mostedhes *n.m* dirt; filth

mosten *n.f* **mostennow** stain

mostya *vb* make dirty; soil

mostys *adj* soiled; contaminated

motorydh *n.m* **motorydhyon** motorist

moutya *vb* sulk

moutyans *n.m* **moutyansow** sulk

movadow *adj* (*spiritually*) movable

movya *vb* move; arouse; incite; motivate; persuade. **es y vovya** emotionally unstable; nervous. **movya nebonan may hwrello neppyth** persuade somebody to do something

movyans *n.m* **movyansow** movement; motivation. **Movyans Skolyow Meythrin** *n.m* Nursery School Movement

mowa *n.m* **mowys** grimace. **gul mowa** *vb* grimace

mowes *n.f* **mowysi** girl; lass

moy *adj, adv* more; another; extra. **byth moy** nor yet; still more. **moy ha moy** increasing(ly). **moy po le** more or less

moyha *adj, adv* most; maximum

mul *n.m* **mules** mule

munys *adj* tiny; little; minute; miniature; small

munysen *n.f* **munysennow** miniature

mus I *adj* mad **II** *n.m* (*offensive*) **musyon** madman

musellek *adj* thick-lipped

muskegi *vb* (*transitive*) madden; derange; drive insane; (*intransitive*) go mad; go insane

muskoges *n.f* **muskogesow** (*offensive*) madwoman; (*female*) lunatic

muskok I *adj* crazy; insane; mad **II** *n.m* (*offensive*) **muskogyon** madman; lunatic

muskotter *n.m* madness; insanity

musur *n.m* **musuryow** measure; moderation. **dres musur** extremely

musura *vb* measure; moderate. **podik-musura** *n.m* measuring jug

musurans *n.m* **musuransow** measurement

musurell *n.f* **musurellow** tape measure

musurys *adj* measured

my *prn* I

myghtern *n.m* **myghternedh** king; (*male*) monarch

myghternes *n.f* **myghternesow** queen; (*female*) monarch

myghterneth *n.f* **myghternethow** kingdom

myghternses *n.m* kingship; monarchy

mygla *vb* cool off

mygyl *adj* lukewarm; tepid; half-hearted

myll *n.f* **mylles** poppy

mylliga *vb* curse; revile

mynchya *vb* play truant

mynchyans *n.m* truancy

mynchyer *n.m* **mynchyoryon** truant

mynn *n.coll* kid goats

mynnas *n.m* **mynasow** purpose; intent; intention

mynnen *n.f* **mynennow** kid goat

mynnes *vb* wish; will; want; intend. **mynnes orth nebonan gul neppyth** wish for somebody to do something

myns I *prn* as many as **II** *n.m* **mynsow** amount; quantity; dimension

mynsek *adj* considerable; sizeable

mynsonieth *n.f* geometry

mynsoniethel *adj* geometric

mynsriv *n.m* **mynsrivow** numerator

mynysen *n.f* **mynysennow** minute

myrgh *n.f* **myrghes** daughter. **myrgh wynn** *n.f* granddaughter. **myrgh veythrin** *n.f* foster-daughter

myser *n.m* **mysoryon** reaper

myshyv *n.m* **myshevys** disaster

mysi *vb* harvest; reap

mysk *n.m* midst. **y'gan mysk** among us. **y'gas mysk** among you (pl). **y'ga mysk** among them
myska *vb* blend; mingle
myskreydhek *adj* hybrid
mystrest *n.m* mistrust

mystrestya *vb* mistrust
myth *n.m* **mythys** myth
mythologieth *n.f* mythology
myttin *n.m* **myttinyow** morning
myttinweyth I *adv* in the morning II *n.m* **myttinweythyow** morning time

N

'n (1) *prn (infixed)* him
'n (2) *art (abbrev)* (= **an**) the. **an gath ha'n ki** the cat and the dog
na (1) I *int* no! II *adv* not. **na X na Y** neither X nor Y. **na hwath** not yet. **na fella** no longer. **na fors** no matter
na (2) *int* no; nay
na (3) *adj (demonstrative)* that. **an gath na** that cat
na² I *cnj* that not; nor II *part (negative verbal particle)* not
Nadelik *n.m* Christmas. **Dydh Nadelik** *n.m* Christmas day. **gwydh Nadelik** *n.coll* Christmas trees. **Nadelik lowen!** Merry Christmas!
nader *n.f* **nadres** adder
nader margh *n.f* dragonfly
naderles *n.m* viper's bugloss
nadh *n.m* chopping
nadha *vb* chop
nag I *cnj* nor II *part* not; that not
na'ga *contr* nor their
na'gan *contr* nor our
na'gas *contr* nor your
nagh *n.m* **naghow** refusal
nagha *vb* deny; decline; object; refuse; renounce
nagonan *prn* no-one; none; not one
nahen *adv* no more
nahyns *adv* not earlier
naker *n.m* **nakrys** kettle-drum
na'm *contr* nor my
namenowgh *adv* rarely; seldom
nameur *adv* not many; not much

namm *n.m* **nammow** spot; stain; blemish; exception. **heb namm** *adv* utterly
namma *vb* spot; stain
namna²(g) *adv* nearly
namnygen *adv* just now
namoy *adv* (not) any more; no more. **nevra namoy** nevermore
naneyl *prn* neither. **na X naneyl Y** neither X nor Y
nans (1) *n.m* **nansow** valley; dale
nans (2) *part* now. **nans yw** ago. **nans yw pymp bledhen** five years ago. **nans yw neppell** not long ago. **nans yw pell** long ago
narkolepsi *n.m* narcolepsy *(med)*
nas *n.f* **nasyow** feature. **fylm nas** *n.m* feature film
naswydh *n.f* **naswedhow** needle
nasya *vb* affect
nath *n.m* **nathes** puffin
na'th⁵ᵃ *contr* nor your *(sg)*
natur *n.f* nature
naturel *adj* natural
natureth *n.f* nature
naw *num* nine
nawves *num* ninth
na'y² *contr* nor his
na'y³ *contr* nor her
neb I *adv* any II *cnj* who III *prn* some. **neb a²** *prn (relative)* who; whom; that. **neb le** anywhere. **neb lies** not many. **neb prys** at any time; sometime. **neb tra** anything. **neb tu** anywhere;

somewhere. **neb tyller** anywhere; somewhere. **neb unn** a particular

nebes I *adj* few; little; slight; some **II** *adv* a little **III** *n.m* few; some. **nebes ha nebes** little by little; piecemeal

nebonan *prn* anyone; anybody; somebody; someone

nebreydh *adj* neuter

nedh *n.coll* nits

nedha *vb* twist

nedhen *n.f* **nedhennow** nit

negedhek *adj* negative

negedhen *n.f* (*photographic*) **negedhennow** negative

negedhys I *adj* apostate **II** *n.m* **negedhysyon** apostate; turncoat

negh *n.m* **neghow** embarassment; fret

neghi *vb* fret

neghus *adj* fretful

negys *n.m* **negysyow** affair; business; errand; transaction. **mones negys** go on an errand. **negys kamm** *n.m* racket; scam

negysyans *n.m* **negysyansow** negotiation

negysyas *vb* negotiate

negysydh *n.m* **negysydhyon** businessman; negotiator

nektar *n.m* **nektars** nectar

nell *n.m* **nellow** power; strength

nemmys *adj* blemished; stained

nen *n.m* **nenyow** ceiling

nenbren *n.m* **nenbrennyer** ridge-pole

neppell *adv* not far. **nans yw neppell** not long ago

neppyth *prn* anything; something

nerth *n.m* **nerthow, nerthyow** might; power; strength; force; energy

nertha *vb* strengthen

nerthedh *n.m* **nerthedhow** power (*physics*)

nerthek *adj* energetic; powerful; robust

nerven *n.f* **nervennow** nerve

nervus *adj* nervous; jittery

nes *adj* nearer; close. **dos nes** come close; approach

nesa *vb* approach

nesadow *adj* approachable

nesarvorel *adj* inshore, nearshore

neshe *vb* approach; near; close

neshevin *n.m* **neshevin** relative; next of kin; (*lexicon*) cognate

neskar *n.m* **neskerens** kin; relation; near relative

nesogas *adj* approximate

nessa *adj* nearer; nearest; next; second; secondary. **pub nessa dydh** every other day

nester *n.m* proximity

-neth *sffx* makes a feminine noun from an adjective

neus *n.coll* threads; yarns

neusen *n.f* **neusennow** thread; yarn

neusenna *vb* thread

neuvell *n.f* **neuvellow** float

neuvella *vb* float

neuvwisk *n.m* swimsuit

neuvya *vb* swim

neuvyer *n.m* **neuvyoryon** swimmer

nev *n.m* **nevow** heaven. **a nev** heavenly

nevek *adj* heavenly

nevra *adv* ever (in the present or future); never (in the present or future). **nevra namoy** nevermore

Nevyon *n.m* Neptune

new *n.f* **newyow** washbasin; sink; trough

newrel *adj* neural

newrologieth *n.f* neurology

newrologydh *n.m* **newrologydhyon** neurologist

newrologyl *adj* neurological

newrosys *n.m* neurosis

newrotek I *adj* neurotic **II** *n.m* **newrotogyon** neurotic

neyj *n.m* **neyjow** flight

neyja *vb* fly; float

neyjer *n.m* **neyjoryon** aviator; flyer

neyth *n.m* **neythow** nest

neythi *vb* nest

neythik *n.m* **neythigow** alcove

ni *prn* we; us; (*enclitic*) we

Nihon *top n.m* Japan

Nihonek *n.m* Japanese language

Nijeri *top n.m* Nigeria

Nijerian *n.m* **Nijerians** Nigerian

nijerian *adj* Nigerian

nikotin *n.m* nicotine

nilon *n.m* nylon. **lodrow nilon** *n.pl* nylons

nith *n.f* **nithow** niece

nitrojen *n.m* (*element*) nitrogen

nivel *n.m* **nivelyow** level; tier. **nivel A** *n.m* A level

niver *n.m* **niverow** number. **niver kesresek** *n.m* serial number. **niver pellgowser** *n.m* phone number

nivera *vb* count; number. **dres nivera** redundant (*supernumerary*)

niverek *adj* numerical

niverell *n.f* **niverellow** counter; counting device

niveren *n.f* **niverennow** numeral

niverennans *n.m* **niverenansow** numbering

niveronieth *n.f* **niveroniethow** arithmetic

niveroniethel *adj* arithmetic

niverus *adj* numerous

niveryans *n.m* **niveryansow** census; count

niwl *n.m* **niwlow** fog; haze; mist

niwlek *adj* misty; hazy; foggy; vague

niwmonia *n.m* (*med*) pneumonia

nobyl I *adj* noble II *n.m* **noblys** noble; nobleman

nogadh *n.m* **nogadhow** (*animal bedding*) litter

Norgagh *top n.m* Norway

Norgaghek *n.m* Norwegian language

norgaghek *adj* Norwegian

Norgaghyas *n.m* **Norgaghysi** Norwegian

normal *adj* normal

normalhe *vb* normalise

normalheans *n.m* **normalheansow** normalisation

normalita *n.m* **normalitys** normality

north *n.m* north. **a'n north** northern

north-est *n.m* north-east

north-west *n.m* north-west

Norvys *n.m* Earth

norvysel *adj* terrestrial

nos (1) *n.f* **nosow** night. **nos da** good night. **derow nos** *n.m* nightfall. **dres nos** overnight. **pows nos** *n.f* nightdress. **pub nos** every night; nightly. **skol nos** *n.f* night school. **yn nos** at night

nos (2) *n.m* **nosow** mark; token

nosedhek *adj* notable

nosweyth I *adv* at night II *n.m* **nosweythyow** night-time

noswikorek *adj* contraband

nosya *vb* notate

nosyans *n.m* **nosyansow** notation

noten *n.f* **notennow** note. **lyver notennow** *n.m* notebook. **noten arghantti** *n.f* banknote

notennyans *n.m* **notenyansow** annotation

noter *n.m* **notoryon** notary; solicitor

noth *adj* bare; naked; nude

nothedh *n.m* nudity

notya *vb* note

notyans *n.m* **notyansow** memo

notyes *adj* (= **notys**) notable

notys *adj* (= **notyes**) notable

nougat *n.m* nougat

novel *n.m* **novelys** novel (*book*)

nowedhi *vb* renew; update

nown *n.m* hunger

nownek *adj* hungry

nownsegves *num* nineteenth

nownsek *num* nineteen

nowedhyans *n.m* **nowedhyansow** innovation

nowodhow *n.pl* news. **nowodhow orth...** news about.... **lyther**

nowodhow *n.m* newsletter. **paper nowodhow** *n.m* newspaper
nowydh *adj, adv* new; fresh; newly; novel. **flamm nowydh, nowydh flamm** brand new. **nowydh genys** newborn. **nowydh gwrys yw genev** I just did it
noy *n.m* **noyens** nephew
nuklerek *adj* nuclear. **atal nuklerek** *n.coll* nuclear waste. **arv nuklerek** *n.f*

nuclear weapon
nuklesen *n.f* **nuklesennow** nucleus (*physics*)
ny² *part* not
nygromons *n.m* necromancy; sorcery
nyhewer *adv* last evening; last night; yesterday evening
nyni *prn* (*emphatic*) we; us
nyns *part* not
nywtron *n.m* **nywtrons** neutron

O

obaya *vb* obey
obayans *n.m* obedience
ober *n.m* **oberow** work; act; deed; exercise. **ober tre** *n.m* homework
oberador *n.m* **oberadoryon** operator
oberedh *n.m* (*in physics*) work
oberen *n.f* **oberennow** task; job
oberer *n.m* **oberoryon** worker
oberi *vb* act; operate; work
oberwas *n.m* **oberwesyon** servant
oberyans *n.m* **oberyansow** operation
objeta *n.m* **objetys** grammatical object
OCD *abbrev* OCD (*med*). **Disordyr Gorgemeryansek Omherdhys** Obsessive Compulsive Disorder
od *n.m* **odys** ode
oferen *n.f* **oferennow** mass; church service; religious offering
oferenni *vb* celebrate mass
offendya *vb* offend
offens *n.m* **offensys** offence
offensus *adj* offensive
offis *n.m* **offisys** office; function; position
offrynna *vb* sacrifice
ogas I *adj* close; near; adjoining **II** *adv* almost; nearly **III** *n.m* vicinity. **ogas dhe²** approximately. **ogas ha** approximately. **ogas ha bledhen** almost a year. **ogas lowr** approximate.

yn ogas nearby. *Personal forms: 1s* **yn ow ogas,** 2s **yn dha ogas,** 3sm **yn y ogas,** 3sf **yn hy ogas,** 1p **yn agan ogas,** 2p **yn agas ogas,** 3p **yn aga ogas**
ogasti *adv* almost; nearly
ogh *int* ugh; oh; alas
oghen *n.pl* oxen
ojyon *n.m* **oghen** ox
O.K. *abbrev* C.E.; A.D.
oker *n.m* (*financial*) interest. **kevradh oker** *n.m* interest rate
oksid *n.m* **oksidys** oxide
oksyjen *n.m* (*element*) oxygen
oktav *n.m* **oktavow** octave
ol *n.m* **olow** trail; track. **ol troos** *n.m* footprint
ola *vb* cry; weep. **ynter hwerthin hag ola** half laughing, half crying
oles *n.f* **olesow** fireplace; hearth. **astel an oles** *n.f* mantelpiece
olew *n.m* **olewow** olive oil
olewi *vb* anoint
olifans *n.m* **olifanses** elephant
oliv *n.coll* olives
oliven *n.f* **olivennow** olive
oll I *adj* all **II** *adv* entirely. **dres oll** particularly; primarily. **kyns oll** notably. **oll a'n gwella** all the best. **pub eur oll** all the time. **oll yn komposter** all right

olldalghus *adj* comprehensive; global

ollgallos *n.m* **ollgallosow** omnipotence

ollgallosek *adj* almighty; omnipotent

ollgemmyn *adj* general

ollvys *n.m* universe

ollvysel *adj* global; universal. **tommheans ollvysel** *n.m* global warming

olva *n.f* **olvaow** weep; wail

om- *prfx* one another; oneself

omach *n.m* **omajys** homage

omajer *n.m* **omajers** vassal; one who pays homage

omaskusya *vb* excuse oneself

omassaya *vb* exercise; test oneself; practise; rehearse

ombareusi *vb* get ready; prepare oneself

ombellhe *vb* distance oneself; withdraw

omberthi *vb* balance

omblegya *vb* bow; back down. **omblegya dhe**[2] give way to

omblegyans *n.m* **omblegyansow** bow

omborth I *adj* balanced; poised **II** *n.m* **omborthow** balance; poise

ombraysya *vb* praise oneself; show off

ombreder *n.m* **ombrederow** meditation

ombrederi *vb* ponder; reflect

ombrevi *vb* prove oneself

ombrofya *vb* apply (*for a post*)

ombrofyans *n.m* **ombrofyansow** application; candidacy

ombrofyer *n.m* **ombrofyoryon** applicant; candidate

omdava *vb* get into contact. **omdava orth** get into contact with

omdenna *vb* withdraw; distance onsef; retire; shrink

omdennans *n.m* **omdenansow** withdrawal; retirement. **gober omdennans** *n.m* pension

omdennys *adj* retired

omdewlel *vb* wrestle; struggle

omdhal *vb* quarrel

omdhalgh *n.m* **omdhalghow** attitude

omdhegi *vb* behave

omdhegyans *n.m* **omdhegyansow** bearing; behaviour; comportment

omdhesedha *vb* correspond; match. **omdhesedha orth** correspond to

omdhidhana *vb* amuse oneself

omdhifuna *vb* wake

omdhigelmi *vb* (*IT*) log out

omdhisevel *vb* trip

omdhiskwedhes *vb* appear; feature

omdhivarva *vb* shave one's beard off

omdhivas *n.m* **omdhivasow** orphan

omdhivasa *vb* orphan

omdhivlamya *vb* apologise

omdhivroa *vb* emigrate

omdhivroans *n.m* **omdhivroansow** emigration

omdhiwiska *vb* undress; strip

omdhiwiskans *n.m* **omdhiwiskansow** strip

omdhon *vb* bear children; be pregnant; conceive a child

omdhoon I *n.m* behaviour **II** *vb* behave; conduct oneself

omdhyghtya *vb* order oneself

omdollans *n.m* **omdollynsi** hallucination (*med*)

omdowl *n.m* wrestling

omdowler *n.m* **omdowloryon** wrestler

omdreylya *vb* revolve; turn around

omdroghya *vb* (*take a bath*) bathe

omfydhyans *n.m* self-confidence

omgavos *vb* find oneself

omgelmi *vb* (*IT*) log in; log on

omgemeres *vb* undertake; take responsibility. **omgemeres rag** become responsible for

omgemeryans *n.m* **omgemeryansow** undertaking; responsibility

omgemeryansek *adj* responsible

omgemeryas *n.m* **omgemerysi** undertaker

omgerensa *n.f* smugness; self-love

omgerensedhek *adj* smug; self-loving; vain

omglewans *n.m* **omglewansow** feeling

omglewansel *adj* sensual

omglewansus *adj* sensuous

omglewes *vb* feel

omgnoukya *vb* (*fight*) scrap

omgomendya *vb* introduce oneself

omgonfortya *vb* comfort oneself

omgregi *vb* hang oneself

omgudha *vb* hide. **omgudha rag** hide from

omguntel *vb* (*intransitive*) assemble; gather

omgussulya *vb* consult; discuss. **omgussulya a-dro dhe'n mater** have a discussion about the issue

omgussulyans *n.m* **omgussulyansow** discussion; dialogue

omhedhi *vb* abstain

omheveli *vb* resemble; take after

omhowla *vb* sunbathe

omhweles *vb* fall down; tip over

omjastya *vb* criticise oneself

omjersya *vb* be at ease. **omjersyewgh!** *int* make yourselves comfortable

omjerya *vb* cheer oneself up

omjunya *vb* (*intransitive*) join; connect

omladh I *n.m* **omladhow** fight; scrap **II** *vb* fight; scrap. **powes-omladh** *n.m* truce

omladha *vb* commit suicide; kill oneself

omladhans *n.m* **omladhansow** suicide

omladhansek *adj* suicidal

omlavar *adj* mute

omlena *vb* adhere. **omlena orth** adhere to

omlenans *n.m* **omlenansow** adherence

omlesa *vb* expand

omlesans *n.m* **omlesansow** expansion

omlesus *adj* expansive

omlet *n.m* **omlettys, omlettow** omelette

omlowenhe *vb* (*intransitive*) celebrate; enjoy oneself; rejoice

omlusek *adj* self-adhesive

omma *adv* here

omoberi *vb* exercise (*physically*)

omres dhe^2 *adj* dependent on. **omres dhe las** alcohol dependent

omrewl *n.f* **omrewlys** self-rule; home-rule

omri *vb* surrender; apply

omrians *n.m* **omriansow** surrender

omsatysfiys *adj* smug; self-satisfied

omsav *n.m* **omsavow** insurrection; insurgency; uprising

omsedhes *n.m* subsidence

omsedhi *vb* subside

omsettya *vb* attack; oppose. **omsettya dhe**^{2} undertake to. **omsettya orth** oppose. **omsettya war**^{2} attack; fall on; raid

omsettyans *n.m* **omsettyansow** attack; onslaught; raid

omsettyans skruth *n.m* **omsettyansow skruth** panic attack

omsettyer *n.m* **omsettyoryon** attacker

omsevel *vb* rise up; rebel; revolt

omsevyans *n.m* **omsevyansow** insurgency

omsevyas *n.m* **omsevysi** insurgent

omsewya *vb* follow; result

omshyndya *vb* self-harm

omshyndyans *n.m* **omshyndyansow** self-harm

omskoodhya *vb* support oneself. **omskoodhya war**^{2} fall back on

omstyryansek *adj* self-explanatory

omsynsi *vb* think oneself to be

omvedhwi *vb* get drunk

omvodhek *adj* selfish

omvodhogeth *n.f* selfishness

omvrewi *vb* fragment

omvrewyans *n.m* **omvrewyansow** fragmentation

omvyska *vb* involve

omvyskans *n.m* **omvyskansow** involvement

omvyskys *adj* involved

omwana *vb* stab oneself

omwaya *vb* move oneself; budge. **skonya omwaya** refuse to budge; dig one's heels in

omwellhe *vb* get over

omwen *vb* wince; wriggle

omwetha *vb* pine away

omwiska *vb* clothe oneself; dress up; get dressed; put on clothes

omwith *n.m* reserve; self-control

omwitha *vb* keep oneself; preserve oneself; protect oneself. **omwitha rag** protect oneself from

omwithek *adj* conservative

omwithys *adj* reserved; restrained

omwodh *adj* self-aware

omwodhvos *n.m* consciousness; self-awareness

omwolghi *vb* wash oneself; bathe oneself. **stevel-omwolghi** *n.f* bathroom

omwovyn *vb* ask oneself; wonder

omwul *vb* pretend; claim to be; turn into

omynvroa *vb* immigrate

omynvroans *n.m* **omynvroansow** immigration

omyttya *vb* omit

on (1) *n.m* **eyn** lamb

on (2) *vb* we are

onan *prn, num* one. **kettep onan** every one

ones *n.f* **onesow** ewe lamb

onest *adj* honest; decent; seemly

onester *n.m* honesty; decency

ongrassyes *adj* graceless; ungrateful; ungracious

-onieth *sffx* study of; science of

onn *n.coll* ash tree

onnen *n.f* **onennow** ash tree

onour *n.m* **onours** honour

onyon *n.coll* onions

onyonen *n.f* **onyonennow** onion

oor *adj* glacial; icy; bitterly cold

oos *n.m* **osow** age; period; epoch; era. **oos-omdenna** *n.m* retirement age. **yn y oos** ever

opera *n.m* **operaow** opera. **opera sebon** *n.m* soap opera

opportunystieth *n.f* opportunism

optycyan *n.m* **optycvans** optician (*commercial*)

or *n.f* **oryon** boundary; border; frontier

ordena *vb* ordain; appoint; arrange; decree; organise

ordenans *n.m* **ordenansow** decree; ordinance

ordyr *n.m* **ordyrs** religious order

organ (1) *n.m* **organs** (*musical instrument*) organ

organ (2) *n.m* **organow** (*anat*) organ. **riyas organow** *n.m* organ donor

organedh *n.m* **organedhow** organism. **organedh varyes yn henynnek** *n.m* genetically modified organism

organek *adj* organic

organs *n.coll* oregano

organs an wreg *n.coll* marjoram

orgelus *adj* arrogant

Oriant *n.m* Orient

orkestra *n.m* **orkestras** orchestra

orlyp *adj* clammy

ors *n.m* **orses** bear. **ors gwynn** polar bear

orsik *n.m* **orsigow** teddy-bear

orth *prp* at; against. **yma'n gador orth an fos** the chair is against the wall. **genys orth** born of. **megys orth** nourished by. **orth an sawgh** by the load. **orth bodh ow brys** intentionally. **orth niver** in number. **orth ow brys** to my mind. **sevel orth** resist; abstain from. *Personal forms: 1s* *orthiv*, 2s *orthis*, 3sm *orto*, 3sf *orti*, 1p *orthyn*, 2p *orthowgh*, 3p *orta*

orthopedek I *adj* orthopaedic **II** *n.f* orthopaedics

orthopedydh *n.m* **orthopedydhyon** orthopaedic surgeon

os *vb* you (sg) are

ost *n.m* **ostys** host; landlord; innkeeper. **ost ayr** *n.m* air steward

ostel *n.f* **ostelyow** hotel; hostel. **ostel yowynkneth** *n.f* youth hostel

ostes *n.f* **ostesow** landlady

ostralek *adj* Australian

Ostrali *top n.f* Australia

Ostralian *n.m* **Ostralians** Australian

Ostri *top n.f* Austria

Ostrian *n.m* **Ostrians** Austrian

ostrian *adj* Austrian

ostya *vb* lodge; accommodate

ostyans *n.m* **ostyansow** accomodation; lodging

ostyas *n.m* **ostysi** guest; lodger

osweyth *n.f* **osweythyow** epoch; era. **Osweyth Kemmyn** Common Era; C.E. **Kyns Osweyth Kemmyn** Before Common Era; B.C.E.

ot *int* here is

otta *int* here is; behold! *Personal forms: 1s* **ottavy**, *2s* **ottajy**, *3sm* **ottava**, *3sf* **ottahi**, *1p* **ottani**, *2p* **ottahwi**, *3p* **ottensi**

ottena *int* there is; look there

ottomma *int* here is; look here

oula *n.m* **oulys** owl

oulya *vb* howl

our *n.m* **ourys** hour; hour's duration. **a-ji dhe our** within an hour. **a'n our** see you later. **hanter-our** half-hour

Ouranos *n.m* Uranus

out *int* out; oh

outray *n.m* **outrayow** outrage. **gans outray** furiously

outraya *vb* outrage

outrayus *adj* outrageous

outya *vb* hoot

ov *vb* I am

ow³ *poss adj* my

ow⁴(**th**) *part* (**+th** *before vowels*) -ing

owgh *vb* you (pl) are

own *n.m* fear; fright; scare; alarm. **gorra own dhe²** scare; frighten. **gorra own yn** alarm. **kemeres own rag** take fright from. **rag own** for fear

own a gethreydh *n.m* homophobia (*fear of*; cf. **kas a gethreydh**)

ownegor a gethreydh *n.m* **ownegoryon a gethreydh** homophobe (*person in fear of*; cf. **kasegor a gethreydh**)

ownek I *adj* afraid; alarmed; cowardly; edgy; fearful; frightened; scared; timid **II** *n.m* **ownogyon** coward

ownek a gethreydh *adj* homophobic (*fearful of*; cf. **kasek a gethreydh**)

ownekhe *vb* intimidate

ownekheans *n.m* **ownekheansow** intimidation

ownus *adj* apprehensive

owr *n.m* (*element*) gold

owr an bobba *n.m* pyrite; fool's gold

owraval *n.m* **owravalow** orange. **sugen owraval** *n.m* orange juice

owravalik *n.m* **owravaligow** kumquat

owrbysk *n.m* **owrbuskes** goldfish

owrek *adj* golden

owr frynkek *n.m* French marigold

owrgi *n.m* **owrgeun** jackal

owrlin *n.m* **owrlinyow** silk. **pryv owrlin** *n.m* silkworm

owrlinus *adj* silky

owrwelen *n.f* **owrwelynni** golden rod

oy *n.m* **oyow** egg. **gwynn oy** *n.m* egg white. **melyn oy** *n.m* egg yolk. **ny dal oy** it isn't worth anything. **ny rov oy** I don't give a damn. **oy bryjys** *n.m* boiled egg. **oy frankres** *n.m* free-range egg. **oy friys** *n.m* fried egg. **oy skramblys** *n.m* scrambled egg

oygel *n.f* **oygellow** ovary

oyl *n.m* **oylys** oil. **podik oyl** *n.m* oil can. **tanker oyl** *n.m* oil tanker

oylek (1) *adj* oily

oylek (2) *n.f* **oylegi** oilfield

oynment *n.m* **oynmentys** ointment

P

pab *n.m* **pabow** pope
pabel (1) *n.f* **pabellow** pavilion
pabel (2) *adj* papal
padel *n.f* **padellow** pan. **padel benn glin** *n.f* kneecap. **padel bonn** *n.f* dustpan. **padel dhorn** *n.f* saucepan. **padel-fria** *n.f* frying pan. **padel horn** *n.f* iron pan. **padel ynken** *n.f* cuttlefish
padellik *n.f* **padelligow** saucer. **padellik-neyja** *n.f* flying saucer; UFO
Pader *n.m* **Paderow** Lord's Prayer
padera *vb* repeat prayers
paderen *n.f* **paderennow** bead
paderow pronter *n.coll* knapweed
padyn *n.m* **padynnow** pad
Pagan *n.m* **Paganys, Paganyon** Pagan
pagan *adj* pagan
Paganieth *n.f* Paganism
paja *n.m* **pajys** page (*boy*)
pal *n.f* **palyow** spade
palas *vb* dig; excavate. **lo-balas** *n.f* trowel. **palas yn-dann** undermine
Palestin *top n.m* Palestine
palestinek *adj* Palestinian
Palestinyas *n.m* **Palestinysi** Palestinian
pali *n.m* velvet; felt
pall *n.m* **pallow** mantle; pall
palmwedhen *n.f* **palmwedhennow** palm tree
palmwydh *n.coll* palm trees
palores *n.f* **paloresow** chough
pals *adj* abundant; copious; numerous; plentiful; many; much; lots (*many of*)
palsi *n.m* **palsis** palsy; paralysis
palster *n.m* **palsteryow** abundance
palsya *vb* paralyse
palsyes *adj* paralysed
palv *n.f* **palvow** palm of hand
palva *vb* stroke; caress
palvala *vb* grope
palvas *n.m* **palvasow** caress; stroke

palys *n.m* **palesys, palesyow** palace
pan *adj* what
pa'n *contr* when… it/him/her
pan² *cnj* when. **byth pan²** *adv* whenever
pana² *adj, prn* what; such. **pana dermyn** when; at which time. **pana lies** how many
panch *n.m* (*drink*) punch
panda *n.m* **pandas** panda
pandra *prn* what
panel *n.m* **panellow** panel
panellya *vb* panel
panes *n.coll* parsnips
panesen *n.f* **panesennow** parsnip
pannweyth *n.coll* textiles
pans *n.m* **pansow** dell; dingle; hollow
paper *n.m* **paperyow** paper. **paper fos** *n.m* wallpaper. **paper gweder** *n.m* sandpaper. **paper grow** *n.m* sandpaper. **paper nowodhow** *n.m* newspaper. **paper privedhyow** *n.m* toilet paper. **paper-skrifa** *n.m* writing paper
papynjay *n.m* **papynjays** parrot
par I *adj* equal II *n.m* **parow** equal; match; sort; type. **a'n par na** that kind of; of that sort. **heb par** unequalled
para *n.m* **parys** gang; group; herd; team; squad. **an para Oll Du** *n.m* the All Blacks. **Para Yeghes an Brys** *n.m* Mental Health Team
parabolek *adj* parabolic
parabolen *n.f* **parabolennow** parable; parabola
parabyl *n.m* **parablys** parable
paradhis *n.f* paradise
paragraf *n.m* **paragrafys, paragrafow** paragraph
paranoyd *adj* paranoid (*med*)
parasitek *adj* parasitic

Para Yeghes an Brys *n.m* Mental Health Team

parchemin *n.m* **parcheminyow** parchment

parde *int* by God!

parder *n.m* **parderyow** equality

pareth *n.f* **parethow** parity

pareusi *vb* prepare; cook; edit; make ready

pargh *vb* endure

park *n.m* **parkow** field; enclosure; park. **park kerri** *n.m* car park. **park-omdhidhana** *n.m* amusement park **park-gwari** *n.m* playing field

parkya (1) *vb* park. **feow-parkya** *n.pl* parking fees

parkya (2) *vb* enclose

parkyans *n.m* parking

parledh *n.m* **parledhow** parlour

parodi *n.m* **parodis** parody

parodia *vb* parody

paros *n.m* **parosyow** screen; party wall

parow *adj* even

parsel *n.m* **parsellow** set of people

parth *n.f* **parthow** part; act; behalf; side; zone. **y'n barth aral** on the other hand

parti *n.m* **partiow** political party. **an Parti Gwithyasel** the Conservative Party. **an Parti Lavur** *n.m* the Labour Party. **an Parti Livrel Gwerinel** *n.m* the Liberal Democratic Party. **an Parti Gwyrdh** the Green Party

parya *vb* couple; pair

parys *adj* ready; handy; convenient; about to. **parys dhe derri yw** it's about to break. **ros parys** *n.f* spare wheel

pas (1) *n.m* **pasow** cough. **losanj pas** *n.m* cough lozenge; cough sweet. **pas garm** *n.m* whooping cough

pas (2) *n.m* **passys** step; pace

pasa *vb* cough

Pask *n.m* Easter. **Pask Byghan** *n.m* Low Sunday. **war Bask** at Easter

passya *vb* pass; go by; overtake

passyes *adj* (= **passys**) past; bygone. **yn termyn eus passyes** in the past; once upon a time

passys *adj* (= **passyes**) past; bygone. **yn termyn eus passys** in the past; once upon a time

past *n.m* **pastow** paste; pastry. **past pyff** *n.m* puff pastry. **past brew** *n.m* short crust pastry

pasta *n.coll* pasta

pastel (1) *n.f* **pastellow** morsel; scrap. **pastel dir** *n.f* smallholding. **pastel vro** *n.f* constituency; district

pastel (2) *n.f* **pastellow** pastel

pasteurya *vb* pasteurise

pasti *n.m* **pastiow** pasty. **pasti kig** *n.m* meat pasty

patatys *n.coll* potatoes

patatysen *n.f* **patatysennow** potato

patent *n.m* **patentys** patent. **patent yn-dann hwithrans** patent pending. **torrva patent** *n.f* patent infringement

patron *n.m* **patronyow** model; pattern

paw *n.m* **pawyow** paw; claw

paw ahwesydh *n.m* delphinium; larkspur

paw bran *n.m* buttercup

pawgen *n.m* **pawgennow** sock; slipper

paw lew *n.f* lady's mantle

paw ors *n.m* acanthus; bear's britches

payn *n.m* **paynys** pain. **payn dens** *n.m* toothache. **payn keyn** *n.m* backache. **payn-merwel** *n.m* capital punishment

paynt *n.m* **payntys, payntow** paint

payntya *vb* paint (*decorate*)

payntyer *n.m* **payntyoryon** (*decorator*) painter

paynya *vb* pain

payon *n.m* **payones** peacock

payoni *vb* show off; strut; swagger

payonyans *n.m* **payonyansow** swagger

pe *vb* pay

peber *n.m* **peboryon** baker

peblys *adj* populated

peder *num, n.f* four

pediatrek I *adj* paediatric **II** *n.f* paediatrics

pedrega *vb* square

pedrek I *adj* square **II pedrogow** *n.m* square

pedren *n.f* **pedrennow,** *dl* **diwbedren** bottom; buttock; haunch

pedrevan *n.f* **pedrevanes** lizard

pedrevanas *vb* crawl

pedri *vb* rot; spoil; corrupt; fester

pega *vb* cover with pitch; tar

pegh *n.m* **peghow** sin; guilt

pegha *vb* sin; offend

peghador *n.m* **peghadoryon** sinner

peghes *n.m* **peghosow** sin

peghus *adj* sinful

pel *n.f* **pelyow** ball; sphere; orb. **gwari pelyow** *n.m* bowling. **pel ayr** *n.f* balloon. **pel dhorn** *n.f* handball (*sport*) **pel droos** *n.f* football. **pel roos** *n.f* netball. **pel vas** *n.f* baseball. **pel ganstel** *n.f* basketball. **pel an norvys** *n.f* globe

peldrosyas *n.m* **peldrosysi** (*professional*) footballer

peldrosyer *n.m* **peldrosyoryon** (*amateur*) footballer

pelikan *n.m* **pelikanes** pelican

pell *adj* distant; far; long; remote. **mos re bell** go too far; exaggerate. **nans yw pell** long ago. **pell alemma** a long way from here

pella I *adj* extreme; further; furthest; utmost **II** *adv* moreover. **na fella** *adv* no further

pellder *n.m* **pellderyow** distance; a long time; remoteness

pellen *n.f* **pellennow** bullet; bag pudding; dumpling

pellennik *n.f* **pellenigow** pill

peller *n.m* **pelloryon** (*witch*) cunning person

pellgewsel *vb* phone

pellgomunyans *n.m* **pellgomunyansow** telecommunicatior.

pellgowsel *n.f* **pellgowsellow** mobile phone

pellgowser *n.m* **pellgowseryow** telephone; phone. **niver pellgowser** *n.m* telephone number

pellhe *vb* move away; send away; banish

pellhwyja *vb* projectile vomit

pellskrifa *vb* fax

pellskrifen *n.f* **pellskrifennow** fax; telegram

pellvotonek *n.m* **pellvotonegi** remote control

pellweler *n.m* **pellweloryow** telescope

pellwolok *n.f* **pellwologow** TV; television. **PW** *abbrev* TV. **pellwolok gapel** cable televisiɔn. **pellwolok lorell** satellite television

pelva *n.f* **pelvaow** bowling green

pelyek *adj* spherical

penans *n.m* penance

Penkost *n.m* pentecost

penkost *n.m* **penkostow** Pentecost; Whitsun

penn *n.m* **pennow** head; end; top. **penn a-rag** *n.m* bow (of a ship). **penn bobba** *n.m* idiot. **penn daras** *n.m* lintel. **penn du** *n.m* blackhead. **Penn Glas** *n.m* 'Obby 'Oss. **penn glin** *n.m* knee-cap. **penn hyns** *n.m* terminal. **penn kales** obstinate; stubborn. **penn medhow** *n.m* drunkard. **penn medhow koth** *n.m* (*colloq*) an old soak. **penn pyst** *n.m* idiot. **penn sagh** *n.m* mumps. **penn tir** *n.m* headland

penn- *prfx* chief; main; premier; principal; top

penn-aghel *n.f* **pennow-aghel** geographical pole. **Penn-Aghel an North** *n.f* the North Pole. **Penn-Aghel an Soth** *n.f* the South Pole

penn barvus *n.m* rockling

penn-bloodh *n.m* **pennow-bloodh** birthday; anniversary

penncita *n.f* **penncitys** capital city

penndegys *adj* confused

penn-dro I *adj* dizzy; giddy; nauseous **II** *n.f* dizziness; giddiness; nausea; vertigo

penn-drog *adj* wicked

penndroppya *vb* nod

penn du *n.m* tadpole

penndyskador *n.m* **penndyskadoryon** principal; headteacher

penneghlek *adj* polar

penneglos *n.f* **penneglosyow** cathedral

pennek *adj* big-headed

pennfenten *n.f* **pennfentynnyow** source

pennfron *n.f* **pennfronnow** muzzle

pennfronna *vb* muzzle

penn glas *n.m* field scabious

penn gwynn *n.m* penguin

pennhembrenkyas *n.m* **pennhembrenkysi** general

pennik lost hir *n.m* **penniges lost hir** long-tailed tit

pennjustis *n.m* **pennjustisyow** chief justice

penn-kook *adj* empty-headed; vacuous

pennkuntelles *n.m* **pennkuntellesow** summit (*meeting*)

pennlinen *n.f* **pennlinennow** heading; headline

pennlugarn *n.m* **pennlugern** headlight

pennmenyster *n.m* **pennmenystrys, pennmenystroryon** Prime Minister; premier

penn-noth *adj* bare-headed

pennobereth *n.f* **pennoberethow** masterpiece

pennow medhow *n.pl* red valerian

pennow medhow gwynn *n.pl* white valerian

penn pali *n.m* **pennow pali** blue tit

penn pali bras *n.m* **pennow pali bras** great tit

penn pali du *n.m* **pennow pali du** coal tit

penn pali gwern *n.m* **pennow pali gwern** marsh tit

pennplas *n.m* **pennplassow** headquarters

pennpusorn *n.m* **pennpusornow** refrain

pennrewl *n.f* **pennrewlys** premise; principle. **pennrewlys** *n.pl* basics

pennrudh *n.m* reedmace

pennser *n.m* **pennseri** architect

pennserneth *n.f* architecture. **pennserneth romanek** *n.f* Romanic architecture. **pennserneth wothek** *n.f* Gothic architecture

pennseviges *n.f* **pennsevigesow** princess

pennsevigeth *n.f* **pennsevigethow** principality

pennsevik *n.m* **pennsevigyon** prince; chief

pennseythen *n.m* (*f*) **pennseythennyow** weekend

pennskav *adj* dizzy

pennskol *n.f* **pennskolyow** university

pennskrif *n.m* **pennskrifow** editorial

pennskrifa *vb* edit

pennskrifer *n.m* **pennskriforyon** editor

penn-sogh *adj* hare-brained

pennti *n.m* **penntiow** cottage

pennyn *n.m* **penynnow** tadpole

pensyon *n.m* **pensyons** pension

pensyonydh *n.m* **pensyonydhyon** pensioner

penys I *n.m* **penysyow** fast **II** *vb* fast

per *n.coll* pears

percevya *vb* perceive

peren *n.f* **perennow** pear

performans *n.m* **performansow** performance

performya *vb* perform

performyer *n.m* **performyoryon** performer

perfydh *adj* perfect. **amser berfydh** *n.f* perfect tense

perfydhder *n.m* perfection

perghen *n.m* **perghennow** owner. **perghen estrigys** *n.m* absentee landlord; second-home owner

perghenegi *vb* take over; claim

perghenna *vb* own; possess

perghennek *n.m* **perghenogyon** owner; proprietor

perghennus *adj* possessive

perghenogeth *n.f* **perghenogethow** ownership; possession

perghenogyl *adj* proprietary

pergherin *n.m* **pergherinyow** pilgrim

pergherinses *n.m* **pergherinsesow** pilgrimage

periodek *adj* periodic. **An Vosen Beriodek** The Periodic Table

perl *n.m* **perlys** pearl

perm *n.m* **permyow** perm

permya *vb* perm

persekutya *vb* persecute

persekutyans *n.m* **persekutyansow** persecution

persil *n.coll* (*plants*) parsley

persilen *n.f* **persilennow** (*plant*) parsley

person *n.m* **persons** person. **person diannedh** *n.m* homeless person

personekheans *n.m* personification

personel *adj* personal

personelhe *vb* customise

personoleth *n.f* **personolethow** personality

perswadus *adj* convincing

perth *n.f* **perthi** (*thicket*) brake; thicket

perthi *vb* bear; endure; put up with; suffer; tolerate. **perthi avi orth** be jealous of; bear malice against. **na borth ahwer!** don't worry! **perthi kov** (a^2) remember. **perthi meth** (a^2) be ashamed (of). **perthi own** (a^2) be afraid (of). **perthi orth** hold out against

perthyans *n.m* patience; endurance; tolerance. **heb perthyans** impatient

perthyer *n.m* **perthyoryon** patient

perthygel *n.m* **perthyglow** particle

perthynek *adj* relative

perthynyans *n.m* **perthynyansow** relationship

peruken *n.f* **perukennow** wig

pervedh *n.m* **pervedhow** inside; interior

pervedhek *adj* indoor; inside; interior; internal **politegieth pervedhek** *n.f* domestic politics

pervynk *n.m* **pervynkys** periwinkle

peryl *n.m* **peryllow, peryllyow** danger; hazard; risk; peril

peryllus *adj* dangerous; hazardous; risky

peryllya *vb* endanger

peryllys *adj* endangered. **eghen beryllys** *n.f* endangered species

pes (1) *adj* paid. **pes da** content; contented; pleased; satisfied. **drog pes** displeased; dissatisfied; in a bad mood

pes (2) *adv* (*before sg. noun*) how many

pesen *n.f* **pesennow** pea

peski *vb* graze

peskweyth *adv* how many times; as often. **peskweyth may**[5] (*followed by a verb*) as often as; whenever

peswar *num, n.m* four

peswardhegves *num* fourteenth

peswardhek *num* fourteen

peswarkorn *n.m* **peswarkern** quadrangle

peswarpaw *n.m* **peswarpawes** newt

peswartenwennel *adj* quadrilateral

peswartrosek *adj* fourfooted

peswar ugens *num* eighty. **deg ha peswar ugens** *num* ninety

peswar ugensves *num* eightieth

peswora *num* fourth

pesya *vb* continue; endure; last

pesyans *n.m* **pesyansow** continuation

petal *n.m* **petalys** petal

petisyon *n.m* **petisyons** petition

petrol *n.m* **petrols** petrol

petrolva *n.f* petrol station; service station

peub *prn* all; everyone; everybody

peul *n.m* **peulyow** pole; stake; post; pylon. **kay peulyow** *n.m* pier

peulge *n.m* **peulgeow** railing

peuns *n.m* **peunsow** pound

p'eur[5] *adv* when

peurell *n.f* **peurellow** browser

peuri *vb* browse; graze

peurva *n.f* **peurvaow** pasture

pewas *n.m* **pewasow** award; prize; reward

piano *n.m* **pianos** piano

pianydh *n.m* **pianydhyon** pianist

pib *n.f* **pibow** pipe. **pibow sagh** *n.pl* bagpipes

piba *vb* pipe

pibell *n.f* **pibellow** pipe

piben *n.f* **pibennow** duct; tube. **piben dhowr** *n.f* hosepipe

pies *n.coll* magpies

piesen *n.f* **piesennow** magpie

piga *vb* sting; goad; incite

pigell *n.f* **pigellow** hoe; pick

pigorn *n.m* **pigern** cone

pigornek *adj* conical

pik-pik *adj* fizzy

piktour *n.m* **piktours** picture

pil *n.m* **pilyow** pile

pildra *n.f* **pildrevow** slum

pilek *adj* heaped

pilen *n.f* **pilennow** rag

pilennek *adj* ragged; tatty

pilya *vb* peel; strip

pilyek I *adj* useless II *n.m* **pilyogyon** spider-crab; useless person

pin *n.coll* pine trees

pinaval *n.m* **pinavalow** pineapple

pinen *n.f* **pinennow** pine tree

pinta *n.m* **pintys** pint

pis *n.m* **pisys** piece

pisa *vb* urinate; pee; piss

pisas *n.m* urine; pee; piss

pistyl *n.m* **pistyllow** little waterfall; spout

pistylla *vb* spout

pisva *n.f* **pisvaow** urinal

pita *n.m* **pitys** pity

pitethus *adj* pitiful

pith *adj* greedy

pithneth *n.f* greed

pitsa *n.m* **pitsas** pizza

piw *prn* who; whom; whose. **piw pynag** whoever

pla *n.m* **plaow** nuisance; pest; plague. **pla gwynn** tuberculosis

plag *n.m* **plagys** plague

plagus *adj* contagious

plagya *vb* afflict; pester; plague

plagys *adj* afflicted; plagued

planet *n.m* **planetys, planetow** planet. **a'n planetys** *adj* planetary

planetva *n.f* **planetvaow** planetarium

plankton *n.coll* plankton

planktonen *n.f* **planktonennow** (individual) plankton

plans *n.m* **plansow** plant

plansa *vb* plant; stick

plas *n.m* **plassow** place; mansion

plasen *n.f* **plasennow** disc; (vinyl) record. **plasen arghansek** *n.f* CD; compact disc. **plasen gales** *n.f* hard disk

plastek I *adj* plastic II *n.m* **plastogow** plastic

plaster *n.m* **plastrow** plaster

plastra *vb* plaster

plat I *adj* flat II *n.m* **platys, platyow** plate. **plat niver** *n.m* number plate

platas *n.m* **platasow** helping; plateful; serving

platinom *n.m* (*element*) platinum

plattya *vb* (*intransitive*) crouch; (*transitive*) flatten

playn I *adj* evident II *n.m* **playnys** (*tool*) plane

playnya *vb* plane

ple[5] *adv* where

pledya *vb* plead

pledyans *n.m* **pledyansow** plea

pleg *n.m* **plegow** bend; crease; fold. **pleg mor** *n.m* bay

plegadow *adj* pleasing

plegell *n.f* **plegellow** folder

plegya (1) *vb* bend; fold; give way; (*gesture*) bow. **plegya tal** frown; knit one's brows

plegya (2) *vb* please. **mar pleg** please. **plegya dhe**[2], **plegya gans** be pleasing to

plegyans *n.m* **plegyansow** tendency; bow

ple'ma *contr* where is

plen *adj* plain. **yeth plen** *n.f* prose

plenta *adj* plenty

plenteth *n.f* plenty; abundance

plentyas *n.m* **plentysi** plaintiff

plesour *n.m* **plesours** pleasure

plesya *vb* please

plesys *adj* pleased

ple'th *contr* where

pleth *n.f* **plethow** plait

pletha *vb* braid; plait

plethys *adj* plaited

plisk *n.coll* shells. **plisk know** *n.coll* nutshells

plisken *n.f* **pliskennow** shell; husk

pliskenna *vb* shell; husk

plit *n.m* **plitys** plight; condition; predicament; situation; state

plomm *n.m* (*element*) lead

plommer *n.m* **plomoryon** plumber

plommwedhek *adj* vertical

plontyans *n.m* propaganda

plos *adj* dirty; filthy; nasty

plosegi *vb* get dirty

plott *n.m* **plottys, plottow** plot

plottya *vb* (*delineate*) plot. **jynn-plottya** *n.m* plotter

ploum *n.coll* plums. **ploum sygh** *n.coll* prunes

ploumen *n.f* **ploumennow** plum

Plouton *n.m* Pluto

plowghya *vb* splash

plustren *n.f* **plustrennow** mole; skin mark

pluv *n.coll* plumage

pluvek *n.f* **pluvogow** cushion; pillow

pluven *n.f* **pluvennow** feather; pen; quill. **hanow pluven** *n.m* pen name. **pluven belvleyn** *n.f* biro; ballpoint pen. **pluven leuvban** *n.f* felt-tip pen. **pluven blomm** *n.f* pencil

pluvennek *adj* feathered

pluw *n.f* **pluwow** parish

pluwek I *adj* parochial II *n.m* **pluwogyon** parishioner

plynch *n.m* **plynchys** wink

plynchya *vb* wink

po *cnj* or. **po... po** *cnj* either... or

pobas *vb* bake

pobel *n.f* **poblow** people

pobla *vb* populate

poblans *n.m* **poblansow** population

poblek *adj* public. **karyans poblek** *n.m* public transport

poblikan *n.m* **poblikans** Roman tax-collector; (*Bible*) publican

pochya *vb* (*cooking*) poach

pocket *n.m* **pocketys, pocketow** pocket

pockya *vb* thrust

poder *adj* rotten

podik *n.m* **podigow** jug. **podik-musura** *n.m* measuring jug. **podik oyl** *n.m* oil can

podkast *n.m* **podkasts, podkastow** podcast

podredha *vb* bruise

podredhek *adj* corrupt, festering

podrek *adj* corrupt; putrid; rotten

podyn *n.m* **podyns** pudding; dessert

pok *n.m* **pokyow** poke; prod

poken I *adv* else II *cnj* or else; otherwise. **poken... po** either... or

pokya *vb* poke; prod

Polak *n.m* **Polakyon** Pole

polat *n.m* **polatys** chap

polici *n.m* **policis** policy

politeger *n.m* **politegoryon** politician

politegieth *n.f* politics. **politegieth a-bervedh** *n.f* domestic politics. **politegieth keswlasek** *n.f* international politics

politek *adj* political

poll (1) *n.m* **pollow** anchorage; pit; pond; pool. **poll holan** *n.m* salt pond. **poll-neuvya** *n.m* swimming pool. **poll pri** *n.m* clay pit. **poll sten** *n.m* tin pit. **poll-troyllya** *n.m* whirlpool

poll (2) *n.m* **pollow** reason; intelligence

pollek *adj* intelligent; brainy

pollen *n.f* **pollennow** puddle

Polonek *n.m* Polish language

polonek *adj* Polish

Poloni *top n.f* Poland

pols *n.m* **polsyow** instant; moment; (*beat*) pulse; short time; while. **dres pols** temporarily. **y'n pols ma** at the moment

polsa *vb* pulse

polsya *vb* polish

polta *adv* a good while

polter *n.m* **polteryow** powder; dust

poltra *vb* (sprinkle with) dust

pomp *n.m* **pompys, pompyow** pump. **pomp petrol** *n.m* petrol pump

pompell *n.f* **pompellow** pump

pompik *n.m* **pompigow** courgette

pompya *vb* pump

pompyon *n.m* **pompyons** pumpkin; gourd; marrow. **pompyon hweg** *n.m* melon

pomster *n.m* **pomsters** quack (*fake doctor*)

ponegi *vb* pollinate

ponn *n.m* dust. **kweth ponn** *n.f* duster. **padel bonn** *n.f* dustpan

ponnek *adj* dusty

pons *n.f* **ponsyow** bridge

ponsfordh *n.f* **ponsfordhow** viaduct

ponvos *n.m* **ponvosow** misery

ponvosek *adj* miserable

ponya *vb* run; trot

ponyans *n.m* run; trot

poos **I** *adj* heavy; (*font*) bold **II** *n.m* **posow** weight; emphasis; importance; pressure. **gorra poos war**^{2} stress

poosa *vb* weigh

pooth *adj* hot; scorching

popa *n.m* **popys** puffin

popet *n.m* **popettys, popettow** doll; puppet

popti *n.m* **poptiow** bakery

por *n.coll* leeks

poran **I** *adv* exactly; just; precisely; quite **II** *adj* precise

por'bugel *n.m* **por'bugeledh** porbeagle

poren *n.f* **porennow** leek

porghel *n.m* **porghelli** young pig. **kig porghel** *n.m* pork

porghel dor *n.m* **porghellow dor** aardvark

porghellik *n.m* **porghelligow** piglet; sucking pig

pornografek *adj* pornographic

pornografieth *n.f* pornography

porpos *n.m* **porposys** purpose

porposya *vb* purpose

porres *adv* absolutely; urgently; of necessity

pors *n.m* **porsys** purse

pors bugel *n.m* shepherd's purse

porsek *n.m* **porsogyon** marsupial

porser *n.m* **porsoryon** bursar

portal *n.m* **portals** portal; porch

portfolio *n.m* portfolio

porth *n.m* **porthow** port; cove; gate; harbour; haven; porch; portal. **porth klos** *n.m* dock. **porth lestri** *n.m* dock

porthadow *adj* tolerable; bearable

porther *n.m* **porthoryon** porter; janitor

porth kov ahanav *n.m* forget-me-not

porthorji *n.m* **porthorjiow** gatehouse; lodge

porthva *n.f* **porthvaow** wharf

portrayans *n.m* **portrayansow** portrait

Portyngal *top n.m* Portugal

Portyngalek *n.m* Portuguese language

portyngalek *adj* Portuguese

Portyngalyas *n.m* **Portyngalysi** Portuguese

porv *n.coll* wick (*of candle*)

porven *n.f* **porvennow** wick (*of candle*). **porven ganabys** *n.f* (*cannabis cigarette*) joint; reefer

posa *vb* lean. **posa war-rag** lean forward

posedhek *adj* positive

posek *adj* important

poslev *n.m* **poslevow** accent; emphasis; stress

posleva *vb* accentuate; emphasise; stress; underline

posna *vb* poison

posnys *adj* poisoned

possybyl *adj* possible

possybylta *n.m* **possybyltas** possibility

post (1) *n.m* post; mail. **erghi der an post** mail order. **karten bost** *n.f* postcard. **kod post** *n.m* postcode. **sodhva bost** *n.f* post office

post (2) *n.m* **postow** post; pillar. **post arwodh** *n.m* sign-post

poster *n.m* **posterow** heaviness; thunder cloud

postya *vb* post; mail

pot *n.m* **potow** kick

potha *vb* heat; scorch

pothhe *vb* heat

pott *n.m* **pottys, pottow** pot. **pott paynt** *n.m* paint pot. **pott te** *n.m* teapot. **pott gwynn** *n.m* hasty-pudding

pottya *vb* lay; put

potya *vb* kick

pow *n.m* **powyow** country; region; land. **Pow Belg** *top n.m* Belgium. **Pow Frynk** *top n.m* France. **Pow Grek** *top* *n.m* Greece. **Pow Sows** *top n.m* England. **Pow Swis** *top n.m* Switzerland

powdir *n.m* countryside

powek *adj* rural

powes I *n.m* **powesow** stop; break; interval; halt; pause; rest; repose II *vb* halt; pause; repose; rest. **powes-omladh** *n.m* truce

powesva *n.f* **powesvaow** resting place

pows *n.f* **powsyow** frock; dress; gown; tunic. **pows nos** *n.f* nightdress; nightie

poynt *n.m* **poyntys, poyntow** point; item. **poynt a skiars** *n.m* maxim. **poynt ha komma** semicolon

poynt gwayn *n.m* break-even

poyntya *vb* point; indicate; punctuate

poyntyans *n.m* **poyntyansow** punctuation

poyson *n.m* **poysons** poison

prag[5] *adv* why; what for. **reson prag** because

praga I *adv* why; what for II *n.m* reason

pragmatek *adj* pragmatic

pragmatieth *n.f* pragmatism

pragmatydh *n.m* **pragmatydhyon** pragmatist

praktis *n.m* **praktisyow** exercise; practice

praktisya *vb* practise; exercise

pramm *n.m* **prammys, prammow** pram

pras *n.m* **prasow** meadow; common pasture

pratt *n.m* **prattys, prattow** lark; trick; prank

prays *n.m* **praysys** praise; compliment

praysya *vb* praise; compliment

preder *n.m* **prederow** thought; worry; anxiety; care

prederi *vb* consider; concentrate; ponder; reflect

prederus *adj* careful; conscientious; considerate; thoughtful; worrying;

anxious

prederyans *n.m* **prederyansow** opinion; reflection

prederys *adj* worried

predheger *n.m* **predhegoryon** ranter; rabble-rouser

predheges *vb* rant

predhek *n.m* **predhegow** rant; noisy speech

pregoth I *n.m* **pregothow** sermon; homily II *vb* preach

pregowther *n.m* **pregowthoryon** preacher

prena *vb* acquire; buy; purchase. **prena kath yn sagh** buy a pig in a poke. **prena neppyth a²** buy something for (a certain price). **prena neppyth orth** purchase something by (a certain quantity)

prenas *n.m* **prenasow** purchase

prenassa *vb* shop; go shopping. **kresen-brenassa** *n.f* shopping centre

prenasser *n.m* **prenassoryon** shopper

prener *n.m* **prenoryon** buyer; purchaser

prenn *n.m* **prennyer** bar; beam; log; timber; *(gambling)* lot. **karghar prenn** *n.m* pillory; stocks. **ser prenn** *n.m* carpenter

prenna *vb* bar; lock

prennek *adj* wooden; woody

prennweyth *n.m* woodwork

prenyas *n.m* **prenysi** professional purchaser

presens *n.m* presence

present *n.m* **presens** present

presentya *vb* present

presentyans *n.m* **presentyansow** presentation

presep *n.m* **presebow** manger

prest I *adj* ever II *adv* always; readily; still

previ *vb* prove; experience; taste; tax; test; try. **previ an perthyans** try one's patience

prevya *vb* experiment

prevyans *n.m* **prevyansow** experience. **heb prevyans** inexperienced

preydh *n.m* **preydhyow** booty; loot; plunder; spoil

preydha *vb* loot; plunder

pri *n.m* **priow** clay; mud. **poll pri** *n.m* **pollow pri** clay pit

pria *vb* daub

prierin *n.m* **prierinyon** pilgrim. **krogen brierin** *n.f* scallop

pries I *n.m* **priosow, dl dewbries** spouse; mate II *adj* married

pri gwynn *n.m* china clay; kaolin

prileghen *n.f* **prileghennow** tile

priosel *adj* conjugal; matrimonial

priosoleth *n.f* matrimony

pris *n.m* **prisyow** price; reputation. **a bris** outstanding; renowned; significant. **a bris isel** cheap. **pris daswerth** *n.m* resale price. **pris viaj** *n.m* fare

prism *n.m* **prismow** prism

prisner *n.m* **prisners, prisnoryon** prisoner

prison *n.m* **prisons, prisonyow** prison; jail; gaol. **tremena termyn yn prison** spend time in prison

prisonya *vb* imprison; incarcerate

prisonyans *n.m* **prisonyansow** imprisonment

prisya *vb* price

privedh *adj* private; personal. **helerghyas privedh** *n.m* private detective; private eye

privedhyow *n.pl* toilet; lavatory. **paper privedhyow** *n.m* toilet paper

privetter *n.m* privacy

priweyth *n.m* pottery; ceramic

priweythen *n.f* **priweyth** ceramic

priweythor *n.m* **priweythoryon** potter

priweythva *n.f* **priweythvaow** pottery; clay-works

professor *n.m* **professoryon** professor

profil *n.m* **profilys** profile

profos *n.m* **profosi** prophet

profya *vb* suggest; offer; propose; bid

profyans *n.m* **profyansow** suggestion; offer; proposal; bid

profyas *n.m* **profysi** bidder

prokurya *vb* procure

prononsya *vb* pronounce

pronter *n.m* **pronteryon** parson; priest; vicar

pronterji *n.m* **pronterjiow** vicarage

prosternya *vb* lay low

Protestant *n.m* **Protestans** Protestant

Protestant *adj* Protestant

protestya *vb* protest

protestyans *n.m* **protestyansow** (*organised*) protest

protestyer *n.m* **protestyoryon** protester

protin *n.m* **protinyow** protein

protokol *n.m* **protokolys** protocol

proton *n.m* **protons** proton

prout *adj* proud; arrogant

prov *n.m* **provow** proof; test. **gul prov** prove

provadow *adj* provable

provia *vb* provide; supply

provians *n.m* **proviansow** provision

provier *n.m* **provioryon** supplier; provider

provyns *n.m* **provynsys** province

prow *n.m* advantage; benefit; profit. **bos meur a brow** come in handy

prowus *adj* beneficial

pryck *n.m* **pryckow** (*degree*) pitch

prydydh *n.m* **prydydhyon** poet

prydydhi *vb* write poetry

prydydhieth *n.f* poetry

prydydhyek *adj* poetic

pryl *n.m* **prylyon** tinstone; cassiterite

pryncipata *n.m* **pryncipatys** principality

prynt *n.m* **pryntys** print

pryntya *vb* print

pryntyans *n.m* **pryntyansow** print-run

pryntyer *n.m* **pryntyoryon** printer (*person or machine*)

prys *n.m* **presyow** time; season. **neb prys** at any time; sometime. **prys boos** *n.m* meal-time. **prys gweli** *n.m* bedtime. **prys te** *n.m* teatime. **y'n gwella prys** fortunately; luckily. **y'n gwettha prys** unfortunately

prysk *n.coll* thicket; shrubs; bushes

prysken *n.f* **pryskennow** shrub; bush

prysweyth *n.m* **prysweythyow** instant; occasion

prysweythyel *adj* momentary; instantaneous

pryv *n.m* **preves, prevyon** worm; crawling animal; grub; insect; bug (*IT*). **pryv del** *n.m* caterpillar. **pryv owrlin** *n.m* silkworm. **pryv prenn** *n.m* woodworm

pryvesek *adj* wormy; verminous

pryvessa *vb* hunt vermin; (*IT*) debug

pryvylej *n.m* **pryvylejys** privilege

PTSD *abbrev* PTSD (*med*). **Disordyr Gwask wosa Skruth** Post-traumatic Stress Disorder

pub *adj* each; every. **dhe bub le** all directions. **pub le** everywhere. **pub huni** everybody. **pub kentel** on every occasion. **pub prys** all the time. **pub termyn** all the time; always. **pub torn** at every turn; every time

pubdedhyek *adj* daily

puber *n.m* **puberyow** pepper

pubermenta *n.f* peppermint

pubonan *prn* everyone; everybody. **pubonan war-barth** all together

pub prys *adv* always

pubra *vb* pepper

pubren *n.f* **pubrennow** bell pepper

pupprys *adv* always

puptra *prn* everything

pur *adj* pure; absolute; accomplished; outright; through and through

pur[2] *adv* very. **pur dha** excellent. **pur lowen** delighted

purek *adj* snotty

purhe *vb* purify; refine

purheans *n.m* **purheansow**
purification
purieth *n.f* purism
Puritan I *adj* Puritan II *n.m* **Puritanyon**
Puritan
Puritanieth *n.f* Puritanism
purpur *adj* purple
purra *adj* thoroughest; veriest; absolute
pursewya *vb* pursue
pursewyans *n.m* **pursewyansow**
pursuit
purva *n.f* **purvaow** refinery
purydh *n.m* **purydhyon** purist
pusketti *n.m* **puskettiow** aquarium
pusorn *n.m* **pusornow** bale; bundle
pusornas *vb* bale
py *prn* which; what
pych *n.m* **pychys** (*musical*) pitch
pycher *n.m* **pychers** pitcher; jug
pychya *vb* pitch; pierce
pychyans *n.m* **pychyansow** piercing
pyckel *n.m* **pyckels** pickle
pyckla *vb* pickle
pyffyer *n.m* **pyffyers** dolphin; porpoise
pyg *n.m* bitumen; pitch; tar
pygans *n.m* means; wherewithal.
war-lergh pygans means-tested
pygemmys *adv* how much
pyjama *n.m* **pyjamas** pyjamas
pyksel *n.m* **pyksels, pykselyow** (*IT*)
pixel
pylla *vb* rifle; fleece; plunder; spoil;
pillage
pyment *n.m* **pymentys** spiced wine
pymp *num* five
pympbys *n.m* **pympbyses** starfish
pympdelen *n.f* cinquefoil
pympel *n.m* **pympellow** pentacle
pympes *num* fifth
pympkorn *n.m* **pympkernow**
pentagon
pymthegves *num* fifteenth
pymthek *num* fifteen

pynag *prn* whoever; whichever;
whatever. **py le pynag** *adv* wherever.
pynag oll *prn* whosoever; whatsoever
pynakyl *n.m* **pynaklys** pinnacle
pyncel *n.m* **pyncels** brush. **pyncel
lagas** *n.m* eye-liner. **pyncel-linenna**
n.m liner
pyncer *n.m* **pynceryow** pincers
pynchya *vb* pinch
pyneyl *prn* whichever; which (*of two*)
pynk hwiban *n.m* **pynkes hwiban**
bullfinch
pynk kemmyn *n.m* **pynkes kemmyn**
chaffinch
pynk menydh *n.m* **pynkes menydh**
brambling
pynn *n.m* **pynnow** pin; peg. **pynn
meus** *n.m* drawing pin
pynna *vb* pin
pyramid *n.m* **pyramidow** pyramid
pyramidek *adj* pyramidal
pyrit *n.m* pyrite; fool's gold
pys *n.coll* peas
pysadow *n.m* prayer
pys an gath *n.coll* birdsfoot trefoil
pyseul *adv* how many. **pyseul a²** how
much (of)
pysi *vb* ask; beg; pray; request. **pysi
gans** pray for. **pysi nebonan a wul
neppyth** ask somebody to do
something. **pysi war²** pray to
pysk *n.m* **puskes** fish
pyskador *n.m* **pyskadoryon** fisherman
pyskador an myghtern *n.m*
pyskadoryon an myghtern
kingfisher
pyskessa *vb* fish. **gwelen-byskessa** *n.f*
fishing rod
pysklyn *n.m* **pysklynnow** fishpond
pysknow *n.coll* peanuts
pysknowen *n.f* **pysknowennow**
peanut
pyskva *n.f* **pyskvaow** aquarium
pyst *n.m* **pystyon** fool. **penn pyst** *n.m*
idiot

pystiga *vb* ache; hurt
pystigys *adj* injured; hurt
pystik *n.m* **pystigow** hurt; lesion
pystol *n.m* **pystolys, pystolow** pistol
pystri *n.m* magic; sorcery
pystria *vb* work magic
pystrier *n.m* **pystrioryon** sorcerer;
  warlock; wizard

pystriores *n.f* **pystrioresow** sorceress
pyth I *n.m* **pythow** thing; possession;
  material; matter; property **II** *prn* what;
  that which. **pyth ha da** possessions.
  python *n.pl* belongings
pythek *adj* concrete
pytt *n.m* **pyttys, pyttow** pit
pywa *vb* own

R

rach *n.m* caution; care; heed. **gans rach**
  careful; carefully
racka *n.m* **rackow** anecdote
racket *n.m* **racketys, racketow** racket;
  bat
radar *n.m* radar
radel *n.coll* scree
radyo *n.m* **radyos, radyoyow** radio
radyologieth *n.f* radiology
radyologiethel *adj* radiological
radyologydh *n.m* **radyologydhyon**
  radiologist
radyovewek *adj* radioactive
radyovewekter *n.m* radioactivity
raff *adj* worthless
rag I *cnj* because; in order to; for **II** *prp*
  for; for the purpose of; from. **ev a**
  omgudhas rag an bleydh he hid
  from the wolf. **rag atti** out of spite.
  rag own in case. **rag tecken**
  momentarily. **rag tro** temporarily.
  Personal forms: 1s **ragov,** *2s* **ragos,** *3sm*
  ragdho, *3sf* **rygdhi,** *1p* **ragon,** *2p*
  ragowgh, *3p* **ragdha**
rag- *prfx* pre-; fore-
ragavon *n.f* **ragavonyow, ragavenow**
  tributary
ragbreder *n.m* **ragbrederow**
  precaution
ragbren *n.m* **ragbrenow** subscription
ragbrena *vb* subscribe

ragbrener *n.m* **ragbrenoryon**
  subscriber
ragdas *n.m* **ragdasow** forefather
ragdir *n.m* foreground
ragdres *n.m* **ragdresow** project
ragdresa *vb* devise a project; project
rager *n.m* **rageryow** preposition; prefix
ragerghi *vb* book; reserve
ragerghys *adj* booked; reserved
ragilow *n.m* **ragilowyow** overture
raglavar *n.m* **raglavarow** introduction;
  preface
raglev *n.m* **raglevow** vote
ragleva *vb* vote
ragleverys *adj* already mentioned
ragnotyans *n.m* **ragnotyansow**
  specification
ragober *n.m* **ragoberow** preparation
ragresegydh *n.m* **ragresegydhyon**
  predecessor
ragresek *vb* pioneer
ragresor *n.m* **ragresoryon** pioneer
ragsel *n.m* **ragselyow** premise
ragskrif *n.m* **ragskrifow** preface
ragvewek *adj* proactive
ragvreus *n.f* **ragvreusow** bias;
  prejudice. **heb ragvreus** unprejudiced
ragvreusek *adj* biased; bigoted;
  prejudiced
ragwir *n.m* **ragwiryow** priority
rahaya *vb* sneeze
rakan *n.m* **rakanow** rake

rakhanow *n.m* **rakhenwyn** pronoun
ralli *n.m* **rallis** rally
rann *n.f* **rannow** share; lot; part; portion; role. **kales rann** *n.f* a hard fate. **kemeres rann** take part; partake; participate. **rann ober** *n.f* task. **rann vrassa a^2** a greater part of; a majority of
ranna *vb* divide; part. **rynnys gans** divided by. **ranna ynter dew** halve
rannans *n.m* **ranansow** division; partition
ranndir *n.m* **ranndiryow** district; region
ranndiryel *adj* regional
ranndra *n.f* **ranndrevow** suburb
rannel *adj* partial
ranngemeryans *n.m* **ranngemeryansow** participle. **ranngemeryans godhevek** *n.m* passive participle
rannji *n.m* **rannjiow** apartment; flat
rannriv *n.m* **rannrivow** fraction
rannskrif *n.m* **rannskrifow** paragraph
rannvro *n.f* **rannvroyow** province; state
rannvroek *adj* provincial
rannwelyek *adj* partially-sighted
rannyeth *n.f* **rannyethow** dialect; idiom
ras *n.m* **rasow** virtue
rasek *adj* graceful; gracious
rask *n.m* **raskow** plane (*tool*)
raska *vb* plane
rastell *n.f* **restell** grill
rastella *vb* grill
rath *n.f* **rathes** rat
ratha *vb* scrape; rasp
rathella *vb* grate
ravna *vb* maraud; mug; ravage
ravnans *n.m* **ravnansow** mugging
ravner *n.m* **ravnoryon** bandit; marauder; mugger
raylya *vb* rail; abuse
r.e. *abbrev* **rag ensampel** e.g.

re (1) *prn* ones. **an re ma** these ones. **an re na** those ones. **re erel** other ones
re^2 (2) *part* (*optative particle*) may. **lowena re'fo** may you be happy (*sg*); (*perfective particle*). **ev re dhyskas Kernewek dres moy es deg bledhen** he has learnt Cornish for more than ten years
re^2 (3) *prp* (*in oaths*) by; upon. **re Jovyn** by Jove
re^2 (4) **I** *adv* too; excessively **II** *prn* too many; too much. **re (a^2)** *adv* too many (of); too much (of)
rebel *n.m* **rebels** rebel; insurgent
rebellya *vb* rebel
rebellyans *n.m* **rebellyansow** rebellion; insurgency; insurrection; revolt; uprising
receva *vb* accept; adopt a motion
reden *n.coll* bracken; ferns
redenen *n.f* **redenennow** fern
reden gols an Werghes *n.coll* maidenhair fern
redigen *n.f* **redigennow** radish
redik *n.coll* radishes
redya *vb* read
redyadow *adj* legible; readable
redyans *n.m* **redyansow** reading
redyer *n.m* **redyoryon** reader
refraynya *vb* refrain
re'gan *contr* (*perfective/optative particle + infixed pronoun 'us'*)
re'gas *contr* (*perfective/optative particle + infixed pronoun 'you (pl)'*)
reken *n.m* **reknow** account; bill; invoice. **heb reken** irrespective. **reken gwerth** *n.m* bill of sale
rekenva *n.f* **rekenvaow** check-out; till
rekna *vb* reckon; calculate; count
reknans *n.m* **reknansow** calculation. **checkya reknans** check a calculation
reknell *n.f* **reknellow** pocket calculator
rekord *n.m* **rekordys** record
rekordya *vb* record

re'm (1) *contr* (*perfective particle +
infixed pronoun 'me'*)

re'm (2) *contr* by my

remedi *n.m* **remedis** solution; remedy.
heb remedi incurable

remenant *n.m* **remenans, remenantys**
remainder; rest. **avel remenant**
residual

remenantel *adj* residual

remm *n.m* rheumatism

remova *vb* budge; (*transitive and
intransitive*) move; remove. **remova
chi** move house

re'n (1) *contr* (*perfective particle +
infixed pronoun 'him; it'*)

re'n (2) *contr* by the

renk *n.m* **renkow, renkyow** rank

renka *vb* arrange; class; rank in order

renkas *n.m* **renkasow** social class

renki *vb* croak; snore

renkyas *n.m* **renkysi** snorer

rennyas *n.m* **renysi** steward

rent *n.m* **rentys, rentow** rent; revenue

reowta *n.m* respect

repentya *vb* repent

repoblek *n.f* **repoblegi** republic

representya *vb* represent

res (1) I *adj* necessary; obligatory II *vb*
need; must. **a res** essential; obligatory.
res porres an absolute necessity. **res
yw dhymm** I must

res (2) *n.m* **resow** race; course; flow.
res a-dro *n.m* roundabout;
merry-go-round; carousel

res (3) *part* (*perfective/optative particle;
used before vowels with* **mos**)

re's (1) *contr* (*perfective/optative particle
+ infixed pronoun 'her', 'it'*)

re's (2) *contr* (*perfective/optative particle
+ infixed pronoun 'them'*)

resa *vb* line up

resayt *n.m* **resaytys, resaytyow** recipe

resegva *n.f* **resegvaow** run; (*race*)
course; career; orbit

resek I *n.m* **resegow** race II *vb* run;
(*liquids and powders*) flow; race. **resek
jynn diwros** *n.m* motocross. **resek
kerri** *n.m* motor racing

resell *n.f* **resellow** cursor

reser *n.m* **resoryon** runner

resin *n.coll* raisins

resinen *n.f* **resinennow** raisin

reski *n.m* **reskeun** hound (*for racing*)

resna *vb* reason

resnadow *adj* reasonable; fair

resnans *n.m* **resnansow** reasoning;
speculation

resnel *adj* rational

reson *n.m* **resons** reason; logic. **dre
reson** because. **herwydh reson**
logical; logically. **reson prag** because

resonus *adj* reasonable

resort *n.m* **resortys** resort

resortya *vb* resortya

rester *n.f* **restri** arrangement; scheme

restorita *n.m* **restoritys** restitution;
amends. **gul restorita** make amends

restra *vb* arrange; organise

restrans *n.m* **restransow** organisation

restren *n.f* **restrennow** (*document*) file

restrenna *vb* (*document*) file

restrenva *n.f* **restrenvaow** filing
cabinet

reswisk *n.m* **reswiskow** track-suit

resyas *n.m* **resyasow** rhythm

resyek *adj* rhythmic

re'th *contr* (*perfective/optative particle +
infixed pronoun 'you (sg.)'*)

reudh *n.m* distress

reudhi *vb* distress

reudhys *adj* distressed

reun *n.m* **reunes, reunyon** seal
(*animal*)

rev *n.f* **revow** oar. **rev dhewbennek** *n.f*
paddle

revedh I *adj* astonishing; surprising II
n.m **revedhow** wonder

reverthi I *n.f* **reverthiow** spring-tide II
vb flood; overwhelm

revrond *adj* reverend

revrons *n.m* respect; reverence. **gul revrons dhe**[2] respect

revya *vb* paddle; row

rew (1) *n.m* **rewyow** ice; frost. **dehen rew** *n.m* ice cream. **kub rew** *n.m* ice cube. **skes rew** *n.m* ice skate

rew (2) *n.m* **rewyow** row; line. **yn rew** successively

rewek *adj* frosty

Rewenys *top n.f* Iceland

Rewenysek *n.m* Icelandic language

rewenysek *adj* Icelandic

Rewenysyas *n.m* **Rewenysysi** Icelander

rewer *n.m* **rewyoryon** freezer

rewi *vb* freeze

rewiva *n.f* **rewivaow** glacier

rewl *n.f* **rewlys** regulation; rule. **rewl voos** *n.f* diet

rewlell *n.f* **rewlellow** ruler (*tool*)

rewlya *vb* rule; control; regulate

rewlyas *n.m* **rewlysi** ruler

rewlys *adj* regular

rewvenydh *n.m* iceberg

rewys *adj* frozen; icy

reydh *n.f* **reydhow** sex

reydhedh *n.f* **reydhedhow** gender

reydhek *adj* sexual

reydhgasek *adj* sexist

reydhgasieth *n.f* sexism

reyn *n.m* **reynys** reign

reynya *vb* reign

reyth I *adj* regular II *n.f* **reythyow** religious law; (*legal*) right. **yn reyth** rightly

ri *vb* give; grant; present. **ri arta** give back. **ri gweres arghans** subsidise; support financially

'Ria *excl* good heavens!

rider *n.m* **ridrow** sieve; colander

ridra *vb* sieve; sift

riel *adj* regal; royal

rim *n.m* **rimyow** rhyme

rimya *vb* rhyme

rin *n.m* **rinyow** mystery

ris *n.coll* rice. **ris bryjys** *n.coll* boiled rice. **ris friys** *n.coll* fried rice. **ris glusek** *n.coll* sticky rice. **ris greun berr** *n.coll* short grain rice. **ris greun hir** *n.coll* long grain rice

risen *n.f* **risennow** grain of rice

riv *n.m* **rivow** number

riva *vb* number

rivell *n.f* **rivellow** dial

riven *n.f* **rivennow** digit

riw *n.f* **riwyow** rise; slope

riyas *n.m* **riysi** donor

ro *n.m* **rohow, royow** gift; present; offering. **ro a natur** *n.m* gift of nature; talent

roas *n.m* **roasow** facility; talent

roasek *adj* talented

robot *n.m* **robotys, robotow** robot

rock *n.m* rock music

rogh *n.m* **roghow** grunt

rogha (1) *vb* grunt

rogha (2) *n.m* **roghys** (*fish*) ray; thornback

rogha bros *n.m* stingray

rol *n.f* **rolyow** list; index; inventory; menu; roll. **rol an warioryon** *n.f* cast (*of a play*). **rol voos** *n.f* restaurant menu. **rol negys** *n.f* agenda

rolas *n.m* **rolasow** catalogue

rolbren *n.m* **rolbrennyer** wooden roller; rolling pin

rolven *n.m* **rolveyn** stone roller

rolwedhen *n.f* **rolwedhennow** (*IT*) menu tree

rolya *vb* roll

Rom *n.m* **Romyon** Roma

romanek *adj* Romanic. **pennserneth romanek** *n.f* Romanic architecture

Romani (1) *top n.f* Romania

Romani (2) *n.m* Romani (*language of Roma people*)

Romanian *n.m* **Romanians** Romanian

Romaniek *n.m* Romanian (*language of Romania*)

romaniek *adj* Romanian

romans *n.m* **romansow** novel

romansek *adj* romantic

romansogeth *n.f* romanticism

romek *adj* Romani

romm *n.m* rum

rond *adj* round; rounded

rondenep *n.m* roundness

ronk I *adj* croaky; hoarse II **ronkow** *n.m* croak; snore. **ronk mernans** *n.m* death rattle

ronsona *vb* ransom

roos *n.f* **rosow** net. **roos fardellow** *n.f* luggage rack

ros (1) *n.coll* roses

ros (2) *n.f* **rosow** wheel. **kador ros** *n.f* wheelchair. **ros-lewya** *n.f* steering wheel. **ros melin** *n.f* mill wheel. **ros parys** *n.f* spare wheel

ros (3) *n.m* **rosyow** hill-spur; promontory; moor

rosella *vb* spin; rotate

rosellans *n.m* **rosellansow** rotation

rosen *n.f* **rosennow** rose

rosen menydh *n.f* peony

rosen wyls *n.f* **rosennow gwyls** dog rose; wild rose (*briar rose*)

ros gwyls *n.coll* dog rose; wild rose (*briar rose*)

rosik *n.f* **rosigow** castor

roskis *n.m* **roskisyow** roller skate

roslyver *n.m* **roslyvrow** netbook (*IT*)

rosmari *n.coll* rosemary

rost *n.m* **rostys** roast

rostell *n.f* **rostellow** skateboard

rostella *vb* skateboard

rostya *vb* roast

rosva *n.f* **rosvaow** avenue; boulevard; promenade

rosweyth *n.m* **rosweythyow** network

rosya *vb* hike; surf (*the internet*)

rosyans *n.m* **rosyansow** hike

roth *n.m* **rothow** shape

rout *n.m* **routys** mob

routabaga *n.m* **routabagys** swede

routh *n.f* **routhow** crowd; throng

routya *vb* lord it over; control

routyell *n.f* **routyellow** router

roweth *n.m* importance; prestige

rubella *n.m* (*med*) rubella (German measles)

rudh *adj* red. **liw rudh** *n.m* blush; red colour. **penn rudh** *n.m* readhead

rudhek *n.m* **rudhogyon** robin

rudhek pilyek *n.m* ragged robin

rudhem *n.m* **rudhemmow** ruby

rudhik *adj* reddish

rudhlas *adj* purple

rudhloos *adj* russet

rudhvelyn *adj* orange

rudhwynn *adj* reddish pink

rudhya *vb* blush; redden

rugbi *n.m* rugby

rugla *vb* rattle

ruglen *n.f* **ruglennow** rattle

rumen *n.f* **rumennow** denomination

run *n.f* **runyow** hillside; slope; rise

rusk *n.coll* peels; barks

ruskek *adj* rough-barked

rusken *n.f* **ruskennow** peel; bark

Russek *n.m* Russian language

russek *adj* Russian

Russi *top n.f* Russia

Russian *n.m* **Russians** Russian

rust *adj* rough

ruta *n.m* meadow rue

rutya *vb* rub

rutyans *n.m* **rutyansow** rub; friction

rutyer *n.m* **rutyeryow** rubber; eraser

ruvanes *n.f* **ruvanesow** queen

ruvanes an koos *n.f* wild clematis (*traveller's joy; old man's beard*)

ruvaneth *n.f* **ruvanethow** kingdom. **Ruvaneth Unys (RU)** *top n.f* United Kingdom (UK)

ryb *adj* beside; near to; next to. **ryb tenewen** alongside. *Personal forms: 1s rybov, 2s rybos, 3sm rybdho, 3sf rybdhi, 1p rybon, 2p rybowgh, 3p rybdha*

rych *adj* rich; sumptuous
rychedh *n.m* **rychedhow** richness
rychhe *vb* enrich
rychys *n.m* riches; wealth
rydh *adj* free
rydhhe *vb* free

rydhses *n.m* freedom; liberty
ryg *n.m* **rygyow** cattle wart
rynni *vb* shiver
rynnys *adj* divided
rypsav *n.m* **rypsavow** lay-by
rys *n.f* **rysyow** ford

S

's *prn* (*infixed, pl*) them; (*infixed, sg*) her; it
sab *n.coll* pine trees; conifers
saben *n.f* **sabennow** pine tree; conifer
sad *adj* constant; earnest; serious; solemn; stable
Sadorn *n.m* Saturday; Saturn
saffir *n.m* **saffiryow** sapphire
safran (1) *n.m* saffron. **tesen safran** *n.f* saffron cake
safran (2) *n.m* crocus
safran an Jowl *n.coll* dodder (*devil's guts; witches hair*)
saga *n.m* **sagas** saga
sagh *n.m* **seghyer** bag; sack. **gwari sagh** *n.m* raffle. **prena kath yn sagh** buy a pig in a poke. **sagh keyn** *n.m* backpack; rucksack. **sagh-koska** *n.m* sleeping bag. **pibow sagh** *n.pl* bagpipes
sagha *vb* (put in a) bag
sakra *vb* consecrate; ordain
sakrifia *vb* sacrifice
sakrifis *n.m* **sakrifisys** sacrifice; sacrificial victim
sakrifisa *vb* sacrifice
salad *n.m* salad
salami *n.m* **salamis** salami
sall *adj* salty
salla *vb* salt; cure; pickle
salm *n.m* **salmow** psalm
salow I *adj* safe; unharmed **II** *adv* safely
salowder *n.m* security; safety
salusi *vb* greet

salvador *n.m* **salvadoryon** saviour
sampel *n.m* **samplow** sample; specimen
sampla *vb* sample
sand *n.m* **sandys** course (of a meal); dish
sandal *n.m* **sandalys** sandal
sans I *adj* holy **II** *n.m* **sens** saint
sansel *adj* saintly; pious
sanshe *vb* sanctify
sansoleth *n.f* sanctity; piety
sarf *n.f* **serf** snake; serpent. **sarf gonna** *n.f* scarf. **sarf-neyja** *n.f* (*toy*) kite
sarfek *adj* serpentine
sarfven *n.m* (*rock*) serpentine
Sarsyn *n.m* (*archaic*) Muslim
satysfia *vb* satisfy
satysfians *n.m* **satysfiansow** satisfaction
sav *n.m* **savow** stand
saven *n.f* **savnow** cleft; gully
savla *n.m* **savleow** standpoint; halt; position; stance; stop. **savla kyttrin** bus stop
savon *n.f* **savonow** standard
savonegi *vb* standardize
savonek *adj* standard
saw (1) *cnj* but; except
saw (2) *adj* safe; secure. **kofer saw** *n.m* safe
sawder *n.m* security; safety. **skwych sawder** *n.m* safety catch
sawen an dhragon *n.m* antirrhinum; snapdragon

sawgh *n.m* **sawghow** burden; load; horse-load. **orth an sawgh** by the load

sawja *n.m* sage (*herb*)

sawment *n.m* therapy

sawna *n.m* **sawnas** sauna

sawor *n.m* **sawaryow** aroma; flavour; taste. **sawor poos** *n.m* nasty smell; stench; odour

sawaren *n.f* **sawrennow** condiment

sawor gwav *n.m* winter savory

sawor hav *n.m* summer savory

sawra *vb* taste

sawrans *n.m* **sawransow** seasoning

sawrek *adj* tasty

sawrys *adj* seasoned; flavoured

sawya *vb* heal; rescue; save. **sawya a**[2] rescue from; heal from. **grugys-sawya** *n.m* lifebelt. **skath-sawya** *n.f* lifeboat. **sawya fas** save face

sawyans *n.m* **sawyansow** rescue

sawyas *n.m* **sawysi** rescuer

se *n.m* **seys, seow** throne; seat

sebon *n.m* **sebonow** soap. **gwari sebon** *n.m* soap opera

sebonas *adj* soapy

seboni *vb* soap

sedh *n.m* **sedhow** dive

sedher *n.m* **sedhoryon** diver. **sedher downvor** *n.m* deep-sea diver

sedhes *n.m* **sedhesow** setting; sinking; submersion

sedhi *vb* dive; submerge; sink; (*sun*) set. **lester-sedhi** *n.m* submarine

segha *vb* dry; wipe

seghans *n.m* **seghansow** wipe

seghen *n.f* **seghennow** dead tree

seghes *n.m* thirst. **bos seghes dhe**[2] thirsty, be thirsty

seghter *n.m* **seghteryow** drought

segi *vb* soak

sel (1) *n.f* **selyow** foundation; base

sel (2) *n.f* **selys, selyow** seal; signet; (*printing*) impression

sel dherivadow *n.f* **selyow derivadow** database

selsigen *n.f* **selsigernow** sausage

selsik *n.coll* sausages

selva *n.f* **selvaow** military base

selven *n.m* **selveyn** foundation stone

selvenel *adj* basic; fundamental

selveneleth *n.f* fundamentalism; extremism

selvenelyas *n.m* **selvenelysi** fundamentalist; extremist

selwel *vb* (*in the context of Christian salvation*) save

selwyans *n.m* **selwyansow** salvation

selwyas *n.m* **selwysi** saviour

selya *vb* establish; found; set up

selyek *adj* basic

semlant *n.m* **semlans** appearance; expression

semli *adj* seemly

sempel *adj* simple; homely; ordinary; plain; primitive

sempelhe *vb* simplify

Sen *n.m* (*title*) Saint

senedh *n.m* **senedhow** parliament. **esel senedh (ES)** *n.m* member of parliament (MP)

senedhek *adj* parlimentary

seni *vb* play (an instrument); ring (a bell); (*transitive and intransitive*) sound

senpeder *n.m* samphire

sens *n.m* **sensys** sense (*anat*)

sensell *n.f* **sensellow** detector; sensor

sensytyvita *n.m* sensitivity

ser *n.m* **seri** craftsperson. **ser prenn** *n.m* carpenter

Serb *n.m* **Serbyon** Serb

Serbek *n.m* Serbian language

serbek *adj* Serbian

Serbi *top* *n.f* Serbia

serfel *n.m* chervil

serri (1) *vb* (*intransitive*) be angry; get angry; (*transitive*) annoy; aggravate;

irritate; make angry. **serri orth** be angry with; get angry with

serri (2) *vb* shut. **serr dha dhiwen!** shut up!

serrys *adj* angry; indignant; vexed

serth *adj* abrupt; vertical; upright; stiff; steep; perpendicular; erect

serthals *n.f* **serthalsyow** precipice

servadow *adj* makeshift; temporary; serviceable

servell *n.f* **servellow** (*IT*) server

servis *n.m* **servisyow** service. **Servis Kenedhlek an Yeghes (NHS)** *n.m* the National Health Service (NHS)

servya *vb* wait upon; serve

servyades *n.f* **servyadesow** waitress

servyas *n.m* **servysi** servant; waiter

servyour *n.m* **servyours** tray

seson *n.m* **sesons, sesonyow** season; period of time. **kleves seson** *n.m* ague

sesya *vb* seize; confiscate; lay hold of; occupy; take prisoner

sesyans *n.m* **sesyansow** occupation

seth (1) *n.f* **sethow** arrow

seth (2) *n.m* **sethow** large jar

setha *vb* shoot

sethas *n.m* **sethasow** jarful

sether *n.m* **sethoryon** archer

sett *n.m* **settys, settow** set; suite. **sett kartennow** *n.m* deck of cards

settya *vb* set; place; put. **settya orth** resist. **settya moos** set the table

settyes *adj* placed

settys *adj* placed

seudh *n.m* **seudhow** (*geographical*) depression

seudhel *n.m* **seudhelyow** heel

seul *prn* so many; so much; whoever

seulabrys *adv* already; formerly; in the past

seuladhydh *adv* long since

sevel *vb* (*intransitive*) stand; arise; get up; rise; halt; (*transitive*) raise up; erect. **sevel orth** resist; abstain from.

sevel orth goheles face up to. **sevel orth hwerthin** keep a straight face

sevellek *n.m* **sevelloges** redwing

sevi *n.coll* strawberries. **kennin sevi** *n.coll* chives

sevia *vb* gather strawberries

sevien *n.f* **seviennow** strawberry

sevur *adj* earnest; serious

sevureth *n.f* severity

sewajya *vb* mitigate

sewen *adj* successful; prosperous

sewena *n.f* success; prosperity; welfare. **heb sewena** unsuccessful; unsuccessfully

seweni *vb* succeed; get on; prosper; thrive; win out

sewenus *adj* successful

sewenyans *n.m* prosperity

sewt *n.m* **sewtys** suit. **sewt kartennow** *n.m* suit of cards

sewya *vb* follow; result. **a sew** following. **sewya dre lagha** sue

sewyans *n.m* **sewyansow** outcome; result; consequence; sequel. **yn sewyans** consequently

seytegves *num* seventeenth

seytek *num* seventeen

seyth *num* seven

seythen *n.f* **seythennyow** week. **an jydh ma war seythen** today week. **pub seythen** *adv* weekly

seythennyek *adj* weekly. **jornal seythennyek** *n.m* weekly

seythves *num* seventh

shackya *vb* shake. **shackya leuv** shake hands

shackyans *n.m* **shackyansow** shake. **shackyans leuv** *n.m* handshake

shafta *n.m* **shaftys** mine-shaft

shakleth *n.m* **shaklethow** milkshake

sham *n.m* shame

shamya *vb* shame

shap *n.m* **shapys** shape. **shap adamant** *n.m* lozenge

shapya *vb* model; shape

sheft *n.m* **sheftys** shaft (*of spear*)

shinya *vb* shine

shoppa *n.m* **shoppys** workshop; shop.
  shoppa ober *n.m* workshop

shora *n.m* **shorys** fit; seizure

shyndya *vb* harm; hurt; impair; injure;
  ruin

shyndyans *n.m* **shyndyansow** injury

shyndys *adj* damaged; hurt; injured

si *vb* fancy

sia *vb* buzz; hiss; rustle

sians *n.m* **siansow** notion

sidhel *n.m* **sidhlow** filter

sidhla *vb* filter; strain

Sikieth *n.f* Sikhism

silikon *n.m* (*element*) silicon

sim *n.m* **simes** monkey

sina *vb* sign

sinans *n.m* **sinansow** signature

sinell *n.f* **sinellow** signal

sinella *vb* signal

sinya *vb* indicate; signal

sira *n.m* **sirys** father; sire. **sira da** *n.m*
  father-in-law. **sira wynn** *n.m*
  grandfather

siw *n.m* **siwyon** bream

skafhe *vb* lighten

skajyn *n.m* **skajynnow** (*offensive*)
  tramp

skala *n.m* **skalys** dish; saucer

skaldya *vb* scald; blight

skaldyans *n.m* **skaldyansow** blight

skalpyon *n.pl* pickles

skampi *n.coll* scampi

skans *n.coll* flakes; scales

skansek *adj* flaky; scaly

skansen *n.f* **skansennow** flakes; scales

skant I *adv* barely; hardly; scarcely;
  scantily **II** *adj* scanty; scarce

skantlowr *adv* barely; hardly; scantily;
  scarcely

skantlyn *n.m* **skantlyns** ruler (*tool*);
  template; pattern

skapya *vb* escape; slip out.
  fordh-skapya *n.f* fire escape; escape
  route

skath *n.f* **skathow** boat. **skath hir** *n.f*
  barge. **skath klos** *n.f* raft.
  skath-revya *n.f* rowboat.
  skath-sawya *n.f* lifeboat. **skath tan**
  n.f motor-boat. **skath-wolya** *n.f*
  sailing boat

skatt I *adj* bankrupt; crushed **II** *n.m*
  skattys, skattow (= **skwatt**) hit;
  blow; slap **III gul skatt** *vb* bankrupt

skattyans *n.m* **skattyansow**
  bankruptcy

skattra *vb* scatter

skav *adj* light; agile; flimsy; nimble;
  slight

skav a'y ligyon *n.m* arum lily (*lords
  and ladies; cuckoo pint*)

skavder *n.m* speed; agility; quickness

skavel *n.f* **skavellow** stool. **skavel
  droos** *n.f* footstool

skavel gronek *n.f* **skavellow kronek**
  toadstool; mushroom

skaw *n.coll* (*trees*) elder. **yrin skaw**
  n.coll elderberry. **gwin skaw** *n.m*
  elderberry wine

skaw dor *n.coll* ground elder

skawen *n.f* **skawennow** (*tree*) elder

skawen an Werghes *n.f* common
  agrimony (*steeples; sticklewort*)

skawen dhu *n.f* hemp agrimony (*holy
  rope*)

skawen gogh *n.f* **skawennow kogh**
  woody nightshade (*bittersweet*)

skaw kogh *n.coll* woody nightshade
  (*bittersweet*)

skenna *n.m* **skennow** tendon

skentel *adj* adept; brainy; clever;
  intelligent; learned; skilled

skentoleth *n.f* wisdom

sker *n.coll* barnacles

skeren *n.f* **skerennow** barnacle

skeri *vb* skim

skes *n.m* **skesow** skate. **skes rew** *n.m* ice skate

skesya *vb* skate. **skesya war rew** ice skate

sketh *n.m* **skethow** strip

skethen *n.f* **skethennow** strip

skethenna *vb* shred; slice; tatter

skethra *vb* lop; prune

skethrek *adj* splintered

skeul *n.f* **skeulyow** ladder; scale. **skeul lovan** *n.f* rope ladder

skeul Varia *n.f* centaury

skeulya *vb* scale

skeus *n.m* **skeusow** reflection; shadow

skeusek *adj* suspicious; shady

skeusen *n.f* **skeusennow** photograph. **skeusen dhewyn-X** *n.f*, **skeusennow dewyn-X** X-ray photograph

skeusenieth *n.f* photography

skeusenner *n.m* **skeusenoryon** photographer

skeusenweyth *n.f* photography

skeusi *vb* escape; evade capture. **skeusi rag** escape from

skevens *n.pl* lungs

skew *n.f* **skewyow** screen. **skew wyns** *n.f* windscreen

ski *n.m* **skis, skiow** ski

skia *vb* ski

skians *n.m* **skiansow** intellect; knowledge; sense; wisdom. **mes a'y skians** out of his mind. **meur y skians** knowledeable. **skians kreftus** *n.m* artificial intelligence

skiansek I *adj* intellectual; intelligent; knowledeable **II** *n.m* **skiansogyon** intellectual

skiber *n.f* **skiberyow** barn

skiens *n.m* **skiensow** science; (*in trad. texts*) knowledge; wisdom

skiensek *adj* scientific

skiensydh *n.m* **skiensydhes** scientist

skientel *adj* intelligent; learned

skila *n.f* **skilys** cause; reason

skinen *n.f* **skinennow** earring

skit *n.m* diarrhoea

skitell *n.f* **skitellow** syringe

skitsofrenek *adj* schizophrenic (*med*)

skitsofrenia *n.m* schizophrenia (*med*)

skitya *vb* inject

skityans *n.m* **skityansow** injection. **skityans petrol** *n.m* fuel injection

sklander *n.m* **sklanderyow** slander; scandal

sklandra *vb* slander; scandalise

skochfordh *n.f* **skochfordhow** alleyway

skochkylgh *n.m* **skochkylghyow** short circuit

skogyn *n.m* **skogynnow** idiot; (*offensive*) half-wit

skol *n.f* **skolyow** school. **lyver skol** schoolbook. **skol elvennek** *n.f* elementary school. **skol gynsa** *n.f* primary school. **skol nessa** *n.f* secondary school. **skol nos** *n.f* night school. **skol ramer** *n.f* grammar school. **skol veythrin** *n.f* nursery school. **skol stat** *n.f* state school. **skol ughel** *n.f* high school

skoler *n.m* **skoloryon** scholar

skolheygel *adj* scholarly

skolheygieth *n.f* scholarship

skolheyk *n.m* **skolheygyon** student; scholar

skolji *n.m* **skoljiow** schoolhouse

skolk *n.m* **skolkyow** sneak

skolkya *vb* sneak

skoll *n.m* rubbish; waste. **tewlel dhe skoll** throw away

skollva *n.f* **skollvaow** wastefulness

skollya *vb* waste; shed; spill; tip. **skollya a-les** disperse. **skollya liv a dhagrow** cry one's eyes out

skollyans *n.m* **skollyansow** spill

skollyek *adj* wasteful

skollyon *n.pl* pieces of junk; slop

skolvaw *n.m* **skolvebyon** schoolboy

skol veythrin *n.f* nursery school

skolvowes *n.f* **skolvowysi** schoolgirl

skombla *vb* defecate (*animals*)

skomm *n.coll* splinter; jetsam

skommen *n.f* **skomennow** chip; splinter. **skommow** *n.pl* wreckage

skon *adv* at once; soon; quickly

skons *n.coll* scones

skonsen *n.f* **skonsennow** scone

skonya *vb* refuse. **acheson rag skonya** *n.m* objection. **skonya a²** abstain from. **skonya gweles** turn a blind eye. **skonya omwaya** refuse to budge; dig one's heels in

skoodh *n.f* **skodhow**, *dl* **diwskodh** shoulder

skoodhya *vb* assist; back; help; second; support

skoodhyans *n.m* **skodhyansow** assistance; help; support. **skoodhyans an bobel** *n.m* grass-roots support

skoodhyer *n.m* **skodhyoryon** supporter; fan; assistant

skoodhyer yeghes *n.m* **skodhyoryon yeghes** health care assistant

skoos *n.m* **skosow** shield

skorn *n.m* **skornys** scorn

skornya *vb* scorn

skornyadow *adj* ridiculous

skorpyonles *n.m* forget-me-not

skorr (1) *n.m* **skorrow** branch

skorr (2) *n.coll* branches; veins of ore

skorrek *adj* branched

skorren *n.f* **skorrennow** (*anat*) vein; branch; vein of ore

skorya *vb* score

skovarn *n.f* **skovornow**, *dl* **diwskovarn** ear; handle (*of a jar*)

skovarnek I *n.m* **skovarnogyon, skovarnoges** hare. **skovarnek Meurth gorbollek** Mad March hare **II** *adj* big-eared

skovarnigow *n.pl* headphones. **skovarnigow munys** earphones

skovva *n.f* **skovvaow** shelter; haven

skowl *n.m* **skowles** (*bird*) kite

skrambla *vb* scramble. **oy skramblys** *n.m* scrambled egg

skravinyas *vb* claw

skriba *n.m* **skribys** scribe

skrif *n.m* **skrifow** article; document. **skrif kott** *n.m* abstract

skrifa *vb* write. **gis-skrifa** *n.m* literary style

skrifedh *n.f* **skrifedhow** writ

skrifen *n.f* **skrifennow** article; document

skrifennyas *n.m* **skrifenysi** secretary

skrifenyaseth *n.f* secretariat

skrifer *n.m* **skriforyon** writer

skriflyver *n.m* **skriflyvrow** notebook

skrifsagh *n.m* **skrifseghyer** briefcase

skrifwas *n.m* **skrifwesyon** clerk

skrifyas *n.m* **skrifysi** (*professional*) writer

skrij *n.m* **skrijow** scream

skrija *vb* scream

skrin *n.f* **skrinyow** screen; monitor

skrinskeusen *n.f* **skrinskeusennow** screenshot

skrinva *n.f* **skrinvaow** gnashing

skriptor *n.m* **skriptors** scripture

skrisel *n.f* **skrisellow** poster

skrolya *vb* scroll

skruth *n.m* **skruthow** shudder; revulsion; panic

skrutha *vb* shudder

skruthus *adj* creepy; ghastly

skruthys *adj* shocked; horrified

skrybla *vb* scribble; doodle

skryblans *n.m* **skryblansow** scribble; doodle

skrynk *n.m* **skrynkow** grin; snarl

skrynkya *vb* grin; snarl

skrypp *n.m* **skryppys, skryppow** wallet

skub *n.m* **skubyon** sweeping

skubell *n.f* **skubellow** broom; brush. **skubell-sugna** *n.f* **skubellow-sugna** vacuum cleaner. **skubell-wolghi** *n.f* **skubellow-golghi** mop

skubellek *adj* rubbishy; trashy

skuber *n.m* **skuboryon** sweeper

skubus *adj* sweeping

skubya *vb* brush; sweep

skubyllen *n.f* **skubyllennow** broom; brush. **skubyllen bast** *n.f* pastry brush. **skubyllen baynt** *n.f* paintbrush. **skubyllen dhens** *n.f* toothbrush

skubyon *n.coll* refuse; sweepings

skubyonen *n.f* **skubyonennow** piece of refuse

skudel *n.f* **skudellow** bowl; dish; plate. **skudel lorell** *n.f* satellite dish

skwardya *vb* rip

skwatt *n.m* **skwattys, skwattow** (= **skatt**) hit; blow

skwattya *vb* hit; smash; squash

skwir I *adj* standard II *n.m* **skwirys** standard; set-square

skwirglassya *vb* stereotype

skwith *adj* weary; tired; sleepy

skwitha *vb* tire; weary

skwithhe *vb* tire

skwithhes *adj* wearied

skwithter *n.m* weariness; fatigue

skwithus *adj* boring; tedious; irksome; tiresome; tiring

skwithys *adj* bored

skwych *n.m* **skwychys** switch; catch; twitch. **skwych sawder** *n.m* safety catch

skwychell *n.f* **skwychellow** (*electric*) switch

skwychella *vb* switch

skwychya *vb* switch; twitch. **skwychya yn farow** switch off. **skwychya yn fyw** switch on

skyll *n.coll* sprouts; shoots

skylla *vb* germinate; sprout; shoot

skyllen *n.f* **skyllennow** sprout; shoot

skyllwyn *adj* whitish

skyrmya *vb* (*swordplay*) fence

skyrrys *adj* splintered

slackya *vb* abate; let up; slacken

sleygh *adj* clever; skilful; competent; skilled

sleyghneth *n.f* skill; dexterity

slim *n.m* **slimys** slime

Slovak *n.m* **Slovakyon** Slovak

slovakek *adj* Slovak

Slovaki *top n.f* Slovakia

Sloven *n.m* **Slovenyon** Slovene

Slovenek *n.m* Slovenian language

slovenek *adj* Slovenian

Sloveni *top n.f* Slovenia

slynk I *adj* slippery II *n.m* **slynkys, slynkow** slide. **karr slynk** *n.m* sleigh

slynkya *vb* glide; drag oneself along

smat *n.m* **smatys** thug; tough guy

snell I *adj* quick; speedy; active II *adv* quickly

snobbyn *n.m* **snobbynnow** snob

snod *n.m* **snodys, snodow** ribbon; tape

socyal *adj* social. **diogeledh socyal** *n.m* social security

socyalieth *n.f* socialism

socyalydh *n.m* **socyalydhyon** socialist

socyalydhek *adj* socialist

socyologieth *n.f* sociology

socyologiethek *adj* sociological

socyologydh *n.m* **socyologydhyon** sociologist

soda *n.m* **sodas** soda

sodha *vb* serve; hold an office

sodhek *n.m* **sodhogyon** officer; official

sodhogel *adj* official

sodhva *n.f* **sodhvaow** office; bureau. **sodhva bost** *n.f* post office. **sodhva doll** *n.f* tax office. **sodhva greslu** *n.f* police station

sodones *n.coll* sultanas

sodonesen *n.f* **sodonesennow** sultana

sodron *n.coll* horse-flies

sodronen *n.f* **sodronennow** horse-fly

sogh (1) *adj* blunt; dull; obtuse. **penn-sogh** *adj* hare-brained

sogh (2) *n.m* **soghyow** ploughshare

soghelin *n.m* **soghelinyow** obtuse angle

sojet *n.m* **sojets** subject (*of a monarch*)

sojeta *n.m* **sojetys** grammatical subject

sokor *n.m* aid

sokra *vb* aid

soled I *adj* solid **II** *n.m* **soledow** solid

solempnita *n.m* **solempnitys** ceremony; solemnity

solempnya *vb* celebrate

solempnyans *n.m* **solempnyansow** celebration

solempnyel *adj* ceremonial

soler *n.m* **soleryow** attic; gallery; loft

solo *n.m* **solos** solo

sols *n.m* **solsow** shilling

solva *n.f* **solvaow** establishment

somm *n.m* **sommow** total; sum

somma *vb* sum

sommen *n.f* **somennow** total; sum

somper *adj* unequalled

sompna *vb* summon

son *n.m* **sonyow** sound; noise. **gas dha son!** shut up! **heb gul son** silently

sona *vb* bless; charm

sonambulism *n.m* somnambulism (*med*); sleepwalking (*colloq*)

sondyans *n.m* **sondyansow** poll

sonek *adj* sonic

sonell *n.f* **sonellow** (*object*) charm

sonet *n.m* **sonettys** sonnet

sonlergh *n.m* **sonlerghyow** soundtrack

sononieth *n.f* acoustics

sononiethel *adj* acoustic

sonskrif *n.m* **sonskrifow** recording

sonskrifa *vb* record (*audio*)

soodh *n.f* **sodhow** employment; occupation; office

soon *n.m* **sonyow** blessing

soov *n.m* suet; tallow

soper *n.m* **soperyow** supper

soprano *n.m* **sopranos** soprano

sopya *vb* sup

sordya *vb* (*transitive*) arouse; evoke; instigate; provoke; (*intransitive*) arise; emerge; mutiny. **sordya marth yn**

nebonan impress somebody. **usi ow sordya** emerging; nascent

sordyans *n.m* **sordyansow** instigation; mutiny; uprising

sorn *n.m* **sornow** corner

sorr *n.m* anger; wrath. **don sorr y'n golon** harbour anger. **kemeres sorr** take umbrage

sorrvan *n.m* indignation

sort (1) *n.m* **sortow** kind; sort; type; variety. **a bub sort** miscellaneous. **a lies sort** varied; heterogeneous

sort (2) *n.m* **sortes** hedgehog

sortya *vb* sort

sos *n.m* friend; mate; pal

sosten *n.m* sustenance; nutrition; foodstuff

sostena *vb* sustain

sostenadewder *n.m* sustainability

sostenadow *adj* sustainable

sotel *adj* crafty; subtle

sotelneth *n.f* subtlety

soth *n.m* south. **a'n soth** southern

soth-est *n.m* south-east

soth-west *n.m* south-west

souba *vb* soak

souben *n.f* **soubennow** morsel

souder *n.m* **soudoryon, soudrys** soldier

souderji *n.m* **souderjiow** barracks

sovran I *adj* sovereign **II** *n.m* **sovrans** sovereign

sovranedh *n.m* sovereignty

sowdhan I *n.m* confusion; bewilderment **II** *adv* **yn sowdhan** astray

sowdhanas *vb* (= **sowdheni**) amaze; be confused; confuse; stupefy; surprise

sowdheni *vb* (= **sowdhanas**) amaze; be confused; confuse; stupefy; surprise

sowdhenys *adj* bewildered; confused

soweth *int* alas; oh dear

sowl *n.coll* stubble; thatch

sowlek *adj* stubbly
sowlenna *vb* thatch
Sows *n.m* **Sowson** Englishman
Sows- *prfx* Anglo-
sows *n.m* **sowsys, sowsow** sauce
Sowses *n.f* **Sowsesow** Englishwoman
Sowsneger *n.m* **Sowsnegoryon**
  English speaker; anglophone
sowsneger *adj* anglophone
Sowsnek *n.m* English language
sowsnek *adj* English
sowsnekhe *vb* anglicise
sowter *n.m* **sowters** psalter
spadha *vb* castrate; neuter; spay
spadhesik *n.m* **spadhesigyon** eunuch
spal *n.m* **spalyow** fine; penalty
spala *vb* fine
spar I *adj* spare **II sparyon** *n.m* spare
  part
sparya *vb* spare; economise
spas *n.m* **spassow** space; opportunity;
  room
spaven *n.f* **spavennow** lull;
  intermission
spavenhe *vb* lull
spavnel *n.f* **spavnellow** lull
Spayn *top n.m* Spain
Spaynek *n.m* Spanish language
spaynek *adj* Spanish
Spaynyer *n.m* **Spaynyoryon** Spaniard
speda *n.f* prosperity
spedhas *n.coll* briars
spedhasen *n.f* **spedhasennow** briar
spedya *vb* succeed; progress; get on.
  spedya marthys da work like a charm
spena *vb* spend; exhaust
spencer *n.m* **spencers** butler
spens *n.m* **spensow** larder
spenys *adj* exhausted
spera *n.m* **sperys** spear
spern *n.coll* thorns. **kurun spern** *n.f*
  crown of thorns; hangover. **spern
  gwynn** *n.coll* hawthorn. **spern du** *coll*
  blackthorn. **spern melen** *n.coll*
  barberries

spernek *adj* thorny
spernen *n.f* **spernennow** thorn
spernen dhu *n.f* **spernennow du**
  blackthorn
spernen wynn *n.f* **spernennow
  gwynn** hawthorn
spik *n.m* **spikys** spike
spinach *n.m* spinach
spis *n.m* **spisys, spisyow** spice
spisa *vb* spice
spisek *adj* spicy
spiser *n.m* **spisoryon** grocer
spisti *n.m* **spistiow** grocery
spit *n.m* spite; malice. **spit dhe**[2] in
  spite of
spitus *adj* spiteful
splander *n.m* gloss; polish
splann I *adj* bright; brilliant; gleaming;
  gorgeous; luminous; shining; superb
  II *int* super! **yn jydh splann** in broad
  daylight
splanna *vb* shine
splannhe *vb* illuminate
splatt *n.m* **splattys, splattow** plot
splattya *vb* (*delineate*) plot
spong *n.m* **spongow** sponge
sport *n.m* **sportys, sportow** sport;
  pastime
sportva *n.f* **sportvaow** stadium
sportyas *n.m* **sportysi** sportsperson
sprall *n.m* **sprallow** inhibition
spralla *vb* inhibit
sprallansedh *n.m* (*in physics*)
  resistance
sprellys *adj* frustrated
sprus *n.coll* kernels
sprusek *adj* nuclear
sprusen (1) *n.f* **sprusennow** kernel;
  pip
sprusen (2) *n.f* **sprusennow** nucleus
  (*biol*)
spryngya *vb* spring up
spyrys *n.m* **spyrysyon** fairy; spirit
spys *n.m* **spysow** period; interval, **a
  verr spys** *adv* soon; shortly

stag (1) I *adj* attached; fixed; stuck **II** *n.m* **stagow** tether. **mos yn stag** get stuck

stag (2) *n.m* **stagow** mire; mud

staga *vb* attach; fix; tether

stagell *n.f* **stagellow** attachment

stamina *n.m* stamina

stamp *n.m* **stampys, stampow** (*postage*) stamp

stampya *vb* stamp

stanch *adj* staunch; waterproof

stanchura *vb* waterproof

stank *n.m* **stankyow** tread; stamp of foot

stankya *vb* tread; trample; stamp

stark *adv* fixedly. **mires stark orth** stare at

stat *n.m* **statys, statow** state; situation; estate. **an Statys Unys** *top n.pl* the United States (*of America*). **stat an les** *n.m* the welfare state

statydh *n.m* **statydhyon** statesman

statydhes *n.f* **statydhesow** stateswoman

statystek *n.f* (*science*) statistics

statystyk *n.m* **statystygyon** statistic

sten *n.m* (*element*) tin

stenek *n.f* **stenegow** stannary

stenor *n.m* **stenoryon** tinner

stenor brith *n.m* **stenores brith** pied wagtail

stenor dowr *n.m* **stenores dowr** grey wagtail

stenor melyn *n.m* **stenores melyn** yellow wagtail

stenus *adj* stannous, tin-bearing

ster *n.coll* stars

steren *n.f* **sterennow** star

steren Maria *n.f* yellow pimpernel

sterennek *adj* starry, spangled

steren Vethlehem *n.f* star of Bethlehem

stergylgh *n.m* **stergylghyow** zodiac

sterji *n.m* **sterjiow** planetarium

sterlester *n.m* **sterlestri** spaceship; starship

steronieth *n.f* astronomy

steroniethel *adj* astronomical

stervarner *n.m* **stervarnoryon** astronaut

steus *n.f* **steusow** course

steuv *n.f* **steuvow** warp

steuvi *vb* warp

stevel *n.f* **stevellow** room. **stevel an klass** *n.f* classroom. **stevel an lys** *n.f* courtroom. **stevel-dhybri** *n.f* dining room. **stevel-omwolghi** *n.f* bathroom. **stevel-wortos** *n.f* waiting room

stevnik *n.f* **stevnigow** palate

stevya *vb* hasten; hurry; rush; dash

stif *n.m* **stifow** jet; squirt

stifa *vb* jet; squirt

stifek *n.m* **stifoges** squid

stifella *vb* spray

stifjyn *n.m* **stifjynnys, stifjynnow** jet engine

stiflinder *n.m* jet lag

stifliv *n.m* jet stream

stiwen *n.m* slap

stiwenna *vb* slap

stlav *adj* lisping

stlavedh I *adj* lisping **II** *n.m* lisp

stlevi *vb* lisp

stock *n.m* **stockys** block

stoff *n.m* **stoffys** material; stuff; substance

stoffki *n.m* **stoffkeur** junkie; addict

stoffya *vb* stuff

stons *n.m* **stonsys** stance; attitude

stoppyer *n.m* **stoppyers** plug

stordi *adj* sturdy

stras *n.m* **strasow** flat valley

strechya *vb* spin out time

strel *n.m* **strelyow** mat; rug

stret *n.m* **stretys, stretow** street. **karr stret** *n.m* tram. **flogh stret** *n.m* street child. **stret unfordh** *n.m* one-way street

stretwikor *n.m* **stretwikoryon** street-trader

stretyn *n.m* **stretynnow** alley; little street

strif *n.m* **strifow** strife; struggle

strifwerth *n.m* **strifwerthow** auction

strifwertha *vb* auction

strifwerther *n.m* **strifwerthoryon** auctioneer

strik I *n.m* **strikys** hyphen **II** *adj* nimble; active

strivya *vb* strive; contend; contest

strivyans *n.m* **strivyansow** contention

striw *n.m* **striwyow** sneeze

striwi *vb* sneeze

strol *n.m* mess; litter; untidiness

strolya *vb* litter

strolyek *adj* dirty; messy

stronk *adj* dirty (*of liquids*)

strooth I *adj* tight; strict; squeezed. **jerkyn strooth** *n.m* straight-jacket **II** *adv* tightly

strotha *vb* bind; restrict; squeeze; wring

strothans *n.m* **strothansow** squeeze

strothys *adj* limited; squeezed

strus *n.m* **strusyow** ostrich

studh *n.m* **studhyow** condition; situation; state; (*IT*) status

studhla *n.m* **studhleow** studio. **studhla drama** *n.m* drama studio

studhva *n.f* **studhvaow** (*room*) study

studhya *vb* study

studhyans *n.m* **studhyansow** (*piece of work*) study. **Studhyans Negys** Business Studies

studhyer *n.m* **studhyoryon** student

studhyus *adj* studious

stumm *n.m* **stummow** bend; turn; turning

stumma *vb* wind; twist; warp. **stumma troha** (*be inclined; move towards*) tend towards

stummans *n.m* **stumansow** tendency

stummys *adj* twisted; warped; gnarled

styr *n.m* **styryow** meaning; sense; significance. **leun a styr** meaningful

styrya *vb* mean; define; explain; gloss; interpret; signify. **henn yw dhe styrya** namely

styryans *n.m* **styryansow** explanation; definition; interpretation. **heb styryans** unaccountable

styryansek *adj* explanatory

styward *n.m* **stywards** steward

stywya *vb* stew

substans *n.f* **substansow** substance

substansek *adj* substantive

sudron *n.coll* drones

sudronen *n.f* **sudronennow** drone

sugal *n.coll* rye. **bara sugal** *n.m* rye bread

sugalen *n.f* **sugalennow** grain of rye

sugen *n.m* **sugenyow** juice; sap; essence. **sugen aval** *n.m* apple juice. **sugen frooth** *n.m* fruit juice. **sugen kig** *n.m* gravy, stock (*meat*). **sugen losow** *n.m* gravy, stock (*vegetable*). **sugen owraval** *n.m* orange juice

sugna *vb* suck; absorb. **skubell-sugna** *n.f* vacuum cleaner

sugnek *adj* juicy

sugnus *adj* succulent

sugra I *n.m* sugar **II** *vb* sugar

Sul *n.m* Sunday

sulfur *n.m* sulphur

Sulweyth I *adv* on a Sunday **II** *n.m* **Sulweythyow** (*time*) Sunday

sur *adj, adv* sure; surely; certain; certainly

surhe *vb* assure; insure

surheans *n.m* **surheansow** insurance

surneth *n.f* **surnethow** certainty

surredi *adv* certainly; surely

Swed *n.m* **Swedys** Swede

Swedek *n.m* Swedish language

swedek *adj* Swedish

Sweden *top n.m* Sweden

Swis *n.m* **Swisys** Swiss (*person*)

swis *adj* Swiss

Swisalmaynek *n.m* Swiss German language

sybwydh *n.coll* fir trees

sybwydhen *n.f* **sybwydhennow** fir tree

syg *n.f* **sygow** attachment; leash; trace (*of a harness*)

syger *adj* slow; idle; lazy; lethargic. **termyn syger** *n.m* leisure

sygera *vb* ooze

sygerneth *n.f* idleness; laziness; lethargy

sygerus *adj, adv* leisurely; at leisure

sygh *adj* arid; dry

sygot *n.m* **sygotow** zygote

syllaben *n.f* **syllabennow** syllable

Syllan *top n.f* Scilly. **Enesow Syllan** *top n.pl* Isles of Scilly

sylli *n.f* **syllies** eel

symfoni *n.m* **symfonis** hurdy-gurdy

synaga *n.m* **synagys** synagogue

syndrom *n.m* **syndromow** syndrome.

syndrom Down *n.m* Down's syndrome

Syndrom Immunodifyk Akwirys *n.m* Acquired Immune Deficiency Syndrom; AIDS

synsans *n.m* siege

synsi *vb* hold; detain; grasp; keep; seize; contain. **syns dha glapp!** shut up! **syns dha vin** shut up! **synsi y'n brys** concentrate on

synsys *adj* held; beholden

synsys dre lagha *adj* sectioned (*med*)

Synt *n.m* (*title*) Saint

Synta *n.f* (*title*) Saint

synthesek *adj* synthetic

syr *n.m* sir

syrra *n.m* **syrrys** sir

system *n.m* **systemow** system

systemasek *adj* systematic

system oberyans *n.m* (*IT*) operating system (OS)

syth *adj* direct; upright

T

ta *prn* (*enclitic, sg*) you

-ta *prn* (*enclitic pronoun*) you (*sg*)

tabb *n.m* **tabbow** tab

tabou I *adj* taboo II *n.m* **tabous** taboo

tabour *n.m* **tabours, tabouryow** drum. **gweskel tabour** beat a drum; drum

tabourer *n.m* **tabouroryon** drummer

tackya *vb* clap. **tackya diwleuv, tackya diwla** clap one's hands

tag *n.m* **tagow** choking

taga *vb* choke; clog; strangle; suffocate

tagles kemmyn *n.m* field bindweed

takla (1) *vb* adorn; deck; furnish; trim

takla (2) *vb* (*football*) tackle

taklans *n.m* **taklansow** (*football*) tackle

taklen *n.f* **taklennow** thing; gear; object

taklow *n.pl* (plural of **tra**) things; items; objects

taksi *n.m* **taksiow** taxi

taktek *n.m* **taktegow** tactics

tal *n.f* (*m*) **talyow** brow; forehead; front; temple

talar *n.m* **talarow** headland (*in a field*)

talas *n.m* **talasow** pavment

talben *n.m* **talbennow** knob

talek I *adj* big-browed II *n.m* **taloges** (*fish*) roach; dace

talenep *n.m* **talenebow** facade

talgam *adj* sullen

talgamma *vb* frown

talgel *n.f* **talgellow** pantry

tallyour *n.m* **tallyours** tray

tallytheren *n.f* **tallytherennow** initial

talsogh I *adj* stupid; dull; unintelligent **II** *n.m* **talsoghyon** dimwit; dullard

talsogha *vb* dumb down

talvedhys *adj* worth

talvesa *vb* to be worth

talvesys *adj* valued; prized

talvos *vb* be priced; rate

talvosek *adj* valuable

talvosogeth *n.f* worth; value; usefulness

Tamar *n.m* Tamar. **Dowr Tamar** *n.m* River Tamar

tamm *n.m* **temmyn** bit; fragment; morsel; piece; scrap. **tamm denti** *n.m* (*food*) delicacy. **tamm ha tamm** bit by bit; gradually; little by little; piecemeal

tamm on *n.m* sea pink; thrift

tan *n.m* **tanyow** fire. **gans tan** alight; on fire. **tan y'n golon** *n.m* enthusiasm

tanbellen *n.f* **tanbellennow** bomb

tanbellenna *vb* bomb

tanbellennik *n.m* **tanbellenigow** explosive shell

tanbren *n.m* **tanbrennyer** match. **kisten danbren** *n.f* matchbox

tanek *adj* fiery

tangasor *n.m* **tangasoryon** firefighter

tanjerin *n.m* **tanjerines** tangerine

tank *n.m* **tankow** tank. **tank puskes** *n.m* fish tank

tanker *n.m* **tankeryow** tanker. **tanker oyl** *n.m* oil tanker. **tanker petrol** *n.m* petrol tanker

tanles *n.coll* rosebay willowherb

tanlu *n.m* **tanluyow** fire brigade

tanow *adj* lean; thin; flimsy; tenuous; rare; scarce

tanowder *n.m* **tanowderyow** thinness; rarity

tanowhe *vb* thin out

tansys *n.m* **tansysyow** bonfire

tanta *vb* court; woo

tanweyth *n.coll* fireworks

tanweythen *n.f* **tanweythennow** firework

tapp *n.m* **tappys, tappow** tap

tar *n.m* tar

taran *n.f* **tarennow** thunder. **taran sonek** *n.f* sonic boom

tarder *n.m* **terder** drill

tardh *n.m* **tardhow** bang; burst; explosion. **tardh taran** *n.m* thunderclap. **tardh dydh** *n.m* daybreak

tardha *vb* (*transitive*) set off; blow up; burst; (*intransitive*) explode; erupt

tardhadow *adj* explosive

tardhans *n.m* **tardhansow** (*volcanic*) eruption

tardhell *n.f* **tardhellow** outlet

tardhik *adj* pop-up

tardra *vb* bore; drill; tap

tarenna *vb* thunder

tarosvan *n.m* **tarosvannow** ghost

tarosvannus *adj* ghostly

tarow *n.m* **terewi** bull

tart *n.m* **tartys** tart

tarten *n.f* **tartennow** tart

tarya *vb* tarry; linger; loaf

tas *n.m* **tasow** father; dad. **Tas Nadelik** *n.m* Father Christmas. **tas besydh** *n.m* godfather. **tas gwynn** *n.m* grandfather

tasegi *vb* patronise

tasegus *adj* condescending; patronising

tasek *n.m* **tasogyon** patron

tasik *n.m* **tasigow** daddy

tasoleth *n.f* fatherhood; paternity. **kummyas tasoleth** *n.m* paternity leave

tasrewl *n.f* **tasrewlys** patriarchy

tassans *n.m* patron saint

tasveth *n.m* **tasvethow** foster-father

tatou *n.m* **tatous** tattoo

tava I *n.m* **tavaow** touch; feel; stroke **II** *vb* touch; feel; stroke. **yn-dann dava** in touch

tavell *n.f* **tavellow** antenna; feeler; probe

taver *n.m* **tavoryon** feeler

tavern *n.m* **tavernyow** tavern; inn

tavernor *n.m* **tavernoryon** bartender; publican; innkeeper

taves *n.m* **tavosow** language; tongue

taves karow *n.m* hart's tongue fern

taves ki *n.m* borage

taves ojyon *n.m* viper's bugloss

tavethli *vb* broadcast

tavlinen *n.f* **tavlinennow** tangent

tavlinennel *adj* tangential

tavol *n.coll* (*plants*) dock

tavol amanyn *n.coll* burdock

tavolen *n.f* **tavolennow** (*plant*) dock

tavosa *vb* scold; tell off

tavosek *adj* talkative; verbose

tavoseth *n.f* idiom; jargon

tavosethek *adj* idiomatic

taw *n.m* silence; quiet

tawel *adj* quiet

tawell *n.f* **tawellow** silencer

tawesek *adj* quiet; taciturn

te *n.m* tea

tebel I *adj* evil; wicked II *n.m* **tebeles** evil person. **an Tebel-El** *n.m* the Devil

tebeldhyghtya *vb* abuse; mistreat; misuse

tebeldhyghtyans *n.m* **tebeldhyghtyansow** abuse; misuse

tebel-el *n.m* devil

tebelfara *vb* misbehave

tebel-hanow *n.m* **tebel-henwyn** bad name; bad reputation

tebelvest *n.m* **tebelvestes** monster

tecken *n.f* **teckennow** moment. **rag tecken** momentarily

teg I *adj* beautiful; fair; fine; handsome; pretty II *adv* quite. **ass yw hemma gwari teg!** what fun!

tegen *n.f* **tegennow** jewel; ornament; pretty thing

tegeyryan *n.m* orchid

tegeyryan gwenen *n.m* bee orchid

tegh *n.m* **teghow** flight; retreat

teghes *vb* flee

tekel *n.m* **tekels** kettle

tekhe *vb* adorn; beautify; decorate

tekka *adj* finer; prettier

teknegieth *n.f* technology

teknegiethel *adj* technological

Teknegieth Kedhlow *n.m* Information Technology

teknegydh *n.m* **teknegydhyon** technician

teknek *n.m* **teknegow** technique

teknogel *adj* technical

teknologieth *n.f* technology

tekst *n.m* **tekstow** text. **messach tekst** *n.m* text message

tekter *n.m* beauty; finery; loveliness. **dre dekter** *adv* gently

tektonek *adj* tectonic

tektonieth *n.f* tectonics

tellek I *adj* pock-marked II *n.m* **tellogyon** pock-marked man; ragamuffin

telli *vb* drill; bore

tellyas *n.m* **tellysi** tax inspector

tellys *adj* holed

telor penndu *n.m* **telores penndu** blackcap

telyn *n.f* **telynnow** harp. **telyn Geltek** *n.f* Celtic harp

telynnek *adj* lyric; lyrical

telynnya *vb* play the harp

telynnyer *n.m* **telynyoryon** harpist

temmik *n.m* **temigow** little bit

tempel *n.m* **templow** temple

templa *n.m* **templys** temple

tempra *vb* moderate; temper

tempredh *n.m* **tempredhow** temperature

tempredhell *n.f* **tempredhellow** thermometer

tempredhlinen *n.f* **tempredhlinennow** isotherm

temprer *n.m* **temproryon** moderator

temprys *adj* moderate

temptya *vb* tempt

temptyans *n.m* **temptyansow** temptation

tender *adj* tender

tenewen *n.m* **tenwennow** side. **linen denewen** *n.f* touch-line. **tenewen an fordh** *n.m* roadside. **ryb tenewen** alongside

tenkys *n.f* **tenkysyow** fate

tenn *n.m* **tennow** pull; tug; shot; (*cigarette*) drag; (*drawing*) plan

tenna *vb* pull; draw; attract; tug; fire; shoot. **tenna dhe²** shoot at. **tenna yn-mes** withdraw (money). **trog-tenna** *n.m* drawer

tennis *n.m* tennis. **tennis moos** *n.m* table tennis

tennlester *n.m* **tennlestri** tug-boat

tennros *n.f* **tennrosow** drag net; pulley

tennva *n.f* strain

tennven *n.m* **tennveyn** magnet; lodestone

tennvenek *adj* magnetic

tennvenieth *n.f* magnetism

tennvenya *vb* magnetise

tennvos *n.m* **tennvosow** attraction

tennvosek *adj* attractive; tempting

tenor *n.m* **tenoryon** tenor

tenva *n.f* **tenvaow** rifle range

ter (1) *adj* clear

ter (2) **I** *adj* insistent **II** *n.m* insistence

ter- *prfx* intermittent

-ter *sffx* makes a masculine noun from an adjective

terabayt *n.m* **terabaytys** terabyte; *abbrev* TB

terder *n.m* eagerness; gusto

terderus *adj* avid

tereylya *vb* alternate

tereylyans *n.m* **tereylyansow** alternation

terghi *vb* coil

tergoska *vb* sleep fitfully

teri *vb* insist

terlemmel *vb* skip; jump about

terlenter *adj* twinkling

terlentri *vb* glisten; sparkle; twinkle

terlesa *vb* diffuse

terlesans *n.m* **terlesansow** diffusion

term *n.m* **termys** term

termonieth *n.f* terminology

termyn *n.m* **termynyow** time; period. **a dermyn dhe dermyn** from time to time. **mes a'y dermyn** untimely. **pub termyn** all the time; always. **termyn a dheu** *n.m* future. **termyn an mis** *n.m* menstruation. **termyn bewnans** *n.m* lifetime. **termyn syger** *n.m* leisure. **(yn) neb termyn** sometime. **yn termyn eus passys** once upon a time

terneyja *vb* flutter

ternos *adv* the day after; the next day. **ternos vyttin** the morning after

ternoth *adj* half naked

terosa *n.m* **terosedhow** disaster

terosus *adj* disastrous

terosva *n.f* **terosvaow** disaster area

terras *n.m* **terrassys; terrassow** terrace

terrer know *n.m* **terroryon know** nuthatch

terri *vb* break; (*of flowers*) pick

terros *n.m* **terrosow** calamity; doom; downfall

terrys *adj* broken

terthen *n.f* **terthennow** fever; temperature

terthennek *adj* feverish

tervans *n.m* **tervansow** tumult; turmoil; riot

tervysk *n.m* **tervyskow** muddle

tervyska *vb* muddle

tes *n.m* heat

tesa *vb* heat

tesek *adj* hot; irritable

tesel *adj* thermal

tesen *n.f* **tesennow** cake. **tesen benn-bloodh** *n.f* birthday cake. **tesen gales** *n.f* biscuit. **tesen geus** *n.f* cheesecake. **tesen safran** *n.f* saffron cake. **tesen vrew** *n.f* shortbread testament *n.m* **testamens** (*Biblical*) testament. **an Testament Koth** *n.m* the Old Testament. **an Testament Nowydh** *n.m* the New Testament

testen *n.f* **testennow** topic; subject

testskrif *n.m* **testskrifow** certificate

teth *n.f* **tethi** udder

tethen *n.f* **tethennow** udder

tetivali *int* what nonsense!

teudh *adj* molten

teudhans *n.m* **teudhansow** solution

teudhi *vb* melt; thaw; dissolve

teudhla *n.m* **teudhleow** foundry

teuregel *adj* parasitic

teurek *n.coll* parasites

teurogen *n.f* **teurogennow** parasite

tevesigieth *n.f* adulthood

tevesik I *adj* adult II *n.m* **tevesigyon** adult

tevi *vb* grow

tevyans *n.m* **tevyansow** growth

tew *adj* fat; bulky; dense. **gober tew** *n.m* gross pay

tewder *n.m* **tewderow** density; thickness; bulk; consistency

tewedh *n.m* **tewedhow** storm

tewedha *vb* weather

tewedhek *adj* weather-beaten

tewedhys *adj* weathered

tewel *vb* be silent

tewes *n.coll* sand. **kastel tewes** *n.m* sandcastle

tewesek *adj* sandy

tewesen *n.f* **tewesennow** grain of sand

tewhe *vb* thicken; fatten

tewl *adj* dark; gloomy; murky; obscure; sombre

tewlder *n.m* darkness

tewlel *vb* throw. **jynn-tewlel** *n.m* projector. **tewlel dhe skoll** throw away. **tewlel dhe-ves** throw away; scrap. **tewlel imach** project a picture. **tewlel towl** make a plan; project. **tewlel yn-mes** throw out

tewlhe *vb* darken

tewlwolow *n.m* dusk; half-light

tewolgow *n.pl* darkness

tewyn *n.m* **tewynnow** dune

teyl *n.m* manure

teylu *n.m* **teyluyow** family. **hanow teylu** *n.m* surname

teyr³ *num, n.f* three

teyrdel *n.coll* trefoil

teyrdelen *n.f* shamrock

teyrgweyth *adv* three times

teyrros *n.f* **teyrrosow** tricycle

teythi *n.pl* attributes; abilities; traits

teythyek I *adj* local; native II *n.m* **teythyogyon** local; native

'th⁵ᵃ *prn* (*infixed, sg*) you; (*poss. adj*) your

thema *n.m* **themys, themow** theme

themasek *adj* thematic

theorem *n.m* **theoremow** theorem

ti (1) I *n.m* **tiow** oath; vow II *vb* swear; vow. **bedhav y di** I dare say

ti (2) *vb* roof

-ti *sffx* building; house

tiek *n.m* **tiogow** farmer

tigen *n.f* **tigennow** handbag

tiger *n.m* **tigres, tigri** tiger

tim *n.m* thyme

tin *n.f* **tinyow** arse. **kraver tin** *n.m* toady; creep

tingogh *n.m* **tingoghes** redstart

tior *n.m* **tioryon** thatcher; slater

tipek *adj* typical

tir *n.m* **tiryow** land. **tir meur** *n.m* mainland. **yn tir** on land

tira *vb* land; come ashore

tiredh *n.m* **tiredhow** territory; region. **an Tiredh a Dhedhewadow** *n.m* the Promised Land

tirlanow *n.m* landfill

tirnos *n.m* **tirnosow** landmark

tirwedh *n.f* **tirwedhow** landscape

titaniom *n.m* (*element*) titanium

titel *n.m* **titlys, titlow** title

tiyas *n.m* **tiysi** juror

tnow *n.m* **tnowi** dale; valley-bottom

to *n.m* **tohow** roof. **keyn to** *n.m* ridge (*of a house*)

tobacko *n.m* tobacco

toch *n.m* **tochys** touch

tochpad *n.m* **tochpadys** touch-pad

tochskrin *n.m* **tochskrinyow** touch-screen

tochya *vb* touch; mention. **ow tochya** concerning; as regards. **tochya pib** light a pipe

tokyn *n.m* **toknys** token; ticket; sign; symbol. **tokyn-mos ha dos** *n.m* return ticket

tokynner *n.m* **tokynoryon** ticket inspector

tokynva *n.f* **tokynvaow** ticket-office

toll (1) *n.m* **tell** hole; burrow; orifice; (*disreptuable nightclub etc.*) dive (*colloq*); opening. **toll alhwedh** *n.m* keyhole. **toll boton** *n.m* button hole. **toll konin** *n.m* rabbit burrow. **toll y'n fos** *n.m* cash dispenser. **toll lavrek** *n.m* (*in trousers*) fly

toll (2) *n.f* **tollow** duty; tax; toll; rate; customs. **kevradh toll** *n.m* tax rate. **sodhva doll** *n.f* tax office. **toll an penn** *n.f* poll tax. **toll annedh** *n.f* property tax. **toll brenas** *n.f* purchase tax. **toll dhaswerth** *n.f* value added tax. **toll dhowr** *n.f* water rate. **toll dir** *n.f* land tax. **toll wober** *n.f* income tax

toll (3) *n.m* deceit; disappointment; fraud. **heb toll na gil** sincerely

tolla *vb* cheat; deceive; delude; kid; mislead

tolladow *adj* taxable

tollborth *n.m* **tollborthow** toll-gate

tollek *adj* holed; leaky; perforated

tollgorn *n.m* **tollgern** flute; cornet. **tollgorn Sowsnek** *n.m* recorder

tolli *vb* tax; levy taxes

tollva *n.f* **tollvaow** toll booth. **Tollva an Wlas** *n.f* Inland Revenue

tollwas *n.m* **tollwesyon** customs officer

tollwisk *n.m* **tollwiskow** disguise; fancy dress

tollwiska *vb* disguise

tollys *adj* cheated; deluded; disappointed

tomder *n.m* heat; warm; warmth

tomm *adj* warm; hot. **dowr tomm** *n.m* brandy. **tomm y woos** hot-blooded

tomma *vb* (*transitive*) warm; (*intransitive*) become warm. **jynn-tomma** *n.m* heater

tommen *n.f* **tomennow** dyke; embankment

tommhe *vb* heat; warm

tommheans *n.m* heating. **tommheans kres** *n.m* central heating

ton *n.m* **tonyow** tone; melody; tune

tonek *adj* tonic. **dowr tonek** *n.m* tonic water

ton-lev *n.m* **ton-levow** intonation; pitch accent

tonn *n.f* **tonnow** wave

tonnas *n.m* **tonasow** tonne

tonnek *adj* wavy

tonnhys *n.m* **tonnhysow** wavelength

tont *adj* cheeky; impertinent; impudent; insolent

tonteth *n.f* impertinence; impudence; insolence

tontya *vb* taunt; tease

tontyans *n.m* **tontyansow** taunt

tonya *vb* tune

toos (1) *n.m* **tosow** tuft; bunch

toos (2) *n.m* dough. **know toos** *n.coll* doughnuts. **toos alamandys** *n.m* marzipan. **toos-gwari** *n.m* playdough

tooth *n.m* speed; hurry. **finweth tooth** *n.f* speed limit

topp *n.m* **toppys, toppow** top; peak; summit

toppyn *n.m* **toppynnow** tip

Tora *n.m* Torah

torek *n.coll* (*arachnids*) mites

torgh (1) *n.f* **tergh** coil; collar; torque

torgh (2) *n.m* **torghes** hog

Tori *n.m* **Toris** Tory

torment *n.m* **tormentys** torment

tormentya *vb* torment

tormentys *adj* afflicted

torn *n.m* **tornys, tornow** tour; turn. **pub torn** at every turn; every time

tornyas *n.m* **tornysi** tourist

tornyaseth *n.f* tourism

torogen *n.f* **torogennow** (*arachnid*) mite

torr (1) *n.m* **torrow** break; fracture

torr (2) *n.f* **torrow** abdomen; belly; stomach; tummy. **torr an dhorn** *n.f* palm of hand

torradow *adj* breakable

torras *n.m* **torrasow** litter (*of animals*)

torrbyff *n.m* **torrbyffow** burp

torrbyffya *vb* burp

torrek *adj* big-bellied; pregnant

torrmen *n.f* saxifrage

torrva *n.f* **torrvaow** breach; breakdown; fracture; rupture. **kert torrva** *n.m* breakdown lorry *m*. **torrva ambos** *n.f* breach of contract. **torrva patent** *n.f* patent infringement. **torrva demedhyans** *n.f* divorce. **torrva gwir-pryntya** *n.f* copyright infringement

torrwynsek *adj* flatulent

torth *n.f* **torthow** loaf. **torth (a) vara** *n.f* loaf of bread

torthel *n.f* **torthellow** bun

tosa *vb* knead

tost *adv* soon

tothya *vb* speed

toul *n.m* **toulys** tool; implement

toulgist *n.f* **toulgistyow** toolbox

toulvarr *n.m* **toulvarrys** (*IT*) toolbar

touna *n.m* **tounas** tuna

tour *n.m* **touryow** tower; keep. **tour korslynk** *n.m* helter skelter. **tour-routya** *n.m* control tower

tourik *n.m* **tourigow** turret

towargh *n.coll* peat

towarghen *n.f* **towarghennow** slab of peat

towel *n.m* **towellow** towel

towl *n.m* **towlow** cast; throw; goal; intention; move (*in a game*); plan; project. **tewlel towl** *vb* make a plan. **towl chons** *n.m* stroke of luck. **towl howl** *n.m* sunstroke. **towl unnik** *n.m* express purpose

towladow *adj* disposable

towlargh *n.m* **towlarghow** budget

towlen *n.f* **towlennow** programme; scheme. **towlen bellwolok** *n.f* television programme

towlenna *vb* (*IT*) program

towlennans *n.m* **towlenansow** planning

towlenner *n.m* **towlenoryon** programmer

towler *n.m* **towloryon** thrower. **towler pel** *n.m* bowler

towlhys *n.m* range of a weapon

tra *n.f* **taklow, traow** thing; item; object. **neb tra** anything. **tra vyth** nothing

trad *n.m* **tradys** trade

trajedi *n.m* **trajediow** tragedy

trajek *adj* tragic

tram *n.m* **tramyow** tram

tramor I *adj* overseas **II** *adv* abroad; overseas

transmyttya *vb* transmit; hand down

transyek *n.m* ecstasy

travalya *vb* travel; labour

trawma *n.m* trauma (*med*)

trayson *n.m* treason

trayta *vb* betray

traytour *n.m* **traytours** traitor

traytouri *n.m* treachery

traytus *adj* treacherous

tre I *n.f* **trevow** farmstead; home; town; village **II** *adv* at home; back. **hel an dre** *n.f* the town hall. **ri tre** give back

trebuchya *vb* (*intransitive*) stumble; totter; fumble; (*transitive*) invert; trip up

trebuchyans *n.m* **trebuchyansow** stumble

trebyl *n.m* **trebylyon** (*music*) treble

tredan *n.m* electricity. **fros tredan** *n.m* electric current. **jagg tredan** *n.m* electric shock

tredanek *adj* electric. **tren tredanek** *n.m* electric train

tredanel *adj* electrical

tredaner *n.m* **tredanoryon** electrician

tredanhe *vb* electrify

tredanva *n.f* **tredanvaow** power plant; power station. **tredanva nuklerek** *n.m* nuclear power station

tredhegves *num* thirteenth

tredhek *num* thirteen

tregeredh *n.f* **tregeredhow** compassion (*loving-kindness*); mercy

tregeredhus *adj* compassionate; sympathetic. **kummyas tregeredhus** *n.m* compassionate leave

tregh *n.m* **treghow** cut; section; slice. **tregh Cesarek** *n.m* Caesarean section

tregher *n.m* **treghoryon** tailor

tregherieth *n.f* tailoring

treghi *vb* cut; slice. **treghi dhe-ves** cut off; amputate

treghys *adj* cut

tregyn *n.m* **tregynnow** drawer

trehwelek *adj* rebellious

trehweles *vb* upset

trehwelus *adj* upsetting

tremen *n.m* **tremenow** passage

tremena *vb* pass; pass away; cross; go by; pass over. **tremena orth** pass by

tremenadow *adj* transitory

tremengummyas *n.m* **tremengumyasow** passport

tremenva *n.f* **tremenvaow** gangway; lobby

Tremenyas *n.m* **Tremenysi** Traveller

tremenyas *n.m* **tremenysi** traveller

tremenys *adj* passed away; deceased; late

tremmliw *n.m* make-up; cosmetics

tremmyn *n.m* **tremynnow** look. **tremmyn settys** *n.m* stare

tren *n.m* **trenow** train. **tren uskis** *n.m* express train

trenja *adv* on the day after tomorrow

trenk *adj* acid; sour; sharp

trenkan *n.m* common sorrel

trenkan an dhavas *n.m* sheep's sorrel

trenkan an koos *n.m* wood sorrel

trenken *n.f* **trenkennow** acid

trenkles *n.m* rhubarb

trenya *vb* train

trenyans *n.m* **trenyansow** training

tresen *n.f* **tresennow** trace; graph

tresennek *adj* graphic

tresor *n.m* **tresorys, tresoryow** treasure

tresorva *n.f* **tresorvaow** treasury

tresorya *vb* treasure

tressa I *adv* thirdly II *num* third. **tressa rann** *n.f* third

trest *n.m* trust; reliance. **Trest Kenedhlek** *n.m* National Trust

trestadow *adj* dependable; trustworthy

trestya *vb* trust. **trestya yn** trust in. **trestya dhe**[2] rely on. **trestya nebonan** trust somebody

tresya *vb* trace

treth *n.m* **trethow** sand; beach; seashore

tretha (1) *vb* ferry

tretha (2) *vb* digest

trethek *adj* sandy

trethor *n.m* **trethoryon** ferryman

trethtegans *n.m* constipation

trethtegys *adj* constipated

trethyas *n.m* **trethysi** passenger

trettya *vb* trample

treudhow *n.m* threshold

treus *adj* stubborn; uppity

treusfurvya *vb* transform

treusi *vb* pass over; cross

treuskorra *vb* transmit; hand down

treuskorrell *n.f* **treuskorrellow** transmitter

treuslinen *n.f* **treuslinennow** diameter

treuspas *n.m* **treuspassow** trespass; offence

treuspassya *vb* trespass

treusperthedh *n.m* conductance

treusperthi *vb* transport; transfer

treusplansa *vb* transplant

treusplansans *n.m* **treusplansansow** transplant

treusporth *n.m* **treusporthow** transport; transfer

treusreydhedhek *adj* transgender

treussplanadow *adj* translucent

treuster *n.m* **treusters, treustrow** cross-beam

treustremen *n.m* **treustremenow** transit

treustremena *vb* transit

treustremenva *n.f* **treustremenvaow** transit area

treustrum *n.m* **treustrummow** bait

treusva *n.f* **treusvaow** crossing. **treusva gerdhoryon** *n.f* pedestrian crossing. **treusva hyns horn** *n.f* level crossing. **treusva labol** *n.f* zebra crossing

treusvewa *vb* survive

treusvewans *n.m* **treusvewansow** survival

treusvysyek *adj* worldwide

treusweladow *adj* transparent

treuswiska *vb* cross-dress

treuswisker *n.m* transvestite

treusworra *vb* transfer

treusworrans *n.m* transfer

treuswrians *n.m* **treuswriansow** transaction

treuswul *vb* transact

trev *n.coll* farmsteads

trevas *n.f* **trevasow** crop; harvest

trevasa *vb* crop; harvest

trevbark *n.m* **trevbarkow** housing estate

treveglos *n.f* **treveglosyow, trevow eglos** village; churchtown

trevek *adj* urban

trevel *adj* urban

trevesiga *vb* settle

trevesigeth *n.f* **trevesigethow** colony; settlement

trevesik *n.m* **trevesigyon** countryman; villager

treveth *n.f* **trevethow** homestead; residence; occasion

trevlu *n.m* **trevluyow** militia

trew *n.m* spittle

trewa *vb* spit

trewesi *adj* forceful

treweythus *adj* occasional; rare

treweythyow *adv* at times; now and again; occasionally; sometimes

trewyas *n.m* spittle

treylouba *vb* stir

treylva *n.f* **treylvaow** modification; turning point

treylya *vb* convert; modify; sprain; turn; translate; wrench. **treylya an keyn orth nebonan** give somebody the cold shoulder. **treylya dhelergh** reverse. **treylya dhe-ves** avert. **treylya dhyworth** turn away from

treylyans *n.m* **treylyansow** conversion; mutation; sprain; translation. **treylyans ger rag ger** *n.m* literal translation. **treylyans U** *n.m* U-turn

treynya *vb* hang back; lag

tri[3] *num, n.m* three

tria *vb* try; test

trial *n.m* **trials** trial

trifel *n.m* **trifellow** trifle (*dessert*)

trig *n.m* low tide

triga *vb* remain; stay; dwell. **bos trigys** reside; live (*at a place*). **yn toll y'n nor yth esa hobbit trigys** in a hole in the ground there lived a hobbit. **bos trigys yn argel** live at the back of beyond

triger *n.m* **trigoryon** inhabitant; dweller. **triger yn ken tyller** non-resident

trigva *n.f* **trigvaow** address; abode; residence; dwelling. **trigva ebost** *n.f* email address

trigys *adj* settled. **bos trigys** live (*at a certain place*)

trihorn *n.m* **trihern** triangle

trihornek *adj* triangular

trilvil[2] *num, n.m* (10^{12}) **trilvilyow** trillion

trist *adj* sad; mournful. **bos trist war-lergh** miss

tristhe *vb* sadden

tristys *n.m* sadness

tri ugens *num* sixty. **deg ha tri ugens** *num* seventy

tri ugensves *num* sixtieth

tro *n.f* **troyow** cycle; turn; occasion; round; (*film*) take. **rag tro** makeshift; temporarily; temporary. **tro askel** *n.f* helicopter. **war neb tro** at any time

trobel *n.m* **troblys, troblow** trouble

trobla *vb* trouble; bother

troblys *adj* troubled

trobol *n.m* **trobollow** whirlpool

troboynt *n.m* **troboyntys, troboyntow** turning point

troboyntel *adj* critical; crucial

trodreghi *vb* circumsize

troer plasen *n.m* **troeryon plasen** record player

trofordh *n.f* **trofordhow** (*signage*) roundabout

trog *n.m* **trogow** case; suitcase; (*car*) boot. **trog-tenna** *n.m* drawer

trogenter *n.f* **trogentrow** screw

trogentra *vb* screw

trogentrell *n.f* **trogentrellow** screwdriver

trogh I *adj* cut; (*of skin, limbs, hearts*) broken; wretched **II** *n.m* **troghow** cut

trogher *n.m* **trogheryow** coulter

troghya *vb* immerse

troghyans *n.m* **troghyansow** immersion

trogylgh *n.m* **trogylghyow** circuit

troha(g) *prp* towards

trolergh *n.m* **trolerghow** footpath

tromm *adj* immediate

trompa *n.m* **trompys** trumpet

tron (1) *n.m* **tronow, tronyow** nose; point (*of land*); snout; trunk (*animal*)

tron (2) *n.m* **tronys** throne. **tron-sedha** *n.m* throne

tron an leugh *n.m* ivy-leaved toadflax (*Kenilworth ivy; mother of thousands*)

tron-droghya *adj* nosy

tronek *adj* curious; nosy

tronekter *n.m* nosiness

trongornvil *n.m* **trongornvil** rhinoceros

tronkys *n.m* bath; ablutions. **gul tronkys** take a bath

troos (1) *n.m* **treys, dl dewdros** foot. **a droos** *adv* on foot. **tros-hys** *n.m* foot (*length*). **ol troos** *n.m* footprint

troos (2) *n.m* **treysi** starling

troos margh *n.m* butterbur

troosnoten *n.f* **troosnotennow** footnote

trop *n.m* **tropys** trope; figure of speech

tropek *adj* tropical

tros *n.m* **trosow** clamour; noise; sound

trosek (1) *adj* noisy

trosek (2) *adj* big-footed

trosell *n.f* **trosellow** pedal

trosella *vb* pedal

trosla *n.m* **trosleow** pedal; treadle; foothold

troswiek *adj* (*of feet*) webbed

trosya *vb* plod

trovan *n.m* **trovannow** tropic

trovannel *adj* tropical

trovya *vb* discover

troyll *n.m* (*f*) **troyllyow** spiral; swirl; ceilidh

troyllya *vb* spin; swirl. **poll-troyllya** *n.m* whirlpool

troyllyek *adj* spiral

tru *int* alas

truan *adj* miserable; wretched; unfortunate

trubyt *n.m* tribute

truedh *n.m* pity. **kemeres truedh (war^2/a^2)** have pity on

truedha *vb* look after; tend

truedhek *adj* pathetic; pitiful; plaintive; sad

trufel *adj* trifling, trivial

trufla *vb* trifle; toy (with)

truflen *n.f* **truflennow** trifle

trumach *n.m* **trumajys, trumajow** voyage

truth *n.m* **truthes, truthow** trout

try- *prfx* triple

tryflek *adj* threefold; treble; triple

trygh I *adj* triumphant; victorious; superior II *n.m* victory; conquest

trygher *n.m* **tryghoryon** victor

tryghi *vb* conquer; vanquish

trymis *n.m* **trymisyow** trimester; quarter (*of a year*)

trymisyek *adj* quarterly

trynn *n.f* **trynnow** fuss

tsunami *n.f* **tsunamiow** tsunami

tu *n.m* **tuyow** direction; side; bearing. **an tu aral** *n.m* the flip side. **tu a-ves** *n.m* exterior

tuberculosis *n.m* tuberculosis (*med*)

tuedh *n.m* **tuedhow** tendency; trend

tuedhder *n.m* orientation. **tuedhder reydhek** sexual orientation

tulyfant *n.m* **tulyfantys** turban. **bleujen tulyfant** *n.f* tulip

turant *n.m* **turans** tyrant; dictator

turantiel *adj* tyrannical; dictatorial

turantieth *n.f* tyranny; dictatorship

turen turk *n.m* **turennow turk** collared dove

Turk *n.m* **Turkys** Turk

Turkek *n.m* Turkish language

turkek *adj* Turkish. **koffi turkek** *n.m* Turkish coffee. **melyssand turkek** *n.m* Turkish delight

Turki *top n.f* Turkey

tus *n.pl* (*plural of den*) people

ty *prn* (*sg*) you. **ty dha honan** yourself

tybel *adj* abstract

tybi *vb* imagine; hold an opinion; fancy

tybieth *n.f* **tybiethow** theory

tybiethel *adj* theoretical

tybyans *n.m* **tybyansow** concept; idea; thought; notion; opinion

tyckli *adj* delicate; problematic

tyckya *vb* tick

tykki Duw *n.m* **tykkiow Duw, tykki Duwes** butterfly. **tykki Duw nos** *n.m* moth

tylda *n.m* **tyldys, tyldow** tent

tyldya *vb* pitch a tent

tyli *vb* owe; reward; pay. **despit heb y dyli** undeserved contempt. **ev a dal gul henna** he should do that. **ny dal mann** it isn't worth anything. **heb tyli** unpaid

tyller *n.m* **tylleryow** location; place; mansion. **tyller havi** *n.m* holiday resort. **tyller vyth** *n.m* nowhere

tynder *n.m* tension; soreness

tynkyal I *n.m* **tynkyalyow** jingle II *vb* jingle

tynn I *adj* cruel; intense; painful; tense; tight; sharp; sore; strict. **pysi tynn** solicit; ask urgently II *adv* tightly

tynnedh *n.m* **tynedhow** intensity

tynnhe *vb* tighten

tynnow *n.pl* tights

tyska *vb* gather corn

tysken *n.f* **tyskennow** sheaf

tythya *vb* hiss

U

ufern *n.m* **ufernyow**, *dl* **dewufern**
ankle
ugens *num* twenty
ugensves *num* twentieth
ugh- *prfx* major; over-; up-
ughboynt *n.m* **ughboyntys,**
ughboyntow maximum; zenith
ughel *adj* high; grand; loud. **ughel y**
dhewfrik stuck up. **yn ughel** aloud
ugheldas *n.m* **ugheldasow** patriarch
ughelder *n.m* height; loudness.
ughelder ebron *n.m* zenith
ugheldir *n.m* **ugheldiryow** highland
ughelgowser *n.m* **ughelgowsoryon**
loudspeaker
ughelhe *vb* highten
ughelhwans *n.m* **ughelhwansow**
ambition
ughelhwansek *adj* ambitious
ughella *adj* higher. **an ughella** highest.
gradh ughella *n.m* superlative
ughelor *n.m* **ugheloryon** noble
ughelvam *n.f* **ughelvammow**
matriarch
ughelvarr *n.m* mistletoe
ughhewol *adj* wide awake
ughkarg *n.m* **ughkargow** upload
ughkarga *vb* upload
ughlamma *vb* high jump
ughradha *vb* upgrade
ughskrif *n.m* superscript
ughsommys *n.m* **ughsommyses**
(*animal*) bat
ughson *n.m* **ughsonyow** ultrasound
ughsonek *adj* ultrasonic
ughviolet *adj* ultraviolet
Ukrayn *top n.f* Ukraine
Ukraynek *n.m* Ukrainian language
ukraynek *adj* Ukrainian
Ukraynian *n.m* **Ukraynians** Ukrainian
un- *prfx* mono-; uni-
undon *adj* monotonous

unfordh *adj* one-way. **stret unfordh**
n.m one-way street
unform *n.m* **unformys** uniform
unigyn *n.m* **unigynnow** individual
unikter *n.m* loneliness
unita *n.m* unity
unlagasek *adj* one-eyed
unn I *num* one II *prn* a certain III *adj*
one; only; sole; single. **a unn eghen**
uniform. **neb unn** a particular
unnegves *num* eleventh
unnek *num* eleven
unnik *adj* individual; only. **towl unnik**
n.m express purpose
unplek *adj* singular
unran *adj* one-piece
unsel *adv* only
unses *n.m* unity; unit
Unsys Yeghes an Brys *n.m* Mental
Health Unit
untu *adj* one-sided; unilateral
unver *adj* agreed; unanimous; in
agreement
unverhe *vb* agree. **gul bos unverhes**
reconcile
unverheans *n.m* **unverheansow**
accordance; agreement; reconciliation;
understanding
unweyth *adv* once; only; incidentally.
unweyth arta once more
unwos *adj* related
unya *vb* unite
unyans *n.m* **unyansow** union. **Unyans**
Europek (UE) *n.m* European Union
(EU)
unyansydh *n.m* **unyansydhyon**
unionist
unyansydhel *adj* unionist
unyent *n.m* **unyentys** ointment
unyethek I *adj* monoglot; monolingual
II *n.m* **unyethogyon** monoglot

unys *adj* united. **an Kenedhlow Unys** *n.pl* the United Nations. **Ruvaneth Unys** *top n.f* United Kingdom. **an Statys Unys** *top n.pl* the United States (*of America*)

ura *vb* lubricate; anoint

uraniom *n.m* (*element*) uranium

uras *n.m* **urasow** salve; lubricant

urdh *n.f* **urdhyow** order

urdhas *n.m* **urdhasow** hierarchy

urdhya *vb* initiate

urdhyans *n.m* **urdhyansow** initiation

urin *n.m* urine

us (1) *n.m* **usow** yell; scream

us (2) *n.m* **usyow, usadow** use; custom; habit

-us *sffx* -ous (*adj. ending*)

usa *vb* yell; scream; bellow

usadow *adj* usual; habitual; routine. **herwydh usadow** *adv* as usual; habitually. **nyns ywa ow usadow** I'm not used to it

usi *vb* (*3s. pres. long form of* **bos**; *used with definite subjects*) is

uskis I *adj* fast; express; quick; rapid; speedy **II** *adv* quickly; speedily

uskisell *n.f* **uskisellow** accelerator

uskishe *vb* accelerate

uskisheans *n.m* **uskisheansow** acceleration

uskitter *n.m* **uskitteryow** velocity

uskittredh *n.m* **uskittredhow** (*physical quantity*) velocity

usya *vb* use; wear out; utilise

usyans *n.m* **usyansow** use. **yn usyans** in use

usyer *n.m* **usyoryon** user

usys *adj* used; accustomed; usual; worn. **bos usys dhe**[2] *vb* tend. **bos usys gans** be accustomed to. **dell yw usys** as usual; usually. **nyns yw usys genev** I'm not used to it

uvel *adj* humble; lowly; modest

uvelder *n.m* humility

uvelhe *vb* humble

V

-va (1) *prn* (*enclitic pronoun*) him

-va (2) *sffx* (*place or abstract idea*)

vandal *n.m* vandal

vandalieth *n.f* vandalism

vandalisa *vb* vandalise

vanylla *n.m* vanilla

varien *n.f* **variennow** variant

variennek *adj* variant

varya *vb* derange; drive insane; madden; change; vary

varyadow *n.m* **varyadowyow** variable

varyans *n.m* **varyansow** variance; variation

varyes *adj* deranged; insane

'vas *adj* beneficial; passable; suitable; serviceable; useful. **nyns yw 'vas** useless. **ny wra 'vas** useless

vayl *n.f* **vaylys** veil

vegan *adj* vegan

veganer *n.m* **veganoryon** vegan

veksya *vb* irk; irritate

vektor *n.m* **vektors, vektorow** vector

venjya *vb* (*transitive*) avenge; *vb* (*intransitive*) take revenge; retaliate

venjyans *n.m* revenge; retaliation; retribution

venym *n.m* **venymyow** poison

venymys *adj* poisonous; toxic

verb *n.f* **verbow** verb

verbel *adj* verbal

versyon *n.m* **versyons** version

vertigo *n.m* vertigo (*med*)

vertu *n.f* **vertus** virtue

vesta *n.m* **vestys** vest

viaj *n.m* **viajys, viajyow** voyage; trip; journey. **hager-viaj** *n.m* bad business. **pris viaj** *n.m* fare

viajya *vb* travel; journey

vil *adj* vile; despicable

vilta *n.f* vileness

virus *n.m* **virusys** virus

Virus Immunodifyk Denel *n.m* Human Immunodeficiency Virus; HIV

visa *n.m* **visas** visa

visach *n.m* **visajys** visage

visour *n.m* **visours** mask; visor

vitamyn *n.m* **vitamynnow** vitamin

vodka *n.m* **vodkas** vodka

volt *n.m* **voltow** volt

voltedh *n.m* **voltedhow** voltage

vota *n.m* **votys** vote

voter *n.m* **votoryon** voter

votya *vb* vote

votyans *n.f* **votyansow** poll

voward *n.m* **vowardys** vanguard

voydya *vb* go away; vanish

vy *prn (enclitic)* I; me

vysytya *vb* visit

vysytyans *n.m* **vysytyansow** visit

vysytyer *n.m* **vysytyoryon** visitor

vyth I *adj* no; not any **II** *adv* none. **ny welis vy golow vyth** I did not see any light. **den vyth** *n.m* nobody. **tra vyth** *n.f* nothing

vytholl *adv* at all; not at all

W

waffer *n.m* **waffers** wafer

waja *n.m* **wajys** perk

walts *n.m* **waltsys** waltz

waltsya *vb* waltz

war *adj* aware; cautious; conscious; wary. **bos war** beware; take precautions

war² *prp* on; upon. **penn war²** superior to. **war an ke** abstaining; on the fence. **war anow** oral. **war dharas** through a door. **war euryow** now and then. **war gamm** backwards. **war yew** onward **war y benn** upside down. *Personal forms: 1s warnav, 2s warnas, 3sm warnodho, 3sf warnedhi, 1p warnan, 2p warnowgh, 3p warnedha*

war-barth *adv* together; jointly. **pubonan war-barth** all together. **war-barth ha** together with

war-dhelergh *adv* back; backwards; to the back

war-ji *adv* inwards

warlena *adv* last year

warleni *adv* last year

war-lergh *prp* after; behind; according to. **gul war-lergh** imitate. *Personal forms: 1s war ow lergh, 2s war dha lergh, 3sm war y lergh, 3sf war hy lergh, 1p war agan lergh, 2p war agas lergh, 3p war aga lergh*

warlinen *adj, adv* online

war-lown *adj* on-site

war-mes *adv* outwards

warn *contr (used in numbers from 21 to 39)* on the

war'n *contr* on the

war-nans I *adv* downwards; downhill **II** *adj* downhill

warneth *n.f* awareness

war-not *adv* at once

war-nuk *adv* by return

war-rag *adv* forwards

war-tu *adv* towards. **war-tu ha(g)** *prp* towards

war-vann *adv* upward, upwards; upstairs; up

war-ves *adv* outside; outwardly

war-wartha *adv* upstairs

war-woles *adv* (*direction*) down; downwards; downstairs; under

warya *vb* watch out; beware

wastya *vb* lay waste

wattedh *n.m* **wattedhow** wattage

weeping *n.f* olva

well! *int* well

west I *n.m* West **II** *adj* western. **a'n west** *adj* western

woles *adj* lower

wolkom I *adj* welcome **II** *n.m* welcome; hospitality

wolkomma *vb* greet; welcome

wolkommus *adj* welcoming; hospitable

wordhi *adj* worthy; honourable

wortalleth *adv* (= **wostalleth**) at first; initially

wortiwedh *adv* (= **wostiwedh**) at last; finally; in the long term; ultimately

wosa *prp* after. **wosa henna** after that; later

wostalleth *adv* (= **wortalleth**) at first; initially

wostaswerth *adj* second-hand

wostiwedh *adv* (= **wortiwedh**) at last; finally; in the long term; ultimately

wrynch *n.m* **wrynchys** deceit; knack; trick (*knack*). **res yw usya wrynch ganso** there's a knack to it

wycket *n.m* **wycketys** wicket

wycketor *n.m* **wycketoryon** wicket keeper

X

X-dewynnya *vb* X-ray

Y

y² *poss. adj* his

y⁵(th) *part* (*verbal particle*)

ya! *int* yes!

yagh *adj* healthy; fine; fit

yaghhe *vb* (*transitive*) cure; heal; (*intransitive*) recover; heal

yaghheans *n.m* **yaghheansow** therapy; recovery

yaghus *adj* healthy; wholesome

yalgh *n.f* **yalghow** purse

-yans *sffx* masculine noun suffix

yar *n.f* **yer** chicken; hen

yaswan *n.f* **yaswanyow** thrill

yaswana *vb* thrill

yaswanus *adj* thrilling

ydhil *adj* feeble; meagre; puny

ydhnik *n.m* **ydhnigow** chick

Yedhow *n.m* **Edhewon** Jew

Yedhowek *adj* Jewish

Yedhowieth *n.f* Judaism

yeghes *n.m* health. **Servis Kenedhlek an Yeghes (NHS)** *n.m* the National Health Service (NHS). **yeghes da!** cheers! **yeghes korfek** *n.m* physical fitness. **yeghes brysel** *n.m* mental health

yeghesek *adj* sanitary

yegheswith *n.m* healthcare

-yer *sffx* human agent

yerji *n.m* **yerjiow** hen-house

yet *n.f* **yetys, yetow** gate; wicket. **yet dhowr** *n.f* lock; flood gate

yeth *n.f* **yethow** language. **yeth an werin** *n.f* informal meeting of

Cornish speakers. **yeth plen** *n.f* prose.
yeth teythyek *n.f* vernacular
language
yethador *n.m* **yethadoryow** grammar
yethonieth *n.f* linguistics
yethoniethel *adj* linguistic
yethor *n.m* **yethoryon** linguist
yeunadow *n.m* **yeunadowyow** craving;
yearning
yeuni *vb* crave; miss; yearn
yew *n.f* **yewow** yoke. **war yew** onward
yeyn *adj* cold
yeynder *n.m* cold (*temperature*)
yeynell *n.f* **yeynellow** fridge;
refrigerator
yeynella *vb* refrigerate
yeynhe *vb* (*transitive*) chill;
(*intransitive*) become cold
yeyn-nowodhow *n.pl* bad news
yfarn *n.m* **yfarnow** hell
yfarnek *adj* hellish
y'ga³ *contr* in their
ygam-ogam *n.m* zigzag
y'gan (1) *contr* in our
y'gan (2) *contr* (*object*) us
y'gas (1) *contr* in your (*pl*)
y'gas (2) *contr* (*object*) you (*pl*)
ygerell *n.f* **ygerellow** opener. **ygerell
gannys** *n.f* tin-opener
ygeri *vb* open; explain
ygeryans *n.m* **ygeryansow** opening
ygerys *adj* opened. **hanter ygerys** ajar;
half opened
ygor *adj* open. **checken ygor** *n.f* blank
cheque
ylyn *adj* clear; limpid; transparent.
gober ylyn *n.m* net pay
y'm (1) *contr* in my
y'm (2) *contr* (*object*) me
yma *vb* there is
ymprovisa *vb* improvise
ymprovisans *n.m* **ymprovisansow**
improvisation
ympynnyon *n.pl* brain. **a'n
ympynnyon** cerebral

yn *prp* in; (*with placenames*) at; into; on.
bys yn all the way to. **yn kosk** asleep;
dormant. **yn le** in place of; instead of.
yn unn² -ing. *Personal forms: 1s* **ynnov**,
2s **ynnos**, *3sm* **ynno**, *3sf* **ynni**, *1p*
ynnon, *2p* **ynnowgh**, *3p* **ynna**
y'n (1) *contr* in the
y'n (2) *contr* (*object*) him; it
yn⁵ *part* -ly. **yn fas** properly. **yn feur**
greatly
yn- *prfx* in-
yn ahwer *adj* distressed (*med*)
yn-bann *adv* up; upward, upwards;
uphill
yn-dann² *prp* under; below; beneath;
underneath. **yn-dann dhor**
underground. **yn-dann dava** in touch.
Personal forms: 1s **yn-dannov**, *2s*
yn-dannos, *3sm* **yn-danno**, *3sf*
yn-danni, *1p* **yn-dannon**, *2p*
yn-dannowgh, *3p* **yn-danna**
yndella *adv* like that. **yndella re bo** *int*
so be it; amen
yndelma *adv* like this
yndelna *adv* like that
yngist *n.f* **yngistyow** (*email*) inbox
yn golow *adv* plainly
yn-hons *adv* over there; yonder
ynia *vb* exhort; incite; press; urge. **ynia
war²** insist on
yniadow I *adj* urgent **II** *n.m* urgency
ynians *n.m* **yniansow** incitement
yniedh *n.m* **yniedhow** impulse
ynjynor *n.m* **ynjynoryon** engineer
ynjynorieth *n.f* engineering
ynk *n.m* ink
yn-kerdh *adv* away. **deun yn-kerdh**
let's be off
yn-kerghyn *prp* around; upon. *Personal
forms: 1s* **yn ow herghyn**, *2s* **yn dha
gerghyn**, *3sm* **yn y gerghyn**, *3sf* **yn hy
herghyn**, *1p* **y'gan kerghyn**, *2p* **y'gas
kerghyn**, *3p* **y'ga herghyn**
ynkerth *n.f* **ynkerthow** acquisition

yn kever *prp* (*used with poss. adjectives, p.8*) concerning; with regard to; regarding. *Personal forms: 1s* **yn ow hever,** *2s* **yn dha gever,** *3sm* **yn y gever,** *3sf* **yn hy hever,** *1p* **y'gan kever,** *2p* **y'gas kever,** *3p* **y'ga hever**

ynkladhva *n.f* **ynkladhvaow** cemetery; graveyard

ynkleudhyans *n.m* **ynkleudhyansow** burial; funeral

ynkleudhyas *vb* bury; inter

ynkleudhyer *n.m* **ynkleudhyoryon** undertaker; funeral director

ynklinya *vb* bow; incline; tilt

ynkorfora *vb* incorporate

ynkorforans *n.m* **ynkorforansow** incorporation

ynkressya *vb* increase; enhance

yn-medh *vb* says; quoth

yn-mes *adv* out; outside; outwards. **yn-mes a²** out of

yn-mysk *prp* amid; among; in the middle of; in the midst of. *Personal forms: 3sm* **yn y vysk,** *3sf* **yn hy mysk,** *1p* **y'gan mysk,** *2p* **y'gas mysk,** *3p* **y'ga mysk**

ynn *adj* narrow

yn-nans *adv* down

yn-nes *adv* closer; nearer

ynni *n.m* **yniow** urge

ynperthi *vb* import

ynporth *n.m* **ynporthow** import

yn-rag *adv* forward; onward; on; ahead. **mos yn-rag** go forward; proceed

yns *vb* they are

ynsidhla *vb* infiltrate

ynsidhlans *n.m* **ynsidhlansow** infiltration

ynsidhler *n.m* **ynsidhloryon** infiltrator; plant

ynspirya *vb* inspire

ynstallya *vb* install

ynstallyans *n.m* **ynstallyansow** installation

ynstruktya *vb* instruct

yntana *vb* excite

yntanus *adj* exciting

yntanys *adj* excited

ynter *prp* (= **yntra**) (*used before vowels*) between. *Personal forms: 1s* **yntredhov,** *2s* **yntredhos,** *3sm* **yntredho,** *3sf* **yntredhi,** *1p* **yntredhon,** *2p* **yntredhowgh,** *3p* **yntredha**

ynterfas *n.m* **ynterfassow** interface

yntirya *vb* bury; inter

yntra *prp* (= **ynter**) (*used before consonants*) between. *Personal forms: 1s* **yntredhov,** *2s* **yntredhos,** *3sm* **yntredho,** *3sf* **yntredhi,** *1p* **yntredhon,** *2p* **yntredhowgh,** *3p* **yntredha**

ynvroyas *n.m* **ynvroysi** immigrant

ynwedh *adv* also; likewise; besides

ynworra *vb* input

ynworrans *n.m* **ynworransow** input

ynyal *adj* deserted; desolate

yogort *n.m* **yogortys, yogortow** yoghurt

yonker *n.m* **yonkers, yonkoryon** youth; youngster

yorgh *n.f* **yorghes** roe-deer

yos *n.m* gruel; puree. **yos avalow** *n.m* apple puree. **yos kergh** *n.m* porridge

you *int* hi; hello

Yow *n.m* Thursday; Jupiter

yow *int* hi; hello

yown *n.m* **yownes** (*fish*) bass

yowynk *adj* young; juvenile

yowynka *adj* younger. **an yowynka** youngest

yowynkhe *vb* rejuvenate; make young

yowynkneth *n.f* youth. **kowethas yowynkneth** *n.m* youth club. **kresen yowynkneth** *n.f* youth centre. **ostel yowynkneth** *n.f* youth hostel

yr *adj* fresh

yredi *adv* readily

yrhe *vb* freshen

ys *n.coll* corn. **ys hweg** *n.coll* maize; sweetcorn. **ys pop** *n.coll* popcorn. **ys rudh** *n.coll* cranberries

-ys (1) *sffx (VA suffix)* -ed (*past participle*)

-ys (2) *sffx (plural suffix; mostly in loan-words)* -(e)s

-ys (3) *sffx (masc. abstract noun suffix)*

y's (1) *contr (object)* her; it

y's (2) *contr (object)* them

ysek *adj* abounding in corn

ysen *n.f* **ysennow** grain of corn. **ysen rudh** *n.f* **ysennow rudh** cranberry

yskans *n.coll* cornflakes

yskansen *n.f* **yskansennow** cornflake

yskar *n.m* sackcloth; sacking; cloth

yskynna *vb* ascend; climb; go up; mount

yskynnans *n.m* take-off

yskynnell *n.f* **yskynellow** elevator; lift

yskynnus *adj* ascending. **yn aray yskynnus** in ascending order

ystyn *vb* extend; put out; pass; reach out; supplement

ystynnans *n.m* **ystynansow** appendix; extension; supplement

ystynnys *adj* extended

y'th[5a] **(1)** *contr* in your (*sg*)

y'th[5a] **(2)** *contr (object)* you (*sg*)

ytho I *adv* therefore **II** *cnj* then; so

yurl *n.m* **yurlys** earl; count

yw *vb* he/she is

Z

zebra *n.m* **zebras** zebra

zombi *n.m* **zombis** zombie

zulu *n.m* **zuluyon** zulu

zynk *n.m* (*element*) zinc

zypp *n.m* **zyppys, zyppow** zip

English - Cornish

A

a *art* (*a certain*) unn
aardvark *n* porghel dor *m*, porghellow dor
abandon *vb* gasa; hepkor; forsakya
abate *vb* bashe; slackya
abattoir *n* latti *m*, lattiow
abbatial *adj* abasel
abbess *n* abases *f*, abasesow
abbey *n* abatti *m*, abattiow
abbot *n* abas *m*, abasow
abbreviate *vb* berrhe
abbreviation *n* berrheans *m*, berrheansow
abdomen *n* torr *f*, torrow
abduct *vb* denladra; (*snatch*) dengibya
abduction *n* denladrans *m*, denladransow; dengibyans *m*, dengibyansow
abhorr *vb* abhorrya
abilities *n* teythi *pl*
ability *n* (*physical*) gallos *m*, gallosow; (*learned*) godhvos *m*, godhvosow
-able *sffx* -adow
able I *adj* abel; **more able** appla **II to be able** gallos; bos abel.
ablutions *n* tronkys *m*
abnormal *adj* anreyth; dinatur
abode *n* trigva *f*, trigvaow; annedh *f*, anedhow
abolish *vb* dilea
abolition *n* dileans *m*, dileansow
abort *vb* astel
about I *adv* (*around*) a-dro; (*at the point of*) parys. **it is about to break** parys dhe derri yw; (*round about*) a-dhedro **II** *prp* a-dro dhe^2
above I *adv* a-ugh **II** *prp* a-ugh dhe^2
abrasive *adj* eskravus
abridge *vb* kothe
abridged *adj* kothes
abroad I *adj* tramor **II** *adv* a-les; (*overseas*) dres mor

abrupt *adj* desempis; serth
absence *n* estrik *m*, estrigow
absent *adj* estrigys
absentee *n* estriger *m*, estrigoryon. **absentee landlord** perghen estrigys *m*, perghennow estrigys
absolute *adj* pur; purra; absolut
absolutely *adv* porres
absolve *vb* assoylya
absorb *vb* lenki; sugna; dena; (*a liquid*) eva; (*a shock or blow*) medhelhe
absorbing *adj* (*interesting*) meur y les; dalghennus
absorption *n* denans *m*
abstain *vb* omhedhi; (*abstain from*) skonya (a^2); (*go without*) sevel orth; (*in a vote*) triga heb votya; bos heb tu
abstaining *adj* war an ke
abstract I *adj* anvateryel; tybel; anpythek **II** *n* berrskrif *m*, berrskrifow; skrif kott *m*, skrifow kott
absurd *adj* fol; gocki
abundance *n* kals *m*, kalsow; lanwes *m*, lanwesow; liester *m*, liesteryow; plenteth *f*; palster *m*, palsteryow
abundant *adj* pals
abuse I *n* tebeldhyghtyans *m*, tebeldhyghtyansow; (*of a substance*) drog-usyans *m*, drog-usyansow **II** *vb* abusya; droghandla; tebeldhyghtya; (*orally*) raylya
abysmal *adj* drog dres eghen
abyss *n* islonk *m*, islonkow
abyssal *adj* islonkel
academic I *adj* akademek **II** *n* akademek *m*, akademogyon
academically *adv* yn akademek
academy *n* akademi *m*, akademiow
acanthus *n* (*bear's britches*) paw ors *m*
accelerate *vb* uskishe
acceleration *n* uskisheans *m*, uskisheansow

accelerator *n* uskisell *f*, uskisellow

accent *n* (*regional accent*) lesyeth *f*, lesyethow; (*in writing*) ughverk *m*, ughverkow; (*stress*) poslev *m*, poslevow; (*pitch accent*) ton-lev *m*, ton-levow. **from your accent** dre dha er

accentuate *vb* posleva

accept *vb* (*receive*) degemeres; receva; (*admit*) amyttya; avowa

acceptable *adj* kemeradow

access I *n* hedhas *m*, hedhasow **II** *vb* drehedhes

accessible *adj* hedhadow

accessory I *adj* gweresek **II** *n* gwereser *m*, gweresoryon

accident *n* droglam *m*, droglammow; gwall *m*, gwallow

accidental *adj* dre wall

accidentally *adv* dre wall

accommodate *vb* (*host*) ostya; (*facilitate*) esya

accommodation *n* (*hosting*) ostyans *m*, ostyansow; (*favour*) esyans *m*, esyansow

accompaniment *n* keveylyans *m*, keveylyansow

accompany *vb* (*accompany someone*) mos gans; mos war-barth ha; (*musically*) keveylya

accomplice *n* keskal *m*, keskalyon

accomplish *vb* kowlwul; kollenwel

accomplished *adj* (*successfully completed*) kowlwrys; (*expert*) perfydh. **an accomplished villain** bilen pur *m*, bilens pur

accomplishment *n* kowlwrians *m*, kowlwriansow; (*attainment*) hedhyans *m*, hedhyansow

accord I *n* akord *m* **II** *vb* (*cause to agree*) akordya; kesseni; (*grant*) grontya; ri. **according to** herwydh; war-lergh. **according to the forecast** herwydh an dhargan

accordance *n* unverheans *m*, unverheansow

account I *n* (*financial*) reken *m*, reknow; akont *m*, akontys, akontow; (*report*) derivadow *m*; derivas *m*, derivasow **II** *vb* akontya; synsi. **account book** lyver akontow *m*, lyvrow akontow. **bank account** akont arghantti *m*, akontys arghantti, akontow arghantti. **by all accounts** dell lever pubonan. **current account** akont kesres *m*, akontys kesres, akontow kesres. **deposit account** akont arghow *m*, akontys arghow, akontow arghow. **of no account** distyr. **on account of** awos; drefen. **take account of** gul vri a²

accountable *adj* akontyadow

accountant *n* akontydh *m*, akontydhyon

accredited *adj* afydhys

accumulate *vb* kreuni; kuntel

accumulator *n* kreunell *f*, kreunellow; kreunyer *m*, kreunyoryon

accuracy *n* kewerder *m*

accurate *adj* kewar; ewn

accurately *adv* yn kewar

accusation *n* kuhudhans *m*, kuhudhansow; kabel *m*, kablow

accuse *vb* kuhudha; kabla

accustomed I *adj* usys **II** *vb* **be accustomed to** bos usys gans

ace *n* onan *m*, onanow

ache I *n* gloos *f*, glosow **II** *vb* pystiga

achieve *vb* kowlwul; kollenwel; hedhes

achievement *n* kowlwrians *m*, kowlwriansow

acid I *adj* trenk **II** *n* trenken *f*, trenkennow; dowr trenk *m*, dowrow trenk

acknowledge *vb* aswon (*admit; accept*) amyttya; avowa; (*express gratitude*) godhvos

acknowledgement *n* aswonvos *m*, aswonvosow

acorn *n* mesen *f*, mesennow; mes *coll.*
  acorn cup byskon mes *f*, byskonyow
  mes
acoustic *adj* sononiethel
acoustics *n* sononieth *f*
acquaintance *n* aswonvos *m*,
  aswonvosow
acquire *vb* kavos; (*buy*) prena
acquisition *n* ynkerth *f*, ynkerthow; tra
  gevys *f*, taklow kevys, traow kevys
acre *n* erow *f*, erewi
acrobat *n* lappyer *m*, lappyoryon
across I *adv* a-dreus II *prp* a-dreus dhe^2;
  dres
acrylic I *adj* akrylek II *n* akrylek *m*,
  akrylogyon
act I *n* ober *m*, oberow; gwrians *m*,
  gwriansow; (*of a play*) parth *f*,
  parthow II *vb* gwari; oberi
action *n* gwrians *m*, gwriansow
activate *vb* bywhe; gorra dhe gerdhes
activated *adj* bywhes
activation *n* bywheans *m*,
  bywheansow; gweythresans *m*,
  gweythresansow
active *adj* byw; gweythresek; strik; snell
activity *n* gwrians *m*, gwriansow;
  aktivita *m*, aktivitys
actor *n* gwarier *m*, gwarioryon
actual *adj* gwir
actually *adv* y'n gwir; yn hwir; yn
  gwiryonedh
acute *adj* (*sharp*) lymm; (*serious*) sevur
A.D. *abbrev* B.A.; Bledhen agan Arlodh
  f; (*Common Age*) O.K.; Osweyth
  Kemmyn *f*; Oos Kemmyn *m*
adamant *adj* adamantek
Adam's apple *n* aval briansen *m*,
  avalow briansen
adapt *vb* aswiwa
adapter *n* aswiwer *m*, aswiworyon
add *vb* keworra
adder *n* nader *f*, nadres
addict *n* stoffki *m*, stoffkeun
addicted to *adj* See: dependent on

addition *n* keworrans *m*, keworransow;
  addyans *m*, addyansow
additional *adj* keworransel
address I *n* (*location*) trigva *f*, trigvaow;
  (*speech*) areth *f*, arethyow II *vb* (*write
  address on*) skrifa trigva war^2; (*speak
  to*) kewsel orth
adept *adj* skentel
adequate *adj* lowr
adhere *vb* glena; omlena. **adhere to**
  glena orth; omlena orth
adherence *n* omlenans *m*, omlenansow
adherent *n* dyskybel *m*, dyskyblon
adhesion *n* arlenans *m*, arlenansow
adhesive I *adj* glenus; glusek II *n* glus
  m, glusow
adjacent *adj* kevogas
adjective *n* hanow gwann *m*, henwyn
  gwann
adjoining *adj* ogas; nessa; yn herwydh
adjust *vb* desedha
adjustment *n* desedhans *m*,
  desedhansow
administer *vb* menystra; governa; (*of
  medicine*) ri
administration *n* menystrans *m*,
  menystransow
administrative *adj* menystrek
administrator *n* menystrer *m*,
  menystroryon
admiration *n* estem *m*
admire *vb* estemya
admission *n* amyttyans *m*,
  amyttyansow
admit *vb* (*acknowledge*) amyttya;
  (*confess*) avowa; meneges; (*let in*)
  degemeres a-berth
admittance *n* kummyas-entra *m*,
  kumyasow-entra. **no admittance**
  entrans difennys
admittedly *adv* res yw avowa
adolescent I *adj* lank; godevesik II *n*
  lank *m*, lankyow
adopt *vb* (*a child*) asvaba; astewis; (*a
  policy or motion*) degemeres; receva

adoption *n* asvabans *m*, asvabansow; astewisyans *m*, astewisyansow.
  adoption agency maynorieth-asvaba *f*, maynoriethow asvaba
adoration *n* gordhyans *m*
adore *vb* gordhya
adorn *vb* afina; tekhe; (*furnish*) takla
Adriatic *n* mor Adriatek *m*
adult I *adj* tevesik **II** *n* tevesik *m*, tevesigyon
adulterer *n* avoutrer *m*, avoutrers, avoutroryon
adulterous *adj* (*approx.*) fals
adultery *n* avoutri *m*
adulthood *n* tevesigieth *f*
advance I *n* avonsyans *m*, avonsyansow **II** *vb* avonsya
advanced *adj* avonsys
advantage *n* les *m*; prow *m*
advantageous *adj* dhe les
advent *n* devedhyans *m*, devedhyansow. **Advent** (*eccles.*) Asvens *m*
adventure *n* aventur *m*, aventurys, aventuryow
adventurous *adj* aventurus
adverb *n* adverb *m*, adverbow; gorer *m*, goreryow
adversary *n* eskar *m*, eskerens
advertise *vb* argemynna
advertisement *n* argemmyn *m*, argemynnow
advice *n* kussul *f*, kussulyow; avis *m*, avisyow
advise *vb* kussulya. **be advised that** bos kussulys a²
adviser *n* kussulyer *m*, kussulyoryon
advisory *adj* kussulyek; a gussul
aerial I *adj* a'n ayr; ayrek **II** *n* ayrlorgh *f* (*m*), ayrlorghow
aerobic *adj* ayrobek
aeroplane *n* jynn ebron *m*, jynnys ebron, jynnow ebron; ayren *f*, ayrennow
aerosol *n* ayrosol *m*, ayrosolys

aesthetic *adj* esthetek
afar *adv* a-bell
affair *n* (*business*) mater *m*, maters, materyow; negys *m*, negysyow; (*relationship*) kerensa gudhys *f*
affect *vb* nasya
affectation *n* maneruster *m*
affected *adj* (*mannerism*) manerus
affection *n* hegaredh *m*
affectionate *adj* hegar
affirm *vb* afia; affirmya
afflict *vb* plagya
afflicted *adj* duwenhes; (*plagued*) plagys; (*tortured*) tormentys
afford *vb* affordya
affordable *adj* affordyadow
afraid I *adj* ownek **II** *vb* **become afraid of** kemeres own rag
Africa *top* Afrika *m*
African I *adj* afrikan **II** *n* Afrikan *m*, Afrikans
aft *adv* (*at the back*) a-dhelergh; (*to the back*) war-dhelergh
after *prp* (*time only*) wosa; (*time and space*) war-lergh
afternoon *n* dohajydh *m*, dohajydhyow; androw *m*, androwyow; (*afternoon-time*) androweyth *m*, androweythyow. **good afternoon** dohajydh da
afternoon-time *adv* dohajydhweyth
afterwards *adv* a-wosa; dres keyn; war-lergh henna
again *adv* arta; das-. **say again** dasleverel. **do again** daswul
against *prp* (*opposition*) erbynn (*spatial*) orth. **against the grain** erbynn an gwias. **against the law** erbynn an lagha. **guard against** gwitha rag
age I *n* oos *m*, osow **II** *vb* kothhe. **old age** henys *m*; kothni *f*
agency *n* mayn *m*, maynys; maynorieth *f*, maynoriethow
agenda *n* rol negys *f*, rolyow negys
agent *n* maynor *m*, maynoryon

aggravate *vb* (*worsen*) gwethhe;
(*irritate*) serri

aggression *n* argas *m*, argasow

aggressive *adj* argasus

aggressor *n* argasor *m*, argasoryon

agile *adj* byw, skav

agility *n* bewder *m*; skavder *m*

agitate *vb* amovya

agitated *adj* amevys; amovyes

agnostic I *adj* agnostek II *n* agnostek *m*,
agnostogyon

ago *adv* nans yw. **long ago** nans yw
pell. **not long ago** nans yw neppell.
three years ago nans yw teyr
bledhen

agony *n* galarow *pl*

agoraphobia *n* (*med*) agorafobia *m*

agree *vb* akordya; (*transitive*) unverhe;
(*intransitive*) bos unver; bos unverhes.
agree with akordya gans; akordya
orth; bos unver gans; bos unverhes
gans; assentya gans. **agree to**
assentya dhe²

agreed *adj* akordys; (*unanimous*) unver

agreement *n* akord *m*; ambos *m*,
ambosow; unverheans *m*,
unverheansow

agricultural *adj* amethel

agriculture *n* ammeth *f*

agrimony, common *n* (*steeples*;
sticklewort) skawen an Werghes *f*

agrimony, hemp *n* (*holy rope*) skawen
dhu *f*

ague *n* kleves seson *m*

ah *int* a

ahead *adv* yn-rag

aid I *n* gweres *m*, gweresow; sokor *m* II
vb gweres; sokra. **first aid** *n* kynweres
m. **hearing aid** klewell *f*, klewellow

AIDS *abbrev* (*med*) AIDS. **Acquired
Immune Deficiency Syndrom**
Syndrom Immunodifyk Akwirys

aim I *n* meder *m*, medrow; (*objective*)
amkan *m*, amkanow; medras *m*,
medrasow II *vb* medra

aimless *adj* antowlek

air I *n* ayr *m* II *vb* ayra. **air
conditioning** *n* ayrewnans *m*,
ayrewnansow *m*, ayrownanjow. **air
steward** *n* ost ayr *m*, ostys ayr

air-borne *adj* (*in flight*) y'n ayr

airborne *adj* (*e.g. disease*) ayr-degys

airline *n* ayrlinen *f*, ayrlinennow

airmail *n* ayrbost *m*. **by airmail** der
ayrbost

airport *n* ayrborth *m*, ayrborthow

airstrip *n* ayrsketh *m*, ayrskethow

airtight *adj* ayrstanch; hermesek

aisle *n* kasel *f*, kaselyow. **aisle seat** *n*
esedh gasel *f*, esedhow kasel

ajar *adj* hanter ygerys

-al *sffx* -el

alarm I *n* (*clock*) difunell *f*, difunellow;
(*warning device*) alarm *m*, alarmow;
(*feeling*) own *m* II *vb* gorra own yn.
burglar alarm alarm ladron *m*,
alarmow ladron. **fire alarm** alarm
tan *m*, alarmow tan

alarm clock *n* difunell *f*, difunellow

alarmed *adj* ownek

alarming *adj* broweghus

alas *int* soweth; tru; ellas; ogh

Albania *top* Albani *f*

Albanian I *adj* albaniek II *n* (*language*)
Albaniek *m*; (*person*) Albanian *m*,
Albanians

albeit *cnj* kyn fo

album *n* albom *m*, albomow; (*book*)
lyver kuntel *m*, lyvrow kuntel;
(*music*) kuntilow *m*, kuntilowyow

alchemist *n* feryl *m*, ferylyow

alchemy *n* alkemi *m*

alcohol *n* las *m*, lasow; alkohol *m*.
alcohol dependency *adj* omres dhe
las

alcoholic I *n* laseger *m*, lasegoryon II
adj lasek

alcoholism *n* (*med*) lasogeth *f*

alcove *n* neythik *m*, neythigow

alder tree *n* gwernen *f*, gwernennow; gwern *coll*

ale *n* korev *m*, korevow *m*

A level *n* nivel A *m*, nivelyow A

algae *n* algi *coll*

algebra *n* aljebra *m*

alias *n* kenhanow *m*, kenhenwyn

alibi *n* alibi *m*, alibis

alien I *adj* estren **II** *n* alyon *m*, alyons; estren *m*, estrenyon

alienate *vb* estrenya

alight I *adj* (*on fire*) gans tan; (*shining brightly*) gans golow **II** *vb* (*dismount*) diyskynna

align *vb* alinya

alignment *n* alinyans *m*, alinyansow

alike *adj* haval; kehaval

alive *adj* byw

alkali *n* lisliwen *f*, lisliwennow

all I *adj* oll **II** *prn* peub. **all the time** pub eur oll. **all the way to** bys yn. **not at all** mann. **the All Blacks** an para Oll Du *m*

allegation *n* kuhudhans *m*, kuhudhansow

allege *vb* kuhudha

alleged *adj* kuhudhys

allergic *adj* allergek

allergy *n* allergedh *m*, allergedhow

alley *n* stretyn *m*, stretynnow

alleyway *n* skochfordh *f*, skochfordhow

all-heal *n* (*common valerian*) medhoges an gors *f*

alliance *n* keffrysyans *m*, keffrysyansow *m*, keffresyanjow

allied *adj* keffrysys

alligator *n* alligator *m*, alligators

alliteration *n* keslytherennans *m*

allow *vb* gasa; alowa

all right *adv* da lowr; oll yn komposter

ally *n* keffrysyas *m*, keffrysysi

almighty *adj* ollgallosek

almond *n* alamand *m*, alamandys, alamandow

almost *adv* (*before an adjective*) ogas; (*before a noun*) ogas ha; (*before a verb*) namna^2; namnag; (*used independently*) ogasti. **he almost won** ev a waynyas ogatti

alms *n* alusen *f*, alusenow

aloes *n* aloes *pl*

aloft *adv* a-vann

alone *adj* possessive adjective + honan

along *adv* a-hys

alongside *adv, prp* ryb tenewen

aloof *adv* a-denewen

aloud *adv* yn ughel

alphabet *n* abecedari *m*, abecedaris; lytherennek *f*, lytherenegi

Alps *top* Alpys *pl*

already *adv* seulabrys

also *adv* ynwedh; keffrys; maga ta

alter *vb* chanjya; dihevelebi

alternate *vb* tereylya

alternation *n* tereylyans *m*, tereylyansow

alternative I *adj* aral; ken **II** *n* ken dewis *m*, ken dewisyow

although *cnj* (*before consonants*) kyn^5; (*before vowels and h-*) kynth

altogether *adv* hys-ha-hys

aluminium *n* (*element*) aluminiom *m*

always *adv* pub prys; pupprys; pub termyn; prest

Alzheimer's disease *n* kleves Alzheimer *m*

amalgam *n* amalgam *m*, amalgamys; kesunses *m*, kesunsesow

amalgamate *vb* kesunya

amaryllis *n* (*Jersey lily*) arlodhesow noth *pl*

amass *vb* gronna

amateur *n* bodhesik *m*, bodhesigyon

amateurish *adj* bodhesik

amaze *vb* gorra marth yn; sowdhanas; sowdheni

amazement *n* marth *m*, marthow

amazing *adj* marthys; anethek

amazingly *adv* marthys

ambassador *n* kannas *f*, kanasow

amber *n* amber *m*, ambrys

ambiguous *adj* amstyryus

ambition *n* ughelhwans *m*, ughelhwansow

ambitious *adj* ughelhwansek

ambulance *n* karr klavji *m*, kerri klavji; ambulans *m*, ambulansys

ambush I *n* kontrewaytyans *m*, kontrewaytyansow **II** *vb* kontrewaytya

amen *int* yndella re bo

amenity *n* (*infrastructure*) isframweyth *m*

amends *n* restorita *m*, restoritys; *n* amendys *pl.* **make amends** gul amendys; gul restorita; astiveri

America *top* Amerika *m*; (*United States of America*) an Statys Unys

American I *adj* amerikanek **II** *n* Amerikan *m*, Amerikanyon. **American football** *n* pel droos amerikanek *f*

amiable *adj* hegar. **amiable towards someone** hegar orth nebonan

amicable *adj* hegar; kuv

amid *prp* yn-mysk

ammunition *n* daffar ladhva *m*

amnesty *n* amnesti *m*, amnestis

among *prp* yn-mysk

amount *n* myns *m*, mynsow

ample *adj* lowr

amplifier *n* argrevell *f*, argrevellow

amplify *vb* moghhe

amplitude *n* heledh *m*, heledhow

amputate *vb* treghi dhe-ves

amuse *vb* didhana. **amuse oneself** omdhidhana

amusement *n* didhan *m*, didhenyow. **amusement park** park-omdhidhana *m*, parkow-omdhidhana

amusing *adj* didhanus

anachronism *n* kammamseren *f*, kammamserennow

anachronistic *adj* kammamseryek

anaemia *n* (*med*) anemia *m*

anaemic *adj* anemek

anaesthetic I *adj* klamderus **II** *n* klamderyas *m*, klamderysi

analogue *adj* analog

analogy *n* analogieth *f*, analogiethow

analyse *vb* dielvenna

analysis *n* dielvennans *m*, dielvenansow

anarchic *adj* direwl

anarchist *n* direwlyas *m*, direwlysi

anarchy *n* direwl *m*

ancestor *n* hendas *m*, hendasow

anchor I *n* ankor *m*, ankoryow **II** ankorya

anchorage *n* ankorva *f*, ankorvaow; poll *m*, pollow. **fleet anchorage** lulyn *f*, lulynnow

anchovy *n* ganowek *m*, ganowogyon

ancient *adj* hen

and *cnj* (*before consonants*) ha; (*before vowels*) hag

anecdote *n* racka *m*, rackow

anemone, wood *n* (*windflower; thimbleweed*) bleujen an gwyns *f*

angel *n* el *m*, eledh

angelic *adj* elek

angelica *n* (*wild celery*) losow eledh *coll*

anger *n* sorr *m*

angle *n* elin *m*, elinyow. **acute angle** lymmelin *m*, lymmelinyow. **obtuse angle** soghelin *m*, soghelinyow. **right angle** elin pedrek *m*, elinyow pedrek

Anglican I *adj* Anglikan **II** *n* Anglikan *m*, Anglikanyon

Anglicanism *n* Anglikanieth *f*

anglicise *vb* sowsnekhe

Anglo- *prfx* Sows-

anglophone I *adj* sowsneger **II** *n* Sowsneger *m*, Sowsnegoryon

angry *adj* serrys. **be angry, get angry, make angry** serri. **get angry with** serri orth

anguish *n* angos *m*; gloos *f*

angular *adj* elinek

animal *n* best *m*, bestes; eneval *m*, enevales; mil *m*, miles. **wild animal** godhvil *m*, godhviles

animate *vb* bywhe

animated *adj* bywhes

animation *n* bywheans *m*, bywheansow

anion *n* anion *m*, anions

ankle *n* ufern *m*, ufernyow, *dl* dewufern

anniversary *n* penn-bloodh *m*, pennow-bloodh. **wedding anniversay** *m* penn-bloodh demedhyans

annotation *n* notennyans *m*, notenyansow

announce *vb* deklarya

annoy *vb* ania; serri

annoying *adj* fyslek. **annoying thing or person** *n* begel *m*, begelyow

annual *adj* bledhynnyek. **annual leave** *n* kummyas bledhynnyek *m*

annually *adv* pub bledhen

Annunciation *n* (*The Feast of the*) Dy'gol Maria mis Meurth *m*

anoint *vb* ura; elia; olewi; anoyntya

anomaly *n* digessenyans *m*, digessenyansow

anonymous *adj* dihanow

anorak *n* anorak *m*, anorakys

anorexia nervosa *n* (*med*) anoreksia nervosa *m*. **a person with anorexia** person gans anoreksia

anorexic *adj* (*med*) anoreksek

another I *adj* aral; ken; moy II *prn* aral. **another one** onan aral; ken onan. **one another** an eyl y gila *m*; an eyl hy ben *f*; *prfx* om-

answer I *n* gorthyp *m*, gorthebow II *vb* gorthebi. **answer back** gorthebi yn tont. **answering machine** jynn-gorthebi *m*, jynnys-gorthebi, jynnow-gorthebi

ant *n* moryonen *f*, moryon

Antarctic *top* Antarktek *m*

antenna *n* tavell *f*, tavellow

anthem *n* antempna *m*, antempnys, antempnow

anti- *prfx* gorth-

anti-clockwise *adj* gorthnaswedhek

antique *n* henbyth *m*, henbython

antirrhinum *n* (*snapdragon*) sawen an dhragon *m*

anus *n* gwenn *m*, gwennow

anxiety *n* ahwer *m*; preder *m*, prederow; fienas *m*, fienasow

anxious *adj* prederus

any I *adj* (*in negative expressions*) vyth II *adv* neb. **I did not see any light** ny welis vy golow vyth

anybody *prn* nebonan

any more *adv* na fella; namoy

anyone *prn* nebonan

anything *prn* (*in positive phrases*) neppyth; neb tra; (*in negative phrases*) tra vyth

anyway *adv* yn neb kas; yn neb fordh

anywhere *adv* neb le; neb tyller; neb tu

apart *adv* a-les

apartment *n* rannji *m*, rannjiow

ape *n* apa *m*, apys

aphid *n* lewen losow *f*, lewennow losow; lew losow *coll*

apologetic *adj* diharesek

apologise *vb* dihares; omdhivlamya

apology *n* dihares *m*, diharesow

apostate I *adj* negedhys II *n* negedhys *m*, negedhysyon

apostle *n* abostol *m*, abesteli

apostrophe *n* kollverk *m*, kollverkys

app *n* (*IT*) app *m*, appow

apparel *n* aparel *m*

apparent *adj* apert; heveladow

apparently *adv* dell hevel

appeal I *n* galow *m*, galowyow; (*law*) appel *m*, appelyow II *vb* gelwel

appear *vb* diskwedhes; omdhiskwedhes

appearance *n* semlant *m*, semlans; mir *m*, mirow

appendix *n* ystynnans *m*, ystynansow

appetite *n* ewl voos *f*, ewlow boos
applaud *vb* gormel
applause *n* gormola *f*, gormoledhow
apple *n* aval *m*, avalow. **crab apple** *n* aval goodh *m*, avalow goodh
apple tree *n* avalen *m*, avalennow; avalwedhen *f*, avalwedhennow; *coll* avalwydh
applicant *n* ombrofyer *m*, ombrofyoryon
application *n* ombrofyans *m*, ombrofyansow
apply *vb* (*bring into operation*) gweytha; (*for a post*) ombrofya; (*oneself*) omri; (*paint etc.*) gorra war^2; gorra dhe^2
appoint *vb* apoyntya; ordena
appointment *n* apoyntyans *m*, apoyntyansow
appreciate *vb* gwerthveurhe
appreciation *n* gwerthveurheans *m*, gwerthveurheansow
apprehensive *adj* ownus
apprentice *n* kynser *m*, kynseri. **smith's apprentice** mab-gov *m*, mebyon-gov
apprenticeship *n* kynserneth *m*, kynsertnethow
approach *vb* dos nes; neshe; nesa
approachable *adj* nesadow
appropriate *adj* gwiw
approval *n* komendyans *m*, komendyansow
approve *vb* komendya. **approved** komendys
approximate *adj* nesogas; ogas lowr
approximately *adv* ogas dhe^2; ogas ha
apricot *n* brykedhen *f*, brykedhennow; brykedh *coll*
April *n* Ebrel *m*; mis Ebrel *m*
apron *n* apron *m*, apronnyow
aquarium *n* pyskva *f*, pyskvaow; pusketti *m*, puskettiow
aquatic *adj* dowrek; a'n dowr
aquilegia *n* (*columbine*) kough damawynn *m*

Arab *n* Arab *m*, Arabyon
Arabia *top* Arabi *m*
Arabian I *adj* arabek **II** *n* Arab *m*, Arabyon
Arabic *n* Arabek
arable *adj* aradow
arbour *n* erber *m*, erberow, erbers
arc *n* gwarak *m*, gwaregow
arch *n* gwarak *f*, gwaregow
archaeological *adj* hendhyskoniethel
archaeologist *n* hendhyskonydh *m*, hendhyskonydhyon
archaeology *n* hendhyskonieth *f*
archaic *adj* hen
archangel *n* arghel *m*, argheledh
archbishop *n* arghepskop *m*, arghepskobow
archer *n* gwareger *m*, gwaregoryon; sether *m*, sethoryon
archery *n* gwaregieth *f*
archipelago *n* enesek *f*, enesegi
architect *n* pennser *m*, pennseri
architecture *n* pennserneth *f*
ardent *adj* gwresek
area *n* arenebedh *m*, arenebedhow; leurnedh *m*, leurnedhow
Argentina *top* Arghantina *f*
Argentinian I *adj* arghantinek **II** *n* Arghantinan *m*, Arghantinans
argue *vb* argya; dadhla; debatya; disputya; kewsel a-dreus. **argue against** argya erbynn; disputya erbynn. **argue with** argya orth; disputya orth. **don't argue!** na gows a-dreus!
argument *n* dadhel *f*, dadhlow; argyans *m*, argyansow
argumentative *adj* kavylek
arid *adj* krin; sygh
arise *vb* sevel; sordya
arithmetic I *adj* niveroniethel **II** *n* niveronieth *f*, niveroniethow
ark *n* argh *f*, arghow. **Noah's Ark** Gorhel Noy. **The Ark of the Covenant** argh kevambos an Arlodh**

arm I *n* (*body part*) bregh *f*, breghow, *dl* diwvregh; (*weapon*) arv *f*, arvow **II** *vb* arva. **take up arms** mos dhe arvow

armature *n* armatur *m*, armaturyow

armchair *n* kador vregh *f*, kadoryow bregh

armed *adj* ervys. **armed to the teeth** ervys bys y'n dhiwen

armour *n* arvwisk *m*. **iron armour** gwisk horn *m*

armpit *n* kasel *f*, kaselyow, *dl* diwgasel

arms *n* arvow *pl*

army *n* lu *m*, luyow

aroma *n* sawor *m*, saworyow; odour *m*, odours

around I *adv* a-dro. **all around** a-derdro **II** *prp* a-dro dhe²; yn-kerghyn

arouse *vb* sordya; movya

arrange *vb* ordena; renka; restra; araya

arrangement *n* aray *m*, arayow; rester *f*, restri

arrest I *n* dalghennas *m*, dalghenasow; **II** *vb* dalghenna. **writ of arrest** kapyas *m*, kapyasow. **cardiac arrest** astel kolon *m*

arrival *n* devedhyans *m*, devedhyansow

arrive *vb* dos; drehedhes

arrogant *adj* gothus; howtyn; orgelus; prout; balgh

arrow *n* seth *f*, sethow

arse *n* tin *f*, tinyow

arsenic *n* (*element*) arsenyk *m*

arson *n* loskrians *m*, loskriansow

arsonist *n* loskrias *m*, loskriysi

art *n* art *m*, artys

article *n* (*text*) erthygel *m*, erthyglow; skrif *m*, skrifow; skrifen *f*, skrifennow. (*grammatical*) ger mell *m*, geryow mell

artificial *adj* kreftus. **artificial intelligence** *n* skians kreftus

artist *n* artydh *m*, artydhyon; (*painter*) lymner *m*, lymnoryon

as I *adv* avel. **I did it as a joke** my a'n gwrug avel ges **II** *cnj* dell². **as I said to him** dell leveris dhodho; **as I believe** dell grysav. **as it seems** dell hevel. **as it were** kepar dell via. **as usual** dell yw usys; herwydh usadow. **as well** maga ta. **be dressed as** bos gwiskys yn. **for as much as** yn mar veur dell². **twice as good** diwweyth mar dha

as… as *cnj* (*with nouns*) mar² … avel. **as white as snow** mar wynn avel ergh; (*with verbs*) mar² … dell². **as simple as it seemed** mar sempel dell hevelis. **as long as** hedre². **as many as** *prn* myns; *adv* kemmys; kekemmys. **as soon as** *adv* kettel². **as quickly as** *adv* kettooth ha

ascend *vb* yskynna; ascendya

ascending *adj* yskynnus. **in ascending order** yn aray yskynnus

ASD *abbrev* (*med*) ASD. **Autism Spectrum Disorder** Disordyr Spektrom Awtystek

ash tree *n* onnen *f*, onennow; onn *coll*; enwydhen *f*, enwydhennow; ennwydh *coll*

ashamed *adj* methek. **be ashamed** kemeres meth

ashen *adj* lusuek

ashes *n* lusu *coll*

ashtray *n* lusuegyn *m*, lusuegynnow

Asia *top* Asi *f*

Asian I *adj* asiek **II** *n* Asian *m*, Asians

aside *adv* a-denewen

ask *vb* (*question*) govyn; (*request*) pysi. **ask a question of someone** govyn orth nebonan. **ask oneself** omwovyn. **ask someone to do something** pysi nebonan a wul neppyth. **ask urgently** pysi tynn

asleep *adj* yn kosk

asparagus *n* merlosowen *f*, merlosowennow; merlosow *coll*

aspen *n* edhlen *f*, edhlennow; edhel *coll*

assassin *n* denledhyas *m*, denledhysi

assemble *vb* (*transitive*) keskorra; (*intransitive*) omguntel

assembly *n* kesva *f*, kesvaow; kuntelles *m* (*f*), kuntellesow

assent *vb* assentya

assessable *adj* assessadow

assist *vb* skoodhya; gweres

assistance *n* skoodhyans *m*, skodhyansow; gweres *m*, gweresow

assistant *n* darbarer *m*, darbaroryon; skoodhyer *m*, skodhyoryon. **health care assistant** skoodhyer yeghes *m*, skodhyoryon yeghes

associate *vb* kowethya. **associate with** kowethya gans

association *n* kowethas *m*, kowethasow

assume *vb* desevos

assumption *n* desev *m*, desevow

assure *vb* afydhya; surhe

aster, autumn *n* (*Michaelmas daisy*) bleujen gool Mighal *f*

asthma *n* (*med*) asthma *m*

asthmatic *adj* (*med*) asthmatek

astonish *vb* gorra marth yn

astonishing *adj* revedh

astray I *adv* yn sowdhan; war stray **II** *vb* **go astray** mos yn sowdhan; sowdhanas; mos war stray; mos dhe stray

astronaut *n* stervarner *m*, stervarnoryon

astronomical *adj* steroniethel

astronomy *n* steronieth *f*

astute *adj* fin; fel

asylum *n* (*place*) meneghiji *m*, meneghijiow; harber *m*, harbers; (*state*) harbereth *f*; meneghi *m*, meneghiow. **political asylum** harbereth wlasek *f*

asymmetrical *adj* digemusur

at *prp* (*spatial*) orth; (*with placenames*) yn; (*temporal*) dhe². **at two in the afternoon** dhe dhiw eur androweyth. **at all** vytholl; banna; mann. **they**

didn't eat at all ny dhyb'sons banna. **it does not concern me at all** ny'm deur mann. **at this time** y'n tor' ma. **at first** wostalleth; wortalleth. **at home** tre. **at last** wortiwedh; wostiwedh. **at sea** yn mor. **at night** yn nos

atheism *n* didhuwieth *f*

atheist *n* didhuwydh *m*, didhuwydhyon; ankrydor *m*, ankrydoryon

atheistic *adj* didhuw

athlete *n* athlet *m*, athletys

athletic *adj* athletek

athletics *n* athletek *pl*

Atlantic *adj* atlantek. **Atlantic Ocean** Keynvor Atlantek *m*

atlas *n* mappalyver *m*, mappalyvrow

atmosphere *n* ayrgylgh *m*

atmospheric *adj* ayrgylghyek

atom *n* atom *m*, atomow

atomic *adj* atomek

atrocious *adj* euthwriansek

atrocity *n* euthwrians *m*, euthwriansow

attach *vb* fastya; staga

attached *adj* stag

attachment *n* syg *f*, sygow; (*to a document or email*) stagell *f*, stagellow

attack I *n* omsettyans *m*, omsettyansow **II** *vb* omsettya war². **heart attack** *n* shora kolon *m*

attacker *n* omsettyer *m*, omsettyoryon

attain *vb* hedhes

attainment *n* drehedhyans *m*, drehedhyansow

attempt I *n* assay *m*, assays; attent *m*, attentys **II** *vb* assaya; hwilas

attend *vb* attendya; (*be present*) bos ena

attendance *n* attendyans *m*, attendyansow

attendant *n* kesservyas *m*, kesservysi

attention I *n* attendyans *m*, attendyansow **II** *vb* **pay attention** attendya

attentive *adj* hewol

attic *n* soler *m*, soleryow

attitude *n* stons *m*, stonsys; omdhalgh *m*, omdhalghow

attorney *n* laghyas *m*, laghysi

attract *vb* tenna

attraction *n* tennvos *m*, tennvosow

attractive *adj* tennvosek

attribute *vb* askrifa

attributed *adj* askrifys

attributes *n* teythi *pl*

auburn *adj* gellrudh

auction I *n* strifwerth *m*, strifwerthow **II** *vb* strifwertha

auctioneer *n* strifwerther *m*, strifwerthoryon

audacity *n* hardhder *m*; bolder *m*

audible *adj* heglew; klewadow

audience *n* goslowysi *pl*

audio-visual *adj* klewwelyek

audit I *n* arhwilyans *m*, arhwilyansow **II** *vb* arhwilas

augment *vb* moghhe

August *n* Est *m*; mis Est *m*

aunt *n* modrep *f*, modrebedh

auntie *n* modrebik *f*, modrebigow

aura *n* awra *m*, awras

austerity *n* dibalster *m*, dibalsteryow

Australia *top* Ostrali *f*

Australian I *adj* ostralek **II** *n* Ostralian *m*, Ostralyans

Austria *top* Ostri *f*

Austrian I *adj* ostrian **II** *n* Ostrian *m*, Ostrians

author *n* awtour *m*, awtours

authoritarian *adj* awtoritaus

authoritarianism *n* awtoritauster *m*

authority *n* awtorita *m*, awtoritas. **on the authority of** herwydh

autism *n* (*med*) awtysm *m*. **a person with autism** person gans awtysm

autistic *adj* (*med*) awtystek

automatic *adj* awtomatek

autumn *n* kynnyav *m*, kynyavow

autumnal *adj* kynyavel

auxiliary *adj* heweres

avail I *n*. **it is of no avail** ny amont **II** *vb* avaylya; amontya

available *adj* kavadow

avalanche *n* erghslynk *m*, erghslynkys, erghslynkow

avenge *vb* diala; venjya

avens, water *n* lesbenigys an dowr *m*

avens, wood *n* lesbenigys an koos *m*

avenue *n* rosva *f*, rosvaow

average I *adj* kresek **II** *n* kresek *m*, kresogow

avert *vb* treylya dhe-ves; didreylya

aviator *n* neyjer *m*, neyjoryon

avid *adj* terderus

avocado *n* avokado *m*, avokados

avoid *vb* avoydya; goheles

avoidable *adj* goheladow

await *vb* gortos

awake *adj* difun. **wide awake** pur dhifun; ughhewol

award *n* pewas *m*, pewasow

aware *adj* war

awareness *n* warneth *f*

away *adv* dhe-ves. **go away!** ke dhe-ves! ke yn-kerdh! **throw away** tewlel dhe-ves; tewlel dhe skoll

awful *adj* euthyk

awfully *adv* euthyk

awkward *adj* kledhek

awl *n* menowes *f*, menowesow

axe *n* bool *f*, bolyow

axis *n* eghel *f*, eghelow

axle *n* aghel *f*, aghlow

azalea *n* azalea *m*, azaleas

B

babble *vb* gerya

baby *n* baban *m*, babanes; flogh
bkghan *m*, fleghes vyghan; babi *m*,
babiow. **baby carriage** kerrik flogh *m*,
kerigow flogh

baby-sit *vb* floghgovia

baby-sitter *n* floghgovier *m*,
floghgovioryon

bachelor *n* bacheler *m*, bachelers.
bachelor's degree bachelerieth *f*,
bacheleriethow

back I *adv* arta; tre; war-dhelergh II *n*
keyn *m*, keynow; kil *m*, kilyer III *vb*
skoodhya. **at the back** a-dhelergh.
back down omblegya. **back off**
kildenna. **back to front** an keyn a-rag.
to the back war-dhelergh

backache *n* payn keyn *m*, paynys keyn

backbone *n* askorn keyn *m*, eskern
keyn

background *n* kilva *f*, kilvaow

backpack *n* sagh keyn *m*, seghyer keyn

backward(s) *adv* war-dhelergh; war
gamm. **backward turn** kildro *f*,
kildroyow

bacon *n* meghin *m*; backen *m*

bacterium *n* egin *m*, eginyow;
bakteriom *m*, bakteria

bad *adj* drog; (*preceding the noun*) hager.
bad deal hager-vargen *m*. **bad deed**
drog-ober *m*, drog-oberow. **bad news**
yeyn-nowodhow *pl*. **bad-tempered**
droktemprys

badge *n* arwodhik *m*, arwodhigow

badger *n* brogh *m*, broghes

badly *adv* yn trog

badminton *n* badminton *m*

bag I *n* sagh *m*, seghyer II *vb* (*put in a
bag*) sagha. **sleeping bag** sagh-koska
m, seghyer-koska

bagpipes *n* pibow sagh *pl*

bail *n* mewgh *m*, mewghyow. **stand
bail** mewghya. **jump bail** gasa
mewgh

bait *n* treustrum *m*, treustrummow

bake *vb* pobas; fornya

baker *n* peber *m*, peboryon

bakery *n* popti *m*, poptiow

balance I *n* kespos *m*, kesposow;
omborth *m*, omborthow; (*device*)
mantol *f*, mantolyow; (*bank account*)
gasadow *m*, gasadowyow II *vb*
omberthi

balanced *adj* omborth

balcony *n* balegva *f*, balegvaow

bald *adj* mool; blogh. **bald person**
penn pilys *m*

bale I *n* pusorn *m*, pusornow II *vb*
pusornas

ball *n* pel *f*, pelyow

ballad *n* ballad *m*, ballads

balloon *n* pel ayr *f*, pelyow ayr

ballot *n* etholans *m*, etholansow

ballpoint pen *n* pluven belvleyn *f*,
pluvennow pelvleyn

balm *n* eli *m*, eliow. **lip balm, lip salve**
eli gweus *m*, eliow gweus

balm, lemon *n* eli lymmaval *m*

balsam, Himalayan *n* basnet gwithyas
m

bamboo *n* korsen Eynda *f*

ban *vb* emskemuna

banana *n* banana *m*, bananas

band *n* bond *m*, bondys, bondow;
(*group*) bagas *m*, bagasow

bandage I *n* lysten *f*, lystennow II *vb*
lystenna

bandit *n* ravner *m*, ravnoryon

bandsaw *n* hesken vond *f*, heskennow
bond

bang *n* (*explosion*) tardh *m*, tardhow;
(*knock*) bonk *m*, bonkys

Bangladesh *top* Bangladesh *m*

banish *vb* pellhe

bank *n* (*money*) arghantti *m*, arghanttiow; (*river bank*) glann *f*, glannow; (*topography*) banken *f*, bankennow. **bank account** akont arghantti *m*, akontow arghantti. **bank balance** gasadow *m*, gasadowyow; kespos arghantti *m*, kesposow arghantti. **bank charges** kostow arghantti *pl*. **bank holiday** dy'gol kemmyn *m*, dy'golyow kemmyn; dy'gol arghantti *m*, dy'golyow arghantti.

banker *n* arghanser *m*, arghansoryon

banknote *n* noten arghantti *f*, notennow arghantti

bankrupt I *adj* skatt II *vb* gul skatt

bankruptcy *n* skattyans *m*, skattyansow

banner *n* baner *m*, baneryow, baners

banquet *n* gwledh *f*, gwledhow; banket *m*, bankettys

baptise *vb* besydhya

baptism *n* besydh *m*, besydhyow

bar I *n* prenn *m*, prennyer; (*pub; law*) barr *m*, barrys II *vb* prenna; barrya

barbaric *adj* barbarek

barbecue *n* barbakoa *m*, barbakoas

barber *n* barbour *m*, barbours

barberry *n* spernen velen *f*, spern melen

bar-code *n* barrgod *m*, barrgodys

bard *n* bardh *m*, berdh

bardic *adj* bardhek

bare I *adj* lomm; (*bald*) mool; blogh; (*naked*) noth II *vb* lommhe. **bare one's teeth** grysla

bare-backed *adj* keyn lomm

barefoot *adj* diarghen; dieskis

bare-headed *adj* penn-noth

bare-legged *adj* fernoth

barely *adv* skant; skantlowr

bareness *n* lomder *m*

bargain I *n* bargen *m*, bargennyow II *vb* bargynnya

barge *n* skath hir *f*, skathow hir

bark (**1**) I *n* (*of a dog*) harth *m*, harthow II *vb* hartha

bark (**2**) *n* (*of a tree*) rusken *f*, ruskennow; rusk *coll*

barley *n* barlys *coll*. **grain of** barlysen *f* barlysennow

barn *n* skiber *f*, skiberyow

barnacle *n* skeren *f*, skerennow; sker *coll*

barometer *n* barometer *m*, barometrow

barracks *n* souderji *m*, souderjiow

barrel *n* balyer *m*, balyeryow

barren *adj* difeyth

barrier *n* lett *m*, lettys, lettow

barrow *n* gravath *f*, gravathow

bartender *n* tavernor *m*, tavernoryon

barter *vb* kesvargynnya

base *n* ben *m*, benyow; goles *m*, golesow; grond *m*, grondys, grondow; sel *f*, selyow. **military base** selva *f*, selvaow

baseball *n* pel vas *f*

bash *vb* dorna; kronkya

bashful *adj* gohelus

basic *adj* selvenel; selyek; elvennek

basics *n* pennrewlys *pl*

basin *n* bason *m*, basonys

basis *n* grond *m*, grondow

basket *n* kanstel *f*, kanstellow; kowel *m*, kowellow; basket *m*, baskettys. **waste-paper basket** atalgist *f*, atalgistyow

basketball *n* pel ganstel *f*

Basque I *adj* baskek II *n* (*language*) Baskek *m*; (*person*) Bask *m*, Baskyon

bass (**1**) I *adj* (*music*) faborden II *n* faborden *m*, fabordenyon. **bass guitar** gitar faborden *m*, gitaryow faborden

bass (**2**) (*fish*) yown *m*, yownes

bastard *n* bastard *m*, bastardyon

bat (**1**) *n* (*animal*) askel groghen *f*, eskelli kroghen; ughsommys *m*, ughsommyses

bat (2) (*sporting*) batt *m*, battys; racket *m*, racketys, racketow

batch *n* bagasik *m*, bagasigow

bath *n* kibel *f*, kibellow; badh *m*, badhys; tronkys *m*

bathe *vb* badhya; (*trans.*) golghi; (*intrans.*) omwolghi; (*take a bath*) omdroghya. **bathing suit** dillas-omvadhya *coll*

bathroom *n* stevel-omwolghi *f*, stevellow-omwolghi; golghva *f*, golghvaow

baton *n* leuvwelen *f*, leuvwelynni

batter (1) *n* (*cooking*) kestew *m*, kestewow

batter (2) *vb* (*beat*) fusta

battery *n* (*electric*) batri *m*, batriow

battle I *n* kas *f*, kasow; batel *f*, batalyow **II** *vb* batalyas

bay (1) *n* (*coastal feature*) pleg mor *m*, plegow mor; baya *m*, bayys; kammas *f*, kamasow

bay (2) *n* (*tree*) baywedhen *f*, baywedhennow; baywydh *coll*

bay (3) *vb* (*hound*) hartha

bazaar *n* basar *m*, basars

B.C. *abbrev* K.O.K.; Kyns Osweyth Kemmyn

B.C.E. *abbrev* K.O.K.; Kyns Osweyth Kemmyn

be *vb* bos; bones. **let's be off** deun yn-kerdh. **the powers that be** an awtoritas *pl*. **so be it** yndella re bo

beach *n* treth *m*, trethow

bead *n* paderen *f*, paderennow

beak *n* gelvin *m*, gelvines

beaker *n* hanaf *m*, hanafow

beam *n* (*wood*) prenn *m*, prennyer. (*light*) dewyn *m*, dewynnow

bean *n* faven *f*, favennow; fav *coll*

bear (1) *n* (*animal*) ors *m*, orses

bear (2) *vb* (*endure*) perthi; godhav; godhevel; (*carry*) don; degi; (*children*) omdhon

bear's britches *n* (*acanthus*) paw ors *m*

bearable *adj* porthadow

beard *n* barv *m*, barvow

bearded *adj* barvus

bearing *n* (*comportment*) omdhegyans *m*, omdhegyansow; (*direction*) tu *m*, tuyow

beast *n* best *m*, bestes

beat *vb* (*strike*) dorna; frappya; gweskel; kronkya; (*with a club*) fusta; (*defeat*) fetha; konkwerrya. **beat a drum** gweskel tabour

beaten *adj* (*struck*) gweskys; (*defeated*) fethys

beautiful *adj* teg

beautify *vb* tekhe; afina

beauty *n* tekter *m*

beaver *n* lostledan *m*, lostledanes; bever *m*, bevers

because *cnj* awos; drefen; rag; dre reson; reson prag

become *vb* dos ha bos; mos ha bos; mos. **become cold** yeynhe. **become hot** tomma. **become tired** skwitha. **I have become old** my re gyllys koth

bed *n* gweli *m*, gweliow

bedding *n* lienyow gweli *pl*

bedroom *n* chambour *m*, chambours

bedsheet *n* lien gweli *m*, lienyow gweli

bedstraw, yellow *n* (*lady's bedstraw*) kala gweli *coll*

bedtime *n* prys gweli *m*, presyow gweli

bee *n* gwenenen *f*, gwenennow; gwenen *coll*

beech *n* fawen *f*, fawennow; faw *coll*

beef *n* kig bewin *m*

beehive *n* kowel gwenen *m*, kowellow gwenen

beer *n* korev *m*, korevow

beet *n* betysen *f*, betysennow; betys *coll*

beetle *n* hwil *m*, hwiles

beetroot *n* betysen rudh *f*, betysennow rudh; betys rudh *coll*

before *prp* (*spatial*) a-dherag; dherag; (*temporal*) kyns. **before now** kyns es lemmyn; **before that** kyns ena

beforehand *adv* dherag dorn; kyns lemmyn

beg *vb* beggya; pysi. **beg mercy from somebody** kria merci war nebonan. **I beg you** my a'th pys

beggar *n* beggyer *m*, beggyers

begin *vb* dalleth

beginner *n* dallether *m*, dallethoryon

beginning *n* dalleth *m*, dallethow; dallathvos *m*, dallathvosow; derow *m*, derowyow

behalf *n* parth *f*, parthow. **on behalf of** a-barth

behave *vb* fara; omdhoon; omdhegi. **behave foolishly** gockia

behaviour *n* omdhoon *m*; fara *m*; omdhegyans *m*, omdhegyansow

behead *vb* dibenna

behind *adv, prp* a-dryv; a-dhelergh

behold I *int* ot; otta; awotta II *vb* mires

beholden *adj* synsys

beige *adj* losvelyn

Belarus *top* Belarus *m*

Belarussian I *adj* belarussek II (*language*) Belarussek *m*; Belarussian *m*, Belarussians

belfry *n* kleghti *m*, kleghtiow

Belgian I *adj* belgek II *n* Belg *m*, Belgyon

Belgium *top* Pow Belg *m*

belief *n* kryjyans *m*, kryjyansow

believe *vb* krysi

bell *n* klogh *m*, klegh. **bell pepper** pubren *f*, pubrennow. **church bell** klogh meur *m*, klegh meur. **small bell** kleghik *m*, kleghigow

belladonna *n* (*deadly nightshade*) morel *m*

bellow *vb* bedhygla; usa

belly *n* torr *f*, torrow

belong *vb* longya

belongings *n* pyth *m*, pythow

beloved I *adj* karadow; meurgerys II *n* kuv *m*, kuvyon

below I *adv* a-woles II *prp* a-woles dhe²; yn-dann². **down below** a-barth a-woles

belt *n* grugys *m*, grugysyow. **seat belt** grugys esedh *m*, grugysyow esedh

bench *n* form *m* (*f*), formys

bend I *n* pleg *m*, plegow; stumm *m*, stummow; kammas *f*, kamasow II *vb* plegya; kromma

beneath *prp* yn-dann². **from beneath** a-dhann²

beneficial *adj* lesel; meur y les *m*; meur hy les *f*; prowus; 'vas

beneficiary I *adj* benfisek II benfisek *m*, benfisogyon

benefit *n* les *m*; prow *m*

benevolence *n* helder *m*

benevolent *adj* hel

bent I *adj* kamm II *prfx* kamm-

berry *n* moren *f*, morennow; mor *coll*

beside *prp* ryb

besides *adv* dres henna; ynwedh; pella

besom *n* banadhlen *f*, banadhel

bespoke *adj* a-vusur

best *adj, adv* (an) gwella. **all the best** oll a'n gwella

bet I *n* kenwostel *m*, kenwostlow II *vb* kenwostla

betony *n* (*wood; purple; bishop's wort*) dagerles *m*

betray *vb* trayta

better *adj, adv* gwell. **far better** milwell

between *prp* (*before consonants*) yntra; (*before vowels*) ynter

beware *vb* bos war; warya

bewildered *adj* sowdhenys

beyond *prp* dres

bezant *n* besont *m*, besons

bias *n* ragvreus *f*, ragvreusow

biased *adj* ragvreusek

Bible *n* Bibel *m*, Biblow

biblical *adj* biblek

bicker *vb* kedrynna

bicycle *n* diwros *f*, diwrosow

bid I *n* profyans *m*, profyansow; kynnik *m*, kynigow **II** *vb* (*at an auction*) profya; kynnik; (*request*) erghi

bidder *n* profyas *m*, profysi

big *adj* bras

big-bellied *adj* torrek

big-browed *adj* talek

big-eared *adj* skovarnek

big-eyed *adj* lagasek

big-footed *adj* trosek

bigger *adj* brassa

biggest *adj* (an) brassa

big-headed *adj* pennek

big-mouthed *adj* ganowek

bigot *n* den ragvreusek *m*, tus ragvreusek

bigoted *adj* ragvreusek

big-tailed *adj* lostek

bile *n* bystel *f*

bilingual *adj* diwyethek

bilingualism *n* diwyethogeth *f*

bill (1) *n* (*financial*) reken *m*, reknow. **bill of sale** reken gwerth *m*, reknow gwerth

bill (2) *n* (*of a bird*) gelvin *m*, gelvines

billion *num* (10^9) bilvil^2 *m*, bilvilyow

bin *n* argh *f*, arghow

binary *adj* dewek

bind I *n* kolm *m*, kolmow **II** *vb* kelmi; strotha; maylya

bindweed, field *n* tagles kemmyn *m*

binge *vb* kwoffi

biodegradable *adj* bewbodradow

biography *n* bewskrif *m*, bewskrifow

biological *adj* bewoniethel

biology *n* bewonieth *f*

bipolar disorder *n* (*med*) disordyr bipolar *m*

birch *n* besowen *f*, besowennow; besow *coll*

bird *n* edhen *f*, ydhyn

biro *n* pluven belvleyn *f*, pluvennow pelvleyn

birth *n* genesigeth *m*, genesigethow; dinythyans *m*, dinythyansow. **give birth** dinythi

birthday *n* penn-bloodh *m*, pennow-bloodh. **birthday cake** tesen benn-bloodh *f*, tesennow penn-bloodh. **birthday card** karten benn-bloodh *f*, kartennow penn-bloodh.

biscuit *n* tesen gales *f*, tesennow kales

bisexual *adj* diwreydhek

bishop *n* epskop *m*, epskobow

bishopric *n* epskobeth *f*, epskobethow

bison *n* bual *m*, bualyon

bit *n* (*morsel*) tamm *m*, temmyn; banna *m*, banaghow; darn *m*, darnow; (*IT*) bytt *m*, byttys, byttow. **a little bit** temmik *m*. **bit by bit** tamm ha tamm

bitch *n* gast *f*, gesti. **son-of-a-bitch** horsen *m*, horsens

bite I *n* brath *m*, brathow **II** *vb* bratha

bitter *adj* hwerow

bitter-sweet *adj* hwerow-hweg

bitumen *n* pyg *m*

bizarre *adj* gorgoynt

black *adj* du. **pitch black** pur dhu. **the All Blacks** an para Oll Du *m*

blackberry *n* moren dhu *f*, morennow du; mor du *coll*

blackbird *n* molgh dhu *f*, molghi du

blackboard *n* bord du *m*, bordow du

blackcap *n* telor penndu *m*, telores penndu

blackcurrant *n* korynt du *m*, koryns du

blacken *vb* duhe

blackhead *n* penn du *m*, pennow dhu

blackish *adj* duik

blacksmith *n* gov *m*, govyon

blackthorn *n* spernen dhu *f*, spernennow du; spern du *coll*

blade *n* lown *m*, lownyow. **blade of grass** gwelsen *f*, gwelsennow

blame I *n* kabel *m*, kablow; blam *m*, blamys **II** *vb* kabla; blamya. **blame somebody for doing something**

blamya nebonan rag ev dhe wul neppyth

blameless *adj* divlam

blanch *vb* kelli liw

blank I *adj* gwag **II** *n* gwagen *f*, gwagennow. **blank cheque** checken ygor *f*, checkennow ygor

blanket *n* lenn *f*, lennow

blazer *n* blaser *m*, blasers

bleat *vb* bryvya

bleed *vb* (*intransitive*) gosa; devera goos; (*transitive*) diwosa

blemish *n* namm *m*, nammow

blemished *adj* nemmys

blend *vb* myska; kemyskya

blended *adj* kemyskys

bless *vb* benyga; sona. **God bless** Dursona

blessed *adj* benygys; gwynn; gwynnvys

blessing *n* bennath *f*, benathow; soon *f*, sonyow

blight I *n* skaldyans *m*, skaldyansow **II** *vb* skaldya

blind I *adj* dall. **blind man's buff** margh dall *m*. **partially sighted** *adj* gowelek. **sight impaired** *adj* gweles aperys **II** *n* (*window blind*) lenn dhu *f*, lennow du **III** *vb* dalla; dallhe

blindness *n* dellni *m*

bliss *n* lowena *f*; joy *m*, joyys

blister *n* gwennen *f*, gwenennow; bothel *f*, bothellow

bloated *adj* kwoffys

block I *n* stock *m*, stockys **II** *vb* lettya

blonde I *adj* melyn **II** *n* melyn hy blew *f*

blood *n* goos *m*, gosow. **blood-red** *adj* kogh. **hardened blood** *n* mol *m*, molyow

bloodline *n* goos *m*, gosow

blood-red *adj* kogh

bloodshed *n* krow *m*

bloodshot *adj* gwythiek

bloody *adj* gosek

blossom I *n* bleujen *f*, bleujyow **II** *vb* bleujyowa

blouse *n* hevis *m*, hevisyow

blow I *n* (*strike*) bomm *m*, bommyn; skwatt *m*, skwattys, skwattow; skatt *m*, skattys, skattow **II** *vb* (*air*) hwytha

blow up *vb* tardha

blue I *adj* glas **II** *vb* (*become green/blue*) glasa

bluebell *n* bleujen an gog *f*, bleujyow an gog

blue tit *n* penn pali *m*, pennow pali

bluish *adj* glasik

blunder I *n* kammwonis *m*, kammwonisyow **II** *vb* kammwonis

blunt *adj* sogh

blush I *n* liw rudh *m*, liwyow rudh **II** *vb* rudhya

blusher *n* liw diwvogh *m*

blustering *adj* hwyflyn

boar *n* badh *m*, badhes

board (*wooden board*) bord *m*, bordys, bordow; (*committee*) kesva *f*, kesvaow. **the Cornish Language Board** Kesva an Taves Kernewek *coll*. **blackboard** *n.m* bord du. **whiteboard** *n.m* bord gwynn. **ironing board** *n.m* bord-hornella. **sideboard** *n.m* bord lestri. **surfboard** *n.m* bord-mordardha

boast I *n* braslavar *m*, braslavarow; bost *m*, bostys, bostow **II** *vb* bostya; fasya

boaster *n* bostyer *m*, bostyoryon; payonyas *m*, payonysi

boat *n* skath *f*, skathow

Boddhisattva *n* Bodisatva *m*, Bodisatvaow

bodhran *n* kroder kroghen *m*, kroder kroghen

body *n* korf *m*, korfow

bog *n* keunegen *f*, keunegennow

bogeyman *n* bocka *m*, bockas, bockyas

boil (1) *vb* bryjyon. **boiled** bryjys. **boiled egg** oy bryjys *m*, oyow bryjys

boil (2) *n* (*med*) hwejalen *f*, hwejalennow

bold *adj* hardh; (*font*) poos

boldness *n* hardhder *m*; bolder *m*

boll *n* bolghen *f*, bolghennow

bolt *n* (*fastening*) ebil *m*, ebilyow. **iron bolt** *n* ebil horn *m*, ebilyow horn

bomb **I** *n* tanbellen *f*, tanbellennow **II** *vb* tanbellenna

bond *n* kevren *f*, kevrennow (*financial*) gorambos *m*, gorambosow; (*bail*) mewgh *m*, mewghyow

bone *n* askorn *m*, eskern

bonfire *n* tansys *m*, tansysyow

bonnet *n* kogh *m*, koghow

bonus *n* bonus *m*, bonusys

book (1) *n* lyver *m*, lyvrow **account book** lyver akontow *m*, lyvrow akontow

book (2) *vb* ragerghi

bookcase *n* argh lyvrow *m*, arghow lyvrow

booked *adj* (*reserved*) ragerghys

booklet *n* lyvryn *f*, lyvrynnow; lyvrik *m*, lyvrigow

bookmark *n* lyvermerk *m*, lyvermerkyow

bookshop *n* lyverji *m*, lyverjiow; gwerthji lyvrow *m*, gwerthjiow lyvrow

boost *vb* kenertha

booster *n* kenerthas *m*, kenerthasow

boot *n* (*footwear*) botasen *f*, botas; *n* (*car*) trog *m*, trogow

booty *n* preydh *m*, preydhyow

borage *n* taves ki *m*

border *n* or *f*, oryon; amal *m*, emlow

bore *vb* (*a hole*) telli; tardra

bored *adj* skwithys

boring *adj* skwithus

born *adj* genys. **born of** genys orth

borough *n* burjestra *f*, burjestrevow

borrow *vb* chevisya; kavos kendon

Bosnia *top* Bosni *f*

Bosnian **I** *adj* bosniek **II** *n* (*person*) Bosnian *m*, Bosnians

boss *n* mester *m*, mestrysi; mestres *f*, mestresow

botanical *adj* losoniethek

botany *n* losonieth *f*

both *adj*, *prp* an dhew *m*; an dhiw *f*

bother **I** *n* grev *m*, grevow; ankombrynsi *m* **II** *vb* ankombra; grevya; trobla

bottle **I** *n* botel *m*, botellow **II** *vb* botella

bottleful *n* botellas *m*, botellasow

bottom *n* (*base*) goles *m*, golesow; (*buttock*) pedren *f*, pedrennow, *dl* diwbedren

boulevard *n* rosva *f*, rosvaow

bounce **I** *n* aslam *m*, aslammow **II** *vb* aslamma

boundary *n* or *f*, oryon

bourgeois *adj* burjesek

bourgeoisie *n* burjeseth *f*

bow (1) **I** *n* (*gesture*) plegyans *m*, plegyansow; omblegyans *m*, omblegyansow **II** *vb* plegya; omblegya; ynklinya

bow (2) (*arc*) gwarak *m*, gwaregow; (*of a ship*) penn a-rag *m*, pennow a-rag

bowl *n* bolla *m*, bollys; skudel *f*, skudellow

bowler (1) *n* (*hat*) hatt bowler *m*, hattys bowler, hattow bowler

bowler (2) *n* towler pel *m*, towloryon bel

bowling *n* gwari pelyow *m*

box (1) *n* kist *f*, kistyow. **small box** *n* kisten *f*, kistennow

box (2) *vb* (*punch*) boksusi

Boxing Day *n* Dy'gol Stefan *m*

boy *n* maw *m*, mebyon

boyfriend *n* karer *m*, karoryon

bra *n* diwvronner *m*, diwronoryon; bra *m*, bras

bracelet *n* armel *m*, armels; breghellik *m*, breghelligow

bracken *n* kranen *f*, kranennow; krann *coll*

255

bracket *n* korbel *m*, korblys;
(*punctuation*) krommvagh *f*,
krommvaghow

brag *vb* fasya

brain *n* ympynnyon *pl*

brainy *adj* pollek; skentel

brake (1) **I** *n* (*vehicle*) fronn *f*, fronnow
II *vb* fronna

brake (2) *n* (*thicket*) perth *f*, perthi

bramble *n* dreysen *f*, dreysennow;
dreys *coll*

brambling *n* pynk menydh *m*, pynkes
menydh

branch *n* skorren *f*, skorrennow; skorr
coll; skorr *m*, skorrow

branched *adj* skorrek

brandy *n* dowr tomm *m*

brass *n* brest *m*

brave *adj* kolonnek; hardh

brawl *vb* freudhi

Brazil *top* Brasil *m*

breach **I** *n* torrva *f*, torrvaow; (*gap*)
bolgh *m*, bolghow; aswa *f*, aswaow **II**
vb bolgha

bread *n* bara *m*. **rye bread** *n* bara sugal
m. **wheaten bread** *n* bara gwaneth *m*

breadcrumb *n* hwigen *f*, hwigennow

breadth *n* les *m*, lesyow

break **I** *n* torr *m*, torrow; (*rest*) powes
m, powesow **II** *vb* terri; krackya

breakable *adj* torradow

breakdown *n* mooth *m*, mothow;
torrva *f*, torrvaow. **breakdown lorry**
n kert torrva *m*, kertow torrva

break-even *n* poynt gwayn *m*

breakfast *n* hansel *m*, hanselyow

breakneck *adj* krackya konna

bream *n* siw *m*, siwyon. **black sea
bream** dama goth *f*, damyow koth.
small bream lommas *m*, lomasow

breast *n* bronn *f*, bronnow, *dl* diwvron;
brest *n.m*, brestys

breastfeed *vb* bronna

breath *n* anal *f*; hwyth *m*, hwethow.
shortness of breath berranal *m*. **short**

of breath *adj* berranellek. **out of
breath** *adj* mes a anal

breathe *vb* anella; hwytha

breathless *adj* dianal

breeze *n* awel glor *f*, awelyow glor

Breton **I** *adj* bretonek **II** (*person*) Breton
m, Bretonyon; (*language*) Bretonek *m*

brew *vb* braga

brewed *adj* bregys

brewer *n* brager *m*, bragoryon

brewery *n* bragji *m*, bragjiow

Brexit *n* Bretenborth *f*; Bretmes *m*

briar *n* spedhasen *f*, spedhasennow;
spedhas *coll*

bribe **I** *n* falsgober *m*, falsgobrow **II** *vb*
falsgobra

brick *n* bryck *m*, bryckys

bride *n* benyn bries *f*, benenes pries

bridegroom *n* gour pries *m*, gwer bries

bridesmaid *n* moren bries *f*, morenyon
pries

bridge *n* pons *m*, ponsyow

brief **I** *adj* berr; kott **II** *n* kenskrif *m*,
kenskrifow

briefcase *n* skrifsagh *m*, skrifseghyer

briefs *n* lavrek byghan *m*, lavrogow
byghan

brigade *n* brigad *m*, brigadow. **fire
brigade** tanlu *m*, tanluyow

bright *adj* splann

brighten *vb* klerhe

brightness *n* splander *m*; golewder *m*

brilliant *adj* splann

brine *n* brin *m*, brinyow

bring *vb* dri

Britain *top* Breten *f*. **Great Britain** *top*
Breten Veur *f*

British *adj* bretennek

Briton *n* Brython *m*, Brythonyon

Brittany *top* Breten Vyghan *f*

brittle **I** *adj* brottel **II** *vb* (*become brittle*)
krina

broach *vb* attamya

broad *adj* efan; ledan. **in broad
daylight** yn jydh splann

broadband *n* bond ledan *m*

broadcast I *n* darlesans *m*, darlesansow **II** *vb* darlesa; tavethli

broccoli *n* broklo *m*, broklos

brochure *n* folennik *f*, folenigow

broken *adj* terrys; (*of skin, limbs, hearts*) trogh

bronchitis *n* bronkitis *m* (*med*)

bronze *n* brons *m*

brooch *n* brocha *m*, brochys

brook *n* gover *m*, goverow

broom *n* skubell *f*, skubellow; (*small brush, mop*) skubyllen *f*, skubyllennow; (*plant*) banadhlen *f*, banadhelennow; banadhel *coll*

broom-brake *n* banadhlek *f*, banadhlegi

brothel *n* horji *m*, horjiow

brother *n* broder *m*, breder

brotherhood *n* brederedh *m*

brother-in-law *n* broder da *m*, breder dha

brow *n* (*forehead*) tal *f* (*m*), talyow

brown *adj* (*light brown*) gell; (*dark brown*) gorm; (*chestnut brown*) gell kesten

brownish *adj* gellik

browse *vb* peuri

browser *n* (*internet*) peurell *f*, peurellow

bruise I *n* brew *m*, brewyon **II** *vb* brewi; podredha

bruised *adj* brew

brush I *n* skubell *f*, skubellow; (*of an artist*) pyncel *f*, pyncels **II** *vb* skuba

Brussels *top* Brussel *m*

brussels sprout *n* kowlik *m*, kowligow; kowlennik *f*, kowlenigow

brutal *adj* milus; garow

brutality *n* miluster *m*; garowder *m*

bryony, black *n* greun an Jowl *coll*

Brythonic *adj* Brythonek

bubble I *n* hwythen *f*, hwythennow **II** *vb* hwythfi

bubbly *adj* hwythennek

bucket *n* kelorn *m*, kelern

buckle I *n* bockyl *m*, bocklys **II** *vb* bockla

Buddhism *n* Boudd:eth *f*

buddhist I *adj* Bouddiek **II** *n* Bouddydh *m*, Bouddydhyon

budge *vb* remova; omwaya

budgerigar *n* budji *m*, budjies

budget *n* bojet *m*, bojettys; towlargh *m*, towlarghow

buffalo *n* bual *m*, bualyon

buffer *n* (*train*) bommell *f*, bomellow

buffet (1) I *n* (*strike*) bommen *f*, bomennow **II** *vb* dreweskel

buffet (2) *n* (*food counter*) buffe *m*, buffes

bug *n* (*insect; IT*) pryv *m*, preves, prevyon

bugle *n* (*flowering plant*) glesin an koos *m*

bugloss, viper's *n* naderles *m*; taves ojyon *m*

build *vb* drehevel; gwruthyl

builder *n* drehever *m*, drehevoryon

building *n* drehevyans *m*, drehevyansow

Bulgaria *top* Bulgari *f*

Bulgarian I *adj* bulgarek **II** *n* (*language*) Bulgarek *f*; Bulgarian *m*, Bulgarians

bulimia nervosa *n* (*med*) bolimia nervosa *m*. **a person with bulimia** person gans bolimia

bulimic *adj* (*med*) bolimek

bulk *n* braster *m*; tewder *m*

bulky *adj* bras; tew

bull *n* tarow *m*, terevi

bullet *n* pellen *f*, pellennow

bulletin *n* bollyn *m*, bollynnow

bullfinch *n* pynk hwiban *m*, pynkes hwiban

bullock *n* lodhen *m*, lodhnow

bully I *n* gormesyer *m*, gormesyoryon **II** *vb* gormesi

bump I *n* bomm *m*, bommyn **II** *vb* bonkya

bun *n* torthel *f*, torthellow

bunch *n* bagas *m*, bagasow; gronn *m*, gronnow; toos *m*, tosow

bundle *n* pusorn *m*, pusornow; gronn *m*, gronnow

bungalow *n* bengalji *m*, bengaljiow

bunk bed *n* gweli bonk *m*, gweliow bonk

buoy *n* morverk *m*, morverkow

burden I *n* begh *m*, beghow; karg *m*, kargow; sawgh *m*, sawghow **II** *vb* beghya

burdensome *adj* beghus

burdock, greater *n* tavol amanyn *coll*; les serghek *m*

bureau *n* burow *m*, burowyow; sodhva *f*, sodhvaow

bureaucracy *n* burokratieth *f*

bureaucrat *n* burokrat *m*, burokratyon

burger *n* borger *m*, borgers. **beef burger** *n* borger bewin *m*, borgers bewin

burglar *n* chilader *m*, chiladron. **burglar alarm** alarm ladron *m*, alarmow ladron

burglary *n* chiladrans *m*, chiladransow

burial *n* ynkleudhyans *m*, ynkleudhyansow

burly *adj* keherek

burn I *n* losk *m*, loskow **II** *vb* leski. **burn up** kowlleski

burnt *adj* leskys

burp I *n* torrbyff *m*, torrbyffow **II** *vb* torrbyffya

burrow *n* toll *m*, tell. **rabbit burrow** toll konin *m*, tell konin

bursar *n* porser *m*, porsoryon

burst I *n* tardh *m*, tardhow **II** *vb* tardha

bury *vb* ynkleudhyas; yntirya

bus *n* kyttrin *m*, kyttrinyow. **bus driver** *n* lewyer kyttrin *m*, lewyoryon kyttrin. **bus station** *n* gorsav kyttrin *m*, gorsavow kyttrin. **bus stop** *n* savla kyttrin *m*, savleow kyttrin; kyttrinva *f*, kyttrinvaow

bush *n* prysken *f*, pryskennow; prysk *coll*

bushy *adj* bosek

bushy-tailed *adj* lostek

business *n* negys *m*, negysyow. **bad business** hager-viaj *m*. **Business Studies** *n* Studhyans Negys *m*

businessperson *n* negysydh *m*, negysydhyon

bustle *vb* fyski

busy *adj* bysi

busybody *n* mellyer *m*, mellyoryon

but *cnj* (*yet*) mes; (*except, save*) saw; lemen

butcher *n* kiger *m*, kigoryon. **butcher's shop** *n* kigti *m*, kigtiow

butler *n* spencer *m*, spencers

butt I (*container*) keryn *f*, kerynyow; (*target*) but *m*, butys **II** *vb* kornya

butter I *n* amanyn *m*, amanynnow **II** *vb* amanynna

butterbur *n* troos margh *m*

buttercup *n* paw bran *m*

butterfly *n* tykki Duw *m*, tykkiow Duw, tykki Duwes

buttock *n* pedren *f*, pedrennow, *dl* diwbedren

button I *n* boton *m*, botonyow **II** *vb* botona. **button hole** *n* toll boton *m*, tell boton. **push a button** pokya boton

buy *vb* prena. **buy a pig in a poke** prena kath yn sagh. **buy back** dasprena. **buy off** falsgobra. **buy on hire purchase** hirbrena. **buy up** kowlbrena

buyer *n* prener *m*, prenoryon

buzz *n* sia. **buzz off!** voyd alemma!; gwayv ow golok!

buzzard *n* bargos *m*, bargoses

by *prp* (*agent*) gans; (*until*) bys; erbynn; (*next to*) ryb. **by bus** yn kyttrin. **by car** yn karr. **by Christmas** erbynn Nadelik. **by day and by night** dres an jydh ha'n nos. **by God** parde; bar' Duw. **by now** erbynn lemmyn. **by rail**

yn tren. **by the load** orth an sawgh.
by the sea ryb an mor. **little by little**
nebes ha nebes
by-election *n* isetholans *m*,
isetholansow

bygone *adj* passys; passyes

bypass *n* fordh dremen *f*, fordhow
tremen

byte *n* bayt *m*, baytys

C

cab *n* taksi *m*, taksiow
cabbage *n* kowlen *f*, kowlennow; kowl
coll
cabin *n* krowji *m*, krowjiow
cabinet *n* (*government*) kabinet *m*,
kabinettys. **bedside cabinet** amari
gweli *f*, amaris gweli. **filing cabinet**
restrenva *f* restrenvaow
cable *n* fun *f*, funyow; kapel *m*, kaplys;
korsen *f*, korsennow. **cable television**
pellwolok gapel *f*
cackle *vb* grega
cacophony *n* hager-dros *f*,
hager-drosow
cactus *n* kaktus *m*, kaktusow
café *n* koffiji *m*, koffijiow
cafeteria *n* koffiva *f*, koffivaow
cage I *n* kowel *m*, kowellow **II** *vb*
kowella; gorra yn kowel
cagey *adj* kelus
cairn *n* karnedh *m*, karnedhow
cake *n* tesen *f*, tesennow. **cake of wax**
koren *f*, korennow. **sweet cake**
gwastel *f*, gwastellow
calamity *n* terros *m*, terrosow
calculate *vb* kalkya; rekna
calculation *n* reknans *m*, reknansow
calculator *n* (*device*) reknell *f*,
reknellow; (*human*) kalkor *m*,
kalkoryon
calendar *n* lyver dedhyow *m*, lyvrow
dedhyow; kalender *m*, kalenderyow
calendula *n* (*common marigold*) les an
gog *m*, losow an gog

calf *n* (*young cattle*) leugh *m*, leughi; (*of
leg*) berr *f*, berrow; garren *f*,
garrennow
call I *n* kri *m*, kriow; galow *m*,
galowyow; (*telephone*) galwen *f*,
galwennow **II** *vb* kria; gelwel. **call
back** daskelwel. **long-distance call**
galow a-bell *m*, galowyow a-bell.
telephone call galow pellgows *m*,
galowyow pellgows
called *adj* (*named*) henwys. **a bloke
called Simon** gwas henwys Simon. **I
am called Meriasek** y'm gylwir
Meryasek
calling *n* galwesigeth *f*, galwesigethow;
galow *m*, galowyow
calm I *adj* kosel; koselek; hebask **II** *n*
kalmynsi *m* **III** *vb* hebaskhe
calorie *n* kalori *m*, kaloris
camel *n* kowrvargh *m*, kowrvergh
camera *n* kamera *m*, kameras; jynn
skeusen *m*, jynnys skeusen, jynnow
skeusen
camp I *n* kamp *m*, kampow **II** *vb*
kampya
campaign I *n* kaskyrgh *m*, kaskyrghow
II *vb* kaskyrghes
campaigner *n* kaskyrgher *m*,
kaskyrghoryon
camphor *n* kamfor *m*
campion, red *n* bleujen gevnisen *f*
campion, white *n* bleujen gevnisen
wynn *f*
can (1) *vb* (*be able to*) gallos. **can you
throw this heavy stone?** a yll'ta

tewlel an men poos ma? (*be qualified to, know how to*) godhvos. **I can speak Cornish** my a wor kewsel Kernewek

can (**2**) **I** *n* (*metal container*) kavas *m*, kavasow; kanna *m*, kannow **II** *vb* kavasa

Canada *top* Kanada *m*

Canadian I *adj* kanadek **II** *n* Kanadian *m*, Kanadians

canal *n* dowrgleudh *m*, dowrgleudhyow

canary *n* kanari *m*, kanaris

cancel *vb* dilea; hedhi

cancer *n* kanker *m*, kankres

candid *adj* apert; frank

candidacy *n* ombrofyans *m*, ombrofyansow

candidate *n* ombrofyer *m*, ombrofyoryon

candle *n* kantol *f*, kantolyow. **candle-stick** *n* kantolbren *m*, kantolbrennyer

candlestick *n* kantolbren *m*, kantolbrennyer

candy-floss *n* komolen sugra *f*; blew sugra *coll*

cane *n* gwelen *f*, gwelynni; lorgh *f* (*m*), lorghow

canine *adj* kius; kepar ha ki

canister *n* kanister *m*, kanisters

cannabis *n* kanabys *coll*

canned *adj* kennys

cannon *n* kanon *m*, kanonyow

canoe *n* kanou *m*, kanouyow

canon *n* chenon *m*, chenons

Canterbury bells *n* klegh an kowr *pl*

cap *n* kappa *m*, kappys, kappow

capability *n* gallos *m*, gallosow

capable *adj* gallosek

capacitance *n* dalghasedh *m*; gavelieth *f*

capacity *n* (*mental ability*) gavel *f*, gavelyow; (*maximum content*) dalghuster *m*

capital *n* (*financial*) chatel *coll*; kevalav *f*. **capital city** penncita *f*, penncitys. **capital punishment** payn-merwel *m*

capitalism *n* chatelydhieth *f*

capitalist *n* chatelydh *m*, chatelydhyon

capsule *n* bolghen *f*, bolghennow

captain *n* kapten *m*, kaptens, kaptenow

caption *n* isskrifik *m*, isskrifigow

captive I *adj* keth **II** *n* keth *m*, kethyon

captivity *n* kethneth *f*

car *n* karr *m*, kerri. **car park** *n* park kerri *m*, parkow kerri. **car wash** *n* golghva gerri *f*, golghvaow kerri. **police car** karr kreslu *m*, kerri kreslu. **driverless car** karr heb lewyer *m*, kerri heb lewyer

caramel *n* karamel *m*, karamels

caravan *n* karavan *m*, karavans

carbohydrate *n* karbohydrat *m*, karbohydratow

carbon *n* (*element*) karbon *m*. **carbon dioxide, CO₂** karbon dioxid

card *n* karten *f*, kartennow. **credit card** *n* karten gresys *f*, kartennow kresys. **cash card** *n* karten vona *f*, kartennow mona. **trump card** karten vudhek *f*, kartennow budhek

cardamom *n* kardamon *coll*

cardiac *adj* a'n golon. **cardiac arrest** *n* astel kolon *m*

cardigan *n* kardigan *m*, kardigans, kardiganow

cardiovascular *adj* kolonwythiek

care I *n* (*keeping*) gwith *m*; (*caution*) rach *m*; (*worry*) preder *m*, prederow **II** *vb* (*care for*) kara. **care for** (*nurse sick people*) gwitha. **care of** (*address*) yn-dann with. **I don't care** ny'm deur. **intensive care** dourwith *m*. **take care!** kemmer with!; kemerewgh with! *pl*

career *n* resegva *f*, resegvaow

carefree *adj* digeudh; divern

careful *adj* prederus; gans rach

carefully *adv* gans rach

careless *adj* dibreder

carer *n* (*of sick people*) gwithyas klevyon *m*, gwithysi glevyon

caress I *n* palvas *m*, palvasow II *vb* palva

cargo *n* karg *m*, kargow

carnal *adj* karnal

carnation *n* kurunik *f*

carnival *n* Gool Enys *m*; karnival *m*

carousel *n* res a-dro *m*, resow a-dro

carpenter *n* ser prenn *m*, seri brenn

carpet *n* leurlen *f*, leurlennow

carriage *n* kocha *m*, kochys

carrion *n* karyn *m*, karynyes

carrot *n* karetysen *f*, karetysennow; karetys *coll*

carrot, wild *n* (*Queen Anne's lace*) las Myghternes Anna *m*

carry *vb* don; degi; (*transport*) karya; (*bear*) perthi. **carry out** gwruthyl

cart *n* kert *m*, kertys, kertow

cartoon *n* komik *m*, komigow

cartridge (*ink*) *n* kisten ynk *f*, kistennow ynk

carve *vb* kervya; (*meat*) treghi kig

case *n* (*box*) trog *m*, trogow; (*circumstance*) kas *m*, kasys; mater *m*, maters, materyow. **in any case** yn neb kas. **in case** rag own; rag dout; les. **in this particular case** y'n kas arbennek ma. **in that case** y'n kas na

cash I *n* mona *coll* II *vb* kashya. **cash card** karten vona *f*, kartennow mona. **cash dispenser** toll y'n fos *m*, tell y'n fos. **petty cash** mannvona *coll*

casket *n* kofryn *m*, kofrynnow

cassiterite *n* pryl *m*, prylyon

cast I *n* towl *m*, towlow; (*of a play*) rol an warioryon *f* II *vb* tewlel; (*hurl*) deghesi. **cast a vote** votya. **cast iron** horn teudhys *m*. **cast out** fesya

castle *n* kastel *m*, kastylli, kestel

castor *n* rosik *f*, rosigow

castrate *vb* spadha

casual *adj* (*informal*) anformel; (*random*) chonsus

casually *adv* yn anfurvus

casualty *n* gwaluster *m*; goliesik *m*, goliesigow

cat *n* kath *f*, kathes

Catalan I *adj* katalorek II *n* (*language*) Katalonek *m*; Katalan *m*, Katalanyon

catalogue *n* menegva *f*, menegvaow; rolas *m*, rolasow

Catalonia *top* Kataloni *f*

cataract *n* (*of eye*) kennen *m*, kenennow

catastrophe *n* gordhroglam *m*, gordhroglammow

catastrophic *adj* gordhroglammek

catch I *n* (*latch*) skwych *m*, skwychys; (*fish etc.*) kachyans *m*, kachyansow; (*snag*) maglen *f*, maglennow II *vb* kachya. **catch fish** pyskessa. **catch mice** legessa. **catch snails** melhwessa

category *n* klass *m*, klassys

caterpillar *n* pryv del *m*, preves del; (*hairy*) kath vlewek *f*, kathes blewek

cathedral *n* penneglos *f*, penneglosyow

Catholic I *adj* Katholik II *n* Katholik *m*, Katholigyon

Catholicism *n* Kathcligieth *f*

cation *n* kation *m*, kations

catmint *n* losowen an gath *f*, losowennow an gath; losow an gath *coll*

catnip *n* losowen an gath *f*, losowennow an gath; losow an gath *coll*

cattle *n* bughes *pl*; (*horned cattle*) gwarthek *coll*. **cattle wart** ryg *m*, rygyow. **cattle prod** gwelen vughes *f*, gwelynni bughes

cauldron *n* kawdarn *m*, kawdarns; chek *m*, chekys

cauliflower *n* kowlvleujen *f*, kowlvleujennow

cause I *n* kaws *m*, kawsys; skila *f*, skilys II *vb* kawsya

causeway *n* kons *m*, konsys, konsow

caution *n* rach *m*; (*warning*) gwarnyans *m*, gwarnyansow

cautious *adj* war

cave *n* fow *f*, fowys; gwag *m*, gwagyon; gogow *f*, gogowyow

cavity *n* kowva *f*, kowvaow

CD *n* plasen arghansek *f*, plasennow arghansek; cidi *m*, cidis

C.E. *abbrev* O.K.; Osweyth Kemmyn *f*

cease *vb* hedhi; astel; cessya; difygya

ceilidh *n* troyll *m* (*f*), troyllyow

ceiling *n* nen *m*, nenyow

celandine, greater *n* gwenolles *m*

celandine, lesser *n* losow lagas *coll*

celebrate *vb* (*serious*) solempnya; (*joyful*) lowender; (*mass*) oferenni; (*party*) kevewya. (*intransitive*) omlowenhe

celebration *n* solempnyans *m*, solempnyansow

celebrity I *adj* goraswonek II *n* goraswonek *m*, goraswonogyon

celery *n* kegisen hweg *f*, kegisennow hweg; kegis hweg *coll*

cell *n* (*prison*) bagh *f*, baghow; (*biology*) kell *f*, kellow, kellyow; log *f*, logow

cellar *n* dorgel *f*, dorgellow; celder *m*, celders

celluloid *n* celluloyd *m*

cellulose *n* cellulos *m*

Celt *n* Kelt *m*, Keltyon

Celtic *adj* Keltek

cement *n* lim *m*

cemetery *n* korflan *f*, korflannow; ynkladhva *f*, ynkladhvaow

census *n* niveryans *m*, niveryansow

centaury *n* skeul Varia *f*

centigrade *n* kanskradh *m*, kanskradhow

centimetre *n* centimeter *m*, centimetrow

central *adj* kres; kresel. **central heating** tommheans kres *m*

centralise *vb* kresenna

centre *n* (*middle*) kres *m*, kresyow; (*building; institution*) kresen *f*,

kresennow; (*rugby player*) kreswas *m*, kreswesyon

centrifugal *adj* kresfoesik

centripetal *adj* kreshwilus

century *n* kansvledhen *f*, kansvledhynnyow

ceramic *n* priweython *f*, priweyth

cereal I *adj* greunek II *n* greunvos *m*, greunvosow

cerebral *adj* a'n ympynnyon

ceremonial *adj* solempnyel

ceremony *n* solempnita *m*, solempnitys

certain *adj* certan; sur; diogel. **a certain one** *prn* unn

certainly *adv* devri; yn tevri; sur; surredi; yn surredi; yn certan

certainty *n* surneth *f*, surnethow

certificate *n* testskrif *m*, testskrifow

certified *adj* destys; certifiys

certify *vb* desta; certifia

chaffinch *n* pynk kemmyn *m*, pynkes kemmyn

chain I *n* kadon *f*, kadonyow; chayn *m*, chaynys II *vb* kadona; chaynya

chainsaw *n* hesken gadon *f*, heskennow kadon

chair I *n* kador *f*, kadoryow II *vb* (*a meeting*) kaderya

chairlift *n* kador-yskynna *f*, kadoryow-yskynna

chairperson *n* kaderyer *m*, kaderoryon

chalet *n* krow prenn *m*, krowyow prenn

chalice *n* kelegel *m*, keleglow

chalk *n* krey *m*, kreyow

challenge I *n* chalenj *m*, chalenjys; er *m* II *vb* chalenjya; erya

chamomile *n* kamilen *f*, kamilennow; kamil *coll*

chance I *n* chons *m*, chonsyow; feus *m*; happ *m*, happys, happow II *vb* chonsya. **by chance** dre happ

change I *n* (*alteration*) chanj *m*, chanjyow; (*money*) mona *coll* II *vb*

chanjya; varya. **changing room** *n*
gwiskva *m*, gwiskvaow

changeable *adj* hedro

channel *n* gooth *f*, gothow; kanel *f*,
kanolyow. **television channel** kanel
bellwolok *f*, kanolyow pellwolok

chaos *n* deray *m*, derays

chap *n* gwas *m*, gwesyon; polat *m*,
polatys

chapel *n* chapel *m*, chapelyow

chaperone *n* gwithyas *m*, gwithysi

character *n* (*quality*) gnas *f*, gnasow;
(*letter*) lytheren *f*, lytherennow

charcoal *n* glowbren *f*, glowbrennyer

charge I *n* (*fee*) kost *m*, kostys, kostow;
(*responsibility*) charj *m*, charjys;
(*electricity*) kargedh *m*, kargedhow **II**
vb (*make responsible*) charjya; (*debit*)
debisya; (*electricity*) karga. **free of
charge** heb kost

charity *n* (*body*) aluseneth *f*,
alusenethow; (*virtue*) cherita *m*;
kerensa *f*; alusen *f*, alusenow

charm I *n* hus *m*, husow; soon *m*,
sonyow; (*item*) sonell *f*, sonellow **II** *vb*
husa; sona. **work like a charm**
spedya marthys da

chart *n* tresen *f*, tresennow

charter *n* chartour *m*, chartours

chase I *n* helgh *m*, helghow **II** *vb*
chassya; helghya; helghi. **chase off**
fesya

chaste *adj* gwar

chastise *vb* chastia

chat I *n* keskows *m*, keskowsow **II** *vb*
keskewsel; kesklappya. **chat room**
keskowsva *f*, keskowsvaow

chatter I *n* klapp *m*; klatter *m* **II** *vb*
klappya; klattra

cheap *adj* a bris isel

cheat *vb* hyga; tolla

cheated *adj* tollys

cheater *n* falswas *m*, falswesyon

cheating *adj* fals

check I *n* lett *m*, lettys, lettow **II** *vb*
checkya; (*hinder*) lettya; (*examine*)
hwithra. **check a calculation** checkya
reknans

check-out *n* rekenva *f*, rekenvaow

checkpoint *n* checkva *f*, checkvaow

check-up *n* hwithrans *m*, hwithransow

cheek *n* bogh *f*, boghow, *dl* diwvogh

cheeky *adj* tont

cheer I *n* cher *m*, cheryow; lowena *f* **II**
vb (*comfort; gladden*) cherya; (*shout
with joy*) garma yn lowen. **cheer
oneself up** omjerya. **cheer up!**
gwellha dha jer!

cheerful *adj* lowenek

cheers! *int* yeghes da!

cheese *n* keus *m*, keusyow. **processed
cheese** keus dyghtys *m*, keusyow
dyghtys

cheesecake *n* tesen geus *f*, tesennow
keus

chef *n* keginer *m*, keginoryon; kog *m*,
kogow

chemical I *adj* kymyk; kymygiethel **II** *n*
kymygen *f*, kymygennow

chemical symbol *n* arwodh
gymygiethel *f*, arwodhyow
kymygiethel

chemist *n* (*dispensing*) kymyst *m*,
kymystyon; (*scientist*) kymygydh *m*,
kymygydhyon. **chemist's shop**
kymyst *m*

chemistry *n* kymygieth *f*

cheque *n* checken *f*, checkennow.
blank cheque checken ygor *f*,
checkennow ygor

cherish *vb* kovia; chersya

cherished *adj* drudh

cherry *n* keresen *f*, keresennow; keres
coll

chervil *n* serfel *m*

chess *n* gwydhbol *m*

chest *n* (*body*) brest *m*, brestys;
diwvron *dl*; (*container*) argh *f*, arghow;
kist *f*, kistyow; kofer *m*, kofrow;

(*money box*) argh vona *f*, arghow mona. **chest of drawers** argh dhillas *f*, arghow dillas

chestnut *n* kestenen *f*, kestenennow; kesten *coll*

chestnut tree *n* kestenwedhen *f*, kestenwedhennow; kestenwydh *coll*

chew *vb* knias. **chew cud** *vb* dasknias

chick *n* mabyar *f*, mabyer; ydhnik *m*, ydhnigow

chicken *n* yar *f*, yer. **chicken meat** kig yar *m*. **chicken shed** krow yer *m*, krowyow yer

chicken-pox *n* brygh yar *f*

chickweed *n* gledh *m*

chief I *prfx* penn- **II** *n* chif *m*, chifys; pennsevik *m*, pennsevigyon

chieftain *n* chyften *m*, chyftens

chiffchaff *n* lawen melyn *m*, lawenes melyn

child *n* flogh *m*, fleghes. **street child** flogh stret *m*, fleghes stret

childlike *adj* floghek

chill I *n* (*infection*) anwos *m*, anwosow; (*temperature*) goyeynder *m* **II** *vb* yeynhe

chilly *adj* (*infection*) anwosek; (*temperature*) goyeyn

chimney *n* chymbla *m*, chymblys

chin *n* elgeth *f*, elgethyow

China *top* China *f*

china clay *n* pri gwynn *m*

Chinese I *adj* chinek **II** *n* (*language*) Chinek *m*

chip I *n* asklosen *f*, asklosennow; asklos *coll*; skommen *f*, skomennow **II** *vb* asklosi. **chip shop** *n* asklotti *m*, asklottiow

chirp *vb* gryllya

chivalry *n* chevalri *m*

chive *n* keninen sevi *f*, keninennow sevi; kennin sevi *coll*

chlorine *n* (*element*) klorin *m*

chocolate *n* choklet *m*, choklets

choice *n* dewis *m*, dewisyow; ethol *m*, etholow

choir *n* keur *m*, keuryow

choke *vb* taga; moga

choking *n* tag *m*, tagow

choose *vb* dewis

choosy *adj* dewisek

chop *vb* divyn; nadha; hackya

chopping *n* nadh *m*

chopstick *n* gwelennik *f*, gwelenigow

chord *n* kord *m*, kordys

chough *n* palores *f*, paloresow

Christ *name* Krist *m*

christen *vb* besydhya; kristonhe

christening *n* besydhyans *m*, besydhyansow

Christian I *adj* Kristyon **II** *n* Kristyon *m*, Kristonyon

Christianity *n* Kristonedh *m*

Christmas *n* Nadelik *m*. **Christmas Day** Dydh Nadelik. **Christmas pudding** podyn Nadelik *m*, podyns Nadelik. **Christmas tree** gwedhen Nadelik *f*, gwydh Nadelik. **Christmas cracker** kracker Nadelik *m*, krackers Nadelik. **Merry Christmas!** Nadelik lowen!

chromatic *adj* kromatek

chrysanthemum *n* boreles *m*, borelesyow

church *n* eglos *f*, eglosyow. **church bell** klogh meur *m*, klegh meur

churchtown *n* treveglos *f*, treveglosyow, trevow eglos

cider *n* cider *m*, ciders

cigar *n* cigar *m*, cigarow

cigarette *n* cigarik *m*, cigarigow

cinema *n* cinema *m*, cinemas

cinnamon *n* kanel *coll*. **cinnamon stick** gwelen ganel *f*

cinquefoil *n* pympdelen *f*

circle *n* kylgh *m*, kylghyow

circuit *n* trogylgh *m*, trogylghyow. **short circuit** skochkylgh *m*, skochkylghyow

circular *adj* kylghek

circumference *n* kehysedh *m*, kehysedhow

circumlocution *n* kylghlavar *m*, kylghlavarow

circumsize *vb* trodreghi

circumstance *n* kesstudh *m*, kesstudhyow; kas *m*. **under the circumstances** y'n kas; y'n kesstudhyow

circus *n* cirk *m*, cirkow

citizen *n* burjes *m*, burjysi

city *n* cita *f*, citys; ker *f*, kerow, keryow. **capital city** penncita *f*, penncitys

civil *adj* civil. **civil rights** gwiryow kemmyn *pl*. **civil servant** gonisek civil *m*, gonisogyon civil

civilian *n* dinasydh *m*, dinasydhyon

civilisation *n* hwarheans *m*, hwarheansow

civilise *vb* hwarhe

civilised *adj* hwarhes

claim I *n* chalenj *m*, chalenjys II *vb* (*assert*) lavasos; (*demand*) perghenegi. **claim to be** omwul

clammy *adj* orlyp

clamour *n* tervans *m*, tervansow; hobadolya *m*, hobadolyas; (*noise*) tros *m*, trosyow

clap *vb* tackya. **clap one's hands** tackya diwleuv; tackya diwla

clarification *n* klerheans *m*, klerheansow

clarify *vb* klerhe

clarity *n* klerder *m*

class I *n* klass *m*, klassys, klassow II *vb* klassya; renka. **social class** renkas *m*, renkasow

classical *adj* klassek

classification *n* klassans *m*, klassansow

classify *vb* klassa

classroom *n* stevel an klass *f*, stevellow an klass

clause *n* kemel *f*, kemellow

claustrophobia *n* (*med*) klawstrofobia *m*

claw I *n* ewin *m*, ewines; kraban *m*, krabanow; (*of crab*) paw *m*, pawyow II *vb* kravas; skravinyas

clay *n* pri *m*. **clay pit** poll pri *m*. **clay-works** *n* priweythva *f*, priweythvaow

claymore *n* kledha meur *m*, kledhedhyow meur

clean I *adj* glan II *vb* glanhe. **clean out** kartha. **come clean** avowa puptra

cleanse *vb* kartha

cleansing *n* karth *m*, karthyon. **ethnic cleansing** karth ethnek *m*, karthyon ethnek

clear I *adj* kler; ter; (*transparent*) ylyn; (*pure*) glan II *vb* klerya

clearly *adv* yn kler

clearway *n* klerfordh *f*, klerfordhow

cleave *vb* folsa

cleavers *n* (*goosegrass; sticky willy*) les serghek byghan *m*

cleft *n* saven *f*, savnow; fols *m*, folsyow

clematis, wild *n* (*traveller's joy; old man's beard*) ruvanes an koos *f*

clergyman *n* klorek *m*, klorogyon

clerk *n* klorek *m*, klorogyon; skrifwas *m*, skrifwesyon

clever *adj* konnyk; skentel; sley

click *vb* klyckya

client *n* kliens *m*, kliensow

cliff *n* als *f*, alsyow; klog *f*, klogow; kleger *m*, klegrow

climate *n* hin *f*, hinyow; ayredh *m*, ayredhow

climatic *adj* hinek

climb *vb* yskynna; krambla

climber *n* krambler *m*, krambloryon

cling *vb* grabalyas

clinic *n* medhegva *f*, medhegvaow

clinical *adj* (*pertaining to a clinic*) medhegvael; (*devoid of emotion*) diamovyans

cloak *n* klok *m*, klokys; mantel *f*, mantylli

clock *n* klock *m*, klockys, klockow

clog *vb* taga

close I *adj* ogas; nes; klos. **come close!** deus nes! **II** *vb* (*shut*) degea; (*approach*) neshe

closed *adj* deges

closely *adv* yn ogas

closer *adv* yn-nes

clot *vb* kowla; mola

cloth *n* kweth *f*, kwethow; lenn *f*, lennow; (*of linen*) lien *m*, lienyow; (*sackcloth*) yskar *m*

clothe *vb* gwiska; kwetha. **clothe oneself** omwiska

clothes *n* dillas *coll*; gwisk *m*. **item of clothing** dillasen *f*, dillasennow. **put on clothes** omwiska

clotted *adj* kowlys; molys. **clotted cream** *n.m* dehen molys

cloud *n* komolen *f*, komolennow; kommol *coll*. **thunder cloud** poster *m*, posterow

cloudless *adj* digommol

cloudy *adj* komolek

clout I *n* (*blow*) klout *m*, kloutys; (*influence*) bri *f* **II** *vb* (*strike*) kloutya

clove *n* (*aromatic bud*) kentrik spis *m*, kentrigow spis; (*of garlic*) ewin *m*, ewines

clover *n* mellyonen *f*, mellyon. **four-leaf clover** mellyonen beder delen *f*, mellyon peder delen

clown *n* lorden *m*, lordenyon

club I *n* (*society*) klub *m*, klubys; (*heavy stick*) fust *f*, fustow **II** *vb* (*beat with a club*) fusta. **go clubbing** klubya

clumsy *adj* kledhek

clutch *vb* grabalyas

co- *prfx* ken-; kes-; kev-

coal *n* glow *coll*

coal tit *n* penn pali du *m*, pennow pali du

coarse *adj* garow

coast *n* arvor *m*, arvoryow; kost *m*, kostys

coastal *adj* arvorel

coat *n* kota *m*, kotys, kotow; mantel *f*, mantylli

coating *n* gwiskas *m*, gwiskasow

cobweb *n* gwias kevnis *m*, gwiasow kevnis

cocaine *n* kokayn *m*

cockerel *n* kulyek *m*, kulyoges

cockles *n* koklysen *f*, koklysennow; koklys *coll*

cockroach *n* hwil du *m*, hwiles du

coconut *n* knowen goko *f*, know koko

cod *n* barvus *m*, barvusi

code *n* kod *m*, kodys; koden *f*, kodennow

coffee *n* koffi *m*, koffiow

coffer *n* argh *f*, arghow; kofer *m*, kofrow; (*small*) kofrik *m*, kofrigow

coffin *n* logel *m*, logelyow

cog *n* dansell *f*, dansellow

cognate I *adj* keslinek **II** *n* neshevin *m*, neshevin

coil I *n* torgh *f*, tergh **II** *vb* terghi

coin *n* bath *m*, bathow

Coke *n* (*beverage*) Kok *m*; Koka-Kola *m*

coke *n* (*treated coal*) kok *coll*

colander *n* rider *m*, ridrow

cold I *n* (*temperature*) yeynder *m*; (*infection*) anwos *m*. **I have a cold** yma anwos warnav **II** *adj* yeyn. **bitterly cold** *adj* oor. **to catch cold** anwosi

coldness *n* (*temperature*) yeynder *m*

collage *n* kollaj *m*, kollajow

collapse I *n* diskar *m*, diskarow **II** *vb* diskara

collar *n* mongel *f*, mongellow; torgh *f*, tergh

collar-bone *n* koloren *f*, kolorennow, *dl* diwgoloren

collared dove *n* turen turk *m*, turennow turk

collate *vb* keskorra

colleague *n* kowethyas *m*, kowethysi

collect *vb* kuntel

collection *n* kuntel *m*, kuntellow

collector *n* kunteller *m*, kuntelloryon

college *n* kolji *m*, koljiow

collide *vb* kesskwattya

collier *n* glowor *m*, gloworyon

colliery *n* glowva *f*, glowvaow

collision *n* kesskwat *m*, kesskwattow

colony *n* trevesigeth *f*, trevesigethow

colostrum *n* godrek *m*

colour I *n* liw *m*, liwyow II *vb* liwa

coloured *adj* liwys; liwek

colourful *adj* liwus

colt *n* ebel *m*, ebeli

coltsfoot *n* losow troos ebel *coll*

columbine *n* (*aquilegia*) kough damawynn *m*

column *n* koloven *f*, kolovennow

com- *prfx* ke-

comb I *n* krib *f*, kribow II *vb* kribas

combination *n* kesunyans *m*, kesunyansow

combine *vb* kesunya

come I *vb* dos; dones II *ppt* (*past participle of dos*) devedhys. **come across** happya war[2]. **come across as** heveli. **come away from** distaga dhyworth. **come and see** dos dhe weles **go back** dehweles. **come in handy** bos meur a brow. **come on!** deun yn-rag. **come round to** dos ha. **come to pass** hwarvos

comeback *n* dehwelans *m*, dehwelans; dehwelyans *m*, dehwelyansow

comedian *n* gesyer *m*, gesyoryon

comedy *n* komedi *m*, komedis

comfort I *n* es *m*; konfort *m*, konforts II *vb* konfortya; (*oneself*) omgonfortya

comfortable *adj* attes. **make yourselves comfortable!** omjersyewgh!

comfrey *n* kolm an askorn *m*

comic I *adj* hwarthus II *n* (*cartoon*) komik *m*, komigow

comma *n* komma *m*, kommas

command I *n* arghadow *m*, arghadowyow; gorhemmyn *m*, gorhemynnow II *vb* erghi

commandment *n* arghadow *m*, arghadowyow. **the Ten Commandments** an Deg Arghadow

commence *vb* dalleth

commendable *adj* komendyadow

comment I *n* kampol *m*, kampollow II *vb* kampolla

commerce *n* kenwerth *m*

commercial *adj* kenwerthel

committee *n* kessedhek *m*, kessedhogow

common *adj* kemmyn

commoner *n* komner *m*, komners

commotion *n* freudh *m*, freudhow

communicate *vb* keskomunya

communication *n* keskomunyans *m*, keskomunyansow

communion I*n* (*of saints*) kowethyans *m*, kowethyansow II *vb* (*take Communion*) komunya **Holy Communion** Komun Sans

communism *n* kemynegoreth *f*

communist I *adj* kemynegorek II *n* kemynegor *m*, kemynegoryon. **the Communist Manifesto** Derivadow an Gemynegoryon *m*

community *n* kemeneth *f*, kemenethow

compact I *adj* kesstrothys II *vb* kesstrotha. **compact disc** plasen arghansek *f*, plasennow arghansek

companion *n* koweth *m*, kowetha; kila *m* (*used only in phrase* **an eyl...y gila**); ben *f* (*used only in phrase* **an eyl...hy ben**)

company *n* kowethyans *m*, kowethyansow; (*crew*) mayni *m*, mayniow; felshyp *m*, felshyps

comparative *adj* kehevelus

compare *vb* heveli; komparya; keheveli

comparison *n* kehevelyans *m*, kehevelyansow

compass *n* (*sea*) mornaswydh *f*,
mornaswydhow

compassion *n* (*loving-kindness*)
tregeredh *f*, tregeredhow

compassionate *adj* tregeredhus.
compassionate leave kummyas
tregeredhus *m*

compatible *adj* kesplegadow

compatriot *n* kestrevesik *m*,
kestrevesigyon

compel *vb* gul dhe^2; konstrina

compensate *vb* astiveri

compensation *n* astiveryans *m*,
astiveryansow

compete *vb* kesstrivya

competent *adj* gallosek; sley

competition *n* kesstrif *m*, kesstrifow

competitive *adj* kesstrivus

competitor *n* kesstriver *m*,
kesstrivoryon

compilation *n* kevernyans *m*,
kevernyansow

compile *vb* kevernya

complain *vb* krodhvolas

complaint *n* krodhvol *m*, krodhvolyow;
gyth *m*, gythyow; (*medical*) kleves *m*,
klevesow

complete I *adj* dien; leun II *vb*
kowlwul; kollenwel

completely I *adv* yn tien II *prfx* (*do
completely*) kowl-; kol-

completeness *n* dieneth *f*

complex *adj* kompleth

complexity *n* komplegeth *f*

complicate *vb* komplekhe

complicated *adj* kompleth

compliment I *n* kortesies *m*,
kortesiesow; prays *m*, praysys II *vb*
praysya

component *n* kesrann *f*, kesrannow

comportment *n* omdhegyans *m*,
omdhegyansow

compose *vb* komposya

composer *n* komposydh *m*,
komposydhyon

composition *n* komposyans *m*,
komposyansow

comprehensible *adj* konvedhadow

comprehensive *adj* kompassus;
olldalghus. comprehensive school
kesskol *f*, kesskolyow

compressor *n* gwaskell *f*, gwaskellow

compromise *n* kesassoylyans *m*,
kesassoylyansow

compulsive *adj* honangonstrinus.
Obsessive Compulsive Disorder
Disordyr Gorgemeryansek
Omherdhys (*med*)

compulsory *adj* konstrinus; res

computer *n* jynn-amontya *m*,
jynnys-amontya, jynnow-amontya

comrade *n* kothman *m*, kothmans;
koweth *m*, kowetha

con- *prfx* ke-; kes-; ken-

concave *adj* kowgrom

conceal *vb* kudha; keles

concealed *adj* kudh

conceive *vb* (*a child*) omdhon; (*an idea*)
koncevya

concentrate *vb* keskreuni; (*mind*)
prederi. concentrate on synsi y'n brys

concept *n* tybyans *m*, tybyansow

concern I *n* bern *m*, bernyow II *vb* (*3s
only*) deur; bern. it is of no concern
ny vern; it does not concern me at all
ny'm deur mann

concerning *prp* a-dro dhe; ow tochya;
(*used with poss. adjectives, p.8*) yn kever

concert *n* keskan *f*, keskanow

conciliatory *adj* akordus

conclude *vb* konkludya

conclusion *n* gorfen *m*, gorfennow

concrete (1) *n* kestevyn *m*,
kestevynnow

concrete (2) *adj* pythek

condensation *n* gluthyans *m*

condescending *adj* tasegus

condiment *n* saworen *f*, saworennow

condition *n* (*premise*) ragsel *m*,
ragselyow; (*state*) studh *m*, studhyow;

plit *m*, plitys
condom *n* haslet *m*, haslettow
conduct I *n* fara *m*; konduk *m* II *vb*
  gidya; hembronk; ledya; (*electricity*)
  kendegi. **conduct an orchestra** gidya
  menestrouthi. **conduct oneself**
  omdhoon
conductance *n* treusperthedh *m*
conductor *n* hembrenkyas *m*,
  hembrenkysi
cone *n* pigorn *m*, pigern
confection *n* kyfeyth *m*, kyfeythyow
conference *n* keskussulyans *m*,
  keskussulyansow
confess *vb* avowa; konfessya; meneges
confession *n* avowans *m*, avowansow
confessor *n* konfessor *m*, konfessors
confide *vb* kyfya
confidence *n* fydhyans *m*; kyfyans *m*
confident *adj* fydhyansek; kyfyansek
confidential *adj* kelyfydhys
confirm *vb* afydhya; fastya; konfirmya
confirmation *n* fastyans *m*, fastyansow
confiscate *vb* sesya
conflict *n* kas *f*, kasow
confluence *n* kemper *m*, kemperyow
conform *vb* kesfurvya
conformist *n* kesfurvyas *m*, kesfurvysi
conformity *n* kesfurvyans *m*
confound *vb* konfondya
confuse (*mix up*) kemyska; (*bewilder*)
  sowdheni; sowdhanas
confused *adj* kemyskys; penndegys;
  sowdhenys
confusion *n* (*state of mind*) sowdhan *m*
congeal *vb* kowla
congest *vb* kreuni; kowla
congestion *n* kowlans *m*, kowlansow
congratulate *vb* keslowenhe
congratulations *n* keslowena *f*
congregation *n* kuntellyans *m*,
  kuntellyansow
congress *n* kuntelles *m* (*f*), kuntellesow
conical *adj* pigornek
conifer *n* saben *f*, sabennow; sab *coll*

conjugal *adj* priosel
conjugate *vb* kesyewa
conjugation *n* kesyewans *m*,
  kesyewansow
connect *vb* (*transitive*) junya;
  (*intransitive*) omjunya
connection *n* (*act of connecting*)
  junyans *m*, junyansow; (*existing link*)
  mell *m*, mellow
conquer *vb* tryghi; fetha; konkwerrya
conqueror *n* fether *m*, fethoryon
conquest *n* trygh *m*, tryghow; fethans
  m, fethansow
conscience *n* kowses *m*, kowsesyow;
  konsyans *m*, konsyansow
conscientious *adj* diwysyk; keskiansek;
  prederus
conscious *adj* war
consciousness *n* omwodhvos *m*. **lose**
  consciousness klamdera
consecrate *vb* sakra
consensual *adj* bodhel
consensus *n* kesakordyans *m*,
  kesakordyansow
consent I *n* bodh *m*, bodhow II *vb*
  assentya
consequence *n* sewyans *m*, sewyansow
consequently *adv* yn sewyans
conservation *n* gwithans *m*
conservative I *adj* gwithyasel; (*in*
  physics) omwithek II *n* (*political*)
  mentenour *m*, mentenouryon,
  mentenours; Tori *m*. Toris. **the**
  Conservative Party *n.m* an Parti
  Gwithyasel
consider *vb* prederi; mires war[2]
considerable *adj* lowr; mynsek
considerate *adj* prederus
consideration *n* avis *m*, avisyow
consist *vb* konsystya
consistency *n* kessenyans *m*; (*of fabric*)
  gwias *m*, gwiasow; tewder *m*,
  tewderow
consistent *adj* kesson. **consistent with**
  yn akord gans

console *n* konsolen *f*, konsolennow.
  video game console konsolen
  wariow *f*
consonant *n* kessonen *f*, kessonennow
consonantal *adj* kessonennel
conspicuous *adj* hewel
conspiracy *n* bras *m*, brasow
conspirator *n* braser *m*, brasoryon
conspire *vb* brasa
constable *n* sodhek an kreslu *m*,
  sodhogoyn an kreslu
constant I *n* (*physics*) divaren *f*,
  divarennow II *adj* sad
constipated *adj* trethtegys
constipation *n* trethtegans *m*
constituency *n* pastel vro *f*, pastellow
  bro
constitution *n* korf lagha *m*, korfow
  lagha
constitutional *adj* korf-laghel
constrain *vb* konstrina
construct *vb* drehevel
construction *n* drehevyans *m*,
  drehevyansow
consult *vb* (*intransitive*) omgussulya;
  (*transitive*) kussulya
consultation *n* kussulyans *m*,
  kussulyansow
consume *vb* konsumya; (*by fire*)
  kowlleski
consumer *n* konsumyer *m*,
  konsumyoryon
consumption *n* konsumyans *m*,
  konsumyansow
contact I *n* kestav *m*, kestavow II *vb*
  kestava. **contact lens** gwedrik kestav
  m, gwedrigow kestav. **get into contact**
  omdava orth
contagious *adj* plagus
contain *vb* synsi
container *n* kofen *f*, kofennow; lestryn
  m, lestrynnow
contaminated *adj* mostys
contemplate *vb* hirbrederi; mires war[2]
contemporary *adj* kevos

contempt *n* dispresyans *m*; fians *m*;
  despit *m* despityow. **undeserved**
  contempt despit heb y dyli
contend *vb* strivya
content (1) *n* dalgh *m*, dalghow
content (2) *adj* pes da
contented *adj* pes da
contention *n* strivyans *m*, strivyansow
contentious *adj* kavylek
contest I *n* kesstrif *m*, kesstrifow II *vb*
  strivya
context *n* kettesten *f*, kettestennow
continent *n* brastir *m*, brastiryow
continental *adj* brastiryel. **continental**
  drift dryftyans an brastiryow *m*
continually *adv* heb hedhi
continuation *n* pesyans *m*, pesyansow
continue *vb* durya; pesya
continuity *n* didorreth *m*
continuous *adj* didor
contour *n* kettres *m*, kettresow
contraband *adj* noswikorek
contraception *n* haslettyans *m*,
  haslettyansow
contraceptive *n* haslet *m*, haslettow
contract *n* ambos *m*, ambosow;
  kevambos *m*, kevambosow. **breach of**
  contract torrva ambos *f*
contraction *n* kotheans *m*, kotheansow
contradict *vb* kontradia
contradiction *n* kontradians *m*,
  kontradiansow
contradictory *adj* kontradiek
contrary *adj* kontrari
contrast *n* gorthwedh *f*, gorthwedhow
contribute *vb* kevri
contribution *n* kevro *m*, kevrohow
contributor *n* kevriyas *m*, kevriysi
contrive *vb* fangla
control I *n* maystri *m* II *vb* rewlya;
  routya; kontrolya. **control tower**
  tour-routya *m*, touryow-routya
controversial *adj* gorthargyadow
controversy *n* gorthargyans *m*,
  gorthargyansow

convenience *n* es *m*. **conveniences** *n.pl*
(*toilets*) privedhyow *pl*
convenient *adj* parys
converge *vb* keskeverya
convergence *n* keskeveryans *m*,
keskeveryansow
convergent *adj* keskeverek
conversation *n* keskows *m*, keskowsow
converse *vb* keskewsel
conversion *n* treylyans *m*, treylyansow
convert *vb* treylya
convex *adj* bothfurvek
conviction *n* kowses *m*, kowsesyow
convince *vb* darbolla
convincing *adj* perswadus
cook I *n* kog *m*, kogow II *vb* kegina;
kegi; (*prepare*) pareusi. **cook the
books** fugya an akontys. **cook up an
excuse** dismygi askus
cooker *n* kogforn *f*, kogfornow
cookery *n* keginieth *f*
cool I *adj* goyeyn II *vb* goyeynhe. **cool
off** mygla
cooperate *vb* kesoberi
cooperation *n* kesoberyans *m*,
kesoberyansow
cooperative *adj* kesoberek
coordinate I *adj* kesordenek II *n*
kesordenek *m*, kesordenogyon III *vb*
kesordena
coordination *n* kesordenans *m*,
kesordenansow
coot *n* dowryar *f*, dowryer
cope *vb* omweres; **cope with** ardyghtya
copious *adj* pals
copper *n* (*element*) kober *m*
copulate *vb* kyjya
copy I *n* dasskrif *m*, dasskrifow;
eylskrif *m*, eylskrifow II *vb* dasskrifa;
eylskrifa; kopia
copyright *n* gwir-pryntya *m*,
gwiryow-pryntya; gwirbryntyans *m*,
gwirbryntyansow. **copyright
infringement** torrva gwir-pryntya *f*,
torrvaow gwir-pryntya

cord *n* korden *f*, kerdyn
cordial *adj* kolonnek
core I *n* kolonnen *f*, kolonennow II *vb*
digolonna
coriander *n* koriander *m*; losowen an
bara *f*
cork I *n* korkyn *m*, korkynnow II *vb*
korkynna
corkscrew *n* alhwedh korkyn *m*,
alhwedhow korkyn
cormorant *n* morvran *f*, morvrini
corn *n* (*cereal*) ysen *f*, ys. **abounding in
corn** *adj* ysek. **corn flakes** yskansen *f*,
yskansennow; yskans *coll*
corner I *n* kornel *f*, kornellow; kornet
m, kornettow; korn *m*, kernow; sorn
m, sornow II *vb* kornella
cornet *n* tollgorn *m*, tollgern
cornflower *n* glasik *m*
Cornicise *vb* Kernewekhe
Cornish *adj* kernewek. **Cornish
language** *n* Kernewek *m*. **Living
Cornish** *n* Kernewek Byw *m*. **Cornish
speaker** Kerneweger *m*,
Kernewegoryon. **I am Cornish**
Kernow ov vy *m*; Kernewes ov vy *f*
Cornishman *n* Kernow *m*, Kernowyon
Cornishwoman *n* Kernewes *f*,
Kernewesow
Cornwall *top* Kernow *f*
coronation *n* kurunyans *m*,
kurunyansow
corporation *n* korforeth *f*, korforethow.
multinational corporation korforeth
lieskenedhlek *f*, korforethow
lieskenedhlek
correct I *adj* ewn II *vb* ewna
correction *n* ewnans *m*, ewnansow
correctness *n* komposter *m*,
komposteryow
correspond *vb* (*writing*) kesskrifa;
(*match*) omdhesedha. **correspond to**
omdhesedha orth
correspondence *n* (*writing*)
kesskrifans *m*, kesskrifansow;

271

(*similarity*) hevelepter *m*, hevelepterow

correspondent *n* kesskrifer *m*, kesskriforyon

corridor *n* kuldremenva *f*, kuldremenvaow

corrosive *adj* kesknius

corrugated *adj* kevryllys

corrupt I *adj* podrek II *vb* legri; pedri

corrupted *adj* legrys

corruption *n* legras *m*, legrasow

corset *n* korset *m*, korsettys

cosmetic I *adj* kosmetek II *n* afinuster *m*, afinusterow; tremmliw *m*, tremmliwyow; liw *m*, liwyow; mingreft *m*. **cosmetic surgery** leuvvedhegneth kosmetek *f*, leuvvedhegnethow kosmetek

cosmic *adj* kosmek

cosmology *n* kosmonieth *f*

cosmos *n* kosmos *m*

cost I *n* kost *m*, kostys, kostow II *vb* kostya. **at all costs** awos eghen

costly *adj* kostek

costume *n* gwiskas *m*, gwiskasow

cosy *adj* klys

cottage *n* pennti *m*, penntiow. **small cottage** dyji *m*, dyjiow

cotton *n* koton *m*, kotenyow. **cotton wool** gwlan koton *coll*

couch I *n* gorwedhva *f*, gorwedhvaow; growedhva *f*, growedhvaow II *vb* gorwedha; growedha

cough I *n* pas *m*, pasow II *vb* pasa. **cough lozenge** losanj pas *m*, losanjys pas. **whooping cough** pas garm *m*

coulter *n* kolter *m*, koltrow; trogher *m*, trogheryow

council *n* kussul *f*, kussulyow; konsel *m*, konsels. **Cornwall Council** Konsel Kernow *m*. **the Cornish Language Council** Kussul an Taves Kernowek *f*

councillor *n* konseler *m*, konseloryon

counsel *n* kussul *f*, kussulyow

count (1) I *n* (*census*) niveryans *m*, niveryansow II *vb* amontya; nivera; rekna

count (2) *n* (*title*) yurl *m*, yurlys

counter (1) *n* (*shop*) komptyer *m*, komptyoryon; (*counting device*) niverell *f*, niverellow; (*in games*) boton *m*, botonyow

counter (2) *vb* (*answer*) gorthebi; (*oppose*) gortheneba

counterfeit I *adj* fug II *vb* fugya

country *n* pow *m*, powyow; bro *f*, broyow; gwlas *f*, gwlasow. **mother country** *n* mammvro *f*, mammvroyow. **open country** mes *m*, mesyow. **pertaining to a country** gwlasek

countryman *n* trevesik *m*, trevesigyon

countryside *n* powdir *m*

county *n* konteth *f*, kontethow

couple I *n* kopel *m*, koplow; dewdhen *m*. **young couple** dewbries *dl* II *vb* parya

coupon *n* kolpon *m*, kolpons

courage *n* kolonekter *m*

courageous *adj* kolonnek

courgette *n* pompik *m*, pompigow

course *n* (*study*) steus *f*, steusow; kors *m*, korsow; (*direction*) hyns *m*, hensyow; (*orbit*) resegva *f*, resegvaow; (*meal*) sand *m*, sandys; (*race*) res *m*, resow. **golf course** gwel golf *m*, gwelyow golf. **in the course of** dres. **of course** heb mar; heb dhout. **of course not** na, yn certan. **race course** resegva *f*, resegvaow

court (1) *n* (*residence*) lys *f*, lysow; (*court of law*) kort *f*, kortys; breuslys *f*, breuslysow

court (2) *vb* (*woo*) tanta

courteous *adj* kortes

courtesy *n* kortesi *m*, kortesis

courtroom *n* stevel an lys *f*, stevellow an lys

courtyard *n* garth *m*, garthow

cousin *n* kenderow *m*, kenderwi; kosin *m*, kosins

cove *n* porth *m*, porthow

cover I *n* gorher *m*, gorheryow; (*of a book*) aden *f*, adenyow; kudhlen *f*, kudhlennow **II** *vb* gorheri; lenni; (*with a cloth*) kwetha

covet *vb* kovaytya

cow *n* bugh *f*, bughes. **calfless cow** gownagh *f*, gownaghes. **cow dung** busel *m*. **dairy cow** bugh-godra *f*, bughes-godra. **little cow** bughik *n* bughigesow *f*

coward *n* ownek *m*, ownogyon; kilgi *m*, kilgeun

cowardice *n* kilgieth *f*

cowardly *adj* ownek

cowboy *n* bughwas *m*, bughwesyon

cowshed *n* bowji *m*, bowjiow

cowslip *n* briallen an gog *f*

crab *n* kanker *m*, kankres

crab-pot *n* kowel kankres *m*, kowellow kankres

crack I *n* krack *m*, krackys **II** *vb* krackya

cradle *n* kowel lesk *m*, kowellow lesk

craft *n* kreft *m*, kreftow

craftsperson *n* kreftor *m*, kreftoryon; ser *m*, seri

crafty *adj* (*wily*) fel; sotel

crag *n* klog *f*, klogow; kleger *m*, klegrow

cramp *n* godramm *m*, godrammow

cranberry *n* kollen aran *f*, kollennow garan; koll garan *coll*; ysen rudh *f*, ysennow rudh; ys rudh *coll*

crane *n* (*bird and machine*) garan *f*, garanes

crane's-bill *n* gelvin garan *m*

cranefly *n* kelyonen aran *f*, kelyon garan

crash *n* bomm *m*, bommyn; (*accident*) droglam *m*, droglammow

crave *n* yeuni

craving *n* ewl *f*, ewlow; yeunadow *m*, yeunadowyow

crawl *vb* pedrevanas; kramya

crayfish *n* gaver vor *f*, gever mor; gryll *m*, gryllys

crayon *n* kreyon *m*, kreyonyow

crazy *adj* muskok

cream *n* dehen *m*, dehennow. **clotted cream** *n.m* dehen molys

cream cake *n* tesen dhehen *f*, tesennow dehen. **sun cream** dehen howl *m*, dehennow howl

crease *n* pleg *m*, plegow

create *vb* gul; gwruthyl

creation *n* gwrians *m*, gwriansow

creative *adj* awenek

creativity *n* awenekter *m*

creator *n* gwrier *m*, gwrioryon; formyer *m*, formyoryon; furvyer *m*, furvyoryon; kreador *m*, kreadors

creature *n* kroadur *m*, kroaduryon

crèche *n* floghva *f*, floghvaow

credible *adj* krysadow

credit *n* kresys *m*. **credit card** karten gresys *f*, kartennow kresys

credulous *adj* hegol

creek *n* heylyn *m*, heylynnow

creep (1) *vb* kramya

creep (2) *n* (*toady*) kraver tin *m*, kravoryon din

creepy *adj* skruthus. **creepy-crawly** (*applied indiscriminately to worms, caterpillars and other insects*) pryv *m*, preves, prevyon

cremate *vb* korfleski

cremation *n* korfloskans *f*, korfloskansow

crescent *n* krommen *f*, kromennow, (*in street signage*) gwarak *f*, gwaregow

cress *n* beleren *f*, belerennow; beler *coll*

cress, garden *n* beler lowarth *coll*

cress, hairy bitter *n* beler hwerow *coll*

crew *n* mayni *m*, mayniow

cricket *n* (*sport*) krycket *m*; (*insect*) gryll *m*, grylles

cricketer *n* gwarier krycket *m*, gwarioryon krycket

crime *n* drogober *m*, drogoberow; galweyth *m*, galweythow; hager-ober *m*, hager-oberow

criminal I *adj* galweythel **II** *n* drogoberor *m*, drogoberoryon

crimp *vb* krygha

crimson *adj* kogh

crisp I *adj* kras **II** *n* (*snack*) kresik *m*, kresigow

critic *n* barner *m*, barnoryon, barneryow; arvreusyas *m*, arvreusysi. **theatre critic** barner gwariva *m*, barnoryon wariva

critical *adj* (*crucial*) troboyntel; (*judgmental*) breusel; (*literary*) krytykel

criticise *vb* (*evaluate*) arvreusi; (*judge*) breusi; krytika; (*find fault*) kabli. **criticise oneself** omjastya

criticism *n* arvreus *f*, arvreusow

critique *n* breusyans *m*, breusyansow

croak I ronk *m*, ronkow **II** *vb* renki

croaky *adj* ronk

Croat *n* Kroat *m*, Kroatyon

Croatia *top* Kroati *f*

Croatian I *adj* kroatek **II** *n* (*language*) Kroatek *m*

crochet *n* krochet *m*, krochetow

crocodile *n* krokodil *m*, krokodiles

crocus *n* safran *m*

cromlech *n* krommlegh *f*, krommleghow

crooked *adj* kamm

crop I (*of a bird*) kroth *f*, krothow; (*harvest*) trevas *f*, trevasow **II** (*cut short*) dibenna; (*harvest*) trevasa

cross I *n* krows *f*, krowsow **II** *vb* (*river, bridge*) tremena; (*stage, room*) treusi

cross-beam *n* treuster *m*, treusters, treustrow

cross-dress *vb* treuswiska

crossing *n* treusva *f*, treusvaow. **level crossing** *n* treusva hyns horn *f*, treusvaow hyns horn. **pedestrian**

crossing treusva gerdhoryon *f*, treusvaow kerdhoryon

crossroads *n* krowsfordh *f*, krowsfordhow

cross-shaped *adj* krowsek

cross-tempered *adj* krowsek

crossword *n* krowseryow *pl*

crotch *n* gowl *f*, gowlow

crouch *vb* plattya

crow *n* bran *f*, brini

crowbar *n* lorgh horn *f* (*m*), lorghow horn

crowd *n* bush *m*, bushys; routh *f*, routhow

crowded *adj* leun a dus. **crowded together** herdhys war-barth

crown *n* kurun *f*, kurunyow

crucial *adj* troboyntel

crucify *vb* krowsya

crude *adj* garow; kriv

crudity *n* krivder *m*

cruel *adj* fell; tynn

cruelty *n* fellder *m*, fellderyow

cruise I *n* morviaj *m*, morviajys, morviajyow **II** *vb* morviajya

cruiser *n* korsyer *m*, korsyoryon

crumb *n* brewyonen *f*, brewyonennow; brewyon *coll*; browsyonen *f*, browsyonennow; browsyon *coll*; (*of bread*) hwigen *f*, hwigennow

crumble *vb* brewi; browsi. **crumbled material** brows *coll*

crunch I *n* krack *m*, krackys **II** *vb* densel

crushed *adj* skatt

crust *n* krestennen *f*, kresten

crustacean *n* krestennek *m*, krestenogyon

crutch *n* kroch *m*, krochys, krochow, *dl* dewgroch

cry I *n* kri *m*, kriow **II** *vb* kria; (*cry out*) leva; (*weep*) ola; devera dagrow; skollya dagrow; dagrewi. **cry one's eyes out** skollya liv a dhagrow. **for crying out loud** awos Duw

crystal *n* gwrys *m*, gwrysow
crystallization *n* gwrysegans *m*,
gwrysegansow
cub *n* kolyn *m*, kelyn. **fox cub** lowarnik
m, lewernigow. **lion cub** lewik *m*,
lewigow
cube *n* kub *m*, kubow
cubic *adj* kubek
cubit *n* kevelin *m*, kevelinyow
cuckoo *n* kog *f*, koges; koukou *f*,
koukous
cucumber *n* kukomber *m*,
kukomberyow
cudgel *n* fust *f*, fustow
cul-de-sac *n* fordh dhall *f*, fordhow dall
culprit *n* drogoberor *m*, drogoberoryon
cultivate *vb* gonis
cultivated *adj* (*of land*) gonedhys
cultural *adj* gonisogethel
culture *n* gonisogeth *f*, gonisogethow.
culture shock *m* dyegrans gonisogeth
cultured *adj* (*of a person*) findhyskys
cumin *n* kumin *coll*
cunning I *adj* kall; konnyk II *n* kalder
m; konnyk *m*
cup *n* hanaf *m*, hanafow. **acorn cup**
byskon mes *f*, byskonyow mes
cupboard *n* amari *f*, amaris
cupful *n* hanafas *m*, hanafasow
curd *n* kowlesen *f*, kowlesennow;
kowles *coll*. **lemon curd** kowles
lymmaval *coll*
curdle *vb* kowla
curdled *adj* kowlys
cure I *n* kur *m*, kurys II *vb* (*restore to
health*) yaghhe; (*preserve*) salla
curiosity *n* (*inquisitiveness*) govynuster
m; (*oddity*) koyntys *f*, koyntysyow
curious *adj* (*strange*) koynt; (*inquisitive*)
govynnus; (*nosy*) tronek
curl I *n* kudyn krullys *m*, kudynnow
krullys II *vb* krullya
curlew *n* gelvinek *m*, gelvinoges,
gelvinogyon
curly *adj* krullys
currant *n* korynt *m*, koryns

currency *n* mona kemmyn *coll*
current *n* fros *m*, frosow. **electric
current** fros tredan *m*, frosow tredan
curriculum *n* kors-dyski *m*,
korsow-dyski
curry *n* kurri *m*, kurris
curse I *n* molleth *f*, mollothow II *vb*
mollethi; miliga
cursed *adj* mollothek
cursor *n* resell *f*, resellow
curtain *n* kroglen *f*, kroglennow
curve I *n* gwarr *f*, gwarrow; krommen *f*,
kromennow II *vb* kamma; kromma
curved *adj* kromm
cushion *n* pluvek *f*, pluvogow
custard *n* kustard *m*
custodian *n* gwithyas *m*, gwithysi
custody *n* gwith *m*. **police custody**
gwith an kreslu *m*
custom *n* maner *f*, maners, manerow;
us *m*, usyow, usadow
customise *vb* personelhe
custom-made *adj* a-vusur
customs *n* toll *f*, tollow. **customs officer**
tollwas *m*, tollwesyon
cut I *adj* trogh; treghys II *n* trogh *m*,
troghow; (*cut of meat*) tregh *m*,
treghow III *vb* treghi
cutlery *n* daffar lymm *m*
cuttable *adj* hedrogh
cut-throat *adj* treghi konna. **cut-throat
competition** kesstrif treghi konna *m*,
kesstrifow treghi konna
cuttlefish *n* padel ynkyn *f*, padellow
ynkyn
cycle I *n* tro *f*, troyow II *vb* (*ride a
bicycle*) diwrosa
cyclist *n* diwroser *m*, diwrosoryon
cyclone *n* gwyns a-dro *m*, gwynsow
a-dro
cylinder *n* hirgrennen *f*, hirgrenennow
cylindrical *adj* hirgren
Czech I *adj* chek II *n* (*language*)
Chekek *m*; (*person*) Chek *m*, Chekyon.
Czech Republic Repoblek Chek *f*

D

dace *n* (*fish*) talek *m*, taloges
dachshund *n* broghki *m*, broghkeun
dad *n* tas *m*, tasow
daddy *n* tasik *m*, tasigow
daffodil *n* lilien Gorawys *f*, liliennow Korawys; lili Korawys *coll*
daft *adj* gocki
daily *adj* dedhyek; pubdedhyek
dainty *adj* denti
dairy *n* leti *m*, letiow. dairy produce askor lethek *m*
daisy *n* kaja *f*, kajow; boreles *m*, borelesyow
daisy, Michaelmas *n* (*autumn aster*) bleujen gool Mighal *f*
daisy, ox-eye *n* kaja vras *f*, kajow bras
dale *n* (*valley*) nans *m*, nansow; (*valley bottom*) tnow *m*, tnowi
dam *n* arge *m*, argeow
damage I *n* damach *m*, damajys; kisyans *m*, kisyansow II *vb* kisya; (*by weather*) arnewa
damaged *adj* shyndys. storm-damaged arnewys
dame *n* dama *f*, damyow
damn I *int* molleth Duw! II *vb* dampnya. I don't give a damn ny rov oy
damp I *adj* glyb II *n* glybor *m*
dance I *n* dons *m*, donsyow II *vb* donsya; karolli
dancer *n* donsyer *m*, donsyoryon
dandelion *n* dans lew *m*, dens lew
Dane *n* Dan *m*, Danyon
danger *n* peryl *m*, peryllow, peryllyow; danjer *m*, danjeryow
dangerous *adj* peryllus; diantel
Danish I *adj* danek II *n* (*language*) Danek *m*
dapple *adj* britha
dappled *adj* brithys

dare I *n* bedhas *m*, bedhasow II *vb* bedha; lavasos. I dare say bedhav y di
daring *adj* bedhek
dark I *adj* tewl II *n* tewolgow *pl*. fear of the dark own rag an tewolgow
darken *vb* tewlhe
darkness *n* tewlder *m*; tewolgow *pl*
darling I *adj* hwegol; keresik II *n* hwegen *f*, hwegennow; melder *m*, melderyow; keresik *m*, keresigyon; kuv kolon *m*, kuvyon kolon; hwegol *m*
dash *vb* fyski; stevya
database *n* sel dherivadow *f*, selyow derivadow
date (1) I *n* (*day*) dydh *m*, dedhyow; (*specific date*) dedhyas *m*, dedhyasow II *vb* (*a person*) mos yn-mes gans; (*a document*) dedhya. date of expiry dedhyas diwedh *m*, dedhyasow diwedh
date (2) *n* (*fruit*) datesen *f*, datesennow; dates *coll*
daub *vb* pria
daughter *n* myrgh *f*, myrghes. daughter-in-law gohydh *f*, gohydhow
dawn *n* bora *m*, boraow
day *n* dydh *m*, dedhyow. day-to-day pub dydh oll. on the day before yesterday *adv* dygynsete. on the day after tomorrow *adv* trenja. once a day unweyth y'n jydh. that will be the day! my a'n krys pan welav! the next day ternos. these days y'n jydh hedhyw. the good old days an hendedhyow brav. Judgement Day Dydh Breus
daybreak *n* tardh dydh *m*, tardhow dydh
daydream I *n* hunros dydh *m*, hunrosow dydh II *vb* hunrosa y'n jydh

daylight *n* golow dydh *m*. **in broad daylight** yn jydh splann

daytime *n* dydhweyth *m*

dazzle *vb* dallhe

dead *adj* marow. **dead end** fordh dhall *f*, fordhow dall

deadly *adj* marwel

deadnettle *n* koog linas *coll*

deaf *adj* bodhar. **become deaf or hearing impaired** *vb* bodhara. **person with hearing impairment** bodharek *m*, bodharogyon. **hearing impaired** *adj* bodharek; klewes aperys

deafen *vb* bodharhe

deal I *n* bargen *m*, bargennyow **II** *vb* bargynnya

dear *adj* keresik; kuv; (*expensive*) kostek; (*in letters*) ker; hweg. **dear George** a Jori ker; a Jori hweg

death *n* mernans *m*, mernansow. **Death** (*personified*) Ankow *m*. **death rate** kevradh mernans *m*, kevradhow mernans. **death rattle** ronk mernans *m*, ronkow mernans

debate I *n* dadhelva *f*, dadhelvaow **II** *vb* dadhla; debatya

debater *n* dadhelor *m*, dadheloryon

debit *vb* debisya

debt *n* kendon *f*, kendonow. **get into debt** kodha yn kendon

debug *vb* (*IT*) pryvessa

decade *n* degvledhen *f*, degvledhynnyow

decadence *n* legras *m*

decay I *n* breynans *m*, breynansow **II** *vb* breyna

decease *vb* merwel

deceased *adj* tremenys

deceit *n* toll *m*; wrynch *m*, wrynchys; gil *m*

deceive *vb* tolla

December *n* Kevardhu *m*; mis Kevardhu *m*

decency *n* onester *m*

decent *adj* onest

decentralise *vb* digresenni

decide *vb* ervira. **I have decided upon** ervirys ov vy dhe

deciduous *adj* kolldhel

decimal *n* degedhek *m*, degedhogow

decipher *vb* digodenni

decision *n* ervirans *m*, erviransow

decisive *adj* ervirus

deck (1) *n* flour *m*, flouryow. **deck of cards** sett kartennow *m*, settys kartennow, settow kartennow

deck (2) *vb* (*adorn*) takla

deck-chair *n* kador creth *f*, kadoryow treth

declaration *n* deklaryans *m*, deklaryansow; diskleryans *m*, diskleryansow

declare *vb* disklerya; deklarya

declension *n* deklinyans *m*, deklinyansow

decline *vb* nagha; deklinya

decode *vb* digodenni

decorate *vb* afina; tekhe

decorative *adj* afinus

decrease I *n* iselheans *m*, iselheansow **II** *vb* iselhe

decree I *n* ordenans *m*, ordenansow **II** *vb* erghi; ordena

decrepit *adj* krebogh

deed *n* (*action*) gwrians *m*, gwriansow; ober *m*, oberow; (*legal document*) chartour *m*, chartours. **bad deed** drog-ober *m*, drog-oberow. **good deed** da-ober *m*, da-oberow

deep *adj* down

deepen *vb* downhe

deep-freeze *vb* downrewi

deep-fry *vb* downfria

deer *n* karow *m*, kerwys

default *n* defowt *m*, defowtow

defeat I *n* fethans *m*, fethansow **II** *vb* fetha; konkwerrya

defeated *adj* fethys

defecate *vb* kawgha; (*animals*) skombla

defect *n* gwall *m*, gwallow; defowt *m*, defowtow

defence *n* defens *m*

defend *vb* defendya; difres

defendant *n* difenner *m*, difenoryon

defender *n* difresyas *m*, difresysi

defer *vb* delatya

defiance *n* defians *m*, defiansow; er *m*

deficiency *n* difyk *m*, difygyow; fowt *m*, fowtys, fowtow

deficient *adj* difygel

deficit *n* difygas *m*, difygasow

defile *vb* defolya

defilement *n* defolyans *m*, defolyansow

define *vb* styrya

definite *adj* devri

definitely *adv* yn tevri

definition *n* styryans *m*, styryansow

deforest *vb* digoswiga

defraud *vb* frowsya

defrost *vb* direwi

defy *vb* defia; erya

degrade *vb* diredhya

degree *n* (*angle or temperature*) gradh *m*, gradhow; (*rank*) degre *m*, degrys. **bachelor's degree** bachelerieth *f*, bacheleriethow. **doctorate** doktourieth *f*, doktouriethow. **master's degree** mestronieth *f*, mestroniethow

delay I *n* ardak *m*, ardagow; delay *m*, delays II *vb* delatya

delegate I *n* kannas *f*, kanasow II *vb* kanasa. **delegate to** gul kannas a^2

delegation *n* kanasedh *m*, kanasedhow

delete *vb* dilea

deletion *n* dileans *m*, dileansow

deliberate *adj* a-borpos

deliberately *adv* a-borpos

delicacy *n* (*tenderness*) bleudhder *m*; (*dainty food*) tamm denti *m*, temmyn denti

delicate *adj* bleudh; denti; fin; tyckli

delicious *adj* dentethyel

delight I *n* delit *m*, delitys II *vb* delitya; didhana; lowenhe

delighted *adj* pur lowen

delightful *adj* hwegol

delinquent *n* drogwas *m*, drogwesyon; felon *m*, felons

deliver *vb* delivra. **deliver from** delivra dhyworth. **deliver up** delivra dhe^2

deliverance *n* delivrans *m*, delivransow

delivery *n* livreson *m*, livresons. **express delivery** livreson uskis *m*, livresons uskis

dell *n* pans *m*, pansow

delphinium *n* (*larkspur*) paw ahwesydh *m*

delude *vb* tolla; flattra

deluded *adj* tollys

deluge *n* liv *m*, livyow; (*heavy shower*) hager-gowas *f*, hager-gowasow

delusion *n* (*med*) kammgrysyans *m*, kammgrysyansow

demand I *n* gorholeth *m*, gorholethow II *vb* demondya

dementia *n* (*med*) dementia *m*

demist *vb* dilughya

democracy *n* gwerinieth *f*, gweriniethow; demokratieth *f*, demokratiethow

democrat *n* gweriniether *m*, gweriniethoryon. **Democrat** (*member of US Democratic party*) Demokrat *m*, Demokratyon

democratic *adj* gwerinel; demokratek

demon *n* jevan *m*, jevanow

demonic *adj* jevanek

Denmark *top* Danmark *m*

denomination *n* (*category*) rumen *f*, rumennow; (*religious*) hanwans *m*, hanwansow

denominator *n* disrannen *f*, disranennow

dense *adj* tew; doos

density *n* tewder *m*, tewderow; (*physics*) dosedh *m*, dosedhow

dent I *n* brall *m*, brallow II *vb* brallya

dental *adj* dynsek

dentist *n* medhek dens *m*, medhogyon dhens

deny *vb* nagha

depart *vb* diberth

department *n* asran *f*, asrannow

departmental *adj* asrannel

departure *n* dibarth *f*, dibarthow

depend *vb*. depend on kregi war². it depends on what you want kregys yw war an pyth a vynnydh

dependable *adj* trestadow

dependent on *adj* omres dhe. he is dependent on drugs omres dhe dhroggys yw ev

depopulated *adj* dibobel

depress *vb* digolenni

depressed *adj* (*colloq*) duwenys I'm feeling a bit depressed today tamm duwenys ov hedhyw

depressing *adj* duwenus that's depressing! ass yw henna duwenus!

depression (1) *n* (*med*) iselweyth *m*; (*colloq; low mood*) cher isel *m*; ki du *m*. she was a bit low yesterday yn cher isel o hi de. he has the black dog (of depression) yma'n ki du warnodho

depression (2) *n* (*economic*) iselweyth *m*, iselweythyow

depression (3) *n* (*topographical*) seudh *m*, seudhow

depth *n* downder *m*, downderyow

deputation *n* kanasedh *m*, kanasedhow

deputy *adj* is-. deputy chairperson iskaderyer *m*, iskaderoryon

derange *vb* varya; muskegi

deranged *adj* varyes

dermatologist *n* medhek kroghen *m*, medhogyon groghen; dermatologydh *m*, dermatologydhyon

dermatology *n* dermatologieth *f*

descant *n* konternot *m*

descend *vb* diyskynna

descending *adj* diyskynnus

describe *vb* deskrifa

description *n* deskrifans *m*, deskrifansow

descriptive *adj* deskrifus

desert (1) *n* (*of a place*) difeyth *m*, difeythyow; difeythtir *m*, difeythtiryow

desert (2) *vb* (*intransitive*) kilfia; (*transitive*) forsakya.

deserted *adj* dibobel; ynyal

deserve *vb* dendyl; dervyn

deservedly *adv* kwit

design I *n* desin *m*, desinyow II *vb* desinya

designer *n* desiner *m*, desinoryon

desirable *adj* desiradow

desire I *n* (*need*) hwans *m*, hwansow II *vb* hwansa

desirous *adj* hwansek

desk *n* desk *m*, deskys, deskow

desolate *adj* (*of a place*) ynyal; (*of a person*) diglon

despair *n* desper *m*

desperate *adj* diglon

desperation *n* diglon *f*

despicable *adj* fiadow; vil

despise *vb* fia; dispresya

despite *n* despit *m*, despityow. in despite of yn despit dhe²

dessert *n* podyn *m*, podyns; melyssand *m*, melyssandys

destine *vb* destna

destined *adj* destnys

destitute *adj* boghosek

destitution *n* boghosogneth *f*

destroy *vb* distrui

destruction *n* diswrians *m*, diswriansow; distruyans *m*, distruyansow

detach *vb* distaga. detach from distaga dhyworth

detached *adj* distag

detail I *vb* manylya II *n* details manylyon *pl*; (*military*) distagyn *f*, distagynnow

detailed *adj* manylys

detain *vb* synsi; karghara

detect *vb* helerghi

detective *n* helerghyas *m*, herlerghysi

detector *n* helerghell *f*, helerghellow; (*sensor*) sensell *f*, sensellow; sensour *m*, sensours

detention *n* kargharans *m*, kargharansow

detergent *n* lin sebon *m*, linyow sebon

deteriorate *vb* gwethhe

deterioration *n* gwethheans *m*, gwethheansow

determine *vb* determya

determined *adj* determys; ervirys

develop *vb* displegya

developing *adj* displegel

development *n* displegyans *m*, displegyansow

deviate *vb* errya

device *n* devis *m*, devisyow

devil *n* dyowl *m*, dyowlow; malan *m*, malanes. **the Devil** *n* an jowl *m*; an tebel-el *f*. **by the Devil** re'n jowl

devise *vb* devisya

devolution *n* digresennans *m*

devolve *vb* digresenni

Devon *top* Dewnens *m*

devour *vb* devorya

dew *n* gluth *m*, gluthow

dexterity *n* sleyneth *f*

diabetes mellitus *n* (*sugar diabetes; med*) diabetes mellitus; (*colloq*) kleves melys *m*

diabetic I *adj* diabetik **II** *n* diabetik *m*, diabetigyon

diagnose *vb* diagnosa

diagnosis *n* diagnosans *m*, diagnosansow

diagonal I *adj* krowslinek **II** *n* krowslinen *f*, krowslinennow

diagram *n* golinyans *m*, golinyansow

dial I *n* rivell *f*, rivellow; dial *m*, dialys **II** *vb* dialya

dialect *n* rannyeth *f*, rannyethow

dialogue *n* (*conversation*) keskows *m*, keskowsow; (*discussion*) omgussulyans *m*, omgussulyansow

diameter *n* treuslinen *f*, treuslinennow

diamond *n* adamant *m*, adamantys, adamantow

diarrhoea *n* skit *m*

diary *n* dydhlyver *m*, dydhlyvrow

dice *n* dis *m*, disyow

dictate *vb* (*impose*) dyghtya; (*to a secretary*) dardhyghtya

dictator *n* turant *m*, turans

dictatorial *adj* turantiel

dictatorship *n* turantieth *f*

dictionary *n* gerylver *m*, gerlyvrow

die *vb* merwel

diesel *n* disel *m*

diet *n* rewl voos *f*, rewlow boos

difference *n* dihevelepter *m*, dihevelepterow; dyffrans *m*, dyffransow

different *adj* ken; dihaval; dyffrans. **different from** dihaval orth; dyffrans orth

difficult *adj* kales

difficulty *n* kaletter *m*, kaletterow; ankombrynsi *m*

diffuse *vb* terlesa

diffusion *n* terlesans *m*, terlesansow

dig *vb* palas. **dig a trench** kleudhya

digest *vb* tretha; goi

digger (*machine*) jynn-palas *m*, jynnys-palas, jynnow-palas

digit *n* riven *f*, rivennow; (*finger*) bys *m*, besies

digital *adj* besyel

dignity *n* dynita *m*

diligence *n* diwysygneth *f*

diligent *adj* diwysyk

dim *adj* godewl

dime *n* demma *m*, demmys

dimension *n* myns *m*, mynsow

dimwit *n* talsogh *m*, talsoghyon

dine *vb* kinyewel; kona. **dining room** *n* stevel-dhybri *f*, stevellow-dybri.

dining car *n* kocha-dybri *m*,
kochys-dybri

dingle *n* gobans *m*, gobansow; pans *m*,
pansow

dinner *n* kinnyow *m*, kinyewow; kon *f*,
konyow

dinosaur *n* arghpedrevan *m*,
arghpedrevanes

diode *n* diod *m*, diodys

diphthong *n* diwvogalen *f*,
diwvogalennow

diploma *n* diplomen *f*, diplomennow

diplomacy *n* lyskanasedh *m*

diplomat *n* lyskannas *f*, lyskanasow

diplomatic *adj* lyskanasek

dipper *n* molgh dhowr *f*, molghi dowr

dipstick *n* gwelen vusur *f*, gwelynni
musur

direct I *adj* didro; syth; **II** *vb*
kevarwodha

direction *n* tu *m*, tuyow

directly *adv* distowgh; hware

director *n* lewydh *m*, lewydhyon;
kevarwodher *m*, kevarwodhoryon

dirt *n* mostedhes *m*

dirty *adj* plos; strolyek; (*of liquids*)
stronk. **make dirty** *vb* mostya. **get
dirty** plosegi

disabled *adj* evredhek. **disabled
person** evredh *m*, evredhyon

disadvantage I *n* anles *m*, anlesow **II**
vb gorra yn-dann anles

disagree *vb* dissentya; disakordya

disagreement *n* disakord *m*,
disakordow

disappoint *vb* diswaytyas

disappointed *adj* diswaytys

disappointing *adj* diswaytus

disappointment *n* diswaytyans *m*,
diswaytyansow; toll *m*

disaster *n* terosa *m*, terosedhow;
myshyv *m*, myshevys. **disaster area**
terosva *f*, terosvaow

disastrous *adj* terosus

disc *n* plasen *f*, plasennow **compact
disc** *n* (*CD*) plasen arghansek *f*,
plasennow arghansek; cidi *m*, cidis

discern *vb* discernya

discharge I *n* diskargans *m*,
diskargansow **II** *vb* diskarga; (*debt*)
akwytya

disciple *n* dyskybel *m*, dyskyblon

discipline *n* dyskybeleth *f*,
dyskybelethow

disclose *vb* diskudha

disclosure *n* diskudhans *m*,
diskudhansow

discontented *adj* drog pes;
diskontentys

discount I *n* diskont *m*, diskontow **II** *vb*
diskontya

discourage *vb* digolenni

discouraging *adj* digolonnus

discover *vb* diskudha; trovya

discovery *n* diskudhans *m*,
diskudhansow

discreet *adj* doth

discriminate *vb* discernya.
discriminate against disfavera.
discriminate in favour of favera

discuss *vb* dadhla; (*have a discussion*)
omgussulya; debatya. **have a
discussion about the issue**
omgussulya a-dro dhe'n mater

discussion *n* dadhel *f*, dadhlow;
omgussulyans *m*, omgussulyansow

disdain *vb* fia

disease *n* dises *m*, disesys

disembark *vb* dilestra

disentangle *vb* digelmi; divagli

disfigure *vb* dihevelebi; hagra

disguise I *n* tollwisk *m*, tollwiskow **II**
vb tollwiska

disgust *vb* divlasa. **be disgusted**
divlasa

disgusting *adj* divlas

dish *n* (*food*) sand *m*, sandow; (*bowl*)
skudel *f*, skudellow, lester *m*, lestri;

(*saucer*) skala *m*, skalys. **wash the dishes** golghi an lestri

dishcloth *n* kweth lestri *m*, kwethow lestri

disheartened *adj* digolennys

dishonest *adj* disonest; gowek; mingow

dishonesty *n* disonester *m*

dishonour I *n* disenor *m*, disenors II *vb* disenora

dishwasher *n* jynn lestri *m*, jynnow lestri

disinfect *vb* diglevesi; disynklevya

disinfectant *n* disynklevyas *m*, disynklevysi

disinfection *n* disynklevyans *m*, disynklevyansow

dislike I *n* kas *m* II *vb* kasa; gohasa

dislocate *vb* (*a joint*) diskevelsi

dismantle *vb* didakla; diswul

dismiss *vb* gordhyllo

disobey *vb* disobaya

disorder *n* deray *m*, derays

dispatch *vb* danvon

disperse *vb* keskar; skollya a-les

dispersion *n* keskar *m*

display I *n* displetyans *m*, displetyansow II *vb* displetya

displease *vb* displesya

displeased *adj* drog pes; displesys

displeasure *n* displesour *m*, displesours; displesyans *m*

disposable *adj* (*impermanent*) towladow

dispose *vb* disposya

disprove *vb* disprevi

dispute I *n* kedrynn *f*, kedrynnow; dadhel *f*, dadhlow; bresel *f*, breselyow II *vb* kedrynna

disquiet I *n* ankres *m*; anes *m*; dises *m* II *vb* ankresya

disrupt *vb* goderri

disruptive *adj* parys dhe ania

dissatisfied *adj* drog pes

dissemble *vb* dissembla

dissent I *n* dissent *m* II *vb* dissentya

dissolve *vb* teudhi

dissonance *n* digessenyans *m*, digessenyansow

distaff *n* kygel *f*, kygelyow

distance I pellder *m*, pellderyow II *vb* **distance oneself** omdenna; avoydya; ombellhe. **long-distance call** galow a-bell *m*, galowyow a-bell

distant *adj* pell

distinct *adj* diblans

distinction *n* (*difference*) dyffrans *m*, dyffransow; (*honour*) bri *f*

distinctive *adj* arbennek; diblans

distinctiveness *n* diblanseth *f*

distress I *n* grev *m*, grevow; reudh *m* II *vb* grevya; reudhi

distressed *adj* reudhys; (*med*) yn ahwer

distressing *adj* grevus

distribute *vb* lesranna

distribution *n* lesrannans *m*, lesranansow

distributor *n* lesrennyas *m*, lesrenysi

district *n* ranndir *m*, ranndiryow; kost *m*, kostys; pastel vro *f*, pastellow bro

disturb *vb* ankresya; ankombra; ania

disturbance *n* ankresyans *m*, ankresyansow

ditch I *n* kleudh *m*, kleudhyow II *vb* (*dig a trench*) kleudhya; (*discard*) hepkor; (*crash-land in water*) dowra

ditty *n* kanik *f*, kanigow

dive I *n* (*submersion*) sedh *m*, sedhow; (*plunge*) lamm penn yn-rag *m*, lammow penn yn-rag; (*disreputable nightclub etc.*) toll *m*, tell (*colloq*) II *vb* (*submerge*) sedhi; (*plunge*) lamma y'n dowr; (*plummet*) kodha

diver *n* sedher *m*, sedhoryon. **deep-sea diver** *n* sedher downvor *m*, sedhoryon dhownvor

divergent *adj* dyffrans

diverse *adj* divers (+*sg. or pl. noun*)

diversity *n* diversita *m*, diversitys

divert *vb* didreylya

divide *vb* ranna. **divided by** rynnys gans

divided *adj* rynnys

division *n* rannans *m*, ranansow

divorce I *n* didhemedhyans *m*, didhemedhyansow; torrva demedhyans *f*, torrvaow demedhyans **II** *vb* didhemedhi

divorced *adj* didhemedhys

dizziness *n* penn-dro *f*

dizzy *adj* pennskav; penn-dro

do *vb* gul. **do for** distrui. **do in** ladha. **do time** spena termyn y'n toll. **do up** fastya. **do without** hepkor

dock (1) *n* (*for ships*) kay *m*, kayys, kayow; porth lestri *n.m.* **docks** *n* porth klos *m*

dock (2) *n* (*plant*) tavolen *f*, tavolennow; tavol *coll*

dockyard *n* lestriva *f*, lestrivaow

doctor *n* (*title*) doktour *m*, doktours; (*medical*) medhek *m*, medhogyon. **doctorate** doktourieth *f*, doktouriethow. **doctor's surgery** *n* medhegva *f*, medhegvaow

doctrine *n* dyskas *m*, dyskasow

document *n* skrif *m*, skrifow; skrifen *f*, skrifennow

documentary *adj* dogvennek

dodder *n* (*devil's guts; witches hair*) safran an Jowl *coll*

dodgems *n* kerri bonk *pl*

dog *n* ki *m*, keun. **male dog** *n* gorgi *m*, gorgeun. **female dog** *n* gast *f*, gesti

dog's mercury *n* mergherles fug *m*

dogfish *n* morgi *m*, morgeun

dole *n* (*benefit*) dol *m*

doll *n* dolli *f*, dolliow; popet *m*, popetow. **doll's house** *n* chi dolli *m*, chiow dolli, treven dolli

dolmen *n* krommlegh *f*, krommleghow

dolphin *n* morhogh *m*, morhoghes; pyffyer *f*, pyffyers

domain *n* arlotteth *f*, arlottethow

domestic *adj* a'n mayni. **domestic politics** politegieth a-bervedh *f*

domesticate *vb* hwarhe

domesticated *adj* hwarhes

dominant *adj* gwarthevyek

dominate *vb* gwarthevya

domination *n* gwarthevyans *m*, gwarthevyansow

dominion *n* mestrynses *m*

domino *n* domino *m*

donate *vb* argevri

donation *n* argevro *m*, argevrohow; doneson *m*, donesonow

done *adj* gwrys. **done for** diswrys

donkey *n* asen *m*, asenes

donor *n* riyas *m*, riysi. **organ donor** riyas organow *m*, riysi organow

doodle I *n* skryblans *m*, skryblansow **II** *vb* skrybla

doom I *n* (*judgment*) breus *f*, breusow; (*fate*) terros *m*, terrosow **II** *vb* breusi

door *n* daras *m*, darasow. **door handle** *n* dornla daras *m*, dornleow daras. **through a door** war dharas

dormant *adj* yn kosk; heb difuna

dormitory *n* koskti *m*, kosktiow

dormouse *n* hunegen *f*, hungennow; hunek *coll*

dosage *n* dognyans *m*, dognyansow

dose I *n* dogen *m*, dognow **II** *vb* dognya

dot *n* dyjyn *m*, dyjynnow. **dots per inch (DPI)** dyjynnow an veusva *pl*

dote *vb* dotya

double I *adj* dewblek **II** *vb* dewblekhe

doubt I *n* dout *m*, doutys; mar *m* **II** *vb* doutya. **without doubt** heb dhout; heb mar

doubtful *adj* doutus

doubtless *adv* heb dhout; heb falladow

dough *n* toos *m*

doughnut *n* knowen doos *f*, knowennow toos; know toos *coll*

dove *n* kolom *f*, kelemmi

down (1) I *adv* yn-nans; war-woles; dhe'n dor **II** *vb* (*food or drink*) lenki.

don't let yourself down! gwith dha hanow da rag meth. **down below** a-barth a-woles. **down-to-earth** heb flows. **down under** yn Ostrali. **dumb down** talsogha. **hand down** treuskorra; transmyttya. **put down** *vb* (*animal*) euthanisya. (*name*) ri y hanow. **shout down** usa a-dreus

down (2) *n* (*fine feathers*) mannbluven *f*, mannbluv

down (3) *n* (*moorland*) goon *f*, gonyow

downfall *n* terros *m*, terrosow

downhill I *adj* war-nans **II** *adv* war-nans

download I *n* iskarg *m*, iskargow **II** *vb* iskarga

downpour *n* hager-gowas *f*, hager-gowasow

downstairs *adv* a-woles; war-woles **downwards** *adv* war-woles; war-nans

dozen *n* dewdhek *m*, dewdhegow

drab *adj* disliw

drag I *n* (*pull*) drayl *m*, draylyow; (*cigarette*) tenn *m*, tennow; (*women's clothes*) kadys *f* **II** *vb* draylya. **an awful drag** ankombrynsi euthyk *m*; **drag net** tennros *f*, tennrosow. **drag oneself along** slynkya. **drag one's feet** delatya. **drag queen** arlodhes kadys *f*, arlodhesow kadys

dragon *n* dragon *f*, dragones

dragonfly *n* nader margh *f*, nadres margh

drama *n* drama *m*, dramas

drama studio *n* studhla drama *m*, studhleow drama

dramatic *adj* dramasek

dramatist *n* dramasydh *m*, dramasydhyon

draw *vb* (*sketch*) delinya; (*pull*) tenna

drawer *n* tregyn *m*, tregynnow; trog-tenna *m*, trogow-tenna

drawing *n* delinyans *m*, delinynansow. **drawing pin** *n* pynn meus *m*, pynnow meus

dream I *n* hunros *m*, hunrosow **II** *vb* hunrosa

dregs *n* godhes *m*

dress I *n* pows *f*, powsyow **II** *vb* gwiska. **dress up** omwiska. **dressing gown** *n* mantel nos *f*, mantylli nos. **fancy dress** *n* gwisk kewewi *m*. **get dressed** omwiska

dresser *n* (*furniture*) lestrier *m*, lestrieryow

drift I *n* dryftyans *m*, dryftyansow **II** *vb* dryftya. **continental drift** dryftyans an brastiryow *m*

driftwood *n* dryftbren *m*, dryftbrennyer

drill I *n* tarder *m*, terder **II** *vb* telli; tardra

drink I *n* diwes *m*, diwosow **II** *vb* eva; (*go drinking*) diwessa. **drinking straw** *n* kalaven-eva *f*, kalavennow-eva

drinkable *adj* evadow

drip (1) *vb* devera

drip (2) *n* (*intravenous therapy; med*) deverell dre wythien *f*, deverellow dre wythien

drive *vb* lewya; lewa; (*animals*) drivya. **drive insane** muskegi; varya. **drive out** helghya; hembronk yn-mes; drivya yn-mes.

drivel I *n* (*drool*) glavor *m*; (*nonsense*) flows *m* **II** *vb* (*drool*) glaveri; (*talk nonsense*) leverel flows

driver *n* lewyer *m*, lewyoryon. **bus driver** *n* lewyer kyttrin *m*, lewyoryon kyttrin. **racing driver** *n* lewyer-resek *m*, lewyoryon-resek. **train driver** *n* lewyer tren *m*, lewyoryon tren. **driverless car** karr heb lewyer *m*, kerri heb lewyer

dromedary *n* dremedal *m*, dremedales

drone *n* sudronen *f*, sudronennow; sudron *coll*

drool I *n* glavor *m* **II** *vb* glaveri

drop I *n* (*fluid*) banna *m*, banaghow; (*of rain*) glawen *f*, glawennow **II** *vb* gasa kodha; droppya

drought *n* seghter *m*, seghteryow

drown *vb* beudhi

drug *n* drogg *m* droggys; droug *m* drougow

druid *n* drewydh *m*, drewydhyon

druidical *adj* drewedhek

drum I *n* tabour *m*, tabouryow II *vb* gweskel tabour

drummer *n* tabourer *m*, tabouroryon

drunk I *adj* medhow II *vb* **get drunk** omvedhwi. **make drunk** medhwi

drunkard *n* penn medhow *m*, pennow medhow

drunkenness *n* medhwynsi *m*; medhwenep *m*

dry I *adj* sygh II *vb* segha. **dry out** desegha. **dry up** desegha; krina.

duchess *n* dukes *f*, dukesow

duchy *n* duketh *f*, dukethow

duck *n* hos *m*, heyji

duckling *n* heyjik *m*, heyjigow

duckweed *n* kenn lynn *coll*; kelynnen *f* kelynnennow; kellyn *coll*

duct *n* piben *f*, pibennow

due *adj* gwaytys

duke *n* duk *m*, dukys

dull *adj* (*blunt*) sogh; (*insipid*) difreth; (*not bright*) disliw; (*unintelligent*) talsogh

dullard *n* (*offensive*) talsogh *m*, talsoghyon

dumb *adj* **see: mute**

dumb down *vb* talsogha

dumpling *n* pellen *f*, pellennow

dune *n* tewyn *m*, tewynnow

dung *n* kawgh *m*

dunnock *n* (*hedge sparrow*) golvan ke *m*, golvanes ke

durable *adj* duryadow

during *prp* dres

dusk *n* tewlwolow *m*; mo *m*, moyow

dusky *adj* godewl

dust I *n* ponn *m*; doust *m*; polter *m*, polteryow II *vb* (*remove dust*) diboltra; (*sprinkle*) poltra

dustbin *n* atalgist *f*, atalgistyow

duster *n* kweth ponn *f*, kwethow ponn

dustpan *n* padel bonn *f*, padellow ponn

dusty *adj* ponnek

Dutch I *adj* iseldiryek II *n* (*language*) Iseldiryek *m*; Iseldiryas *m*, Iseldirysi

duty *n* (*responsibility*) dever *m*, deverow; (*tax*) toll *f*, tollow

duvet *n* kolghes *f*, kolghesow

dwarf *n* korr *m*, korryon

dwell *vb* triga

dweller *n* triger *m*, trigoryon

dwelling *n* annedh *f*, anedhow; trigva *f*, trigvaow. **winter dwelling** gwavos *f*, gwavosow

dye I *n* liw *m*, liwyow II *vb* liwa

dyed *adj* liwys; liwek

dyer's greenweed *n* korrvanadhel owr *coll*

dyke *n* (*embankment*) tommen *f*, tomennow; (*slang: lesbian*) lesbianes *f*, lesbianesow

dynamic *adj* dynamek

dynamics *n* dynamegieth *f*

dynamite I *n* dynamit *m* II *vb* dynamitya

dynamo *n* dynamo *m*, dynamoyow

dyslexia *n* (*med*) dysleksia *m*. **a person with dyslexia** person gans dysleksia

dysmorphia *n* (*med*) dysmorfia *m*

E

each *adj* pub; kettep
eager *adj* freth. **I am eager to meet her**
  mall yw genev hy metya
eagerness *n* frethter *m*; mall *m*; terder
  m
eagle *n* er *m*, eryon, eres
ear *n* skovarn *f*, skovornow, *dl*
  diwskovarn
earl *n* yurl *m*, yurlys
early *adv* a-varr; a-brys. **not earlier**
  nahyns
earn *vb* dendyl
earnest *adj* diwysyk; sad; sevur
earnings *n* gober *m*, gobrow
earphones *n* skovarnigow munys *pl*
earring *n* bysow skovarn *m*, bysowyer
  skovarn; skinen *f*, skinennow
Earth *n* (*planet*) (an) Norvys *m*
earth *n* dor *m*, doryow
earthquake *n* dorgrys *m*, dorgrysyow
earthwork *n* dorge *m*, dorgeow
earthworm *n* bulugen *f*, bulugennow;
  buluk *coll*
earwig *n* gorlosten *f*, gorlostennow;
  gorlost *coll*
ease I *n* es *m* II *vb* esya; heuthhe. **at
  ease** attes. **be at ease** omjersya. **put at
  ease** esya. **make ill at ease** disesya
easel *n* margh-skrifa *m*, mergh-skrifa
easier *adj* esya
east *n* est *m*; howldrehevel *m*
Easter *n* Pask *m*. **at Easter** war Bask
easterly *adj* a-dhia an est
eastern *adj* a'n est; a'n howldrehevel
eastwards *adj* war-tu ha'n est
easy *adj* es; (*comfortable*) attes
eat *vb* dybri
eating disorder *n* disordyr dybri *m*
echo I *n* (*general*) dasson *m*,
  dassonyow; (*of voice*) daslev *m*,
  daslevow II *vb* dasseni
eclipse *n* difyk *m*, difygyow

ecologist *n* ekologydh *m*,
  ekologydhyon
ecology *n* ekologieth *f*
economic *adj* erbysek
economical *adj* erbysus
economics *n* erbysieth *f*
economise *vb* erbysi; sparya
economist *n* erbysydh *m*, erbysydhyon;
  ekonomydh *m*, ekonomydhyon
economy *n* erbysiedh *m*; ekonomieth *f*
ecstasy *n* transyek *m*; gorawen *f*
ecstatic *adj* gorawenus
-ed *sffx* -ys
edge *n* amal *m*, emlow
edgy *adj* ownek; frommus
edible *adj* dybradow
edit *vb* (*publication*) pennskrifa;
  pareusi; (*alter*) chanjya; golegi
edition *n* dyllans *m*, dyllansow
editor *n* (*person*) pennskrifer *m*,
  pennskriforyon. (*software*) chanjyell *f*,
  chanjyellow
editorial *n* pennskrif *m*, pennskrifow
educate *vb* adhyski; ri dyskans (dhe²)
educated *adj* dyskys
education *n* adhyskans *m*,
  adhyskansow
educational *adj* adhyskansek
eel *n* sylli *f*, syllies
effect I *n* effeyth *m*, effeythyow II *vb*
  effeythi. **Doppler effect** effeyth
  Doppler *m*. **greenhouse effect** effeyth
  chi gweder *m*
effective *adj* effeythus
efficiency *n* effeythadewder *m*
efficient *adj* effeythadow
effort *n* assay *m*, assays
e.g. *abbrev* r.e.; rag ensampel
egg *n* oy *m*, oyow. **egg cup** hanaf oy *m*,
  hanafow oy; **egg white** gwynn oy *m*,
  gwynnow oy; **egg yolk** melyn oy *m*,
  melynyow oy. **free range-egg** oy

frankres *m*, oyow frankres. **lay eggs** dedhwi. **not worth an egg** ny dal oy

Egypt *top* Ejyp *m*

Egyptian I *adj* ejyptek **II** *n* (*language*) Ejyptek *m*; (*person*) Ejyptyon *m*, Ejyptyonyon

eight *num* eth

eighteen *num* etek

eighteenth *num* etegves; *abbrev* 18ves

eighth *num* ethves; *abbrev* 8ves

eightieth *num* peswar ugensves; 80ves

eighty *num* peswar ugens

eisteddfod *n* esedhvos *m*, esedhvosow

either... or *cnj* po... po; poken... po

eject *vb* estewlel

elastic *adj* gwedhyn; elastek

elasticity *n* gwedhynder *m*, gwedhynderow

elbow *n* elin *m*, elinyow, *dl* dewelin

elder I *adj* kottha; henavek **II** *n* (*person*) henavek *m*, henavogyon **III** *n* (*tree*) skawen *f*, skawennow; skaw *coll*

elderberry wine *n* gwin skaw *m*

elder, ground *n* skaw dor *coll*

elderly I *adj* henavek **II** *n* tus henavek *pl*

elder tree *n* skawen *f*, skawennow; skaw *coll*

eldest *adj* an kottha

elect *vb* etholi

elected *adj* etholys

election *n* etholans *m*, etholansow

elector *n* etholer *m*, etholoryon

electric *adj* tredanek. **electric current** fros tredan *m*, frosow tredan

electrical *adj* tredanel

electrician *n* tredaner *m*, tredanoryon

electricity *n* tredan *m*

electrify *vb* tredanhe

electron *n* elektron *m*, elektrons

electronic *adj* elektronek

element *n* elven *f*, elvennow

elemental *adj* elvennel

elementary *adj* elvennek

elephant *n* olifans *m*, olifanses

elevator *n* yskynnell *f*, yskynellow

eleven *num* unnek

eleventh *num* unnegves; *abbrev* 11ves

elf *n* korrigan *m*, korriganes

eliminate *vb* defendya; dilea

elimination *n* dileans *m*, dileansow

elk *n* kowrgarow *m*, kowrgerwys

ellipse *n* hirgylgh *m*, hirgylghyow

elliptical *adj* hirgylghek

elm *n* elowen *f*, elowennow; elow *coll*. **elm grove** elowek *f*. elowegi

else I *adv* ken **II** *cnj* poken

email I *n* ebost *m*, ebostow. **email address** trigva ebost *f* **II** *vb* ebostya

embankment *n* tommen *f*, tomennow

embarassment *n* negh *m*, neghow; ankombrynsi *m*

embarrassed *adj* ankombrys

embarrassing *adj* ankombrus; methus

embassy *n* kanaseth *f*, kanasethow; (*building*) kanatti *m*, kanattiow

emblem *n* arwodh *f*, arwodhyo

emblematic *adj* arwodhek

embrace I *n* byrlans *m*, byrlansow **II** *vb* byrla

embroider *vb* brosya

embroidery *n* brosweyth *m*

emerald *n* (*gem*) gwerem *m*, gweremmow

emerge *vb* dos yn-mes; sordya

emergency *n* goredhom *m*, goredhommow. **emergency exit** mallborth *m*, mallborthow

emerging *adj* usi ow sordya

emigrant *n* divroyas *m*, divroysi

emigrate *vb* omdhivroa

emigration *n* omdhivroans *m*, omdhivroansow

eminent *adj* flour

emotion *n* amovyans *m*, amovyansow

emotionless *adj* diamovyans

emperor *n* emperour *m*, emperours

emphasis *n* poslev *m*, poslevow; poos *m*, posow

emphasise *vb* posleva

empire *n* emperoureth *f,* emperourethow

employ *vb* arveth

employee *n* arvethesik *m,* arvethesigyon

employer *n* arvethor *m,* arvethoryon

employment *n* soodh *f,* sodhow

empress *n* emperes *f,* emperesow

emptiness *n* gwakter *m*

empty I *adj* gwag **II** *vb* gwakhe

empty-headed *adj* penn-koog

enable *vb* gallosegi

enamel I *n* emayl *m;* enamel *m* **II** *vb* emaylhe; enamelhe

encamp *vb* kampya; gwersella

encampment *n* kampva *f,* kampvaow; gwersellans *m,* gwersellansow

enchant *vb* husa; gorhana

enchanted *adj* husys

enchantment *n* hus *m,* husow

encircle *vb* kylghya

enclose *vb* degea. **enclose with a hedge or fence** *vb* keas; parkya

enclosed *adj* klos

enclosure *n* garth *m,* garthow; park *m,* parkow; hay *f,* hayow

encode *vb* kodenni

encounter I *n* metyans *m,* metyansow **II** *vb* metya (orth); dos erbynn; dierbynna

encyclopaedia *n* godhoniador *m,* godhoniadoryon

end I *n* diwedh *m,* diwedhow; penn *m,* pennow; fin *f,* finyow **II** *vb* diwedha; finsya. **dead end** fordh dhall *f,* fordhow dall. **end to end** hys-ha-hys

endanger *vb* peryllya. **endangered species** eghen beryllys *f,* eghennow peryllys

endangered *adj* peryllys

endeavour I *vb* assaya **II** *n* attent *m,* attentys

ended *adj* gorfennys

ending *n* diwedhva *f,* diwedhvaow

endless *adj* didhiwedh; dibenn

endurance *n* perthyans *m,* perthyansow

endure *vb* (*last*) pesya; (*tolerate*) perthi; durya; pargh

enemy *n* eskar *m,* eskerens; envi *m*

energetic *adj* nerthek

energy *n* nerth *m,* nerthow, nerthyow; (*physics*) nerthedh *m,* nerthedhow

engaged *adj* (*to be married*) ambosys

engagement *n* (*to be married*) ambos demedhyans *m,* ambosow demedhyans

engine *n* jynn *m,* jynnys, jynnow. **engine house** *n* jynnji *m,* jynnjiow

engineer *n* ynjynor *m,* ynjynoryon

engineering *n* ynjynorieth *f*

England *top* Pow Sows *m;* Pow an Sowson *m*

English I *adj* sowsnek **II** *n* (*language*) Sowsnek *m.* **English speaker** *n* Sowsneger *m,* Sowsnegoryon

Englishman *n* Sows *m,* Sowson

Englishwoman *n* Sowses *f,* Sowsesow

engrave *vb* gravya

enhance *vb* (*improve*) gwellhe; (*increase*) ynkressya

enjoy *vb* bos da gans. **enjoy oneself** omlowenhe. **enjoy yourself!** omlowenha! **I enjoy** Da yw genev

enjoyable *adj* heudhadow

enjoyment *n* lowender *m*

enlarge *vb* brashe

enlighten *vb* golowi

enlightenment *n* golowyans *m*

enmity *n* avi *m;* eskarogeth *f,* eskarogethow; eskerensa *f*

enormity *n* kowrogeth *f,* kowrogethow

enormous *adj* kowrek

enough *adj* lowr. **good enough** da lowr

enquire *vb* govyn

enquiry *n* govynadow *m.* **enquiry office** *n* govynva *f,* govynvaow

enrage *vb* serri; gorra konnar yn

enrich *vb* rychhe

ensure *vb* surhe

enter *vb* entra
enterprise *n* aventur *m*, aventuryow
entertain *vb* didhana
entertainer *n* didhaner *m*,
  didhanoryon
entertaining *adj* didhan
entertainment *n* didhan *m*; (*an*
  entertainment) didhanedh *m*
enthusiasm *n* tan y'n golon *m*
enthusiastic *adj* gwresek; krisek
entice *vb* dynya
entire *adj* dien; kowal
entirely *adv* oll; kowal; yn tien
entomology *n* hweskeronieth *f*
entrance *n* entrans *m*, entransow
envelope *n* maylyer *m*, maylyers
envious *adj* avius
environment *n* kerghynnedh *m*,
  kerghynedhow
environmental *adj* kerghynedhel
environmentalist *n* kerghynedhor *m*,
  kerghynedhoryon
environs *n* kerghyn *m*, kerghynnow
envy *n* avi *m*
enzyme *n* ensaym *m*, ensaymyow
epic I *adj* epyk II *n* epyk *m*, epygys
epilepsy *n* (*med*) epilepsi *m*
epistle *n* epystyl *m*, epystlys
epoch *n* osweyth *f*, osweythyow; oos *m*,
  osow
equal I *adj* par; kehaval II *n* par *m*,
  parow. without equal dibarow
equality *n* parder *m*, parderyow
equate *vb* keheveli
equation *n* kehavalen *f*, kehavalennow
equator *n* kehysedh *m*, kehysedhow
equilibrium *n* kespos *m*, kesposow;
  komposter *m*, komposteryow
equinox *n* kehysnos *f*, kehysnosow
equip *vb* darbari; hernessya
equipment *n* daffar *m*. put on
  equipment hernessya
equipped *adj* darbarys
equivalent I *adj* kemmys. equivalent
  to kemmys ha

era *n* osweyth *f*, osweythyow; oos *m*,
  osow
eradicate *vb* diwreydhya
erase *vb* defendya
eraser *n* rutyer *m*, rutyeryow
erasure *n* defendyans *m*,
  defendyansow
erect I *adj* a'y sav; sevys; serth II *vb*
  sevel; drehevel
erection *n* drehevyans *m*,
  drehevyansow
erosion *n* esknians *m*
erotic *adj* erotek
err *vb* (*in deed*) kammwul; (*in thought*)
  kammdybi
errand *n* negys *m*, negysyow. go on an
  errand mones negys
erroneous *adj* kamm
error *n* kamm *m*, kammow; (*in deed*)
  kammwrians *m*, kammwriansow; (*in*
  thought) kammdybyans *m*,
  kammdybyansow
erudite *adj* dyskys
erupt *vb* tardha
eruption *n* tardhans *m*, tardhansow
eryngo *n* (*sea holly*) morgelyn *coll*
-(e)s *sffx* (*plural suffix*) -ys
escalator *n* jynn-yskynna *m*,
  jynnys-yskynna, jynnow-yskynna
escallonia *n* kewydh rudh *coll*
escape I *n* diank, diankow II *vb* diank;
  skeusi; skapya. escape from skeusi
  rag. fire escape, escape route
  fordh-skapya *f*, fordhow-skapya
esoteric *adj* esoterek; kevrinek
especially *adv* yn arbennek
espionage *n* aspians *m*, aspiansow
essay *n* assay *m*, assays
essence *n* sugen *m*, sugenyow
essential *adj* a res; essensek
essentially *adv* yn essensek
establish *vb* selya; fastya; fondya
establishment *n* fondyans *m*,
  fondyansow; solva *f*, solvaow

estate *n* stat *m*, statys; (*property*) perghenogeth *m*. **feudal estate** fe *m*, feow. **housing estate** trevbark *m*, trevbarkow

esteem **I** *n* bri *f*; breus ughel *f*; estem *m* **II** *vb* estemya

estimate **I** *n* (*numerical*) dismygriv *m*, dismygrivow **II** *vb* estemya

Estonia *top* Estoni *f*

Estonian **I** *adj* estoniek **II** *n* (*language*) Estoniek; (*person*) Estonian *m*, Estonians

estuary *n* heyl *m*, heylyow

etc. *abbrev* (*et cetera*) h.e.; hag erel

eternal *adj* heb dhiwedh; dibenn; bythkwethek

ethereal *adj* digorf

ethical *adj* ethegel

ethics *n* ethek *f*

ethnic *adj* ethnek. **ethnic cleansing** karth ethnek *m*, karthyon ethnek

ethnicity *n* hil *f*, hilyow

eunuch *n* spadhesik *m*, spadhesigyon

Europe *top* Europa *m*

European **I** *adj* europek **II** *n* European *m*, Europeanyon. **European Parliament** Eurosenedh *m*. **European Union (EU)** Unyans Europek (UE) *m*

euthanise *vb* euthanisya

evade *vb* kavanskeusa; (*evade capture*) skeusi

evaluate *vb* arvreusi

evaluation *n* arvreusyans *m*, arvreusyansow

evaporate *vb* ethenna

even **I** *adj* (*balanced*) kompes; (*numbers*) parow **II** *adv* hogen. **get even** diala

evening *n* gorthugher *m*, gorthugherow. **evening time** gorthugherweyth. **this evening** haneth. **last evening** nyhewer

event *n* hwarvos *m*, hwarvosow; darvos *m*, darvosow; kentel *m*, kentelyow

eventually *adv* wortiwedh; wostiwedh

ever **I** *adj* prest **II** (*in the past*) bythkweth; bykken; bynari; bynitha; (*in the present or future*) nevra

evergreen *adj* bythlas

everlasting *adj* bythkwethek

evermore *adv* bys vykken; bys vynari; rag nevra vynitha

every *adj* pub; kettep. **every day** pub dydh; keniver dydh. **on every occasion** pub kentel. **every time** pub torn

everybody *prn* peub; pubonan; pub huni; keniver

everyone *prn* pubonan; peub; keniver

everything *prn* puptra

everywhere *adv* pub le

evidence *n* dustuni *m*

evident *adj* playn; apert

evil *adj* drog; tebel; tebel-. **evil person** *n* tebel *m*, tebeles

evoke *vb* sordya

ewe *n* davas *f*, deves. **ewe lamb** *n* ones *f*, onesow

exact *adj* kewar

exactly *adv* poran

exaggerate *vb* gorliwa; mos re bell

exaggeration *n* gorliwans *m*, gorliwansow

examination *n* apposyans *m*, apposyansow. **oral examination** apposyans war anow *m*, apposyansow war anow. **medical examination** hwithrans medhek *m*, hwithransow medhek. **written examination** apposyans skrifys *m*, apposyansow skrifys

examine *vb* eksamnya; (*test by questions*) apposya

examiner *n* arholyas *m*, arholysi; eksamnyer *m*, eksamnyoryon

example *n* ensampel *m*, ensamplys, ensamplow

excavate *vb* palas; kleudhya; kowa

excavation *n* kowans *m*, kowansow

excellent *adj* pur dha; kooth

except *cnj* marnas; saw; a-der
exception *n* namm *m*, nammow
exceptional *adj* ankoth
excessively *adv* re
exchange I *n* keschanj *m*, keschanjyow **II** *vb* keschanjya
excite *vb* yntana
excited *adj* yntanys
exciting *adj* yntanus
exclude *vb* keas mes; ekskludya
exclusive *adj* ekskludus
excommunicate *vb* emskemuna
excrement *n* kawgh *m*
excretion *n* kawghans *m*
excuse I *n* askus *m*, askusyow **II** *vb* askusya. **excuse oneself** omaskusya
execute *vb* eksekutya; (*carry out*) kowlwul
execution *n* eksekutyans *m*, eksekutyansow
exercise I *n* assay *m*, assays; ober *m*, oberow; praktis *m*, praktisyow **II** *vb* (*practise*) praktisya; (*physical*) omoberi; (*try out*) assaya; (*test oneself*) omassaya
exhaust I *n* gorvok *m*, gorvogow **II** *vb* spena. **exhaust pipe** *n* piben worvok *f*, pibennow gorvok
exhausted *adj* spenys
exhibit *n* diskwedhyn *f*, diskwedhynnow
exhibition *n* diskwedhyans *m*, diskwedhyansow
exhort *vb* keski; ynia
exist *vb* bos; eksistya
existence *n* bosva *f*, bosvaow
exit *n* (*e.g. of an actor*) kwytyans *m*, kwytyansow; (*of a building*) mesporth *m*, mesporthow. **fire exit** mesporth tan *m*, mesporthow tan. **emergency exit** mallborth *m*, mallborthow
exotic *adj* eksotek
expand *vb* efani; lesa; (*intransitive*) omlesa

expansion *n* efanyans *m*; lesans *m*, lesansow; omlesans *m*, omlesansow
expansive *adj* omlesus
expect *vb* (*hope for*) gwaytyas; (*assume*) desevos
expected *adj* gwaytys
expel *vb* estewlel
expelled *adj* estewlys
expense *n* kost *m*, kostys, kostow
expensive *adj* kostek
experience I *n* prevyans *m*, prevyansow; eksperyans *m*, eksperyansow **II** *vb* previ
experienced *adj* eksperyansys
experiment I *n* arbrev *m*, arbrovow **II** *vb* arbrevi; prevya
experimental *adj* arbrovel
expert *n* konnyk *m*, konygyon
expertise *n* konegeth *f*
expire *vb* diwedha; (*breathe out*) anella mes; (*die*) merwel
expiry *n* diwedhans *m*, diwedhansow. **date of expiry** dedhyas diwedh *m*, dedhyasow diwedh
explain *vb* styrya; displegya; ygeri
explanation *n* styryans *m*, styryansow; displegyans *m*, displegyansow
explanatory *adj* displegyansek; styryansek
explode *vb* tardha
explosion *n* tardh *m*, tardhow
explosive I *n* devnydh-tardha *m*, devnydhyow-tardha **II** *adj* hedardh; tardhadow
export I *n* esporth *m*, esporthow **II** *vb* esperthi
expose *vb* diskudha
exposed *adj* diglos
express I *adj* ekspres, uskis **II** *vb* (*put in words; state*) meneges; gorra yn geryow; (*squeeze out*) gwaska yn-mes. **express delivery** livreson uskis *m*, livresons uskis. **express purpose** towl unnik *m*. **express train** tren uskis *m*, trenow uskis

expression *n* (*of speech*) lavar *m*,
lavarow; (*on face*) semlant *m*, semlans
extend *vb* ystyn
extended *adj* ystynnys
extension *n* ystynnans *m*, ystynansow
extent *n* hys *m*
exterior I *adj* a-ves II *n* tu a-ves *m*
external *adj* a-ves
extinguish *vb* difudhi
extinguisher *n* difudhell *f*, difudhellow
extra I *adj* moy II *adv* moy; dres henna
extraordinary *adj* dres eghen; koynt
extreme *adj* pella; diwettha
extremely *adv* fest; dres eghen; dres
musur
extremism *n* seveneleth *f*
extremist *n* sevenelyas *m*, sevenelysi

eye I *n* lagas *m*, lagasow, *dl* dewlagas II
vb lagatta. **private eye** helerghyas
privedh *m*, helerghysi brivedh. **turn a
blind eye** skonya gweles. **one-eyed**
adj unlagasek
eyeball *n* aval lagas *m*, avalow lagas
eyebright *n* kannlagas *m*
eyebrow *n* abrans *m*, abransow, *dl*
dewabrans
eyelash *n* blewen lagas *f*, blewennow
lagas; blew lagas *coll*
eyelid *n* kroghen lagas *f*, kreghyn lagas
eye-liner *n* pyncel lagas *m*, pyncels
lagas
eye-shadow *n* liw lagas *m*, liwyow
lagas
eyesore *n* hakter *m*

F

fable *n* henhwedhel *m*, henhwedhlow
fabric *n* gwias *m*, gwiasow
fabulous *adj* marthys; anethek
fabulously *adv* marthys
facade *n* talenep *m*, talenebow
face I *n* bejeth *f*, bejethow; enep *m*,
enebow; fas *m*, fassow; greuv *m*,
greuvow II *vb* enebi. **face down** gul
maystri war[2]. **face paint** paynt bejeth
m, payntys bejeth, payntow bejeth.
face up to sevel orth goheles. **foolish
face** folenep *m*, folenebow. **fly in
the face of** erya. **keep a straight face**
sevel orth hwerthin. **save face** sawya
fas
facility *n* (*talent*) roas *m*, roasow;
(*equipment*) komodyta *m*, komodytys;
(*amenity*) isframweyth *m*
facing *prp* a-dal
facsimile *n* eylskrif *m*, eylskrifow
fact *n* feth *m*, fethow; fakt *m*, faktys
factor *n* elven *f*, elvennow
factory *n* gweythva *f*, gweythvaow

factual *adj* fethyel; gwiryonedhek
faculty (*mental*) teythi *pl*; (*university*)
kevasran *f*, kevasrannow
fade *vb* disliwa
faeces *n* kawgh *m*
fail I *n* fall *m*; falladow *m*, falladowyow
II *vb* fyllel; difygya. **fail somebody**
fyllel dhe[2]. **without fail** heb falladow;
heb fyllel
failing *n* defowt *m*, defowtow
failure *n* fall *m*; falladow *m*,
falladowyow; defowt *m*, defowtow
faint I *adj* gwann; faynt II *n* klamder *m*,
klamderyow III *vb* klamdera. *adj*
liable to faint, feeling faint
klamderek
fair (1) *adj* (*attractive*) teg; gwynn;
(*colouring*) melyn; (*just*) ewn;
resnadow
fair (2) *n* (*fayre*) fer *m*, feryow; (*feast*)
gool *m*, golyow
fairground *n* ferla *m*, ferleow
fairly *adv* (*equitably*) yn ewn

(*reasonably*) nebes

fairness *n* ewnhynseth *f*; ewnder *m*

fairy *n* spyrys *m*, spyrysyon; fay *f*, fayys. **fairy tale** hwedhel a'n dus vyghan *m*, hwedhlow a'n dus vyghan

faith *n* fydh *f*, fedhyow; fay *m*

faithful *adj* len; lel

faithfully *adv* yn lel. **yours faithfully** yn lel

faithless *adj* dislen

fake I *adj* fug II *vb* fugya

falcon *n* falghun *m*, falghunes

fall I *n* kodh *m*, kodhow II *vb* kodha. **fall apart** diskara. **fall back on** omskoodhya war². **fall behind** kodha dhelergh. **fall down** omhweles. **fall flat** kodha yn plat. **fall for a trick** bos tollys. **fall for somebody** kara nebonan yn fol. **fall on** (*encounter*) dos erbynn; (*attack suddenly*) omsettya war². **fall out over** strivya a-dro dhe². **fall short** difygya; fyllel. **fall unconscious** klamdera

fallow *adj* (*unploughed*) anerys

false *adj* fals

falsify *vb* falshe

falter *vb* hockya

fame *n* bri *f*; gerda *m*

familiar I *adj* aswonys II *n* (*demon or spirit*) bocka dov *m*

family *n* teylu *m*, teyluyow

famous *adj* a vri; gerys-da

fan (1) I *n* (*device*) gwynsell *f*, gwynsellow II *vb* gwynsella; fanya

fan (2) *n* (*supporter*) skoodhyer *m*, skodhyoryon

fancy I *n* sians *m*, siansow II *vb* si; tybi. **fancy dress** tollwisk *m*, tollwiskow; giswisk *m*

fantastic *adj* (*imaginative*) fantasiek; (*superb*) gorwiw

fantasy *n* fantasi *m*, fantasis

far *adj* pell. **far better** milwell. **far worse** milweth

fare (1) *n* (*transportation fee*) pris viaj *m*, prisyow viaj

fare (2) *n* (*food*) boos *m*, bosow

fare (3) *vb* fara

farewell *int* farwell

farm I *n* bargen tir *m*, bargenys tir, bargennyow tir II *vb* gonis tir; amethi. **home farm** hendra *f*, hendrevow. **small farm** godrev *f*, godrevi

farmer *n* tiek *m*, tiogow

farmhouse *n* chi tiek *m*, chiow tiek, treven tiek

farming *n* ammeth *f*. **organic farming** ammeth organek *f*

farmstead *n* tre *f*, trevow; trev *coll*

farrier *n* ferror *m*, ferroryon

fart I *n* bramm *m*, bremmyn II *vb* bramma

farther *adj* pella

farthest *adj* (an) pella

fascinate *vb* dynya

fascinating *adj* dynyansek; meur y dhynyans *m*; meur hy dynyans

fascination *n* dynyans *m*, dynyansow

fascist I *adj* faskor II *n* faskor *m*, faskoryon

fashion *n* gis *m*, gisyow. **according to the fashion** herwydh an gis. **follower of fashion** holyer gis *m*, holyoryon is. **out of fashion** mes a'n gis

fashionable *adj* herwydh an gis

fast (1) *adj* uskis

fast (2) I *n* penys *m*, penysyow II *vb* penys

fasten *vb* fastya

fastidious *adj* denti

fat I *n* blonek *m*, blonegow II *adj* tew

fatal *adj* marwel

fate *n* feus *m*; destnans *m*; tenkys *f*, tenkysyow. **a hard fate** kales rann *f*

father I *n* tas *m*, tasow; sira *m*, sirys. **Father Christmas** Tas Nadelik *m* II *vb* bos tas dhe²

fatherhood *n* tasoleth *f*

father-in-law *n* hwegron *m*, hwegronyon; sira da *m*, sirys da

fatigue *n* skwithter *m*

fatten *vb* tewhe

fatty *adj* berrik

fault I *n* fowt *m*, fowtys, fowtow **II** *vb* blamya; kabli. **find fault with** blamya; kabli

favour I *n* favour *m*, favours **II** *vb* favera. *prp* **in favour of** a-barth

favourable *adj* faverus

favourite *adj* moyha kerys; drudh

fax I *n* pellskrifen *f*, pellskrifennow **II** *vb* pellskrifa

fear I *n* own *m* **II** *vb* doutya. **fear of the dark** own rag an tewolgow. **for fear** rag own; rag dout. **I shouted for fear that you would fall** my a armas rag own ty dhe godha

fearful *adj* ownek

fearless *adj* diown; kolonnek; hardh

fearlessness *n* diownekter *m*

feast I *n* gool *m*, golyow; (*convivial event, party*) kevewi *m*, kevewiow; kenwes *m*, kenwesow **II** *vb* golya. **feast-day** dy'gol *m*

feat *n* gwrians dres eghen *m*

feather *n* pluven *f*, pluvennow

feathered *adj* pluvennek

feature I *n* nas *f*, nasyow **II** *vb* omdhiskwedhes. **feature film** fylm nas *m*, fylmow nas

February *n* Hwevrer *m*; mis Hwevrer *m*; Hwevrel *m*; mis Hwevrel *m*

federal *adj* keffrysek; federal

fee *n* fe *m*, feow; gober *m*, gobrow. **parking fees** feow-parkya *pl*. **tuition fees** feow dyskans *m*

feeble *adj* difreth; gwann; ydhil

feed *vb* maga; boosa

feedback I *n* dasliv *m* **II** *vb* dasliva

feel I *n* tava *m*, tavaow **II** *vb* (*sense*) klewes; (*be aware*) omglewes; (*be of opinion*) synsi; (*touch*) tava

feeler *n* tavell *f*, tavellow; taver *m*, tavoryon

feeling *n* omglewans *m*, omglewansow

feign *vb* fugya

feint *n* fug *m*, fugyow

feldspar *n* gwrysven *m*, gwrysveyn

feline *adj* kathek; kepar ha kath

fellow *n* gwas *m*, gwesyon

fellows *n* (*peers*) hynsa *pl*

fellowship *n* kowethas *m*, kowethasow; felshyp *m*, felshyps

felon *n* felon *m*, felons

felt (*material*) *n* pali *m*

female I *n* benynreydh *f*, benynreydhow **II** *adj* benow

feminine *adj* gwregel; (*grammatical gender*) benow. **feminine noun** ger benow *m*

feminism *n* benelegorieth *f*

feminist I *n* benelegor *m*, benelegoryon **II** *adj* benelek

fence (1) I *n* (*enclosure*) kloos *f*, klosyow; ke *m*, keow **II** *vb* keas. **on the fence** (*also fig.*) war an ke

fence (2) *vb* (*swordplay*) skyrmya

fence (3) *vb* (*receive or sell stolen goods*) fensya

fennel *n* fenoghel *f*

fern *n* redenen *f*, redenennow; reden *coll*

fern, hart's tongue *n* taves karow *m*

fern, maidenhair *n* reden gols an Werghes *coll*

fern, male *n* marghredenen *f*

ferric *adj* hornek

ferry I *n* kowbal *m*, kowbalow **II** *vb* tretha. **ferry crossing** *n* kowbalhyns *m*, kowbalhensyow

ferryman *n* trethor *m*, trethoryon

fertile *adj* frothus; feyth

fester *vb* pedri

festering *adj* podredhek

festival *n* gool *m*, golyow

fetch *vb* kerghes

fetter I *n* karghar *m*, kargharow **II** *vb* karghara

feudal *adj* fewdal. **feudal estate** fe *m*, feow

fever *n* terthen *f*, terthennow. **scarlet fever** kleves kogh *m*

feverfew *n* lesderth *m*

feverish *adj* terthennek

few I *adj* boghes; nebes **II** *n* nebes *m*

fewer *adj* le

fiancé *n* gour ambosys *m*, gwer ambosys

fiancée *n* benyn ambosys *f*, benyn ambosys

fickle *adj* hedro

fiction *n* fugieth *f*

fiddle (1) I *n* (*instrument*) fyll *m*, fyllys, fyllow **II** *vb* (*play musical instrument*) fyllya

fiddle (2) I *n* (*swindle*) hyg *f*, hygow **II** *vb* hyga

fiddler *n* (*musician*) fyller *m*, fylloryon

fiddlesticks! *int* bramm an gath!

fidget *vb* fysla

fie *int* fi; agh

fief *n* fe *m*, feow

field I *n* park *m*, parkow; gwel *m*, gwelyow **II** *vb* mesya

fieldfare *n* molgh las *f*, molghi glas

fiend *n* jevan *m*, jevanow

fiendish *adj* jevanek

fierce *adj* fell; fers; goodh; gwyls; garow

fifteen *num* pymthek

fiery *adj* tanek

fifteenth *num* pymthegves; *abbrev* 15ves

fifth *num* pympes; *abbrev* 5es

fiftieth *num* hanterkansves; *abbrev* 50ves

fifty *num* hanterkans, hanterkansow; deg ha dew ugens

fig *n* figysen *f*, figysennow, figys *coll*

fight I *n* omladh *m*, omladhow **II** *vb* omladh; (*do battle*) batalyas. **fight against** batalyas orth

fighter *n* kasor *m*, kasoryon

figure I figur *m*, figurys; (*form*) furv *f*, furvow; form *m* (*f*). formys **II** *vb* figura; (*form*) furvya. **figure of speech** trop *m*, tropys. **figure out** dismygi

file (1) I *n* (*document*) restren *f*, restrennow **II** *vb* restrenna. **filing cabinet** restrenva *f*, restrenvaow. **filename** (*IT*) hanow restren *m*, henwyn restren

file (2) I *n* (*tool*) liv *f*, livyow **II** *vb* livya

fill I *n* lanwes *m*; leunder *m*; gwalgh *m* **II** *vb* lenwel; leunhe. **fill up** kollenwel. **fill with** lenwel a²; **have one's fill of** kavos y walgh a²

film I (*cinema*) fylm *m*, fylmow; (*covering*) kennen *f*, kenennow **II** *vb* (*make a film*) fylmya. **coat with film** kenna

filter I *n* sidhel *m*; sidhlow **II** *vb* sidhla

filth *n* lastedhes *m*; mostedhes *m*

filthy *adj* plos

fin *n* askel *f*, eskelli

final *adj* finek; finel

finally *adv* wortiwedh; wostiwedh

financial *adj* arghansel

find *vb* kavos. **find oneself** omgavos. **find out** dismygi

fine I *adj* (*refined*) fin; (*beautiful*) teg; (*excellent*) brav; (*healthy*) yagh **II** *n* (*penalty*) spal *m*, spalyow **III** *vb* (*penalise*) spala

finer *adj* tekka

finery *n* tekter *m*

finger *n* bys *m*, besies. **index finger** bys rag *m*, besies rag. **middle finger** bys kres *m*, besies kres. **ring finger** bys bysow *m*, besies bysow. **little finger** bys byghan *m*, besies byghan *m*

fingernail *n* ewin *m*, ewines

finish I *n* gorfen *m*, gorfennow **II** *vb* gorfenna; finsya

finished *adj* gorfennys

Finland *top* Fynndir *m*

Finn *n* Fynn *m*, Fynnys

Finnish I *adj* fynnek **II** *n* Fynnek *m*

fir tree *n* sybwydhen *f*, sybwydhennow; sybwydh *coll*

fire I *n* tan *m*, tanyow **II** *vb* (*a weapon*) tenna; (*dismiss*) gordhyllo. **fire brigade** tanlu *m*, tanluyow. **fire engine** jynn tan *m*, jynnys tan, jynnow tan. **fire escape** fordh-skapya *f*, fordhow-skapya. **on fire** gans tan

firefighter *n* tangasor *m*, tangasoryon

fireplace *n* oles *f*, olesow

firewood *n* keunysen *f*, keunysennow; *coll* keunys

firework *n* tanweythen *f*, tanweythennow; tanweyth *coll*

firm *adj* (*steadfast*) fyrv

first *num* kynsa; *abbrev* 1a. **at first** wostalleth; wortalleth. **first aid** kynweres *m*

fish I *n* pysk *m*, puskes **II** *vb* pyskessa. **fish for compliments** hwilas gormola. **fish for salmon** eghoka. **fishing boat** kok *m*, kokow. **fishing rod** gwelen-byskessa *f*, gwelynni-pyskessa. **fish market** marghas puskes *f*, marghasow puskes. **fish tank** tank puskes *m*, tankow puskes

fishbone *n* dren *m*, dreyn

fisherman *n* pyskador *m*, pyskadoryon

fish-hook *n* higen *f*, higennow

fishing boat *n* kok *m*, kokow

fishpond *n* pysklyn *m*, pysklynnow

fissure *n* fols *m*, folsyow

fist *n* dorn *m*, dornow, *dl* dewdhorn

fistful *n* dornas *m*, dornasow

fit (1) I *adj* (*suitable*) gwiw; (*healthy*) yagh **II** *vb* desedha

fit (2) *n* (*seizure; outburst*) shora *m*, shorys. **have a fit** kavos kren

fitness *n* (*suitability*) gwiwder *m*; (*physical*) yeghes korfek *m*

five *num* pymp

fix *vb* (*fasten, affix*) staga; (*repair*) ewnhe

fixed *adj* stag

fixedly *adv* stark

fizzy *adj* pik-pik

flag *n* baner *m*, baneryow, baners

flake I *n* skansen *f*, skansennow; skans *coll*; lown *m*, lownyow **II** *vb* lownya

flaky *adj* skansek; lownek

flame *n* flamm *m*, flammow; fagel *f*, faglow

flamingo *n* flamek *m*, flameges

flammable *adj* helosk; loskadow

flap I *n* lappa *m*, lappys **II** *vb* flappya

flash I *n* lughesen *f*, lughesennow **II** *vb* lughesi

flask *n* kostrel *m*, kostrels. **vacuum flask** kostrel gwakter *m*

flaskful *n* kostrelas *m*, kostrelasow

flat I *adj* plat; gwastas **II** *n* (*building*) rannji *m*, rannjiow

flatten *vb* plattya

flatter *vb* fekla

flattering *adj* fekyl

flattery *n* feklans *m*

flatulent *adj* torrwynsek

flavour *n* sawor *m*, saworyow; blas *m*, blasow

flavoured *adj* sawrys

flawless *adj* dinam

flax *n* linen *f*, linennow; lin *coll*

flay *vb* diruska

flea *n* hwannen *f*, hwanennow; hwann *coll*

flee *vb* fia; fia dhe'n fo; teghes

fleece I *n* knew *m*, knewyow **II** *vb* (*defraud*) pylla

fleet *n* lu lestri *m*, luyow lestri

flesh *n* kig *m*, kigyow. **in the flesh** yn kig yn kneus

flexibility *n* gwedhynder *m*

flexible *adj* gwedhyn; hebleth

flicker I *n* flyckrans *m*, flyckransow **II** *vb* flyckra

flies *n* (*in trousers*) toll lavrek *m*, tell lavrek

flight *n* neyj *m*, neyjow; (*escape*) tegh *m*, teghow. **take flight** fia dhe'n fo

flimsy *adj* skav; tanow

fling *vb* deghesi; tewlel

flint *n* kelester *m*, kelesteryow; flynt *m*, flyntys

flip I *n* klout skav *m*, kloutys skav **II** *vb* treylya. **egg flip** medh oy *f*. **the flip side** an tu aral *m*

flipper *n* botasen balvek *f*, botasennow palvek; botas palvek *coll*

flirt *vb* flyrtya

float I *n* (*fishing*) neuvell *f*, neuvellow **II** *vb* neuvella; neyja

flock I *n* flock *m*, flockys; (*animals*) gre *f*, greow; (*birds*) hes *f*, hesow **II** *vb* hesya

flog *vb* kastiga

flood I *n* liv *m*, livow; lanwes *m* **II** *vb* liva; reverthi. **flood gate** yet dhowr *f*, yetys dowr, yetow dowr

floodgate *n* livyet *f*, livyetow

floodlights *n* livwolowys *pl*

floor *n* leur *m*, leuryow. **ground floor** leur a-woles *m*

flour *n* bleus *m*, bleusyow

flourish *vb* (*succeed*) seweni; (*blossom*) bleujyowa; (*grow*) tevi; (*plants*) glasa

floury *adj* bleusek

flow I *n* fros *m*, frosow; res *m*, resow **II** *vb* frosa; (*liquids and powders*) resek

flower I *n* bleujen *f*, bleujyow; flour *m*, flourys. **flower bed** *n* bleujyowek *f*, bleujyowegi **II** *vb* bleujyowa

flu *n* flou *f*

fluency *n* frethter *m*

fluent *adj* freth

fluff *n* mannbluven *f*, mannbluv

fluffy *adj* mannbluvek

fluid I *adj* linyel **II** *n* lin *m*, linyow

fluorite *n* (*mineral*) kann *m*

fluorspar *n* kann *m*

flush I *n* flosh *m*, floshys **II** *vb* floshya; kartha

flute *n* pib *m*, pibow; tollgorn *m*, tollgern

flutter *vb* terneyja

fly I *n* (*insect*) kelyonen *f*, kelyonennow; kelyon *coll*; (*in trousers*) toll lavrek *m*, tell lavrek **II** *vb* neyja. **bluebottle fly** *n* kelyonen gig *f*

flyer (*aviator*) neyjer *m*, neyjoryon; (*leaflet*) folennik *f*, folenigow

flying saucer *n* padellik-neyja *f* padelligow-neyja

foam *n* ewonen *f*, ewonennow; ewon *coll*. **shaving foam** ewon-divarva *coll*

foamy *adj* ewonek

focus I *n* fog *f*, fogow **II** *vb* fogella. **out of focus** mes a fog. **sharp focus** fog lew

focussed *adj* fogellys

fog *n* niwl *m*, niwlow

foggy *adj* niwlek

fold I *n* pleg *m*, plegow **II** *vb* plegya

folder *n* plegell *f*, plegellow

folding *adj* heblek

folk *n* gwerin *f*. **folk song** *n* kan werin *f*, kanow gwerin

folklore *n* lien gwerin *m*

follow *vb* (*physical*) holya; (*outcome*) sewya; omsewya

follower *n* holyer *m*, holyoryon

following *adj* (*which follows*) a sew

folly *n* folneth *f*; gockineth *f*; folenep *m*, folenebow

fond *adj* karadow

fondle *vb* chersya

font *n* (*in church*) besydhven *m*, besydhveyn; (*in document*) font *m*, fontys. **bold font** font poos *m*. **italic font** font italek *m*

food *n* boos *m*, bosow

foodstuff *n* sosten *m*

fool *n* bobba *m*, bobbys; gocki *m*, gockies; pyst *m*, pystyon

foolish *adj* fol; gocki. **foolish face** folenep *m*, folenebow. **behave foolishly** *vb* gockia

foolishness *n* folneth *f*; folenep *m*, folenebow

fool's gold *n* *mineral* pyrit *m*; owr an bobba *m*

foot *n* (*anat*) troos *m*, treys, *dl* dewdros. **on foot** *adv* a droos; (*base*) ben *m*, benyow; (*length*) tros-hys *m*, treys-hys

football *n* pel droos *f*, pelyow troos

footballer *n* peldrosyer *m*, peldrosyoryon; (*professional*) peldrosyas *m*, peldrosysi

foothold *n* trosla *f*, trosleow

footnote *n* troosnoten *f*, troosnotennow

footpath *n* trolergh *m*, trolerghow; kerdhva *f*, kerdhvaow

footprint *n* ol troos *m*, olow troos

footstool *n* skavel droos *f*, skavellow troos

for *cnj, prp* rag. **as for** ow tochya. **as for him** yn y^2 gever. **for breakfast** dhe hansel. **for ever** bys vykken. **for three months** trymis. **for shame!** rag meth! **look for** hwilas. **thank you for** meur ras a^2. **what for?** Praga?

forbid *vb* difen

force *n* nerth *m*, nerthow, nerthyow; fors *m*, forsow; (*in physics*) forsedh *m*

forceful *adj* trewesi; krev

forceless *adj* dinerth

ford *n* rys *f*, rysyow

fore- *prfx* ar-; dar-

forecast I *n* dargan *f*, darganow II *vb* dargana

forefather *n* hendas *m*, hendasow; ragdas *m*, ragdasow

forefinger *n* bys rag *m*, besies rag

foreground *n* ragdir *m*

forehead *n* tal *f* (*m*), talyow

foreign *adj* estren; astranj

foreigner *n* estren *m*, estrenyon

forename *n* hanow kynsa *m*, henwyn kynsa

forenoon *n* kynseghwa *m*

forest *n* koos *m*, kosow; koswik *f*, koswigow. **rain forest** koswik law *f*, koswigow glaw

forester *n* forster *m*, forstoryon

forever *adv* bys vykken; bys vynari; bys vynitha; rag nevra vynitha

forewarn *vb* darweri

forge I *n* gelforn *f*, gelfornow; govel *f*, goveli II *vb* (*form metal*) govelya; (*counterfeit; falsify*) fugya

forgery *n* fug *m*, fugyow; fugyans *m*, fugyansow

forget *vb* ankevi. **forget it!** gwra/gwrewgh y ankevi!

forgetfulness *n* ankov *m*, ankovyow

forget-me-not *n* skorpyonles *m*; porth kov ahanav *m*

forgive *vb* gava. **forgive somebody** gava dhe nebonan

forgiveness *n* gevyans *m*, gevyansow

fork *n* (*tool*) forgh *f*, fergh; (*Y-shape*) gowl *f*, gowlow

forked *adj* gowlek

form I *n* (*shape*) furv *f*, furvow; form *m* (*f*), formys II *vb* furvya; formya

formal *adj* formel

format I *n* (*IT*) furvas *m*, furvasow II *vb* furvasa

former *adj* kyns. **the former** an pyth kampollys kynsa

formerly *adv* seulabrys; kyns

forsake *vb* forsakya

fort *n* din *m*, dinyow; dinas *m*, dinasow. **hill fort** ker *f*, kerow, keryow; kastel *m*, kastylli, kestel

forthwith *adv* a-dhesempis; 'dhesempis; dison

fortieth *num* dew ugensves; *abbrev* 40ves

fortified *adj* (*of a building*) dinek; (*strengthened*) krefhes

fortnight *n* diw seython; hanter-mis *m*, hanter-misyow

fortress *n* din *m*, dinyow; ker *f*, kerow, keryow

fortunate *adj* feusik; gwynnvys

fortunately *adv* y'n gwella prys

fortune *n* fortun *m*, fortunnyow; feus *m*

fortune-teller *n* kolyek *m*, kolyogyon

forty *num* dew ugens

forward *adv* a-rag; yn-rag. **go forward** mos yn-rag. **lean forward** posa war-rag

forwards *adv* war-rag

fossil *n* menhesen *f*, menhesennow

foster *vb* maga; meythrin

foster-daughter *n* myrgh veythrin *f*, myrghes meythrin

foster-father *n* tasveth *m*, tasvethow

foster-mother *n* mamveth *f*, mamvethow

foster-son *n* mab meythrin *m*, mebyon veythrin

foul *adj* hager

foul-mouthed *adj* droktavosek

found *vb* selya; fondya; grondya

foundation *n* fondyans *m*, fondyansow; (*basis*) grond *m*, grondys, grondow; sel *f*, selyow. **foundation stone** selven *m*, selveyn. **lay foundations** fondya; grondya

foundry *n* teudhla *m*, teudhleow

fountain *n* fenten *f*, fentynnyow

four *num* peswar *m*; peder *f*

fourfooted *adj* peswartrosek

fourteen *num* peswardhek

fourteenth *num* peswardhegves; 14ves

fourth *num* peswora; *abbrev* 4a

fox *n* lowarn *m*, lewern. **fox cub** *n* lowarnik *m*, lewernigow

foxglove *n* manek lowarn *f*, manegow lowarn

fraction *n* rannriv *m*, rannrivow

fracture *n* torrva *f*, torrvaow; torr *m*, torrow

fragile *adj* hedor

fragment I *n* darn *m*, darnow; tamm *m*, temmyn **II** *vb* omvrewi

fragmentary *adj* dernigel; kepar ha brewyon

fragmentation *n* omvrewyans *m*, omvrewyansow

frail *adj* brottel; gwann

frame I *n* fram *m*, framyow **II** *vb* framya

France *top* Pow Frynk *m*

franchise *n* franchis *n*, franchisow

frank *adj* frank

frankincense *n* frankincens *m*

fraud *n* (*deceit*) toll *m*; fraws *m*; (*person*) falswas *m*, falswesyon

fraudulent *adj* frawsus

fray *vb* freudha

freckle *n* brithen *f*, brithennow

freckled *adj* brithennek

free I *adj* rydh; frank **II** *vb* (*set free, deliver*) rydhhe; delivra; (*cut loose*) lewsel. **free of charge** heb kost. **go free** bos delivrys. **is this table free?** usi nebonan orth an voos ma? **set free** delivra dhe wari

freedom *n* frankedh *m*; rydhses *m*

free-range *adj* frankres. **free-range egg** oy frankres *m*, oyow frankres

freeze *vb* rewi

freezer *n* rewer *m*, rewyoryon

freight *n* fres *m*; karg *m*, kargow

French I *adj* frynkek **II** *n* (*language*) Frynkek *m*

French person *n* Frynk *m*, Frynkyon

frequency *n* menowghter *m*, menowghteryow; (*physics*) menowghedh *m*, menowghedhyow

frequent I *adj* menowgh **II** *vb* daromres

frequently *adv* yn fenowgh

fresh *adj* fresk; yr; (*new*) nowydh; (*brand new*) flamm nowydh; (*of food*) kro; (*raw, uncooked*) kriv

freshen *vb* yrhe

fret I *n* negh *m*, neghow; fienasow *pl* **II** *vb* neghi

fretful *adj* neghus

friction *n* rutyans *m*

Friday *n* Gwener *f*; dy'Gwener *m*. **Good Friday** *n* dy'Gwener an Grows *m*. **Friday night** dy'Gwener dhe nos

fridge *n* yeynell *f*, yeynellow

fried *adj* friys. **fried egg** *n* oy friys *m*, oyow friys

friend *n* koweth *m*, kowetha; kowethes *f*, kowethesow; kothman *m*, kothmans; (*mate*) sos *m*, sos

friendless *adj* digoweth

friendly *adj* kowethek

friendship *n* kowethegeth *f*

frieze *n* hirskeusen *f*, hirskeusennow

fright *n* own *m*. **take fright from** kemeres own rag

frighten *vb* gorra own dhe²

frightened *adj* ownek

frightful *adj* grysel; euthyk

frock *n* pows *f*, powsow

frog *n* kwilkyn *m*, kwilkynnyow

from *prp* dhyworth; dyworth; a²; (*since*) a-dhia². **from beneath, from under** a-dhann². **from here** alemma; (*from there*) alena. **from now on** alemma rag. **from on, from over, from on top of** a-dhywar²; dhywar²; dywar²

front I *adj* a-rag II *n* tal *f* (*m*), talyow; (*front of body*) greuv *m*, greuvow. **back to front** an keyn a-rag. **in front** *adv* a-rag. **in front of** a-dherag

frontier *n* or *f*, oryon

frost *n* rew *m*, rewyow

frosty *adj* rewek

froth I *n* ewon *coll*; II *vb* ewoni

frothy *adj* ewonek

frown *vb* talgamma; brendya; plegya tal

frozen *adj* rewys

fruit *n* frothen *f*, frothennow; frooth *coll*; frut *m*, frutys. **fruit juice** *n* sugen frooth *m*, sugenyow frooth

frustrated *adj* sprellys

fry *vb* fria. **frying pan** *n* padel-fria *f*, padellow-fria; leswedh *m*, leswedhow; lecher *m*, lechers

fuchsia *n* droppys kogh *coll*

fuck I *n* kyjyans *m*, kyjyansow II *vb* kyjya

fuel *n* keunysen *f*, keunysennow; *coll* keunys

fugitive I *adj* foesik II *n* foesik *m*, foesigyon

-ful *sffx* -as, -asow

fulfil *vb* kewera; kowlwul; komposa; kollenwel

fulfilment *n* keweras *m*

full *adj* leun. **full of** leun a²

full-grown *adj* kowldevys

fullness *n* leunder *m*

fumble *vb* trebuchya

fume I *n* mog *m* II *vb* megi

fun *n* delit *m*; gwari *m*, gwariow. **make fun of** gul ges a². **what fun!** ass yw hemma gwari teg!

function *n* (*office*) offis *m*, offisys

functional *adj* gweythresek

fund I *n* arghas *m*, arghasow II *vb* arghasa; provia arghans rag

fundamental *adj* selvenel

fundamentalism *n* selveneleth *f*

fundamentalist *n* selvenelyas *m*, selvenelysi

funding *n* arghasans *m*

funeral *n* galarans *m*, galaransow; (*burial*) ynkleudhyans *m*, ynkleudhyansow; (*cremation*) korfloskans *m*, korfloskansow

funeral director *n* dyghtyer galar *m*, dyghtyoryon alar

fungus *n* fong *m*, fongow

funny *adj* hwarthus

furious *adj* koneryek

furiously *adv* gans outray

furnace *n* fog *f*, fogow

furnish *vb* mebla; takla

furniture *n* mebel *m*

further *adj* pella. **any further** (*usually in negative sentences*) na³ fella. **without further ado** heb na hirra lavarow

furthest *adj* pella

fury *n* konnar *f*

furze *n* (*gorse*) eythinen *f*, eythinennow; eythin *coll*

fuse *n* lesken *f*, leskennow

fusion *n* kesteudhans *m*, kesteudhansow

fuss I *n* trynn *f*, trynnow **II** *vb* fysla

fussy *adj* (*making a fuss*) fyslek;

(*fastidious*) denti

futile *adj* euver

futon *n* fouton *m*, foutonyow

future *n* termyn a dheu *m*, termynyow a dheu

future tense *n* amser a dheu *f*

G

gabble *vb* klappya

gadfly *n* kelyonen vargh *f*, kelyonennow margh; kelyon margh *coll*

Gael *n* Godhal *m*, Godhyli

Gaelic I *adj* godhalek **II** *n* (*language*) Godhalek *m*

gain I *n* gwayn *m*, gwaynyow; les *m* **II** *vb* gwaynya. **gain a reputation** kavos hanow

galaxy *n* galaksi *m*, galaksiow

gale *n* awel *f*, awelyow

gall *n* bystel *f*

gallery *n* (*balcony*) soler *m*, soleryow; (*exhibition room*) mirva *f*, mirvaow

gallon *n* gallon *m*, gallons

gallows *n* krogbren *m*, krogbrennyer; kloghbren *m*, kloghbrennyer

galore *adj* lowr a². **prizes galore** lowr a bewasow

gamble *vb* hapwari

game (1) *n* (*play*) gwari *m*, gwariow. **board game** *n* gwari bord *m*, gwariow bord. **card game** *n* gwari kartennow *m*, gwariow kartennow. **Olympic Games** *n* Gwariow Olympek *pl*. **role playing game (RPG)** *n* gwari rol *m*, gwariow rol; gwari rann *m*, gwariow rann. **video game** *n* gwari gwydhyow *m*, gwariow gwydhyow. **play a double game** gwari gans gwelen dhewblek

game (2) *n* (*live quarry*) gam *m*; (*meat*) helgik *m*

game (3) *adj* (*bold*) hardh

gang *n* para *m*, parys; bagas *m*, bagasow

gangster *n* bilen *m*, bilens

gangway *n* tremenva *f*, tremenvaow

gaol *n* prison *m*, prisonyow

gaoler *n* jayler *m*, jaylers

gap *n* bolgh *m*, bolghow; aswa *f*, aswaow

garage *n* karrji *m*, karrjiow

garden I *n* lowarth *m*, lowarthyow **II** *vb* lowartha. **kitchen garden** *n* erber *m*, erberow, erbers

gardener *n* lowarther *m*, lowarthoryon

garish *adj* gorliwys

garlic *n* keninen *f*, keninennow; kennin *coll*

garlic, wild *n* (*ramsons*) koos kennin *coll*; (*three-cornered leek*) kennin trihornek *coll*

garrison *n* garnisyon *m*, garnisyons

gas *n* gass *m*, gassys

gasp *vb* dyena

gastritis *n* (*med*) gastritis *m*

gate *n* yet *f*, yetys, yetow; porth *m*, porthow. **flood gate** yet dhowr *f*, yetys dowr, yetow dowr

gatehouse *n* porthorji *m*, porthorjiow

gather *vb* (*transitive*) kuntel; (*intransitive*) omguntel. **gather acorns** mesa. **gather apples** avalowa. **gather

berries mora. **gather corn** tyska. **gather firewood** keunyssa. **gather flowers** terri. **gather honey** mela. **gather mussels** meskla. **gather nuts** knowa. **gather seaweed** gomonna. **gather strawberries** sevia

gatherer *n* kunteller *m*, kuntelloryon

gaudy *adj* gorliwys

gauntlet *n* manek blat *f*, manegow plat

gay *adj* (*joyful*) lowenek; (*homosexual*) kethreydhek; havalreydhek

gaze *vb* lagatta

gear *n* (*equipment*) taklen *f*, taklow; daffar *m*; (*clothes*) aparel *m*; (*mechanical*) maglen *f*, maglennow. **change gear** maglenna

gearstick *n* gwelen vaglen *f*, gwelynni maglen

gel *n* jell *m*, jellow

gelatine *n* jell *m*, jellow

gem *n* gemm *m*, gemmow

gender *n* reydhedh *m*, reydhedhow

gender dysphoria *n* dysforia reydhedh *m*

general (1) *adj* (*universal*) ollgemmyn. **general practitioner** medhek mayni *m*, medhogyon vayni

general (2) *n* (*army*) pennhembrenkyas *m*, pennhembrynkysi

generally *adv* dre vras

generate *vb* dinythi

generation *n* (*process*) dinythyans *m*, dinythyansow; (*of people in family*) henedh *m*, henedhow

generator *n* dinythor *m*, dinythoryon. **electric generator** *n* dinythor tredan *m*, dinythoryon tredan

generosity *n* helder *m*

generous *adj* hel

genetic *adj* genynnek. **genetically modified organism** *n* organedh varyes yn henynnek *m*, organedhow varyes yn henynnek

genie *n* bocka lugarn *m*, bockas lugarn, bockyas lugarn

genius I *n* (*especially gifted person*) awenydh *m*, awenydhyon; (*bordering on madness*) gorbollek *m*, gorbologyon **II** *adj* (*bordering on madness*) gorbollek

genre *n* eghen *f*, eghennow

gentle *adj* hweg; jentyl

gentleman *n* den jentyl *m*, tus jentyl

gentlewoman *n* benyn jentyl *f*, benenes jentyl

gently *adv* yn kosel; dre dekter

gents *n* (*signage*) gwer *pl*

genuine *adj* lel; gwir; gwiryon

geographical *adj* doroniethel

geography *n* doronieth *f*

geological *adj* dororiethel

geologist *n* dororydh *m*, dororydhyon

geology *n* dororieth *f*

geometric *adj* mynsoniethel

geometry *n* mynsonieth *f*

germ *n* (*microbe*) korrbryv *m*, korrbryves, korrbryvyon

German I *adj* almaynek **II** *n* (*German language*) Almaynek *m*; (*German person*) Alman *m*, Almanyon. **German shepherd dog** ki bleydh *m*, keun bleydh

Germany *top* Almayn *m*. **Federal Republic of Germany** Republik Keffrysek Almayn *m*

germinate egina; skylla

get *vb* kavos; (*obtain*) kerghes. **get about** mos a-dro. **get along** (*move*) kerdhes. **get angry with** serri orth. **get back** daskavos. **get cracking** dalleth. **get dressed** omwiska. **get drunk** omvedhwi. **get even** diala. **get ill** kodha klav. **get into debt** kodha yn kendon. **get on** (*progress*) spedya; seweni. **get out of here!** voyd alemma! **get out of my sight!** gwayv ow golok! **get over** omwellhe. **get ready** ombareusi. **get round to** kavos chons dhe². **get wind of something**

klewes son a neppyth. **get up** sevel. **I have** my a'm beus. **get out** gwayvya

ghastly *adj* euthyk; skruthus

ghetto *n* getto *m*, gettos

ghost *n* tarosvan *m*, tarosvannow. **good ghost** *n* bocka gwynn *m*, bock(y)as wynn. **bad ghost** *n* bocka du *m*, bock(y)as dhu. **ghost train** *n* tren tarosvan *m*, trenow tarosvan. **give up the ghost** daskor y enev

ghostly *adj* tarosvannus

giant **I** *adj* kowrek; kowr- **II** kowr *m*, kewri

gibbet *n* krogla *m*, krogleow

giddiness *n* penn-dro *f*

giddy *adj* penn-dro

gift *n* ro *m*, rohow, royow

gifted (*talented*) konnyk

gigabyte *n* gigabayt *m*, gigabaytys; *abbrev* GB

gigantic *adj* kowrek

gill *n* (*respiratory organ*) brynken *f*, brynkennow; brynk *coll*

gillyflower *n* (*stock*) knowdhel *coll*

gin *n* (*drink*) jynevra *m*

ginger *n* jynjyber *coll*; jynjer *coll*

giraffe *n* jiraf *m*, jirafes

girdle *n* grugys *m*, grugysyow; kengrel *f*, kengrellow; kyngel *f*, kynglow

girl *n* mowes *f*, mowysi

girlfriend *n* kares *f*, karesow

give *vb* ri. **give back** ri tre; ri arta. **given that** a-ban². **give off** (*sound*) seni; (*smell*) flerya. **give over** cessya. **give or take** a-dro dhe². **give trouble** gul trobel. **give up** daskor; hepkor. **give way** plegya

glacial *adj* oor

glacier *n* rewiva *f*, rewivaow

glad *adj* lowen; heudh; heudhik. **be glad** heudhi; heuthhe

gladden *vb* heuthhe

glade *n* lannergh *m*, lanerghi

gladiolus *n* lilien gledha *f*, liliennow kledha; lili kledha *coll*

glamour *n* (*magic*) hus *m*

gland *n* gwagren *f*, gwagrennow

glass *n* (*material; mirror*) gweder, gwedrow; (*vessel*) gwedren *f*, gwedrennow

glasses *n* dewweder *dl*

glassful *n* gwedrennas *f*, gwedrenasow

gleam *vb* lentri

gleaming *adj* lentrus; splann

glen *n* glynn *m*, glynnow

glide *vb* slynkya

glisten *vb* terlentri

glittering *adj* dewynnek

gloat *vb* gorawena

global *adj* (*worldwide*) ollvysel; dres oll an bys; (*comprehensive*) olldalghus. **global warming** tommheans ollvysel *m*

globe *n* pel an norvys *f*, pelyow an norvys

gloom *n* (*darkness*) tewlder *m*

gloomy *adj* tewl; trist

glorious *adj* gormoledhek; gloryus

glory *n* glori *m*; golewder *m*; gordhyans *m*; gormola *f*

gloss **I** *n* lenter *m*; splander *m* **II** *vb* gorra lenter war²; (*explain*) styrya. **lip gloss** lenter gweus *m*

glove *n* manek *f*, manegow

glow **I** *n* golow *m*, golowys **II** *vb* golowi

glue **I** *n* glus *m*, glusow **II** *vb* glusa

gluttonous *adj* kowlek

gnarled *adj* stummys

gnashing *n* skrinva *f*, skrinvaow

gnat *n* gwibesen *f*, gwibes

gnome *n* korrik *m*, korrigow; (*mine spirit*) knoukyer *m*, knoukyers; (*goblin*) bocka *m*, bock(y)as. **garden gnome** korrik lowarth *m*, korrigow lowarth

go *vb* (*move; travel*) mos; (*function*) oberi. **go along** (*cooperate*) kesoberi. **go away** mos dhe-ves; avodya. **go back** dehweles. **go by** (*be called*) bos henwys; (*pass*) passya; tremena. **go**

down diyskynna. **go mad** dotya; muskegi; varya. **go missing** mos dhe goll. **go on an errand** mones negys. **go out** mos yn-mes; (*of a flame*) merwel. **go over to** treusi dhe. **go up** yskynna

goad I *n* bros *m*, brosow II *vb* brosa; piga

goal *n* (*object; target*) amkan *m*, amkanow; kosten *f*, kostennow; towl *m*, towlow; medras *m*, medrasow; (*sports*) gol *m*, golyow

goalkeeper *n* gwithyas gol *m*, gwithysi wol

goat *n* gaver *f*, gever, gyvres. **he-goat** *n* bogh *m*, boghes

goatee *n* barv gaver *m*, barvow gaver

goblin *n* bocka *m*, bock(y)as

god *n* duw *m*, duwow; (*Jewish, Christian & Muslim God*) Duw *m*. **God bless!** Dursona! Duw re sonno!

godchild *n* flogh besydh *m*, fleghes vesydh

goddess *n* duwes *f*, duwesow

godfather *n* tas besydh *m*, tasow vesydh

godless *adj* didhuw

godmother *n* mamm vesydh *m*, mammow besydh

goggle-eyed *adj* lagasek

gold *n* (*element*) owr *m*

goldcrest *n* lawen krib owr *m*, lawenes krib owr

golden *adj* owrek; owryek

golden rod *n* owrwelen *f*, owrwelynni

goldfinch *n* melynek penn rudh *m*, melynoges penn rudh

goldfish *n* owrbysk *m*, owrbuskes

golf *n* golf *m*. **golf course** gwel golf *m*, gwelyow golf

gone *adj* gyllys

good *adj* da; (*morally good; respectable*) mas. **good day** dydh da; durdadhehwi. **good morning** myttin da. **good evening** gorthugher da.

good heavens re Varia; 'Ria. **good night** nos da; Durnostadha

goodbye I *int* (*sg*) Duw genes; dha weles; farwell dhis; (*pl*) Duw genowgh; agas gweles; farwell dhywgh II *n* farwell *m*. **wave goodbye** gwevya farwell. **wave!** (*imp*) gwev!

goodness *n* dader *m*. **goodness knows** Duw hepken a wor

goods *n* gwara *coll*; (*possessions*) pyth ha da

goose *n* goodh *f*, godhow

gooseberry *n* growsen *f*, growsennow; grows *coll*. **gooseberry bush** growsvos *m*, growsvosow

goosegrass *n* (*cleavers; sticky willy*) les serghek byghan *m*

gore *n* krow *m*

gorge (1) *n* (*ravine*) islonk *m*, islonkow; kownans *m*, kownansow

gorge (2) *vb* kwoffi

gorgeous *adj* splann

gorilla *n* gorylla *m*, gorylles

gorse *n* (*furze*) eythinen *f*, eythinennow; eythin *coll*

gorseth *n* gorsedh *f*, gorsedhow. **The Cornish Gorseth** Gorsedh Kernow *f*

gory *adj* gosek

gosling *n* godhik *m*, godhigow

gospel *n* aweyl *f*, aweylys, aweylyow

gossamer *n* gweun *m*

gossip I *vb* kyhwedhla; kesklappya yn unn sklandra; esedha war skavel an gow II *n* kyhwedhel *m*, kyhwedhlow

Gothic I *adj* gothek II *n* (*language*) Gothek *m*. **Gothic architecture** pennserneth wothek *f*

gourd *n* pompyon *m*, pompyons

govern *vb* governa

government *n* governans *m*, governansow

gown *n* pows *f*, powsyow; **dressing gown** mantel nos *f*, mantylli nos

grace *n* gras *m*, grassow

graceful *adj* grassyes; rasek

graceless *adj* diras; ongrassyes

gracious *adj* deboner; grassyes; rasek

graciousness *n* jentylys *m*

grade I *n* gradh *m*, gradhow **II** *vb* gradhegi

gradual *adj* gradhel

gradually *adv* tamm ha tamm

graduate I *n* gradhesik *m*, gradhesigyon **II** *vb* gradhya

graduation *n* gradhyans *m*, gradhyansow

grail *n* gral *m*

grain *n* greunen *f*, greunennow; greun *coll*

grammar *n* (*system of rules*) gramer *m*, grameryow; gramasek *f*, gramasegow; (*book*) yethador *m*, yethadoryow

grammatical *adj* gramasek

gram *n* gramm *m*, grammow

granary *n* greunva *f*, greunvaow; greunji *m*, greunjiow

grand *adj* bryntin; brav; meur; ughel. **grand piano** *n* piano bras *m*, pianos bras

grandchild *n* flogh gwynn *m*, fleghes wynn

granddaughter *n* myrgh wynn *f*, myrghes gwynn

grandfather *n* tas gwynn *m*, tasow wynn; sira wynn *m*, sirys wynn

grandmother *n* mamm wynn *f*, mammow gwynn; dama wynn *f*, damyow gwynn

grandparents *n* kerens wynn

grandson *n* mab wynn *m*, mebyon wynn

grange *n* greunji *m*, greunjiow

granite *n* growan *m*, growenyow

grant I *n* gront *m*, grontys, grontow **II** *vb* grontya; ri

grape *n* grappa *m*, grappys, grappow

grapefruit *n* aval paradhis *m*, avalow paradhis

graph *n* tresen *f*, tresennow

graphic *adj* tresennek

graphical *adj* grafegel. **graphical user interface (GUI)** ynterfas usyer grafegel *m*, ynterfassow usyer grafegel; *abbrev* YUG

graphics *n* grafek *f*, grafegow

grasp I *n* dalghen *f*, dalghennow; gavel *f*, gavelyow **II** *vb* dalghenna; synsi

grass *n* gwels *coll*. **blade of grass** *n* gwelsen *f*, gwelsennow. **grass-roots support** *n* skoodhyans an bobel *m*

grassy *adj* gwelsek

grate *vb* rathella

grateful *adj* grasek

gratis *adj* didal

grave *n* bedh *m*, bedhow

gravel *n* grow *coll*; (*piece of*) growen *f*, growennow

gravelly *adj* growynnek

gravestone *n* men bedh *m*, meyn bedh

graveyard *n* korflan *f*, korflannow; ynkladhva *f*, ynkladhvaow; bedhros *f*, bedhrosow

gravity *n* gravedh *m*, gravedhow

gravy *n* (*meat*) sugen kig *m*, sugenyow kig; (*vegetable*) sugen losow *m*, sugenyow losow

graze *vb* peuri; peski

grease *n* blonek *m*, blonegow

greasy *adj* blonegek

great I *adj* meur **II** *int* splann! bryntin!

great-aunt *n* gorvodrep *f*, gorvodrebedh

Great Britain *top* Breten Veur *f*

great-hearted *adj* meurgolonnek

greatly *adv* yn feur; yn fras

great tit *n* penn pali bras *m*, pennow pali bras

great-uncle *n* gorewnter *m*, gorewntres

Greece *top* Pow Grek *m*; Gres *f*

greed *n* krefni *f*; pithneth *f*

greedy *adj* kraf; pith

Greek I *adj* grek **II** *n* (*language*) Greka *m*; (*person*) Grek *m*, Grekys

green I *adj* (*natural*) glas; (*artificial*) gwyrdh; gwer **II** *n* (*colour*) liw glas *m*; (*grass*) glesyn *m*, glesynnow **III** (*become green/blue*) *vb* glasa. **bowling green** pelva *f*, pelvaow. **dark green** *adj* dulas. **light green** *adj* gwerwyn. **the Green Party** an Parti Gwyrdh. **the Greens** *n* an Re Wyrdh *pl*

greenfinch *n* melynek banal *m*, melynoges banal

greengrocer *n* gwerther losow *m*, gwerthoryon losow

greenhouse *n* chi gweder *m*, chiow gweder; treven gweder. **greenhouse effect** effeyth chi gweder *m*

greenish *adj* gwerik

greet *vb* dynerghi; haylya; salusi; wolkomma

greeting *n* dynnargh *m*, dynarghow. **greetings** *n* gorhemynadow *pl*; *idiom* lowena dhis! (*sg*); lowena dhywgh! (*pl*)

gregarious *adj* kowethus

grey *adj* loos; (*also: blue, green*) glas

griddle *n* men-pobas *m*, meyn-pobas

grief *n* duwon *m*; galar *m*, galarow; anken *m*, ankenyow; keudh *m*, keudhow. **without grief** *adj* dialar

grievance *n* grevons *m*, grevonsys. **he nurses a grievance** yma grevons dhodho

grieve *vb* grevya; keudhi; (*afflict*) duwenhe; (*mourn*) duwena; galari

grieved *adj* duwenhes

grievous *adj* ankensi

grill I *n* rastell *f*, restell; **II** *vb* rastella

grim *adj* asper; fell; garow

grimace I *n* mowa *m*, mowys **II** *vb* gul mowa

grin I *n* skrynk *m*, skrynkow **II** *vb* grysla; skrynkya

grind *vb* mala; melyas

grinder *n* (*tool*) malell *f*, malellow; (*person*) maler *m*, maloryon

grip I *n* dalghen *f*, dalghennow; krapp *m* **II** *vb* dalghenna

gritty *adj* growynnek

groan I *n* hanas *m*, hanasow **II** *vb* hanasa

groat *n* grot *m*, grotys

grocer *n* spiser *m*, spisoryon

groceries *n* gwara boos *coll*

grocery *n* spisti *m*, spistiow

groin *n* kedhorva *f*, kedhorvaow

groove *n* kleudhik *m*, kleudhigow

grope *vb* palvala

gross *adj* (*repulsive*) divlas

ground I *n* (*surface of the earth*) dor *m*, doryow; (*floor*) leur *m*, leuryow; (*soil*) gweres *m*, gweresow **II** *vb* (*touch the ground; base on; connect to the ground*) grondya. **from the ground up** a'n dalleth. **ground floor** leur a-woles *m*. **to the ground** dhe'n dor

grounds *n* (*dregs*) godhes *m*

groundsel *n* madra *m*, madrow

group I *n* para *m*, parys; bagas *m*, bagasow **II** *vb* gorra yn bagas

grove *n* kelli *f*, kelliow

grovel *vb* kramya

grow *vb* tevi. **grow up** adhvesi

growl I *n* grommyans *m*, grommyansow **II** *vb* grommya

growth *n* tevyans *m*, tevyansow

grub *n* pryv *m*, preves

gruel *n* yos *m*

grumble I *n* krodhvol *m*, krodhvolow **II** *vb* krodhvolas

grumbling *adj* krodhek

grunt I *n* rogh *m*, roghow **II** *vb* rogha

guarantee I *n* mewgh *m*, mewghyow **II** *vb* mewghya

guard I *n* gwith *m*; (*person*) gwithyas *m*, gwithysi **II** *vb* gwitha

guardian *n* gwithyas *m*, gwithysi

Guernsey *top* Gwernenys *f*

guess *vb* dismygi

guest *n* gwester *m*, gwestoryon; ostyas *m*, ostysi

guesthouse *n* gwesti *m*, gwestiow

guide I *n* kevarwodher *m*,
  kevarwodhoryon; gid *m*, gidys II *vb*
  kevarwodha; gidya

guidebook *n* gidlyver *m*, gidlyvrow

guile *n* gil *m*

guilt *n* (*law*) kabluster *m*; (*moral*) pegh
  m

guilty *adj* kablus. **not guilty** ankablus

guinea pig *n* hogh Gyni *m*, hoghes
  Gyni

guise *n* gis *m*

guitar *n* gitar *m*, gitaryow. **electric
  guitar** *n* gitar tredanek *m*, gitaryow
  tredanek

gulf *n* morblek *m*, morblegow

gull *n* golan *f*, golanes

gully *n* saven *f*, savnow

gum (1) *n* (*anat*) kig dens *m*, kigyow
  dens

gum (2) *n* (*substance*) glus *m*, glusow

gun *n* gonn *m*, gonnys

gunner *n* gonner *m*, gonoryon

gust *n* kowas wyns *f*, kowasow gwyns;
  hwaff *m*, hwaffys

gusto *n* terder *m*. **with gusto** yn freth

gut *n* kolodhyonen *f*, kolodhyonennow;
  kolodhyon *coll*

gutter *n* londer *m*, londrys

guy *n* den *m*, tus; gwas *m*, gwesyon.
  tough guy *n* smat *m*, smatys

gymnasium *n* hel sport *f*, helyow sport

gymnastics *n* gymnastek *m*; lappyans
  m. **perform gymnastics** lappya

gynaecological *adj* bengorfoniethel

gynaecologist *n* bengorfydh *m*,
  bengorfydhyon

gynaecology *n* bengorfonieth *f*

Gypsy *n* Jypson *m*, Jypsonyon. (*see also:
  Roma, Traveller*)

gypsy *adj* jypsonek

H

habit *n* us *m*, usyow, usadow;
  (*garment*) goon *m*, gonyow

habitable *adj* anedhadow

habitat *n* bewva *f*, bewvaow

habitual *adj* usadow

hack *vb* hackya. **hack off** hackya
  dhe-ves

haddock *n* korrvarvus *m*, korrvarvusi

haemorrhoids *n* kleves marghogyon *m*

hag *n* gwragh *f*, gwraghes

hail (1) I (*weather*) *n* keser *coll* II *vb* gul
  keser

hail (2) *vb* (*greet*) haylya

hailstone *n* keseren *f*, keserennow

hair *n* blewen *f*, blewennow; blew *coll*;
  gols *coll*; (*lock of*) kudyn *m*,
  kudynnow

hair stylist *n* gisyer gols *m*, gisyoryon
  wols

hairy *adj* blewek

hake *n* densek *m*, densoges

half *n* hanter *m*, hanteryow. **go halves
  with** mos hanter ha hanter gans. **half
  laughing half crying** ynter hwerthin
  hag ola

half-brother *n* hanter-broder *m*,
  hanter-breder

half-hearted *adj* mygyl

half-hour *n* hanter-our *m*, hanter-ourys

half-light *n* tewlwolow *m*

halfpenny *n* demma *m*, demmys

half-sister *n* hanter-hwor *f*,
  hanter-hwerydh

half-wit *n* (*offensive*) skogyn *m*,
  skogynnow

halibut *n* meurlith *f*, meurlithes

hall *n* hel *f*, helyow. **the town hall** hel
  an dre *f*

hallowed *adj* benygys

hallucination *n* (*med*) omdollans *m*, omdollynsi

halt I *n* hedh *m*, hedhow; savla *f*, savleow; (*rest*) powes *m*, powesow **II** *vb* hedhi; powes; sevel

halve *vb* hantera; ranna ynter dew

ham *n* mordhos hogh *f*

hammer I *n* morthol *m*, mortholyow **II** *vb* mortholya

hammered *adj* mortholys

hamper *vb* ankombra

hamster *n* hamster *m*, hamsters

hand *n* leuv *f*, leuvyow, *dl* diwleuv, diwla; dorn *m*, dornow, *dl* dewdhorn. **hand-luggage** *n* fardellow dorn *pl*. **left hand** dorn kledh *m*. **on the other hand** y'n fordh aral; y'n barth aral. **right hand** dorn dyghow *m*. **shake hands** shackya leuv

handbag *n* tigen *f*, tigennow

handball *n* (*sport*) pel dhorn *f*; (*offence in football*) dornbel *f*, dornbelyow

handbook *n* kowethlyver *m*, kowethlyvrow; dornlyver *m*, dornlyvrow

hand down *vb* transmyttya; treuskorra

hand-eye coordination *n* kesordenans dorn-lagas *m*

handful *n* dornas *m*, dornasow

handicapped *adj* see: disabled

handicraft *n* dornweyth *m*, dornweythyow; kreft *f*, kreftow

handkerchief *n* lien dorn *m*, lienyow dorn

handle I *n* dornla *m*, dornleow; (*of a knife*) karn *m*, karnow; (*of a jar*) skovarn *f*, skovornow **II** *vb* handla

handling *n* handlans *m*, handlansow

handshake *n* shackyans leuv *m*, shackyansow leuv

handsome *adj* teg

handwriting *n* dornskrifans *m*, dornskrifansow

handy *adj* (*convenient*) parys; (*skilled*) konnyk

hang I *n* krog *f*, krogow **II** *vb* kregi. **get the hang of** konvedhes. **hang back** treynya. **hang oneself** omgregi. **hang out the washing** lesa an golgh

hang-glide *vb* ayrgregi

hangover *n* (*headache*) kurun spern *m*, kurunyow spern

haphazard *adj* hwymm-hwamm

happen *vb* hwarvos; darvos. **happen to** dos ha. **what's happening?** pandr'a hwer?

happening *n* hwarvos *m*, hwarvosow

happily *adv* yn lowen

happiness *n* lowena *f*

happy *adj* lowen; lowenek

harbour I *n* porth *m*, porthow **II** *vb* goskeusi. **harbour anger** don sorr y'n golon

hard *adj* kales. **a hard fate** kales rann *f*. **hard disk** *n* plasen gales *f*, plasennow kales

hardback *n* lyver kudhlen gales *m*, lyvrow kudhlen gales

hardly *adv* (+ *neg.*) skant; skantlowr. **I can hardly believe it** skant ny'n krysav

hardness *n* kaletter *m*

hardware *n* kalesweyth *m*

hard-working *adj* diwysyk

hare *n* skovarnek *m*, skovarnogyon, skovarnoges. **Mad March hare** skovarnek Meurth gorbollek

harebell *n* klogh an eos *m*, klegh an eos

hare-brained *adj* penn-sogh

harm I *n* dregyn *m*, dregynnow; drog *m*, drogow **II** *vb* shyndya

harmful *adj* dregynnus

harmless *adj* didhregynnus

harmonica *n* harmonika *m*, harmonikas

harmonics *n* kessenegow *pl*

harmonious *adj* kesson

harmonise *vb* kesseni

harmony *n* kessenyans *m*,
kessenyansow

harness *n* hernes *m*, hernessow. **put on
a harness** hernessya

harp *n* telyn *f*, telynnow. **Celtic harp**
telyn Geltek *f*, telynnow Keltek. **play
the harp** telynnya

harpist *n* telynnyer *m*, telynyoryon

harrow *vb* klosya

harsh *adj* asper; garow; hwerow; lymm

harvest I *n* trevas *f*, trevasow II *vb*
trevasa; kynyas; mysi

haste *n* fisten *m*; fysk *m*; mall *m*. **make
haste** fistena

hasten *vb* fistena; stevya

hasty *adj* fysk

hat *n* hatt *m*, hattys, hattow.
broad-brimmed hat diber dowr *m*,
dibrow dowr

hate I *n* kas *m* II *vb* kasa. **I hate** kas yw
genev vy

hateful *adj* kasadow

hatred *n* kas *m*

haughty *adj* howtyn

haul *vb* halya

haulage *n* halyans *m*, halyansow

haunch *n* mordhos *f*, mordhosow; *dl*
diwvordhos; pedren *f*, pedrennow, *dl*
diwbedren

have *vb* kavos; (*own*) pywa. **be had up**
bos dres dherag an justis. **have a bath**
omdroghya; gul tronkys. **have a meal**
kavos boos. **have to** (*must*) bos res
dhe² … a² …. **have someone on**
flattra. **I have** (**in my possession**)
y'm beus; yma dhymm. **I have a cold**
yma anwos warnav. **I will have that**
my a'm bydh henna. **I have with me**
yma genev

haven *n* porth *m*, porthow; por' *m*,
porthow; harber *m*, harbers; (*shelter*)
skovva *f*, skovvaow

hawk *n* hok *m*, hokys

hawthorn *n* spernen wynn *f*,
spernennow gwynn; spern gwynn
coll

hay *n* gora *m*. **new-mown hay** foon *m*

haystack *n* das wora *f*, deys gora

hazard *n* peryl *m*, peryllow, peryllyow

hazardous *adj* argollus; peryllus

haze *n* niwl *m*, niwlow

hazel tree *n* kollen *f*, kollennow; koll
coll

hazelnut *n* knowen goll *f*, knowennow
koll; know koll *coll*

hazy *adj* niwlek

he *prn* ev; (*enclitic*) e, ev; va

head *n* penn *m*, pennow

headache *n* drog penn *m*, drogow penn

heading *n* (*textual*) titel *m*, titlys, titlow;
pennlinen *f*, pennlinennow

headland *n* penn tir *m*, pennow tir; (*in
a field*) talar *m*, talarow

headlight *n* pennlugarn *m*, pennlugern

headline *n* pennlinen *f*, pennlinennow

headphones *n* skovarnigow *pl*

headquarters *n* pennplas *m*,
pennplassow

headteacher *n* penndyskador *m*,
penndyskadoryon

headway *n* avonsyans *m*, avonsyansow

heal *vb* yaghhe; sawya

health *n* yeghes *m*. **good health!
cheers!** yeghes da! **the National
Health Service (NHS)** Servis
Kenedhlek an Yeghes (NHS) *m*

health care assistant *n* skoodhyer
yeghes *m*, skodhyoryon yeghes

healthcare *n* yegheswith *m*

healthy *adj* (*not ill*) yagh;
(*health-giving*) yaghus

heap *n* bern *m*, bernyow; graghel *f*,
graghellow; kals *m*, kalsow

heaped *adj* graghellys; pilek

hear *vb* klewes. **hear about** klewes a².
hear from klewes gans

hearing *n* (*sense*) klew *m*; (*legal*)
goslowva *f*, goslowvaow. **hearing aid**
klewell *f*, klewellow. **hearing**

impaired *adj* bodharek; klewes aperys

heart *n* kolon *f*, kolonnow

heart attack *n* shora kolon *m*

hearth *n* oles *f*, olesow; eth *m*, ethys; fog *f*, fogow

heartless *adj* dibita

heartsease *n* (*wild pansy*) losowen an drynsys *f*

hearty *adj* kolonnek

heat **I** *n* tomder *m*; tes *m* **II** *vb* tommhe; tesa; pothhe; potha

heater *n* jynn-tomma *m*, jynnys-tomma, jynnow-tomma

heath *n* grug *m*, grugow. **Cornish heath** kekesow *coll*

heather *n* grug *m*, grugow

heating *n* tommheans *m*. **central heating** tommheans kres *m*

heave **I** *n* halyans *m*, halyansow **II** *vb* halya

heaven *n* nev *m*, nevow

heavenly *adj* nevek; a nev

heaviness *n* poster *m*, posterow

heavy *adj* poos

hedge **I** *n* ke *m*, keow; (*low or broken down hedge*) gorge *m*, gorgeow **II** *vb* keas

hedged *adj* kes; keek

hedgehog *n* sort *m*, sortes

heed **I** *n* fors *m*; rach *m* **II** *vb* kola orth; bos war. **take heed** kemeres with

heel *n* gwewen *f*, gwewennow, *dl* diwwewen; seudhel *m*, seudhelyow. **head over heels** dres penn ha diwskovarn. **dig one's heels in** skonya omwaya

height *n* ughelder *m*; (*high place*) ardh *m*, ardhow

heir *n* er *m*, erys; her *m*, heryon

held *adj* synsys

helicopter *n* tro askel *f*, troyow askel

hell *n* yfarn *m*, yfarnow. **a hell of a noise** tros yfarnek *m*

hellebore *n* kraban an ors *m*

hellish *adj* yfarnek

hello *int* hou; yow

helmet *n* basnet *m*, basnettys, basnettow

helmsman *n* lewydh *m*, lewydhyon

help **I** *int* harow! **II** *n* gweres *m*; skoodhyans *m*, skodhyansow **III** *vb* gweres; gul gweres dhe[2]; skoodhya. **help me** (*sg*) gweres vy; (*pl*) gweresewgh vy. **help somebody do something** gweres nebonan ow kul neppyth. **help yourself** tann dhis dha honan

helper *n* gwereser *m*, gweresoryon

helpful *adj* heweres; gweresek

helping *n* platas *m*, platasow

helpless *adj* diweres

helter skelter *n* tour korslynk *m*, touryow korslynk

hemi- *prfx* hanter-

hemlock *n* kegisen *f*, kegisennow; kegis *coll*

hemp, Indian *n* kewarghen *f*, kewarghennow; kewargh *coll*

hen *n* yar *f*, yer. **free-range hen** yar frankres *f*, yer frankres

henbane *n* gahen *f*

hence *adv* ahanan; alemma.

hen-house *n* yerji *m*, yerjiow

hepatitis *n* (*med*) hepatitis *m*

her *prn* (*infixed*) 's; *poss. adj* hy[3]. **by her** gensi. **for her** rygdhi. **of her** anedhi. **to her** dhedhi. **with her** gensi

herb *n* erba *m*, erbys; losowen *f*, losow

herb-Robert *n* les Robin *m*

herd **I** *n* gre *f*, greow; para *m*, parys **II** *vb* bugelya

here *adv* omma. **from here** alemma. **here is** otta; ottomma

heresy *n* er *m*

heritage *n* ertach *m*, ertajys. **Cornish Heritage** Ertach Kernow *m*

hermetic *adj* hermesek

hero *n* gorour *m*, gorwer

heron *n* kerghydh *f*, kerghydhyon

herring *n* hernen wynn *f*, hernennow gwynn; hern gwynn *coll*

herself *prn* hy honan

hesitate *vb* hockya

hesitation *n* hockyans *m*, hockyansow

heterogeneous *adj* a lies eghen; a lies sort

heterosexual I *adj* kenreydhek **II** *n* kenreydhor *m*, kenreydhoryon

hexagon *n* hweghkorn *m*, hweghkernow

hi *int* hou; yow

hibiscus *n* kowrvalow *m*, kowrvalowyow

hiccup I *n* hick *m*, hickow **II** *vb* hickas

hidden *adj* kudh; kel

hide (1) *n* (*skin*) kroghen *f*, kreghyn

hide (2) *vb* (*transitive* (*hide something/someone*)) kudha; keles; (*intransitive* (*hide oneself*)) omgudha. **hide from** (*transitive*) kudha rag; (*intransitive*) omgudha rag

hideous *adj* hager

hideout *n* kovva *f*, kovvaow; kudhva *f*, kudhvaow; kel *m*, kelyow

hierarchy *n* urdhas *m*, urdhasow

high *adj* ughel. **high jump** *vb* ughlamma. **high place** *n* ardh *m*, ardhow

higher *adj* ughella; (*in placenames*) gwartha

highest *adj* (an) ughella

highland *n* ugheldir *m*, ugheldiryow

highlight *vb* golowboyntya

highten *vb* ughelhe

highway *n* fordh veur *f*, fordhow meur

hike I *n* gwandrans *m*, gwandransow; rosyans *m*, rosyansow **II** *vb* gwandra; rosya

hilarious *adj* pur hwarthus

hill *n* bre *f*, breow; bronn *f*, bronnow; (*big hill*) menydh *m*, menydhyow. **hill fort** ker *f*, kerow, keryow; kastel *m*, kastylli, kestel

hillside *n* run *f*, runyow

hill-spur *n* ros *m*, rosyow

hilltop *n* topp menydh *m*, toppys menydhyow, toppow menydhyow

him *prn* ev; -va; (*infixed*) 'n. **by him** ganso. **for him** ragdho. **of him** anodho. **to him** dhodho. **with him** ganso

Himalayan balsam *n* basnet gwithyas *m*

himself *prn* y honan

hinder *vb* lettya

Hinduism *n* Hindieth *f*

hinge *n* medynor *f*, medynoryow

hint I *n* hynt *m*, hyntys **II** *vb* hyntya

hip *n* klun *f*, klunyow, *dl* diwglun

hippopotamus *n* dowrvargh *m*, dowrvergh

hire I *n* arveth *m*, arvethow **II** *vb* (*employ*) arveth; (*rent*) gobrena. **hire purchase** hirbren *m*, hirbrenyow. **on hire purchase** yn hirbren

his *poss. adj* y²

hiss *vb* tythya; sia

historian *n* istorior *m*, istorioryon

historical *adj* istorek

history *n* istori *m*

hit I *n* skwatt *m*, skwattys, skwattow; skatt *m*, skattys, skattow **II** *vb* gweskel; skwattya

hitchhike *vb* meusya

hitherto *adv* bys dhe'n eur ma; kyns lemmyn

HIV *abbrev* (*med*) HIV. **Human Immunodeficiency Virus** Virus Immunodifyk Denel

hoarse *adj* hos; kreg; ronk

hobby *n* hobi *m*, hobis

hobby-horse *n* hobihors *m*, hobihorsys; ('*Obby 'Oss*) Penn Glas *m*

hockey *n* hocki *m*

hoe I *n* kravell *f*, kravellow; (*pick*) pigell *f*, pigellow **II** *vb* kravellas

hog *n* hogh *m*, hoghes; torgh *m*, torghes

hogweed *n* kegis an mogh *coll*

hold I *n* dalghen *f*, dalghennow **II** *vb* synsi. **hold out against** perthi orth. **hold an office** sodha

holdall *n* kroder kroghen *m*, krodrow kroghen

holding *n* dalghennas *m*, dalghenasow

hole *n* toll *m*, tell

holed *adj* tollek; tellys

holiday *n* dy'gol *m*, dy'golyow. **holiday home** havos *f*, havosow; chi golyow *m*, chiow golyow

hollow I *adj* kow; gwag **II** *n* kew *f*, kewyow; kow *f*, kowyow; pans *m*, pansow; gobans *m*, gobansow

hollowed *adj* kowesik

holly *n* kelynnen *f*, kelynnennow; kelyn *coll*

holly, sea *n* (*eryngo*) morgelyn *coll*

hollyhock *n* malowen lowarth *f*

holocaust *n* loskaberth *m*, loskaberthow

holograph *n* holograf *m*, holografow

holy *adj* sans. **the Holy Spirit** an Spyrys Sans

homage *n* omach *m*, omajys. **one who pays homage** omajer *m*, omajers

home *n* tre *f*, trevow. **at home** tre; y'n chi. **from home** a-dre. **holiday home** chi golyow *m*, chiow golyow; havos *f*, havosow. **go home** mos tre. **care home** annedh witha *f*, anedhow gwitha

homeless *adj* diannedh; disklos; disto. **homeless person** *n* person diannedh *m*

homely *adj* sempel; diflows

home-made *adj* gwrys y'n chi

homemaker *n* gwas ti *m*, gwesyon chi; gwre'ti *f*, gwragedh chi

home-rule *n* omrewl *f*, omrewlys

homesick *adj* hirethek

homesickness *n* hireth *f*

homestead *n* treveth *f*, trevethow

homewards *adv* dhe-dre

homework *n* ober tre *m*, oberow tre

homicide *n* denladh *m*, denladhow

homily *n* pregoth *m*, pregothow; homeli *m*, homelis

homophobe *n* (*person in fear of*) ownegor a gethreydh *m*, ownegoryon a gethreydh; (*hater of*) kasegor a gethreydh *m*, kasegoryon a gethreydh

homophobia *n* (*fear of*) own a gethreydh *m*; (*hate of*) kas a gethreydh *f*

homophobic *adj* (*fearful of*) ownek a gethreydh; (*hateful of*) kasek a gethreydh

homophone *n* kethsonek *f*, kethsonegow

homosexual I *adj* kethreydhek; havalreydhek **II** *n* kethreydhor *m*, kethreydhoryon; havalreydhor *m*, havalreydhoryon

honest *adj* onest

honesty (1) *n* onester *m*

honesty (2) *n* (*plant*) bath arghans *m*

honey *n* mel *m*

honeycomb *n* kriben vel *f*, kribennow mel

honeyed *adj* melys

honeymoon *n* mis mel *m*

honeysuckle *n* gwydhvosen *f*, gwydhvosennow; gwydhvos *coll*

honour I *n* enor *m*, enorys; onour *m*, onours **II** *vb* enora

honourable *adj* enorys; enoradow; wordhi

honoured *adj* enorys

hood *n* hod *m*, hodys; kugol *m*, kugollow; kogh *m*, koghow. **riding hood** huk *f*, hukys

hoodie *n* hodik *m*, hodigow

hoof *n* karn *m*, karnow

hook I *n* higen *f*, higennow; bagh *f*, baghow **II** *vb* higenna

hoop *n* kylgh *m*, kylghyow

hoop-la *n* kylghigow *pl*

hoot *vb* outya; kernya

hop (1) I *n* lamm *m*, lammow **II** *vb* lamma; lemmel; kronogas

hop (2) *n* (*plant*) hopysen *f*, hopysennow

hope I *n* govenek *m*, govenegow **II** *vb* gwaytyas; bos govenek dhe. **I hope** yma govenek dhymm; govenek a'm beus

hopeless *adj* anwovenek

hops *n* hopys *coll*

horehound *n* les loos *m*

horizon *n* gorwel *f*, gorwelyow

horizontal *adj* gorwelyek

horn *n* korn *m*, kern, *dl* dewgorn

horned *adj* kornek

horrible *adj* euthyk

horribly *adv* euthyk

horrified *adj* skruthys

horror *n* euth *m*

horse *n* margh *m*, mergh. **horse trading** (*fig.*) bargynnya

horse-fly *n* sodronen *f*, sodronennow; sodron *coll*

horse-load *n* sawgh *m*, sawghow

horse-power *n* marghnerth *m*, marghnerthow

horseradish *n* marghredik *m*, marghredigow

horseshoe *n* horn margh *m*, horn mergh

horsetail *n* (*plant*) lost margh *m*

hosepipe *n* piben dhowr *f*, pibennow dowr

hospitable *adj* degemerus; hel; wolkommus

hospital *n* klavji *m*, klavjiow

hospitality *n* gwestva *f*; helder *m*; wolkom *m*

host *n* ost *m*, ostys

hostage *n* gostel *m*, gostlow

hostel *n* ostel *m*, ostelyow

hostile *adj* eskarek

hot *adj* tesek; pooth; (*warm*) tomm; (*extremely hot; blazing*) bros. **hot chocolate** choklet tomm *m*

hot-blooded *adj* tomm y woos

hotel *n* ostel *m*, ostelyow

hot-pot *n* (*meat*) avalow dor ha kig *coll*; (*vegetable*) avalow dor ha losow *coll*

hound *n* hond *m*, hons; (*hunting*) helgi *m*, helgeun; (*racing*) reski *m*, reskeun

hour *n* (*o'clock*) eur *f*, euryow; (*duration*) our *m*, ourys. **within an hour** a-ji dhe our

hourly *adj*, *adv* herwydh an our. **hourly rate** eurdal *m*, eurdalow

house *n* chi *m*, chiow, treven. **country house** manerji *m*, manerjiow. **detached house** chi unnik *m*, chiow unnik, treven unnik. **full house** (*poker*) gwariji leun *m*; dornas leun *m*. **move house** remova chi. **semi-detached house** gevelji *m*, geveljiow. **set up house** dalleth triga

household *n* mayni *m*, mayniow

house martin *n* chikog *f*, chikoges

housewife *n* gwre'ti *f*

housework *n* lavur tre *m*, lavuryow tre

hovel *n* krowji *m*, krowjiow

hover *vb* bargesi

how I *adv* (*before conjugated verbs*) fatel[2]; (*in other positions*) fatla **II** *int* ass; assa[2] **III** *cnj* dell[2]. **how fine the weather is** ass yw brav an gewer. **how nice of you** ass os ta kuv. **how are you** (*sg*) fatla genes; (*pl*) fatla genowgh **how come** prag. **how many** pana lies; py lies; pes. **how many times** peskweyth. **how much** pygemmys. **how often** py lies termyn; pana lies gweyth

however *adv* byttegyns

howl *vb* oulya

hug I *n* byrlans *m*, byrlansow **II** *vb* byrla

huge *adj* kowrek; bras dres eghen

hull *n* kogh *m*, koghow

hum *vb* hwyrni

human I *n* den *m*, tus **II** *adj* denel

humanitarian *adj* dengerensedhek

humanity *n* denses *m*

humankind *n* mab den *m*; denses *m*

humble I *adj* uvel **II** *vb* uvelhe
humid *adj* leyth
humility *n* uvelder *m*
humorous *adj* hwarthus
humour *n* hwarthuster *m*
hump *n* both *f*, bothow; bothen *f*,
 bothennow
Hundred *n* (*administrative division*)
 keverang *f*, keverangow
hundred *num* kans *m*, kansow. **a**
 hundred times kanskweyth
hundredfold *adv* kansplek
hundredth *num* kansves *m*, kansvesow;
 abbrev 100ves
Hungarian I *adj* hungarek **II** *n*
 (*language*) Hungarek *m*; (*person*)
 Hungarian *m*, Hungarians
Hungary *top* Hungari *m*
hunger *n* nown *m*
hungry *adj* nownek; gwag. **I am**
 hungry nown a'm beus; gwag ov vy;
 yma nown dhymm
hunt I *n* helgh *m*, helghow **II** *vb*
 helghya; helghi
hunter *n* helghor *m*, helghoryon
hurdy-gurdy *n* symfoni *m*, symfonis
hurl *vb* deghesi; hurlya
hurler *n* hurlyer *m*, hurlyoryon
hurling *n* (*game*) hurlya *m*
hurry I *n* fisten *m*; tooth *m*; fysk *m* **II** *vb*
 fistena; fyski; stevya. **hurry up** (*sg*)

fisten; (*pl*) fistenewgh. **I am in a**
 hurry mall yw genev
hurt I *adj* pystigys; shyndys **II** *vb*
 shyndya; pystiga; (*intrans.*) glosa **III**
 n pystik *m*, pystigow; drog *m*, drogow
husband *n* gour *m*, gwer; gourti *m*
hush *int* (*sg*) taw; taw tavas; (*pl*)
 tewewgh; tewewgh tavas
husk I *n* plisken *f*, pliskennow **II** *vb*
 pliskenna
hut *n* krow *m*, krowyow; (*rough or*
 ruined hut) krellas *m*, krellow
hybrid *adj* myskreydhek
hydraulic *adj* hidrolek
hydroelectric *adj* dowrdredanek
hydrogen *n* (*element*) hidrojen *m*
hydromel *n* medh *m*
hymn *n* hymna *m*, hymnys
hyperactive *adj* gorvewek
hyperlink *n* gorgevren *f*,
 gorgevrennow
hyphen *n* strik *m*, strikys
hypnotic *adj* huskoskek
hypocrisy *n* fayntys *m*
hypocrite *n* fekler *m*, fekloryon; fekyl
 fals *m*
hypocritical *adj* fekyl cher
hypothesis *n* godybieth *f*,
 godybiethow
hypothesise *vb* godybi

I

I *prn* my; (*enclitic*) vy
-ic *sffx* -ek
ice *n* rew *m*. **ice cream** dehen rew *m*.
 ice cube kub rew *m*, kubow rew. **ice**
 skate *n* skes rew *m*, skesow rew; *vb*
 skesya war rew
iceberg *n* rewvenydh *m*
Iceland *top* Rewenys *f*
Icelander *n* Rewenysyas *m*, Rewenysysi

Icelandic *n* (*language*) Rewenysek *m*
icicle *n* kleghien *f*, kleghiennow; kleghi
 coll
icon *n* ikon *m*, ikonys; (*computer*
 desktop) arwodhik *m*, arwodhigow;
 (*representation of a Saint*) delow *f*,
 delowyow
iconic *adj* ikonek
icy *adj* rewys; oor

idea *n* tybyans *m*, tybyansow

ideal I *adj* delvrysek **II** *n* delvrys *m*, delvrysyow

ideally *adv* y'n gwella kas

identical *adj* kethsam

identity *n* honanieth *f*, honaniethow

idiom *n* (*turn of phrase*) lavar *m*, lavarow; (*peculiar style of expression*) tavoseth *f*; (*regional variety*) rannyeth *f*, rannyethow

idiomatic *adj* tavosethek

idiot *n* bobba *m*, bobbys; penn bobba *m*, pennow bobba; penn pyst *m*, pennow pyst; skogyn *m*, skogynnow. **you goggle-eyed idiot** ty penn bobba lagasek

idle *n* diek; syger. **idle talk** flows *m*

idleness *n* sygerneth *f*

if *cnj* a^4; (*before consonants*) mar^4; mara^4; (*before vowels*) mars; maras; (*unlikely conditions*) a^4; (*negative*) mar ny^2

ignorance *n* fowt dyskans *m*, fowtys dyskans

ignorant *adj* heb dyskans

ignore *vb* sevel orth aswon; skonya aswon

-ile *sffx* -el

ill *adj* (*sick*) klav; (*bad*) drog. **fall ill** kodha klav

illegal *adj* anlaghel; erbynn an lagha

illegitimate *adj* direyth

illiteracy *n* anlettryseth *f*

illiterate *adj* anlettrys

illness *n* klavder *m*; kleves *m*, klevesow

illuminate *vb* golowi; splannhe; (*artistically*) afina

illusion *n* hus *m*, husow. **create an illusion** husa

illustrate *vb* lymna

illustration *n* lymnans *m*, lymnansow

illustrator *n* lymner *m*, lymnoryon

image *n* imach *m*, imajys; hevelep *m*, hevelebow; aven *m*, avenyow

imagery *n* delwedh *m*

imaginary *adj* dismygel

imagination *n* dismygyans *m*, dismygyansow; (*poetic*) awen *f*

imagine *vb* desevos; dismygi; koncevya; tybi

imbalance *n* angespos *m*, angesposow

imitate *vb* gul war-lergh

imitation *n* gwrians war-lergh *m*, gwriansow war-lergh

immature *adj* anadhves

immediate *adj* desempis; tromm

immediately *adv* a-dhesempis; a-dhistowgh; hware; heb lett

immense *adj* kowrek

immerse *vb* troghya

immersion *n* troghyans *m*, troghyansow

immigrant *n* ynvroyas *m*, ynvroysi

immigrate *vb* omynvroa

immigration *n* omynvroans *m*

imminent *adj* degynsywek

immoral *adj* anvas

immorality *n* anvaseth *f*, anvasethow

immortal *adj* anvarwel

immune *adj* (*legal*) antavadow; (*med*) immun

immunisation *n* (*med*) immunheans *m*

immunise *vb* (*med*) immunhe

immunity *n* (*med*) immunedh *m*

impair *vb* aperya; shyndya

impassable *adj* hepfordh

impatient *adj* heb perthyans

impede *vb* lettya

impend *vb* degynsywa

impending *adj* degynsywek

imperfect *adj* anperfydh. **imperfect tense** amser anperfydh *f*

imperial *adj* emperourethek

imperialism *n* emperouregieth *f*

imperialistic *adj* emperouregek

impersonal *adj* dibersonel

impertinence *n* tonteth *f*

impertinent *adj* tont

implement I *n* toul *m*, toulys **II** *vb* kowlwul

implementation *n* gweythresans *m*, gweythresansow

implore *vb* konjorya

imply *vb* goblegi

impolite *adj* diskortes

import I *n* ynporth *m*, ynporthow **II** *vb* ynperthi

importance *n* bri *f*; poos *m*; les *m*; roweth *m*

important *adj* posek; bysi. **it's important for you to go** bysi yw dhis mos

impossible *adj* analladow; anpossybyl; na yll bos

impostor *n* falswas *m*, falswesyon

impoverish *vb* boghosekhe

impoverished *adj* boghosek

impractical *adj* (*person*) kledhek y dowlow *m*; kledhek hy thowlow *f*; (*thing*) kales dhe wul

imprecise *adj* andhiblans

impress I *n* merk *m*, merkys; stampa *m*, stampys **II** *vb* merkya; stampya. **be impressed by** bos kemerys gans. **impress somebody** sordya marth yn nebonan

impression *n* (*printing*) sel *f*, selys, selyow; (*retained effect or feeling*) argraf *m*, argrafyow; (*pressure*) gwaskans *m*, gwaskansow; (*humorous imitation*) gwrians war-lergh *m*, gwriansow war-lergh

imprison *vb* prisonya; karghara

imprisonment *n* prisonyans *m*, prisonyansow; kargharans *m*, kargharansow

improbable *adj* diwirhaval

improper *adj* anwiw

improve *vb* (*transitive and intransitive*) gwellhe

improvement *n* gwellheans *m*, gwellheansow

improvisation *n* ymprovisans *m*, ymprovisansow; (*music, theatre etc.*) dismygwari *m*, dismygwariow

improvise *vb* ymprovisa; (*music, theatre etc.*) dismygwari

impudence *n* tonteth *f*

impudent *adj* tont

impulse *n* yniedh *m*, yniedhow

impulsive *adj* fysk

in *prp* yn. **in agreement with** unver gans. **in front of** a-rag. **in place of** yn le. **in the** y'n. **in the vicinity of** yn herwydh. **in three days' time** godreva; godrevedh. **in which way** pana vaner. **is he in?** usi ev yn tre?

in- *prfx* yn-

inaccessible *adj* anhedhadow

inaccuracy *n* ankewerder *m*

inaccurate *adj* ankewar

inactive *adj* anweythresek

inbox *n* (*email*) yngist *f*, yngistyow

incapable *adj* anteythi; diallos

incarcerate *vb* karghara; prisonya

incarceration *n* kargharans *m*, kargharansow

inception *n* dalleth *m*, dallethow

incessantly *adv* heb lett

inch *n* meusva *f*, meusvaow

incident *n* hwarvedhyans *m*, hwarvedhyansow

incidental *adj* hwarvosek

incidentally *adv* dre happ; unweyth

incinerate *vb* gorleski; kowlleski

incineration *n* gorlosk *m*

incinerator *n* gorloskell *f*, gorloskellow

incite *vb* movya; ynia; piga

incitement *n* ynians *m*, yniansow

incline I *n* goleder *f*, goledrow **II** *vb* ynklinya

include *vb* komprehendya

inclusive *adj* dalghus

inclusivity *n* dalghuster *m*

incognito I *adj* yn-dann hanow fug **II** *n* hanow fug *m*, henwyn fug

income *n* gober *m*, gobrow

incompatible *adj* ankesplegadow

incompetent *adj* diallos

incomplete *adj* andhien

incomprehensible *adj* ankonvedhadow

inconvenience I *n* ankombrynsi *m*; dises *m*, disesys II *vb* ankombra

inconvenient *adj* ankombrus

incorporate *vb* ynkorfora

incorporation *n* ynkorforans *m*, ynkorforansow

incorrect *adj* anewn; ankewar

increase *vb* kressya; ynkressya; moghhe

increased *adj* kressys

increasing *adj* usi owth ynkressya; moy ha moy

increasingly *adv* moy ha moy

incredible *adj* digrysadow

incubate *vb* kovia

incurable *adj* dieli; heb remedi

indecent *adj* lewd

indeed *adv* devri; yn tevri; fest

independence *n* anserghogeth *f*

independent *adj* anserghek

indescribable *adj* andheskrifadow

index *n* menegva *f*, menegvaow; rol *f*, rolyow

India *top* Eynda *f*

Indian I *adj* eyndek II *n* Eyndek *m*, Eyndogyon

indicate *vb* kevarwodha; meneges; poyntya; sinya

indication *n* menek *m*, menegow

indicative *adj* menegek. **indicative mood** gis menegek *m*

indignant *adj* serrys

indignation *n* sorrvan *m*

indirect *adj* andhidro

indistinct *adj* diskler; andhiblans

individual I *adj* unnik II *n* unigyn *m*, unigynnow

indolence *n* diekter *m*

indoor *adj* pervedhek

indoors *adv* a-bervedh; a-ji

inductance *n* dynedh *m*

industrial *adj* diwysyansel

industrious *adj* diwysyk

industry *n* diwysyans *m*, diwysyansow; hwel ober *m*, hwelyow ober

ineffective *adj* aneffeythus

inefficient *adj* aneffeythus

inequality *n* dibarder *m*, dibarderyow

inexpensive *adj* a bris isel

inexperienced *adj* heb prevyans

inexpert *adj* digreft

infamous *adj* drog gerys

infamy *n* bismer *m*, bismeras

infant *n* fleghik *m*, fleghesigow, fleghigyow

infect *vb* klevesi

infected *adj* klevesys

infection *n* klevesans *m*, klevesansow

infectious *adj* klevesus

inferior *adj* isella; gweth

infiltrate *vb* ynsidhla

infiltration *n* ynsidhlans *m*, ynsidhlansow

infiltrator *n* (*infiltrator*) ynsidhler *m*, ynsidhloryon

infinite *adj* didhiwedh

infinitive *n* hanow-verb *m*, henwyn-verb

infinity *n* didhiwedhter *m*

inflame *vb* fagla

inflammation *n* fagel *f*, faglow

inflate *vb* (*with gas*) hwytha

inflation *n* (*with gas*) hwythans *m*, hwythansow

inflexibility *n* diwedhynder *m*

inflexible *adj* diwedhyn

influence I *n* delanwes *m*, delanwesow; awedhyans *m*, awedhyansow II *vb* delenwel; awedhya

influenza *n* flou *f*

inform *vb* derivas; kedhla. **inform somebody** derivas dhe nebonan; derivas orth nebonan

informal *adj* anformel

information *n* kedhlow *pl*

Information Technology *n* Teknegieth Kedhlow *m*

infrared *adj* isrudh

infrastructure *n* isframweyth *m*

infrequent *adj* anvenowgh

-ing *sffx* (*before consonants*) ow[4]; (*before vowels*) owth; yn unn[2]

ingredient *n* devnydh *m*, devnydhyow

inhabit *vb* anedhi

inhabitable *adj* anedhadow

inhabitant *n* triger *m*, trigoryon; anedhyas *m*, anedhysi

inhabited *adj* anedhys

inherit *vb* herya; erita

inhibit *vb* spralla

inhibition *n* sprall *m*, sprallow

inhospitable *adj* didhynnargh

initial **I** *adj* kynsa **II** *n* tallytheren *f*, tallytherennow

initially *adv* wostalleth; wortalleth

initiate *vb* urdhya

initiation *n* urdhyans *m*, urdhyansow

inject *vb* skitya

injection *n* skityans *m*, skityansow. **fuel injection** skityans petrol

injure *vb* hodya; shyndya

injured *adj* hodys; pystigys; shyndys

injury *n* shyndyans *m*, shyndyansow; goli *m*, goliow

injustice *n* anjustis *m*

ink *n* ynk *m*

inlet *n* logh *m*, loghow

inn *n* tavern *m*, tavernyow; hostelri *m*, hostelriow

inner *adj* nessa dhe'n kres

innkeeper *n* ost *m*, ostys; tavernor *m*, tavernoryon

innocent **I** *adj* ankablus; (*naive*) inocent **II** *n* inocent *m*, inocens

innovation *n* nowedhyans *m*, nowedhyansow

inorganic *adj* anorganek

input **I** *n* ynworrans *m*, ynworransow **II** *vb* ynworra

inquire *vb* govyn

inquiry *n* govynadow *m*

inquisitive *adj* govynnus

insane *adj* muskok; varyes. **go insane** muskegi. **drive insane** muskegi; varya

insanity *n* muskotter *m*

insect *n* pryv *m*, preves; hweskeren *f*, hweskerennow; hwesker *coll*

insecticide *n* gorthpryv *m*, gorthpryvyow

insecure *adj* andhiogel

insecurity *n* andhiogeledh *m*, andhiogeledhow

insensitive *adj* tew y groghen

insert *vb* gorra a-bervedh

inshore *adj* nesarvorel

inside **I** *adj* pervedhek **II** *adv* a-bervedh; a-ji **III** pervedh *n.m*, pervedhow **IIV** *prp* a-bervedh yn; a-ji dhe[2]

insignificance *n* fowt styr *m*; fowt bri *m*

insignificant *adj* distyr

insincere *adj* fals

insincerity *n* falsuri *m*

insipid *adj* difreth

insist *vb* teri. **insist on** ynia war[2]

insistence *n* ter *m*; er *m*

insistent *adj* ter

insolence *n* tonteth *f*

insolent *adj* tont

insomnia *n* (*med*) insomnia *m*; (*colloq*) anhun *m*

insomniac *adj* anhunek

inspect *vb* hwithra; eksamnya

inspection *n* hwithrans *m*, hwithransow

inspector *n* hwithrer *m*, hwithroryon

inspiration *n* awen *f*

inspire *vb* ynspirya; aweni

install *vb* ynstallya; settya yn y dyller

installation *n* ynstallyans *m*, ynstallyansow

instance *n* gweyth *f*, gweythyow; ensampel *m*, ensamplys, ensamplow. **for instance** rag ensampel

instant **I** *adj* desempis **II** *n* pols *m*, polsyow; prysweyth *m*, prysweythyow. **instant coffee** koffi desempis *m*. **instant message** *n* messach desempis *m*, messajys desempis

instantaneous *adj* prysweythyel

instantly *adv* a-dhesempis; kettooth ha'n ger

instead *adv* yn le. **instead of her** yn hy le

instigate *vb* sordya

instruct *vb* dyski; ynstruktya

instruction *n* dyskans *m*, dyskansow

instructions *n* danvonadow *pl*

instructor *n* dyskador *m*, dyskadoryon; dyskadores *f*, dyskadoresow

instrument *n* (*means*) mayn *m*, maynys; (*music*) daffar ilow *m*

instrumental *adj* maynek

insufficient *adj* anlowr

insular *adj* enesek

insulate *vb* enesega

insulation *n* enysegans *m*, enysegansow

insult I *n* despit *m*, despitys; arvedhen *f*, arvedhennow II *vb* despitya; arvedh

insulting *adj* arvedhus

insurance *n* surheans *m*, surheansow

insure *vb* surhe

insurgency *n* omsav *m*, omsavow; omsevyans *m*, omsevyansow; rebellyans *m*, rebellyansow

insurgent *n* omsevyas *m*, omsevysi; rebel *m*, rebels

insurrection *n* omsav *m*, omsavow; omsevyans *m*, omsevyansow; rebellyans *m*, rebellyansow

integer *n* kowlniver *m*, kowlniverow

integrity *n* ewnhynseth *f*

intellect *n* skians *m*, skiansow

intellectual I *adj* skiansek II *n* skiansek *m*, skiansogyon

intelligence *n* poll *m*, pollow

intelligent *adj* skentel; skientel; skiansek; pollek

intend *vb* mynnes

intense *adj* tynn; glew

intensity *n* krevder *m*, krevderyow; tynnedh *m*, tynedhow; glewder *m*, glewderyow

intensive *adj* dour. **intensive care** dourwith *m*

intent *n* mynnas *m*, mynasow

intention *n* mynnas *m*, mynasow; towl *m*, towlow; brys *m*, brysyow

intentional *adj* a-borpos

intentionally *adv* a-borpos; orth bodh ow brys

inter *vb* (*bury*) ynkleudhyas; yntirya

interactive *adj* kesvewek

inter-Celtic *adj* keskeltek

intercept *vb* kontrewaytya

interception *n* kontrewaytyans *m*, kontrewaytyansow

interchange I *n* keschanj *m*, keschanjyow II *vb* keschanjya

interchangeable *n* keschanjadow

intercourse *n* daromres *m*, daromresow. **sexual intercourse** daromres karnal *m*; kyjyans *m*, kyjyansow. **have sexual intercourse** kyjya

interest I *n* (*concern*) bern *m*, bernyow; les *m*; (*financial*) oker *m* II *vb* (*3s only*) deur. **it does not interest me** ny'm deur; **see if it interests you** mir mara'th teur. **interest rate** kevradh oker *m*, kevradhow oker

interesting *adj* didheurek; dhe les; lesek

interface *n* ynterfas *m*, ynterfassow

interfere *vb* mellya

interference *n* mellyans *m*, mellyansow

interior I *adj* pervedhek II *n* pervedh *m*, pervedhow

intermittent *adj*, *prfx* ter-

internal *adj* pervedhek

international *adj* keswlasek

internet *n* kesroswey-h *m*. **surf the internet** rosya an kesrosweyth

interpret *vb* styrya

interpretation *n* styryans *m*, styryansow

interpreter *n* latimer *m*, latimers

interrogate *vb* apposya

interrupt *vb* goderri; *(speech)* kewsel a-dreus

interrupted *adj* goderrys

interruption *n* godor *m*, godorrow

interval *n* *(short break)* powes *m*, powesow; *(period)* spys *m*, spysow

interview I *n* keswel *f*, keswelyow **II** *vb* kesweles

intimidate *vb* ownekhe

intimidation *n* ownekheans *m*, ownekheansow

into *prp* yn

intolerable *adj* anporthadow; diwodhav

intolerance *n* fowt perthyans *m*

intonation *n* ton-lev *m*, ton-levow

intoxicate *vb* medhwi

intoxicated *adj* medhow

intoxication *n* medhwenep *m*

intravenous *adj* dre wythien. **drip** *n* *(intravenous therapy; med)* deverell dre wythien *f*, deverellow dre wythien

intricate *adj* gwius

introduce *vb* komendya. **introduce oneself** omgomendya

introduction *n* *(people)* komendyans *m*, komendyansow; *(book)* raglavar *m*, raglavarow

invalid I *adj* *(false)* drog; *(incapacitated)* klav **II** *n* klav *m*, klevyon

invasion *n* goryskyn *m*, goryskynnow

invent *vb* devisya; dismygi

invention *n* dismygyans *m*, dismygyansow

inventor *n* deviser *m*, devisoryon

inventory *n* rol *f*, rolyow

inversion *n* gorthtro *f*, gorthtroyow

invert *vb* gorra an pyth a-wartha dhe woles; trebuchya

invest *vb* kevarghewi

investigate *vb* hwithra

investigative *adj* hwithrus

investment *n* kevarghow *m*, kevarghowyow

invincible *adj* antryghadow

invisibility *n* anweladewder *m*

invisible *adj* anweladow

invitation *n* galow *m*, galowyow

invite *vb* gelwel

invoice *n* reken *m*, reknow

involve *vb* omvyska

involved *adj* omvyskys

involvement *n* omvyskans *m*, omvyskansow

inwards *adv* war-ji

ion *n* ion *m*, ionow

ionic *adj* ionek

Ireland *top* Iwerdhon *f*

iris *n* *(yellow flag)* elestren *f*, elester

Irish I *adj* iwerdhonek **II** *n* *(language)* Iwerdhonek; Godhalek Iwerdhon *m*

Irishman *n* Godhal *m*, Godhyli

irk *vb* ania; veksya

irksome *adj* skwithus

iron I *adj* hornek **II** *n* *(element)* horn *m*; *(laundry)* hornell *f*, hornellow **III** *vb* hornella. **cast iron** horn teudhys *m*. **iron armour** gwisk horn *m*. **ironing board** *n* bord-hornella *m*, bordys-hornella, bordow-hornella

ironic *adj* ironek

ironmonger *n* horner *m*, hornoryon

irony *n* gesedh *m*, gesedhow

irrational *adj* direson

irreducible *adj* anlehadow

irrefutable *adj* annaghadow; na yll bos disprevys

irregular *adj* avrewlys; direwl; digompes

irregularity *n* digomposter *m*, digomposteryow; direwl *m*

irrelevant *adj* heb bri

irreproachable *adj* divlam

irrespective *adj* heb reken. **irrespective of** na fors pyneyl

irresponsible *adj* dibreder

irrigate *vb* dowrhe
irritable *adj* krowsek
irritate *vb* serri; veksya
-ish *sffx* -ek
Islam *n* Islam *m*
Islamic *adj* Islamek
island *n* enys *f*, enesow
Isle of Man *top* Manow *f*; Enys
  Vanow *f*
Isles of Scilly *top* Syllan *f*; Enesow
  Syllan *pl*
islet *n* enesik *f*, enesigow
isobar *n* isobar *m*, isobarow
isogloss *n* isogloss *m*, isoglossow
isolate *vb* enyshe
isolated *adj* enyshes
isolation *n* (*state*) enysekter *m*;
  (*process*) enysheans *m*, enysheansow
isotherm *n* tempredhlinen *f*,
  tempredhlinennow
isotope *n* isotop *m*, isotopow
isotopic *adj* isotopek
Israel *top* Israel *m*

Israeli I *adj* israelyek **II** *n* Israelyas *m*,
  Israelysi
issue I *n* (*publication*) dyllans *m*,
  dyllansow; (*topic*) mater *m*, maters **II**
  vb dyllo
it *prn* ev *m*; va *m*; (*after imperatives*) e *m*;
  hi *f*; (*object*) 'n *m*; 's *f*
Italian I *adj* italek **II** *n* (*language*) Italek
  m; (*person*) Italian *m*, Italians
italic *adj* (*font*) italek
Italy *top* Itali *m*
itch I *n* debron *m*, debronow; kos *f*,
  kosow **II** *vb* debreni; kosa
item *n* (*on a list*) poynt *m*, poyntys,
  poyntow; (*thing*) tra *f*, taklow, traow
iterative *adj* daswriansek
itself *prn* ev y honan *m*; hi hy honan
ivory *n* dans olifans *m*
ivy *n* idhyowen *f*, idhyowennow;
  idhyow *coll*
ivy, Kenilworth *n* (*ivy-leaved toadflax;*
  mother of thousands) tron an leugh *m*

J

jab *n* gwan *f*, gwanyow
jack *n* (*playing card*) gwas *m*, gwesyon
jackal *n* owrgi *m*, owrgeun
jackass *n* margh asen *m*, mergh asen
Jack-by-the-hedge *n* (*garlic mustard*)
  Jakka a'n ke *m*
jackdaw *n* chogha *m*, choghys
jacket *n* jerkyn *m*, jerkyns, jerkynnow
jack-in-the-box *n* jowl-lemmel *m*,
  jowlow-lemmel
jagged *adj* densek
jail *n* prison *m*, prisonyow
jailer *n* jayler *m*, jaylers
jam *n* (*preserve*) kyfeyth *m*, kyfeythyow.
  traffic jam *n* daromdak *m*,
  daromdagow
janitor *n* porther *m*, porthoryon

January *n* Genver *m*; mis Genver *m*
Japan *top* Nihon *m*
Japanese *n* (*language*) Nihonek *m*
jar (1) *n* (*large vessel*) seth *m*, sethow.
  small jar jarrik *m*, jarrigow
jar (2) *n* (*shock*) jagg *m*, jaggys
jarful *n* sethas *m*, sethasow
jargon *n* tavoseth *f*
jaundice *n* kleves melyn *m*
jaundiced *adj* melynik
jaw *n* awen *f*, awenow, *dl* diwawen; gen
  f, genyow, *dl* diwen; grudh *f*, grudhow;
  challa *m*, challys; chal *m*, chalys
jawbone *n* challa *m*, challys
jay *n* kegin *f*, kegines
jazz *n* jazz *m*
jealous *adj* gorvynnek; avius. **be**

jealous of someone perthi avi orth nebonan

jealousy *n* avi *m*

jeans *n* jins *pl*; lavrek jin *m*, lavrogow jin

jeep *n* jip *m*, jipys

jeer I *n* ges *m*, gesyow **II** *vb* gesya

jelly *n* kowlesen *f*, kowles

jellyfish *n* morgowlesen *f*, morgowlesennow; morgowles *coll*

jerkin *n* jerkyn *m*, jerkynnow, jerkyns

Jersey *top* Jersenys *f*

jersey *n* gwlanek *m*, gwlanogow

jest I *n* jest *m*, jestys **II** *vb* jestya

jet (1) I *n* (*stream*) stif *m*, stifow; (*plane*) jett *m*, jettys, jettow **II** *vb* stifa. **jet engine** stifjyn *m*, stifjynnys, stifjynnow. **jet lag** stiflinder *m*. **jet stream** stifliv *m*

jet (2) *n* (*mineral*) men du *m*

jet-black *adj* morel

jetsam *n* skommen *f*, skomennow; skomm *coll*

jetty *n* kay *m*, kayys, kayow

Jew *n* Yedhow *m*, Yedhewon

jewel *n* tegen *f*, tegennow; jowel *m*, jowelys

jewellery *n* gemmweyth *m*; tegennow *pl*

Jewish *adj* Yedhowek

jig *n* (*dance*) jyg *m*, jygyow; (*movement*) kryghlam *m*, kryghlammow

jigsaw *n* (*puzzle*) gwari mildam *m*, gwariow mildam

jingle I *n* tynkyal *m*, tynkyalyow; (*as part of advertisement*) kanik *f*, kanigow **II** *vb* tynkyal

jittery *adj* doutys; nervus

job *n* oberen *f*, oberennow

jog *vb* goresek

jogger *n* goreser *m*, goresoryon

join *vb* (*transitive*) junya; (*intransitive*) omjunya

joint *n* mell *m*, mellow; kevals *m*, kevalsyow; (*cannabis cigarette*) porven ganabys *f*, porvennow kanabys

jointed *adj* mellek

jointly *adv* war-barth

joke I *n* ges *m*, gesyow **II** *vb* gul ges

joker *n* gesyer *m*, gesyoryon

jolly *adj* jolif; lowenek

jolt I *n* jagg *m*, jaggys **II** *vb* kryghylli

journal *n* jornal *m*, jornalys

journalist *n* jornalyas *m*, jornalysi

journey I *n* viaj *m*, viajys, viajow; kerdh *m*, kerdhow **II** *vb* viajya

jowl *n* chal *m*, chalys

joy *n* lowena *f*, lowenedhow; joy *m*, joyys

joyful *adj* heudh; lowenek

jubilant *adj* gormoledhek

Judaism *n* Yedhowieth *f*

judge I *n* breusyas *m*, breusysi; barner *m*, barnoryon, barneryow **II** *vb* breusi; barna

judgement *n* breus *f*, breusow

judgmental *adj* breusel

judo *n* judo *m*

jug *n* podik *m*, podigow; pycher *m*, pychers. **measuring jug** podik-musura *m*, podigow-musura

juggle *vb* joglya

juggler *n* jogler *m*, joglers, jogloryon

jugular *adj* a'n konna. **jugular vein** gwythien an konna *f*

juice *n* sugen *m*, sugenyow. **apple juice** sugen aval *m*. **fruit juice** sugen frooth *m*. **orange juice** sugen owraval *m*

juicy *adj* sugnek

July *n* Gortheren *m*; mis Gortheren *m*

jumble I (*mixture*) kemmysk *m*, kemyskow; (*old clothes*) *n* hendhillasen *f*, hendhillasennow; hendhillas *coll* **II** *vb* kemyska. **jumble sale** basar *m*, basars

jump I *n* lamm *m*, lammow **II** *vb* lamma; lemmel. **jump about** terlemmel. **jump bail** gasa mewgh.

jump over dreslemmel. **jump ship** kilfia. **jump the queue** dreslemmel an lost

jumper (1) *n* (*athlete*) lammer *m*, lamoryon

jumper (2) *n* (*sweater*) gwlanek *m*, gwlanogow

junction (*road*) fordh dhibarth *f*, fordhow dibarth; (*streams*) kemper *m*, kemperyow

June *n* Metheven *m*; mis Metheven *m*

jungle *n* gwylgos *m*, gwylgosow; jangal *m*, janglow

juniper *n* merywen *f*, merywennow; meryw *coll*

junk *n* atal *coll*; skollyon *pl*. **junk food** *n* boos atal *m*

junkie *n* (*colloq; person with drug dependency*) stoffki *m*, stoffkeun

Jupiter *n* Yow *m*; Jovyn *m*; Jubyter *m*

juridical *adj* justisek; a'n lagha

jurisdiction *n* arlottes *m*

juror *n* tiyas *m*, tiysi

jury *n* dewdhek person *pl*

just I *adj* ewn; poran; ewnhynsek **II** *adv* (*only*) hepken. **just as** kepar dell[2]; par dell[2]. **just as it is** par dell yw. **just now** namnygen. **I have just done it** nowydh gwrys yw genev

justice *n* (*virtue*) ewnder *m*; justis *m*; (*magistrate*) justis *m*. justisyow. **chief justice** *n* pennjustis *m*, pennjustisyow

justifiable *adj* avowadow

justify *vb* avowa; justifia

jute *n* (*fabric*) jouta *m*

jutting *adj* balek

juvenile *adj* yowynk

K

kale *n* kowlen *f*, kowlennow; kowl *coll*

kangaroo *n* kangarou *m*, kangarous

kaolin *n* pri gwynn *m*

karate *n* karate *m*

kayak *n* kayak *m*, kayakys, kayagow

keel *n* keyn *m*, keynow

keen *adj* (*sharp*) lymm; (*eager*) hwansek. **I am keen to** mall yw genev a[2]

keenness *n* mall *m*, mallow

keep I *n* (*castle*) tour *m*, touryow **II** *vb* gwitha; synsi. **keep a promise** kewera. **keep in touch** kestava. **keep oneself** omwitha. **keep to a rule** synsi rewl. **keep up** kesstrivya

keeper *n* gwithyas *m*, gwithysi

keepsake *n* kovro *m*, kovrohow

kelp *n* gomonen *f*, gomonennow; gommon *coll*

Kenilworth ivy *n* (*ivy-leaved toadflax; mother of thousands*) tron an leugh *m*

kennel *n* kiji *m*, kijiow; (*kennels*) keunva *f*, keunvaow

kerchief *n* lien *m*, lienyow

kernel *n* sprusen *f*, sprusennow; sprus *coll*

ketchup *n* kechap *m*

kettle *n* kalter *f*, kaltoryow; tekel *m*, tekels; (*cooking vessel*) chek *m*, chekys. **tea kettle** *n* chek te *m*, chekys te. **put the kettle on** gorra an galter dhe vryjyon

kettle-drum *n* naker *m*, nakrys

kettleful *n* kalteras *m*, kalterasow

key *n* (*lock*) alhwedh *m*, alhwedhow; (*typing*) alhwedhen *f*, alhwedhennow

keyboard *n* alhwedhell *f*, alhwedhellow; bysowek *f*, bysowegi

keyhole *n* toll alhwedh *m*, tell alhwedh

keyword *n* ger alhwedh *m*, geryow alhwedh

kick I *n* pot *m*, potow **II** *vb* potya

kid I *n* (*child*) flogh *m*, fleghes; (*goat*) mynnen *f*, mynennow; mynn *coll* **II** *vb* gul ges; tolla. **are you kidding?** esos ta ow kul ges?

kidnap *vb* denladra; (*snatch*) dengibya

kidnapping *n* denladrans *m*, denladransow; dengibyans *m*, dengibyansow;

kidney *n* loneth *f*, lonethi. **steak and kidney pie** hogen vewin ha loneth *f*, hogennow bewin ha loneth

kill *vb* ladha. **kill oneself** omladha

killed *adj* ledhys

killer *n* ladher *m*, ladhoryon; denledhyas *m*, denledhysi; (*professional or hired*) ledhyas *m*, ledhysi

killing *n* ladhva *f*, ladhvaow

killjoy *n* ledhyas lowena *m*, ledhysi lowena

kiln *n* oden *f*, odenyow

kilobyte *n* kilobayt *m*, kilobaytys; *abbrev* KB

kilocalorie *n* kilokalori *m*, kilokaloris

kilogramme *n* kilogram *m*, kilogrammow; *abbrev* kg

kilometre *n* kilometer *m*, kilometrow; *abbrev* km

kilt *n* losten albanek *f*, lostennow albanek; losten vrith *f*, lostennow brith. **Cornish kilt** losten vrith kernewek *f*, lostennow brith kernewek

kin *n* neskar *m*, neskerens. **next of kin** neshevin *m*, neshevin

kind (1) *adj* (*amiable*) hegar; hweg; kuv. **kind regards** gorhemynadow a'n gwella. **be so kind as to** dell y'm kyrri

kind (2) *n* (*variety*) eghen *f*, eghennow; kinda *m*, kindys. **that kind of** a'n par na

kind of (*sort of*) *adj* nebes

kindle *vb* dewi; enowi

kindly *adj* hegar; kolonnek

kindness *n* kuvder *m*

kinetic *adj* kinetyk

king *n* myghtern *m*, myghternedh. **king size** kowrek

kingdom *n* gwlaskor *f*, gwlaskordhow; myghterneth *f*, myghternethow; ruvaneth *f*, ruvanethow. **United Kingdom** *top* Ruvaneth Unys *f*; Gwlaskor Unys *f*

kingfisher *n* pyskador an myghtern *m*, pyskadoryon an myghtern

kingship *n* myghternses *m*

kiosk *n* kiosk *m*, kioskys

kiss I *n* amm *m*, ammow; bay *m*, bayow **II** *vb* amma; baya. **kiss somebody** amma dhe nebonan. **kiss me!** amm dhymm!

kit *n* daffar *m*

kitchen *n* kegin *f*, keginow. **kitchen dresser** *n* lestrier *m*, lestrieryow. **kitchen garden** erber *m*, erberow, erbers

kite *n* (*bird*) skowl *m*, skowles; (*toy*) sarf-neyja *f*, serf-neyja

kitten *n* kathik *m*, kathigow

knack *n* wrynch *m*. **there's a knack to it** res yw usya wrynch ganso

knapweed *n* paderow pronter *coll*

knave *n* (*playing card*) gwas *m*, gwesyon

knead *vb* tosa

knee *n* glin *m*, glinyow, *dl* dewlin. **knee-cap** *n* penn glin *m*, pennow glin; padel benn glin *f*, padellow penn glin

kneel *vb* mos war benn dewlin

kneeling *adj* war benn glin

knickers *n* islavrek *m*, islavrogow

knife *n* kollell *f*, kellylli. **pocket knife** kellyllik *f*, kellylligow

knife-handle *n* karn kollan *m*, karnow kollan

knight *n* marghek *m*, marghogyon

knit *vb* gwia. **knit one's brows** plegya tal

knitwear *n* dillas-gwia *coll*

knob *n* talben *m*, talbennow

knock I *n* bonk *m*, bonkys; knouk *m*, knoukys **II** *vb* bonkya; knoukya; frappya. **knock-out competition** kesstrif-dilea *m*, kesstrifow-dilea

knocker *n* (*mine spirit*) knoukyer *m*, knoukyers; kravlost *m*, kravlostow; (*door*) morthol daras *m*, mortholow daras

knot I *n* kolm *m*, kolmow; kolmen *f*, kolmennow **II** *vb* kelmi

knotty *adj* kolmek

know *vb* (*know how to*) godhvos; (*recognise*) aswon

know-how *n* godhvos *m*

knowledge *n* skians *m*, skiansow; aswonvos *m*, aswonvosow; godhvos *m*, godhvosow

knowledgeable *adj* skiansek; meur y skians *m*; meur hy skians *f*; meur aga skians *pl*

known *adj* aswonys; godhvedhys. **well known** godhvedhys yn ta

knuckle *n* mell dorn *m*, mellow dorn

Korea *top* Korea *f*. **North Korea** Korea Gledh *f*. **South Korea** Korea Dhyghow *f*

Korean I *adj* koreek **II** *n* (*language*) Koreek; (*person*) Korean *m*, Koreans

kumquat *n* owravalik *m*, owravaligow

L

label I *n* label *m*, labelyow **II** *vb* staga label orth

laboratory *n* arbrovji *m*, arbrovjiow; hwilva *f*, hwilvaow

laborious *adj* lavurus

labour I *n* hwel *m*, hwelyow; lavur *m*, lavuryow; (*childbirth*) gwelivos *m* **II** *vb* lavurya; gonis; travalya. **go into labour** gwelivesi. **Labour Party** Parti Lavur *m*

labourer *n* lavuryas *m*, lavurysi

labour intensive *adj* gorlavurus

lace I *n* las *m*, lasow **II** *vb* lasya

lack I *n* fowt *m*, fowtys **II** *vb* fyllel. **tra vyth ny fyll dhyn** we don't lack anything; we have everything we need

lad *n* maw *m*, mebyon

ladder *n* skeul *f*, skeulyow

ladies *n* (*signage*) benenes *pl*

ladle *n* lo ledan *f*, loyow ledan

lady *n* arlodhes *f*, arlodhesow

lady's mantle *n* (*plant*) paw lew *f*

ladybird *n* bughik Dhuw *f*, bughigesow Duw

lag *vb* treynya

lager *n* korev gwann *m*, korevow gwann *m*

lair *n* kovva *f*, kovvaow; kudhva *f*, kudhvaow

lake *n* lynn *f*, lynnyn

lamb *n* on *m*, eyn

lame *adj* kloppek. **person with a limp** kloppek *m*, kloppogyon

lameness *n* klefni *m*

lament I *n* kynvan *m*, kynvannow **II** *vb* kyni; galari

lamentation *n* kynvan *m*, kynvannow

lamp *n* lugarn *m*, lugern. **lamp-post** *n* golowbren *m*, golowbrennyer

lampoon *vb* gul ges a²

land I *n* tir *m*, tiryow, (*country*) bro *f*, broyow; (*nation*) gwlas *f*, gwlasow; (*region*) pow *m*, powyow **II** *vb* tira. **Land's End** Penn an Wlas *m*. **on land** yn tir. **the Promised Land** an Tiredh a Dhedhewadow *m*

landfill *n* tirlanow *m*

landlady *n* ostes *f*, ostesow

landlord *n* ost *m*, ostys

landmark *n* tirnos *m*, tirnosow

landscape *n* tirwedh *f*, tirwedhow

lane *n* bownder *f*, bownderyow

language *n* taves *m*, tavosow; yeth *f*, yethow

lantern *n* lugarn *m*, lugern; lantern *m*, lanterns

lap (1) *n* (*anat*) barlen *f*, barlennow

lap (2) *vb* lapya

laptop *n* barlennell *f*, barlenellow

larch *n* larchwedhen *f*, larchwedhennow; larchwydh *coll*

lard *n* blonek *m*, blonegow

larder *n* spens *m*, spensow

large *adj* bras; meur

lark (1) *n* (*bird*) ahwesydh *m*, ahwesydhes

lark (2) *n* (*prank*) pratt *m*, prattys, prattow

larkspur *n* (*delphinium*) paw ahwesydh *m*

laryngitis *n* (*med*) larynjitis *m*

larynx *n* (*med*) larynks *m*

lass *n* moren *f*, morenyon; mowes *f*, mowysi

last I *adj* diwettha **II** *vb* pesya; durya. **at last** wostiwedh; wortiwedh. **last night** nyhewer. **last week** y'n seythen usi passy(e)s. **last year** warlena; warleni

lasting *adj* duryadow

late I *adj* diwedhes; helergh; (*deceased*) tremenys **II** *adv* a-dhiwedhes

lately *adv* a-dhiwedhes; a-gynsow; a-lergh

later I *adj* diwettha **II** *adv* wosa henna. **see you later** (*sg*) dha weles; (*pl*) agas gweles; a'n our

latest *adj* diwettha

Latin I *adj* latinek **II** *n* (*language*) Latin *m*

latitude *n* efander *m*

latter *adj* diwettha. **the latter** an pyth kampollys diwettha

Latvia *top* Latvi *f*

Latvian I *adj* latviek **II** *n* (*language*) Latviek *m*; (*person*) Latvian *m*, Latvians

laud I *n* lawd *m*, lawdys **II** *vb* lawdya

laugh I *n* hwarth *m*, hwarthow **II** *vb* hwerthin

laughable *adj* hwarthus

laughter *n* hwarth *m*, hwarthow

launch *vb* lonchya; (*put to sea*) mora

laundry *n* golghti *m*, golghtiow

lava *n* lava *m*

lavatory *n* attesva *f*, attesvaow; privedhyow *pl*

lavender *n* lavant *m*

lavish *adj* gorhel

law *n* lagha *f*, laghys; (*act*) reyth *f*, reythyow. **court of law** breuslys *f*, breuslysyow; kort *f*, kortys. **lynch law** lagha an lovan *f*. **religious law** lay *f*, layys; reyth *f*, reythyow

lawful *adj* herwydh an lagha; laghel

lawless *adj* dilagha

lawn *n* glesin *m*, glesinyow

lawn-mower *n* jynn glesin *m*, jynnys glesin, jynnow glesin

lawsuit *n* ken *m*, kenyow

lawyer *n* laghyas *m*, laghysi

lax *adj* logh

laxity *n* logheth *f*

lay I *adj* leg **II** *vb* laya; pottya; (*eggs*) dedhwi. **lay hands on** dalghenna. **lay hold of** sesya. **lay low** prosternya. **lay open** apertya. **lay waste** wastya

lay-by *n* rypsav *m*, rypsavow

layer *n* gwiskas *m*, gwiskasow

layout *n* aray *m*, arayys, arayow; delinyans *m*, delinyansow

lay person *n* leg *m*, legyon

laziness *n* diekter *m*; sygerneth *f*; diegi *m*

lazy *adj* diek; syger

lead (1) I *n* (*electrical*) led *m*, ledyow; (*for a dog*) lesh *m*, leshyow **II** *vb* hembronk; ledya

lead (2) *n* (*element*) plomm *m*

leader *n* hembrenkyas *m*, hembrenkysi; ledyer *m*, ledyoryon

leaf *n* (*of plants*) delen *f*, delyow; del *coll*; (*page*) folen *f*, folennow; (*paper*) lyven *f*, lyvennow

leafless *adj* didhelen

leaflet *n* folennik *f*, folenigow

leafy *adj* delek; delennek; delyowek

league *n* (*union*) kesunyans *m*, kesunyansow

leak I *n* dowrfols *m*, dowrfolsyow II *vb* devera; dyllo dowr

leaky *adj* tollek

lean (1) *adj* tanow; (*of meat*) kogh

lean (2) *vb* posa. **lean forward** posa war-rag

leap I *n* lamm *m*, lammow II *vb* lamma; lemmel. **leap year** bledhen lamm *f*, bledhynnyow lamm

learn *vb* dyski. **learn from someone** dyski gans nebonan

learned *adj* dyskys; skentel

learner *n* dysker *m*, dyskoryon

learning difficulty *n* (*med*) kaletter dyski *m*, kaletterow dyski. **a person with a learning difficulty** person gans kaletter dyski

learning disability *n* (*med*) evredhder dyski *m*, evredhderow dyski. **a person with learning disabilities** person gans evredhderow dyski

leash *n* lesh *m*, leshyow; syg *f*, sygow

least *adj* lyha. **at least** dhe'n lyha

leather I *adj* ledhrek II *n* ledher *m*, ledhrow

leave I *n* kummyas *m*, kumyasow II *vb* gasa; (*depart*) diberth. **annual leave** *n* kummyas bledhynnyek *m*. **carer's leave** *n* kummyas gwithyas *m*. **compassionate leave** *n* kummyas tregeredhus *m*. **maternity leave** *n* kummyas mamoleth *m*. **parental leave** *n* kummyas kerensel *m*. **paternity leave** *n* kummyas tasoleth *m*

leaven *n* gwel *m*, gwelow

Lebanese I *adj* lebanek II *n* (*person*) Lebanyas *m*, Lebanysi

Lebanon *top* Lebanon *m*

lecture I *n* areth *f*, arethyow II *vb* arethya

lecturer *n* arethor *m*, arethoryon

leek *n* poren *f*, porennow; por *coll*

leek, three cornered *n* (*wild garlic*) kennin trihornek *coll*

left *adj* (*remaining*) gesys; (*opposite of right*) kledh. **on the left of** a-gledh dhe[2]

left-handed *adj* kledhek

leg *n* garr *f*, garrow, *dl* diwarr

legal *adj* laghel

legend *n* henhwedhel *m*, henhwedhlow

legible *adj* lennus; redyadow

legion *n* lyjyon *m*, lyjyons

leisure *n* termyn syger *m*. **at leisure** sygerus

leisurely *adv* sygerus

lemon *n* lymmaval *m*, lymmavalow. **lemon curd** *n* kowles lymmaval *coll*

lend *vb* ri kendon. **lend something to someone** ri neppyth yn kendon dhe nebonan

length *n* hys *m*, hysow; hirder *m*, hirderyow. **at length** dhe-hys. **of the same length as** kehys ha

lengthen *vb* hirhe

lenite *vb* medhelhe

lenition *n* (*2nd state mutation*) medhelheans *m*, medhelheansow

lens *n* gwedrik *m*, gwedrigow; lens *f*, lensow. **contact lens** *n* gwedrik kestav *m*, gwedrigow kestav

Lent *n* Korawys *m*

leopard *n* lewpard *m*, lewpardes

leper *n* klavorek *m*, klarvorogyon; leper *m*, lepers

leprosy *n* lovryjyon *pl*; klavor *m*; kleves bras *m*

lesbian I *adj* lesbian II *n* lesbianes *f*, lesbianesow

lesion *n* pystik *m*, pystigow

less *adv, adj, prn* le

lessen *vb* lehe

lesser *adj* le

lesson *n* dyskans *m*, dyskansow; kentel *m*, kentelyow

lest *cnj* dout; rag own. **take care lest you fall** (*mind you don't fall*) kemmer with rag own ty dhe godha

let *vb* (*allow*) gasa; (*prevent*) lettya. **don't let yourself down** gwith dha hanow da rag meth. **let up** slackya. **let me help you** gas vy dhe'th gweres

lethargic *adj* syger

lethargy *n* diegi *m*; sygerneth *f*

letter *n* (*epistle*) lyther *m*, lytherow; (*character*) lytheren *f*, lytherennow

letterbox *n* kist lytherow *f*, kistyow lytherow

lettuce *n* letusen *f*, letusennow; letus *coll*

level I *adj* kompes; leven II *n* nivel *m*, nivelyow III *vb* komposa; levenhe. **be level with** bos kompes gans

lever *n* kolpes *m*, kolpesow

lewd *adj* lewd

lexicon *n* gerlyver *m*, gerlyvrow

liability *n* kendon *f*, kendonow

liaise *vb* keskelmi. **liaise with** keskelmi orth

liar *n* gowek *m*, gowygyon. **you are just liars** nyns owgh lemen gowygyon

libel I *n* kabel *m*, kablow II *vb* kabla

liberal *adj* (*generous*) hel; (*tolerant*) livrel. **Liberal Democratic Party** *n* Parti Livrel Gwerinel *m*. **the LibDems** *n* an re LivWer *pl*

liberate *vb* livra

liberated *adj* livrys; dhe wari

liberation *n* livreson *m*, livresons

liberty *n* frankedh *m*; rydhses *m*

librarian *n* lyveryas *f*, lyverysi

library *n* lyverva *f*, lyvervaow

licence *n* leshyans *m*, leshyansow; kummyas *m*, kumyasow. **driving licence** *n* kummyas-lewya *m*, kumyasow-lewya

lichen *n* fongalgi *coll*

lick *vb* lapya

lid *n* gorher *m*, gorheryow

lie (1) I *n* (*untruth*) gow *m*, gowyow II *vb* gowleverel; leverel gow. **barefaced lie** gow diveth *m*, gowyow diveth

lie (2) *vb* (*recline*) gorwedha; growedha

lieutenant *n* leftenant *m*, leftenants

life *n* bewnans *m*, bewnansow

lifebelt *n* grugys-sawya *m*, grugysyow-sawya

lifeboat *n* skath-sawya *f*, skathow-sawya

lifestyle *n* bewedh *m*, bewedhow

lifetime *n* termyn bewnans *m*, termynyow bewnans

lift I *n* (*elevator*) yskynnell *f*, yskynellow; (*in a car*) gorrans *m*, gorransow II *vb* drehevel. **give a lift** ri gorrans. **thumb a lift** diskwedhes an meus

light (1) *adj* (*not heavy*) skav

light (2) I *n* golow *m*, golowys II *vb* (*fire*) gorra tan yn; (*candle, lamp, cigarette etc.*) enowi. **light up** golowi

lightbulb *n* bollen *f*, bollennow

lighten (1) *vb* (*make less heavy*) skafhe

lighten (2) *vb* (*illuminate*) golowi

lighter *n* enowell *f*, enowellow; kuner *m*, kunoryon

lighterage *n* morgaryans *m*

lighthouse *n* golowji *m*, golowjiow

lighting *n* golowyans *m*, golowyansow

lightning *n* lughes *coll*. **bolt of lightning** lughesen *f*, lughesennow

like (1) I *adj* haval; hevelep II *prp* avel; kepar (ha). **like hell** malbew damm. **like that** yndella; yndelna. **like this** yndelma

like (2) *vb* kara. **be liked by** bos da gans. **I like** da yw genev

likelihood *n* gwirhevelepter *m*

likely *adj* gwirhaval

liken *vb* heveli

likeness *n* hevelep *m*, hevelebow. **in the likeness of** yn hevelep a²; yn hevelep dhe²

likewise *adv* keffrys; ynwedh

lily *n* lilien *f*, liliennow; lili *coll*. **lily of the valley** losowen an hav *f*, losow an hav

lily, arum *n* (*lords and ladies; cuckoo pint*) skav a'y ligyon *m*

limb *n* esel *m*, eseli

lime *n* (*fruit*) limaval *m*, limavalow

limelight *n* kalghwolow *m*, kalghwolowyow. **in the limelight** yn lagas an bys

limestone *n* kalgh *m*

limit I *n* fin *f*, finyow; finweth *f*, finwethow II *vb* finwetha

limited *adj* strothys

limp *vb* kloppya. **walk with a limp** kerdhes yn unn gloppya; bos kloppek. **limping person** kloppek *m*, kloppogyon

limpet *n* brenigen *f*, brenigennow; brennik *coll*

limpid *adj* ylyn

line *n* linen *f*, linennow; lin *m*, linyow; (*row*) rew *m*, rewyow. **bottom line** lin goles *m*. **line up** *vb* resa

linear *adj* linyek

linen *n* lien *m*, lienyow

linesman *n* linenner *m*, linenoryon

ling *n* (*heather*) grug *m*, grugow

linger *vb* tarya

ling-fish *n* lenes *f*, lenesow

linguist *n* yethor *m*, yethoryon

linguistic *adj* yethoniethel

linguistics *n* yethonieth *f*

lining *n* ispan *m*, ispannow

link I *n* (*of a chain*) mell *m*, mellow; (*tie*) kolm *m*, kolmow; (*internet*)

kevren *f*, kevrennow II *vb* (*transitive*) keskelmi; junya

linnet *n* linek rudh *m*, linoges rudh

lintel *n* penn daras *m*, pennow daras

lion *n* lew *m*, lewyon; lion *m*, lions. **lion cub** lewik *m*, lewesigow. **lion tamer** dover lewyon *m*, dovoryon lewyon

lioness *n* lewes *f*, lewesow

lip *n* gweus *f*, gweusyow, *dl* diwweus. **lip balm** eli gweus *m*, eliow gweus. **lip gloss** lenter gweus *m*. **lip salve** eli gweus *m*, eliow gweus

lipstick *n* liw gweus *m*, liwyow gweus; minliw *m*, minliwyow

liquid I *adj* linyel II *n* lin *m*, linyow. **washing-up liquid** (*detergent*) lin sebon *m*, linyow sebon

liquor *n* las *m*, lasow

lisp I *n* stlavedh *m* II *vb* stlevi

lisping *adj* stlav; stlavedh

list *n* rol *f*, rolyow

listen *vb* goslowes. **listen to** goslowes orth

listener *n* goslowyas *m*, goslowysi

lit *adj* golowys; enowys; gans golow; gans tan

literacy *n* lettryseth *f*; gallos redya *coll*

literal *adj* ger rag ger. **literal translation** treylyans ger rag ger

literary *adj* liennek

literate *adj* lettrys

literature *n* lien *m*, liennow

lithium *n* (*element*) lithiom *m*

Lithuania *top* Lithuani *f*

Lithuanian I *adj* lithuaniek II *n* (*language*) Lithuaniek *m*; (*person*) Lithuanian *m*, Lithuanians

litre *n* liter *m*, litrow

litter I *n* (*transportation*) gravath *f*, gravathow; (*animal bedding*) nogadh *m*, nogadhow; (*animal brood*) torras *m*, torrasow; (*rubbish*) strol *m* II *vb* strolya

little I *adj* byghan; boghes; munys II **a little** *adv* nebes III *n* nebes *m*. **little**

son maban *m*, mebyn. **little by little** nebes ha nebes; tamm ha tamm

live I *adv* (*event*) yn fyw **II** *vb* (*be alive*) bewa; (*at a place*) bos trigys. **he lives in St. Ives** yma ev trigys yn Porth Ia. **live together** kesvewa. **live at the back of beyond** bos trigys yn argel. **live on something** bewa orth neppyth

liveliness *n* bewder *m*

lively *adj* byw; bewek; (*quick*) buan

liver *n* avi *m*, aviow

living I *adj* byw **II** *n* bewnans *m*, bewnansow. **earn a living** dendyl bewnans. **among the living** yn-mysk an re vyw. **where are you living?** ple'th os ta trigys? **within living memory** a-ji dhe gov den. **Living Cornish** Kernewek Byw

living-room *n* esedhva *f*, esedhvaow

lizard *n* pedrevan *f*, pedrevanes

load I *n* karg *m*, kargow; sawgh *m*, sawghow; begh *m*, beghow **II** *vb* karga; beghya

loaded *adj* kergys

loaf (1) *n* (*of bread*) torth *f*, torthow

loaf (2) *vb* (*waste time*) tarya

lobby I *n* (*pressure group*) bagas gwaskas *m*, bagasow gwaskas; (*corridor*) tremenva *f*, tremenvaow **II** *vb* gwaska

lobe *n* lappa *m*, lappys

lobster *n* legest *m*, legesti

local I *adj* teythyek; leel **II** *n* teythyek *m*, teythyogyon

localism *n* leelieth *f*

locality *n* tyller *m*, tylleryow

locate *vb* desedha

location *n* tyller *m*, tylleryow

lock I *n* (*on a door*) floren *f*, florennow; (*water*) yet dhowr *f*, yetys dowr; (*of hair*) kudyn *m*, kudynnow **II** *vb* (*with key*) alhwedha; (*with bar*) prenna

locker *n* amari *m*, amaris

locket *n* florennik *f*, florenigow

locust *n* lokust *m*, lokustes

lodestone *n* (*magnet*) tennven *m*, tennveyn

lodge I (*gatehouse*) porthorji *m*, porthorjiow; (*of a secret organisation*) kevrinva *f*, kevrinvaow **II** *vb* ostya

lodger *n* ostyas *m*, ostysi

lodging *n* ostyans *m*, ostyansow

loft *n* soler *m*, soleryow

lofty *adj* ardhek

log I *n* prenn *m*, prennyer; kyf *m*, kyfyon **II** *vb* (*log in*) omgelmi; (*log out*) omdhigelmi

logic *n* reson *m*; lojyk *m*

logical *adj* herwydh reson; herwydh lojyk

logistics *n* logystek *f*

loiter *vb* krowdra

London *top* Loundres *m*

London pride *n* kowlen S. Padrek *f*

loneliness *n* hireth *f*; (*of a place*) unikter *m*

lonely *adj* (*friendless*) digoweth; (*longing*) hirethek; (*place*) pell dhyworth tus

long *adj* hir; pell. **all day long** dres an jydh. **as long as** hedre[2]. **in the long term** war an diwedh; wostiwedh; wortiwedh. **long ago** nans yw pell; pell dhe'n eur ma; termyn pell alemma. **long-distance call** galow a-bell *m*, galowyow a-bell. **no longer** na fella

longer *adj* hirra

longest *adj* (an) hirra

long-haired *adj* blewek; hir y vlew *m*; hir hy blew *f*; hir aga blew *pl*

longing I *adj* hirethek **II** *n* hireth *f*, hirethow

long-sighted *adj* hirwelyek

long-standing *adj* hen

longstone *n* menhir *m*, menhiryon

long-winded *adj* hir y gows *f*; hir hy hows *f*; hir aga hows *pl*

look I (*gaze*) golok *f*, gologow; tremmyn *m*, tremynnow; (*appearance*) mir *m*, mirow **II** *vb* mires. **look after** gwitha war²; truedha. **look at** mires orth. **look down on** dispresya. **look for** hwilas. **look here** *int* ottomma. **look into** hwithra. **look out** kemeres with. **look there** *int* ottena. **look upon** mires war²

loose *adj* lows

loosen *vb* lewsel

loosestrife, purple *n* krowles purpur *m*

loosestrife, yellow *n* krowles melyn *m*

loot I *n* preydh *m*, preydhyow **II** *vb* preydha

lop *vb* skethra

lord I *n* arlodh *m*, arlydhi **II** *vb* **lord it over** routya. **House of Lords** Chi an Arlydhi. **Lord's Prayer** Pader *m*, Paderow

lorry *n* kert *m*, kertow. **lorry driver** lewyer kert *m*, lewyoryon gert

lose *vb* (*mislay; be deprived of*) kelli; (*be defeated*) fyllel. **lose consciousness** klamdera. **lose out on** fyllel a²

loser *n* kollor *m*, kolloryon

loss *n* koll *m*, kollow; kolles *f*, kollesow; (*defeat*) fall *m*, fallow. **danger of loss** argol *m*. **state of loss** kolva *f*, kolvaow

lost *adj* kellys. **be lost** mos dhe goll

lot (1) *n* (*share*) rann *f*, rannow; (*gambling*) prenn *m*, prennyer

lot (2) *prn* (*a lot of*) meur a² (*before pl. noun*); lies (*before sg. noun*)

lotion *n* lin *m*, linyow

lots *adj* (*many of*) pals (*after pl. noun*)

lottery *n* gwari dall *m*, gwariow dall

loud *adj* ughel; heglew

loudness *n* ughelder *m*, ughelderyow

loudspeaker *n* ughelgowser *m*, ughelgowsoryon

lounge *n* esedhva *f*, esedhvaow

lovage *n* gwyles *m*, gwylesow

love I *n* kerensa *f*. (*terms of endearment*) melder *m*, melderyow **II** *vb* kara.

love-sick klav dre gerensa

love-in-a-mist *n* glas an niwl *m*

loveliness *n* tekter *m*

lovely *adj* teg

lover *n* karer *m*, karoryon; karores *f*, karoresow

loving *adj* karadow; kerensedhek; kuv

low *adj* isel

lower I *adj* woles; is- **II** *adv* a-woles; a-is **III** *vb* iselhe

lowest *adj* (an) isella

lowly *adj* uvel

loyal *adj* lel

Loyalist *n* Lelyas *m*, Lelysi

loyalty *n* lelder *m*; leowta *m*

lozenge *n* losanj *m*, losanjys; (*shape*) shap adamant *m*; (*sweet*) hwegen *f*, hwegennow. **cough lozenge** losanj pas *m*, losanjys pas

lubricant *n* uras *m*, urasow

lubricate *vb* ura; louba

luck *n* chons *m*, chonsyow; happ *m*, happys; feus *m*. **bad luck** mewl *m*. **good luck!** chons da!

luckily *adv* y'n gwella prys

lucky *adj* feusik; gwynnvys. **lucky for me!** gwynn ow bys!

ludicrous *adj* hwarthus

luggage *n* fardellow *pl*. **luggage rack** roos fardellow *f*, rosow fardellow

lukewarm *adj* mygyl; godom

lull I *n* spaven *f*, spavennow; spavnel *f*, spavnellow **II** *vb* spavenhe; koselhe; lolla

lullaby *n* hungan *f*, hunganow

luminous *adj* golow; splann. **luminous intensity** krevder golow *m*

lump *n* bothen *m* (*f*), bothennow

lunar *adj* lorel

lunatic I *adj* (*offensive*) muskok; lorek; badus **II** *n* muskok *m*, muskogyon; muskoges *f*, muskogesow; lorek *m*, lorogyon

lunch I *n* li *f*, livyow; liv *f*, livyow; (*picnic lunch*) kroust *m*, kroustyow **II** *vb* livya

lungs *n* skevens *pl*

lust *n* lust *m*, lustys

lute *n* lut *m*, lutys

luxuriant *adj* fethus

luxurious *adj* gorlanwesek

luxury *n* gorlanwes *m*, gorlanwesow

-ly *sffx* yn⁵

lying (1) *adj* (*dishonest*) gowek; mingow

lying (2) *adj* (*reclining*) a'y worwedh; a'y wrowedh

lynch *vb* lynchya. **lynch law** lagha an lovan *f*

lyric *adj* telynnek

lyrical *adj* telynnek

lyrics *n* geryow *pl*

M

Macedonia *top* Makedoni *f*

Macedonian I *adj* makedoniek **II** *n* (*language*) Makedoniek; (*person*) Makedonian *m*, Makedonians

machine *n* jynn *m*, jynnys, jynnow. **answering machine** jynn-gorthebi *m*, jynnys-gorthebi, jynnow-gorthebi. **ticket machine** jynn tokyn *m*, jynnys tokyn, jynnow tokyn. **washing machine** jynn-golghi *m*, jynnys-golghi, jynnow-golghi

machinery *n* jynnweyth *f*, jynnweythow

mackerel *n* brithel *m*, brithyli

macro- *prfx* kowr-

mad *adj* fol; mus; muskok. **go mad** dotya; muskegi

madam *n* madama *f*, madamys

madden *vb* muskegi; varya

made *adj* gwrys

madman *n* (*offensive*) mus *m*, musyon; muskok *m*, muskogyon; fol *m*, felyon

madness *n* muskotter *m*

madwoman *n* (*offensive*) muskoges *f*, muskogesow

magazine *n* (*periodical*) lyver termyn *m*, lyvrow termyn

magenta *adj* majenta

maggot *n* kontronen *f*, kontronennow; kontron *coll*

magic *n* hus *m*, husow; pystri *m* **work magic** *vb* pystria

magical *adj* hudel

magician *n* huder *m*, hudoryon

magistrate *n* justis *m*, justisyow

magnanimous *adj* meur y golon *m*; meur hy holon *f*; meur aga holon *pl*

magnet *n* tennven *m*, tennveyn

magnetic *adj* tennvenek

magnetise *vb* tennvenya

magnetism *n* tennvenieth *f*

magnificent *adj* brasoberys

magpie *n* piesen *f*, piesennow; pies *coll*

maid *n* maghteth *f*, maghtethyon

maiden *n* maghteth *f*, maghtethyon

mail I *n* post *m* **II** *vb* postya. **mail order** erghi der an post

main *adj* penn-

mainland *n* tir meur *m*; dor bras *m*

mainly *adv* dre vras

maintain *vb* mentena; mentenya

maintainer *n* mentenour *m*, mentenouryon, mentenours

maintenance *n* mentons *m*. **maintenance costs** *n* kostow mentons *pl*

maize *n* hwegys *coll*; ys hweg *coll*

majestic *adj* meuredhek

majesty *n* brastereth *f*; meuredh *m*

major *adj* brassa; meur-²; ugh-²

majority n rann vrassa f, rannow brassa

make vb gul; gwruthyl. **make a plan** tewlel towl. **make amends** gul amendys; gul restorita; astiveri. **make angry** serri. **make haste** fistena. **make right** ewna; amendya. **make use of** gul devnydh a². **make somebody do something** gul dhe nebonan gul neppyth

maker n gwrier m, gwrioryon

makeshift adj servadow; rag tro

make-up n liw bejeth m; afinuster m, afinusterow; mingreft m; tremmliw m, tremmliwyow. **put on make-up** gorra liw dhe'n bejeth

malady n kleves m, klevesow

malaria n (med) malaria m

male I adj gorow; gour-² **II** n gorreydh m

malice n atti m; avi m; spit m. **bear malice against** perthi avi orth

malicious adj drogbrederys

mallet n morben m, morbennow

mallow, common n malowen f, malowennow; malow coll

mallow, marsh n malowen geunek f

malt n brag m, bragow

Malta top Malta m

Maltese I adj maltek **II** n (language) Maltek m; (person) Maltyas m, Maltysi

mammal n bronnvil m, bronnviles

mammalian adj bronnvilek

Man top Manow f; (Isle of Man) Enys Vanow f

man n (human being) den m, tus; (male) gour m, gwer; (husband) gour m, gwer; (servant) gwas m, gwesyon. **good man** den mas m, tus vas; densa m. **man and woman** den ha benen. **man-at-arms** den arvow m, tus arvow. **to the last man** yn kettep gwas

manage vb (run) dyghtya; menystra; (cope) ardyghtya; omweres

management n dyghtyans m, dyghtyansow; menystrans m,

menystransow

manager n dyghtyer m, dyghtyoryon

mandible n grudh f, grudhow; challa m, challys

mandrake n mandragora m

mane n mong f, mongow

manga n (Japanese comic) manga m, mangas

manger n presep m, presebow

mango n mango m, mangos

mangy adj lovrek

manhandle vb handla yn harow

mania n (colloq) konnar f; (med) mania m

maniac n (offensive) lorek m, lorogyon

manic adj (med) manek

manifest adj hewel

manifestation n heweledh m, heweledhow

manifesto n derivadow m. **the Communist Manifesto** Derivadow an Gemynegoryon m

manipulate vb handla

manipulation n handlans m, handlansow

mankind n mab den m

manly adj gourel

mannequin n manykyn m (f), manykyns

manner n kor m, korow; maner f, maners, manerow; fordh f, fordhow

manor n maner m, maners, manoryow. **manor house** manerji m, manerjiow

mansion n mansyon m, mansyons; plas m, plassow; tyller m, tylleryow

manslaughter n denladh m, denladhow. **commit manslaughter** denladha

mantelpiece n astel an oles f, astellow an oles

mantle n mantel f, mantylli; pall m, pallow

manual I adj (by hand) dre dhorn; dornel **II** n (handbook) kowethlyver m,

333

kowethlyvrow; dornlyver *m*, dornlyvrow

manufacture I *n* gwrians *m*, gwriansow **II** *vb* gwruthyl

manufacturer *n* gwrier *m*, gwrioryon

manure *n* teyl *m*; mon *m*

manuscript *n* dornskrif *m*, dornskrifow

Manx I *adj* manowek **II** *n* (*language*) Manowek

many I *adj* (*before sg. noun*) lies; lower; (*before pl. noun*) meur a^2; kals a^2; (*after pl. noun*) pals; polta. **many people** lies huni; lies den. **many times** lieskweyth. **how many times** pana lies gweyth **II** *prn* lies. **as many** keniver. **as many as** kemmys. **how many** pana lies; pes; py lies; pyseul. **so many** keniver. **too many** re **III** *adv* **not many** nameur

map *n* mappa *m*, mappys, mappow

maple *n* gwinwelen *f*, gwinwelennow; gwinwel *coll*

maraud *vb* ravna

marauder *n* ravner *m*, ravnoryon

marble *n* (*rock*) marbel *m*; (*toy*) marblen *f*, marblennow; kalesen *f*, kalesennow

March *n* Meurth *m*; mis Meurth *m*

march I *n* keskerdh *m*, keskerdhow **II** *vb* keskerdhes

mare *n* kasek *f*, kasegi

margarine *n* margarin *m*

margin *n* amal *m*, emlow

marginal *adj* amalek

marigold *n* les an gog *m*, lesyow an gog

marigold, common *n* (*calendula*) les an gog *m*, losow an gog

marigold, French *n* owr frynkek *m*

mariner *n* marner *m*, marners, marnoryon; morwas *m*, morwesyon

maritime *adj* morek; a'n mor; arvor

marjoram *n* organs an wreg *coll*

mark I *n* merk *m*, merkys; nos *m*, nosow **II** *vb* merkya. **quotation mark** merk devyn *m*, merkys devyn

market I *n* marghas *f*, marghasow **II** *vb* marghasa. **fish market** marghas puskes *f*, marghasow puskes. **market garden** lowarth losow *m*, lowarthyow losow. **market place** marghasva *f*, marghasvaow. **stock market** marghas stock *f*, marghasow stock

marketable *adj* marghasadow

marketing *n* marghasans *m*

marking *n* markyans *m*, markyansow

marmalade *n* kyfeyth owraval *m*, kyfeythyow owraval

marram grass *n* hesk an tewes *coll*

marriage *n* demedhyans *m*, demedhyansow

married *adj* demedhys; pries. **married couple** dewbries *dl*

marrow *n* (*bone*) mer *m*; (*vegetable*) pompyon *m*, pompyons

marry *vb* demedhi

Mars *n* Meurth *m*

marsh *n* hal *f*, halow; gwernen *f*, gwernennow; gwern *coll*; keunek *f*, keunegi

marshy *adj* gwernek

marsupial *n* porsek *m*, porsogyon

martian *adj* meurthek

martyr I *n* merther *m*, mertheryon **II** *vb* mertherya

marvel *n* aneth *m*, anethow; marthus *m*, marthusyon, marthusi, marthusow

marvellous *adj* marthys; barthusek

marvellously *adv* marthys

Marxism *n* Marksydhieth *f*

Marxist I *adj* marksydhek **II** *n* marksydh *m*, marksydhyon

marzipan *n* toos alamandys *m*

mascara *n* liw blew lagas *m*

mascot *n* maskot *m*, maskotys

masculine *adj* (*manly*) gourel; (*grammatical*) gorow

mash *vb* brewi

mask *n* mask *m*, maskow; visour *m*, visours

mason *n* mason *m*, masons

masonry *n* menweyth *m*

mass (1) *n* (*bunch*) bush *m*, bushys; (*physical*) gronnedh *m*

mass (2) *n* (*church service*) oferen *f*, oferennow

massacre *n* gorladhva *f*, gorladhvaow

massage I *n* leuvtosans *m*, leuvtosansow **II** *vb* leuvtosa

massive *adj* kowrek

mast *n* gwern *f*, gwernow

master *n* mester *m*, mestrysi; arlodh *m*, arlydhi. **master's degree** mestronieth *f*, mestroniethow

masterpiece *n* pennobereth *f*, pennoberethow

mastery *n* maystri *m*

mat *n* strel *m*, strelyow

match (1) I *n* (*equal*) par *m*, parow **II** *vb* omdhesedha

match (2) *n* (*fire starter*) tanbren *m*, tanbrennyer

match (3) *n* (*sports*) fyt *m*, fyttys, fyttow

matchbox *n* kisten danbren *m*, kistennow tanbren

mate *n* (*spouse*) pries *m*, priosow, *dl* dewbries; (*friend*) sos *m*, sos; koweth *m*, kowetha; kothman *m*, kothmans; (*on ship*) brennyas *m*, brenysi

material *n* daffar *coll*; stoff *m*, stoffys; devnydh *m*, devnydhyow; pyth *m*, pythow

maternal *adj* mammel

maternity *n* mamoleth *f*. **maternity leave** kummyas mamoleth *m*. **maternity ward** diberthva vamoleth *f*

mathematics *n* awgrym *m*

matriarch *n* ughelvam *f*, ughelvammow

matriarchy *n* mammrewl *f*, mammrewlys

matrimonial *adj* priosel

matrimony *n* priosoleth *f*

matt *adj* avlenter

matter I *n* mater *m*, maters, materyow; pyth *m*, pythow **II** *vb* bernya. **it doesn't matter** ny vern; **it doesn't matter to me** ny'm deur. **no matter** na fors. **what's the matter?** pandr'yw an mater?

mattress *n* matras *m*, matrassow

mature I *adj* adhves **II** *vb* adhvesi

Mauritius *top* Enys Morris *f*

maxim *n* poynt a skians *m*, poyntys a skians, poyntow a skians

maximize *vb* (*IT*) kowlvoghhe

maximum I *adj* moyha **II** *n* ughboynt *m*, ughboyntys, ughboyntow

May *n* Me *m*; mis Me *m*. **May Day** Kala' Me *m*

may *part* re². **may you be happy** (*sg*) re bi lowen; lowena re'fo; (*pl*) re bowgh lowen; lowena re'gas bo; **may he never die** bynner re varwo

maybe *adv* martesen

mayor *n* mer *m*, meryon. **home of the mayor** merji *m*, merjiow

maypole *n* besowen Hav *f*, besowennow Hav

me *prn* (*enclitic*) vy; -ma; (*infixed*) 'm; (*object*) vy; (*emphatic*) evy. **by me** genev. **for me** ragov. **of me** ahanav. **to me** dhymm. **with me** genev

mead *n* (*drink*) medh *m*

meadow *n* pras *m*, prasow; budhyn *m*, budhynnow

meadowsweet *n* medhles *m*

meagre *adj* ydhil

meal *n* (*repast*) boos *m*, bosow. **have a meal** kavos boos. **meal taken to work** kroust *m*, kroustyow

meal-time *n* prys boos *m*, presyow boos

mean (1) *vb* styrya

mean (2) I *adj* (*average*) kresek **II** *n* mayn *m*, maynys

mean (3) *adj* (*cruel*) fell

meander *vb* kogrenni

meaning *n* styr *m*, styryow

meaningful *adj* leun a styr

means *n.pl* (*method*) mayn *m*; (*funds*) pygans *m*. **by means of** der; dre²

means-tested *adj* war-lergh pygans

meantime *n* kettermyn *m*. **in the meantime** y'n kettermyn; ha henna ow kortos

meanwhile *adv* y'n kettermyn

measles *n* brygh rudh *f*. **German measles** brygh Almayn *f*

measure I *n* musur *m*, musuryow **II** *vb* musura. **tape measure** *n* musurell *f*, musurellow

measured *adj* musurys

measurement *n* musurans *m*, musuransow

meat *n* kig *m*, kigyow. **minced meat** brewgik *m*; kig divynys *m*

mechanic *n* jynnweythor *m*, jynnweythoryon; jynner *m*, jynoryon

mechanical *adj* jynnweythek

mechanics *n* mekanek *f*

mechanism *n* jynnweyth *f*, jynnweythow

medal *n* medalen *f*, medalennow

medallion *n* medalen vras *f*, medalennow bras

meddle *vb* mellya

meddler *n* mellyer *m*, mellyoryon

median *n* kresriv *m*, kresrivow

mediator *n* medhador *m*, medhadoryon; mayn *m*, maynys

medical *adj* medhegel

medication *n* medhegneth *f*, medhegnethow

medicinal *adj* medhegiethel

medicine *n* (*medication*) medhegneth *f*, medhegnethow; (*science*) medhegieth *f*; (*arch*) fysek *f*

medieval *adj* kresosel

mediocre *adj* da lowr; heb meur a vri

meditation *n* ombreder *m*, ombrederow

Mediterranean *adj* kresvorek. **the Mediterranean Sea** an Kresvor *m*

medium I *adj* kresek; kreswedhek **II** *n* mayn *m*, maynys

meek *adj* hwar; klor

meet *vb* metya; dos erbynn. **meet someone** metya nebonan; (*pre-arranged*) metya gans nebonan; (*encounter*) metya orth nebonan

meeting *n* kuntelles *m* (*f*), kuntellesow; metyans *m*, metyansow. **meeting of bards** gorsedh *f*, gorsedhow

mega- *prfx* kowr-

megabyte *n* megabayt *m*, megabaytys

megalith *n* men bras *m*, meyn bras

megaphone *n* korn-kewsel *m*, kern-kewsel

melancholic *adj* moredhek

melancholy *n* moredh *m*, moredhow

mellow *adj* adhves

melodious *adj* melodius

melody *n* melodi *m*, melodis; ton *m*, tonyow

melon *n* melon *m*, melonyow; pompyon hweg *m*, pompyons hweg

melt *vb* teudhi

member *n* esel *m*, eseli

membership *n* eseleth *f*, eselethow

membrane *n* kennen *f*, kenennow

memento *n* kovro *m*, kovrohow, kovroyow

memo *n* notyans *m*, notyansow

memorable *adj* hegov

memorial *n* men kov *m*, meyn kov

memorise *vb* kevenna

memory *n* kov *m*, kovyow. **memory stick** *n* kyv kov *m*, kyvyon kov. **in memory of** er kov. **within living memory** a-ji dhe gov den

men *n.pl* (*males*) gwer *pl*; (*people*) tus *pl*; (*servants*) gwesyon *pl*

menace *vb* braggya

mend *vb* ewna

menhir *n* menhir *m*, menhiryon

menopause *n* menopos *m*

menstruation *n* amseryow *pl*; (*colloq*) termyn an mis *m*; misyow *pl*

mental *adj* brysel

mental health *n* yeghes brysel *m*

Mental Health Team *n* Para Yeghes an Brys *m*

Mental Health Unit *n* Unsys Yeghes an Brys *m*

mention I *n* kampol *m*, kampollow; menek *m*, menegow **II** *vb* kampolla; meneges; tochya. **already mentioned** *adj* ragleverys

menu *n* (*in a restaurant*) rol voos *f*, rolyow boos; (*IT*) rol *f*, rolyow. **menu tree** (*IT*) *n* rolwedhen *f*, rolwedhennow

meow I *n* miow *m* **II** *vb* miowal

merchandise *n* gwaren *f*, gwarennow; gwara *coll*

merchant *n* marchont *m*, marchons; marghador *m*, marghadoryon; (*hawker*) gwikor *m*, gwikoryon. **merchant ship** gorhel kenwerth *m*, gorholyon kenwerth

merciless *adj* didrueth

mercury *n* (*element*) arghans byw *m*

Mercury *n* (*planet*) Mergher *m*

mercy *n* tregeredh *f*, tregeredhow; merci *m*. **beg mercy from somebody for something** kria merci war nebonan rag neppyth. **have mercy on** kemeres merci a²

merge *vb* kesunya

meridian I *adj* meridian **II** *n* meridian *m* meridians

merit I *n* merit *m*, meritys **II** *vb* dendyl; dervyn

mermaid *n* morvoren *f*, morvoronyon

merry *adj* lowenek; heudh. **merry-go-round** *n* res a-dro *m*, resow a-dro. **merry Christmas!** Nadelik lowen!

mess *n* strol *m*; deray *m*, derays. **in a mess** yn deray

message I *n* messach *m*, messajys **II** *vb* messajya. **instant message** *n* messach desempis *m*, messajys desempis. **text**

message *n* messach tekst *m*, messajys tekst

messenger *n* kannas *f*, kanasow

messiah *n* messias *m*, messiasow

messianic *adj* messianek

messy *adj* strolyek

metabolic *adj* metabolek

metabolism *n* metaboledh *m*, metaboledhow

metal *n* alkan *m*, alkenyow; metol *m*, metelyow

metallic *adj* metelyek

metaphor *n* metafor *m*, metaforow

meteorite *n* men kowas *m*, meyn kowas

meteorological *adj* keweroniethel

meteorology *n* keweronieth *f*

method *n* method *m*, methodys

methodical *adj* methodek

Methodist I *adj* Methodek **II** *n* Methodydh *m*, Methodydhyon

metre *n* meter *m*, metrow; *abbrev* m

metropolis *n* gorcita *f*, gorcitys

mew *vb* miowal

Mexican I *adj* meksikan **II** *n* (*person*) Meksikan *m*, Meksikans

Mexico *top* Meksiko ·n

Michaelmas daisy *n* (*autumn aster*) bleujen gool Mighal *f*

micro- *prfx* korr-

microbe *n* korrbryv *m*, korrbryves, korrbryvyon

microphone *n* korrgowsell *f*, korrgowsellow

microscope *n* korrwelell *f*, korrwelellow

microscopic *adj* korrwelek

microwave *n* korrdon *f*, korrdonnow. **microwave oven** forn gorrdon *f*; (*colloq*) forn byng *n.f*

mid *adj* kres

midday *n* hanter-dydh *m*, hanter-dedhyow

midden *n* byjyon *m*, byjyons

middle *n* kres *m*, kresyow. **in the middle of** yn-mysk

midge *n* gwibesen *f*, gwibesennow; gwibes *coll*

midget I *adj* korr-; pur vyghan II *n* korr *m*, korres

midnight *n* hanter-nos *f*, hanter-nosow

midst *n* mysk *m*. **in the midst of** yn-mysk

Midsummer *n* Golowan *m*

midway *adv* dhe hanter an fordh

midwife *n* gwelivedhes *f*, gwelivedhesow

might *n* gallos *m*, gallosow; nerth *m*, nerthow, nerthyow

mighty *adj* gallosek

migraine *n* megrim *m*

migrant *n* divroek *m*, divroegyon

migrate *vb* divroa

migration *n* divroans *m*, divroansow

milady *n* madama *f*, madamys

mild *adj* klor; (*mild-mannered*) hwar

mildew *n* kewni *coll*

mile *n* mildir *m*, mildiryow

militant I *adj* breselek; kasorek II breseler *m*, breseloryon

military I *adj* kasorek II *n* lu *m*, luyow

militia *n* trevlu *m*, trevluyow

milk I *n* leth *m*, lethow II *vb* godra. **curdled milk** leth kowlys *m*. **first milk** (*colostrum*) godrek *m*. **sweet milk** levrith *m*. **skimmed milk** leth didhehen *m*. **unpasteurised milk** leth kriv *m*. **milkshake** shakleth *m*, shaklethow

milkmaid *n* lethwreg *f*, lethwragedh

milkman *n* gwerther leth *m*, gwerthoryon leth; lethwas *m*, lethwesyon

milkwort, common *n* lethles *m*

milky *adj* lethek. **Milky Way** *n* Hyns Sen Jamys *f*

mill *n* melin *f*, melinyow. **mill wheel** ros melin *m*, rosow melin. **pepper mill** melin buber *f*, melinyow puber. **water mill** melin dhowr *f*, melinyow dowr

millennium *n* milvledhen *f*, milvledhynnyow

miller *n* meliner *m*, melinoryon

millhouse *n* melinji *m*, melinjiow

millimetre *n* milimeter *m*, milimetrow; *abbrev* mm

million *num* milvil² *m*, milvilyow; milyon *m*, milyonow. **a million times** milvilweyth

millionaire *n* milvilwas *m*, milvilwesyon

millionth *num* milvilves; *abbrev* 1,000,000ves

mime I *n* mim *m*, mimyow II *vb* mimya

mimic I *n* mim *m*, mimyow II *vb* mimya

mince *vb* divyn. **minced meat** kig divynys *m*; brewgik *m*

mincemeat *n* (*sweet*) brewvos *m*

mind I *n* brys *m*, brysyow II *vb* gwaytyas; gorwitha. **I don't mind** ny vern dhymm; ny'm deur. **never mind** na fors; ny vern. **state of mind** cher *m*, cheryow. **to my mind** orth ow brys

mine (1) *prn* ow huni. **it's mine** dhymm yw; my a'n pyw *m*; my a's pyw *f*. **the victory was mine** an trygh eth genev

mine (2) *n* bal *m*, balyow. **mine waste** atal *coll*. **opencast mine** mongleudh *m*, mongleudhyow. **coffin mine** koghyn *m*, koghynnow

miner *n* den bal *m*, tus val

mineral *n* moon *m*, monow. **mineral water** dowr ewonek *m*

mine-work *n* hwel *m*, hwelyow

mingle *vb* kemyska; myska

mini- *prfx* korr-

miniature I *adj* korr-; munys II *n* munysen *f*, munysennow

minimal *adj* ispoyntel; lyha

minimalism *n* ispoyntegieth *f*

minimise *vb* (*IT*) kowllehe

minimum I *adj* lyha II *n* ispoynt *m*, ispoyntys, ispoyntow. **minimum**

wage gober ispoyntel *m*

mining *n* balweyth *m*

minister *n* menyster *m*, menystrys, menystroryon. **Prime Minister** pennmenyster *m*, pennmenystrys, pennmenystroryon

ministry *n* menystrans *m*, menystransow

minor I *adj* le **II** *n* minor *m*, minors; (*underage*) flogh yn-dann oos *m*, fleghes yn-dann oos

minority *n* minoryta *m*, minorytys. **a minority of** an byghanna rann a². **ethnic minority** minoryta ethnek *m*, minorytys ethnek

minstrel *n* menstrel *m*, menstrels

minstrelsy *n* menestrouthi *m*

mint (1) *n* (*herb*) menta *f*

mint (2) *n* (*money*) batti *m*, battiow; bathva *f*, bathvaow

mint, apple *n* menta aval *f*

mint, water *n* menta an dowr *f*

minus *prp* (*mathematical operator*) marnas

minute (1) *adj* munys

minute (2) I *n* (*time*) mynysen *f*, mynysennow; (*of meeting*) kovnotyans *m*, kovnotyansow **II** *vb* (*a meeting*) kovnotya

minx *n* flownen *f*

miracle *n* marthus *m*, marthusyon, marthusi, marthusow; merkyl *m*, merklys. **miracle play** gwari mir *m*, gwariow mir

miraculous *adj* barthusek

mirage *n* miraj *m*, mirajys

mire *n* leysek *f*, leysegi; stag *m*, stagow

mirror *n* gweder-mires *m*, gwedrow-mires

mirth *n* lowender *m*

misbehave *vb* tebelfara

miscellaneous *adj* divers (*followed by sg. or pl. noun*); a bub sort

mischief *n* dregyn *m*, dregynnow

mischievous *adj* dregynnus

misdeed *n* kammweyth *m*

misdemeanour *n* drog-ober *m*, drog-oberow

miser *n* erbysyas *m*, erbysysi; kraf *m*, krefyon

miserable *adj* galarek; law; moredhek; truan; ponvosek

miserly *adj* kraf

misery *n* anken *m*, ankenyow; ponvos *m*, ponvosow

misfortune *n* anfeus *m*

mishandle *vb* droghandla

mishap *n* droglam *m*, droglammow

misjudge *vb* kammvreusi

mislead *vb* kammledya; decevya; tolla

misogynist *n* kasegor benynreydh *m*, kasegoryon venynreydh

misogyny *n* kas a venynreydh *f*

Miss *n* (*girls*) Mestresik *f*, Mestresigow; (*arch*) damsel *f*, damsels; (*adult women*) Mestres *f*, Mestresow; *abbrev* Mres *f*

miss *vb* bos fowt a²; fyllel; (*fail to hit*) fyllel a weskel; (*miss somebody*) yeuni war-lergh; bos trist war-lergh. **I miss you** Yth yeunav war dha lergh. **something is missing** yma fowt a neppyth; neppyth a fyll

mission *n* kanaseth *f*, kanasethow

mist *n* niwl *m*, niwlow. **thick mist** kowas niwl *f*, kowasow niwl

mistake *n* kammgemeryans *m*, kammgemeryansow

mistaken *adj* kammdybys; kammgemerys

Mister *n* Mester *m*, Mestrysi

mistle thrush *n* molgh gerdhin *f*, molghes kerdhin

mistletoe *n* ughelvar *m*

mistreat *vb* tebeldhyghtya

mistress *n* arlodhes *f*, arlodhesow; (*lady of the house*) mestres *f*, mestresow

mistrust I *n* mystrest *m* **II** *vb* mystrestya

misty *adj* niwlek

misunderstand *vb* kammgonvedhes
misuse I *n* tebeldhyghtyans *m*,
tebeldhyghtyansow II *vb*
tebeldhyghtya; kammusya
mite (1) *n* (*arachnid*) torogen *f*,
torogennow; torek *coll*
mite (2) *n* (*bit*) dyjyn *m*, dyjynnow
mitigate *vb* lehe; sewajya
mix I *n* kemmysk *m*, kemyskow;
kabolva *f*, kabolvaow II *vb* kemyska;
kaboli
mixed *adj* kemyskys
mixer *n* kemysker *m*, kemyskoryon;
(*gadget*) kemyskell *f*, kemyskellow
mixture *n* kemyskans *m*, kemyskansow
moan I *n* kynvan *m*, kynvannow II *vb*
kyni; (*complain*) krodhvolas
mob *n* rout *m*, routys
mobile *adj* gwayadow
mobile phone *n* klappkodh *f*,
klappkodhow; pellgowsel *f*,
pellgowsellow
mock *vb* gesya; gul ges. **mock
someone** gul ges a nebonan
mockery *n* ges *m*, gesyow
model I *n* (*representation*) patron *m*,
patronyow; (*fashion*) model gis *m*,
modelys is II *vb* shapya
modem *n* modem *m*, modems
moderate I *adj* klor; temprys II *vb*
tempra; musura
moderation *n* musur *m*, musuryow
moderator *n* temprer *m*, temproryon
modern *adj* arnowydh
modernisation *n* arnowydhheans *m*,
arnowydhheansow
modernise *vb* arnowydhhe
modest *adj* uvel; isel; klor
modesty *n* klorder *m*
modification *n* treylva *f*, treylvaow;
chanjyans *m*, chanjyansow
modify *vb* treylya; chanjya
moist *adj* leyth; glyb
moisten *n* leytha; glybya; dowrya
moisture *n* glybor *m*

molar *n* kildhans *m*, kildhens
Moldavian I *adj* moldavek II *n*
Moldavek *m*; (*person*) Moldavian *m*,
Moldavians
Moldova *top* Moldova *f*
mole (1) *n* (*animal*) godh *f*, godhow
mole (2) *n* (*on skin*) plustren *f*,
plustrennow
molecule *n* molekulen *f*,
molekulennow
molest *vb* disesya
molten *adj* teudh
moment *n* pols *m*, polsyow; tecken *f*,
teckennow. **at the moment** y'n pols
ma; y'n tor' ma
momentarily *adj* rag pols; rag tecken
momentary *adj* prysweythyel
momentum *n* momentom *m*
monarch *n* myghtern *m*, myghternedh,
myghternyow; myghternes *f*,
myghternesow
monarchy *n* myghternses *m*
monastery *n* managhti *m*, managhtiow
monastic *adj* managhek
Monday *n* Lun *m*; dy'Lun *m*. **Monday
night** dy'Lun dhe nos
monetary *adj* monesek
money *n* mona *coll*; arghans *m*. **money
box** *n* argh vona *f*, arhgow mona;
kofrik erbys *m*, kofrigow erbys
monitor *n* (*prefect*) gorwolyas *m*,
gorwolysi; (*IT*) skrin *f*, skrinyow
monk *n* managh *m*, menegh
monkey *n* sim *m*, simes
monkshood *n* (*wolf's bane*) kugol an
managh *m*; losow an bleydh *coll*
mono- *prfx* un-
monoglot I *adj* unyethek II *n* unyethek
m, unyethogyon
monolingual *adj* unyethek
monologue *n* kows unn den *m*,
kowsow unn den
monopoly *n* monopolegieth *f*,
monopolegiethow; monopoli *m*,
monopolis

340

monotonous *adj* undon

monster *n* euthvil *m*, euthviles; tebelvest *m*, tebelvestes

month *n* mis *m*, misyow

monthly *adj* misyek; misek

monument *n* men kov *m*, meyn kov

mood *n* cher *m*, cheryow; (*grammar*) gis *m*, gisyow. **in a bad mood** drog pes. **in a good mood** pes da. **indicative mood** gis menegek *m*. **subjunctive mood** gis islavarek *m*

moody *adj* brottel y jer *m*; brottel hy cher *f*; brottel aga cher *pl*

moon *n* loor *f*, loryow

moor *n* (*marsh*) hal *f*, halow; (*upland*) goon *f*, gonyow; ros *m*, rosyow

moorhen *n* lagyar *f*, lagyer

mop *n* skubell-wolghi *f*, skubellow-golghi

moped *n* hwil tan *m*, hwiles tan

moral I *adj* mas **II** *n* dyskans *m*, dyskansow

morality *n* maseth *f*, masethow

morals *n* maners *pl*; manerow *coll*

more *adj, adv* moy. **not any more** (*with negation*) namoy. **more and more** moy ha moy. **more or less** moy po le. **more than** moy ages; moy es. **no more** nahen. **once more** unweyth arta. **still more** byth moy

moreover *adv* keffrys; hagensoll; hagoll; pella

morning *n* myttin *m*, myttinyow; (*duration*) myttinweyth *m*, myttinweythyow. **good morning** myttin da. **in the morning** myttinweyth. **morning star** (*Venus*) Borlowen *f*. **morning time** myttinweyth *m*. **morning twilight** boragweyth *f*. **the morning after** ternos vyttin. **this morning** hedhyw vyttin; an myttin ma. **yesterday morning** de vyttin

morsel *n* tamm *m*, temmyn; pastel *f*, pastellow; souben *f*, soubennow

mortal *adj* marwel

mortgage I *n* marwostel *m*, marwostlow **II** *vb* marwostla

mosaic *n* brithweyth *m*, brithweythyow

mosque *n* mosk *m*, moskow

mosquito *n* moskito *m*, moskitos

moss *n* kewni *coll*

mossy *adj* kewniek

most *adj, adv* moyha. **at most** dhe'n moyha. **for the most part** dre vras

motel *n* karrostel *m*, karrostelyow

moth *n* godhan *m*, godhanes; tykki Duw nos *m*, tykkiow Duw nos, tykki Duwes nos

mother *n* mamm *f*, mammow; dama *f*, damyow

motherhood *n* mamoleth *f*

mother-in-law *n* hweger *f*, hwegrow

motherland *n* mammvro *f*, mammvroyow

motion *n* gwayans *m*. gwayansow; (*at a meeting*) avis *m*, avisyow

motivate *vb* movya

motivation *n* movyans *m*, movyansow

motive *n* acheson *m*, achesonys, achesonyow

motocross *n* resek jynn diwros *m*

motor *n* jynn *m*, jynnys, jynnow

motorbike *n* jynn diwros *m*, jynnow diwros

motor-boat *n* skath tan *f*, skathow tan

motor-car *n* karr tan *m*, kerri tan

motorcycle *n* jynn diwros *m*, jynnow diwros

motorist *n* motorydh *m*, motorydhyon

motorway *n* gorfordh *f*, gorfordhow

mottle *vb* britha

mottled *adj* brithys

mould (1) *n* (*fungus*) kosk *m*

mould (2) *n* (*casting*) furv *f*, furvow, furvyow; form *m* (*f*,, formys

mouldy *adj* loos. **go mouldy** koska; losi

mound *n* krug *m*, krugow; bern *m*, bernyow

mount *vb* yskynna; krambla

mountain *n* menydh *m*, menydhyow

mountaineer *n* menedhyer *m*, menedhyoryon

mountaineering *n* menedhorieth *f*

mountainous *adj* menedhyek

mourn *vb* galari; kyni

mournful *adj* trist

mourning *n* kynvan *m*, kynvannow

mouse *n* logosen *f*, logos

moustache *n* minvlew *coll*

mouth *n* (*anat*) ganow *m*, ganowow; min *m*, minow, minyow, minyon; (*of a river*) aber *m*, aberyow. **mouth organ** *n* harmonika *m*, harmonikas

mouthful *n* ganowas *m*, ganowasow

movable *adj* gwayadow; (*spiritually*) movadow

move I *n* gwaya *m*, gwayow; (*in a game*) towl *m*, towlow II *vb* (*move about*) remova; gwaya; (*spiritually; emotionally*) movya; (*stir*) styrrya; (*move oneself*) omwaya. **move away** pellhe. **move house** remova chi

movement *n* gwayans *m*, gwayansow; (*also political*) movyans *m*, movyansow; (*in music*) kors *m*, korsow. **Nursery School Movement** Movyans Skolyow Meythrin *m*

movie *n* fylm *m*, fylmow

mow *vb* felghya

mower *n* felghell *f*, felghellow

Mr *abbrev* Mester *m*; *abbrev* Mr

Mrs *abbrev* Mestres *f*; *abbrev* Mres

Ms *abbrev* Mestres *f*; *abbrev* Mres

much I *adj* lower; meur a²; (*after pl. noun*) pals II *adv* polta. **not much** nameur. **as much as** kekemmys ha. **for as much as** yn mar veur dell². **how much (of)** pygemmys; pyseul (a²). **so much** kemmys; seul. **too much (of)** re (a²)

mud *n* leys *m*, leysyow; pri *m*, priow; stag *m*, stagow

muddle I *n* tervysk *m*, tervyskow II *vb* tervyska

muddy *adj* leysek

mug *n* (*cup*) kruskyn *m*, kruskynnow; (*visage*) bejeth *f*, bejethow

mugger *n* ravner *m*, ravnoryon

mugwort *n* loos les *coll*

mule *n* mul *m*, mules

mullein, great *n* (*common; woolly; Aaron's rod*) gwlanik *m*

mullet *n* (*fish*) meyl *m*, meyli

multi- *prfx* lies-

multicoloured *adj* liesliw

multicultural *adj* liesgonisogethek

multifunctional *adj* lieskweythresek

multilateral *adj* liestu

multilingual *adj* liesyethek

multinational *adj* lieskenedhlek. **multinational corporation** korforeth lieskenedhlek *f*, korforethow lieskenedhlek

multiple *adj* liesplek; liesek

multiplication *n* liesheans *m*, liesheansow

multiplicity *n* liester *m*, liesteryow

multiplier *n* liesheor *m*, liesheoryon

multiply *vb* lieshe. **multiplied by** lieshes gans

multipurpose *adj* liesporpos

multi-storey *adj* liesleur

multi-talented *adj* liesroasek

mum *n* (*mother*) mamm *f*, mammow

mumble I *n* kows diskler *m*, kowsow diskler II *vb* kewsel yn tiskler

mummy *n* (*mother*) mammik *f*, mamigow

mumps *n* penn sagh *m*

munch *vb* densel

municipality *n* burjestra *f*, burjestrevow

murder I *n* moldrans *m*, moldransow II *vb* moldra; ladha

murdered *adj* ledhys; moldrys

murderer *n* moldrer *m*, moldroryon; denledhyas *m*, denledhysi; ladher *m*, ladhoryon

murky *adj* tewl

murmur I *n* hanas *m*, hanasow **II** *vb* hanasa

muscle *n* keheren *f*, keherennow; keher *coll*

muscular *adj* keherek

muse *n* awen *f*

museum *n* gwithti *m*, gwithtiow

mushroom *n* skavel gronek *f*, skavellow kronek

music *n* ilow *f*; (*instrumental*) menestrouthi *m*

musical I *adj* ilowek **II** *n* (*play*) ilowari *m*, ilowariow; gwari ilow *m*, gwariow ilow

musician *n* ilewydh *m*, ilewydhyon; (*minstrel*) menstrel *m*, menstrels

Muslim I *adj* Moslem; Islamek **II** *n* Moslem *m*, Moslemyon; (*archaic*) Sarsyn *m*, Sarsyns

mussel I *n* mesklen *f*, mesklennow; meskel *coll* **II** *vb* **gather mussels** meskla

must *vb* bos res dhe² **I must** res yw

dhymm

mustard *n* (*condiment*) kedhow *m*

mustard, garlic *n* (*Jack-by-the-hedge*) Jakka a'n ke *m*

mustard, white *n* (*yellow*) kedhow *m*

mutation *n* treylyans *m*, treylyansow

mute *adj* omlavar; avlavar

mutiny I *n* sordyans *m*, sordyansow **II** *vb* sordya

mutton *n* kig davas *m*

mutual *adj* ken-; kes-; an eyl y gila *m*; an eyl hy ben *f*

muzzle I *n* (*nose*) dewfrik *dl*; (*over an animal's mouth*) pennfron *f*, pennfronnow; (*of a gun*) ganow *m* **II** *vb* pennfronna

my *poss. adj* ow³

myself *prn* ow honan

mysterious *adj* kevrinek

mystery *n* kevrin *m*, kevrinyow; rin *m*, rinyow

myth *n* myth *m*, mythys

mythology *n* mythologieth *f*

N

nail I *n* (*carpentry*) kenter *f*, kentrow; (*fingers or toes*) ewin *m*, ewines **II** *vb* kentra; (*with many nails*) kentrewi. **nail scissors** *n* gwelsigow ewin *pl*. **nail… to…** kentra… orth…. **nail varnish** gwernis ewin *f*, gwernisyow ewin

naive *adj* anfel

naked *adj* noth; lomm. **half naked** ternoth

name I *n* hanow *m*, henwyn **II** *vb* henwel. **bad name** tebel-hanow *m*, tebel-henwyn. **call by name** gelwel orth y hanow. **in the name of** a-barth. **pen name** hanow pluven *m*, henwyn pluven. **put your name down** ri dha

hanow. **stage name** hanow gwari *m*, henwyn gwari. **what is your name?** pyth yw dha hanow? **my name is Jori** Jori yw ow hanow

named *adj* henwys

nameless *adj* dihanow

namely *adv* henn yw; henn yw dhe styrya

nanny *n* magores *f*, magoresow. **nanny goat** gaver *f*, gever

nap I *n* gogosk *m*, gogoskow **II** *vb* gogoska

nape *n* (*anat*) kil *m*, kilyer

napkin *n* lien diwla *m*, lienyow diwla; kwethyn *m*, kwethynnow

nappy *n* lien baban *m*, lienyow baban

narcissus *n* fionen *f*, fionennow; fion *coll*

narcolepsy *n* (*med*) narkolepsi *m*

narrate *vb* hwedhla

narration *n* hwedhlans *m*, hwedhlansow; derivas *m*, derivasow

narrative I *adj* hwedhlek **II** *n* hwedhel *m*, hwedhlow

narrator *n* hwedhlor *m*, hwedhloryon

narrow *adj* kul; ynn

nascent *adj* usi ow sordya

nasturtium *n* kappa kornhwilen *m*, kappys kornhwilen

nasty *adj* drog; plos; bystyon; (*preceding the noun*) hager

nation *n* kenedhel *f*, kenedhlow. **the United Nations** an Kenedhlow Unys *pl*

national *adj* kenedhlek

nationalise *vb* kenedhlegi

nationalised *adj* kenedhlegys

nationalism *n* kenedhlegieth *f*

nationalist *n* kenedhloger *m*, kenedhlogoryon

nationality *n* kenedhlogeth *f*, kenedhlogethow

native I *adj* genesik; teythyek **II** *n* genesik *m*, genesigyon; teythyek *m*, teythyogyon. **native to Cornwall** a Gernow

natural *adj* gnasek; naturel

nature *n* (*natural world*) natur *f*; (*personality*) gnas *f*, gnasow; (*human nature*) natureth *f*

naturist *n* diwiskydh *m*, diwiskydhyon

naughty *adj* drog

nausea *n* penn-dro *f*

nauseous *adj* penn-dro

navel *n* begel *m*, begelyow

navelwort *n* (*pennywort*) krampothen vowysi *f*, krampothennow mowysi; krampoth mowysi *coll*

navigable *adj* hefordh

navy I *n* morlu *m*, morluyow **II** *adj* (*colour*) mordu

near I *adj* nes; ogas **II** *vb* neshe. **near at hand** dhe dhorn. **near to** ogas dhe²; ryb

nearby *adv* yn ogas; dhe dhorn

nearer I *adj* nessa **II** *adv* yn-nes

nearest *adj* nessa

nearly *adv* ogasti; pur ogas; (*used before a verb*) namna²; namnag

neat *adj* kempen

neatly *adv* yn kempen

necessary *adj* res. **absolutely necessary** res porres. **if necessary** mars yw res; mar po res

necessity *n* edhom *m*, edhommow. **of necessity** porres

neck *n* konna *m*, konaow

necklace *n* delk *m*, delkow

necktie *n* kolm konna *m*, kolmow konna

necromancy *n* nygromons *m*

nectar *n* nektar *m*, nektars

need I *n* edhom *m*, edhommow **II** *vb* bos edhom a²; bos res dhe². **I need it** yma edhom dhymm anodho; **I need to do it** res yw dhymm y wul

needle *n* naswydh *f*, naswedhow

needy I *adj* edhommek **II** *n* (*needy person*) edhommek *m*, edhomogoyon

negative I *adj* negedhek **II** *n* (*photographic*) negedhen *f*, negedhennow

neglect I *n* dispresyans *m*, dispresyansow; gwall *m*, gwallow **II** *vb* dispresya

negotiate *vb* negysyas; bargynnya

negotiation *n* negysyans *m*, negysyansow

negotiator *n* negysydh *m*, negysydhyon

neigh *vb* kryghias

neighbour *n* kentrevek *m*, kentrevogyon

neighbourhood *n* kentreveth *f*, kentrevethow

neither *prn* naneyl. **neither... nor...** na... na...; naneyl... na...

nephew *n* noy *m*, noyens

Neptune *n* Nevyon *m*

nerve *n* nerven *f*, nervennow

nervous *adj* nervus

nest I *n* neyth *m*, neythow **II** *vb* neythi

net *n* roos *f*, rosow. **drag net** tennros *f*, tennrosow

netball *n* pel roos *f*

netbook *n* (*IT*) roslyver *m*, roslyvrow

Netherlands *top* Iseldiryow *pl*

nettle *n* linasen *f*, linasennow; linas *coll.* **bed of nettles** linasek *f*, linasegi

network *n* rosweyth *m*, rosweythyow

neural *adj* newrel

neurological *adj* newrologyl

neurologist *n* newrologydh *m*, newrologydhyon

neurology *n* newrologieth *f*

neurosis *n* newrosys *m*

neurotic I *adj* newrotek **II** *n* newrotek *m*, newrotogyon

neuter I *adj* (*grammatical gender*) direydh; nebreydh **II** *vb* (*of animals*) spadha

neutral *adj* diduel; heptu

neutrality *n* heptueth *f*

neutron *n* nywtron *m*, nywtrons

never *adv* (*in the past*) bythkweth; (*in the present or future*) nevra; (*negative optative*) bynner. **may he never do...** bynner re wrello.... **never mind** ny vern

nevermore *adv* (*with negation*) nevra namoy

nevertheless *adv* byttegyns

new *adj* nowydh

newborn *adj* nowydh genys

newly *adv* nowydh

news *n* nowodhow *pl*. **news about...** nowodhow orth...

newsagent *n* gwerther jornalys *m*, gwerthoryon jornalys

newsletter *n* lyther nowodhow *m*, lytherow nowodhow

newspaper *n* paper nowodhow *m*, paperyow nowodhow

newt *n* peswarpaw *m*, peswarpawes

New Zealand *top* Mordir Nowydh *m*

next *adj* nessa. **next to** nes dhe[2]; ryb. **next door** y'n nessa chi. **next year** nessa bledhen; an vledhen usi ow tos. **the next day** ternos. **the next morning** ternos vyttin

nice *adj* hweg

nicotine *n* nikotin *m*

niece *n* nith *f*, nithow

Nigeria *top* Nijeri *m*

Nigerian I *adj* nijerian **II** *n* (*person*) Nijerian *m*, Nijerians

night *n* nos *f*, nosow; (*duration; night-time*) nosweyth *m*, nosweythyow. **at night** nosweyth. **in the night** yn termyn an nos. **last night** nyhewer. **just before night falls** haneth dhe nos

nightclub *n* klub nos *m*, klubys nos

nightdress *n* pows nos *f*, powsyow nos

nightfall *n* derow nos *m*

nightingale *n* eos *f*, eosow

nightjar *n* churra nos *m*, churrys nos; dorhok *m*, dorhokys

nightly *adv* pub nos

nightmare *n* hulla *m*, hullevow; hunlev *m*, hunlevow. **Night Mare** *f* (*Montol character*) Kasek Nos

night school *n* skol nos *f*, skolyow nos

nightshade, deadly *n* (*belladonna*) morel *m*

nightshade, woody *n* (*bittersweet*) skawen gogh *f*, skawennow kogh; skaw kogh *coll*

nightshirt *n* krys nos *m*, krysyow nos

nil *n* mann *m*

nimble *adj* skav; strik

nine *num* naw

nineteen *num* nownsek

nineteenth *num* nownsegves; *abbrev* 19ves

ninetieth *num* degves ha peswar ugens; *abbrev* 90ves

ninety *num* deg ha peswar ugens

ninth *num* nawves; *abbrev* 9ves

nip I *n* gwask *f*, gwaskow **II** *vb* gwaska

nipple *n* hwennen *f*, hwenennow

nit *n* nedhen *f*, nedhennow; nedh

nit-pick *vb* folsa blew

nitrogen *n* (*element*) nitrojen *m*

no I *adv* na; vyth **II** *int* na!; na^2 + *verb*; **no longer** na fella. **no matter** na fors. **no more** nahen; namoy. **no smoking** megi difennys

noble I *adj* nobyl **II** *n* ughelor *m*, ugheloryon; nobyl *m*, noblys

nobody *prn* den vyth *m*

nod *vb* penndroppya

noise *n* tros *m*, trosyow; son *m*, sonyow

noiseless *adj* didros

noisy *adj* trosek

nomad *n* gwandryas *m*, gwandrysi

nominally *adv* yn hanow

non- *prfx* an-; di-

non-alcoholic *adj* dilasek; medhel

non-aligned *adj* heptu

non-conformist *n* dissentyer *m*, dissentyoryon

none *prn* nagonan; vyth

nonetheless *adv* byttele

non-resident II *adj* trigys yn ken tyller **II** *n* triger yn ken tyller *m*

nonsense *n* flows *m*. **what nonsense!** tetivali!

non-standard *adj* diskwir

non-stop *adj* heb hedhi

non-violent *adj* kosel; difreudh

nook *n* kil *m*, kilyer

noon *n* hanter-dydh *m*, hanter-dedhyow

no-one *prn* nagonan

nor *cnj* (*before consonants*) na; (*before vowels*) nag. **nor yet** byth moy

normal *adj* normal

normalisation *n* normalheans *m*, normalheansow

normalise *vb* normalhe

normality *n* normalita *m*, normalitys

north *n* gogledh *f*; north *m*; kledhbarth *f*. **on the north side** *adv* a-gledhbarth

north-east *n* north-est *m*

northerly *adj* a-dhia an north

northern *adj* a'n north; a'n gledhbarth

northwards *adj* war-tu ha'n north

north-west *n* north-west *m*

Norway *top* Norgagh *m*

Norwegian I *adj* norgaghek **II** *n* (*language*) Norgaghek *m*; (*person*) Norgaghyas *m*, Norgaghysi

nose *n* tron *m*, tronow, tronyow; frigow *pl*; dewfrik *dl*

nosiness *n.m* tronekter

nostalgia *n* hireth *f*, hirethow

nostril *n* frig *m*, frigow, *dl* dewfrik

nosy *adj* tronek; tron-droghya

not *part* (*in most main clauses*) ny^2; nyns; (*with imperatives and in relative clauses*) na^2; nag. **and not** a-der. **not at all** vytholl. **not earlier** nahyns. **not far** neppell. **not one** nagonan. **not yet** na hwath. **that not** na^2; nag. **not many, not much** *adv* nameur

notable *adj* notys; notyes; nosedhek

notably *adv* kyns oll

notary *n* noter *m*, notoryon

notate *vb* nosya

notation *n* nosyans *m*, nosyansow

note I *n* noten *f*, notennow **II** (*remark*) notya; (*be aware of*) attendya; (*notice*) merkya; (*observe*) avisya. **take note of** merkya

notebook *n* lyver notennow *m*, lyvrow notennow; skriflyver *m*, skriflyvrow

nothing *prn* tra vyth *f*; mann *m*. **nothing doing!** chons vyth!

notice I *n* (*advertisement*) argemmyn *m*, argemynnow **II** *vb* merkya; attendya. **take notice of** gul vri orth. **I didn't take notice** ny wrug evy attendya.

until further notice erna vo klewys neppyth ken

noticeable *adj* hewel

notify *vb* gwarnya

notion *n* tybyans *m*, tybyansow; sians *m*, siansow; devis *m*, devisyow

nougat *n* nougat *m*

nought *n* mann

noun *n* hanow *m*, henwyn

nourish *vb* maga

novel I *adj* nowydh **II** *n* romans *m*, romansow; novel *m*, novelys

November *n* Du *m*; mis Du *m*

novice *n* dallether *m*, dallethoryon

now *adv* lemmyn; y'n eur ma. **from now on** alemma rag. **now and again** treweythyow. **now and then** war euryow. **up till now** bys y'n eur ma

nowadays *adj* y'n jydh hedhyw

nowhere *adv* tyller vyth

nuclear *adj* (*biol*) sprusek; (*physics*) nuklerek. **nuclear waste** atal nuklerek *coll*. **nuclear weapon** arv nuklerek *f*, arvow nuklerek. **nuclear power station** tredanva nuklerek *f*, tredanvaow nuklerek

nucleus *n* (*biol*) sprusen *f*, sprusennow; (*physics*) nuklesen *f*, nuklesennow

nude *adj* noth; lomm

nudism *n* diwiskieth *f*

nudist *n* diwiskydh *m*, diwiskydhyon

nudity *n* nothedh

nuisance *n* (*annoying thing*) pla *m*, plaow; (*annoying thing or person*) begel *m*, begelyow

numb *adj* ewinrewys

number I *n* niver *m*, niverow; riv *m*, rivow; (*quantity*) myns *m*, mynsow **II** *vb* nivera; riva. **in number** orth niver.

number plate plat niver *m*, platys niver, platyow niver. **random number** happriv *m*, happrivow. **serial number** niver kesresek *m*, niverow kesresek. **telephone number** niver pellgowser *m*, niverow pellgowser

numbering *n* niverennans *m*, niverenansow

numbness *n* ewinrew *m*

numeral *n* niveren *f*, niverennow

numerator *n* mynsriv *m*, mynsrivow

numerical *adj* niverek

numerous *adj* niverus; (*preceding a sg. noun*) lies; (*following a pl. noun*) pals

nun *n* lenes *f*, lenesow

nunnery *n* lenji *m*, lenjiow

nurse I *n* (*hospital*) klavjior *m*, klavjioryon; (*children*) klavjior fleghes *m* **II** *vb* (*sick people*) gwitha; (*children*) maga; (*breastfeed*) bronna. **wet nurse** mammeth *f*, mamethow

nursery *n* meythrinva *f*, meythrinvaow. **nursery school** sko veythrin *f*, skolyow meythrin

nurture I *n* magereth *f* **II** *vb* maga

nut *n* knowen *f*, knovwennow; know *coll*

nuthatch *n* terrer know *m*, terroryon know

nutmeg *n* knowen muskat *f*, knowennow muskat; know muskat *coll*

nutrition *n* megyans *m*; sosten *m*, sostenow

nutritious *adj* magus

nutshell *n* plisken krowen *f*, plisk know

nuzzle *vb* minya

nylon *n* nilon *m*

nylons *n* lodrow nilon *pl*

O

O *part* (*vocative particle*) A^2

oak *n* derowen *f*, derowennow; derow *coll*; dar *m*, deri

oar *n* rev *f*, revow

oat flake *n* kerghen *f*, kerghennow

oath *n* ti *m*, tiow; li *m*, liow

oats *n* kergh *coll*. **porridge oats** yos kergh

obedience *n* gostytter *m*; obayans *m*

obedient *adj* gostyth

obese *adj* berrik

obey *vb* obaya

object (1) *n* (*thing*) taklen *f*, taklennow; tra *f*, traow, taklow; (*goal*) medras *m*, medrasow; (*grammar*) objeta *m*, objetys

object (2) *vb* nagha

objection *n* acheson rag skonya *m*, achesonys rag skonya, achesonyow rag skonya

objective *n* amkan *m*, amkanow

obligation *n* ambos *m*, ambosow

obligatory *adj* a res

oblong *adj* hirbedrek

obscene *adj* lewd

obscenity *n* lewdnes *m*, lewdnessys

obscure *adj* tewl; ankler

obsequious *adj* goruvel

observant *adj* (*watchful*) hwithrus; (*diligent*) diwysyk

observation *n* aspians *m*, aspiansow

observe *vb* aspia; avisya; mires orth

obsessed *adj* gorgemerys

obsession *n* gorgemeryans *m*

obsessive behaviour *n* fara gorgemeryansek *m*

obstacle *n* lett *m*, lettys, lettow

obstinate *adj* gorth; penn kales

obstruction *n* lett *m*, lettys, lettow

obtain *vb* kavos

obtuse *adj* sogh

obvious *adj* apert; hewel

occasion *n* (*occurrence*) treveth *f*, trevethow; tro *f*, troyow; prysweyth *m*, prysweythyow; (*cause*) acheson *m*, achesonys, achesonyow. **on every occasion** pub kentel

occasional *adj* treweythus

occasionally *adv* treweythyow

occupation *n* (*job*) soodh *f*, sodhow; (*conquest*) sesyans *m*, sesyansow; (*of a building*) anedhyans *m*, anedhyansow

occupy *vb* (*a building*) kavanedhi; (*conquer*) sesya

occur *vb* hwarvos

occurrence *n* hwarvedhyans *m*, hwarvedhyansow

OCD *abbrev* (*med*) OCD. **Obsessive Compulsive Disorder** Disordyr Gorgemeryansek Omherdhys

ocean *n* keynvor *m*, keynvoryow; mor bras *m*, moryow bras. **Atlantic Ocean** Keynvor Atlantek *m*. **Indian Ocean** Keynvor Eyndek *m*. **Pacific Ocean** Keynvor Hebask *m*

o'clock *n* eur *f*

octave *n* oktav *m*, oktavow; ethves *m*, ethvesow

October *n* Hedra *m*; mis Hedra *m*

octopus *n* kollell-lesa *f*, kellylli-lesa

odd *adj* (*strange*) koynt; (*number*) dibarow

oddity *n* koyntys *f*, koyntysyow

odds *n* chons *m*, chonsyow

ode *n* od *m*, odys

odour *n* eth *m*, ethow; ethen *f*, ethennow; (*food*) blas *m*, blasow; (*stench*) fler *m*, fleryow; sawor poos *m*, saworyow poos

of *prp* a^2. **of this kind** a'n par ma. **by means of** der. **for the purpose of** rag. **for the sake of** awos; rag kerensa a^2. **in memory of** er kov. **in place of** yn le. **in spite of** awos; spit dhe^2. **in the**

middle of yn-mysk. **in the name of** a-barth (dhe²). **in the presence of** a-rag. **instead of** yn le. **lots of** meur a²; (*following pl. nouns*) pals. **masses of** bush a². **on behalf of** a-barth (dhe²). **out of** yn-mes a²

off I *adj* (*switched off*) marow **II** *adv* dhe-ves; yn-kerdh. **a mile off** mildir alemma. **chase off** fesya. **buzz off!** gwayv ow golok! **right off** heb lett; kyns es hedhi. **show off** payoni; ombraysya. **switch off** skwychya yn farow; skwychya yn-mes; ladha. **the milk is off** an leth yw kowlys. **tell off** keredhi; tavosa; keski

offence *n* offens *m*, offensys; treuspas *m*, treuspassow

offend *vb* offendya; (*commit a crime or sin*) pegha; (*disgust*) divlasa

offensive *adj* divlas; offensus

offer I *n* profyans *m*, profyansow; kynnik *m*, kynigow **II** *vb* profya; kynnik

offering *n* ro *m*, rohow, royow; (*religious context*) oferen *f*, oferennow

office *n* (*workplace*) sodhva *f*, sodhvaow; burow *m*, burowyow; (*job*) soodh *f*, sodhow; (*function*) offis *m*, offisys. **post office** *n* lytherva *f*, lythervaow. **tax office** sodhva doll *f*, sodhvaow toll. **the Post Office** Sodhva an Post *f*

officer *n* sodhek *m*, sodhogyon

official I *adj* sodhogel **II** *n* sodhek *m*, sodhogyon

offline *adj, adv* IT dhywarlinen

offside *adj* war an tu kamm

offspring *n* agh *f*, aghow

often *adv* menowgh; yn fenowgh; lieskweyth. **as often as** (*followed by a verb*) peskweyth may⁵ (th)

oggy *n* hogen *f*, hogennow; kofen *f* kofennow

oh *int* (*alas*) out; agh; ogh. **oh dear!** soweth! **oh hell!** jowl!

oil *n* oyl *m*, oylys. **olive oil** olew *m*, olewow. **oil can** podik oyl *m*, podigow oyl. **oil tanker** tanker oyl *m*, tankeryow oyl

oilfield *n* oylek *f*, oylegi

oily *adj* oylek

ointment *n* eli *m*, eliow; unyent *m*, unyentys; oynment *m*, oynmentys

OK *adj* da lowr

old *adj* koth; (*preceding the noun*) hen. **grow old** kothhe. **old age** henys *m*; kothni *f*

older *adj* kottha

oldest *adj* (an) kottha

oleander *n* bayrosen *f*, bayrosennow; bayros *coll*

olive *n* oliven *f*, olivennow; oliv *coll*. **olive oil** olew *m*, olewow

omelette *n* omlet *m*, omlettys, omlettow; krampothen oyow *f*, krampoth oyow

omen *n* kool *f*, koylow

omit *vb* omyttya

omnipotence *n* ollgallos *m*

omnipotent *adj* ollgallosek

on I *adj* (*switched on*) byw **II** *adv* (*forward*) a-rag; yn-rag **III** *prp* war²; (*of clothing*) a-dro dhe². **the shoes on your feet** an eskisyow a-dro dhe'th treys. **come on** (*2s*) deus yn-rag; (*2p*) dewgh yn-rag. **from now on** alemma rag. **go on** (*2s*) ke yn-rag; (*2p*) kewgh yn-rag. **have somebody on** gul ges a nebonan. **on behalf of** a-barth (dhe²). **on foot** a-droos. **on land** yn tir. **on land and sea** yn tir hag yn mor. **on purpose** a-borpos. **on Sunday** Sulweyth. **on the** (*used in numbers from 21 to 39*) warn. **on the bottom** a-woles. **on the contrary** dhe'n kontrari; yn gortherep; y'n kontrari part. **on the left** a-gledh. **on the right** a-dhyghow. **on the other hand** y'n fordh aral; y'n barth aral. **on time** a-brys; a-dermyn. **on top** a-wartha.

switch on enowi; skwychya yn fyw.
they're on to me ymons war ow lergh
once *adv* unweyth. **once more** arta. **at once** desempis; hware; skon; war-not. **once upon a time** yn termyn eus passy(e)s

one I *num* (*independent*) onan; (*before a noun*) unn **II** *prn* onan; (*used after pub, lies, and kettep*) huni. **another one** onan aral; ken aral. **not one** nagonan. **one of two** eyl. **one another** an eyl y gila *m*; an eyl hy ben *f*; (*reciprocal prefix*) om-. **one by one** an eyl wosa y gila *m*; an eyl wosa hy ben *f*. **other ones** re erel; ken re. **that one** henna *m*; honna *f*. **the one** an onan; an huni; (*referring to a person*) neb. **the ones** an re. **the other ones** an re erel; an ken re. **these ones** an re ma. **this one** hemma *m*; homma *m*. **those ones** an re na

one-piece *adj* unrann

onerous *adj* beghus

oneself *prfx* om-

one-sided *adj* untu

one-way *adj* unfordh. **one-way street** stret unfordh *m*, stretys unfordh, stretow unfordh

onion *n* onyonen *f*, onyonennow; onyon *coll*

online *adj*, *adv* (*IT*) warlinen

only I *adj* unnik; unn **II** *adv* hepken; yn unnik; unweyth; (*with negation*) marnas; unsel **III** *cnj* (*save*) lemen **I have only two books.** Yma dew lyver dhymm hepken. **if I could only have...** unweyth a kaffen.... **only child** flogh unnik *m*

onomatopoeia *n* ger herwydh son *m*

onset *n* dallathvos *m*, dallathvosow

on-site *adj* war-lown

onslaught *n* omsettyans *m*, omsettyansow

onward *adv* yn-rag; war yew

ooze *vb* sygera

opaque *adj* diskler

open I *adj* ygor; (*of land*) gwastas **II** *vb* ygeri

opened *adj* ygerys

opener *n* ygerell *f* ygerellow

opening *n* (*act of opening*) ygeryans *m*, ygeryansow; (*aperture*) bolgh *m*, bolghow; (*beginning*) dalleth *m*, dallethow; (*orifice*) toll *m*, tell

openly *adv* apert; yn ygor

opera *n* gwari kan *m*, gwariow kan; opera *m*, operaow. **soap opera** opera sebon *m*, operaow sebon

operate *vb* oberi

operating system *n* (*IT*) system oberyans *m*

operation *n* oberyans *m*, oberyansow

operator *n* oberador *m*, oberadoryon

ophthalmologist *n* medhek lagasow *m*, medhogyon lagasow

ophthalmology *n* medhegieth lagasow *f*

opinion *n* avis *m*, avisyow; breus *f*, breusow; brys *m*, brysyow; tybyans *m*, tybyansow; kussul *f*, kussulyow; prederyans *m*, prederyansow. **give an opinion** ri breus. **hold an opinion** tybi. **in my opinion** orth ow brys

opponent *n* erbynner *m*, erbynoryon

opportunism *n* opportunystieth *f*

opportunity *n* chons *m*, chonsyow; spas *m*, spassow

oppose *vb* enebi; gortheneba; omsettya orth

opposite I *adj* konter **II** *n* kontrari *m*, kontraris; konter *m*, konters **III** *prp* a-dal

opposition *n* enebieth *f*; gorthter *m*

oppress *vb* arwaska; kompressa

oppression *n* arwask *m*, arwaskow; kompressyans *m*, kompressyansow

optician *n* (*commercial*) optycyan *m*, optycyans

option *n* dewis *m*, dewisyow

optional *adj* a-dhewis; dre dhewis; dewisel

optionally *adv* a-dhewis

or *cnj* po. **either... or** po... po; poken... po. **or else** poken

oral *adj* der anow; war anow. **oral examination** apposyans war anow *m*, apposyansow war anow

orange I *adj* (*colour*) rudhvelyn **II** *n* (*fruit*) owraval *m*, owravalow

oration *n* areth *f*, arethyow

orator *n* arethor *m*, arethoryon; dadhelor *m*, dadheloryon

orb *n* pel *f*, pelyow

orbit I *n* resegva *f*, resegvaow **II** *vb* resek a-dro (dhe²)

orchard *n* avalennek *f*, avalenegi; avallan *f* avallannow

orchestra *n* orkestra *m*, orkestras

orchid *n* tegeyryan *m*

orchid, bee *n* tegeyryan gwenen *m*

ordain *vb* apoyntya; sakra; ordena

order I *n* (*arrangement*) aray *m*, arayys, arayow; (*command*) gorhemmyn *m*, gorhemynnow; (*purchase*) arghadow *m*, arghadowyow; (*organisation*) urdh *f*, urdhyow; (*rank*) order *m*, orders; (*religious*) ordyr *m*, ordyrs **II** *vb* (*arrange in order*) araya; kempenna; (*command*) gorhemmyn; (*request; purchase*) erghi. **in ascending order** yn aray yskynnus. **in chronological order** yn aray termyn. **in descending order** yn aray diyskynnus. **in order to** rag. **mail order** erghi der an post. **order oneself** omdhyghtya

orderly *n* (*attendant*) kempenner *m*, kempenoryon

ordinance *n* ordenans *m*

ordinary *adj* kemmyn; sempel

oregano *n* organs *coll*

organ *n* (*musical instrument*) organ *m*, organs; (*anat*) organ *m*, organow. **mouth organ** *n* harmonika *m*, harmonikas

organic *adj* organek. **organic farming** ammeth organek *f*

organisation *n* (*body*) kowethyans *m*, kowethyansow; (*arrangement*) restrans *m*, restransow. **United Nations Organisation (UNO)** Kowethyans an Kenedhlow Unys (KKU) *m*

organise *vb* restra; ordena

organism *n* organedh *m*, organedhow

Orient *n* Oriant *m*

orientation *n* tuedhder *m*

orifice *n* toll *m*, tell

origin *n* devedhyans *m*, devedhyansow; dalleth *m*, dallethow; dallathvos *m*, dallathvosow

original I *adj* derowel; gwreydhek **II** *n* mammfurv *f*, mammfurvow, mammfurvyow; (*of a text*) mammskrif *m*, mammskrifow

originally *adv* y'n dalleth

originate *vb* dalleth

ornament I *n* tegen *f*, tegennow **II** *vb* afina

ornamental *adj* afinus

orphan I *n* omdhivas *m*, omdhivasow **II** *vb* omdhivasa

orthodox *adj* ewngryjyk

orthography *n* lytherenieth *f*

orthopaedic *adj* orthopedek

orthopaedic surgeon *n* orthopedydh *m*, orthopedydhyon

orthopaedics *n* orthopedek *f*

oscillation *n* daromres *m*, daromresow

ostrich *n* strus *m*, strusyow

other *adj* aral, erel; (*preceding a noun*) ken. **another one** onan aral; ken onan. **each other** an eyl y gila *m*; an eyl hy ben *f*. **every other day** (*every second day*) pub nessa dydh; (*every day but not today*) pub dydh aral *m*. **on the other hand** y'n fordh aral; y'n barth aral. **the one... the other** an eyl y gila *m*; an eyl hy ben *f*. **the other ones** an re erel

otherwise I *adv* yn ken maner; ken; kontrari. **I cannot do otherwise**

(than)... Ny allav gul ken (es)... **II**
cnj poken. **otherwise I will go** poken
yth av

otter *n* dowrgi *m*, dowrgeun

our *poss. adj* agan

ourselves *prn* agan honan

out I *adv* mes; yn-mes **II** *int* out. **cast
out** fesya. **cry out** garma. **get out of
my sight!** gwayv ow golok! **have a
tooth out** kavos dans tennys yn-mes.
out cold diswar. **out-and-out** purra.
out of yn-mes a². **out of focus** mes a
fog. **out of sight** mes a wel. **put out**
(*expel*) gorra yn-mes; (*extend*) ystyn;
(*extinguish*) difudhi. **run out** (*of
something*) difygya. **throw out** tewlel
yn-mes

outbox *n* (*IT*) meskist *f*

outcast *n* gal *m*, galyon, galow; adla *m*,
adlyon

outcome *n* sewyans *m*, sewyansow;
diwedh *m*, diwedhow

outfit *n* aparel *m*

outing *n* diskeverans *m*, diskeveransow

outlaw *n* adla *m*, adlyon

outlet *n* tardhell *f*, tardhellow

outlook *n* gologva *f*, gologvaow

output I *n* eskorrans *m*, eskorransow **II**
vb eskorra

outrage I *n* outray *m*, outrayow **II** *vb*
outraya

outrageous *adj* outrayus

outright *adj* pur

outside I *adj* a-ves **II** *adv* yn-mes; mes;
(*looking*) war-ves **III** *prp* a-der; a-ves
dhe²; yn-mes a². **outside the town**
a-ves dhe'n dre

outsider *n* estren *m*, estrenyon

outskirts *n* oryon *pl*

outspoken *adj* freth

outstanding *adj* a bris; dres eghen;
meur y vri

outwardly *adv* war-ves

outwards *adv* war-ves; yn-mes

oval I *adj* hirgylghek **II** *n* hirgylgh *m*,
hirgylghyow

ovary *n* oygel *f*, oygellow

ovation *n* garm wormola *f*, garmow
gormola

oven *n* forn *f*, fornow. **microwave oven**
forn gorrdon *f*, fornow korrdon

over I *adj* (*ended*) diwedhys; gorfennys
II *adv* (*in a higher place*) a-ugh **III** *prp*
dres. **go over** tremena. **over a
hundred** moy es kans. **over here** hons
omma. **over there** hons; yn-hons. **tip
over** omhweles

over- *prfx* gor-; ugh-

overboard *adv* mes a'n lester

overcast *adj* gorgomolek

overcharge *vb* gorharga

overcome I *adj* fethys **II** *vb* fetha

overconfidence *n* gorfydhyans *m*,
gorfydhyansow

overconfident *adj* gorfydhyansek

overdo *vb* gorwul

overeat *vb* gordhybri; kwoffi

overflow *vb* fenna; gorfrosa

overgrow *vb* gordevi

overgrown *adj* gordevys

overlap I *n* gorgudhans *m*,
gorgudhansow **II** *vb* gorgudha

overload I *n* gorvegh *m*, gorveghyow **II**
vb gorveghya; gorharga

overlook *vb* (*fail to notice*) fyllel gweles;
(*look over from above*) mires dres

overnight *adv* dres nos

overpopulated *adj* gorbeblys

overseas *adv* tramor; dres mor

oversee *vb* gorweles

overseer *n* gorwolyas *m*, gorwolysi

oversight *n* ankov *m*, ankovyow

overspend *adj* gorspena

overtake *vb* passya

overthrow *vb* domhwel

overtime *n* gordermyn *m*

overture *n* ragilow *m*

overview *n* gorwolok *f*, gorwologow

overweight *adj* borr

overwhelm *vb* reverthi
owe *vb* tyli
owl *n* oula *m*, oulys; kowan *f*,
    kowannow
own I *vb* pywa; perghenna **II** *adj* honan.
    my own ow honan. **my own book** ow
    lyver ow honan
owner *n* perghennek *m*, perghenogyon;
    perghen *m*, perghennow
ownership *n* perghenogeth *f*,
    perghenogethow

ox *n* ojyon *m*, oghen. **young ox** lodhen
    m, lodhnow; lonn *m*, lonnow
oxen *n* oghen *pl*
oxide *n* oksid *m*, oksidys. **carbon
    dioxide, CO_2** karbon dioxid *m*.
    carbon monoxide, CO karbon
    unnoxid *m*
oxygen *n* (*element*) oksyjen *m*
oyster *n* estren *f*, estrennow; ester *coll*
oyster-bed *n* estrek *f*, estregi

P

pace *n* kammen *f*, kamennow; pas *m*,
    passys
Pacific Ocean *n* Keynvor Hebask *m*
pacifism *n* kresydhieth *f*
pacifist *n* kresydh *m*, kresydhyon
pacify *vb* koselhe; hebaskhe
pack *vb* fardella
package I *n* fardel *m*, fardellow **II** *vb*
    fardella
packet *n* fardellik *m*, fardelligow
pact *n* ambos *m*, ambosow
pad *n* padyn *m*, padynnow
paddle I *n* rev dhewbennek *f*, revow
    dewbennek **II** *vb* revya
paediatric *adj* pediatrek
paediatrician *n* medhek fleghes *m*,
    medhogyon fleghes
paediatrics *n* pediatrek *f*
Pagan *n* Pagan *m*, Paganys, Paganyon
pagan *adj* pagan
Paganism *n* Paganieth *f*
page (1) *n* (*book*) folen *f*, folennow
page (2) *n* (*boy*) paja *m*, pajys
pager *n* galwydh *m*, galwydhyon
paginate *vb* folenna
pagination *n* folennans *m*
paid *adj* pes
pail *n* kelorn *m*, kelern

pain I *n* payn *m*, paynys; dolor *m*,
    dolors **II** *vb* paynya
painful *adj* tynn; (*mentally*) ankensi
painless *adj* dibayn
paint I *n* liw *m*, liwyow; paynt *m*,
    payntys **II** *vb* (*a picture*) lymna;
    (*decorate*) payntya; (*to colour*) liwa.
    paint box *n* kisten liwyow *f*,
    kistennow liwyow. **paint pot** *n* pott
    paynt *m*, pottys paynt, pottow paynt.
    face paint *n* paynt bejeth *m*, payntys
    bejeth, payntow bejeth
paintbrush *n* skubyllen baynt *f*,
    skubyllennow paynt
painter *n* (*artist*) lymner *m*, lymnoryon.
    (*decorator*) payntyer *m*, payntyoryon
painting *n* liwans *m*, liwansow;
    liwyans *m*, liwyansow; lymnans *m*,
    lymnansow
pair I *n* kopel *m*, koplow; dewdhen *m*
    II *vb* parya
pal *n* sos *m*
palace *n* palys *m*, palesys, palesyow
palatable *adj* blesys da
palate *n* stevnik *f*, stevnigow
pale I *adj* disliw; gwannliwek **II** *vb* kelli
    liw
Palestine *top* Palestin *m*

353

Palestinian I *adj* palestinek **II** *n* Palestinyas *m*, Palestinysi

palette *n* liwvord *m*, liwvordow

pall *n* pall *m*, pallow

palm *n* (*of hand*) palv *f*, palvow; torr an dhorn *f*, torrow an dorn

palm-tree *n* palmwedhen *f*, palmwedhennow; palmwydh *coll*

palsy *n* palsi *m*, palsis

pamper *vb* chersya re; gorjersya

pamphlet *n* folennik *f*, folenigow

pan *n* padel *f*, padellow. **frying pan** *n* padel-fria *f*, padellow-fria; leswedh *m*, leswedhow; lecher *m*, lechers. **iron pan** padel horn *f*, padellow horn

pancake *n* krampothen *f*, krampoth

panda *n* panda *m*, pandas

pane *n* kwarel *m*, kwarels

panel I *n* panel *m*, panellow **II** *vb* panellya

pang *n* gloos *f*, glosow

panic I *n* skruth *m*, skruthow; euth *m* **II** *vb* kemeres skruth; kemeres euth. **panic attack** omsettyans skruth *m*, omsettyansow skruth

pansy, garden *n* melion lowarth *coll*

pansy, wild *n* (*heartsease*) losow an Drynsys *coll*

pansy, yellow *n* melionen velyn *f*, melionennow melyn; melion melyn *coll*

pant *vb* dyena

panties *n* lavrek byghan *m*, lavrogow byghan

pantomime *n* gwari mus *m*, gwariow mus

pantry *n* talgel *f*, talgellow

pants *n* (*underpants*) lavrek byghan *m*, lavrogow byghan; islavrek *m*, islavrogow

papal *adj* pabel

paper *n* paper *m*, paperyow. **paper chain** *n* kadon baper *f*, kadonyow paper. **paper hat** *n* hatt paper *m*, hattys paper, hattow paper. **paper**

tissue lien paper *m*, lienyow paper.

toilet paper paper privedhyow.

writing paper paper-skrifa

paperback *n* lyver kudhlen vedhel *m*, lyvrow kudhlen vedhel

parable *n* parabyl *m*, parablys; parabolen *f*, parabolennow

parabola *n* parabolen *f*, parabolennow

parabolic *adj* parabolek

parachute *n* lammlen *f*, lammlennow

paradise *n* paradhis *f*

paragraph *n* rannskrif *m*, rannskrifow; paragraf *m*, paragrafys, paragrafow

parallel *adj* keslinek; kettuel

parallelogram *n* kettuelen *f*, kettuelennow

paralyse *vb* palsya

paralysed *adj* palsyes

paralysis *n* palsi *m*, palsis

paranoid *adj* (*med*) paranoyd

parasite *n* teurogen *f*, teurogennow; teurek *coll*

parasitic *adj* teuregel; parasitek

parasol *n* howllen *f*, howllennow

parcel *n* fardel *m*, fardellow

parch *vb* krasa

parched *adj* kras

parchment *n* parchemin *m*, parcheminyow

pardon I *n* gevyans *m*, gevyansow **II** *vb* gava

parent *n* kar *m*, kerens

parental *adj* a'n gerens; kerensel. **parental leave** *n* kummyas kerensel *m*

parenthesis *n* krommvagh *f*, krommvaghow

parents *n* kerens *pl*

parish *n* pluw *f*, pluwow

parishioner *n* pluwek *m*, pluwogyon

parity *n* pareth *f*, parethow

park I *n* park *m*, parkow **II** *vb* parkya. **car park** *n* park kerri *m*, parkow kerri

parking *n* parkyans *m*. **parking fees** feow-parkya *pl*. **no parking** parkya difennys

parliament *n* senedh *m*, senedhow.
The Cornish Stannary Parliament
Konsel Stenegow Kernow *m*. **member
of parliament (MP)** esel senedh *m*,
eseli senedh; *abbrev* ES
parliamentary *adj* senedhek
parlour *n* parledh *m*, parledhow
parochial *adj* pluwek
parody I *n* parodi *m*, parodis **II** *vb*
parodia
parrot *n* papynjay *m*, papynjays
parsley *n* persilen *f*, persilennow; persil
coll
parsley, cow *n* kegis an vugh *coll*
parsnip *n* panesen *f*, panesennow;
panes *coll*
parson *n* pronter *m*, pronteryon
part I *n* rann *f*, rannow; darn *m*,
darnow; parth *f*, parthow **II** *vb*
diberth; (*disperse*) keskar; (*divide*)
ranna. **for the most part** dre vras.
take part kemeres rann. **a greater
part of** brassa rann a^2
partake *vb* kemeres rann. **partake in**
bos kevrennek a^2
partial *adj* rannel
partially-sighted *adj* rannwelyek
participant *n* kevrennek *m*,
kevrenogyon
participate *vb* kemeres rann; bos
kevrennek. **participate in** bos
kevrennek a^2
participating *adj* kevrennek
participle *n* ranngemeryans *m*,
ranngemeryansow. **passive participle**
ranngemeryans godhevek *m*,
ranngemeryansow godhevek
particle *n* perthygel *m*, perthyglow
particular *adj* arbennek. **a particular
one** neb unn
particularly *adv* dres oll; yn arbennek
parting *n* keskar *m*
partition *n* rannans *m*, ranansow
partner *n* keskoweth *m*, keskowetha;
kespar *m*, kesparow

partnership *n* keskowethyans *m*,
keskowethyansow. **The Cornish
Language Partnership** (*name of
organisation*) Keskowethyans an Yeth
Kernewek *m*
partridge *n* grugyar *f*, grugyer
party I *n* (*celebration*) kevewi *f*,
kevewiow; (*political*) parti *m*, partis,
partiow **II** *vb* (*hold a party*) kevewya
pass *vb* (*pass by*) tremena; (*time*)
passya; (*pass something to somebody*)
ystyn. **come to pass** hwarvos. **pass
away** (*die*) merwel; tremena. **pass by**
tremena orth. **pass over** treusi;
tremena
passable *adj* (*navigable*) hefordh;
(*satisfactory*) 'vas; da lowr
passage *n* tremen *m*, tremenow
passenger *n* trethyas *m*, trethysi.
passenger ship gorhel trethysi *m*,
gorholyon trethysi
passive *adj* godhevek; godhevus
passport *n* tremengummyas *m*,
tremengumyasow
password *n* ger-tremena *m*,
geryow-tremena
past I *adj* passys; passyes **II** *n* termyn
eus passy(e)s **III** *pro* dres. **in the past**
seulabrys; yn termyn eus passy(e)s;
last week y'n seythen usi passy(e)s
pasta *n* pasta *coll*
paste *n* past *m*, pastow
pastel *n* pastel *f*, pastellow
pasteurise *vb* pasteurya
pastime *n* gwari *m*, gwariow; sport *m*,
sportys, sportow
pastor *n* bugel *m*, bugeledh
pastry *n* hogen *f*, hogennow; past *m*,
pastow. **puff pastry** past pyff *m*. **short
crust pastry** past brew *m*
pasture *n* peurva *f*, peurvaow.
common pasture pras *m*, prasow
pasty *n* pasti *m*, pastiow. **meat pasty**
pasti kig *f*, pastiow kig. **vegetable
pasty** pasti losow *f*, pastiow losow

patch I *n* klout *m*, kloutys **II** *vb* kloutya

patent I *adj* apert **II** *n* patent *m*, patentys. **patent infringement** torrva patent *f*, torrvaow patent. **patent pending** patent yn-dann hwithrans

paternity *n* tasoleth *f*. **paternity leave** kummyas tasoleth *m*

path *n* hyns *m*, hensyow

pathetic *adj* truedhek

patience *n* perthyans *m*

patient I *adj* godhevus; meur y berthyans *m*; meur hy ferthyans *f*; meur aga ferthyans *pl* **II** *n* godhevyas *m*, godhevysi; perthyer *m*, perthyoryon

patriarch *n* ugheldas *m*, ugheldasow

patriarchy *n* tasrewl *f*, tasrewlys

patriot *n* gwlaskarer *m*, gwlaskaroryon

patriotic *adj* gwlaskar

patriotism *n* gwlaskerensa *f*

patron *n* tasek *m*, tasogyon. **patron saint** *n* tassans *m*, tassens

patronise *vb* tasegi

patronising *adj* tasegus

pattern *n* skantlyn *m*, skantlyns; patron *m*, patronyow

pause I *n* powes *m*, powesow; hedh *m*, hedhow **II** *vb* powes; hedhi

pave *vb* konsya

pavement *n* kons *m*, konsys, konsow

pavilion *n* pabel *f*, pabellow

paw *n* paw *m*, pawyow

pawn I *n* gostel *m*, gostlow **II** *vb* gostla. **pawn something for** gostla neppyth a²

pay I *n* gober *m*, gobrow **II** *vb* tyli; (*pay for*) pe; (*buy*) prena. **pay attention** attendya. **pay off** akwytya. **sick pay** gober kleves. **gross pay** gober tew *m*, gobrow tew. **net pay** gober ylyn *m*, gobrow ylyn

payment *n* talas *m*, talasow

pea *n* pesen *f*, pesennow; pys *coll*

peace *n* kres *m*

peaceful *adj* hebask

peach *n* aval gwlanek *m*, avalow gwlanek

peacock *n* payon *m*, payones

peak *n* bleyn *m*, bleynyow; topp *m*, toppys, toppow

peanut *n* knowen dhor *f*, knowennow dor; know dor *coll*; pysknowen *f*, pysknow

pear *n* peren *f*, perennow; per *coll*

pearl *n* perl *m*, perlys

peasant *n* gwerinor *m*, gwerinoryon

peat *n* towargh *coll*

pebble *n* bilien *f*, biliennow; bili *coll*; kelester *m*, kelesteryow

peculiar *adj* koynt

pedal I *n* trosell *f*, trosellow; trosla *f*, trosleow **II** *vb* trosella

peddler *n* gwikor *m*, gwikoryon; marchont *m*, marchons

pedestrian *n* kerdher *m*, kerdhoryon. **pedestrian crossing** treusva gerdhoryon *f*, treusvaow kerdhoryon

pedigree *n* aghskrif *m*, aghskrifow

pee I *n* pisas *m* **II** *vb* pisa

peel I *n* rusken *f*, ruskennow; rusk *coll*; kenn *m*, kennow **II** *vb* diruska; pilya

peeler *n* (*tool*) diruskell *f*, diruskellow

peep (1) *n* (*sound*) gik *m*, gikys

peep (2) *vb* (*look*) gyki. **not a peep** na gik na mik

peer *n* (*equal; friend*) koweth *m*, kowetha; kowethes *f*, kowethesow

peers *n* hynsa *pl*; (*Lords Temporal*) arlydhi *pl*

peg *n* ebil *m*, ebilyow, ebilyer; pynn *m*, pynnow. **peg out the washing** lesa an golgh

pelican *n* pelikan *m*, pelikanes

pen *n* pluven *f*, pluvennow. **felt-tip pen** *n* pluven leuvban *f*, pluvennow leuvban. **pen name** hanow pluven *m*, henwyn pluven

penalty *n* spal *f*, spalyow

penance *n* penans *m*

pence *n* dinerow *pl*

pencil *n* pluven blomm *f*, pluvennow plomm

penetrate *vb* dewana; kropya

penguin *n* penn gwynn *m*, pennow gwynn

peninsula *n* konna tir *m*, konaow tir

penis *n* kalgh *f*, kalghyow

penknife *n* kollell bleg *f*, kellylli pleg

penny *n* (*coin*) dineren *f*, dinerennow; (*unit of currency*) diner *m*, dinerow

pennyroyal *n* menta riel *f*

pennywort *n* (*navelwort*) krampothen vowesi *f*, krampothennow mowysi; krampoth mowysi *coll*; (*ivy-leaved toadflax*) tron an leugh *m*

pension *n* gober omdennans *m*, gobrow omdennans; pensyon *m*, pensyons

pensioner *n* pensyonydh *m*, pensyonydhyon

pentacle *n* pympel *m*, pympellow

pentagon *n* pympkorn *m*, pympkernow

Pentecost *n* penkost *m*

peony *n* rosen menydh *f*

people *n* (*nation*) pobel *f*, poblow; (*persons*) tus *pl*. **common people** gwerin *f*; an gemmyn *pl*

pepper **I** *n* puber *m*, puberyow **II** *vb* pubra. **bell pepper** pubren *f*, pubrennow

peppermint *n* pubermenta *f*

per *prp* dre²; der. **per capita** an penn. **per kilometre** an kilometer

perceive *vb* percevya; (*notice*) merkya; (*sense*) klewes

percent *n* kansran *f*, kansrannow

percentage *n* kansran *f*, kansrannow

percussion *n* frappyans *m*

percussive *adj* frappyansek

perdition *n* argol *m*

perfect *adj* perfydh; flour

perfection *n* perfydhder *m*; keweras *m*

perfidious *adj* fekyl

perforated *adj* tollek

perforation *n* kraw *m*, krawyow

perform *vb* performya; gwruthyl

performance *n* gwryth *f*, gwrythow; gwrythyans *m*, gwrythyansow; performans *m*, performansow

performer *n* gwarier *m*, gwarioryon; performyer *m*, performyoryon

perhaps *adv* martesen

peril *n* peryl *m*, peryllow, peryllyow

perimeter *n* kylghvusur *m*, kylghvusuryow

period *n* (*age*) oos *m*, osow; (*menstrual*) amseryow *m*; (*colloq*) termyn an mis *m*; (*of time*) seson *m*, sesons, sesonyow; spys *m*, spysow; termyn *m*, termynyow

periodic *adj* periodek. **The Periodic Table** *n* An Vosen Beriodek *f*

periodical *n* lyver termyn *m*, lyvrow termyn

periodically *adv* a dermyn dhe dermyn

peripheral *adj* amalek

periphery *n* amal *m*, emlow

periwinkle *n* pervynk *m*, pervynkys

perjure *vb* gowlia

perjury *n* gowli *m*

perk *n* waja *m*, wajys

perm **I** *n* perm *m*, permyow **II** *vb* permya

permanent *adj* fast

permeate *vb* dewana

permission *n* kummyas *m*, kumyasow; gront *m*, grontys, grontow. **with your permission** der dha gummyas (*sg*); der agas kummyas (*pl*)

permit **I** *n* kummyas *m*, kumyasow **II** *vb* gasa; alowa

perpendicular *adj* serth

perpetual *adj* heb hedhi; anhedhek

perpetually *adv* pub eur; anhedhek; heb hedhi

persecute *vb* persekutya

persecution *n* persekutyans *m*, persekutyansow

person *n* den *m*, tus; person *m*, persons; (*physical body*) korf *m*, korfow

personal *adj* personel; (*private*) privedh

personality *n* personoleth *f*, personolethow

personality disorder *n* (*med*) disordyr personoleth *m*

personification *n* personekheans *m*

perspire *vb* hwysa

persuade *vb* dri; movya. **persuade somebody to do something** movya nebonan may hwrello neppyth

perverse *adj* gorth

pessimist *n* gwethafor *m*, gwethaforyon

pessimistic *adj* gwethafor

pest I *n* pla *m*, plaow; ball *f*, ballow II *int* mal

pester *vb* plagya

pet I *adj* dov II *n* (*tame animal*) eneval dov *m*, enevales dov; (*endearment*) hwegen *f*, hwegennow III *vb* chersya

petal *n* petal *m*, petalys; delen vleujen *f*, del bleujyow

petition I *n* govenek *m*, govenogow; petisyon *m*, petisyons II *vb* govenegi

petrify *vb* menhe

petrol *n* petrol *m*; menoyl *m*. **petrol pump** *n* pomp petrol *m*, pompys petrol, pompyow petrol. **petrol station** *n* petrolva *f*, petrolvaow. **petrol tanker** *n* tanker petrol *m*, tankeryow petrol

petticoat *n* golesen *f*, golesennow

petty *adj* mann²-

Pharaoh *n* Faro *m*, Faros

pharmacist *n* kymyst *m*, kymystyon

pharmacy *n* (*shop*) kymyst *m*

phase *n* (*e.g. of the Moon*) gwedh *f*, gwedhow

pheasant *n* fesont *m*, fesons

philosopher *n* filosofer *m*, filosofers

philosophical *adj* filosofek

philosophy *n* filosofieth *f*, filosofiethow

phobia *n* (*med*) fobia *m*. **a person with a phobia** person gans fobia

phone I *n* pellgowser *m*, pellgowseryow II *vb* pellgewsel. **phone call** *n* galow pellgows *m*, galowyow pellgows

phosphorus *n* (*element*) fosforos *m*

photocopier *n* liesskrifell *f*, liesskrifellow

photocopy I *n* liesskrif *m*, liesskrifow II *vb* liesskrifa

photograph *n* skeusen *f*, skeusennow

photographer *n* skeusenner *m*, skeusenoryon

photography *n* skeusenieth *f*; skeusenweyth *f*

photosynthesis *n* lughwrians *m*

phrase *n* lavaren *f*, lavarennow

physical *adj* fisegel

physician *n* medhek *m*, medhogyon

physics *n* fysegieth *f*

pianist *n* pianydh *m*, pianydhyon

piano *n* piano *m*, pianos

pick (1) *n* (*tool*) pigell *f*, pigellow

pick (2) I *n* (*selection*) *n* dewis *m*, dewisyow II *vb* (*choose*) dewis; (*collect; e.g. flowers*) kuntel; terri

pickle I *n* pyckel *m*, pyckels; skalpyon *pl* II *vb* salla; pyckla

picnic *n* kroust *m*, kroustys, kroustyow

picture *n* imach *m*, imajys; (*picture*) lymnans *m*, lymnansow; liwans *m*, liwansow; liwyans *m*, liwyansow

pie *n* hogen *f*, hogennow. **steak and kidney pie** hogen vewin ha loneth *f*, hogennow bewin ha loneth

piece *n* tamm *m*, temmyn; darn *m*, darnow; pis *m*, pisys

piecemeal *adj, adv* nebes ha nebes; tamm ha tamm

pier *n* kay peulyow *m*, kayys peulyow, kayow peulyow

pierce *vb* gwana; pychya

piercing I *adj* (*sharp*) lymm II *n* (*body modification*) pychyans *m*, pychyansow

piety *n* sansoleth *f*

pig *n* hogh *m*, hoghes; (*young pig*) porghel *m*, porghelli. **pigs** *n* mogh *pl.* **buy a pig in a poke** prena kath yn sagh

pigeon *n* kolom *f*, kelemmi

piggy bank *n* kofrik erbys *m*, kofrigow erbys

piglet *n* porghellik *m*, porghelligow

pignut *n* keler *coll*

pigsty *n* krow mogh *m*, krowyow mogh

pike *n* (*fish*) densek dowr *m*, densoges dowr

pilchard *n* hernen *f*, hern

pile *n* pil *m*, pilyow; bern *m*, bernyow

piles *n.pl* (*haemorrhoids*) kleves marghogyon *m*

pilgrim *n* pergherin *m*, pergherinyow; prierin *m*, prierinyon

pilgrimage *n* pergherinses *f*, pergherinsesow

pill *n* pellennik *f*, pellenigow

pillar *n* koloven *f*, kolovennow; post *m*, postow

pillory I *n* karghar prenn *m*, kargharow prenn II *vb* karghara

pillow *n* pluvek *f*, pluvogow

pilot *n* lewyader *m*, lewyadoryon

pimpernel, scarlet *n* brathles *m*

pimpernel, yellow *n* steren Maria *f*

pimple *n* kuriek *m*, kuriogas, kuriegi

pin I *n* pynn *m*, pynnys, pynnow II *vb* pynna. **rolling pin** rolbren *m*, rolbrennyer

pincers *n* pyncer *m*, pynceryow

pinch *vb* pynchya

pine (1) *n* (*tree*) pinen *f*, pinennow; pin *coll*; saben *f*, sabennow; sab *coll*

pine (2) *vb* (*long for*) omwetha; kemeres tristys

pineapple *n* pinaval *m*, pinavalow

pine-cone *n* aval saben *m*, avalow saben

pink *adj* (*pale*) gwynnrudh; (*reddish*) rudhwynn. (*flesh-coloured*) kigliw

pinnacle *n* pynakyl *m*, pynaklys

pint *n* pinta *m*, pintys

pioneer I *n* ragresor *m*, ragresoryon II *vb* ragresek

pious *adj* sansel

pip *n* sprusen *f*, sprusennow; sprus *coll*

pipe I *n* pib *f*, pibow; pibell *f*, pibellow II *vb* piba

pipit, meadow *n* bonnik *m*, bonniges

piracy *n* morladrynsi

pirate *n* morlader *m*, morladron

piss I *n* pisas *m* II *vb* pisa

pistol *n* pystol *m*, pystolys, pystolow

pit *n* pytt *m*, pyttys, pyttow; poll *m*, pollow. **clay pit** *n* poll pri *m*, pollow pri

pitch I *n* (*bitumen*) pyg *m*; (*degree*) pryck *m*, pryckow; (*music*) pych *m*, pychys II *vb* pychya; (*throw*) tewlel; (*cover with pitch*) pega; (*pitch a tent*) tyldya. **pitch accent** tonlev *m*, tonlevow. **pitch black** pur dhu

pitcher *n* pycher *m*, pychers

pitiful *adj* pitethus; truedhek

pitiless *adj* dibita

pity *n* truedh *m*; pita *m*, pitys. **have pity on** kemeres truedh war[2]; kemeres truedh a[2]

pixel *n* pyksel *m*, pyksels, pykselyow

pizza *n* pitsa *m*, pitsas

placate *vb* diserri; koselhe

place I *n* tyller *m*, tylleryow; le *m*, leow; plas *m*, plassow II *vb* gorra; settya. **high place** ardh *m*, ardhow. **Playing Place** (*plen-an-gwary*) plen an gwari *m*, plenys an gwari. **in place of** yn le. **take place** hwarvos

placed *adj* settyes; settys

plague I *n* plag *m*, plagys; pla *m*, plaow; ball *f*, ballow; *int* malbew II *vb* plagya

plagued *adj* plagys

plaice *n* lith *f*, lithes

plain I *adj* (*unadorned*) plen; (*level*) leven; gwastas; kompes; (*simple*) sempel II n plen m, plenys. **plain to see** apert

plainly adv apert; efan; yn golow

plaintiff n plentyas m, plentysi

plaintive adj truedhek

plait I n pleth f, plethow II vb pletha

plaited adj plethys

plan I n (project) towl m, towlow; (drawing) tenn m, tennow II vb tewlel towl; towla; devisya

plane (1) I n (tool) rask f, raskow; playn m, playnys II vb (carpentry) raska; playnya

plane (2) (aircraft) jynn ebron m, jynnys ebron, jynnow ebron; ayren f, ayrennow

planet n planet m, planetys, planetow

planetarium n planetva f, planetvaow; sterji m, sterjiow

planetary adj a'n planetys

plank n astel f, estyl

plankton n planktonen f, planktonennow; plankton coll

planning n towlennans m, towlenansow

plant (1) I n (botanical) losowen f, losow; les m, lesyow; plans m, plansow (infiltrator) ynsidhler m, ynsidhloryon II vb plansa; (sow) hasa; (establish) fastya. **gather plants** losowa

plant (2) n (factory) gweythva f, gweythvaow; (equipment) daffar m. **power plant** tredanva f, tredanvaow

plantain, broad-leaved n les hynsledan m, losow hynsledan

plantain, ribwort n hynsledan pymp gwythien m

plaster I n plaster m, plastrow II vb plastra

plastic I adj hebleth; plastek II n plastek m, plastogow

plate n plat m, platys, platyow; skudel f, skudellow. **number plate** plat niver m, platys niver, platyow niver

plateful n platas m, platasow

platform n (railway) kay m, kayys, kayow; (rostrum) arethva f, arethvaow; bynk f, bynkyow

platinum n (element) platinom m

plausibility n gwirhevelepter m

plausible adj gwirhaval

play I n gwari m, gwariow II vb (a game) gwari; (an instrument) seni; (a wind instrument) hwytha. **miracle play** gwari mir m, gwariow mir. **playing place** n (plen-an-gwary) plen an gwari m, plenys an gwari

playdough n toos-gwari m

player n gwarier m, gwarioryon

playground n garth-gwari m, garthow-gwari

playing field n park-gwari m, parkow-gwari

playlist n kanrol f, kanrolyow

playwright n dramatydh m, dramatydhyon

plea n pledyans m, pledyansow; klem m, klemys

plead vb pledya

pleasant adj hweg; hegar

please I int mar pleg; (sg) dre dha vodh; my a'th pys; (pl) dre'gas bodh; my a'gas pys II vb plesya; plegya (dhe^2)

pleased adj pes da; plesys

pleasing adj hweg; jentyl; plegadow. **be pleasing to** plegya dhe^2; plegya gans

pleasure n plesour m, plesours; delit m, delitys

pleb n (offensive) chorl m, chorlys

plebeian n komner m, komners

pledge I n arwostel m, arwostlow; gaja m, gajys II vb arwostla

plentiful adj pals

plenty I adj lowr; plenta II n plenteth f. **plenty of** lowr a^2 (followed by pl. noun); lies (followed by sg. noun). **in plenty** lowr

pliable adj gwedhyn; hebleth

pliers *n* geveligow *pl*

plight *n* plit *m*, plitys

plod *vb* trosya

plot I *n* (*conspiracy*) bras *m*, brasow; (*ground*) splatt *m*, splattys, splattow; (*of a story*) plott *m*, plottys, plottow **II** (*conspire*) brasa; (*delineate*) plottya; splattya

plotter *n* (*conspirator*) braser *m*, brasoryon; (*device*) jynn-plottya *m*, jynnow-plottya

plough I *n* arader *m*, ereder **II** *vb* aras

ploughed *adj* erys

ploughman *n* araderor *m*, araderoryon; hedhlor *m*, hedhloryon. **ploughman's lunch** li araderor

ploughshare *n* sogh *m*, soghyow

plug I *n* stoppyer *m*, stoppyers; (*electrical*) ebilyer *m*, ebilyers, ebilyorow **II** *vb* ebilya

plum *n* ploumen *f*, ploumennow; ploum *coll*

plumage *n* pluv *coll*

plumber *n* plommer *m*, plomoryon

plump *adj* berrik

plunder I *n* preydh *m*, preydhyow **II** *vb* preydha

pluperfect *adj* gorberfydh

plural I *adj* liesek **II** *n* liesplek *m*, liesplegow

plurality *n* liester *m*, liesteryow

plus *prp* (*mathematical operator*) ha; hag (*before vowels*)

Pluto *n* Plouton *m*

pneumonia *n* (*med*) niwmonia *m*

poach *vb* (*steal game*) ladra helgik; (*cook*) pochya

pocket *n* pocket *m*, pocketys, pocketow. **pocket calculator** *n* reknell *f*, reknellow. **pocket knife** kellyllik *f*, kellylligow

pock-marked *adj* tellek. **pock-marked person** tellek *m*, tellogyon

podcast *n* podkast *m*, podkasts, podkastow

poem *n* bardhonek *m*, bardhonogow; kan *f*, kanow

poet *n* prydydh *m*, prydydhyon; (*bard*) bardh *m*, berdh

poetic *adj* prydydhyek

poetry *n* bardhonieth *f*; prydydhieth *f*. **write poetry** *vb* prydydhi

point I *n* poynt *m*, poyntys, poyntow; (*tip of an object*) bleyn *m*, bleynyow; (*of land*) tron *m*, tronyow **II** (*indicate*) poyntya; (*sharpen*) bleynya

poise *n* omborth *m*, omborthow

poised *adj* omborth

poison I *n* gwenon *m*, gwenenyow; venym *m*, venymyow; poyson *m*, poysons **II** *vb* posna

poisoned *adj* posnys

poisonous *adj* gwenonek; venymys

poke I *n* pok *m*, pokyow **II** *vb* pokya. **buy a pig in a poke** prena kath yn sagh

Poland *top* Poloni *m*

polar *adj* penneghlek. **polar bear** *n* ors gwynn *m*, orses gwynn

Pole *n* Polak *m*, Polakyon

pole *n* gwelen *f*, gwelynni; peul *m*, peulyow; lorgh *f* (*m*), lorghow; (*of a cart*) gwelen garr *f*, gwelynni karr; (*geographical*) penn-aghel *m* (*f*), pennow-aghel, penn-aghlow. **the North Pole** Penn-Aghel an North *m* (*f*); **the South Pole** Penn-Aghel an Soth *m* (*f*)

police *n* kreslu *m*. **police car** *n* karr kreslu *m*, kerri kreslu. **police station** *n* sodhva greslu *f*, sodhvaow kreslu

police officer *n* gwithyas kres *m*, gwithysi gres

policy *n* polici *m*, policis

Polish I *adj* polonek **II** *n* Polonek *m*

polish I *n* splander *m* **II** *vb* polsya. **polish with wax** kora. **nail polish** gwernis ewin *f*, gwernisyow ewin

polite *adj* kortes

political *adj* politek. **political asylum** harbereth wlasek *f*

politician *n* politeger *m*, politegoryon

politics *n* politegieth *f*

poll *n* (*election*) votyans *m*, votyansow; (*survey*) sondyans *m*, sondyansow

pollinate *vb* ponegi

pollute *vb* defolya

polluter *n* defolyer *m*, defolyoryon

pollution *n* defolyans *m*, defolyansow

polyanthus *n* (*garden primrose*) briallen lowarth *f*, briallennow lowarth

polymath *n* liesroasek *m*, liesroasogyon

pomegranate *n* greunaval *m*, greunavalow

pond *n* lagen *f*, lagennow; poll *m*, pollow

ponder *vb* prederi; ombrederi

pony *n* hoba *m*, hobas

pool *n* poll *m*, pollow. **swimming pool** *n* poll-neuvya *m*, pollow-neuvya

poor *adj* boghosek. **poor person** boghosek *m*, boghosogyon

popcorn *n* ys pop *coll.* **kernel of popcorn** ysen bop *f*

pope *n* pab *m*, pabow

poppy *n* myll *f*, mylles

popular *adj* (*of the people*) gwerinek; (*liked*) gerys-da

populate *vb* pobla

populated *adj* peblys

population *n* poblans *m*, poblansow

pop-up *adj* tardhik

porbeagle *n* por'bugel *m*, por'bugeledh

porch *n* portal *m*, portals; (*usually used in plural*) porth *m*, porthow

pork *n* kig mogh *m*; kig porghel *m*

pornographic *adj* pornografek

pornography *n* pornografieth *f*

porpoise *n* morhogh *m*, morhoghes; pyffyer *m*, pyffyers

porridge *n* yos kergh *m*

port *n* porth *m*, porthow; (*especially in place-names*)

portable *adj* degadow

portal *n* porth *m* porthow; portal *m*, portals

porter *n* porther *m*, porthoryon

portfolio *n* portfolio *m*

portion *n* darnas *m*, darnasow; rann *f*, rannow

portly *adj* korfek

portrait *n* portrayans *m*, portrayansow

Portugal *top* Portyngal *m*

Portuguese I *adj* portyngalek II *n* (*language*) Portyngalek *m*; (*person*) Portyngalyas *m*, Portyngalysi

position *n* le *m*, leow; savla *m*, savleow; gre *m*, greys; (*office*) offis *m*, offisys

positive *adj* posedhek

posperity *n* sewena *f*

possess *vb* perghenna; pywa

possession *n* perghenogeth *f*, perghenogethow; pyth *m*, pythow

possessive *adj* perghennus

possibility *n* possybylta *m*, possybyltas

possible *adj* possybyl; galladow

possibly *adv* martesen

post (1) I *n* (*mail*) post *m* II *vb* postya. **post office** sodhva bost *f*, sodhvaow post

post (2) *n* (*pole*) peul *m*, peulyow

postage *n* lytherdol *m*, lytherdollow. **postage stamp** *n* stamp *m*, stampys, stampow

postcard *n* karten bost *f*, kartennow post

postcode *n* kod post *m*, kodys post

poster *n* skrisel *f*, skrisellow

postman *n* lytherwas *m*, lytherwesyon

postpone *vb* delatya

postwoman *n* lythervowes *f*, lythervowysi

pot *n* pott *m*, pottys, pottow

potato *n* aval dor *m*, avalow dor; patatysen *f*, patatysennow; patatys *coll.* **mashed potato** aval dor brewys *m*, avalow dor brewys. **potato chip** *n* asklosen *f*, asklos. **potato crisp** *n* kresik *m*, kresigow

potent *adj* gallosek

potential I *adj* galladow **II** *n* galladewder *m*, galladewderyow

potter *n* priweythor *m*, priweythoryon

pottery *n* (*craft*) priweyth *m*; (*factory*) priweythva *f*, priweythvaow

pound *n* (*currency & weight*) peuns *m*, peunsow

pour *vb* diveri

poverty *n* boghosogneth *f*

powder *n* polter *m*, polteryow. **washing powder** *n* lisiw *m*, lisiwyow

power *n* gallos *m*, gallosow; nell *m*, nellow; nerth *m*, nerthow; (*in physics*) gallosedh *m*. **power plant** tredanva *f*, tredanvaow. **nuclear power station** tredanva nuklerek *f*, tredanvaow nuklerek

powerful *adj* gallosek; nerthek; kevothek; krev

powerless *adj* diallos; dinerth

pox *n* brygh *f*, breghi

practical *adj* hewul

practice *n* praktis *m*, praktisyow

practise *vb* praktisya; omassaya

pragmatic *adj* pragmatek

pragmatism *n* pragmatieth *f*

pragmatist *n* pragmatydh *m*, pragmatydhyon

praise I *n* gormola *f*, gormoledhow; prays *m*, praysys **II** *vb* gormel; praysya. **praise oneself** ombraysya

pram *n* pramm *m*, prammys, prammow; gweli ros *m*, gweliow ros

prank *n* pratt *m*, prattys, prattow

prawn *n* bibyn bubyn *m*, bibynes bubyn

pray *vb* pysi. **pray for** pysi gans. **pray to** pysi war[2]

prayer *n* pysadow *m*. **Lord's Prayer** Pader *m*, Paderow

pre- *prfx* rag-; ar-; dar-

preach *vb* pregoth

preacher *n* pregowther *m*, pregowthoryon

precaution *n* ragbreder *m*, ragbrederow. **take precautions** bos war

precious *adj* drudh; ker

precipice *n* kleger *m*, klegrow; serthals *f*, serthalsyow; lammleder *f*, lammledrow

precipitation *n* kodhans *coll*

precipitous *adj* deserth

precise *adj* poran

precisely *adv* poran

predecessor *n* ragresegydh *m*, ragresegydhyon

predicament *n* plit *m*, plitys

predict *vb* dargana; darleverel

predictable *adj* darganadow

prediction *n* dargan *f*, darganow

preface *n* raglavar *m*, raglavarow; ragskrif *m*, ragskrifow; kynsskrif *m*, kynsskrifow

prefer *vb* bos gwell gans. **she prefers** gwell yw gensi

preference *n* (*IT*) dewisyans *m*, dewisyansow

prefix *n* rager *m*

pregnant *adj* gans flogh; torrek. **be pregnant** omdhon

prehistoric *adj* kynsistorek

prejudice *n* ragvreus

prejudiced *adj* ragvreusek

premier I *adj* penn- **II** *n* pennmenyster *m*, pennmenystrys, pennmenystroryon

premise *n* ragsel *m*, ragselyow; pennrewl *f*, pennrewlys

preparation *n* darbar *m*, darbarow; ragober *m*, ragoberow. **in preparation for** erbynn

prepare *vb* pareusi; darbari; fyttya; para. **prepare oneself** ombareusi

prepared *adj* darbarys

preposition *n* rager *m*, rageryow

preposterous *adj* avresnel

prescriptive *adj* gorhemynnek

presence *n* lok *m*; presens *m*; golok *f*, gologow. **in the presence of** a-rag; yn lok

present I *adj* a-lemmyn **II** *n* (*offering*) ro *m*, rohow, royow; present *m*, presens; (*the present time*) an termyn a-lemmyn **III** *vb* (*give*) ri; presentya; (*introduce*) komendya. **at present** y'n eur ma

present tense *n* amser a-lemmyn *f*

presentation *n* presentyans *m*, presentyansow

presently *adv* hware

preserve *vb* gwitha; omwitha; (*foods*) kyfeythya. **preserve from** gwitha rag

preserves *n.pl* (*jam*) kyfeyth *m*, kyfeythow

preside *vb* kaderya

president *n* lewydh *m*, lewydhyon

press I *n* gwask *f*, gwaskow **II** *vb* gwaska; (*clothes*) levna; (*urge*) ynia. **cheese press** keuswask *f*, keuswaskow. **printing press** gwask-pryntya *f*, gwaskow-pryntya. **the Press** an Wask *f*

pressing *adj* bysi; res porres

pressure *n* poos *m*, posow; (*in physics*) gwaskedh *m*

prestige *n* roweth *m*

presume *vb* bedha; lavasos. **presumed guilty** kablus bedhys. **presumed innocent** ankablus bedhys

presumption *n* bedhekter *m*, bedhekteryow

pretend *vb* fekla; omwul

prettier *adj* tekka

pretty *adj* teg. **pretty thing** tegen *f*, tegennow

prevent *vb* lettya; lesta. **prevent somebody from doing something** lesta nebonan rag gul neppyth

prevention *n* lestans *m*

preview *n* kynwel *f*, kynwelyow

previous *adj* kyns

price I *n* pris *m*, prisyow; gwerth *f*, gwerthow **II** *vb* prisya. **be priced**

talvos

prick I (*pierce*) *n* bros *m*, brosow; gwan *f*, gwanyow **II** *vb* brosa

pride *n* gooth *m*

priest *n* pronter *m*, pronteryon

primarily *adv* dres oll; y'n kynsa le

primary *adj* kynsa

primitive *adj* sempel

primrose, garden *n* (*polyanthus*) briallen lowarth *f*, briallen lowarth

primrose, wild *n* briallen *f*, briallennow; brialli *coll*

prince *n* pennsevik *m*, pennsevigyon

princess *n* pennseviges *f*, pennsevigesow

principal I *adj* penn- **II** *n* (*head teacher*) penndyskador *m*, penndyskadoryon

principality *n* pennseviges *f*, pennsevigethow; pryncipata *m*, pryncipatys

principle *n* pennrewl *f*, pennrewlys

print I *n* prynt *m*, pryntys **II** *vb* pryntya. **print-run** pryntyans *m*, pryntyansow

printer *n* pryntyer *m*, pryntyoryon

priority *n* ragwir *m*, ragwiryow

prism *n* prism *m*, prismow

prison *n* prison *m*, prisons, prisonyow

prisoner *n* prisner *m*, prisners, prisnoryon. **take prisoner** sesya

privacy *n* privetter *m*

private *adj* privedh

privilege *n* pryvylej *m*, pryvylejys

prize *n* pewas *m*, pewasow

prized *adj* talvesys

proactive *adj* ragvewek

probable *adj* gwirhaval

probably *adv* dell hevel

probe I *n* tavell *f*, tavellow **II** *vb* (*examine*) hwithra; (*insert*) kropya

problem *n* kudyn *m*, kudynnow; kaletter *m*, kaletterow

problematic *adj* tyckli

procedure *n* dyghtyans *m*, dyghtyansow. **routine procedure** dyghtyans kemmyn proceed *vb* mos yn-rag

process I *n* argerdh *m*, argerdhow II *vb* argerdhes

processed *adj* dyghtys. **processed cheese** keus dyghtys *m*, keusyow dyghtys

procession *n* keskerdh *m*, keskerdhow

proclaim *vb* gwarnya

proclamation *n* gwarnyans *m*, gwarnyansow

procrastinate *vb* hirviga; delatya

procure *vb* (*obtain*) gwaynya, kavos; (*pimp*) prokurya

prod I *n* pok *m*, pokyow II *vb* pokya. **cattle prod** gwelen vughes *f*, gwelynni bughes

produce I *n* askor *m* II *vb* askorra

producer *n* askorrer *m* askorroryon

product *n* askorras *m*, askorrasow

production *n* askorrans *m*

profession *n* galwesigeth *f*, galwesigethow

professional I *adj* galwesik II *n* galwesik *m*, galwesigyon

professor *n* professor *m*, professoryon

profile *n* profil *m*, profilys

profit I *n* les *m*; budh *m*, budhow; prow *m* II *vb* gwaynya

profitable *adj* lesek

profitless *adj* diles

program *vb* (*IT*) towlenna

programme *n* towlen *f*, towlennow. **televison programme** towlen bellwolok *f*, towlennow bellwolok

programmer *n* towlenner *m*, towlenoryon

progress I *n* avonsyans *m*, avonsyansow II *vb* avonsya; spedya

prohibit *vb* difen

prohibited *adj* difennys

project (1) *n* ragdres *m*, ragdresow; (*plan*) towl *m*, towlow;

project (2) *vb* tewlel; ragdresa; (*a picture*) tewlel imach; (*plan*) tewlel towl

projector *n* jynn-tewlel *m*, jynnow-tewlel

prole *n* (*offensive*) chorl *m*, chorlys

proletarian *adj* gwerinek

proletariat *n* gwerin *f*

promenade *n* kerdhva *f*, kerdhvaow; rosva *f*, rosvaow

prominence *n* (*geographical*) bann *m*, bannow; (*fame*) bri *f*

prominent *adj* (*geographically*) bannek; (*famous*) a vri

promise I *n* ambos *m*, ambosow; dedhewadow *m*, dedhewadowyow II *vb* ambosa; dedhewi. **an unkept promise** ambos heb keweras. **the Promised Land** an Tiredh a Dhedhewadow *m*

promontory *n* ros *m*, rosyow

promote *vb* avonsya

promotion *n* avonsyans *m*, avonsyansow

prompt *vb* lostleverel

promptly *adv* a-boynt

pronoun *n* rakhanow *m*, rakhenwyn

pronounce *vb* leverel; prononsya

pronunciation *n* leveryans *m*, leveryansow

proof *n* prov *m*, provow

propaganda *n* plontyans *m*

proper *adj* ewn

properly *adv* yn fas

property *n* pyth *m*, pythow; kerth *f*, kerthow

prophecy *n* dargan *f*, darganow

prophet *n* profos *m*, profosi

proportion *n* kemusur *m*, kemusuryow

proportional *adj* kemusurel

proposal *n* profyans *m*, profyansow

propose *vb* profya

proposition *n* kynnik *m*, kynigow

proprietary *adj* perghenogyl

proprietor *n* perghennek *m*, perghenogyon

prose *n* yeth plen *f*

prosecute *vb* darsewya

prosecution *n* darsewyans *m*,
darsewyansow
prosecutor *n* darsewyas *m*, darsewysi
prosper *vb* seweni
prosperity *n* speda *f*; sewena *f*;
sewenyans *m*
prosperous *adj* sewen
prostitute *n* hora *f*, horys
protect *vb* difres; gwitha. **protect from**
gwitha rag. **protect oneself from**
omwitha rag
protection *n* difresyans *m*,
drifresyansow
protein *n* protin *m*, protinyow
protest **I** *vb* protestya; (*complain*)
krodhvolas **II** protestyans *m*,
protestyansow; krodhvol *m*,
krodhvolow
Protestant **I** *adj* Protestant **II** *n*
Protestant *m*, Protestans
protester *n* protestyer *m*, protestyoryon
protocol *n* protokol *m*, protokolys
proton *n* proton *m*, protons
prototype *n* kenwra *m*, kenwraow
protuberant *adj* bothek
proud *adj* gothus; prout
provable *adj* provadow
prove *vb* previ; gul prov. **prove oneself**
ombrevi
provection *n* (*4th state mutation*)
kalesyans *m*
proverb *n* henlavar *m*, henlavarow;
lavar koth *m*, lavarow koth
proverbial *adj* henlavarek; a'n lavar
koth
provide *vb* provia
provider *n* provier *m*, provioryon
province *n* rannvro *f*, rannvroyow;
provyns *m*, provynsys
provincial *adj* rannvroek
provision *n* provians *m*, proviansow;
darbar *m*, darbarow; daffar *m*
provocation *n* brosans *m*, brosansow
provocative *adj* a wra sordya
provoke *vb* brosa; sordya

proximity *n* nester *m*
prudence *n* dothter *m*
prudent *adj* dooth; fur
prune (1) *n* ploumen sygh *f*, ploum
sygh
prune (2) *vb* skethra
psalm *n* salm *m*, salmow
psalter *n* sowter *m*, sowters
pseudo- *prfx* fug-[2]
pseudonym *n* leshanow *m*, leshenwyn
psyche *n* brys *m*, brysyow
psychiatrist *n* medhek brys *m*,
medhogyon vrys
psychological *adj* brysoniethel
psychologist *n* brysonydh *m*,
brysonydhyon
psychology *n* brysonieth *f*
PTSD *abbrev* (*med*) PTSD.
Post-traumatic Stress Disorder
Disordyr Gwask wosa Trawma
pub *n* diwotti *m*, diwottiow; barr *m*,
barrys
puberty *n* kedhorieth *f*
pubic *adj* kedhorek. **pubic hair**
kedhoren *f*, kedhorennow; kedhor *coll*
pubis *n* kedhorva *f*, kedhorvaow
public **I** *adj* poblek **II** *n* **the public** an
bobel *m*; an werin *f*
publican *n* (*innkeeper*) tavernor *m*,
tavernoryon; (*Bible: Roman
tax-collector*) poblikan *m*, poblikans
publicity *n* argemynnans *m*,
argemynansow
publicly *adv* yn poblek; a-rag tus
publish *vb* dyllo
publisher *n* dyller *m*, dylloryon
puce *adj* gellburpur
pudding *n* podyn *m*, podyns; (*dessert*)
melyssand *m*, melyssandys. **bag
pudding** pellen *f*, pellennow. **black
pudding** gosogen *f*, gosogennow.
hog's pudding gosogen wynn *f*,
gosogennow gwynn. **bread pudding**
podyn bara *m*, podyns bara.
Christmas pudding podyn Nadelik

m, podyns Nadelik. **hasty-pudding** pott gwynn *m*, pottys gwynn, pottow gwynn

puddle *n* pollen *f*, pollennow; lagen *f*, lagennow

puerile *adj* floghel

puff I *n* hwyth *m*, hwethow **II** *vb* hwytha

puffin *n* nath *m*, nathes; popa *m*, popys

puffy *adj* hwythek

puke *vb* hwyja

pull I *n* tenn *m*, tennow **II** *vb* tenna

pulley *n* tennros *f*, tennrosow

pullover *n* gwlanek *m*, gwlanogow

pulse I *n* (*beat*) pols *m*, polsyow **II** *vb* polsa

pump I *n* pomp *m*, pompys, pompyow; pompell *f*, pompellow **II** *vb* pompya. **petrol pump** pomp petrol *m*, pompys petrol, pomypow petrol

pumpkin *n* pompyon *m*, pompyons

pun I *n* gwari war eryow *m*, gwariow war eryow **II** *vb* gwari war eryow

punch (1) I *n* (*blow*) bomm; hwaff *m*, hwaffys **II** *vb* boksusi; dorna; hwaffa

punch (2) *n* (*drink*) panch *m*

punctual *adj* a-boynt

punctually *adv* a-boynt

punctuate *vb* poyntya

punctuation *n* poyntyans *m*, poyntyansow

pungency *n* mosokter *m*

pungent *adj* flerys; mosek

punish *vb* kessydhya

punishment *n* kessydhyans *m*, kessydhyansow

puny *adj* ydhil

pupil *n* (*student*) dyskybel *m*, dyskyblon; (*of the eye*) byw an lagas *m*, bewyow an lagas

puppet *n* popet *m*, popettys, popettow

puppy *n* kolyn *m*, kelyn

purchase I *n* prenas *m*, prenasow **II** *vb* prena. **hire purchase** hirbren *m*, hirbrenyow

purchaser *n* prener *m*, prenoryon; (*professional*) prenyas *m*, prenysi

pure *adj* pur; glan

puree *n* yos *m*. **apple puree** yos avalow *m*

purge I *n* karth *m*, karthyon **II** *vb* kartha

purification *n* purheans *m*, purheansow

purify *vb* purhe

purism *n* purieth *f*

purist *n* purydh *m*, purydhyon

Puritan I *adj* Puritan **II** *n* Puritan *m*, Puritanyon

Puritanism *n* Puritanieth *f*

purple *adj* purpur; glasrudh; rudhlas

purpose I *n* porpos *m*, porposys; mynnas *m*, mynasow **II** *vb* porposya. **express purpose** towl unnik *m*. **on purpose** a-borpos

purposely *adv* a-borpos

purse *n* pors *m*, porsys; yalgh *f*, yalghow

pursue *vb* helghya; pursewya

pursuer *n* helghyas *m*, helghysi

pursuit *n* pursewyans *m*, pursewyansow

push I *n* herdhyans *m*, herdhyansow **II** *vb* herdhya. **push a button** pokya boton

push-chair *n* kador herdhya *f*, kadoryow herdhya

put *vb* gorra; pottya; settya. **put back** delatya. **put down** (*animal*) euthanisya. **put forward** profya. **put in order** araya. **put on** (*activate*) gweytha; (*clothes*) gwiska; (*a show*) gwruthyl. **put your name down** ri dha hanow. **put out** (*expel*) tewlel yn-mes; (*extend*) ystyn; (*extinguish*) difudhi; (*publish*) dyllo. **put somebody's mind at rest** hebaskhe nebonan. **put together** framya; keskorra; komposya. **put up with** perthi

putrid *adj* podrek; breyn

pyjamas *n* pyjama *m*, pyjamas; dillas nos *coll*

pylon *n* peul *m*, peulyow

pyramid *n* pyramid *m*, pyramidow

pyramidal *adj* pyramidek

pyrite *n* pyrit *m*; owr an bobba *m*

Q

quack I *n* (*fake doctor*) pomster *m*, pomsters II *vb* kwackya

quadrangle *n* peswarkorn *m*, peswarkern

quadrant *n* kwadrant *m*, kwadrantys

quadrilateral *adj* peswartenwennel

quaint *adj* koynt

Quaker *n* Krener *m*, Krenoryon

qualification *n* kwalifians *m*, kwalifiansow; (*restriction*) strothans *m*, strothansow; (*suitability*) gwiwder *m*

qualify *vb* kwalifia; (*restrict*) strotha; (*be suitable*) bos gwiw

quality *n* gnas *f*, gnasow

quantity *n* myns *m*, mynsow

quarrel I *n* kedrynn *f*, kedrynnow; dalva *f*, dalvaow II *vb* kedrynna; omdhal

quarry *n* mengleudh *m*, mengleudhyow

quarry worker *n* mengleudhyer *m*, mengleudhyoryon

quarter I *n* (*fraction; region*) kwarter *m*, kwartrys (*of year*) trymis *m*, trymisyow; (*mercy*) tregeredh *f*, tregeredhow II *vb* kwartrona

quarterly *adj* trymisyek

quartz *n* kannven *m*, kannveyn

quaver *n* kwaver *m*, kwaveryow

quay *n* kay *m*, kayys, kayow

queen *n* myghternes *f*, myghternesow; ruvanes *f*, ruvanesow

Queen Anne's lace *n* (*wild carrot*) las Myghternes Anna *m*

quench *vb* (*thirst*) disegha

query I *n* govyn *m*, govynnow II *vb* govyn

quest *n* hwithrans *m*, hwithransow

question I *n* govyn *m*, govynnow II *vb* govyn. **test by questions** apposya

questionnaire *n* govynador *m*, govynadoryon

queue I *n* lost *m*, lostow II *vb* gul lost; lostya. **jump the queue** dreslemmel an lost

quibble I *n* folsans blew *m*, folsansow blew II *vb* folsa blew

quick *adj* uskis; snell; buan

quicken *vb* (*accelerate*) uskishe

quickly *adv* skon; uskis; (yn) skav; snell

quickness *n* skavder *m*

quiet I *adj* kosel; tawesek; dison; tawel II *n* kosoleth *f*; taw *m*. **keep quiet** taw taves

quieten *vb* koselhe

quietness *n* kosoleth

quill *n* pluven *f*, pluvennow

quilt *n* kolghes *f*, kolghesow

quit *vb* kwytya

quite *adv* (*precisely*) poran; (*rather*) lowr; (*very*) glan; teg

quiz *n* kwys *m*, kwysyow

quotation *n* devyn *m*, devynnow. **quotation mark** merk devyn *m*, merkys devyn

quote I *n* devyn *m*, devynnow II *vb* devynna

quoth *vb* yn-medh; 'medh

R

rabbit *n* konin *m*, konines

rabble-rouser *n* predheger *m*,
predhegoryon

rabid *adj* koneryek

race (1) I *n* (*competition*) resek *m*,
resegow; res *m*, resow II *vb* resek

race (2) *n* (*ethnicity*) agh *f*, aghow; hil
m, hilyow. human race mab den *m*

racial *adj* aghel

racing *n* resek *m*. car racing *n* resek
kerri. racing car *n* karr-resek *m*,
kerri-resek. racing driver
lewyer-resek *m*, lewyoryon-resek

racism *n* hilgasieth *f*

racist I *n* hilgasydh *m*, hilgasydhyon II
adj hilgasek

rack *n* kloos *f*, klosyow. luggage rack
roos fardellow *f*, rosow fardellow

racket (1) *n* (*bat*) racket *m*, racketys,
racketow

racket (2) *n* (*noise*) habadolya *m*

racket (3) *n* (*scam*) negys kamm *m*,
negysyow kamm

radar *n* radar *m*

radial *adj* gwradhel

radiant *adj* dewynnek

radiate *vb* dewynnya

radiation *n* dewynnyans *m*,
dewynynansow

radiator *n* dewynnell *f*, dewynellow

radical I *adj* gwreydhyel II *n*
gwreydhyolydh *m*,
gwreydhyolydhyon

radicalise *vb* gul gwreydhyel

radicalism *n* gwreydhyoleth *f*

radio *n* radyo *m*, radyos, radyoyow

radioactive *adj* radyovewek

radioactivity *n* radyovewekter *m*

radiological *adj* radyologiethel

radiologist *n* radyologydh *m*,
radyologydhyon

radiology *n* radyologieth *f*

radish *n* redigen *f*, redigennow; redik
coll

radius *n* asen *f*, asennow

raffle *n* gwari sagh *m*, gwariow sagh

raft *n* skath klos *f*, skathow klos

rafter *n* kebren *f*, kebrennow

rag *n* pilen *f*, pilennow

ragamuffin *n* tellek *m*, tellogyon

rage I *n* konnar *f*; koler *m* II *vb* koneri

ragged *adj* pilennek

ragged robin *n* rudhek pilyek *m*

ragwort *n* madra bras *m*, madrow bras

raid I *n* omsettyans *m*, omsettyansow
II *vb* omsettya war^2

rail I *n* kledhren *f*, kledhrennow II *vb*
deraylya; raylya

railing *n* peulge *m*, peulgeow

railway *n* hyns horn *m*, hensyow horn.
railway station *n* gorsav *m*, gorsavow

rain I *n* glaw *m* II *vb* gul glaw. rain
forest koswik law *f*, koswigow glaw

rainbow *n* kammneves *f*,
kammnevesow

raincoat *n* kota glaw *m*, kotys glaw;
mantel law *f*, mantylli glaw

rainfall *n* glawas *m*

rainy *adj* glawek

raise *vb* (*lift; build*) drehevel; (*raise a
child*) maga; meythrin. raise up sevel

raisin *n* resinen *f*, resinennow; resin *coll*

rake *n* rakan *m*, rakanow

rally *n* (*of cars*) ralli *m*, rallis

ram *n* (*animal*) hordh *m*, hordhes

ramsons *n* (*wild garlic*) koos kennin *coll*

random *adj* chonsus. random number
happriv *m*, happrivow

range *n* (*reach*) efander *m*; (*of a weapon*)
towlhys *m*; (*of animals*) gwandrans *m*,
gwandransow. mountain range
kadon *f*, kadonyow. rifle range tenva
f, tenvaow

rank (1) I *n* (*order*) renk *m*, renkow, renkyow; degre *m*, degrys **II** *vb* (*in order*) renka

rank (2) *adj* (*noxious*) mosek

ransom I *n* daspren *m*, dasprenyow **II** *vb* dasprena; ronsona

rant I *n* predhek *m*, predhegow **II** *vb* predheges

ranter *n* predheger *m*, predhegoryon

rape I *n* argasreydh *f*, argasreydhow **II** *vb* argasreydhya

rapeseed *n* (*oilseed rape*) ervinik *m*, ervinigow

rapid *adj* uskis

rapist *n* argasreydher *m*, argasreydhoryon

rare *adj* (*uncommon*) tanow; treweythus; (*lightly cooked*) gosek

rarely *adv* namenowgh

rarity *n* tanowder *m*, tanowderyow

rascal *n* jowdyn *m*, jowdyns; drog-polat *m*, drog-polatys; lorel *m* lorels

rash (1) *adj* (*reckless*) dibreder

rash (2) *n* (*on skin*) brygh *m*, breghi

rasp *vb* ratha

raspberry *n* avanen *f*, avanennow; avan *coll*

rat *n* rath *f*, rathes

rate I *n* (*mathematical*) kevradh *m*, kevradhow; (*tax*) toll *f*, tollow **II** *vb* talvos. **at any rate** yn neb kas. **death rate** kevradh mernans *m*, kevradhow mernans. **hourly rate** eurdal *m*, eurdalyow. **monthly rate** mistal *m*, mistalyow. **water rate** *n* toll dhowr *f*, tollow dowr. **tax rate** kevradh toll *m*, kevradhow toll

rather *adv* kyns. **rather than** a-der. **I'd rather** gwell via genev

ratification *n* fastheans *m*, fastheansow

ratify *vb* fasthe

ratio *n* komparriv *m*, komparrivow

ration I *n* ewnran *f*, ewnrannow **II** *vb* ewnranna

rational *adj* resnel

rattle I *n* ruglen *f*, ruglennow **II** *vb* rugla. **death rattle** ronk mernans *m*, ronkow mernans

ravage *vb* ravna

raven *n* bran vras *f*, brini bras; marghvran *f*, marghvrini

ravenous *adj* nownek bras

ravine *n* kownans *m*, kownansow

raw *adj* kriv

rawness *n* krivder *m*

ray (1) *n* (*of light*) dewyn *m*, dewynnow

ray (2) *n* (*fish*) rogha *m*, roghys; karleyth *f*, karleythow. **starry ray** grija *m*, grijow

razor *n* alten *f*, altennow

razor-fish *n* kelligen *f*, kelligi; kellik *coll*

re- *prfx* das-

reach I *n* drehedhyans *m*, drehedhyansow **II** *vb* drehedhes; hedhes. **reach out** ystyn

reachable *adj* a yll bos hedhys; hedhadow

react *vb* dasoberi

reaction *n* dasoberyans *m*, dasoberyansow

reactor *n* dasoberor *m*, dasoberoryon. **nuclear reactor** dasoberor nukler *m*, dasoberoryon nukler

read *vb* redya; (*aloud*) lenna

readable *adj* redyadow

reader *n* redyer *m*, redyoryon; (*aloud*) lenner *m*, lenoryon

readily *adv* prest; yredi; heb ahwer

reading *n* redyans *m*, redyansow

reading difficulty *n* kaletter redya *m*, kaletterow redya. **a person with reading difficulites** person gans kaletterow redya

ready *adj* parys. **make ready** pareusi

real *adj* gwir

realise *vb* aswon; konvedhes

realistic *adj* gwirvosek

reality *n* gwirvos *m*, gwirvosow

really *adv* dhe wir; heb wow; yn tevri

realm *n* gwlaskor *f*, gwlaskordhow

reap *vb* mysi

reaper *n* myser *m*, mysoryon. **The Grim Reaper** Ankow

rear *vb* (*raise a child*) maga; meythrin

reared *adj* megys

reason I *n* (*cause*) acheson *m*, achesonys, achesonyow; skila *f*, skilys; kaws *m*, kawsys; praga *m*; (*logic*) reson *m*, resons; poll *m*, pollow **II** *vb* resna

reasonable *adj* resnadow; resonus

reasoning *n* resnans *m*, resnansow

rebel I *n* rebel *m*, rebels **II** *vb* rebellya; omsevel

rebellion *n* rebellyans *m*, rebellyansow

rebellious *adj* trehwelek

rebuke *vb* keredhi

recall *vb* (*call back*) daskelwel; (*remember*) perthi kov (a^2)

recede *vb* kila

receipt *n* (*written*) akwytyans *m*, akwytyansow

receive *vb* degemeres; kemeres

recent *adj* a-dhiwedhes

recently *adv* a-dhiwedhes; a-gynsow; a-lergh; nyns yw neb pell

reception *n* kemeryans *m*, kemeryansow; degemeryans *m*, degemeryansow. **reception area** *n* degemerva *f*, degemervaow

recession *n* kilans *m*, kilansow

recipe *n* resayt *m*, resaytys, resaytyow

recitation *n* dyth *m*, dythow

recite *vb* dythya

reckon *vb* rekna

recline *vb* gorwedha; growedha

reclusive *adj* ankarus

recognise *vb* aswon

recollect *vb* perthi kov a^2

recollection *n* kov *m*, kovyow

recommend *vb* komendya

recommendation *n* komendyans *m*, komendyansow

reconcile *vb* unverhe; gul bos unverhes

reconciliation *n* unverheans *m*, unverheansow

reconstruct *vb* dastrehevel

reconstruction *n* dastrehevyans *m*, dastrehevyansow

record I *n* (*document*) kovadh *m*, kovadhow; (*sport etc.*) rekord *m*, rekordys; (*disc*) plasen *f*, plasennow **II** *vb* rekordya; (*document*) kovadha; (*sound*) sonskrifa. **record player** *n* troer plasen *m*, troeryon plasen

recorder *n* (*musical instrument*) tollgorn Sowsnek *m*, tollgern Sowsnek

recording *n* sonskrif *m*, sonskrifow

recover *vb* (*get back*) daskavos; (*from an illness*) yaghhe

recovery *n* yaghheans *m*, yaghheansow

rectangle *n* hirbedrek *m*, hirbedrogow

rectangular *adj* hirbedrek

recycle *vb* eylgylghya

recycling *n* eylgylghyans *m*

red *adj* rudh

redden *vb* rudhya

reddish *adj* rudhik

redeem *vb* dasprena

redemption *n* daspren *m*, dasprenyow

redhead *n* penn rudh *m*, pennow rudh

redo *vb* daswul

redstart *n* tingogh *m*, tingoghes

reduce *vb* lehe; byghanhe

redundant *adj* (*supernumerary*) dres nivera; (*from employment*) anarvethys; (*colloq*) tewlys a-ves

redwing *n* sevellek *m*, sevelloges

reed *n* korsen *f*, korsennow; *coll* kors

reed bed *n* korsek *f*, korsegi; keunegen *f*, keunegennow

reed bunting *n* golvanek kors *m*, golvanoges kors

reedmace *n* lost an gath *m*; pennrudh *m*

reedy *adj* korsek

reef *n* krib *f*, kribow

reefer *n* (*cannabis cigarette*) porven ganabys *f*, porvennow kanabys

re-examination *n* dashwithrans *m*, dashwithransow

re-examine *vb* dashwithra

reference *n* kampollans *m*, kampollansow

refine *vb* afina; purhe

refined *adj* afinys; fin

refinery *n* purva *f*, purvaow

reflect *vb* (*throw back light*) dastewynnya; (*think upon*) prederi; ombrederi

reflection *n* skeus *m*, skeusow; (*consideration*) prederyans *m*, prederyansow

reform *n* amendyans *m*, amendyansow. **sweeping reforms** amendyansow ledan *pl*

refrain (1) *n* (*of a song*) pennpusorn *m*, pennpusornow

refrain (2) *vb* (*desist*) refraynya

refresh *vb* disegha

refrigerate *vb* yeynella

refrigerator *n* yeynell *f*, yeynellow

refuge *n* argel *f*, argelyow; meneghi *m*, meneghiow; harber *m*, harbers

refusal *n* nagh *m*, naghow

refuse (1) *vb* (*deny*) nagha; denagha; skonya

refuse (2) *n* (*waste*) atal *coll*; skubyonen *f*, skubyonennow; skubyon *coll*

refute *vb* konkludya

regal *adj* riel

regard I *n* govis *m*, govisyon II *vb* mires orth. **best regards** gorhemynadow a'n gwella

regarding *prp* (*used with poss. adjectives, p.8*) yn kever

region *n* ranndir *m*, ranndiryow; tiredh *m*, tiredhow; pow *m*, powyow

regional *adj* ranndiryel

register *vb* kovskrifa

registration *n* kovskrifans *m*, kovskrifansow. **car registration number** *m* niver kovskrifans karr

registry *n* kovskrifla *m*, kovskrifleow

regret I *n* edrek *m*, edregow II *vb* edrega. **I regret** Yma edrek dhymm

regretful *adj* edregus

regular *adj* rewlys; reyth

regularly *adv* yn fenowgh

regulate *vb* rewlya

regulation *n* rewl *f*, rewlys

rehab *n* dassev *m*. **he's gone into rehab** yma ev yn dassev lemmyn

rehabilitation *n* dassevelyans *m*. **it's a rehabilitation centre** kresen dhassevelyans yw

rehearsal *n* assay *m*, assays

rehearse *vb* omassaya

reign I *n* reyn *m*, reynys II *vb* reynya

reindeer *n* karow ergh *m*, kerwys ergh

reject *vb* denagha

rejoice *vb* lowenhe; (*intransitive*) omlowenhe. **rejoice!** omlowenha!

rejuvenate *vb* yowynkhe

relate *vb* (*tell*) derivas; (*establish a relationship*) keskelmi

related *adj* kelmys; (*by blood*) unwos

relation *n* (*family member*) kar *m*, kerens; kares *f*, karesow; (*near relative*) neskar *m*, neskerens; (*next of kin*) neshevin *m*, neshevin

relationship *n* (*social*) kowethyans *m*, kowethyansow; (*familial*) kolm goos *m*, kolmow goos; (*correlation*) perthynyans *m*, perthynyansow

relative I *adj* perthynek II *n* kar *m*, kerens; kares *f*, karesow. (*near relative*) neskar *m*, neskerens; (*next of kin*) neshevin *m*, neshevin

relax *vb* diskwitha

relaxation *n* diskwithans *m*

relaxing *adj* diskwithus

release I *n* livreson *m*, livresons; (*publication*) dyllans *m*, dyllansow II *vb* (*set free*) livra; (*publish*) dyllo

relevance *n* bri *f*

relevant *adj* a vri

reliable *adj* lel; diogel

reliance *n* trest *m*

relic *n* (*of saint*) krer *m*, kreryow

relief *n* difres *m*, difresow; difresyans *m*, difresyansow

relieve *vb* difres. **relieve someone of something** difres nebonan a neppyth

religion *n* kryjyans *m*, kryjyansow

religious *adj* kryjyk

relinquish *vb* hepkor

reload *vb* daskarga

reluctant *adj* anvodhek; hell. **I am reluctant to…** poos yw genev

reluctantly *adv* a'y anvodh

rely *vb* trestya; fydhya. **rely on** fydhya war^2; trestya dhe^2

remain *vb* gortos; (*stay*) triga

remainder *n* remenant *m*, remenantys, remenans

remake I *n* daswrians *m*, daswriansow **II** *vb* daswul

remarkable *adj* marthek; marthys

remarkably *adv* marthys

remedy *n* remedi *m*, remedis

remember *vb* perthi kov (a^2); kofhe

remind *vb* kofhe

remote *adj* pell. **remote control** *n* pellvotonek *m*, pellvotonegi

remoteness *n* enysekter *m*; pellder *m*

remove *vb* dilea; remova

remunerate *vb* gobra

remuneration *n* gober *m*, gobrow

rename *vb* dashenwel

renationalised *adj* daskenedhlegys

render *vb* ri

renew *vb* nowedhi

renounce *vb* nagha

renowned *adj* a bris; a vri; gerys-da

rent I *n* rent *m*, rentys, rentow **II** *vb* gobrena

repair I *vb* ewnhe; ewna **II** *n* ewnheans *m*, ewnheansow; ewnans *m*, ewnansow

repay *vb* attyli

repayment *n* attal *m*, attelyow. **as repayment** yn attal

repeat I *n* (*broadcasting*) dastarlesans *m*, dastarlesansow **II** *vb* (*do again*) gul arta; (*say again*) dasleverel. **repeat prayers** padera

repent *vb* kodha yn edrek; repentya

repentant *adj* egregus

replace *vb* aslea

repletion *n* gwalgh *m*

reply I *n* gorthyp *m*, gorthebow **II** *vb* gorthebi

report I *n* derivas *m*, derivasow **II** *vb* derivas

reporter *n* derivador *m*, derivadoryon

repose I *n* powes *m*, powesow **II** *vb* powes; diskwitha

represent *vb* (*depict*) delinya; (*speak for*) representya; kanasedhi

reprint I *n* daspryntyans *m*, daspryntyansow **II** *vb* daspryntya

reproach *vb* keredhi

reproduction *n* dinythyans *m*, dinythyansow; (*copy*) daswrians *m*, daswriansow

reptile *n* kramvil *m*, kramviles

reptilian *adj* kramvilek

republic *n* repoblek *m*, repoblegi

reputation *n* bri *f*; pris *m*, prisyow. **gain a reputation** kavos hanow. **good reputation** ger da *m*. **bad reputation** tebel-hanow

request I *n* govyn *m*, govynnow **II** *vb* govyn; pysi

require *vb* erghi. **require of someone** mynnes orth nebonan

resale *n* daswerth *f*, daswerthow. **resale price** pris daswerth *m*

rescue I *n* sawyans *m*, sawyansow **II** *vb* sawya

rescuer *n* sawyas *m*, sawysi

research *n* hwithrans *m*, hwithransow

researcher *n* hwithrer *m*, hwithroryon

resell *vb* daswertha

reseller *n* daswerther *m*, daswerthoryon

resemblance *n* hevelep *m*, hevelebow

resemble *vb* omheveli dhe[2]; bos haval dhe[2]. **he resembles you** haval yw ev dhis

resembling *adj* haval

reserve I *n* (*stockpile*) kreun *m*, kreunyow; (*reservation of land*) gwithva *f*, gwithvaow; (*self-control*) omwith *m* **II** *vb* (*keep back*) gwitha; gorra a-denewen; (*book a seat, room etc.*) ragerghi. **nature reserve** gwithva natur *f*, gwithvaow natur

reserved *adj* (*booked*) ragerghys; (*restrained*) omwithys

reservoir *n* kreun *m*, kreunyow

reset *vb* dassettya

resettle *vb* dasanedhi

reside *vb* bos trigys

residence *n* trigva *f*, trigvaow; treveth *f*, trevethow

residential *adj* anedhys; anedhel. **non-residential** heb bos anedhys

residual *adj* remenantel; avel remenant

residue *n* gasadow *m*, gasadowyow

resin *n* glus *m*, glusow

resist *vb* sevel orth; settya orth

resistance *n* defens *m*, defensow; (*in physics*) sprallansedh *m*

resolve *vb* ervira; digelmi

resonant *adj* heglew

resort I *n* resort *m*, resortys; (*holiday place*) tyller havi *m*, tylleryow havi **II** *vb* resortya. **as a last resort** fowt fordh aral

resource I *n* (*resources*) asnodhow *pl* **II** *vb* provia arghans rag

resourceful *adj* amkanus

respect I *n* reowta *m*; revrons *m* **II** *vb* gordhya; gul revrons dhe[2]. **with respect to her** yn hy[3] hever

respectful *adj* mas

respiration *n* anallans *m*

respite *n* hedh *m*, hedhow

respond *vb* gorthebi

response *n* gorthyp *m*, gorthebow

responsibility *n* omgemeryans *m*, omgemeryansow; charj *m*, charjys. **take responsibility** omgemeres

responsible *adj* omgemeryansek. **become responsible for** omgemeres rag

responsive *adj* gorthebus

rest I *n* (*relaxation*) powes *m*; (*remainder*) remenant *m*, remenantys, remenans **II** *vb* diskwitha; powes

restaurant *n* bosti *m*, bostiow

restful *adj* kosel

resting place *n* powesva *f*, powesvaow

restitution *n* restorita *m*, restoritys

restless *adj* dibowes

restore *vb* daskor; astiveri

restrain *vb* fronna; chastia

restrained *adj* fronnys; (*reserved; self-controlled*) omwithys

restraint *n* fronn *m*, fronnow

restrict *vb* fronna; strotha

restriction *n* fronnans *m*, fronansow

result I *n* sewyans *m*, sewyansow **II** *vb* sewya; omsewya

resume *vb* daskemeres

resurgence *n* dastardh *m*, dastardhow

resurrect *vb* dasserghi

resurrection *n* dasserghyans *m*, dasserghyansow

retail I *n* daskwerthans *m*, daskwerthansow **II** *vb* daskwertha

retailer *n* daskwerther *m*, daskwerthoryon

retain *vb* gwitha

retainer *n* gwithyas *m*, gwithysi

retaliate *vb* venjya; dasarvedh

retaliation *n* venjyans *m*, venjyansow

retention *n* gwith *m*

retinue *n* koskor *pl*

retire *vb* omdenna

retired *adj* omdennys

retirement *n* omdennans *m*, omdenansow. **retirement age** oos-omdenna *m*

retract *vb* denagha

retreat I *n* tegh *m*, teghow; kilden *m*, kildennow; (*secluded place*) argel *f*, argelyow **II** *vb* kildenna

retribution *n* dial *m*; venjyans *m*

retrospect *n* golok war-dhelergh *f*

return I *n* dehwelans *m*, dehwelansow; dehwelyans *m*, dehwelyansow **II** *vb* (*come back*) dehweles; (*give back*) daskor; ri arta. **by return** war-nuk. **many happy returns!** penn-bloodh lowen dhis ha meur anedha! **return ticket** tokyn-mos ha dos *m*, toknys-mos ha dos

reunification *n* dasunyans *m*, dasunyansow

reunify *vb* dasunya

reveal *vb* diskudha

revelation *n* diskwedhyans *m*, diskwedhyansow; diskudhans *m*, diskudhansow

revenge *n* dial *m*; venjyans *m*. **take revenge** diala; venjya

revenue *n* rent *m*, rentys, rentow. **Inland Revenue** Tollva an Wlas *f*

reverence *n* revrons *m*

reverend *adj* revrond

reverie *n* hunros dydh *m*, hunrosow dydh

reversal *n* kildro *f*, kildroyow

reverse I *n* kil *m*, kilyer **II** *vb* gorthtreylya; treylya dhelergh. **reverse gear** maglen dhelergh *f*

review I *n* daswel *f*, daswelyow; (*critique*) breusyans *m*, breusyansow; (*re-examination*) dashwithrans *m*, dashwithransow **II** *vb* dasweles; (*re-examine*) dashwithra

revile *vb* kabli; mylliga

revise *vb* dasweles; amendya

revision *n* daswel *f*, daswelyow

revival *n* dasserghyans *m*, dasserghyansow

revive *vb* dasserghi. **Revived Cornish** Kernewek Dasserghys *m*

revolt I *n* rebellyans *m*, rebellyansow; domhwelans *m*, domhwelansow **II** *vb* domhwel; omsevel

revolting *adj* (*disgusting*) kasadow; divlas

revolution *n* (*political*) domhwelans *m*, domhwelansow; (*mechanical*) hweldro *f*, hweldroyow

revolutionary I *adj* domhwelus **II** *n* domhweler *m*, domhweloryon

revolve *vb* omdreylya

revulsion *n* skruth *m*, skruthow. **feel revulsion** divlasa

reward I *n* (*wages*) gober *m* gobrow; (*prize*) pewas *m*, pewasow **II** *vb* tyli; gobra. **give a reward to** ri pewas dhe[2]

rewrite I *n* dasskrif *m*, dasskrifow **II** *vb* dasskrifa

rhetorical *adj* arethek

rheumatism *n* galar eseli *m*; kleves eseli *m*; remm *m*

rhinoceros *n* trongornvil *m*, trongornviles

rhubarb *n* trenkles *m*

rhyme I *n* rim *m*, rimyow **II** *vb* rimya

rhythm *n* resyas *m*, resyasow

rhythmic *adj* resyek

rib *n* asen *f*, asennow; asowen *f*, asowennow; asow *coll*

ribbed *adj* asennek

ribbon *n* snod *m*, snodys, snodow

rice *n* ris *coll*. **boiled rice** ris bryjys *coll*. **grain of rice** risen *f*, risennow. **fried rice** ris friys *m*. **long grain rice** ris greun hir *coll*. **short grain rice** ris greun berr *coll*. **sticky rice** ris glusek *coll*

rich *adj* (*all senses*) rych; (*wealthy*) golusek. **rich person** golusek *m*, golusogyon

riches *n* rychys *m*

richness *n* rychedh *m*, rychedhow

rick *n* das *f*, deys

rid *vb* kartha

riddance *n* delivrans *m*, delivransow.
  good riddance to him! gwyns teg
  a-dryv dhodho!
riddle (1) *n* (*puzzle*) dismyk *m*,
  dismygow
riddle (2) *n* (*strainer*) kroder *m*,
  krodrow
ride I *n* (*on a horse*) marghogeth *f*,
  marghogethow; (*lift in a car*) gorrans
  m, gorransow **II** *vb* (*a horse*)
  marghogeth; (*a bike*) diwrosa; (*in a
  car*) mos yn karr
rider *n* marghek *m*, marghogyon
ridge *n* drumm *m*, drummyow; keyn *m*,
  keynow; kriben *m*, kribennow; (*of a
  roof*) keyn to *m*, keynow to
ridge-pole *n* nenbren *m*, nenbrennyer
ridicule I *n* ges *m*, gesyow **II** *vb* gul ges
  a²
ridiculous *adj* hwarthus; skornyadow
riding *n* marghogeth *f*. **riding hood**
  huk *f*, hukys. **Little Red Riding
  Hood** Huk Vyghan Rudh *f*
rifle (1) *vb* (*fleece, plunder*) pylla
rifle (2) *n* (*gun*) gonn hir *m*, gonnys hir.
  rifle range *n* tenva *f*, tenvaow
rift *n* fols *m*, folsyow
right I *adj* (*morally*) kompes; (*true*)
  gwir; (*correct*) ewn; (*suitable*) gwiw;
  (*exact*) kewar; (*opposite to left*) dyghow
  II *n* gwir *m*, gwiryow; (*legal*) reyth *m*,
  reythyow. **on the right** a-dhyghow.
  set right amendya; ewna. **you are
  right** ewn os ta *sg*; ewn owgh hwi *pl*
right-handed *adj* dyghow
rightly *adv* yn ewn; yn reyth
rigorous *adj* dour
ring (1) *n* (*jewellery*) bysow *m*,
  bysowyer; (*circle, hoop*) kylgh *m*,
  kylghyow. **ring finger** *n* bys bysow *m*
ring (2) *vb* (*a bell*) seni
ringmaster *n* mester cirk *m*, mestrysi
  cirk
riot *n* tervans *m*, tervansow
rip *vb* skwardya

ripe *adj* adhves
ripen *vb* adhvesi
ripeness *n* adhvetter *m*
rise I *n* (*slope*) run *f*, runyow; riw *f*,
  riwyow **II** *vb* sevel. **rise up** omsevel
risk *n* peryl *m*, peryllow, peryllyow;
  argol *m*
risky *adj* peryllus
ritual I *adj* devosek; devosel **II** *n* devos
  f, devosow
river *n* avon *f*, avonyow; (*in names of
  rivers*) dowr *m*, dowrow. **River Tamar**
  Dowr Tamar
river-mouth *n* heyl *m*, heylyow; (*in
  place-names*) aber *m*, aberyow
roach *n* (*fish*) talek *m*, taloges
road *n* fordh *f*, fordhow; hyns *m*,
  hensyow. **ancient track** henfordh *f*,
  henfordhow
road-block *n* fordhlett *m*, fordhlettys,
  fordhlettow
roadside *n* tenewen an fordh *m*,
  tenwennow an fordhow
roast I *n* rost *m*, rostys **II** *vb* rostya
rob *vb* ladra
robber *n* lader *m*, ladron
robbery *n* (*individual crime*) ladrans *m*,
  ladransow; (*in general*) ladrynsi *m*
robin *n* rudhek *m*, rudhogyon
robot *n* robot *m*, robotys, robotow
robust *adj* nerthek; krev
rock (1) *n* (*stone*) karrek *f*, kerrek,
  karrygi
rock (2) *vb* leska. **rocking horse** *n*
  margh-leska *m*, mergh-leska. **rock
  music** rock *m*; ilow rock *m*
rocket *n* (*missile*) fusen *f*, fusennow
rocket, field *n* (*yellow rocket*) mellyon
  an Werghes *coll*
rockling *n* penn barvus *m*, pennow
  barvus
rock-pile *n* karn *m*, karnow
rocky *adj* karnek; karnedhek
rod *n* gwelen *f*, gwelynni. **fishing rod** –
  gwelen-byskessa *f*, gwelynni-pyskessa

roe-deer *n* yorgh *f*, yorghes

rogue *n* drogwas *m*, drogwesyon; adla *m*, adlyon

role *n* rann *f*, rannow

roll I *n* (*list; roll of paper*) rol *f*, rolyow; (*bread*) bara byghan *m* **II** *vb* rolya. **rolling pin** rolbren *m*, rolbrennyer

roller *n* (*wooden*) rolbren *m*, rolbrennyer; (*stone*) rolven *m*, rolveyn; (*in a car wash*) jynn-rolya *m*, jynnys-rolya, jynnow-rolya. **roller skate** roskis *m*, roskisyow

Roma *n* Rom *m*, Romyon. (*see also: Gypsy, Traveller*)

Romani I *adj* romek **II** *n* (*language*) Romani *m*

Romania *top* Romani *f*

Romanian I *adj* romaniek **II** *n* (*language*) Romaniek; (*person*) Romanian *m*, Romanians

Romanic *adj* romanek. **Romanic architecture** pennserneth romanek *f*

romantic *adj* romansek

romanticism *n* romansogeth *f*

roof I *n* to *m*, tohow **II** *vb* ti

rook *n* bran dre *f*, brini tre

room *n* (*in a building*) stevel *f*, stevellow; (*space*) spas *m*, spassow. **bathroom** stevel-omwolghi *f*, stevellow-omwolghi. **dining room** stevel-dhybri *f*, stevellow-dybri. **living room** *n* esedhva *f*, esedhvaow. **sitting room** *n* esedhva *f*, esedhvaow. **smallest room** (*toilet; colloq*) stevel-vyghan *f*, stevellow-byghan. **waiting room** *n* stevel-wortos *f*, stevellow-gortos

root *n* gwreydhen *f*, gwreydh. **square root** gwreydhen bedrek *f*, gwreydhennow pedrek

rope *n* lovan *f*, lovanow. **rope ladder** *n* skeul lovan *f*, skeulyow lovan

rose *n* rosen *f*, rosennow; ros *coll*

rose, dog *n* (*wild rose; briar rose*) rosen wyls *f*, rosennow gwyls; ros gwyls *coll*

rose, wild *n* (*dog rose; briar rose*) rosen wyls *f*, rosennow gwyls; ros gwyls *coll*

rosemary *n* rosmari *coll*

rot I *n* breynder *m* **II** *vb* breyna; pedri

rotate *vb* rosella

rotation *n* rosellans *m*, rosellansow

rotten *adj* poder; podrek; breyn

rough *adj* garow; rust

rough-barked *adj* ruskek

rougher *adj* garwa

roughest *adj* (an) garwa

roughness *n.m* garowder

round I *adj* rond; krenn **II** *adv* a-dro **III** *n* tro *f*, troyow; kylgh *m*, kylghyow **IV** *prp* a-dro dhe^2

roundabout *n* (*traffic*) fordh a-dro *f*, fordhow a-dro; (*signage*) trofordh *f*, trofordhow; (*play equipment*) res a-dro *m*, resow a-dro

rounded *adj* rond; kromm

roundness *n* rondenep *m*

router *n* (*WLAN*) routyell *f*, routyellow

routine *adj* kemmyn; usadow. **routine procedure** dyghtyans kemmyn

row (1) *n* (*disturbance*) hobadolya *m*, hobadolyas

row (2) *n* (*line*) rew *m*, rewyow

row (3) *vb* (*paddle*) revya

rowan tree *n* kerdhinen *f*, kerdhinennow; kerdhin *coll*

rowboat *n* skath-revya *f*, skathow-revya

royal *adj* riel

rub I *n* rutyans *m*, rutyansow **II** *vb* rutya

rubber *n* (*material*) glus gwedhyn *m*, glusow gwedhyn; (*eraser*) rutyer *m*, rutyeryow

rubbish *n* atal *coll*; skoll *m*; (*verbal*) flows *m*. **rubbish tip** byjyon *m*, byjyons

rubbishy *adj* skubellek

rubella *n* (*med; colloq German measles*) rubella *m*

ruby *n* rudhem *m*, rudhemmow

rucksack *n* sagh keyn *m*, seghyer keyn

rudder *n* lew *m*, lewyow

rude *adj* diskortes

rue, meadow *n* ruta *m*

rug *n* strel *m*, strelyow

rugby *n* rugbi *m*

ruin I *n* (*building*) magor *f*, magoryow; kryllas *m*, kryllasow; (*financial*) diswrians *m* **II** *vb* shyndya

ruined *adj* diswrys

rule (1) I (*regulation*) *n* rewl *f*, rewlys **II** *vb* rewlya

rule (2) *n* (*drawing tool*) linennell *f*, linenellow

ruler (1) *n* (*measuring tool*) rewlell *f*, rewlellow; skantlyn *m*, skantlyns

ruler (2) *n* (*head of state*) rewlyas *m*, rewlysi

rum *n* dowr tomm molas *m*; romm *m*

rumour *n* kyhwedhel *m*, kyhwedhlow

rumple *vb* krygha

run I *n* resegva *f*, resegvaow; ponyans *m* **II** *vb* (*of liquids or powder; also figuratively*) resek; (*of persons or animals*) ponya; (*a program; transitive*) eksekutya. **run away** (*escape*) diank;

(*flee*) fia (dhe'n fo). **run into debt** mos a-berth yn kendon. **run out (of something*) difygya. **run through** berya

runaway I *adj* foesik **II** *n* foesik *m*, foesigyon

runner *n* reser *m*, resoryon

runway *n* hyns-tira *m*, hensyow-tira

rupture *n* torrva *f*, torrvaow

rural *adj* powek

rush (1) I *n* (*hurry*) fysk *m* **II** *vb* fistena; fyski; stevya

rush (2) (*plant*) bronnen *f*, bronennow; bronn *coll*

rushed *adj* fysk

russet *adj* rudhloos

Russia *top* Russi *f*

Russian I *adj* russek **II** (*language*) Russek *m*; Russian *m*, Russians

rust I *n* gossen *f* **II** *vb* gosseni

rustle *vb* sia

rustproof *adj* diogel rag gossen

rusty *adj* gossenek

ruthless *adj* dibita

rye *n* sugal *coll*. **grain of rye** sugalen *f*, sugalennow. **rye bread** *n* bara sugal *m*

S

sack *n* sagh *m*, seghyer

sackcloth *n* yskar *m*

sacking *n* yskar *m*

sacrifice I *n* sakrifis *m*, sakrifisys **II** *vb* sakrifia; sakrifisa; (*eccles*) offrynna

sad *adj* trist; (*pitiful*) truedhek

sadden *vb* tristhe; duwena; duwenhe

saddened *adj* tristhes; duwenhes

saddle I *n* diber *m*, dibrow **II** *vb* dibra

sadly *adv* truan; yn truan; truedhek; yn truedhek

sadness *n* tristys *m*; duwon *m*

safe I *adj* (*protected*) salow; saw **II** *n* (*strongbox*) kofer saw *m*, kofrow saw.

safe and sound diogel ha kosel

safeguard *vb* gwitha; diogeli

safely *adv* yn salow; heb danjer

safety *n* sawder *m*; salowder. **safety catch** skwych sawder *m*, skwychys sawder. **safety belt** grugys diogeledh *m*, grugysyow diogeledh

saffron *n* safran *m*. **saffron cake** *n* tesen safran *f*, tesennow safran

saga *n* saga *m*, sagas

sage (1) I *adj* (*prudent*) dooth **II** *n* (*wise person*) dooth *m*, dothyon

sage (2) *n* (*herb*) sawja *m*

sail I *n* gool *m*, golyow **II** *vb* golya.

sailing ship gorhel golyow *m*, gorholyon golyow

sailor *n* marner *m*, marners, marnoryon; golyer *m*, golyoryon

Saint *n* (*title*) Sen *m*; Synt *m*; Synta *f*; *abbrev* S.

saint *n* sans *m*, sens

St John's Wort *n* losow S. Jowan *coll*.

saintly *adj* sansel

sake *n* kerensa *f*. **for the sake of** rag kerensa; a-barth; awos. **for God's sake** a-barth Duw

salad *n* salad *m*, saladys

salami *n* salami *m*, salamis

salary *n* gober *m*, gobrow

sale *n* (*event*) gwerth *f*, gwerthow; (*act of selling*) gwerthas *m*, gwerthasow. **for sale** dhe wertha

salesperson *n* gwerther *m*, gwerthoryon; marchont *m*, marchons

salmon *n* eghek *m*, eghoges, eghogyon

salt I *n* holan *coll*, **II** *vb* salla. **grain of salt** holanen *f*, holanennow. **salt water** *n* hyli *m*; dowr sall *m*

salty *adj* holanek; sall

salvation *n* selwyans *m*, selwyansow

salve *n* eli *m*, eliow; uras *m*, urasow; ismegen *f*, ismegennow; ismek *coll*. **lip balm, lip salve** eli gweus *m*, eliow gweus

same *adj* keth; an unn. **the same as** an keth ha. **the same one** an keth onan. **the same length as** kehys ha. **at the same time** yn kettermyn

samphire *n* senpeder *m*

samphire, rock *n* fenoghel mor *m*

sample I *n* sampel *m*, samplow **II** *vb* sampla

sanctify *vb* sanshe

sanctity *n* sansoleth *f*; benesikter *m*

sanctuary *n* meneghiji *m*, meneghijiow

sand *n* tewes *coll*; treth *m*, trethow. **grain of sand** tewesen *f*, tewesennow

sandal *n* sandal *m*, sandalys

sandcastle *n* kastel tewes *m*, kastylli tewes

sandpaper *n* paper gweder *m*; paper grow *m*

sandstone *n* kragen *f*, kragennow; krag *coll*

sandwich *n* baramanyn *m*, baramanynnow

sandy *adj* tewesek; trethek

sanitary *adj* yeghesek

sap *n* sugen *m*, sugenyow

sapphire *n* saffir *m*, saffiryow

sardine *n* (*pilchard*) hernen *m*, hernennow hern *coll*; (*preserved*) fumado *m*, fumados

satellite *n* (*artificial*) lorell *f*, lorellow; (*moon*) loor *f*, loryow. **satellite television** *f* pellwolok lorell

satellite dish *n* skudel lorell

satire *n* ges a'n jydh *m*, gesyow a'n jydh

satisfaction *n* satysfians *m*, satysfiansow

satisfied *adj* pes da

satisfy *vb* kollenwel bodh; satysfia

Saturday *n* Sadorn *m*; dy'Sadorn *m*. **Saturday night** dy'Sadorn dhe nos

Saturn *n* (*god or planet*) Sadorn

sauce *n* sows *m*, sowsys, sowsow

saucepan *n* padel dhorn *f*, padellow dorn

saucer *n* padellik *f*, padelligow; skala *m*, skalys

sauna *n* sawna *m*, sawnas

sausage *n* selsigen *f*, selsigennow; selsik *coll*

savage I *adj* gwyls; garow **II** *n* gwyls *m*, gwylsyon

save I *vb* (*rescue*) sawya; (*keep*) difres; (*money*) erbysi; (*in the context of Christian salvation*) selwel **II** *cnj* (*save*) lemen

savings *n* erbysyon *pl*

saviour *n* selwyas *m*, selwysi; salvador *m*, salvadoryon

savory, summer *n* sawor hav *m*

savory, winter *n* sawor gwav *m*

savvy I *adj* fel

saw I *n* hesken *f*, heskennow **II** *vb* heskenna. **bow saw** hesken warak *f*, heskennow gwarak. **chain saw** hesken gadon *f*, heskennow kadon

sawdust *n* bleus hesken *m*

saw-grass *n* hesken *f*, heskennow; hesk *coll*

saxifrage *n* torrmen *f*

say *vb* leverel. **say again** dasleverel. **he says** yn-medh ev

saying *n* lavar koth *m*, lavarow koth; dyth *m*, dythow

scab *n* kragh *m*, kreghi

scabious, devil's bit *n* glaswenon *m*

scabious, field *n* penn glas *m*

scald *vb* skaldya

scale (1) I *n* (*system of fixed intervals*) skeul *f*, skeulyow **II** *vb* skeulya; krambla

scale (2) I *n* (*of fish*) skansen *f*, skans **II** *vb* (*remove scales*) diskansa

scales *n.pl* (*weighing*) mantol *f*, mantolyow

scallop *n* krogen brierin *f*, kregyn prierin

scaly *adj* skansek

scam *n* negys kamm *m*, negysyow kamm

scampi *n* skampi *coll*

scan I *n* arhwilyans *m*, arhwilyansow **II** *vb* arhwilas

scandal *n* bismer *m*, bismeras; sklander *m*, sklanderyow

scandalise *vb* gul bismer dhe²; sklandra

scanner *n* arhwilell *f*, arhwilellow. **flatbed scanner** arhwilell weli *f*, arhwilellow gweli

scantily *adv* skant; skantlowr

scanty *adj* skant

scar I *n* kreythen *f*, kreythennow; kreyth *coll* **II** *vb* kreythya

scarce *adj* skant; tanow

scarcely *adv* skant; skantlowr

scarcity *n* tanowder *m*, tanowderyow

scare I *n* own *m* **II** *vb* gorra own dhe²

scarecrow *n* bocka *m*, bockas, bockyas

scared *adj* ownek. **I am scared** yma own dhymm

scarf *n* lien konna *m*, lienyow konna; sarf gonna *f*, serf konna

scarlet *adj* kogh. **scarlet fever** kleves kogh *m*

scarper *vb* gwayvya

scatter *vb* (*intransitive*) keskar; (*transitive*) skattra

scattering *n* keskar *m*

scene *n* gwel *f*

scent *n* eth *m*, ethow; ethen *f*, ethennow

sceptic *n* diskryjyk *m*, diskryjygyon

sceptical *adj* diskryjyk; anhegol

scheme I *n* (*arrangement*) rester *f*, restri; (*plan*) towlen *f*, towlennow **II** *vb* devisya; tewel towl

schizophrenia *n* (*med*) skitsofrenia *m*. **a person with schizophrenia** person gans skitsofrenia

schizophrenic *adj* (*med*) skitsofrenek

scholar *n* skoler *m*, skoloryon; skolheyk *m*, skolheygyon

scholarly *adj* skolheygel; dyskys bras

scholarship *n* skolheygieth *f*

school *n* skol *f*, skolyow; (*of whales*) hes *f*, hesow. **elementary school** skol elvennek *f*, skolyow elvennek. **grammar school** skol ramer *f*, skolyow gramer. **primary school** skol gynsa *f*, skolyow kynsa. **secondary school** skol nessa *f*, skolyow nessa. **high school** skol ughel *f*, skolyow ughel. **nursery school** skol veythrin *f*, skolyow meythrin. **state school** skol stat *f*, skolyow stat

schoolbook *n* lyver skol *m*, lyvrow skol

schoolboy *n* skolvaw *m*, skolvebyon

schoolgirl *n* skolvowes *f*, skolvowysi

schoolhouse *n* skolji *m*, skoljiow

science *n* skiens *m*, skiensow;
godhonieth *f*, godhoniethow

scientific *adj* skiensek; godhoniethek

scientist *n* skiensydh *m*, skiensydhyon;
godhonydh *m*, godhonydhyon

Scilly *top* Syllan *f*. **Isles of Scilly**
Enesow Syllan *pl*

scimitar *n* kledha kromm *m*,
kledhedhyow kromm

scissors *n* gwelsigow *pl*

scold *vb* tavosa; keredhi

scone *n* skonsen *f*, skonsennow; skons
coll

scorch *vb* gorleski; potha

scorching *adj* pooth

score *vb* skorya

scorn I *n* skorn *m*, skornys II *vb*
skornya

Scot *n* Alban *m*, Albanyon

Scotland *top* Alban *m*

Scottish *adj* albanek

scoundrel *n* drog-polat *m*,
drog-polatys

scout I *n* aspier *m*, aspioryon II *vb* aspia

scramble *vb* skrambla. **scrambled egg**
oy skramblys *m*, oyow skramblys

scrap (1) I (*small piece*) *n* tamm *m*,
temmyn; pastel *f*, pastellow II *vb*
(*discard*) tewlel dhe-ves. **scrap heap**
dralva *f*, dralvaow. **scrap iron** horn
koth *m*. **scrap paper** paperyow koth *pl*

scrap (2) I *n* (*fight*) omladh *m*,
omladhow II *vb* omgnoukya; omladh

scrape *vb* kravas; kravellas; ratha; (*file*)
livya. **scrape the bottom of the
barrel** kravas goles an balyer

scratch I *n* kravas *m*, kravasow II *vb*
kravas. **start from scratch** dalleth heb
tra vyth

scream I *n* skrij *m*, skrijow; us *m*, usow
II *vb* skrija; usa

scree *n* radel *coll*

screen *n* (*partition*) paros *m*, parosyow;
(*IT*) skrin *f*, skrinyow; (*for
concealment*) skew *f*, skewyow

screenshot *n* skrinskeusen *f*,
skrinskeusennow

screw I *n* trogenter *f*, trogentrow II *vb*
trogentra (*copulate*) kyjya

screwdriver *n* trogentrell *f*,
trogentrellow

scribble I *n* skryblans *m*, skryblansow
II *vb* skrybla

scribe *n* skriba *m*, skribys

scripture *n* skriptor *f*, skriptors

scrofula *n* kleves an myghtern *m*

scroll *vb* skrolya

scrub (1) *n* (*vegetation*) krann *coll*

scrub (2) *vb* kartha

scrubby *adj* krannek

scruple *n* dout *m*, doutys; danjer *m*,
danjeryow

sculpt *vb* gravya

sculptor *n* gravyer *m*, gravyoryon

sculpture *n* gravyans *m*, gravyansow

scum *n* (*film on liquid*) kenn *m*, kennow;
(*filth*) lastedhes *m*

scummy *adj* kennek

sea *n* mor *m*, moryow. **put to sea** mora.
sea urchin morsort *m*. **the Black Sea**
an Mor Du *m*

sea pink *n* (*thrift*) bryton *coll*; tamm
on *m*

seagull *n* golan *f*, golanes

seakale *n* morgowl *coll*

seal (1) *n* (*animal*) reun *m*, reunes,
reunyon

seal (2) I *n* (*document*) sel *f*, selys,
selyow II *vb* selya

seaman *n* marner *m*, marners,
marnoryon

search I *n* hwithrans *m*, hwithransow;
(*chase; frantic search*) helgh *m*,
helghow II *vb* hwilas; hwithra

sea-sedge *n* moresken *f*, moreskennow;
moresk *coll*

seashore *n* (*seaside*) morrep *m*,
morrebow; (*beach*) treth *m*, trethow

season *n* seson *m*, sesons, sesonyow;
prys *m*, presyow

seasoned *adj* sawrys

seasoning *n* sawrans *m*, sawransow

seat *n* esedh *f*, esedhow; kador *f*, kadoryow; se *m*, seys, seow. **aisle seat** esedh gasel *f*, esedhow kasel. **seat belt** grugys esedh *m*, grugysyow esedh. **window seat** *n* esedh fenester *f*, esedhow fenester

seated *adj* esedhys

seawave *n* mordon *f*, mordonnow

seaway *n* morfordh *f*, morfordhow

seaweed *n* gomonen *f*, gomonennow; gommon *coll*

secluded *adj* argelys; klos. **secluded spot** tyller klos

second I *n* (*unit of time*) eylen *f*, eylennow II *num* nessa; eyl III *vb* eylya; skoodhya.

secondary *adj* nessa

second-hand *adj* wostaswerth

second-home owner *n* perghen estrigys *m*, perghennow estrigys

secret I *adj* kel; kevrinek; kudh II *n* kevrin *m*, kevrinyow. **in secret** yn-dann gel

secretariat *n* skrifenyaseth *f*

secretary *n* skrifennyas *m*, skrifenysi

secretly *adv* yn-dann gel. **it was decided secretly** ervirys veu yn-dann gel

section *n* tregh *m*, treghow. **Caesarean section** *n* tregh Cesarek

sectioned *adj* (*med*) synsys dre lagha

secure I *adj* diogel; saw II *vb* diogeli; fastya

security *n* diogeledh *m*; sawder *m*; salowder *m*

sedge *n* hesk *coll*

sediment I *n* godhes *m*, godhosow II *vb* **deposit sediment** godhesa

sedimentary *adj* godhosek

see *vb* gweles

seed *n* hasen *f*, hasennow; has *coll*. **sow seed** gonis has

seek *vb* hwilas

seem *vb* heveli. **as it seems** dell hevel

seemingly *adv* dell hevel

seemly *adj* onest; semli

segregate *vb* diberth

seize *vb* dalghenna; sesya; synsi

seizure *n* shora *m*, shorys. **shora kolon** heart attack

seldom *adv* namenowgh; boghes venowgh

select *vb* dewis

selection *n* dewis *m*, dewisyow

self I *prp* honan II *prfx* om-

self-adhesive *adj* omlusek

self-aware *adj* omwodh

self-awareness *n* omwodhvos *m*

self-confidence *n* omfydhyans *m*

self-control *n* omwith *m*

self-explanatory *adj* omstyryansek

self-harm I *n* omshyndyans *m*, omshyndyansow II *vb* omshyndya

self-heal *n* (*plant*) medhoges las *f*

selfish *adj* omvodhek; honanus

selfishness *n* omvodhogeth *f*; honanuster *m*; kovaytys *m*

self-love *n* omgerensa *f*

self-loving *adj* omgerensedhek

self-rule *n* omrewl *f*, omrewlys

self-satisfied *adj* omsatysfiys

sell *vb* gwertha. **sell for** gwertha a^2. **sell wholesale** kowlwertha

seller *n* gwerther *m*, gwerthoryon

semester *n* hweghmis *m*, hweghmisyow

semi- *prfx* hanter-

semibreve *n* hanterbrev *m*, hanterbrevow

semicircle *n* hanterkylgh *m*, hanterkylghyow

semicolon *n* poynt ha komma

semifinal *n* hantergwari *m*, hantergwariow

seminar *n* kesareth *f*, kesarethyow

semi-vowel *n* hanterbogalen *f*, hanterbogalennow

send *vb* danvon. **send away** pellhe

senile *adj* gyllys pur goth

senior I *adj* kottha; henavek **II** *n* henavek *m*, henavogyon

sense I *n* (*wisdom*) skians *m*, skiansow; (*sight, smell etc.*) sens *m*, sensys; (*meaning*) styr *m*, styryow **II** *vb* (*perceive*) klewes

senseless *adj* diboll

sensibility *n* finder *m*

sensible *adj* fur

sensitive *adj* kroghendanow; fin

sensitivity *n* sensytyvita *m*

sensor *n* sensell *f*, sensellow

sensual *adj* omglewansel

sensuous *adj* omglewansus

sentence I *n* (*grammatical*) lavar *m*, lavarow; (*law*) breus *f*, breusow **II** *vb* breusi

separate I *adj* diberthys; diblans **II** *vb* diberth; (*disentangle*) digelmi; divagli

separately *adv* dibarow

separateness *n* diblanseth *f*

separation *n* dibarth *f*, dibarthow; keskar *m*

separatism *n* keskarieth *f*

separatist *n* keskarydh *m*, keskarydhyon

September *n* Gwynngala *m*; mis Gwynngala *m*

sequel *n* sewyans *m*, sewyansow

sequence *n* kevres *m*, kevresow; holyans *m*, holyansow

sequential *adj* kevresek

Serb *n* Serb *m*, Serbyon

Serbia *top* Serbi *f*

Serbian I *adj* serbek **II** *n* (*language*) Serbek *m*

serene *adj* hebask

serial *adj* kevresek; a-gevres. **serial number** niver kesresek *m*, niverow kesresek

series *n* kevres *m*, kevresyow

serious *adj* sad; sevur

seriously *adv* yn sad; yn sevur; (*indeed*) devri; yn tevri

sermon *n* pregoth *m*, pregothow

serpent *n* sarf *f*, serf (*in the Book of Genesis*) hager-bryv *m*, hager-breves, hager-brevyon

serpentine I (*rock*) *n* sarfven *m*, sarfveyn **II** (*sinuous*) *adj* sarfek

servant *n* gwas *m*, gwesyon; servyas *m*, servysi; oberwas *m*, oberwesyon; gonisek *m*, gonisogyon

serve *vb* dyghtya; (*in employment*) servya; sodha

server *n* (*IT*) servell *f*, servellow

service *n* servis *m*, servisyow; (*labour*) gonis *m*, gonisyow. **service station** petrolva *f*, petrolvaow. **the National Health Service (NHS)** Servis Kenedhlek an Yeghes (NHS) *m*

serviceable *adj* servadow; 'vas

servile *adj* keth

serving *n* platas *m*, platasow

session *n* esedhek *m*, esedhogow; (*eisteddfod*) esedhvos *m*, esedhvosow

set I *n* sett *m*, settys, settow; (*of people*) parsel *m*, parsellow; (*theatre*) desedhva *f*, desedhvaow **II** *vb* settya; gorra; (*sun*) sedhi. **set aside** gorra a-denewen. **set back** gorra a-dhelergh. **set free** delivra. **set in** dalleth. **set up** selya. **set off** (*leave*) gasa; **set off** (*gun*) tenna; (*explosives*) tardha; (*trap*) diantel. **set out** gorra yn-mes. **set right** ewna. **set up house** dalleth triga

set-square *n* skwir *m*, skwirys

setting *n* sedhes *m*, sedhesow

settle *vb* (*inhabit*) anedhi; triga; (*on new land*) trevesiga; (*argument*) ervira

settled *adj* (*inhabited*) trigys

settlement *n* trevesigeth *f*, trevesigethow

seven *num* seyth

seventeen *num* seytek

seventeenth *num* seytegves; *abbrev* 17ves

seventh *num* seythves; *abbrev* 7ves

seventieth *num* degves ha tri ugens; *abbrev* 70ves

seventy *num* deg ha tri ugens

several *adj* (*with sg*) lies; (*with pl*) meur a^2; (*a few*) nebes

severe *adj* sevur; a-has; kales

severity *n* sevureth *f*; hardigras *m*

sew *vb* gwrias

sewing *n* gwrias *m*. **sewing machine** jynn-gwrias *m*, jynnys-gwrias, jynnow-gwrias

sex *n* reydh *f*; (*activity*) daromres karnal *m*

sexism *n* reydhgasieth *f*

sexist *adj* reydhgasek

sexual *adj* reydhek; karnal

sexual orientation *n* tuedhder reydhek *m*

shackle I *n* karghar *m*, kargharow II *vb* karghara

shade I *n* goskes *m*; goskotter *m* II *vb* goskeusi

shadow *n* skeus *m*, skeusow

shady *adj* skeusek

shaft *n* gwelen *f*, gwelynni; (*of spear*) sheft *m*, sheftys; (*mine*) shafta *m*, shaftys

shake I *n* kren *m*, krenyow II *vb* krena; shackya. **we shook hands** ni a shackyas leuv

shall *vb* **I shall go** my a; my a vynn mos; my a wra mos

shallow *adj* bas

shame I *n* meth *f*, methow; sham *m*; (*pity*) dieth *m* II *vb* shamya. **it's a shame** dieth yw; soweth. **for shame!** rag meth!

shamed *adj* methys

shameful *adj* methus

shameless *adj* diveth

shamrock *n* teyrdelen *f*

shape I *n* furv *f*, furvow; form *m* (*f*), formys; roth *m*, rothow; shap *m*, shapys II *vb* furvya; formya; shapya

share I *n* kevren *f*, kevrennow; rann *f*, rannow II *vb* kevrenna. **share in** bos kevrennek a^2

shareholder *n* kevrannor *m*, kevranoryon

shark *n* morvleydh *m*, morvleydhes

sharp *adj* (*pointed*) lymm; tynn; (*taste or smell*) hwerow; trenk; (*intense*) glew. **sharp focus** fog lew

sharpen *vb* bleynya; lymma

shave *vb* divarva **shave one's beard off** omdhivarva. **shaving foam** ewon-divarva *coll*

she *prn* hi; (*enclitic*) hi

sheaf *n* tysken *f*, tyskennow

shear *vb* (*fleece*) knyvyas

shears *n* gwelsow *pl*

shed (1) *n* (*outbuilding*) krow *m*, krowyow

shed (2) *vb* (*cast off*) skollya; devera. **shed tears** dagrewi; devera dagrow; skollya dagrow

sheep *n* davas *f*, deves

sheep-cot *n* krow deves *m*, krowyow deves

sheepdog *n* ki deves *m*, keun deves

sheet *n* (*bed*) lien gweli *m*, lienyow gweli; (*paper*) folen *f*, folennow

shelf *n* estyllen *f*, estyllennow

shell I *n* (*carapace*) krogen *f*, kregyn; (*egg*) plisken *f*, plisk; (*bomb*) tanbellennik *m*, tanbellenigow II *vb* (*remove shell*) pliskenna

shelter I *n* skovva *f*, skovvaow II *vb* klesa

shepherd *n* bugel *m*, bugeledh

shepherd's purse *n* pors bugel *m*

shepherdess *n* bugeles *f*, bugelesow

shield *n* skoos *m*, skosow

shift *n* (*work*) kor *m*, korow

shilling *n* sols *m*, solsow

shine I *n* lenter *m* II *vb* splanna; golowi; shinya

shining *adj* splann

ship *n* gorhel *m*, gorholyon; lester *m*, lestri. **merchant ship** gorhel kenwerth *m*, gorholyon kenwerth. **sailing ship** gorhel golyow *m*, gorholyon golyow. **passenger ship** gorhel trethysi *m*, gorholyon trethysi

shipload *n* gorhelas *m*, gorhelasow

shipment *n* gorhelas *m*, gorhelasow

shirt *n* krys *m*, krysyow; hevis *m*, hevisyow. **T-shirt** krys T *m*

shit I *n* kawgh *m* II *vb* kawgha

shiver *vb* deglena; krena; rynni

shoal *n* hes *f*, hesow

shock I *n* (*jolt*) jagg *m*, jaggys; (*electric*) jagg tredan *m*, jaggys tredan. **culture shock** *m* dyegrans gonisogeth II *vb* dyegri

shocked *adj* dyegrys; skruthys

shoe I *n* eskis *f*, eskisyow II *vb* (*horse*) hernya. **put on shoes** arghena

shoot (1) *vb* (*gun*) tenna; (*bow and arrow*) setha; (*net*) tewlel roos; (*film*) fylmya

shoot (2) I *n* (*sprout*) egin *m*, eginyow; skyllen *f*, skyll II *vb* egina; skylla

shoot at *vb* tenna dhe². **shoot somebody** (*with a bullet*) gweskel nebonan gans pellen; (*with an arrow*) gweskel nebonan gans seth

shop I *n* (*store*) gwerthji *m*, gwerthjiow; (*workshop*) shoppa *m*, shoppys II *vb* prenassa; (*at a market*) marghasa

shopper *n* prenasser *m*, prenassoryonow

shopping centre *n* kresen-brenassa *f*, kresennow-prenassa

shore *n* (*seaboard*) morrep *m*, morrebow; (*river bank*) glann *f*, glannow

short *adj* kott; berr. **fall short** difygya; fyllel. **short circuit** skochkylgh *m*, skochkylghyow. **short time** pols *m*, polsyow

shortbread *n* tesen vrew *f*, tesennow brew

shortcrust *n* kresten vrew *f*

shorten *vb* berrhe; kothe

shortening *n* kotheans *m*, kotheansow

shortly *adv* a verr spys; kyns neppell; kott termyn

shorts *n* lavrek berr *m*, lavregow berr; lavrek kot *m*, lavregow kot

short-sighted *adj* berrwelyek

shot *n* tenn *m*, tennow

shoulder *n* skoodh *f*, skodhow, *dl* diwskodh. **give somebody the cold shoulder** treylya an keyn orth nebonan. **hard shoulder** glann gales *f*, glannow kales. **soft shoulder** glann vedhel *f*, glannow medhel

shout I *n* kri *m*, kriow; garm *f*, garmow II *vb* garma; kria

shove *vb* herdhya

show I *n* diskwedhyans *m*, diskwedhyansow II *vb* diskwedhes. **show off** payoni; ombraysya

shower I *n* kowas *f*, kowasow II *vb* kowesi

showery *adj* kowasek

shred *vb* skethenna

shrewd *adj* fel

shrimp *n* bibyn bubyn *m*, bibynes bubyn

shrine *n* krerva *f*, krervaow

shrink *vb* omdenna; lehe

shrub *n* prysken *f*, pryskennow; prysk *coll*

shudder I *n* skruth *m*, skruthow II *vb* skrutha

shut I *adj* deges; klos II *vb* degea; serri; keas. **shut up!** serr dha dhiwen! syns dha glapp! taw taves! gas dha son!

shy *adj* gohelus

sick *adj* klav. **sick pay** gober kleves *m*, gobrow kleves. **take sick** kodha klav

sickness *n* klavder *m*: kleves *m*, klevesow

side *n* tu *m*, tuyow; tenewen *m*, tenwennow; parth *f*, parthow; (*edge*) amal *m*, emlow. **reverse side** gorthenep *m*, gorthenebow

sideboard *n* bord lestri *m*, bordys lestri, bordow lestri

sidelong *adv* a-denewen

siege *n* synsans *m*

sieve I *n* rider *m*, ridrow; (*coarse/garden*) kroder *m*, krodrow; (*large*) kasyer *m*, kasyerow **II** *vb* ridra

sift *vb* krodra; ridra

sigh I *n* hanas *m*, hanasow **II** *vb* hanasa

sight *n* golok *f*, gologow; (*view*) gwel *f*, gwelyow. **get out of my sight!** gwayv ow golok! **partially sighted** *adj* gowelek. **sight impaired** *adj* gweles aperys

sign I *n* arwodh *f*, arwodhyow; tokyn *m*, toknys **II** *vb* sina

signal I *n* arwodh *f*, arwodhyow; *n* sinell *f* sinellow **II** *vb* sinya; sinella

signature *n* sinans *m*, sinansow

signet *n* (*seal*) sel *f*, selys

significance *n* styr *m*, styryow

significant *adj* a bris; a vri

signify *vb* styrya

sign-post *n* post arwodh *m*, postow arwodh

Sikhism *n* Sikieth *f*

silence *n* taw *m*. **silence! be quiet!** taw taves!

silencer *n* tawell *f*, tawellow

silent I *adj* didros; tawesek **II** (*to be silent*) *vb* tewel

silently *adv* heb gul son; heb gul gik na mik

silicon *n* (*element*) silikon *m*

silk *n* owrlin *m*, owrlinyow

silkworm *n* pryv owrlin *m*, preves owrlin, prevyon owrlin

silky *adj* owrlinus

silly *adj* gocki

silver *n* (*element*) arghans *m*

silvery *adj* arghansek

similar *adj* haval; hevelep

similarity *n* hevelepter *m*

similarly *adv* yndella; yn kepar maner

simile *n* komparyans *m*, komparyansow

simmer *vb* govryjyon

simple *adj* sempel; (*easy*) es

simplify *vb* sempelhe

simply *adv* yn sempel; dre vaner es

simultaneous *adj* kettermynyek

sin I *n* pegh *m*; peghes *m*, peghosow **II** *vb* pegha

since *cnj* (*followed by a verb*) a-ban^2; a-dhia ban^2; (*followed by a noun*) a-dhia. **long since** seuladhydh

since then *adv* alena rag

sincere *adj* gwiryon; kolonnek

sincerely *adv* heb toll na gil. **yours sincerely** dhis yn lel

sinful *adj* peghus

sing *vb* kana

singer *n* kaner *m*, kanoryon

single I *adj* unn; unnik; (*unmarried*) andhemedhys **II** *prn* onan. **not a single one** (*people*) nagonan; (*things*) tra vyth. **I didn't see a single one** ny welis vy nagonan

singular *adj* unplek

sink (1) *n* new *f*, newyow

sink (2) *vb* sedhi

sinking *n* sedhes *m*, sedhesow

sinner *n* peghador *m*, peghadoryon

sir *n* syrra *m*, syrrys; (*title*) syr *m*

sire *n* sira *m*, sirys

siskin *n* melynek gwern *m*, melynoges gwern

sister *n* hwor *f*, hwerydh

sit *vb* esedha

site *vb* lea

situation *n* le *m*, leow; desedhans *m*, desedhansow; plit *m*, plitys; studh *m*, studhyow; stat *m*, statys, statow

six *num* hwegh

sixpence *n* hwedner *m*

sixteen *num* hwetek

sixteenth *num* hwetegves; *abbrev* 16ves

sixth *num* hweghves; *abbrev* 6ves

sixtieth *num* tri ugensves; *abbrev* 60ves

sixty *num* tri ugens

size *n* braster *m*, brasterow; myns *m*, mynsow

sizeable *adj* lowr; mynsek

skate I *n* skes *m*, skesow II *vb* skesya. **ice skate** *n* skes rew *m*, skesow rew; *vb* skesya war rew. **roller skate** *n* roskis *m*, roskisyow

skateboard I *n* rostell *f*, rostellow II *vb* rostella

sketch I *n* delinyans *m*, delinyansow; linennans *m*, linenansow II *vb* linenna

ski I *n* ski *m*, skiow, skis II *vb* skia. **ski pole** *n* gwelen ski *f*, gwelynni ski

skilful *adj* sleygh

skill *n* sleyghneth *f*

skilled *adj* sleygh; konnyk; skentel

skim *vb* (*milk*) didhehenna; (*movement*) skeri; (*digging; mining*) gobalas. **skimmed milk** leth didhehen *m*

skin I *n* kroghen *f*, kreghyn; kneus *coll*; (*on milk*) kenn *m* II *vb* diruska; kroghena

skinny *adj* kennek; kronek; (*bony*) askornek

skip (1) *vb* (*jump*) terlemmel; (*with a rope*) lemmel lovan. **skip it!** gwra y ankevi! (*sg*); gwrewgh y ankevi! (*pl*)

skip (2) *n* (*container*) kibel *f*, kibellow

skipping rope *n* lovan lemmel *f*, lovanow lemmel

skirt *n* losten *f*, lostennow

skull *n* klopen *m*, klopennow; krogen benn *f*, kregyn penn

sky *n* ebron *f*, ebronyow

skylark *n* ahwesydh *m*, ahwesydhes

slack *adj* lows

slacken *vb* slackya

slam I *n* bomm *m*, bommyn II *vb* deghesi gans tros ha nell; degea gans tros bras. **slam on the brakes** gweskel an fronn

slander I *n* sklander *m*, sklanderyow II *vb* sklandra; esedha war skavel an gow

slang *n* isyeth *f*, isyethow

slap I *n* skatt *m*, skattys, skattow; stiwen *m* II *vb* stiwenna; hwattya; skwattya

slapdash *adj* hwymm-hwamm

slate I *n* leghen *f*, leghennow; legh *coll*; kyllasen *f*, kyllas II *vb* (*roof with slate*) kylasenna

slater *n* tior *m*, tiorycn

slaughter I *n* ladhva *f*, ladhvaow II *vb* ladha

slave I *n* keth *m*, kethyon II *vb* (*toil*) lavurya

slavery *n* kethneth *f*

sleep I *n* kosk *m* II *vb* koska. **sleeping bag** sagh-koska *m*, seghyer-koska. **sleep fitfully** tergoska. **put to sleep** *vb* (*animal*) euthanisya

sleepless *adj* difun; digosk

sleepwalk *vb* (*colloq*) koskkerdhes *For clinically diagnosed sleepwalking see: somnambulism*

sleepy *adj* hunyek; skwith

sleeve *n* breghel *m*, bregholow

sleigh *n* draylell *f*, draylellow; karr slynk *m*, kerri slynk

slender *adj* moon; tanow; (*narrow*) ynn; kul

slice I *n* tregh *m*, treghow II *vb* treghi; skethenna

slide I *n* slynk *m*, slynkys, slynkow II *vb* slynkya

slight I *adj* (*small*) boghes; nebes; skav II *n* (*spurn*) dispresyans *m*, dispresyansow III *vb* dispresya

slightly *adv* boghes; nebes

slim *adj* moon; tanow; (*narrow*) ynn; kul

slime *n* leys *m*, leysyow; slim *m*, slimys

slimy *adj* loubek

slip I *n* (*undergarment*) golesen *f*, golesennow; *n* (*of paper*) folennik *f*, folenigow; darn paper *m*, darnow paper II *vb* slynkya. **slip out** skapya

slipper *n* pawgen *m*, pawgennow
slippery *adj* slynk
slobber I *n* glavor *m* II *vb* glaveri
slobbering *adj* glavorek
sloe *n* eyrinen *f*, eyrinennow; eyrin *coll*
slogan *n* (*battle cry*) garm vresel *f*, garmow bresel; (*advertising slogan*) garm-argemynna *f*, garmow-argemynna
slope I *n* leder *f*, ledrow; run *f*, runyow; riw *f*, riwyow II *vb* ledri
sloping *adj* ledrek
sloth *n* (*animal*) lentvil *m*, lentviles; (*laziness*) diegi *m*
Slovak I *adj* slovakek II *n* (*language*) Slovakek *m*; (*Slovak person*) Slovak *m*, Slovakyon
Slovakia *top* Slovaki *f*
Slovene *n* (*person*) Sloven *m*, Slovenyon; (*language*) Slovenek *m*
Slovenia *top* Sloveni *f*
Slovenian *adj* slovenek
slow I *adj* lent; syger II *vb* (*slow down*) lenthe
slowly *adv* yn lent
sludge *n* loub *m*, loubyow
slug *n* melhwen *f*, melhwennow; (*sometimes snail*) melhwesen *f*, melhwes; (*small slug*) gluthvelhwen *f*, gluthvelhwennow
slum *n* pildra *f*, pildrevow
sly *adj* fel; kall
slyness *n* kalder *m*; felder *m*
small *adj* byghan; munys
smaller *adj* byghanna; le
smallholding *n* pastel dir *f*, pastellow tir
smallpox *n* brygh *f*, breghi
smart (1) *adj* skentel; konnyk (*neat*) fethus; brav; fin
smart (2) *vb* gloosa
smash *vb* skwattya
smear I *n* drogurans *m*, droguransow II *vb* drogura

smell I *n* blas *m*, blasow; sawor *m*, saworyow; (*stink*) fler *m*, fleryow II *vb* blasa; (*sense*) klewes; (*stink*) flerya; mosegi
smelly *adj* flerys; mosek
smile I *n* minhwarth *m*, minhwarthow II *vb* minhwerthin
smith *n* gov *m*, govyon
smoke I *n* mog *m* II *vb* megi; (*smoke a pipe*) tochya pib. **no smoking** megi difennys
smooth I *adj* leven; gwastas II *vb* levena
smoothie *n* levenek *f*, levenegow
smug *adj* omsatysfiys; omgerensedhek
smuggle *vb* franklondya
smuggler *n* gwikor frank *m*, gwikoryon frank
smugness *n* omgerensa *f*
snack *n* kroust *m*, kroustyow, kroustys; tamm *m*, temmyn
snail *n* bulhorn *m*, bulhornes; (*sometimes slug*) melhwesen *f*, melhwes. **catch snails** *vb* melhwessa
snail-like *adj* melhwesek
snake *n* sarf *f*, serf
snapdragon *n* (*antirrhinum*) sawen an dhragon *m*
snarl I *n* skrynk *m*, skrynkow II *vb* grysla; deskerni; skrynkya
snatch *vb* kibya
sneak I *n* skolk *m*, skolkyow II *vb* skolkya
sneeze I *n* striw *m*, striwyow II *vb* striwi; rahaya
sniff I *n* frikhwyth *m*, frikhwythow II *vb* frikhwytha
snipe *n* (*bird*) kiogh *f*, kioghyon; gaver hal *f*, gyvres hal, gever hal
snivel *vb* mera
snob *n* snobbyn *m*, snobbynnow
snore I *n* ronk *m*, ronkow II *vb* renki
snorer *n* renkyas *m*, renkysi
snotty *adj* purek
snout *n* tron *m*, tronow
snow I *n* ergh *coll* II *vb* gul ergh

snowdrop *n* bleujen ergh *f*, bleujennow ergh; bleujyow ergh *coll*

snowfall *n* kodh ergh *m*, kodhow ergh

snowflake *n* erghen *f*, erghennow

snowman *n* den ergh *m*, tus ergh

snowy *adj* erghek

snug *adj* klys. **make snug** klysa

so I *adv* mar² **II** *cnj* ytho; rag henna. **she is so pretty** mar deg yw hi. **so much** kemmys; **thus** yndella. **so that** may⁵; (*before vowel*) mayth. **so I see** dell welav. **so what?** pandr'a vern?

soak I *n* **an old soak** (*drunkard; colloq*) penn medhow koth *m* **II** *vb* gwlyghi; segi; souba

soap I *n* sebon *m*, sebonow **II** *vb* seboni. **soap opera** *n* gwari sebon *m*

soapy *adj* sebonas

sober *adj* (*solemn*) sad; (*not drunk*) divedhow

sociable *adj* kowethyadow

social *adj* kowethasek; socyal. **social security** diogeledh socyal *m*

socialism *n* socyalieth *f*

socialist I *adj* socyalydhek **II** *n* socyalydh *m*, socyalydhyon

society *n* kowethas *m*, kowethasow

sociological *adj* socyologiethek

sociologist *n* socyologydh *m*, socyologydhyon

sociology *n* socyologieth *f*

sock *n* lodrik *m*, lodrigow; (*leather sock, slipper*) pawgen *m*, pawgennow

socket *n* kraw *m*, krawyow

soda *n* soda *m*, sodas

sofa *n* gweli dydh *m*, gweliow dydh

soft *adj* medhel; (*tender*) bleudh; (*of sound*) isel

soften *vb* bleudhya; medhelhe

softness *n* bleudhder *m*

software *n* (*IT*) medhelweyth *m*

soil I *n* (*earth*) gweres *m*, gweresow **II** *vb* (*befoul*) mostya; kagla

soiled *adj* los; mostys

solar *adj* howlek

soldier *n* souder *m*, soudoryon, soudrys

sole I *adj* unn; unnik **II** *n* (*foot*) godhen *m*, godhnow; (*shoe*) goles eskis *m*. **the sole heir** an er unnik

solemn *adj* sad

solemnity *n* solempnita *m*, solempnitys

solicit *vb* pysi tynn

solicitor *n* noter *m*, notoryon

solid I *adj* soled **II** *n* soled *m*, soledow

solo I *adj* y honan **II** *n* (*performance*) solo *m*, solos

soluble *adj* (*chemistry*) hedeuth; (*of a problem*) assoyladow

solution *n* men *m*, menys; remedi *m*, remedis; (*of problem*) digolm *m*, digolmow; (*chemistry*) teudhans *m*, teudhansow

solve *vb* digelmi; assoylya

sombre *adj* tewl

some I *adj* nebes **II** *prn* neb; re; rann **III** *n.m* nebes **some of them** rann anedha; re anedha

somebody *prn* nebonan

somehow *adv* war neb kor; neb maner; neb fordh

someone *prn* nebonan. **someone or other** mab y dhama *m*, myrgh hy dama *f*. **the burglary was done by someone or other** an ladrans a veu gwrys gans mab y dhama

something *prn* neppyth

sometime *adv* neb prys; (yn) neb termyn

sometimes *adv* treweythyow

somewhere *adv* neb tyller; neb le; neb tu

somnambulism *n* (*med*) sonambulism *m*

son *n* mab *m*, mebyon. **grandson** *n* mab wynn *m*, mebyon wynn. **little son** maban *m*, mebyn; meppik *m*, meppigow. **son-in-law** *n* deuv *m*, deuvyon

song *n* kan *f*, kanow. **folk song** *n* kan werin *f*, kanow gwerin

sonic *adj* sonek. **sonic boom** taran sonek *f*

sonnet *n* sonet *m*, sonettys

soon *adv* hware; skon; yn skon; tost; a verr spys. **as soon** kettooth; kettost. **as soon as** kettooth ha; kettost ha

sooner *adj* kyns. **the sooner the better** dhe skonna dhe well

soot *n* hudhygel *m*

soothe *vb* hebaskhe; koselhe

sooty *adj* hudhyglek

soprano *n* soprano *m*, sopranos

sorcerer *n* pystrier *m*, pystrioryon

sorceress *n* pystriores *f*, pystrioresow

sorcery *n* pystri *m*; hus *m*; nygromons *m*

sore I *adj* tynn II *n* goli *m*, goliow

soreness *adj* tynnder

sorrel, common *n* trenkan *m*

sorrel, sheep's *n* trenkan an dhavas *m*

sorrel, wood *n* trenkan an koos *m*

sorrow *n* anken *m*, ankenyow; keudh *m*; duwon *m*

sorrowful *adj* ahwerek; moredhek

sorry I *adj* edrygys; keudhesik II *int* (*apologies*) diharesow! **be sorry** kemeres duwon. **I am sorry** drog yw genev; edrek a'm beus. **make sorry** keudhi

sort I *n* eghen *f*; sort *m*, sortow; par *m*, parow II *vb* digemyska; sortya. **of that sort** a'n par na. **sort out** handla; komposa

soul *n* enev *f*, enevow

sound I *n* son *m*, sonyow; (*noise*) tros *m*, trosyow II *vb* seni

soundless *adj* dison

soundtrack *n* sonlergh *m*, sonlerghyow

soup *n* kowl *m*, kowlow

sour *adj* trenk

source *n* (*of stream*) pennfenten *f*, pennfentynnyow; (*derivation*) devedhyans *m*

south *n* soth *m*; dyghow *m*; dyghowbarth *f*. **on the south side** a-dhyghowbarth

south-east *n* soth-est *m*

southerly *adj* a-dhia an soth

southern *adj* a'n soth; a'n dhyghowbarth

southwards *adv* war-tu ha'n soth

south-west *n* soth-west *m*

souvenir *n* kovro *m*, kovrohow, kovroyow

sovereign I *adj* sovran II *n* sovran *m*, sovrans

sovereignty *n* sovranedh *m*

sow (1) *vb* (*seed*) hasa. **sow seed** gonis has

sow (2) *n* (*swine*) gwis *f*, gwisi; banow *f*, banowes, bynewi

space *n* spas *m*; efander *m*; (*astronomy*) efanvos *m*. **space bar** *n* (*on a keyboard*) barren spas *f*, barrennow spas

space bar *n* barren spas *f*, barrennow spas

spaceship *n* sterlester *m*, sterlestri

spade *n* pal *f*, palyow

Spain *top* Spayn *m*

Spaniard *n* Spaynyer *m*, Spaynyoryon

Spanish I *adj* spaynek II *n* (*language*) Spaynek

spanner *n* alhwedh know *f*, alhwedhow know

spare I *adj* (*extra*) spar; (*reserve*) difresek II *vb* sparya. **spare part** spar *m*, sparyon. **spare wheel** ros parys *f*, rosow parys

spark *n* elven *f*, elvennow

sparkle *vb* terlentri

sparkling *adj* gwryghonek

sparrow *n* golvan *m*, golvanes. **house sparrow** (*dunnock*) golvan chi *m*, golvanes chi

sparse *adj* tanow

spasm *n* gloos *f*, glosow

spay *vb* spadha

speak *vb* kewsel; klappya. **speak to** kewsel orth. **speak on behalf of** kewsel gans. **well spoken of** gerys-da

speaker *n* kowser *m*, kowsoryon; (*orator*) arethor *m*, arethoryon

spear I *n* guw *m*, guwow; spera *m*, sperys **II** *vb* guwa

spearmint *n* menta wuwdhel *f*

special *adj* arbennek

specialist *n* arbeniger *m*, arbenigoryon

species *n* eghen *f*, eghennow

specific *adj* komparek

specification *n* ragnotyans *m*, ragnotyansow

specimen *n* sampel *m*, samplow

speck *n* dyjyn *m*, dyjynnow

spectacles *n* dewweder *dl*

spectator *n* mirer *m*, miroryon

speculate *vb* (*theorise*) desevos; (*financially*) aventurya

speculation *n* (*theorising*) resnans *m*, resnansow; aventur *m*, aventurys, aventuryow

speech *n* (*address*) areth *f*, arethyow; (*faculty*) kows *m*; (*noisy*) predhek *m*, predhegow

speechless *adj* dilavar

speed I *n* tooth *m*; skavder *m* **II** *vb* tothya; spedya. **speed limit** finweth tooth *f*, finwethow tooth

speedily *adv* uskis

speedwell *n* (*plant*) leslesa *m*

speedy *adj* uskis

spell (1) *vb* (*orthography*) lytherenna

spell (2) *n* (*magic*) hus *m*, husow

spell (3) *n* (*period*) kors *m*, korsow

spellbound *adj* husys

spelling *n* lytherenans *m*

spend *vb* spena

sperm *n* hasen *f*, hasennow; has *coll*

sphere *n* pel *f*, pelyow

spherical *adj* pelyek

spice I *n* spis *m*, spisys, spisyow **II** *vb* spisa. **spiced wine** pyment *m*, pymentys

spicy *adj* spisek

spider *n* kevnisen *f*, kevnis. **spider web** gwias kevnis *m*, gwiasow kevnis

spider-crab *n* pilyek *m*, pilyogyon

spike I *n* kenter *f*, kentrow; kolgh *m*, kolghow; spik *m*, spikys **II** *vb* kentra. **spike a drink** krefhe diwes

spill I *n* skollyans *m*, skollyansow **II** *vb* skollya; (*blood*) devera

spin *vb* troyllya; rosella

spinach *n* spinach *m*

spinal *adj* a'n keyn

spine *n* mell keyn *m*, mellow keyn

spiral I *adj* troyllyek **II** *n* troyll *m* (*f*), troyllyow

spirit *n* spyrys *m*, spyrysyon

spit *vb* trewa

spite *n* atti *m*; spit *m*. **in spite of** spit dhe[2]. **out of spite** rag atti

spiteful *adj* spitus

spittle *n* trew *m*; trewyas *m*

splash I *n* lagyans *m* **II** *vb* lagya; plowghya

spleen *n* felgh *f*, felghyow

splendid *adj* splann; bryntin

splint *n* astel *f*, estyl

splinter *n* skommen *m*, skomennow

splintered *adj* skyrrys; skethrek

split I *n* fols *m*, folsyow **II** *vb* folsa; (*go away quickly*) gwayvya

splitting *n* folsans *m*, folsansow

spoil I (*loot*) preydh *m*, preydhyow **II** *vb* (*plunder*) pylla; (*ruin*) diswul; (*decay*) pedri; (*a child*) gorbeski

sponge *n* spong *m*, spongow

spoon *n* lo *f*, loyow

sport *n* sport *m*, sportys, sportow

sportsperson *n* sportyas *m*, sportysi

spot I *n* (*stain*) namm *m*, nammow; (*pimple*) kuriek *m*, kuriogas, kuriegi; brygh *f*, breghi (*place*) tyller *m*, tylleryow **II** *vb* namma

spotless *adj* dinam

spotted *adj* breghys

spouse *n* pries *m*, priosow

spout I *n* pistyl *m*, pistyllow II *vb* pistylla

sprain I *n* treylyans *m*, treylyansow II *vb* treylya

spray *vb* stifella

spread I *n* lesans *m*, lesansow II *vb* lesa. **spread the washing** (*hang out the washing*) lesa an golgh

spreadsheet *n* leslen *f*, leslennow

sprig *n* barren *f*, barrennow

spring (1) *n* (*season*) gwenton *m*

spring (2) *n* (*source generally and water source*) fenten *f*, fentynnyow

spring (3) *vb* (*jump*) lamma; lemmel. **spring up** spryngya

sprout I *n* skyllen *f*, skyllennow; skyll *coll* II *vb* skylla. **brussels sprout** kowlik *m*, kowligow; kowlennik *f*, kowlenigow

spurge, sea *n* flammgos an mor *m*

spurge, sun *n* flammgos an howl *m*

spurge, wood *n* flammgos an ke *m*

squad *n* para *m*, paraow

squall *n* hager-awel *f*, hager-awelyow

square I *adj* pedrek II *n* pedrek *m*, pedrogow III *vb* pedrega

squash *vb* gwaska; skwattya

squeak I *n* mik *m*, mikow II *vb* gwighal

squeeze I *n* gwaskans *m*, gwaskansow; strothans *m*, strothansow II *vb* gwaska; strotha; gwrynnya

squeezed *adj* strooth; strothys

squeezing *n* gwaskans *m*, gwaskansow

squid *n* stifek *m*, stifoges

squirrel *n* gwiwer *m*, gwiweres, gwiwerow

squirt I *n* stif *m*, stifow II *vb* stifa

stab *vb* berya; gwana. **stab oneself** omwana

stability *n* krefter *m*; faster *m*

stable (1) *adj* (*steady*) fast; sad

stable (2) *n* (*for horses*) marghti *m*, marghtiow

stack I *n* das *f*, deys II *vb* dasa

stadium *n* sportva *f*, sportvaow

staff *n* (*employees*) mayni *coll*; (*rod*) lorgh *f*, lorghow; lath *f*, lathow

stag *n* karow *m*, kerwys

stage *n* gwariva *f*, gwarivaow. **stage name** hanow gwari *m*, henwyn gwari

stain I *n* namm *m*, nammow; mosten *f*, mostennow II *vb* namma

stained *adj* nemmys

stair *n* gris *m*, grisyow, grisys

stake *n* peul *m*, peulyow

stakeholder *n* kevrennek *m*, kevrenogyon

stalemate *n* methardak *m*, methardagow

stalk *n* garen *f*, garennow; **straw stalk** gwelen gala *f*, gwelynni kala

stamina *n* stamina *m*

stamp I *n* (*postage*) stamp *m*, stampys, stampow; (*of foot*) stank *m*, stankyow II *vb* stampya; (*with foot*) stankya. **stamp out** diwreydhya

stance *n* stons *m*, stonsys; savla *m*, savleow

stand I *n* sav *m*, savow II *vb* sevel; (*bear, suffer*) perthi. **stand against** sevel orth. **stand aside** *vb* sevel a-denewen. **stand out** *vb* sevel yn-mes. **stand up** *vb* sevel yn-bann. **I can't stand it** ny allav y berthi

standard I *adj* savonek; skwir II *n* savon *f*, savonow; skwir *m*, skwirys; (*flag*) baner *m*, baneryow

standardise *vb* savonegi

standing *adj* a'y sav

standpoint *n* savla *m*, savleow

stannary *n* stenek *f*, stenegow

stanza *n* gwers *f*, gwersyow

stapler *n* jynn-krommgentra *m*, jynnys-krommgentra, jynnow-krommgentra

star *n* steren *f*, sterennow; ster *coll*

star of Bethlehem *n* steren Vethlehem *f*

stare I *n* tremmyn settys *m*, tremynnow settys II *vb* lagatta; mires stark. **stare**

at lagatta orth; mires stark orth

starfish *n* pympbys *m*, pympbyses

starling *n* troos *m*, treysi

starry *adj* sterennek

starship *n* sterlester *m*, sterlestri; gorhel efander *m*, gorholyon efander

start I dalleth *m*, dallethow; *n* derow *m*, derowyow **II** *vb* dalleth

starve *vb* (*die of hunger*) famya (*intrans.*); merwel dre nown. **I'm starving** gwag ov vy

state I *n* stat *m*, statys, statow; (*condition*) plit *m*, plitys; studh *m*, studhyow; (*country*) gwlas *f*, gwlasow; (*province*) rannvro *f*, rannvroyow **II** *vb* meneges. **the United States** an Statys Unys *pl*

statement *n* menegyans *m*, menegyansow; derivas *m*, derivasow

statesman *n* statydh *m*, statydhyon

stateswoman *n* statydhes *f*, statydhesow

station *n* savla *m*, savleow; (*bus, train*) gorsav *m*, gorsavow. **police station** sodhva greslu *f*, sodhvaow kreslu

statistic *n* statystyk *m*, statystygyon. **science of statistics** statystek *f*

statue *n* imach *m*, imajys; delow *m*, delowyow

status *n* (*IT*) studh *m*, studhyow; (*rank*) gre *m*, greys

staunch *adj* stanch

stay *vb* (*wait*) gortos; (*dwell*) triga

steady *adj* fast

steak *n* tregh kig *m*, treghow kig

steal *vb* ladra

steam I *n* ethen *f*, ethennow; eth *m* **II** *vb* ethenna

steamship *n* gorhel tan *m*, gorholyon tan

steel *n* dur *m*

steep *adj* serth; (*colloq*) krackya konna

steer *vb* lewa; lewya. **steering wheel** ros-lewya *f*, rosow-lewya

stem *n* ben *m*, benyow; garr *f*, garrow

stench *n* fler *m*, fleryow; sawor poos *m*, saworyow poos

step *n* (*grade*) gradh *m*, gradhow; (*pace*) kamm *m*, kammow; kammen *f*, kamennow; pas *m*, passys; (*stair*) gris *m*, grisyow, grisys

stepbrother *n* lesvroder *m*, lesvreder

stepchild *n* lesflogh *m*, lesfleghes

stepdaughter *n* elses *f*, elsesow

stepfather *n* lestas *m*. lestasow; altrow *m*, altrowyon

stepmother *n* altrewen *f*, altrewenyow; lesvam *f*, lesvammow

stepsister *n* leshwor *f*, leshwerydh

stepson *n* els *m*, elsyon

stereotype *vb* skwirglassya

stew I *n* bros *m*, brosow **II** *vb* stywya; hirvryjyon

steward *n* rennyas *m*. renysi; styward *m*, stywards

stick (1) I *n* gwelen *f*, gwelynni; lath *f*, lathow **II** *vb* (*thrust into*) plansa

stick (2) *vb* (*adhere*) glena; staga. **glena orth** glena orth. **get stuck** mos yn stag

sticker *n* glenysen *f*, glenysennow

sticky *adj* glusek

stiff *adj* (*inflexible*) diwedhyn; (*hard*) kales; (*straight*) serth

still (1) *adj* kosel

still (2) *adv* hwath; hogen; prest. **still more** byth moy

stillness *n* kalmynsi *m*; kosoleth *f*

sting I *n* gwan *f*, gwanyow **II** *vb* gwana; piga

stingray *n* rogha bros *m*, roghys bros

stink I *n* fler *m*, fleryow; mosokter *m* **II** *vb* flerya; mosegi

stinking *adj* mosek; flerys

stir I (*uproar*) *n* habadolya *m* **II** *vb* kaboli; treylouba; (*cause a stir*) gul habadolya

stitch I *n* gwri *m*, gwriow **II** *vb* gwrias; brosya

stitchwort, greater *n* boos nader *m*

stitchwort, lesser *n* lagasow kathes *m.pl*

stock (1) *n* (*gillyflower*) knowdhel *coll*

stock (2) *n* (*meat*) sugen kig *m*, sugenyow kig; (*vegetable*) sugen losow *m*, sugenyow losow

stocking *n* loder *m*, lodrow

stockpile *n* kreun *m*, kreunyow

stocks *n.pl* (*pillory*) karghar prenn *m*, kargharow prenn

stock-still *adj* heb gul gik na mik

stolen *adj* ledrys

stomach *n* (*anat. organ*) sagh boos *m*, seghyer boos; (*abdomen generally*) torr *f*, torrow

stone I *n* men *m*, meyn; (*in the body*) mantedh *coll* **II** *vb* labedha. **standing stone** menhir *m*, menhiryon. **Stone Age** Oos an Men *m*

stonecrop, biting *n* bewles hwerow *coll*

stone-dead *adj* devarow

stool *n* skavel *f*, skavellow

stop I *n* (*for bus, train etc.*) savla *m*, savleow; hedhas *m*; (*rest*) powes *m*, powesow **II** *vb* (*intransitive*) hedhi; (*transitive*) astel; (*prevent*) lettya; sevel orth

stoppage *n* astel *m*, astelyow

stopwatch *n* hedheuryer *m*, hedheuryerow

store *n* (*storehouse*) gwithva *m*, gwithvaow; (*shop*) gwerthji *m*, gwerthjiow

storehouse *n* gwithva *f*, gwithvaow

storey *n* leur *m*, leuryow

storm I *n* hager-awel *f*, hager-awelyow; tewedh *m*, tewedhow **II** *vb* arnewa. **storm-damaged** arnewys

story *n* hwedhel *m*, hwedhlow; drolla *m*, drollys

straight *adj* kompes; ewn. **straight away** *adv* a-dhesempis; dihwans; distowgh

straight-edge *n* (*rule*) linennell *f*, linenellow

straightforward *adj* diflows; didro

straight-jacket *n* jerkyn strooth *m*, jerkyns strooth, jerkynnow strooth

strain I *n* tennva *f* **II** *vb* (*filter*) sidhla

strainer *n* kroder *m*, krodrow

strange *adj* astranj; estren; koynt; (*unknown*) ankoth

stranger *n* estren *m*, estrenyon; alyon *m*, alyons

strangle *vb* taga

straw *n* kala *coll*; (*stalk*) gwelen gala *f*, gwelynni kala; kalaven *f*, kalavennow. **drinking straw** kalaven-eva *f*, kalavennow-eva

strawberry *n* sevien *f*, sevi

streak I *n* ribin *m*, ribins, ribinow **II** *vb* britha

streaked *adj* brith

stream *n* gover *m*, goverow

street *n* stret *m*, stretys, stretow. **little street** stretyn *m*, stretynnow. **one-way street** stret unfordh *m*, stretys unfordh, stretow unfordh. **street child** flogh stret *m*, fleghes stret

street-trader *n* stretwikor *m*, stretwikoryon

strength *n* nerth *m*, nerthow; krevder *m*, krevderyow; krefter *m*, krefteryow; nell *m*, nellow

strengthen *vb* krefhe; nertha

stress I *n* gwask *f*, gwaskow; (*emphasis*) poslev *f*, poslevow **II** *vb* gorra poos war²; (*emphasise*) posleva

stressful *adj* ankensi; tynn; ahas

stretch *vb* tenna; ystyn

stretcher *n* gravath *f*, gravathow

strict *adj* tynn; strooth; hardh

stride *n* kamm *m*, kammow

strife *n* strif *m*, strifow

strike (1) *vb* (*hit*) gweskel; frappya; kronkya; dorna

strike (2) *vb* (*suspension of work*) astel ober

string *n* korden *f*, kerdyn

stringently *adv* hardlych

strip I *n* sketh *m*, skethow; skethen *f*, skethennow; (*removal of clothes*) omdhiwiskans *m*, omdhiwiskansow **II** *vb* destryppya; pilya; (*take off clothes*) omdhiwiska. **strip bare** lommhe

striped *adj* brith; labol

strive *vb* strivya

stroke I *n* bommen *f*, bomennow; kronk *m*, kronkys; (*caress*) palvas *m*, palvasow **II** *vb* tava; palva. **stroke of luck** towl chons *m*, towlow chons

strong *adj* krev

structural *adj* kesweythel; framweythel

structure I *n* kesweyth *m*, kesweythow **II** *vb* framya; araya

struggle I *n* strif *m*, strifow **II** *vb* omdewlel; omladh; gwynnel

strut *vb* payoni

stubble *n* sowl *coll*

stubbly *adj* sowlek

stubborn *adj* gorth; treus; penn kales. **he is stubborn** kales yw y benn

stubbornness *n* gorthter *m*; er *m*

stuck *adj* stag. **get stuck** mos yn stag. **stuck up** ughel y dhewfrik

student *n* studhyer *m*, studhyoryon; skolheyk *m*, skolheygyon

studio *n* studhla *m*, studhleow

studious *adj* studhyus

study I *n* studhyans *m*, studhyansow; (*room*) studhva *f*, studhvaow **II** *vb* studhya

stuff I *n* daffar *m*; *n* devnydh *m*, devnydhyow; stoff *m*, stoffys **II** *vb* stoffya

stuffy *adj* klos

stumble I trebuchyans *m*, trebuchyansow **II** *vb* trebuchya

stun *vb* basa; gul dhe glamdera

stupefy *vb* sowdhanas; sowdheni

stupendous *adj* gorvarthys

stupid *adj* gocki; talsogh

stupidity *n* gockineth *f*

sturdy *adj* stordi

sty *n* krow *m*, krowyow. **pigsty** *n* krow mogh *m*, krowyow mogh

style *n* gis *m*, gisyow; (*manner*) kor *m*, korow. **literary style** gis-skrifa *m*, gisyow-skrifa

stylish *adj* herwydh an gis

sub- *prfx* is-

subject *n* (*topic*) testen *f*, testennow; mater *m*, materow, maters; (*academic*) devnydh *m*, devnydhyow; (*of monarch*) sojet *m*, sojets; (*grammar*) sojeta *m*, sojetys

subjunctive *adj* islavarek. **subjunctive mood** gis islavarek *m*

sublime *adj* gorughel

submarine *n* lester-sedhi *m*, lestri-sedhi

submerge *vb* sedhi

submersion *n* sedhes *m*, sedhesow

subscribe *vb* ragbrera

subscriber *n* ragbrerer *m*, ragbrenoryon

subscript *n* isskrif *m*

subscription *n* ragbren *m*, ragbrenow

subsequent *adj* iskevresek

subside *vb* omsedhi

subsidence *n* omsedhes *m*

subsidiary I *adj* gweresek **II** *n* iskowethyans *m*, iskowethyansow

subsidise *vb* ri gweres arghans

subsidy *n* arghans-gweres *m*, arghansow-gweres

substance *n* substans *f*, substansow; stoff *m*, stoffys

substandard *adj* issavonek

substantial *adj* krev; meur

substantive I *adj* substansek **II** *n* (*grammar*) hanow *m*, henwyn

subtitle I *n* istitel *m*, istitlow, istitlys **II** *vb* istitla

subtle *adj* sotel

subtlety *n* sotelneth *f*

subtract *vb* istenna; kemeres a^2

subtraction *n* istennans *m*, istenansow

suburb *n* ranndra *f*, ranndrevow; mestrev *f*, mestrevow

succeed *vb* seweni; spedya (*follow*) dos war-lergh

success *n* sewena *f*

successful *adj* sewen; sewenus

successive *adj* an eyl wosa y gila

successively *adv* yn rew

successor *n* er *m*, erys

succulent *adj* sugnus

such *adj, prn* (*like*) kepar ha; avel; a'n par na; pana². **such an idea!** pana dybyans!

suck *vb* sugna; dena. **sucking pig** porghellik *m*, porghelligow

sudden *adj* tromm

suddenly *adv* distowgh; a-dhesempis

sue *vb* sewya dre lagha

suet *n* soov *m*

suffer *vb* perthi; godhav; godhevel

suffering *n* godhevyans *m*

sufficient *adj* lowr a²

sufficiently *adv* lowr

suffocate *vb* taga

sugar I *n* sugra *m* II *vb* sugra. **sugar beet** *n* betysen sugra *f*, betysennow sugra; betys sugra *coll*

suggest *vb* profya; kussulya; gorra yn-rag

suggestion *n* profyans *m*, profyansow; kussul *f*, kussulyow

suicidal *adj* omladhansek

suicide *n* omladhans *m*, omladhansow. **commit suicide** omladha

suit I *n* (*clothes*) sewt *m*, sewtys; dillas *coll*, dillasen; (*law*) ken *m*, kenyow II *vb* desedha. **suit of cards** sewt kartennow *m*, sewtys kartennow

suitable *adj* gwiw; 'vas

suitcase *n* trog *m*, trogow

suite *n* (*series; music*) kevres *m*, kevresyow; (*set*) sett *m*, settys; (*retinue*) koskor *pl*

sulk I *n* moutyans *m*, moutyansow II *vb* moutya

sullen *adj* talgam

sulphur *n* (*element*) loskven *m*, loskveyn; sulfur *m*

sultana *n* (*fruit*) sodonesen *f*, sodonesennow; sodones *coll*

sum I *n* sommen *f*, somennow; somm *m*, sommow II *vb* somma

summarise *vb* berrskrifa

summary *n* berrskrif *m*, berrskrifow

summer I *n* hav *m*, havow, havyow II **pass the summer** *vb* havi

summery *adj* havek

summit (1) *n* penn *m*, pennow; gwartha *m*, gwarthevyon; barr *m*, barrow; topp *m*, toppys, toppow

summit (2) *n* (*meeting*) pennkuntelles *m*, pennkuntellesow

summon *vb* sompna; gelwel

sumptuous *adj* rych

sun *n* howl *m*, howlyow

sunbathe *vb* omhowla

sunburn *n* howllosk *m*, howlloskow

sunburnt *adj* howlleskys

Sunday *n* Sul *m*; dy'Sul *m*. **Sunday night** *n* dy'Sul dhe nos. **Low Sunday** Pask Byghan *m*

sundew *n* eylesen *f*, eylesennow; eyles *coll*

sunflower *n* bleujen an howl *f*

sunglasses *n* howlwedrow *pl*

sunhat *n* hatt howl *m*, hattow howl, hattys howl

sunny *adj* howlyek

sunrise *n* howldrehevel *m*, howldrehevelyow

sunset *n* howlsedhes *m*

sunstroke *n* towl howl *m*, towlow howl

suntan *n* liw howl *m*, liwyow howl

sup *vb* sopya

super *int* splann! marthys da!

superb *adj* bryntin; splann

superficial *adj* arenebel

superfluous *adj* dres edhom

superintend *vb* avisya

superintendant *n* avisyer *m*, avisyoryon

superior *adj* gwell; trygh. **superior to** gwell es

superlative I *adj* ughella **II** *n* gradh ughella *m*, gradhow ughella

supermarket *n* gorvarghas *f*, gorvarghasow

supernatural *adj* gornaturel

superscript *n* ughskrif *m*

superstition *n* hegoledh *m*, hegoledhow

superstitious *adj* hegol

supervise *vb* gorweles; menystra

supervision *n* menystrans *m*, menystransow

supervisor *n* gorwolyas *m*, gorwolysi

supper *n* soper *m*; kon *f*. **supper time** prys soper

supple *adj* gwedhyn; hebleth

supplement I *n* (*to a book*) ystynnans *m*, ystynansow; (*to diet*) keworrans *m*, keworransow **II** *vb* ystyn; keworra

supplementary *adj* keworransus

suppleness *n* gwedhynder *m*

supplier *n* provier *m*, provioryon

supply *vb* provia

support I *vb* skoodhya; (*financially*) ri gweres arghans. **support oneself** omskoodhya. **support together** kesskoodhya **II** *n* skoodhyans *m* skodhyansow. **mutual support** kesskoodhyans

supporter *n* skoodhyer *m*, skodhyoryon

suppose *vb* desevos; tybi. (**as**) **I suppose** dell dybav

supposedly *adv* yn tesevek

supremacy *n* gwarthevyans *m*

supreme *adj* gorughel

sure *adj* sur; diogel

surely *adv* sur; diogel; yn surredi; yn tiogel

surf I *n* mordardh *m* **II** *vb* mordardha. **surf the internet** rosya an

kesrosweyth

surface *n* enep *m*, enebow; arenep *m*, arenebow

surfboard *n* bord-mordardha *m*, bordow-mordardha

surgeon *n* leuvvedhek *m*, leuvvedhogyon

surgery *n* (*place*) medhegva *f*, medhegvaow; (*treatment*) leuvvedhegneth *f*, leuvvedhegnethow

surgical *adj* leuvvedhegel

surname *n* hanow teylu *m*, henwyn teylu

surpass *vb* gorbassya

surprise I *n* marth *m*, marthow **II** *vb* sowdhanas

surprising *adj* revedh

surprisingly *adv* marthys; yn farthys

surreal *adj* gorwir

surrender I *n* omrians *m*, omriansow **II** *vb* omri

surround *vb* bos yn-kerghyn; mos yn-kerghyn; kerghynna

surveillance *n* aspians *m*

survey I *n* arhwithrans *m*, arhwithransow **II** *vb* arhwithra

survival *n* treusvewans *m*, treusvewansow

survive *vb* treusvewa; durya

survivor *n* duryer *m*, duryoryon

susceptible *adj* gostydh

suspect I *adj* gogrysek **II** *n* gogrysek *m*, gogrysogyon **III** *vb* gogrysi; drogdybi; doutya

suspend *vb* (*hang*) kregi; (*interrupt; abort; cease*) astel

suspense *n* fienasow *pl*

suspension *n* (*construction; hanging*) krog *f*, krogow; kregans *m*, kregansow; (*interruption*) astel *m*, astelyow; (*chemical*) dalghennans *m*, dalghenansow

suspicion *n* gogrys *m*; dout *m*

suspicious *adj* gogrysus; skeusek. **to be suspicious** *vb* gogrysi; bos skeus dhe nebonan a neppyth. **I'm suspicious of her** yma skeus dhymm anedhi

sustain *vb* sostena

sustainability *n* sostenadewder *m*

sustainable *adj* sostenadow

sustenance *n* sosten *m*

swagger I *n* payonyans *m*, payonyansow II *vb* payoni

swallow (1) *n* (*bird*) gwennel *f*, gwenili

swallow (2) *vb* lenki; kolenki

swamp I *n* gwernen *f*, gwernennow; gwern *coll* II *vb* beudhi; liva

swampy *adj* gwernek

swan *n* alargh *m*, elergh

swank I *n* (*boaster*) bostyer *m*

swap I *n* keschanj *m*, keschanjyow II *vb* keschanjya

swarm *n* hes *f*, hesow

swear *vb* (*take an oath*) lia; ti; (*use bad language*) mollethi

sweat I *n* hwys *m* II *vb* hwysa. **sweat gland** gwagren hwys *f*, gwagrennow hwys

sweatshirt *n* krys hwys *m*, krysyow hwys

Swede *n* (*nationality*) Swed *m*, Swedys

swede *n* (*vegetable*) routabaga *m*, routabagys

Sweden *top* Sweden *m*

Swedish I *adj* swedek II *n* (*language*) Swedek *m*

sweep *vb* skubya

sweeper *n* skuber *m*, skuboryon

sweeping I *adj* skubus; ow skuba II *n* skub *m*, skubyon. **a sweeping statement** derivas ledan *m*. **sweeping reforms** amendyansow ledan *pl*

sweet I *adj* hweg II *n* hwegyn *m*, hwegennow. **very sweet** melys. **cough sweet** losanj pas *m*, losanjys pas

sweetcorn *n* hwegys *coll*; ys hweg *coll*

sweeten *vb* hwekhe; melyshe

sweetest *adj* hwegol

sweetheart *n* keresik *m*, keresigyon; kuv kolon *m*, kuvyon kolon

sweetness *n* melder *m*, melderyow

sweetshop *n* gwerthji hwegennow *m*, gwerthji hwegennow

swell *vb* hwedhi

swelling *n* bothen *f*, bothennow; hwedh *m*, hwedhow

swift I *adj* uskis; skav II *n* gwennel dhu *f*, gwenili du

swim *vb* neuvya. **swimming pool** *n* poll-neuvya *m*, pollow-neuvya

swimmer *n* neuvyer *m*, neuvyoryon

swimsuit *n* neuvwisk *m*; dillas-neuvya *coll*

swindle I *n* hyg *f*, hygow II *vb* hyga

swine *n* hogh *m*, hoghes; mogh *pl*

swing I *n* lesk *m*, leskow; lesk lovan *m* II *vb* leska

swirl I *n* troyll *m* (*f*), troyllyow II *n* troyllya

Swiss I *adj* swis II *n* (*person*) Swis *m*, Swisys. **Swiss German** Swisalmaynek *m*

switch I *n* skwychell *f*, skwychellow; skwych *m*, skwychys II *vb* skwychya; skwychella. **switch off** skwychya yn farow. **switch on** skwychya yn fyw

Switzerland *top* Pow Swis *m*

swollen *adj* kwoffys

swoon I *n* klamder *m*, klamderyow II *vb* klamdera

sword *n* kledha *m*, kledhedhyow. **wield a sword** *vb* kledhya

syllable *n* syllaben *f*, syllabennow

syllabus *n* dyskevres *m*, dyskevresow

symbol *n* arwodh *f*, arwodhyow; tokyn *m*, toknys

symbolic *adj* arwodhek

symbolise *vb* arwedhya

symbolism *n* arwodhogeth *f*

symmetrical *adj* kemusur

symmetry *n* kemusur *m*, kemusuryow

sympathetic *adj* keskolonnek; keskodhevek; tregeredhus

sympathy *n* keskolonekter *m*; tregeredh *f*; truedh *m*

symptom *n* arwodh *f*, arwodhyow; sin *m*, sinys, sinyow

synagogue *n* synaga *m*, synagys

synchronise *vb* kettermynegi

syndrome *n* syndrom *m*, syndromow; kleves *m*, klevesow. **Down's syndrome** syndrom Down *m*

synonym *n* ger kesstyr *m*, geryow kesstyr

synonymous *adj* kesstyr

synthetic *adj* synthesek

syringe *n* skitell *f*, skitellow

syrup *n* melysugen *m*, melysugenyow

system *n* kevreyth *m*, kevreythyow; system *m*, systemow

systematic *adj* systemasek

T

tab *n* tabb *m*, tabbow

table *n* moos *f*, mosow; bord *m*, bordys, bordow. **set the table** settya moos

tablecloth *n* lien moos *m*, lienyow moos

tablespoon *n* lo vras *f*, loyow bras

tablet *n* (*medicine*) pellennik *m*, pellenigow; (*IT*) leghen *f* leghennow

table tennis *n* tennis moos *m*

tabletop *n* bord *m*, bordow

taboo **I** *adj* tabou **II** *n* tabou *m*, tabous

taciturn *adj* tawesek

tack **I** *n* (*nail*) kentrik *m*, kentrigow **II** *vb* (*nail*) kentra orth

tackle (1) *n* (*outfit; gear*) aparel *m*, aparels

tackle (2) **I** *n* (*football*) taklans *m*, taklansow **II** *vb* takla

tackle (3) *vb* (*attempt*) attamya

tact *n* dothenep *m*; dothter *m*

tactful *adj* doth

tactic *n* taktek *m*, taktegow

tactless *adj* didhoth

tadpole *n* pennyn *m*, penynnow; penn du *m*, pennow du

tail *n* lost *m*, lostow

tailor *n* tregher *m*, treghoryon

tailoring *n* tregherieth *f*

take **I** *n* (*film*) tro *f*, troyow; (*fishing; hunting*) kachyans *m*, kachyansow **II** *vb* kemeres; (*e.g. a drink*) kavos; (*capture; confiscate*) sesya; (*pick out*) dewis. **it takes** (*it requires*) res yw. **take a bath** gul tronkys. **take a day off** kemeres dy'gol. **take after** omheveli dhe². **take along with** (*bring*) dri. **take a rest** powes. **take a seat** esedha. **take away** gorra dhe-ves. **take by surprise** sowdhanas. **take back** daskemeres. **take care** kemeres with. **take care of** gwitha; gorra with a². **take for granted** degemeres puptra avel neppyth dendylys; triga heb aswon gras a dra vyth. **take medicine** lenki medhegneth. **take off** (*clothes*) diwiska; omdhiwiska (*aeroplane*) yskynna. **take over** (*acquire, claim*) perghenegi. **take place** hwarvos. **take prisoner** sesya. **take revenge** diala. **take sick** kodha klav. **take someone, give a lift** gorra nebonan. **take that!** *int* (*sg*) tann henna! (*pl*) tannewgh henna! **take the side of** assentya gans. **take up** (*absorb*) lenki; (*accept*) degemeres; (*enter into a profession*) dos ha bos; mos ha bos; (*lift*) drehevel; (*shorten*) berrhe. **take up arms** mos dhe arvow

take-off *n* yskynnans *m*

tale *n* hwedhel *m*, hwedhlow; kedhel *m*, kedhlow. **fairy tale** hwedhel a'n dus vyghan *m*, hwedhlow a'n dus vyghan;

folk tale drolla *m*, drollow. **tell tales** hwedhla

talent *n* roas *m*, roasow; ro a natur *m*, rohow a natur, royow a natur

talented *adj* roasek

talk I *n* kows *m*, kowsow **II** *vb* kewsel; klappya. **it's all talk!** nyns yw marnas flows! **idle talk** flows *m*. **talk together** *vb* (*converse*) keskewsel

talkative *adj* tavosek

tall *adj* ughel; hir

tallness *n* ughelder *m*; hirder *m*

tallow *n* soov *m*

tally I *n* kevriv *m*, kevrivow **II** *vb* kevriva

talon *n* ewin *m*, ewines

tame I *adj* dov; hwar **II** *vb* dova; dovhe

tan I *adj* (*brown*) gell **II** *n* (*suntan*) liw howl *m* **III** *vb* (*sunburn*) howlleski; (*leather*) dyghtya kreghyn; (*beat*) kronkya

tangent *n* tavlinen *f*, tavlinennow

tangential *adj* tavlinennel

tangerine *n* tanjerin *m*, tanjerines

tangle *vb* maglenna; magli; dreysa

tank I *n* tank *m*, tankow. **fish tank** tank puskes *m*, tankow puskes. **petrol tank** tank petrol *m*, tankow petrol. **water tank** dowrargh *m*, dowrarghow **II** *vb* lenwel an tank. **fill up** (*petrol*) kollenwel an tank; (*alcohol*) omvedhwi

tanker *n* (*ship*) tanker *m*, tankeryow. **oil tanker** *n* tanker oyl *m*, tankeryow oyl

tanned *adj* (*sunburnt*) howlleskys

tansy *n* boton owr *m*, botonyow owr

tap I *n* tapp *m*, tappys, tappow **II** *vb* tardra

tape *n* snod *m*, snodys. **tape measure** musurell *f*, musurellow

tapestry *n* (*embroidered*) brosweyth *m*; (*woven*) brithlen *f*, brithlennow

tar I *n* pyg *m*; tar *m* **II** *vb* pega

target I *n* kosten *f*, kostennow **II** *vb* kostenna

tarry *vb* tarya

tart *n* tart *m*, tartys; tarten *f*, tartennow

tartan *n* brith *coll*

task *n* ober *m*, oberow; oberen *f*, oberennow; rann ober *f*, rannow ober

taste I *n* (*flavour*) blas *m*, blasow; sawor *m*, saworyow; (*aesthetic judgment*) discernyans *m*, discernyansow **II** *vb* blasa; sawra; (*try*) previ; (*have a distinct flavour*) bos gans sawer

tasteless *adj* anvlasus

tasty *adj* sawrek

tatter *vb* skethenna

tattoo *n* korfliw *m*, korfliwyow; tatou *m*, tatous

tatty *adj* pilennek

taunt I *n* tontyans *m*, tontyansow **II** *vb* tontya

tavern *n* tavern *m*, tavernyow; diwotti *m*, diwottiow; barr *m*, barrys; hostelri *m*, hostelriow

tax I *n* toll *f*, tollow **II** *vb* (*levy taxes*) tolli; (*try*) previ. **income tax** toll wober *f*, tollow gober. **land tax** toll dir *f*. **poll/council tax** toll an penn *f*, tollow an penn. **purchase tax** toll brenas *f*, tollow prenas. **stamp duty** toll stamp *f*, tollow stamp. **tax inspector** tellyas *m*, tellysi. **tax office** sodhva doll *f*, sodhvaow toll. **tax one's patience** previ an perthyans. **value added tax** toll dhaswerth *f*. **tax rate** kevradh toll *m*, kevradhow toll

taxable *adj* tolladow

tax-free *adj* didoll; heb toll

taxi *n* taksi *m*, taksiow

tea *n* te *m*. **tea-towel** *n* kweth te *f*, kwethow te

teach *vb* dyski. **teach someone to do something** dyski dhe² nebonan gul neppyth

teacher *n* dyskador *m*, dyskadoryon; dyskadores *f*, dyskadoresow

teaching *n* dyskas *m*; (*lesson*) dyskans *m*

teacup *n* hanaf te *m*, hanafow te *m*

team *n* para *m*, parys; bagas *m*, bagasow

teapot *n* pott te *m*, pottys te, pottow te

tear (1) *n* (*weeping*) dagren *f*, dagrennow; dager *m*, dagrow. **shed tears** devera dagrow; skollya dagrow; dagrewi

tear (2) *vb* (*rip*) skwardya

teardrop *n* dagren *f*, dagrennow

tease *vb* tontya; gul ges a^2

teasel *n* kribellow *f.pl*

teaspoon *n* lo de *f*, loyow te

teaspoonful *n* loyas te *f*, loyasow te

teat *n* hwennen *f*, hwenennow

teatime *n* prys te *m*

technical *adj* teknogel

technician *n* teknegydh *m*, teknegydhyon

technique *n* teknek *m*, teknegow

technological *adj* teknegiethel

technology *n* teknologieth *f*; teknegieth *f*

tectonic *adj* tektonek

tectonics *n* tektonieth *f*

teddy-bear *n* orsik *m*, orsigow

tedious *adj* skwithus

tedium *n* hirneth *f*

teenage *adj* degowek

teenager *n* degowek *m*, degowogyon

teetotal *adj* lasnaghus

teetotaller *n* lasnagher *m*, lasnaghoryon

telecommunication *n* pellgomunyans *m*, pellgomunyansow

telegram *n* pellskrifen *f*, pellskrifennow

telephone I *n* pellgowser *m*, pellgowseryow **II** *vb* pellgewsel. **telephone call** galow pellgows *m*, galowyow pellgows. **telephone number** *n* niver pellgowser *m*, niverow pellgowser

telescope *n* pellweler *m*, pellweloryow

televise *vb* darlesa

television *n* pellwolok *f*, pellwologow. **television channel** kanel bellwolok *f*, kanolyow pellwolok. **television programme** towlen bellwolok *f*, towlennow pellwolok

tell *vb* derivas; leverel; kedhla. **tell off** keredhi; tavosa; keski. **tell tales** hwedhla

temper I *n* (*disposition*) gnas *f*, gnasow **II** *vb* tempra

temperature *n* tempredh *m*, tempredhow; (*fever*) terthen *f*

tempest *n* hager-awel *f*, hager-awelyow

template *n* skantlyn *m*, skantlyns

temple (1) *n* (*place of worship*) tempel *m*, templow; templa *m*, templys

temple (2) *n* (*anat*) er *m*, eryow, *dl* dewer; tal *f* (*m*), talyow

temporarily *adv* dres pols; rag tro

temporary *adj* anbarghus; servadow; rag tro

tempt *vb* temptya; godhynya

temptation *n* temptyans *m*, temptyansow

tempting *adj* dynyek; tennvosek; (*enticing*) dynyansek

ten *num* deg

tenant *n* (*of hired property*) gobrener *m*, gobrenoryon

tend *vb* (*be inclined; move towards*) stumma troha; (*habit*) bos usys dhe^2; (*a patient*) gwitha; truedha

tendency *n* stummans *m*, stumansow; plegyans *m*, plegyansow; (*trend*) tuedh *m*, tuedhow

tender *adj* tender; bleudh

tenderness *n* bleudhder *m*

tendon *n* skenna *m*, skennow

tennis *n* tennis *m*

tenor *n* (*singing voice*) tenor *m*, tenoryon

tense (1) *adj* tynn

tense (2) *n* (*of verbs*) amser *f*, amseryow. **present tense** *n* amser a-lemmyn *f*. **imperfect tense** *n* amser anperfydh *f*. **perfect tense** *n* amser berfydh *f*. **pluperfect tense** *n* amser worberfydh *f*. **future tense** *n* amser a dheu *f*. **preterite tense** *n* amser dremenys *f*

tension *n* tynder *m*

tent *n* tylda *m*, tyldys, tyldow. **pitch a tent** *vb* tyldya

tentative *adj* a-gynnik

tenth *num* degves; *abbrev* 10ves

tenuous *adj* tanow

tepid *adj* mygyl

terabyte *n* terabayt *m*, terabaytys; *abbrev* TB

term *n* (*word*) ger *m*, geryow; term *m*, termys; (*academic*) termyn *m*; (*trimester*) trymis *m*, trymisyow

terminal *n* penn hyns *m*, pennow hyns

terminate *vb* gorfenna

terminology *n* termonieth *f*

terrace *n* terras *m*, terrassys, terrassow

terrestrial *adj* norvysel

terrible *adj* euthyk

terribly *adv* euthyk

terrific *adj* (*of size*) marthys bras; (*excellent*) splann; (*horrible*) euthyk

terrified *adj* ownek; dyegrys

terrify *vb* broweghi; euthega

territory *n* tiredh *m*, tiredhow

terror *n* euth *m*; euthekter *m*; browagh *m*, browaghow

terrorise *vb* broweghi

terrorism *n* broweghereth *f*

terrorist *n* broweghyas *m*, broweghysi

test I *n* prov *m*, provow; (*formal examination*) apposyans *m*, apposyansow II *vb* previ; tria; apposya

testament *n* (*Biblical*) testament *m*. **the New Testament** an Testament Nowydh *m*. **the Old Testament** an Testament Koth *m*

testicle *n* kell *f*, kellow, kellyow, *dl* diwgell

testify *vb* dustunia; desta

testimony *n* dustuni *m*, dustuniow

testy *adj* krowsek

tether I *n* stag *m*, stagow II *vb* staga

text *n* tekst *m*, tekstow. **text message** *n* messach tekst *m*, messajys tekst

text-book *n* dysklyver *m*, dysklyvrow

textile *n* pannweythen *f*, pannweyth

texture *n* gwiasedh *m*, gwiasedhow

than I *prp* ages II *cnj* es dell[2]

thank *vb* grassa; godhvos gras dhe[2]. **thank God!** meur ras dhe Dhuw! dhe Dhuw re bo grassys! **thank you!** meur ras dhis! meurastaji! **thank you very much!** (*informal*) meur ras bras! (*formal*) meur ras dhis/dhywgh yn feur. **thank you for ...** meur ras dhis/dhywgh a[2] ...

thankfully *adj* (*used with poss. adj, see p.9*) gwynn ... bys. **thankfully, everyone was OK** gwynn aga bys, pubonan o da lowr

thanks *n* gras *m*, grassow. **give thanks for** godhvos gras a[2]

that I *adj* (*demonstrative*) an ... na. **that man** an den na. II *prn* henna *m*; honna *f*; (*used before* **yw** *and* **o**) henn *m*; honn *f*; (*relative*) neb a[2]; a[2] III *cnj* y[5]; yth; dell[2]. **that not** na[2] (g). **that which** an pyth. **so that** rag may[5]; mayth

thatch I *n* sowl *coll* II *vb* sowlenna

thatcher *n* tior *m*, tioryon

thaw *vb* teudhi

the *art* an. **in the** y'n. **of the** a'n. **to the** dhe'n

theatre *n* gwariva *f*, gwarivaow; gwariji *m*, gwarijiow. **open-air theatre** *n* plen an gwari *m*, plenys an gwari

theatrical *adj* gwarijiel

theft *n* ladrynsi *m*; (*individual crime*) ladrans *m*

their *poss. adj* aga[3]

theirs *prn* dhedha; aga re *pl*. **it's theirs** i a'n pyw

them *prn* aga³; 'ga³; (*infixed*) 's. **by them** gansa. **for them** ragdha. **of them** anedha. **with them** gansa. **to them** dhedha

thematic *adj* themasek

theme *n* thema *m*, themys, themow

themselves *prn* aga honan

then I *adv* ena; y'n eur na II *cnj* ytho

theologian *n* duwonydh *m*, duwonydhyon

theology *n* duwonieth *f*

theorem *n* theorem *m*, theoremow

theoretical *adj* tybiethel

theory *n* tybieth *f*, tybiethow

therapy *n* yaghheans *m*, yaghheansow; sawment *m*; dyghtyans *m*, dyghtyansow

there *adv* ena. **from there, thence** *adv* alena. **to there, thither** *adv* dhi; di

thereabouts *adv* a-derdro

thereafter *adv* wosa henna

thereby *adv* dre henna; gans henna

therefore *adv* rag henna; alena; ytho

thermal *adj* tesel

thermometer *n* tempredhell *f*, tempredhellow

these I *adj* (*demonstrative*) an … ma II *prn* an re ma

they *prn* i; (*enclitic*) i

thick *adj* tew. **thick mist** kowas niwl *f*, kowasow niwl

thicken *vb* tewhe

thicket *n* prysk *m*, pryskys; perth *f*, perthi

thick-lipped *adj* tew y dhiwweus; musellek

thickness *n* tewder *m*

thief *n* lader *m*, ladron

thieve *vb* ladra

thigh *n* mordhos *f*, mordhosow, *dl* diwvordhos

thimble *n* byskon *f*, byskonyow

thin *adj* tanow; moon

thin out *vb* tanowhe

thing *n* taklen *f*, taklow; tra *f*, traow; pyth *m*, pythow

think *vb* tybi; prederi; (*believe*) krysi. **think of** (*remember*) perthi kov a². **think oneself to be** *vb* omsynsi

thinness *n* tanowder *m*, tanowderyow

third I *num* tressa II *n* tressa rann *f*; *abbrev* 3a. **the third day from now** *adv* godreva; godrevedh

thirdly *adv* tressa

thirst *n* seghes *m*

thirsty, be thirsty *adj* bos seghes dhe². **I am thirsty** yma seghes dhymm; seghes a'm beus

thirteen *num* tredhek

thirteenth *num* tredhegves; *abbrev* 13ves

thirtieth *num* degves warn ugens; *abbrev* 30ves

thirty *num* deg warn ugens

this I *adj* (*demonstrative*) an … ma II *prn* hemma *m*; homma *f*. **this is …** hemm yw … *m*; homm yw … *f*

thistle *n* askallen *f*, askallennow; askal coll

thistle, field *n* askallen bras *f*, askallennow pras

thistle, milk *n* askallen leth *f*, askallennow leth

thistle, sow *n* askallen vogh *f*, askallennow mogh

thither *adv* di; dhi

thorn *n* dren *m*, dreyn; (*bush*) spernen *f*, spern

thornback *n* rogha *m*, roghys; grija *m*, grijow

thorny *adj* drenek; spernek

thorough *adj* dien; kowal; leun

thoroughest *adj* purra

thoroughfare *n* fordh lan *f*, fordhow glan

thoroughly *adv* kowal; yn tien

those I *adj* (*demonstrative*) an … na II *prn* an re na. **all those who** seul a²; kemmys a²

though *cnj* kyn⁵; (*before vowels and h-*) kynth

thought *n* preder *m*, prederow; tybyans *m*, tybyansow

thoughtful *adj* prederus

thoughtless *adj* dibreder

thousand *num* mil² *m*, milyow

thousand times *adv* milweyth

thousandfold *adj* milblek

thousandth *num* milves; *abbrev* 1000ves

thrash *vb* dorna

thread I *n* neusen *f*, neusennow; neus *coll* **II** *vb* neusenna

threat *n* godros *m*, godrosow; braslavar *m*, braslavarow; (*danger*) peryl *m*, peryllyow

threaten *vb* godros; braggya

threatening *adj* godrosus

three *num* tri³ *m*; teyr³ *f*. **in three days time** *adv* godreva; godrevedh. **three times** *adv* teyrgweyth

threefold *adj* tryflek

thresh *vb* fusta

thresher *n* jynn-fusta *m*, jynnys-fusta, jynnow-fusta

threshold *n* treudhow *m*

thrift (1) *n* (*sea pink*) bryton *coll*; tamm on *m*

thrift (2) *n* (*saving money*) erbys *m*, erbysyow

thrill I *n* yaswan *f*, yaswanyow **II** *vb* yaswana

thrilling *adj* yaswanus

thrive *vb* seweni

throat *n* briansen *f*, briansennow

throne *n* tron *m*, tronys; se *m*, seys, seow

throng *n* routh *f*, routhow

through *prp* dre²; der; dres. **run through** berya. **through a door** war dharas. **through and through** pur

throughout *prp* dre bub rann; (*over all*) dres

throw I *n* towl *m*, towlow **II** *vb* tewlel. **throw away** *vb* tewlel dhe-ves; tewlel

dhe skoll; **throw down** *vb* disevel. **throw out** tewlel yn-mes. **throw up** *vb* (*vomit*) hwyja. **throw violently** deghesi

thrower *n* towler *m*, towloryon

thrush *n* molgh *f*, molghi. **song thrush** molgh loos *f*, molghi loos. **mistle thrush** molgh gerdhin *f*, molghes kerdhin

thrust *vb* herdhya; pockya

thug *n* bilen *m*, bilens; smat *m*, smatys

thuggish *adj* bilen

thumb *n* meus *m*, meusi; bys bras *m*, besies bras

thump I *n* kronk *m*, kronkys **II** *vb* kronkya; dorna

thunder I *n* taran *f*, tarennow **II** *vb* tarenna

thunderclap *n* tardh taran *m*, tardhow taran

thunderstruck *adj* dyegrys

Thursday *n* Yow *m*; dy'Yow *m*; **Thursday night** *n* dy'Yow dhe nos

thus *adv* (*like this*) yndelma; y'n fordh ma; (*like that*) yndella; y'n fordh na

thwart *vb* lesta

thyme *n* tim *m*

thyme, wild *n* kosfinellen *f*, kosfinellennow; kosfinel *coll*

tiara *n* kurunik *f*, kurunigow

tick I *n* (*short moment*) tecken *f*, teckennow **II** *vb* tyckya. **what makes you tick?** fatel usi dha vrys ow kweytha?

ticket *n* tokyn *m*, toknys. **ticket inspector** *n* tokynner *m*, tokynoryon. **ticket-office** *n* tokynva *f*, tokynvaow. **ticket machine** *n* jynn tokyn *m*, jynnow tokyn, jynnys tokyn. **return ticket** tokyn-mos ha dos *m*, toknys-mos ha dos

tickle *vb* debreni; kosa

ticklish *adj* hegos

tide *n* lanwes mor *m*; mortid *m*, mortidys. **high tide** *n* morlanow *m*, morlanowyow; lanow *m*, lanowyow.

low tide *n* trig *m*; mordrik *m*.

neap-tide *n* marvor *m*; marowvor *m*.

spring-tide *n* reverthi *f*, reverthiow; gorlanwes *m*, gorlanwesow

tidy I *adj* kempen; glanyth **II** *vb* kempenna

tie I *n* kolm *m*, kolmow; (*necktie*) kolm konna *m*, kolmow konna **II** *vb* kelmi. **tie... to...** kelmi... orth...

tier *n* nivel *m*, nivelyow

tiger *n* tiger *m*, tigres, tigri

tight *adj* tynn; strooth

tighten *vb* tynnhe; fastya

tightly *adv* yn tynn; yn strooth

tightrope *n* lovan dynn *f*, lovanow tynn

tightrope walker *n* kerdher lovan *m*, kerdhoryon lovan

tights *n* tynnow *pl*

tile *n* prileghen *f*, prileghennow

till (1) (= **until**) **I** *prp* bys; (*with nouns*) bys yn; (*with pronouns*) bys dhe² **II** *cnj* bys pan²; bys may⁵; (*before a consonant*) erna²; (*before a vowel*) ernag. **until next time!** bys dhe'n nessa tro!

till (2) *n* (*for paying*) rekenva *f*

till (3) *vb* (*work land*) gonis

tilt I *n* goleder *f*, goledrow **II** *vb* ynklinya

timber *n* (*beam*) prenn *m*, prennyer

time *n* termyn *m*, termynyow; prys *m*, presyow. **a long time ago** nans yw termyn hir. **a short time** pols *m*, polsyow. **a short time ago** a-gynsow. **at any time** war neb tro; neb prys. **at the same time** yn kettermyn. **at times** treweythyow. **a long time** pellder. **a very long time** hirneth *f*. **time-line** linen dermyn *f*. **by the time** erbynn. **in time** a-dermyn. **once upon a time** yn termyn eus passys. **on time** a-dermyn; a-brys. **three times** teyrgweyth. **what is the time** py eur yw. **spin out time** *vb* strechya

timely *adv* a-brys

timetable *n* euryador *m*, euryadoryow; rol dermynyow *f*, rolyow termynyow

timid *adj* gohelus; ownek

tin *n* (*element*) sten *m*; (*vessel, can*) kanna *m*, kannys, kannow; kavas *m*, kavasow. **tin-opener** *n* ygerell gannys *f*, ygerellow kannys

tin-bearing *adj* stenus

tinner *n* (*miner*) stenor *m*, stenoryon

tinstone *n* pryl *m*, prylyon

tint I *n* arliw *m*, arliwyow **II** *vb* arliwa

tiny *adj* munys

tip (1) I *n* (*point*) bleyn *m*, bleynyow; toppyn *m*, toppynnow **II** *vb* bleynya

tip (2) I *n* (*money*) grastal *m*, grastalyow **II** *vb* ri grastal

tip (3) I *n* (*tilt*) goleder *f*, goledrow **II** *vb* ynklinya; (*rubbish*) skollya. **rubbish tip** byjyon *m*, byjyons. **tip over** omhweles

tipsy *adj* govedhow

tire *vb* skwitha; skwithhe

tired *adj* skwith

tiresome *adj* skwithus

tiring *adj* skwithus

tissue *n* (*paper handkerchief*) lien paper *m*, lienyow paper

tit, long-tailed *n* pennik lost hir *m*, penniges lost hir

tit, marsh *n* penn pali gwern *m*, pennow pali gwern

titanium *n* (*element*) titaniom *m*

tithe *n* dega *m*, degedhow. **pay tithe** degevi

title *n* titel *m*, titlys, titlow

to *prp* dhe²; (*towards*) war-tu ha(g). **up to** bys; bys yn; bys dhe². **to the place** (*thither*) bys di

toad *n* kronek *m*, kronoges; kronek du *m*. **little toad** *n* kronegyn *m*, kronegynnow

toadflax, common *n* (*yellow*) lin gwyls *m*

toadflax, ivy-leaved *n* (*Kenilworth ivy; mother of thousands*) tron an leugh *m*

toadstool *n* skavel gronek *f*, skavellow kronek

toady *n* kraver tin *m*, kravoryon din

toast I *n* krasen *f*, krasennow; *n.coll* kras **II** *vb* krasa

toasted *adj* kras; kresys

toaster *n* krasell *f*, krasellow

tobacco *n* tobacko *m*

today *adv* hedhyw

toe *n* bys troos *m*, besies troos

toenail *n* ewin *m*, ewines

toffee *n* klyjien *f*, klyjiennow; klyji *coll*

together *adv* war-barth; ken-; kes-; kev-. **all together** pubonan war-barth. **together with** war-barth ha

toil I *n* lavur *m*; lavuryans *m* **II** *vb* lavurya

toilet *n* (*lavatory*) attesva *f*, attesvaow; privedhyow *pl*. **urinal** pisva *f*, pisvaow. **toilet paper** *n* paper privedhyow *m*

token *n* tokyn *m*, toknys; nos *m*, nosow

tolerable *adj* porthadow

tolerance *n* perthyans *m*, perthyansow

tolerant *adj* meur y berthyans *m*; meur hy ferthyans *f*; meur aga ferthyans *pl*

tolerate *vb* perthi; godhav; godhevel

toll *n* (*tax*) toll *f*, tollow

toll booth *n* tollva *f*, tollvaow

toll-gate *n* tollborth *m*, tollborthow

tomato *n* aval kerensa *m*, avalow kerensa

tomb *n* logel *m*, logelyow; bedh *m*, bedhow

tombstone *n* men bedh *m*, meyn bedh

tomorrow *adv* a-vorow. **on the day after tomorrow** *adv* trenja. **tomorrow morning** ternos vyttin

tone *n* ton *m*, tonyow; son *m*, sonyow

tongs *n* gevel *f*, gevelyow

tongue *n* taves *m*, tavosow. **mother tongue** *n* mammyeth *f*, mammyethow

tonic *adj* tonek. **tonic water** dowr tonek *m*

tonight *adv* haneth

tonne *n* tonnas *m*, tonasow

tonsil *n* kilwagren *f*, kilwagrennow

tonsillitis *n* (*med*) tonsilitis *m*

too *adv* (*also*) ynwedh; maga ta; keffrys; (*too far, too great etc.*) re[2]. **too many, too much** *adv* re (a[2]). **too much money** re a vona; re a arghans. **too many people** re a dus

tool *n* toul *m*, toulys

toolbar *n* (*IT*) toulvarr *m*, toulvarrys

toolbox *n* toulgist f, toulgistyow

tooth *n* dans *m*, dens. **back tooth** dans dhelergh *m*, dens dhelergh. **armed to the teeth** ervys bys y'n dhiwen. **bare one's teeth** grysla. **canine tooth** dans lagas *m*, dens lagas. **front tooth** dans rag *m*, dens rag. **milk tooth** dans-sugna *m*, dens-sugna. **wisdom tooth** dans keyn *m*, dens keyn. **have a tooth out** kavos dans tennys yn-mes

toothache *n* drog dans *m*, drogow dans; payn dens *m*, paynys dens

toothbrush *n* skubyllen dhens *f*, skubyllennow dens

toothpaste *n* dehen dens *m*

toothy *adj* dynsek

top I *adj* gwartha; penn- **II** *n* penn *m*, pennow; topp *m*, toppys, toppow **III** *vb* (*crop*) dibenna; (*excel; dominate*) fetha. **off the top of one's head** heb pareusi. **on top** a-wartha. **on top of** a-wartha dhe[2]. **on top of the world** gwynn y vys *m*. **top up** arlenwel

topic *n* testen *f*, testennow

tor *n* karn *m*, karnow

Torah *n* Tora *m*

torch *n* faglen *f*, faglennow

torment I *n* torment *m*, tormentys **II** *vb* tormentya

torque *n* torgh *f*, tergh

torrent *n* keynres *m*, keynresyow

tortoise *n* kronek ervys *m*, kronogow ervys; melhwioges *f*, melhwiogesow; kroban *m*, krobanes

torture I *n* torment *m*, tormentys **II** *vb* tormentya

Tory *n* Tori *m*, Toris

total I *adj* (*whole*) kowal; (*complete*) leun **II** *n* somm *m*, sommow; sommen *f*, somennow

totally *adv* yn tien

totter *vb* trebuchya

touch I *n* toch *m*, tochys; (*sense*) tava *m*, tavow **II** *vb* tava; tochya. **in touch** yn-dann dava. **keep in touch with** kestava gans

touch-line *n* linen denewen *f*, linennow tenewen

touch-pad *n* tochpad *m*, tochpadys

touch-screen *n* tochskrin *m*, tochskrinyow

tough *adj* kales

tour *n* torn *m*, tornys, tornow

tourism *n* tornyaseth *f*

tourist *n* tornyas *m*, tornysi; (*summer visitor*) havyas *m*, havysi; (*offensive*) moryonen *f*, moryonennow; moryon *coll*

tow *vb* halya

towards I *adv* war-tu **II** *prp* war-tu ha(g); (*before consonants*) troha; (*before vowels*) trohag

towel *n* towel *m*, towellow; mantel *m*, mantylli

tower *n* tour *m*, touryow

town *n* tre, trev *f*, trevow. **the town council** *n* konsel an dre *m*. **town councillor** *n* konseler a'n dre *m*. **the town hall** *n* hel an dre *f*. **in town** y'n dre

townsperson *n* burjes *m*, burjysi

toxic *adj* gwenonek; venymys

toy I *n* gwariell *f*, gwariellow; tegen *f*, tegennow **II** *vb* trufla. **toy-shop** *n* gwerthji gwariellow *m*, gwerthjiow gwariellow

trace I *n* (*art*) tresen *f*, tresennow; (*track*) lergh *m*, lerghow; (*harness*) syg *f*, sygow; (*link*) kadon *f*, kadonyow **II** *vb* tresya

track I *n* (*trace*) lergh *m*, lerghow; ol *m*, olow; (*footstep*) kamm *m*, kammow **II** *vb* helerghi

trackless *adj* hepforch

track-suit *n* reswisk *m*, reswiskow

tractor *n* jynn-tenna *m*, jynnys-tenna, jynnow-tenna

trade I *n* (*commerce*) kenwerth *m*, kenwerthow; trad *m*, tradys; (*handcraft*) kreft *f*, kreftow **II** *vb* kenwertha; marghasa. **trade union** kesunyans lavur *m*, kesunyansow lavur

trader *n* gwikor *m*, gwikoryon; marchont *m*, marchons

tradition *n* hengov *m*, hengovyow

traditional *adj* hengovek

traffic *n* daromres *m*, daromresow. **traffic lights** *n* golowys fordh *pl*. **traffic jam** *n* daromdak *m*, daromdagow

tragedy *n* trajedi *m*, trajediow

tragic *adj* trajek

trail *n* lergh *m*, lerghow; ol *m*, olow

trailer *n* draylyer *m*, draylyoryon

train (1) *n* (*railway*) tren *m*, trenow. **train driver** lewyer tren *m*, lewyoryon tren. **train journey** viaj tren *m*, viajyow tren, viajys tren

train (2) *vb* dyski; trenya. **train somebody to do something** dyski dhe nebonan gul neppyth

trainer *n* (*teacher*) dyskador *m*, dyskadoryon; dyskadores *f*, dyskadoresow; (*shoe*) eskis sport *f*, eskisyow sport

training *n* trenyans *m*, trenyansow

trait *n* gnasen *f*, gnasennow; (*attributes, pl.*) teythi *pl*

traitor *n* traytour *m*, traytours

tram *n* karr stret *m*, kerri stret; tram *m*, tramyow

tramp *n* (*offensive*) gwyll *m*, gwyllyow; skajyn *m*, skajynnow; loselwas *m*, loselwesyon

trample *vb* stankya; trettya

tranquil *adj* kosel

tranquiliser *n* kalmydh *m*, kalmydhyon

tranquility *n* kosoleth *f*; kalmynsi *m*

transact *vb* treuswul

transaction *n* treuswrians *m*, treuswriansow; negys *m*, negysyow

transfer I *n* treusporth *m*, treusporthow; treusworrans *m*, treusworransow II *vb* treusperthi; treusworra

transform *vb* treusfurvya

transgender *adj* treusreydhedhek

transit I *n* treustremen *m*, treustremenow II *vb* treustremena. **transit area** treustremenva *f*, treustremenvaow

transitory *adj* tremenadow; brottel

translate *vb* treylya

translation *n* treylyans *m*, treylyansow

translucent *adj* treussplanadow

transmission *n* treuskorrans *m*, treuskorransow; danvonadow *m*

transmit *vb* treuskorra; transmyttya

transmitter *n* treuskorrell *f*, treuskorrellow

transparent *adj* treusweladow; boll; ylyn

transplant I *n* treusplansans *m*, treusplansansow II *vb* treusplansa

transport I *n* treusporth *m*, treusporthow; karyans *m*, karyansow II *vb* treusperthi; karya. **public transport** karyans poblek *m*

transvestite *n* treuswisker *m*

trap I *n* maglen *f*, maglennow II *vb* maglenna; bagha

trapdoor *n* lo an jowl *f*, loyow an jowl

trashy *adj* skubellek

trauma *n* (*med*) trawma *m*

travel *vb* viajya; (*on foot*) travalya

Traveller *n* Tremenys *m*, Tremenysi. (*see also: Gypsy, Roma*)

traveller *n* tremenys *m*, tremenysi

tray *n* servyour *m*, servyours; tallyour *m*, tallyours

treacherous *adj* traytus; fals; gowek

treachery *n* falsuri *m*; traytouri *m*

tread I *n* stank *m*, stankyow II *vb* stankya

treadle *n* trosla *f*, trosleow

treason *n* trayson *m*

treasure I *n* tresor *m*, tresorys, tresoryow II *vb* tresorya

treasurer *n* alhwedhor *m*, alhwedhoryon

treasury *n* tresorva *f*, tresorvaow

treat *vb* dyghtya

treated *adj* dyghtys

treatment *n* dyghtyans *m*

treaty *n* kevambos *m*, kevambosow

treble I *adj* tryflek II *n* (*music*) trebyl *m*, trebylyon

tree *n* gwedhen *f*, gwedhennow; gwydh *coll*. **apple tree** avalen *f*, avalennow. **Christmas tree** gwedhen Nadelik *f*, gwydh Nadelik. **dead tree** seghen *f*, seghennow

treecreeper *n bird* kramyerik *m*, kramyeriges

trefoil *n* teyrdel *coll*

trefoil, birdsfoot *n* pys an gath *coll*

tremble *vb* krena

trend *n* tuedh *m*, tuedhow

trespass I *n* treuspas *m*, treuspassow; kammweyth *m* II *vb* kammdremena; treuspassya

trespasser *n* kammdremener *m*, kammdremenoryon

trial *n* (*test*) prov *m*, provow; (*law*) trial *m*, trials; (*attempt*) assay *m*, assays

triangle *n* trihorn *m*, trihern

triangular *adj* trihornek

tribal *adj* lothel

tribe *n* looth *m*, lothow; kordh *m*, kordhow

tributary *n* ragavon *m*, ragavonyow, ragavenow

tribute *n* trubyt *m*

trick I *n* (*prank*) pratt *m*, prattys, prattow; (*cheat*) hyg *f*, hygow; (*dodge*) kast *m*, kastys; (*knack*) wrynch *m*, wrynchys **II** *vb* gul pratt; hyga; kastya

trickle *vb* devera

tricky *adj* (*delicate*) tyckli; (*dodgy*) kastek

tricycle *n* teyrros *f*, teyrrosow

trifle I *n* (*small matter*) truflen *f*, truflennow; (*dessert*) trifel *m*, trifellow **II** *vb* trufla

trifling *adj* trufel

trillion *num* (10^{12}) trilvil^2 *m*, trilvilyow

trim I *adj* taklys yn ta **II** *vb* godreghi; takla; dyghtya

trimester *n* trymis *m*, trymisyow

trip I *n* viaj *m*, viajyow, viajys **II** *vb* omdhisevel; (*trip up*) disevel; trebuchya

tripe *n* (*organ meat*) klout bolghen *m*; (*nonsense*) flows *m*

triple *adj* try-; tryflek

triumphant *adj* gormoledhek; trygh

trivial *adj* trufel; anposek

trolley *n* karigell *f*, karigellow

troop *n* lu *m*, luyow; koskor *pl*; mayni *m*, mayniow

trope *n* trop *m*, tropys

tropic *n* trovan *m*, trovannow

tropical *adj* trovannel; tropek

trot I *n* ponyans *m* **II** *vb* ponya

trouble I *n* ahwer *m*; kedrynn *f*; trobel *m*, troblys, troblow **II** *vb* trobla; serri. **give somebody trouble** grevya dhe nebonan. **what's the trouble with you?** pandr'a hwer dhis?

troubled *adj* troblys

troublesome *adj* fyslek

trough *n* hester *m*, hesteryow; new *f*, newyow

trousers *n* lavrek *m*, lavrogow

trout *n* truth *m*, truthes, truthow

trowel *n* lo-balas *f*, loyow-palas

truancy *n* mynchyars *m*

truant I *n* mynchyer *m*, mynchyoryon **II** *vb* (*play truant*) mynchya

truce *n* powes-omladh *m*, powesow-omladh

truck *n* kert *m*, kertys, kertow

true *adj* gwir

truly *adv* devri; yn tevri; dhe wir; yn hwir; heb wow

trumpet *n* hirgorn *m*, hirgern; trompa *m*, trompys

trunk *n* (*tree*) ben *m*, benyow; (*box*) kofer *m*, kofrow; (*animal*) tron *m*, tronow; (*car boot*) tog *m*, trogow

trust I *n* trest *m*; fydhyans *m* **II** *vb* trestya dhe^2; (*have faith*) fydhya; (*lend ear, entrust*) kola. **National Trust** Trest Kenedhlek *m*. **trust me!** trest dhymm! **trust in** trestya yn

trustworthy *adj* trestadow

trusty *adj* lel

truth *n* gwiryonedh *m*, gwiryonedhow; gwir *m*, gwiryow

truthful *adj* gwiryon

try I *n* assay *m*, assays **II** *vb* hwilas; assaya; previ; tria

T-shirt *n* krys T *m*, krysyow T

tsunami *n* tsunami *f*, tsunamiow

tub *n* kibel *f*, kibellow; keryn *f*, kerynyow. **hot tub** kibel domm *f*, kibellow tomm

tube *n* piben *f*, pibennow. **the Tube** *n* (*London Underground*) an Bib *f*

tuberculosis *n* (*colloq*) pla gwynn *m*; (*med*) tuberculosis *m*

Tuesday *n* Meurth *m*; dy'Meurth *m*. **Tuesday night** *n* dy'Meurth dhe nos

tuft *n* toos *m*, tosow

tug I *n* tenn *m*, tennow; krog *f*, krogow **II** *vb* tenna

tug-boat *n* tennlester *m*, tennlestri**

tug-of-war *n* kesstrif-tenna *m*, kesstrifow-tenna

tuition *n* dyskans *m*, dyskansow.
  tuition fees feow dyskans *m*

tulip *n* bleujen tulyfant *f*, bleujyow tulyfant

tumble I *n* kodh *m*, kodhow **II** *vb* kodha

tumbler *n* (*glass*) gwedren *f*, gwedrennow

tummy *n* torr *m*, torrow

tumour *n* hwedh *m*, hwedhow

tumult *n* tervans *m*, tervansow

tumulus *n* krug *m*, krugow

tuna *n* touna *m*, tounas

tune I *n* ton *m*, tonyow **II** *vb* tonya

tuneless *adj* didon

tunic *n* pows *f*, powsyow

tunnel *n* kowfordh *f*, kowfordhow

turban *n* tulyfant *m*, tulyfantys

turf *n* kesen *f*, kesennow; kesow *coll*

Turk *n* Turk *m*, Turkys

Turkey *top* Turki *f*

turkey *n* yar Gyni *f*, yer Gyni

Turkish I *adj* turek **II** *n* (*language*) Turek *m*. **Turkish coffee** koffi turek *m*, koffiow turek. **Turkish delight** melyssand turek *m*, melyssandys turek

turmoil *n* tervans *m*, tervansow

turn I *n* (*of wheel; in taking turns*) tro *f*, troyow; torn *m*, tornys; stumm *m*, stummow **II** *vb* treylya. **at every turn** pub torn. **backward turn** kildro *f*, kildroyow. **U-turn** treylyans U *m*, treylyansow-U. **turn around** omdreylya. **turn away from** treylya dhyworth. **turn back** dehweles. **turn into** omwul. **turn off** (*switch*) skwychya yn-mes; skwychya yn farow; ladha. **turn on** (*switch*) skwychya yn fyw; enowi. **do a good turn** gul torn da

turncoat *n* negedhys *m*, negedhysyon

turning *n* stumm *m*, stummow.
  turning point troboynt *m*, troboyntys,

troboyntow; treylva *f*, treylvaow

turnip *n* ervinen *f*, ervinennow; ervin *coll*

turret *n* tourik *m*, tourigow

turtle *n* morgroban *m*, morgrobanes

tutor *n* dyskador *m*, dyskadoryon; dyskadores *f*, dyskadoresow

tutorial I *adj* dyskansus **II** *n* dyskans *m*, dyskansow

TV *n* pellwolok *f*, pellwologow; (*abbrev*) PW

twelfth *num* dewdhegves; *abbrev* 12ves

twelve *num* dewdhek

twentieth *num* ugensves; *abbrev* 20ves

twenty *num* ugens

twenty-first *num* kynsa warn ugens

twice *adv* diwweyth

twig *n* barren *f*, barrennow

twiggy *adj* barrek

twilight *n* mo *m*. **morning twilight** boragweyth *f*

twin I *n* gevel *m*, gevellyon, gevellas **II** *vb* (*towns*) gevella

twinkle *vb* terlentri

twinkling *adj* terlenter

twinned *adj* (*towns*) gevellys

twist *vb* gwia; kamma; stumma; (*spin, braid*) nedha; (*coil*) terghi

twisted *adj* stummys

twitch I *n* skwych *m*, skwychys **II** *vb* skwychya

two *num* dew^2 *m*; diw^2 *f*

twofold *adj* dewblek

type I *n* (*kind*) eghen *f*, eghennow; sort *m*, sortow; par *m*, parow **II** *vb* jynnskrifa

typewrite *vb* jynnskrifa

typewriter *n* jynn-skrifa *m*, jynnys-skrifa, jynnow-skrifa

typical *adj* tipek

typist *n* jynnskrifer *m*, jynnskriforyon

tyrannical *adj* turantiel

tyrannise *vb* gul maystri war^2

tyranny *n* turantieth *f*

tyrant *n* turant *m*, turans

tyre *n* bonden *f*, bondennow

U

udder *n* teth *f*, tethi; tethen *f*, tethennow
UFO *n* tra neyja anaswonys (TNA) *f*; (*flying saucer*) padellik-neyja *f*, padelligow-neyja
ugh *int* ogh
uglier *adj* hakkra
ugliest *adj* (an) hakkra
uglify *vb* hagra
ugliness *n* hakter *m*
ugly *adj* hager. **make ugly** hagra
Ukraine *top* Ukrayn *f*
Ukrainian I *adj* ukraynek II *n* (*language*) Ukraynek *m*; (*person*) Ukraynian *m*, Ukraynians
ulcer *n* goli byw *m*, goliow byw
ultimate *adj* diwettha
ultimately *adv* wortiwedh; wostiwedh; war an diwedh
ultrasonic *adj* ughsonek
ultrasound *n* ughson *m*, ughsonyow
ultraviolet *adj* ughviolet
umbrella *n* glawlen *f*, glawlennow
un- *prfx* an-; di-; dis-; heb
unable *adj* diallos; (*unable to speak*) omlavar; (*unable to move*) stag; anteythi
unabridged *adj* heb kotheans
unacceptable *adj* ankemeradow
unaccompanied *adj* y honan oll *m*; hy honan oll *f*
unaccountable *adj* (*unanswerable*) diambos; (*unexplained*) heb styryans
unalike *adj* ankespar
unanimous *adj* keskolon; unver
unattached *adj* anstag
unavoidable *adj* anwoheladow
unaware *adj* diswar
unbalanced *adj* diomborth
unbearable *adj* anporthadow
unbeatable *adj* antryghadow
unbelievable *adj* ankrysadow

unbelieving *adj* ankryjyk
unbroken *adj* anterrys
uncertain *adj* ansur; ansertan; diantel
uncertainty *n* ansurneth *f*, ansurnethow
uncivil *adj* didhoth
uncle *n* ewnter *m*, ewntres
unclean *adj* avlan
unclear *adj* diskler; andhiblans; ankler
uncomfortable *adj* anes
uncommon *adj* ankemmyn
unconcealed *adj* digudh
unconcerned *adj* divern
unconscious *adj* (*fainting*) klamderek; (*unaware*) diswar. **fall unconscious** klamdera
unconsciously *adv* heb godhvos
unconstitutional *adj* erbynn korf an lagha
uncooked *adj* kriv
uncover *vb* diskudha; (*betray*) diskevra
undeniable *adj* anaghadow
under I *adv* (*location*) a-woles; (*direction*) war-woles II *prp* yn-dann^2. **from under** *prp* a-dhann^2
underdeveloped *adj* re voghes y dhisplegyans
undergraduate I *adj* isradhek II isradhesik *m*, isradhesigyon
underground *adj* yn-dann dhor. **London Underground** an Bib *f*
underhand *adj* kudhoberys
underline *vb* islinya; (*stress*) posleva
undermine *vb* palas yn-dann
underneath I *adv* a-woles II *prp* yn-dann^2
underpants *n* islavrek *m*, islavrogow
understand *vb* konvedhes
understanding *n* (*comprehension*) konvedhes *m*; (*agreement*) unverheans *m*, unverheansow; akord *m*

undertake *vb* omgemeres. **undertake to** omsettya dhe²

undertaker *n* omgemeryas *m*, omgemerysi; (*funeral director*) ynkleudhyer *m*, ynkleudhyoryon

undertaking *n* omgemeryans *m*, omgemeryansow; charj *m*, charjys

underwater *adj* yn-dann dhowr

underwear *n* dillas nessa *m*

undesirable *adj* andhesiradow

undeveloped *adj* heb displegya

undo *vb* (*destroy*) diswul; (*untie*) digelmi

undoing *n* diswrians *m*, diswriansow

undone *adj* diswrys; (*e.g. a knot*) digelmys

undoubted *adj* andhoutys

undoubtedly *adv* heb dhout

undress *vb* diwiska; omdhiwiska

undrinkable *adj* anevadow

unearthly *adj* annorel

uneasy *adj* anes

unelected *adj* anetholys

unemployed *adj* diweyth; heb hwel

unemployment *n* diweythieth *f*. **unemployment benefit** gober diweythieth *m*, gobrow diweythieth

unequal *adj* dispar

unequalled *adj* heb par; somper

uneven *adj* ankompes; digompes

unexpected *adj* anwaytys

unfailing *adj* anfalladow

unfair *adj* anewn

unfaithful *adj* dislen

unfamiliar *adj* anaswonys

unfasten *vb* difastya

unfavourable *adj* disfaverus

unfold *vb* (*develop*) displegya; (*show*) displetya; (*spread*) lesa

unfortunate *adj* truan; anfeusik

unfortunately *adv* y'n gwettha prys

unfriendly *adj* anhwek; diguv

unfurnished *adj* gwag; heb mebel

ungracious *adj* ongrassyes

ungrateful *adj* ongrassyes

unhappy *adj* anlowen

unharmed *adj* salow; dibystik

unhealthy *adj* anyagh

unholy *adj* ansans

unhurt *adj* dibystik

uni- *prfx* un-

uniform I *adj* unform; a unn eghen **II** *n* unform *m*, unformys

unilateral *adj* untu

unimpaired *adj* anaperys

unimportant *adj* diboos; anposek

uninhabitable *adj* ananedhadow

uninhabited *adj* ananedhys

unintelligent *adj* diskians

unintentional *adj* didowl

uninterrupted *adj* anwoderrys

union *n* kesunyans *m*, kesunyansow; unyans *m*, unyansow. **European Union** Unyans Europek *m*. **trade union** kesunyans lavur *m*, kesunyansow lavur

unionist I *adj* unyansydhel **II** *n* (*trade unionist*) esel a gesunyans lavur *m*, eseli a gesunyans lavur; (*party political*) unyansydh *m*, unyansydhyon

unique *adj* unnik; dibarow; heb parow

unit *n* (*mathematics, physics*) unses *m*; (*teaching*) dyskans *m*

unite *vb* unya; kesunya; kyjya

united *adj* unys. **the United Nations (UN)** an Kenedhlow Unys (KU) *pl*. **the United States (US)** an Statys Unys (SU) *pl*. **the United Kingdom (UK)** an Ruvaneth Unys (RU) *f*

unity *n* unses *m*; unita *m*

universal *adj* ollvysel

universe *n* ollvys *m*

university *n* pennskol *f*, pennskolyow

unjust *adj* anewn; kammhynsek; anjust

unkind *adj* anhwek; diguv; dignas

unknown *adj* ankoth; anwodhvedhys

unlawful *adj* anlaghel; erbynn an lagha

unless *cnj* marnas

unlike *adj* dihaval

unlikely *adj* diwirhaval. **it's unlikely** skant ny yll bos

unlimited *adj* heb finweth; difinweth

unload *vb* diskarga

unlock *vb* dialhwedha

unlucky *adj* anfeusik

unmarried *adj* dibries; andhemedhys

unnatural *adj* dignas; dinatur

unnecessary *adj* heb res

unoccupied *adj* (*not employed*) heb hwel; (*vacant*) gwag; (*uninhabited*) diannedh

unofficial *adj* ansodhogel

unopened *adj* anygerys

unopposed *adj* dienebys

unpack *vb* difardella; (*unload*) diskarga

unpaid *adj* heb tyli

unpleasant *adj* divlas; disawor

unplug *vb* disebilya

unpopular *adj* ankerys

unpredictable *adj* andharganadow

unprejudiced *adj* heb ragvreus

unprotected *adj* diwith

unqualified *adj* anwiw

unquestionably *adv* heb dhout

unravel *vb* freudha

unreasonable *adj* anresnadow; avresonus

unrecognised *adj* anaswonys

unrelated (*separate*) ankelmys; diblans; (*not relatives*) heb bos unwos

unreliable *adj* andhiogel

unrest *n* ankres *m*

unrestrained *adj* difron

unrighteous *adj* kammhynsek

unripe *adj* kriv; anadhves

unroll *vb* dirolya

unsafe *adj* diantel

unsatisfactory *adj* dilowr; anplegadow

unsatisfied *adj* diskontentys

unscrew *vb* didrogentra

unseen *adj* diwel

unsettle *vb* ankombra

unskilled *adj* digreft

unstable *adj* diantel. **emotionally unstable** es y vovya *m*; es hy movya *f*

unsteady *adj* diantel

unsuccessful *adj* heb sewena

unsuitable *adj* anwiw

untethered *adj* anstag

untidiness *n* strol *m*

untidy *adj* ankempen; digempen

untie *vb* digelmi

untied *adj* digelmys

until (= **till** (**1**)) **I** *prp* bys; (*with nouns*) bys yn; (*with pronouns*) bys dhe[2] **II** *cnj* bys pan[2]; bys may[5]; (*before a consonant*) erna[2]; (*before a vowel*) ernag. **until next time!** bys dhe'n nessa tro!

untimely *adj* mes a'y dermyn

untouchable *adj* antavadow

untrue *adj* anwir

untruth *n* anwirder *m*; gow *m*, gowyow

untruthful *adj* gowek

unusual *adj* koynt; anusadow

unveil *vb* dislenni

unwary *adj* diswar

unwelcome *adj* didhynnargh

unwell *adj* anyagh; klav

unwilling *adj* anvodhek

unwise *adj* anfur; dibreder

unworthy *adj* anwiw

unwrap *vb* dismaylya

up *adv* yn-bann; war-vann. **stand up!** sav yn-bann! **speak up!** kows yn ughel! **is she up yet?** usi hi a'y sav hwath? **up the street** an stret yn-bann. **up to date** arnowydh. **what's up?** pandr'a hwer?

update *vb* nowedhi

upgrade *vb* gwellhe; (*IT*) ughradha

uphill *adv* yn-bann; war venydh

upload I *n* (*IT*) ughkarg *m*, ughkargow **II** *vb* ughkarga

upon *prp* war[2]; orth; yn-kerghyn; (*in oaths*) re[2]. **once upon a time** yn termyn eus passy(e)s

upper *adj* gwartha**

uppity *adj* gorth; treus

upright *adj* serth; syth; (*morally*) ewnhynsek

uprising *n* sordyans *m*, sordyansow; omsav *m*, omsavow; rebellyans *m*, rebellyansow

uproar *n* habadolya *m*

upset I *adj* distemprys II *vb* distrempra; (*turn upside-down*) disevel; trehweles

upsetting *adj* trehwelus

upside-down *adv* (an pyth) a-wartha dhe-woles; war y benn

upstairs I *adv* war-vann; war-wartha

upwards *adv* war-vann; yn-bann

uranium *n* (*element*) uraniom *m*

Uranus *n* Ouranos *m*

urban *adj* trevek; trevel

urchin *n*. **sea urchin** morsort *m*

urge I *n* ynni *m*, yniow II *vb* ynia

urgency *n* yniadow *m*

urgent *adj* yniadow; ter. **it is urgent** res porres yw

urgently *adv* porres. **ask urgently** pysi tynn

urinal *n* pisva *f*, pisvaow

urinate *vb* pisa

urine *n* pisas *m*; urin *m*

us *prn* ni; (*infixed*) 'gan; (*emphatic*) nyni. **by us** genen. **for us** ragon. **to us** dhyn. **of us** ahanan. **with us** genen

use I *n* devnydh *m*, devnydhyow; us *m*, usyow, usadow; usyans *m*, usyansow II *vb* usya. **in use** yn usyans. **make use of** gul devnydh a². **put to good use** gul devnydh da a²

used *adj* usys; devnydhys. **I'm not used to it** nyns yw ev ow usadow. **I used to do it** my a'n gwre

useful *adj* dhe les; 'vas

usefulness *n* les *m*; talvosogeth *f*

useless *adj* pilyek; diles. **useless person** (*offensive*) pilyek *m*, pilyogyon

user *n* devnydhyer *m*, devnydhyoryon; usyer *m*, usyoryon. **username** hanow usyer *m*. **user-friendly** heweres. **user identity** honanieth usyer *f*, honaniethow usyoryon

usual *adj* usys; usadow. **as usual** herwydh usadow; dell yw usys

usually *adv* herwydh usadow; dell yw usys

utensil *n* lester *m*, lestri

uterus *n* brys *m*, brysyow

utilise *n* devnydhya; gul devnydh a²; usya

utility *n* les *m*, lesow

utmost *adj* pella

utter I *adj* pur; dien; kowal II *vb* leverel

utterance *n* lavar *m*, lavarow

utterly *adv* glan; kowal; yn tien; heb namm

V

vacancy *n* gwagla *m*, gwagleow

vacant *adj* gwag

vacate *vb* gwakhe

vacation *n* dy'gol *m*, dy'golyow

vaccinate *vb* bryghlina

vaccination *n* bryghlinans *m*, bryghlinansow

vaccine *n* bryghlin *m*, bryghlinyow

vacuous *adj* penn-koog

vacuum *n* gwagva *f*, gwagvaow; gwakter *m*, gwakteryow. **vacuum cleaner** *n* skubell-sugna *f*, skubellow-sugna. **vacuum flask** kostrel gwakter *m*, kostrels gwakter

vagabond *n* brybour *m*, brybours

vagina *n* kons *f*, konsow, konsyow

vagrant *n* gwyll *m*, gwyllyow; lorel *m* lorels

vague *adj* diskler; niwlek

vain *adj* (*fruitless*) koog; (*full of oneself*) omgerensedhek

vale *n* nans *m*, nansow

valerian, common *n* (*all-heal*) medhoges an gors *f*

valerian, red *n* pennow medhow *m.pl*

valerian, white *n* pennow medhow gwynn *m.pl*

valid *adj* ewn; a vri

validate *vb* komposa

validity *n* komposter *m*, komposteryow

valley *n* nans *m*, nansow. **deep wooded valley** glynn *m*, glynnow. **flat valley** stras *m*, strasow. **small valley** golans *m*, golansow

valley-bottom *n* tnow *m*, tnowi

valour *n* kolonekter *m*

valuable *adj* a bris; talvosek

value *n* bri *f*; talvosogeth *f*, talvosogethow. **value added tax** toll dhaswerth *f*

valued *adj* talvesys

valueless *adj* diwerth; euver

valve *n* klapes *m*, klapesow

van *n* kertik *m*, kertigow

vandal *n* vandal *m*, vandals

vandalise *vb* vandalisa

vandalism *n* vandalieth *f*

vanguard *n* voward *m*, vowardys

vanilla *n* vanylla *m*

vanish *vb* mos mes a wel; voydya

vanquish *vb* fetha; tryghi; konkwerrya; overkomya

vapour *n* ethen *f*, ethennow

variable I *adj* chanjus II *n* varyadow *m*, varyadowyow

variance *n* varyans *m*, varyansow

variant I *adj* variennek II *n* varien *f*, variennow

variation *n* varyans *m*, varyansow

varied *adj* a lies eghen; a lies sort; divers (*followed by sg. or pl. noun*)

variety *n* eghen *f*, eghennow; sort *m*, sortow

various *adj* divers (*followed by sg. or pl. noun*); dyffrans (+ *pl. noun*); liesek

varnish I *n* gwernis *f*, gwernisyow II *vb* gwernisya. **nail varnish** gwernis ewin *f*, gwernisyow ewin

vary *vb* treylya; varya

vase *n* lester bleujyow *m*, lestri bleujyow; lester flourys *m*, lestri flourys

vassal *n* omajer *m*, omajers

vast *adj* efan; bras dres eghen

vat *n* keryn *f*, kerynyow

vault *n* dorgel *f*, dorgellow

veal *n* kig leugh *m*

vector *n* vektor *m*, vektors, vektorow

vegan I *adj* vegan II *n* veganer *m*, veganoryon

vegetable *n* losowen gegin *f*, losow kegin

vegetarian I *n* losoweger *m*, losowegoryon II *adj* losowek

vegetation *n* glasneth *f*; losowedh *m*

vehicle *n* karr *m*, kerri

veil *n* vayl *f*, vaylys; kudhlen *f*, kudhlennow

veiled *adj* kudhys

vein *n* (*blood-vessel*) gwythien *f*, gwythi; (*stream*) gooth *f*, gothi; (*of tin ore*) skorren *f*, skorrennow

velocity *n* uskitter *m*, uskitteryow; (*physical quantity*) uskittredh *m*, uskittredhow

velvet I *adj* a bali II *n* pali *m*

vend *vb* gwertha

vendor *n* gwerther *m*, gwerthoryon

ventilate *vb* ayrella

ventilation *n* ayrellans *m*, ayrellansow

ventilator *n* ayrell *f*, ayrellow

venture I *n* aventur *m*, aventurys, aventuryow II *vb* bedha; lavasos

venue *n* le *m*, leow

Venus *n* Gwener *f*; (*as morning star*) Borlowen

verb *n* verb *f*, verbow

verbal *adj* (*spoken*) der anow; war anow; (*about verbs*) verbel; (*about words*) geryel

verbose *adj* tavosek; gerennek. **be verbose** gerya

verbosity *n* gerenogeth *f*

verdict *n* breus *f*, vreusow; ervirans *m*, erviransow

verge *n* (*general*) amal *m*, emlow; (*roadside*) glann fordh *f*, glannow fordh

veriest *adj* purra

verify *vb* komposa; gwirya; gwirhe

vermin I *n* lastedhes *m* **II hunt vermin** *vb* pryvessa

verminous *adj* pryvesek

vernacular *adj* teythyek. **vernacular language** *n* yeth teythyek *f*, yethow teythyek

vernal *adj* gwentonel

versatile *adj* lieskonnyk

verse *n* gwers *f*, gwersyow

version *n* versyon *m*, versyons

versus *prp* erbynn

vertical *adj* plommwedhek; serth

vertigo *n* (*colloq*) penn-dro *f*; (*med*) vertigo *m*

very *adv* pur^2; fest. **very good** pur dha

vessel *n* lester *m*, lestri

vest *n* vesta *m*, vestys

vestry *n* gwiskti *m*, gwisktiow

vetch, common *n* gwegbys an park *coll*

vetch, yellow *n* gwegbys melyn *coll*

veterinarian *n* milvedhek *m*, milvedhogyon; medhek bestes *m*, medhogyon vestes

veterinary *adj* milvedhegiethel

vexed *adj* serrys

via *prp* dre^2; (*before vowel*) der

viaduct *n* ponsfordh *f*, ponsfordhow

vibrate *vb* krena

vibration *n* krenans *m*, krenansow

vicar *n* pronter *m*, pronteryon

vicarage *n* pronterji *m*, pronterjiow

vice (1) *n* (*moral weakness*) drogedh *m*, drogedhow

vice (2) *n* (*tool*) bis *f*, bisyow

vice (3) *adj* (*deputy*) is-

vice-chairperson *n* iskaderyer *m*, iskaderyoryon

vice-president *n* islewydh *m*, islewydhyon

vicinity *n* ogas *m*; kerghyn *m*, kerghynnow

vicious *adj* hegas

victim *n* fethesik *m*, fethesigow; (*sacrificial*) sakrifis *m*, sakrifisys

victor *n* trygher *m*, tryghoryon; fether *m*, fethoryon

victorious *adj* budhek; budhogel; fethek; trygh

victory *n* trygh *m*. **the victory was mine** an trygh eth genev

victuals *n* viktuals *pl*

video *n* gwydhyow *m*, gwydhyowyow

view *n* gwel *f*, gwelyow; golok *f*, gologow

viewpoint *n* gwelva *f*, gwelvaow

vigil *n* gool *m*, golyow

vigilant *adj* hewol

vigorous *adj* freth

vigorously *adv* gans meur a gris

vigour *n* kris *m*

vile *adj* kasadow; vil

vileness *n* kasadewder *m*; vilta *f*

village *n* trev *f*, trevow; treveglos *f*, treveglosyow, trevow eglos; gwig *f*, gwigow; tre *f*, trevow

villager *n* trevesik *m*, trevesigyon

villain *n* bilen *m*, bilenys; gal *m*, galyon, galow

villainous *adj* bilen

vine *n* gwinbren *m*, gwinbrennyer

vinegar *n* aysel *m*

vineyard *n* gwinlan *f*, gwinlannow

violence *n* garowder *m*; freudh *m*, freudhow

violent *adj* garow; gwyls; freudhek

violet I *adj* (*colour*) glasrudh; purpur **II**
n (*flower*) melionen *f*, melionennow;
melion *coll*

violet, dog *n* melion an ki *coll*

violet, marsh *n* melion an gors *coll*

violet, sweet *n* melionen velyseth *f*,
melionennow melyseth; melion
melyseth *coll*

violin *n* krowd *m*, krowdys; fyll *m*,
fyllys, fyllow

virgin I *adj* gwyrgh **II** *n* gwerghes *f*,
gwerghesow

virile *adj* gourel

virtual *adj* gowir. **virtual reality** *n*
gwirvos gowir *m*

virtue *n* vertu *f*, vertus; ras *m*, rasow

virtuous *adj* ewnhynsek; mas; glan

virus *n* virus *m*, virusys

visa *n* visa *m*, visas

visage *n* bejeth *f*, bejethow; visach *m*,
visajys; fas *m*, fassow

visibility *n* gweladewder *m*

visible *adj* gweladow

vision *n* (*sense*) golok *f*; (*apparition*,
imagination) gwelesigeth *f*,
gwelesigethow; besyon *m*, besyons;
gwel *f*, gwelyow

visit I *n* godrik *m*, godrigow; vysytyans
m, vysytyansow **II** *vb* godriga;
vysytya

visitor *n* godriger *m*, godrigoryon;
vysytyer *m*, vysytyoryon

visor *n* visour *m*, visours

visual *adj* gwelesek

vital *adj* bewek

vitamin *n* vitamyn *m*, vitamynnow

vivid *adj* glew

vocabulary *n* gerva *f*, gervaow

vocal *adj* dre lev; levyel

vocalic *adj* bogalek

vocation *n* galwesigeth *f*,
galwesigethow; galow *m*, galowyow

vocational *adj* galwansek

vodka *n* vodka *m*, vodkas

voice *n* lev *m*, levow

voicemail *n* levbost *m*, levbostow

volcanic *adj* loskvenydhyek

volcano *n* loskvenydh *m*,
loskvenydhyow; menydh tan *m*,
menydhyow tan

volt *n* volt *m*, voltow

voltage *n* voltedh *m*, voltedhow

volume *n* (*spatial*) dalghedh *m*; (*book*)
kevrol *f*, kevrolyow; (*sound*) ughelder

voluntary *adj* bodhek; a-vodh

volunteer I *n* bodhek *m*, bodhogyon **II**
vb bodhegi

vomit *vb* hwyja; (*projectile*) pellhwyja

vote I *n* raglev *m*, raglevow; vota *m*,
votys **II** *vb* ragleva; votya

voter *n* voter *m*, votoryon

vouch *vb* avochya

vow I *n* ti *m*, tiow **II** *vb* ti

vowel *n* bogalen *f*, bogalennow

voyage *n* viaj *m*, viajyow, viajys; (*sea*
voyage) trumach *m*, trumajys,
trumajow

vulgar *adj* isel; kemmyn

vulnerable *adj* goliadow

vulture *n* hok karyn *m*, hokys karyn

W

wad *n* (*cloth*) klout *m*, kloutys; (*of spit*)
klott *m*, klottys, klottow

waddle *vb* hoskerdhes

wafer *n* waffer *m*, waffers

waffle *vb* flowsa

wage I *n* gober *m*, goborow **II** *vb* gostla.
wage war gostla bell

wager I *n* kenwostel *m*, kenwostlow **II**
vb kenwostla

wagon *n* karven *f*, karvenow

wagtail, grey *n* stenor dowr *m*, stenores dowr

wagtail, pied *n* stenor brith *m*, stenores brith

wagtail, yellow *n* stenor melyn *m*, stenores melyn

wail I *n* olva *f*, olvaow **II** *vb* kyni

waist *n* kres *m*, kresyow

waistcoat *n* kryspows *f*, kryspowsyow

wait *vb* gortos. **waiting room** stevel wortos *f*, stevellow gortos

waiter *n* servyas *m*, servysi

waitress *n* servyades *f*, servyadesow

waive *vb* gwayvya

wake *n* gool *m*, golyow

wake up *vb* difuna

Wales *top* Kembra *f*

walk I *n* kerdh *m*, kerdhow **II** *vb* kerdhes

walker *n* kerdher *m*, kerdhoryon

wall *n* fos *f*, fosow. **party wall** *n* paros *m*, parosyow

wallet *n* skrypp *m*, skryppys, skryppow

wallflower *n* bleujen fosow *f*

wallop I *n* kronk *m*, kronkys **II** *vb* kronkya

wallpaper *n* paper fos *m*, paperyow fos; paper paros *m*, paperyow paros

walnut *n* knowen Frynk *f*, know Frynk

walrus *n* morvugh *f*, morvughes

waltz I *n* walts *m*, waltsys **II** *vb* waltsya

wand *n* gwelen *f*, gwelynni. **magic wand** gwelen hus *f*, gwelynni hus

wander *vb* gwandra

wanderer *n* gwandryas *m*, gwandrysi

wandering *adj* gwandrek

want I *n* (*desire*) hwans *m*, hwansow; edhom *m*, edhommow **II** *vb* mynnes; (*desire*) bos hwans dhe[2]. **I want it** yma hwans dhymm anodho; hwans a'm beus anodho

war *n* (*armed conflict*) kas *f*, kasow; bell *m*; (*dispute*) bresel *f*, breselyow. **go to**

war *vb* breseli; mos dhe'n gas. **wage war** gostla bell

ward *n* diberthva *f*, diberthvaow

warden *n* gwithyas *m*, gwithysi

wardrobe *n* dillasva *f*, dilasvaow

ware *n* (*merchandise*) gwaren *f*, gwarennow; gwara *coll*

warehouse *n* gwaraji *m*, gwarajiow

warfare *n* breselyans *m*

warlock *n* pystrier *m*, pystrioryon

warm I *adj* tomm **II** *n* tomder *m* **III** *vb* tomma; tommhe

warmth *n* tomder *m*

warn *vb* gwarnya

warning *n* gwarnyans *m*, gwarnyansow

warp I *n* steuv *f*, steuvow **II** *vb* steuvi; stumma

warped *adj* stummys

wart *n* gwenogen *f*, gwenogennow. **cattle wart** ryg *m*, rygyow. **warts and all** yn despit dhe'n fowtow

wary *adj* war

wash I *n* golgh *m* **II** *vb* golghi. **wash oneself** *vb* omwolghi. **wash up, wash the dishes** *vb* golghi an lestri

washable *adj* golghadow

washbasin *n* new *f*, newyow

washing *n* golgh *m*, golghow; golghas *m*, golghasow. **washing machine** *n* jynn-golghi *m*, jynnys-golghi, jynnow-golghi. **washing powder** *n* lisiw *m*, lisiwyow. **hang out the washing** lesa an golgh

washing-up liquid *n* golghlin *m*, golghlinyow; lin sebon *m*

wasp *n* goghien *f*, goghiennow; goghi *coll*

waste I *adj* gwast; (*land*) difeyth **II** *n* (*rubbish, squandering*) skoll *m*, skollyon; atal *coll* **III** *vb* skollya; gwastya. **waste time** gwibessa

wasteful *adj* skollyek

wastefulness *n* skollva *f*, skollvaow

wasteland *n* difeyth *m*, difeythyow

watch I *n* (*vigil*) gool *m*, golyow; (*timepiece*) euryor *f*, euryoryow **II** *vb* (*look at*) mires orth. **watch out** gwaytyas; kemeres with; warya. **watch over** gwitha war[2]. **watch television** mires orth an bellwolok. **keep watch** golyas

watchdog *n* golgi *m*, golgeun

water I *n* dowr *m*, dowrow **II** *vb* dowra; dowrhe. **water tank** dowrargh *m*, dowrarghow

water-colour *n* dowrliw *m*, dowrliwyow

watercress *n* beler dowr *coll*

waterfall *n* dowrlam *m*, dowrlammow. **little waterfall** pistyl *m*, pistyllow

waterproof I *adj* stanch **II** *vb* stanchura

water vole *n* dowrrath *f*, dowrrathes

watery *adj* dowrek; deverel; devrek

wattage *n* wattedh *m*, wattedhow

wave I *n* (*water*) tonn *f*, tonnow; (*hand*) gwevyans *m*, gwevyansow **II** *vb* gwevya. **wave!** (*imp*) gwev! **she gave him a wave** hi a ros gwevyans dhodho

wavelength *n* tonnhys *m*, tonnhysow

wavy *adj* tonnek

wax I *n* kor *coll* **II** *vb* kora. **cake of wax** koren *f*, korennow

way *n* fordh *f*, fordhow; hyns *m*, hensyow; (*customary practice*) fordh usadow *f*; (*manner*) maner *f*, manerow; (*style, fashion*) gis *m*, gisyow. **all the way to** bys yn. **a long way from here** pell alemma. **be on one's way** mos y'n fordh. **give way to** omblegya dhe[2]. **in this way** yndelma. **in that way** yndella; yndelna. **in any way** war neb kor. **make way for** gasa spas dhe[2]. **no way!** gwra y ankevi! (*sg*), gwrewgh y ankevi! (*pl*); kammen vyth! **on the way out** ow mos yn-mes. **this way out** (*signage*) fordh yn-mes. **way back** (*in time*) nans yw pell

we *prn* ni; (*enclitic*) ni

weak *adj* gwann

weaken *vb* gwanna; gwannhe; bleudhya

weak-hearted *adj* gwann y golon

weakness *n* gwander *m*

wealth *n* pyth *m*, pythow; rychys *m*. **worldly wealth** pythow an bys *pl*

wealthy *adj* golusek. **wealthy person** golusek *m*, golusogyon

weapon *n* arv *f*, arvow

wear *vb* gwiska; bos gwiskys yn. **wear off** gwannhe. **wear out** usya

wearied *adj* skwithhes

weariness *n* skwithter *m*

weary I *adj* skwith **II** *vb* skwitha

weather I *n* kewer *f*; awel *f*, awelyow **II** *vb* tewedha. **bad weather** *n* hager-awel *f*. **fine weather** *n* kewer deg *f*. **weather a storm** dos dre hager-awel

weather-beaten *adj* tewedhek

weathered *adj* tewedhys

weave *vb* gwia

weaver *n* gwiader *m*, gwiadoryon

web *n* gwias *m*, gwiasow. **spider web** gwias kevnis *m*, gwiasow kevnis. **World Wide Web** *n* gwias treusvysek *m*

webbed *adj* gwiek; (*feet*) troswiek

webmail *n* gwiaspost *m*, gwiaspostow

webmaster *n* gwiasvester *m*, gwiasvestrysi

website *n* gwiasva *f*, gwiasvaow

wedding *n* demedhyans *m*, demedhyansow. **wedding anniversay** *m* penn-bloodh demedhyans

wedge I *n* genn *m*, gennow **II** *vb* genna

Wednesday *n* Mergher *m*; dy'Mergher *m*. **Wednesday night** dy'Mergher dhe nos

weed *n* hwennen *f*, hwenennow; hwenn *coll*

weedy *adj* hwennek

week *n* seythen *f*, seythennyow. **today week** an jydh ma war seythen. **last week** y'n seythen usi passy(e)s

weekday *n* dy'gweyth *m*, dedhyow gweyth

weekend *n* pennseythen *m* (*f*), pennseythennyow

weekly I *adj* seythennyek **II** *adv* pub seythen **III** *n* (*publication*) jornal seythennyek *m*, jornals seythennyek

weep I *n* olva *f*, olvaow **II** *vb* ola; devera dagrow; skollya dagrow; dagrewi. **cry one's eyes out** skollya liv a dhagrow

weevil *n* gwedhan *m*, gwedhanes

weigh *vb* poosa

weight *n* poos *m*, posow

weird *adj* koynt

weirdness *n* koyntys *f*, koyntysyow

welcome I *n* dynnargh *m*, dynarghow; wolkom *m* **II** *adj* wolkom **III** *vb* dynerghi; wolkomma. **welcome to Cornwall** Kernow a'gas dynnergh. **you're welcome** wolkom os (*sg*), wolkom owgh (*pl*)

welcoming *adj* wolkommus

welfare *n* sewena *f*; les *m*. **the welfare state** stat an les *m*

well (1) I *adj* yagh; yn poynt da. **I am well** yn poynt da ov; yagh ov **II** *adv* yn ta. **well done** gwrys yn ta **III** *int* well! **as well as** keffrys ha. **get well** gwellhe; yaghhe. **very well** pur dha. **well advised** fur. **well balanced** kompes. **well behaved** doth. **well deserved** dendylys yn ta. **well paid** gobrys yn ta. **well preserved** gwithys yn ta. **well spoken of** gerys-da. **well-to-do** rych lowr

well (2) *n* (*spring*) fenten *f*, fentynnyow

well-intentioned *adj* masvresek

Welsh I *adj* Kembrek **II** *n* (*language*) Kembrek *m*

Welshman *n* Kembro *m*, Kembroyon

Welshwoman *n* Kembres *f*, Kembresow

wench *n* moren *f*, morenyon

werewolf *n* gourvleydh *m*, gourvleydhes

West *n* west *m*; howlsedhes *m*; gorlewin *f*

westerly *adj* a-dhia an west

Western *n* (*film*) fylm bughwas *m*, fylmow bughwas

western *adj* west; a'n west; a'n howlsedhes

westwards *adv* war-tu ha'n west

wet I *adj* glyb **II** *vb* glybya. **wet nurse** mammeth *f*, mammethow

wetness *n* glybor *m*

whale *n* morvil *m*, morviles

wharf *n* porthva *f*, porthvaow; kay gwara *m*, kayys gwara, kayow gwara

what I *adj* pan; pana[2] **II** *prn* pyth; pandra; py **III** *int* dar. **what for?** prag[5]; praga

whatever *prn* pynag (oll); pynag oll dra; pyseul a[2]. **whatever may be** pypynag y fo

whatsoever *prn* pynag oll

wheat *n* gwaneth *coll*

wheel *n* ros *f*, rosow. **spare wheel** ros parys *f*, rosow parys. **steering wheel** ros-lewya *f*, rosow-lewya

wheelbarrow *n* gravath ros *f*, gravathow ros

wheelchair *n* kador ros *f*, kadoryow ros

when I *adv* p'eur[5] **II** *cnj* pan[2]; pana dermyn; neb

whence *adv* a-ble[5]

whenever *adv* byth pan[2]; peskweyth may[5]

where I *adv* ple[5]; (*before a vowel*) ple'th; py; (*before a vowel*) pyth **II** *cnj* (*before a consonant*) le may[5]; (*before a vowel*) le mayth; py tyller

wherever *adv* py le pynag; (*direction*) pynag oll fordh

wherewithal *n* pygans *m*

whether *cnj* bo; po; mar[4]; mars

420

which *prn* (*interrog.*) py; (*of two*) pyneyl; piw a². **that which** an pyth; an dra; (*relative particle*) a²; (*with prepositions*) may⁵

whichever *prn* pynag (oll); pyneyl

while I *cnj* hedre²; (*before a consonant*) ha; (*before a vowel*) hag II *n* pols *m*; prys *m*; tecken *f*. **a good while** *adv* polta. **a little while ago** *adv* a-gensow. **while I was at school** pan esen y'n skol

whim *n* sians *m*, siansow

whip I *n* hwypp *m*, hwyppys, hwyppow II *vb* hwyppya; (*cream etc.*) forlya; dornella

whirlpool *n* poll-troyllya *m*, pollow-troyllya; trobol *m*, trobollow

whisk I *n* forlell *f*, forlellow; dornell *f*, dornellow II *vb* forlya; dornella

whisker *n* minvlewen *f*, minvlewennow

whiskey *n* dowr tomm Iwerdhon *m*

whisky *n* dowr tomm Alban *m*; hwiski *m*, hwiskiow; gwires Alban *m*

whisper I *n* hanas *m*, hanasow; hwystren *f*, hwystrennow II *vb* hwystra; hanasa

whistle I *n* (*sound*) hwibanans *m*; (*whiz*) hwiban *m*; (*instrument*) hwythell *f*, hwythellow; hwibanowl *f*, hwibanowlow II *vb* hwibana. **let's wet our whistles!** glybyn agan min!

white *adj* gwynn. **bright white** *adj* kann. **egg white** gwynn oy *m*, gwynnow oy

whiteboard *n* bord gwynn *m*, bordow gwynn

whiteness *n* gwynder *m*

whitethroat *n* konna gwynn *m*, konaow gwynn

whiting *n* (*fish*) gwynnek *m*, gwynoges

whitish *adj* skyllwyn; gwynnik

Whitmonday *n* Dy'Lun Penkost *m*

Whitsun *n* penkost *m*, penkostow

who, whom I *prn* (*personal*) piw II *prn* (*relative*) a²; neb a²; (*perfective*) re² III

cnj neb

whoever *prn* pynag (oll); piw pynag; seul

whole I *adj* (*healthy*) yagh; salow; (*complete*) kowal; dien; (*prefixed*) kowl-; kol- II *n* myns oll *m*. **the whole** an … oll; oll an; **as a whole, on the whole** dre vras

wholemeal *n* bleus leun *m*; bleus gell *m*. **wholemeal bread** bara leun *m*

wholesale *adj* kowlwerth. **sell wholesale** kowlwertha

wholesome *adj* yaghus

wholly *adv* yn tien; oll; (*as prefix*) kowl-; kol-

whom *prn* neb; piw

whoop I *garm f*, garmow II *vb* garma. **whooping cough** pas garm *m*

whose *prn* piw. **whose car is this?** dhe biw usi an karr ma? **he's the man whose father is in London** ev yw an den mayth usi y das yn Loundres

whosoever *prn* pynag oll

why I *adv* prag⁵; praga II *int* dar

wick *n* porven *f*, porvennow; porv *coll*; bouben *f*, boubennow

wicked *adj* drog; kammhynsek; tebel; penn-drog

wickedness *n* drokter *m*; drokoleth *m* (*f*)

wicket *n* (*door*) darasik *m*, darasigow; (*gate*) yet *f*, yetys, yetow; (*cricket*) wycket *m*, wycketys. **wicket keeper** wycketor *m*, wycketoryon

wide *adj* ledan; efan. **wide awake** *adj* pur dhifun

widen *vb* ledanhe

widow *n* gwedhwes *f*, gwedhwesow

widowed *adj* gwedhow

widower *n* gwedhow *m*, gwedhowyon

width *n* les *m*; lester *m*

wield a sword *vb* kledhya

wife *n* gwreg *f*, gwragedh

WiFi *n* DiWi *m* (*abbrev. of diwiver*)

wig *n* peruken *f*, perukennow

421

wild *adj* gwyls; goodh. **wild animal** godhvil *m*, godhviles

wilderness *n* gwylvos *m*, gwylvosow

wildlife *n* godhvewnans *m*

will I *n* bolonjedh *m*, bolonjedhow; bodh *m*, bodhow; (*testament*) kemynskrif *m*, kemynskrifow **II** *vb* mynnes. **I will go home** my a wra mos tre; **do what you will** gwra kepar dell vynni

willing *adj* bodhek. **if you are willing** mars yw dha vodh

willow *n* helygen *f*, helygennow; helyk *coll*

willowherb *n* helygles *coll*

willowherb, broad-leaved *n* helygles ledan *coll*

willowherb, hoary *n* helygles denti *coll*

willowherb, rosebay *n* tanles *coll*

win I *n* gwayn *m*, gwaynyow **II** *vb* gwaynya. **win out** seweni

wince *vb* omwen

winch *n* gwyns *f*, gwynsys

wind (1) *n* awel *f*, awelyow; gwyns *m*, gwynsow

wind (2) *vb* (*turn*) stumma. **wind up** flattra

windmill *n* melin wyns *f*, melinyow gwyns

window *n* fenester *f*, fenestri

windowed *adj* fenestrek

windscreen *n* skew wyns *f*, skewyow gwyns. **windscreen wiper** disegher *m*, diseghoryon

windsurfing *n* astelwolyans *m* **go windsurfing** *vb* astelwolya

windy *adj* gwynsek; awelek

wine *n* gwin *m*, gwinow. **red wine** *n* gwin rudh *m*. **white wine** *n* gwin gwynn *m*. **spiced wine** pyment *m*, pymentys

wing *n* askel *f*, eskelli

winged *adj* askellek

wingless *adj* diaskellek

wink I *n* gwynk *m*, gwynkow; plynch *m*, plynchys **II** *vb* gwynykya; plynchya. **wink at** gwynkya orth; plynchya orth

winner *n* gwaynyer *m*, gwaynyoryon

winning I *adj* a wayn **II** *n* gwayn *m*, gwaynyow

winnings *n* gwaynyow *pl*

winter *n* gwav *m*, gwavow. **all winter** dres an gwav. **in winter** y'n gwav. **pass the winter** gwavi. **winter dwelling** gwavos *f*, gwavosow. **winter solstice** howlsav an gwav *m*

wintry *adj* gwavek

wipe I *n* seghans *m*, seghansow **II** *vb* segha

wiper *n* disegher *m*, diseghoryon

wire *n* gwivren *f*, gwivrennow; gwiver *coll*

wireless *adj* diwiver

wisdom *n* furneth *m*; skentoleth *f*; skians *m*. **wisdom tooth** dans keyn *m*, dens keyn

wise *adj* fur

wish I *n* hwans *m*; bolonjedh *m*; bodh *m*, bodhow. **with all good wishes** gans pub bolonjedh da **II** *vb* mynnes; bos hwansek. **I wish** my a garsa. **wish for somebody to do something** mynnes orth nebonan gul neppyth

wishbone *n* askorn bolonjedh *m*, eskern bolonjedh

witch *n* gwragh *m*, gwraghes. **cunning person** peller *m*, pelloryon

with *prp* gans. **along with** a-barth dhe[2]. **with me** genev. **with you** (*sg*) genes; (*pl*) genowgh. **with him** ganso. **with her** gensi. **with us** genen. **with them** gansa

withdraw *vb* (*intransitive*) omdenna; kildenna; ombellhe; (*transitive: retract*) denagha; (*transitive: money*) tenna yn-mes

withdrawal *n* omdennans *m*, omdenansow; kildennans *m*, kildenansow

wither *vb* gwedhra

withered *adj* gwedhrys

within I *prp* a-ji dhe[2]; yn; a-berth yn; (*of time*) kyns penn **II** *adv* a-ji. **within a week** kyns penn seythen. **within living memory** a-ji dhe gov den

without *prp* heb; di-; a-der. **without doubt** heb dhout; heb mar. **without further ado** heb na hirra lavarow. **without me** hebov. **without you** (*sg*) hebos. **without him** hebdho. **without her** hebdhi. **without us** hebon. **without you** (*pl*) hebowgh. **without them** hebdha

witness I *n* (*testimony*) dustuni *m*, dustuniow; (*person*) dustunier *m*, dustunioryon **II** *vb* desta; dustunia

wits *n* konnyk *m*; skians *m*. **out of his wits** mes a'y skians

witty *adj* didhan; didhanus; hwarthus

wizard *n* pystrier *m*, pystrioryon

woe *n* gew *m*, gewow. **woe is me!** *int* go vy!

wolf *n* bleydh *m*, bleydhi

wolf's bane *n* (*monkshood*) losow an bleydh *coll*, kugol an managh *m*

wolframite *n* kall *m*, kallow

woman *n* benyn *f*, benenes

womankind *n* benynreydh *f*

womb *n* brys *m*, brysyow

wonder I *n* aneth *m*, anethow; marth *m*, marthow; revedh *m*, revedhow **II** *vb* omwovyn. **I wonder** (*have doubt*) yma dout dhymm; (*surprised*) marth yw genev. **wonder at** gul aneth a[2]

wonderful *adj* marthys; barthusek

wonderfully *adv* marthys

woo *vb* tanta

wood *n* (*forest*) koos *m*, kosow; (*material*) prenn *m*, prennyer

woodcock *n* kevelek *m*, keveloges

wooded *adj* gwydhyel

wooden *adj* prenn; a brenn; prennek

woodland *n* gwedhek *f*, gwedhegi

woodlouse *n* gwragh oles *f*, gwraghes oles

woodpecker *n* kasek koos *f*, kasegi koos. **great spotted woodpecker** kasek koos bras *f*, kasegi koos bras. **lesser spotted woodpecker** kasek koos byghan *f*, kasegi koos byghan

woodruff, sweet *n* kala hweg *coll*

woodwork *n* prennweyth *m*

woodworm *n* pryv prenn *m*, preves prenn, prevyon prenn

woody *adj* prennek; (*many trees*) kosek

wool *n* gwlan *coll*

woollen *adj* gwlanek

woolly *adj* gwlanek

word *n* ger *m*, geryow

work I *n* hwel *m*, hwelyow; ober *m*, oberow; (*labour*) lavur *m*; gonis *m*, gonisyow; (*shift of*) kor *m*, korow; (*in physics*) oberedh *m* **II** *vb* gul hwel; lavurya; oberi. **set to work** gweytha. **working animal** best hwel *m*, bestes hwel. **work-day, working day** gweyth *m*, gweythyow. **homework** ober tre *m*

workbench *n* bynk *f*, bynkyow

worker *n* gweythor *m*, gweythoryon; oberer *m*, oberoryon

workman *n* oberwas *m*, oberwesyon; gwas hwel *m*, gwesyon hwel; gweythor *m*, gweythoryon

workmanship *n* kreft *f*, kreftow

workshop *n* hwelji *m*, hweljiow; shoppa ober *m* shoppys ober

world *n* bys *m*, bysow. **the world** an bys; an nor; an norvys

world-famous *adj* meurgerys dres oll an bys

worldwide *adj* dres oll an bys; treusvysyek

worm *n* pryv *m*, preves, prevyon; (*earthworm*) bulugen *f*, bulugennow; buluk *coll*

wormy *adj* pryvesek

worn *adj* usys

worn-out *adj* lavurys

worried *adj* prederys

worry I *n* preder *m*, prederow **II** *vb* ania. **don't worry!** na borth ahwer!

worrying *adj* prederus

worse *adj* (*cmp*) gweth; lakka. **far worse** milweth

worsen *vb* gwethhe

worship I *n* gordhyans *m*; gologhas *m*; (*honorific title*) worshyp *m* **II** *vb* gordhya

worst *adj* (an) gwettha; (an) lakka

worth I *adj* talvedhys. **it isn't worth much** ny dal nameur; **it is not worth anything at all** ny dal mann; ny dal oy **II** *n* talvosogeth *f*; pris *m* **III** *vb*. **to be worth** talvesa

worthiness *n* gwiwder *m*

worthless *adj* diwerth; euver; koog; raff (*preceds the noun*)

worthy *adj* gwiw; wordhi

wound I *n* goli *m*, goliow **II** *vb* golia

wrap *vb* maylya

wrapping *n* maylyans *m*, maylyansow

wrasse *n* gwragh *f*, gwraghes

wrath *n* sorr *m*

wreath *n* garlont *f*, garlons

wreck *n* gwreck *m*, gwreckys

wreckage *n* skommow *pl*

wren *n* gwrannen *f*, gwranennow

wrench I *n* (*tool*) alhwedh know *m*, alhwedhow know **II** *vb* treylya

wrestle *vb* omdewlel

wrestler *n* omdowler *m*, omdowloryon

wrestling *n* (*sport*) omdowl

wretched *adj* truan; trogh; (*unlucky*) anfeusik; (*hateful*) hegas

wriggle *vb* omwen

wring *vb* strotha; gwrynnya

wrinkle *vb* krygha

wrinkled *adj* krebogh

wrist *n* konna bregh *m*, konaow bregh

writ *n* skrifedh *f*, skrifedhow. **writ of arrest** kapyas *m*, kapyasow

write *vb* skrifa; (*by hand*) dornskrifa; (*typewrite*) jynnskrifa

writer *n* skrifer *m*, skriforyon; (*professional*) skrifyas *m*, skrifysi; (*author*) awtour *m*, awtours

writing *n* skrif *m*, skrifow

wrong I *adj* (*incorrect*) kamm; (*mistaken*) kammgemerys; (*bad*) drog **II** *n* drokoleth *m* (*f*); kamm *m*, kammow **III** *vb* droga; gul kamm erbynn; dregynna **IV** *prfx* kamm-; drog-; drok-

X

X-ray I *n* dewyn-X *m*, dewynnow-X. **X-ray photograph** *n* skeusen dhewyn-X *f*, skeusennow dewyn-X **II** *vb* X-dewynnya

Y

-y *sffx* -ek

yacht *n* lester-gwari *m*, lestri-gwari

yard *n* (*measure*) lath *f*, lathow. **half a yard** *n* kevelin *m*, kevelinyow; (*enclosure*) lann *f*, lannow; garth *m*, garthow

yardarm *n* dela *f*, deledhow

yarn *n* (*strand of fibres*) neusen *f*, neusennow; *coll* neus; (*story*) drolla *m*, drollys. **spin a yarn** (*tell a story*) derivas drolla

yarrow *n* minfel *m*

yawn *vb* deleva; dianowi

year *n* bledhen *f*, bledhynnyow. **all the year round** dres oll an vledhen. **before the year is out** kyns penn bledhen. **last year** warlena. **leap year** bledhen lamm *f*, bledhynnyow lamm. **next year** nessa bledhen; an vledhen usi ow tos. **this year** hevlena; hevleni. **years of age** bloodh *m*

yearly I *adj* bledhynnyek II *adv* a'n vledhen; pub bledhen

yearn *vb* yeuni; bos hirethek. **yearn for** bos hirethek war-lergh; yeuni *followed by direct object*

yearning I *adj* hirethek II *n* yeunadow *m*, yeunadowyow; hireth *f*, hirethow

yeast *n* burm *coll*

yell I *n* kri *m*, kriow; garm *f*, garmow; us *m*, usow II *vb* (*shout*) garma; usa; (*cry out*) kria

yellow *adj* melyn

yellowhammer *n* melynek eythin *m*, melynoges eythin

yellowish *adj* melynik

yes *int* ya!; ea! **yes, certainly!** dhe wir!

yesterday I *n* de *m* I *adv* de. **day before yesterday** dygynsete. **yesterday evening** *adv* nyhewer. **yesterday morning** de vyttin

yet *adv* hwath. **nor yet** byth moy. **not yet** na hwath

yew *n* ewinen *f*, ewinennow; ewin *coll*

yield *vb* (*give way*) plegya; (*give up*) hepkor

yoghurt *n* yogort *m*, yogortys, yogortow

yoke *n* yew *f*, yewow

yolk *n* melyn oy *m*, melynyow oy

yonder I *adj* enos; nos II *adv* eno; enos; hons; yn-hons

you *prn* (*sg*) ty; (*pl*) hwi; (*enclitic, sg*) jy; ta; (*enclitic, pl*) hwi; (*infixed, sg*) 'th^{5a}; (*infixed, pl*) 'gas. **by you** (*sg*) genes; (*pl*) genowgh. **for you** (*sg*) ragos; (*pl*) ragowgh. **of you** (*sg*) ahanas; (*pl*) ahanowgh. **to you** (*sg*) dhis; (*pl*) dhywgh. **with you** (*sg*) genes; (*pl*) genowgh

young *adj* yowynk. **when I was young** ha my yowynk; pan en vy yowynk. **make young** *vb* yowynkhe

younger *adj* yowynka

youngest *adj* (an) yowynka

youngster *n* yonker *m*, yonkers, yonkoryon

your *poss. adj* (*sg*) dha^2; (*pl*) agas

yourself *prn* dha honan. (*colloq, critical*) mab dha dhama *m*, myrgh dha dhama *f*. **after all, you are yourself** wosa all, mab dha dhama os

yourselves *prn* agas honan

youth *n* (*young age*) yowynkneth *f*; (*young person*) yonker *m*, yowynkes; (*young man*) den yowynk *m*; (*young woman*) benyn yowynk *f*; (*young people*) tus yowynk *pl*. **youth hostel** *n* ostel yowynkneth *f*. **youth club** *n* kowethas yowynkneth *m*

youthful *adj* yowynk

Z

zeal *n* diwysykter *m*

zealous *adj* diwysyk

zebra *n* zebra *m*, zebras. **zebra crossing** *n* treusva labol *f*, treusvaow labol

zenith *n* ughelder ebron *m*; ughboynt *m*

zero *num* mann *m*

zigzag I *n* kammdro *f*, kammdroyow;

ygam-ogam *m* **II** *vb* kammdreylya
zinc *n* (*element*) zynk *m*
zip *n* zypp *m*, zyppys, zyppow
zodiac *n* stergylgh *m*, stergylghyow
zombie *n* zombi *m*, zombis
zone *n* parth *f*, parthow
zoo *n* milva *f*, milvaow

zoological *adj* miloniethel
zoology *n* milonieth *f*
zoom in *vb* moghhe
zoom out *vb* lehe
Zulu *n* Zulu *m*, Zuluyon
zygote *n* sygot *m*, sygotow

Notes

Notes

Notes

Notes

Notes

Notes